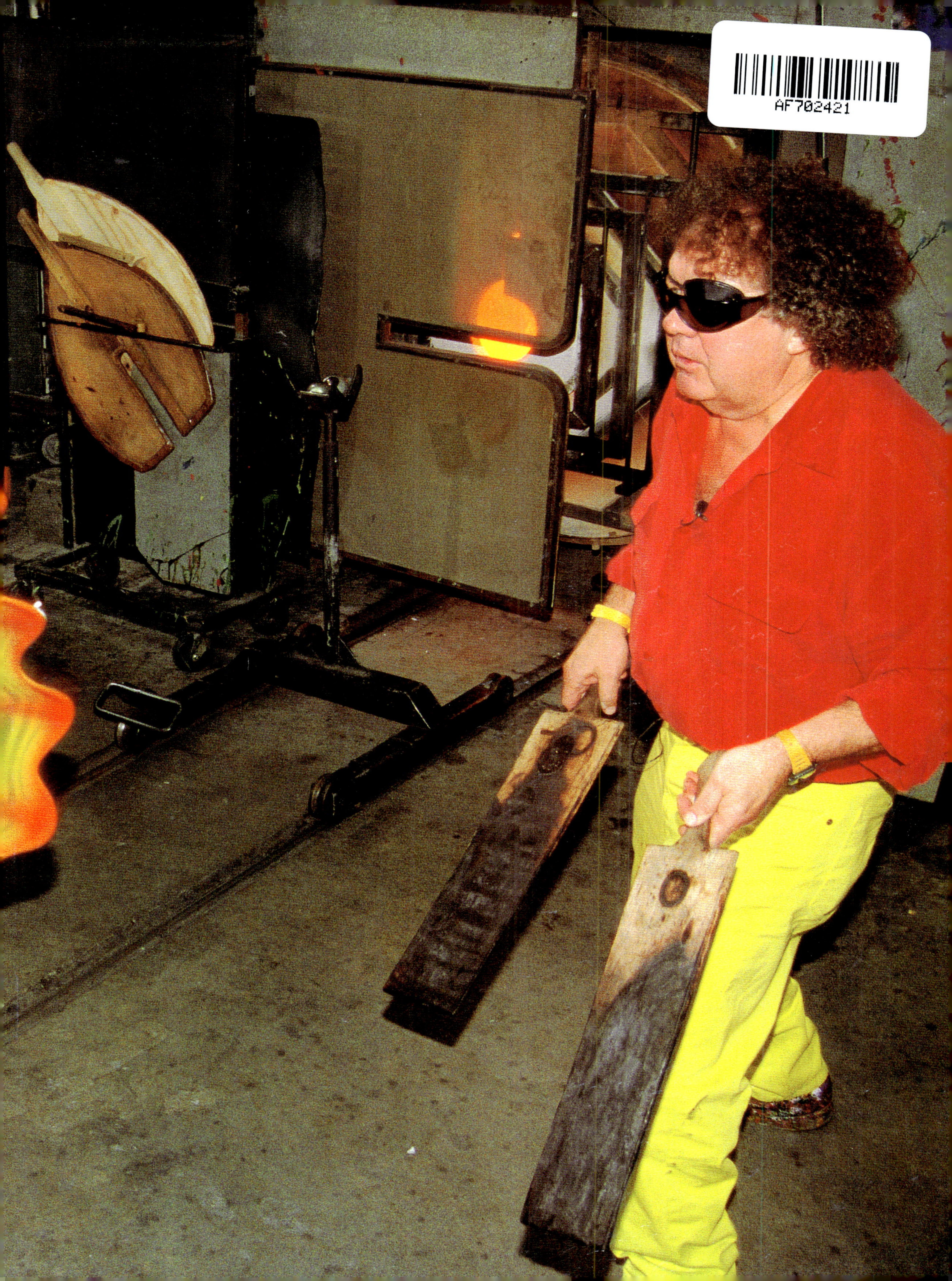

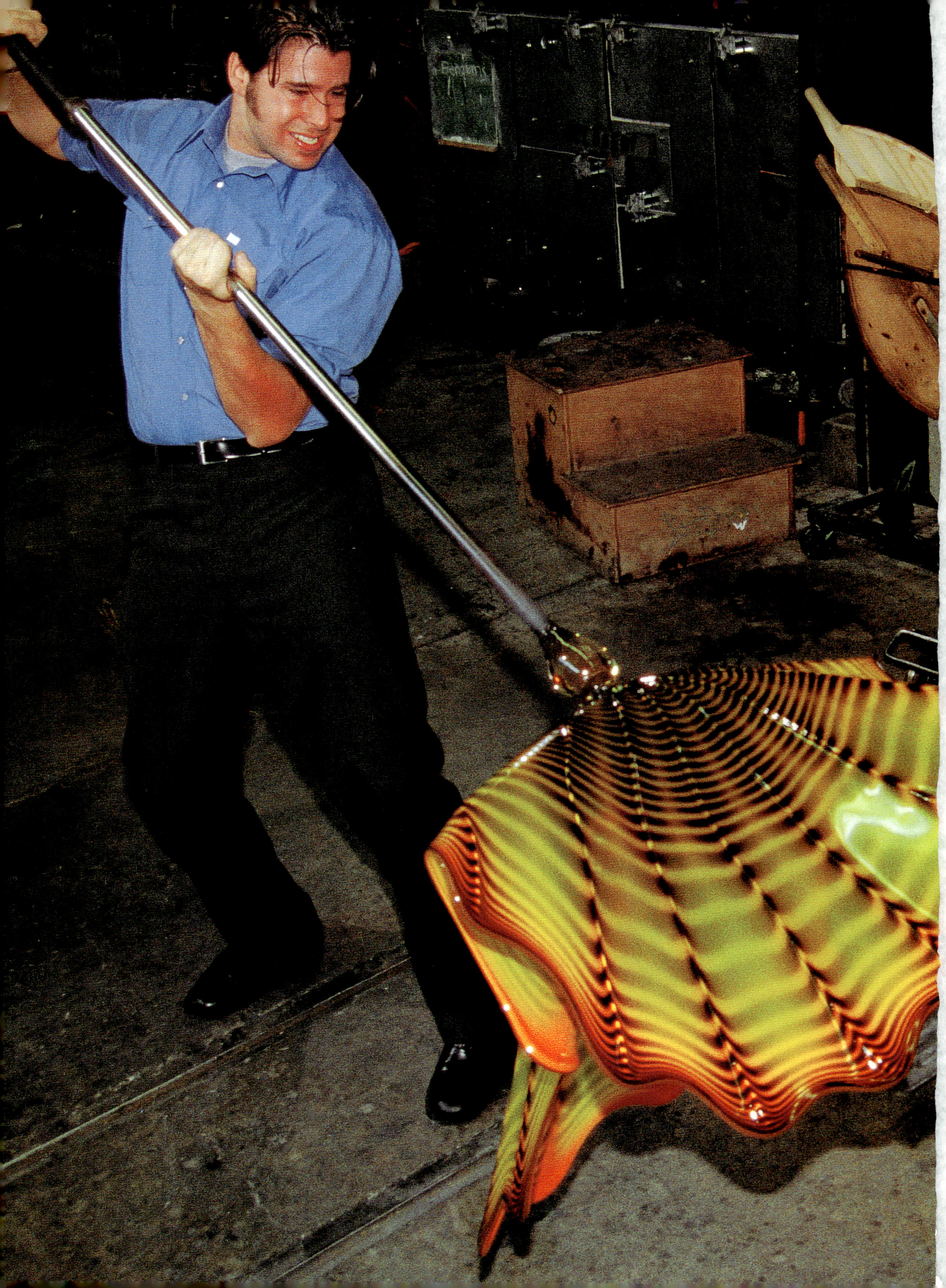

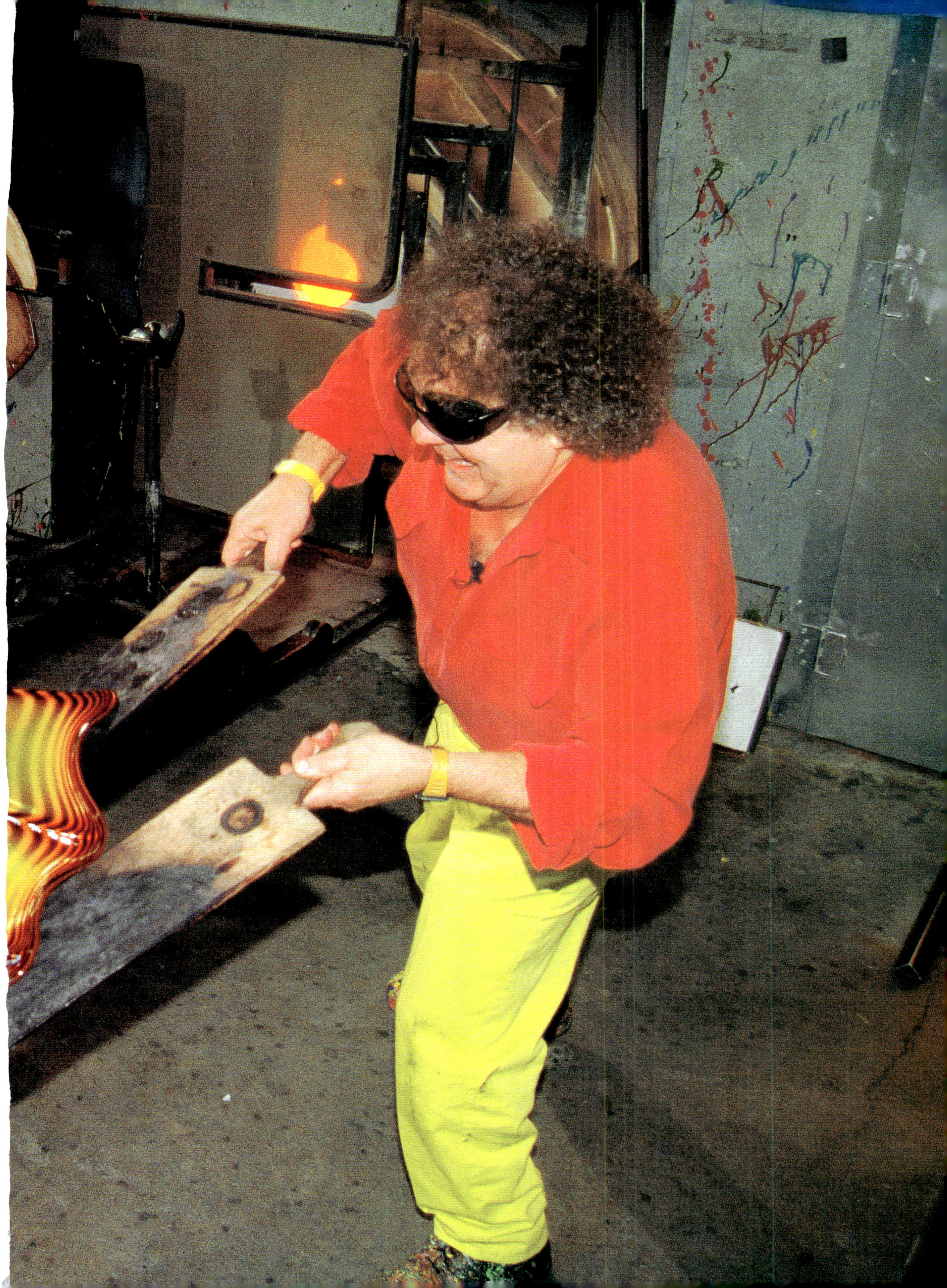

for Jackson

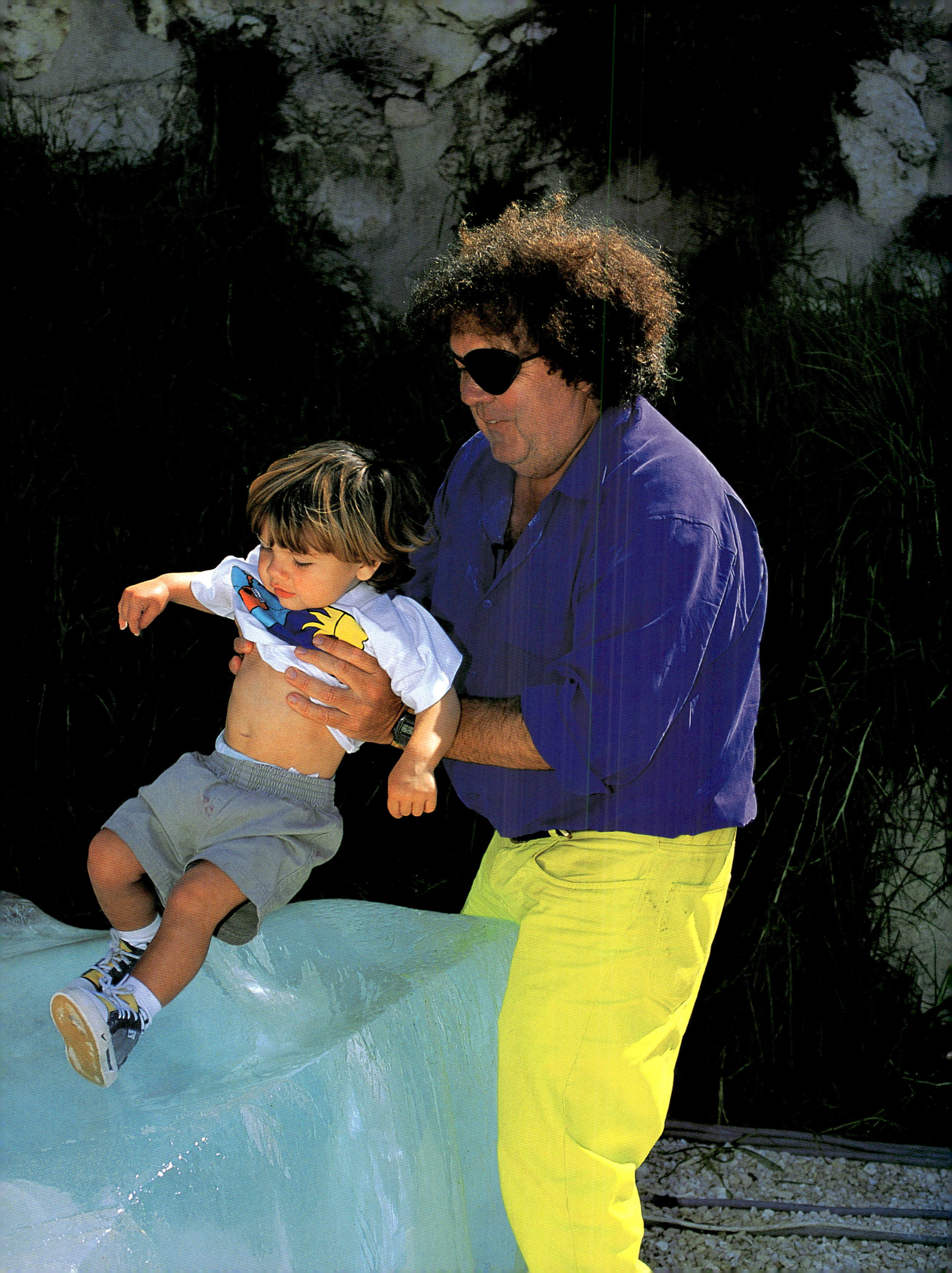

Chihuly

Projects

By Dale Chihuly

Essays by Barbara Rose and Dale Lanzone

Contents

1 Rhode Island School of Design, Providence

2 Artpark, Lewiston, New York

3 Shaare Emeth Synagogue, St. Louis

4 Saint Peter's Church, New York City

5 Seattle Art Museum

6 MacMillan Residence, Indian Wells, California

7 Stewart Williams House, Palm Springs, California

8 Albright-Knox Art Gallery, Buffalo, New York

9 Pillsbury Mansion, Wayzata, Minnesota

10 Honolulu Academy of Arts

11 100,000 Pounds of Ice and Neon, Tacoma, Washington

12 Rose Window, Minneapolis Institute of Arts

13 Joslyn Art Museum, Omaha, Nebraska

14 Lismore Castle, Ireland

15 Union Station, Tacoma, Washington

16 Bellagio, Las Vegas

17 Malina Window, Detroit, Michigan

18 Lautner House, Palm Springs, California

19 The Boathouse, Seattle

20 Icicle Creek Chandelier, Leavenworth, Washington

21 LongHouse, East Hampton, New York

22 Vianne, France

23 The News Tribune, Tacoma, Washington

24 Victoria and Albert Museum, London

25 Chrysler Museum of Art, Norfolk, Virginia

26 Atlantis, Paradise Island, Bahamas

27 Monterrey, Mexico

28 Nuutajärvi, Finland

29 Niijima Glass Art Center, Niijima, Japan

30 Ukai Museum, Hakone, Japan

31 Benaroya Hall, Seattle

32 Chihuly in the Light of Jerusalem 2000

33 Jerusalem Wall of Ice

34 Chihuly Bridge of Glass

Dale Chihuly's Paradise Regained by Barbara Rose

Dale Chihuly occupies a unique position in the history of contemporary art. His work is immensely popular with the general public, which usually disdains the avant-garde. At the same time, some of the most important art critics, art historians, and museum curators have acclaimed its brilliance, quality, and inventiveness. His material is glass, which is traditionally associated with the decorative arts, by definition subservient to architecture, and with closed vessels and containers or precious small-scale objects. Yet Chihuly has broken through these limitations and literally changed the definition of glass. He has found ways of creating huge environments and theatrical happenings with this intransigent and fragile material by stretching its unique properties in unprecedented ways.

By now, there is a substantial body of literature covering the three decades of Chihuly's art. Curiously, however, of all of the various appraisals of his work, no two are similar. Indeed, it seems that each critic or writer has his or her own Dale Chihuly. For Matisse scholar Jack Cowart, Chihuly follows Matisse's path of high decoration, as seen in Matisse's brilliantly colored late cutouts and the stained glass of the chapel at Vence. For psychoanalytically oriented critic Donald Kuspit—who has written the most complex and incisive interpretation of the artist's achievement—Chihuly reconciles the reality principle with the pleasure principle. Kuspit sees Chihuly as an artist capable of returning us to the state of innocent wonder of childhood. Other historians cite Chihuly's many layered references to other civilizations, such as the ancient Persian and the Renaissance Venetian traditions, as well as to other cultures, such as those of the Native Americans with whom he has had direct experience. All note his obvious references to nature and to natural processes, which is the inescapable core of his imagery.

Naturally, my Dale Chihuly is different from all of the above, although he shares characteristics with previous descriptions of his means and objectives. My Dale Chihuly is a mischievous, cunning, inspired shaman—a magician, a contemporary Merlin, a Ken Kesey Merry Prankster who produces the psychedelic experience of a magical, glowing, and sparkling, brilliantly alive panorama without drugs. This enchanted glass world has as much to do with Alice in Wonderland and the Wizard of Oz as it does with the great Renaissance and Baroque festivals that sovereigns arranged to entertain their courts and subjects.

I see Chihuly as something like an artistic Superman—capable of crossing boundaries, crashing through barriers, destroying stereotypes, linking continents—a larger-than-life savior who revived an ancient and dying tradition by transplanting it from the Old World to the New. Chihuly is the only artist, outside of Robert Rauschenberg perhaps, who manages actually to live out the sixties dream of making environmental art for the people and of connecting groups in communal situations. He does this by using technology as a tool to take us back to nature. In this sense, Chihuly's work has elements and aspirations in common with those of the artists connected with Experiments in Art and Technology, founded in the 1960s by Robert Rauschenberg and Billy Kluver (and also including Claes Oldenburg and Robert Whitman).

While reading the by-now-abundant literature on Chihuly, I was surprised by how many of the writers and curators who had supported his art were people I personally admired, such as Patterson Sims, Walter Darby Bannard, and the late Henry Geldzahler and David Bourdon. All had turned their backs on the narrow academic road of deconstructionist, neo-Marxist, and gender-based criticism now fashionable in the academies. And, of course, Chihuly himself had veered away from his initial conceptual origins in the direction of a bold and generous art that speaks directly to the public in a language that everyone can understand.

The global range of Chihuly's peripatetic activities and his ability to achieve huge and complex projects outside the closed mandarin circle of the official art world parallel that of Christo and Jean Claude. However, unlike their projects, his have no specific political or strategic goals. Like them, he manages his own oeuvre, essentially transcending the petty mechanics of the art world. And like their work, his installations are double-edged and multilayered, capable of being interpreted in a variety of sometimes contradictory ways.

In Chihuly's case, however, one cannot really speak of iconography or political content. The extravagance and theatricality of his site-specific installations are really challenged only by the brilliance and daring of Frank Stella's recent eccentric and clashing architecturally inspired works. Lacking Stella's aggression and confrontational hostility, however, Chihuly's environments, although they share a similar urge to the high decoration characteristic of Islamic and

Baroque architecture, are surely more user-friendly. Perhaps because he was trained as an interior designer, Chihuly became accustomed early on to working with rather than against architects.

Like Stella, Chihuly is an immensely successful public artist, capable of filling huge spaces with works of art, produced by teams of collaborators, that provide maximum stimulation and surprise to the public. Both produce sensations of wonder and awe that recall the efforts of the Counter-Reformation to throw off the cold hand of theory-laden Mannerism in order to address the masses directly with a theatrical and spectacular art that had emotional as well as visual impact. However, if Stella aims to be the Michelangelo of postmodernism, Chihuly would just as soon bring Cellini to the people, a more democratic and probably more realizable goal.

Chihuly's environments are intensely present in their colors and dramatic formats. They invite us to surrender to and drown in their weird beauty rather than to stand apart from them. They never demand that their forms or iconography be dissected. If they lack the avant-garde's detachment from the public, they are also devoid of its hostility and indigestibility. In his wildly imaginative fantastic installations, Chihuly creates a total world, a *Gesamtkunstwerk,* which one enters to be hypnotized and seduced. His is an artificial paradise located somewhere between the languorous, opium-induced synesthesia of Symbolism and the jeweled fairy-tale caves of Ali Baba. It is a world of visions and epiphanies, of illusions and chimera made real and literal. All-encompassing and thoroughly engaging, it is a world of pure sensuous and optical delight, in which one can float and dream.

I do not see Chihuly's exotic environments, however, as related to the transcendence from the material world to any sublime spiritual state, even though there are undeniable echoes of Romanticism in their fantastical quality. Our response to these forms, so frequently evocative of undersea life with its crystalline and coral formations or of the denseness and exoticism of lush tropical forests, is not to transcend them but to drown in them or to be lost and physically disoriented. The reaction is more bodily than spiritual, more like the sense one has of plunging into one of Monet's late *Nymphaea* paintings to join the banks of water lilies. It is an experience of immersion quite at odds with the subject-object division that characterizes worshiping the aesthetic icons in the ivory tower of the modern museum, where art is cut off from every other kind of experience.

Chihuly's shimmering glass installations create the pleasure and release of a bodily freedom that permits us to feel unanchored, liberated both from gravity and from the familiar boring and colorless shapes and experiences of everyday reality. There is more than a little of the poet in Chihuly. However, the poetry he evokes is the rapturous dreamworld of Coleridge and Blake rather than the nostalgia of Baudelaire and the fin de siècle Symbolists, to whom many writers have linked him. The Symbolists were basically depressed escapists nostalgic for Paradise Lost, never believing it could be regained. In their visionary and ecstatic quality, Chihuly's environments have more to do with the innocence of the epiphany than with the decadence of disappointment and loss. He has the gift of restoring to us what contemporary culture robs us of: delight, wonder, amazement.

One way to see Chihuly is as the anti-Mondrian, the archenemy of Constructivism, with its geometric grids channeling the masses into the productive order of modular repetition. Chihuly's forms are neither static nor solid but transparent, translucent and wavy, changeable and iridescent. They cannot be reduced to gestalts or static images. Their vital energy expands and explodes the fundamental spherical or cylindrical shapes of blown glass into eccentric and unforeseen new forms. These flickering and incandescent, expanding, permuted forms defy the limitations of geometry and stasis and of stable immutable structure.

Engulfed in Chihuly's glowing, effervescent, intensely patterned environments streaming with colored light, we find ourselves inside Kublai Khan's pleasure dome, ecstatically disoriented and hypnotically deranged citizens of Xanadu. We are returned to that state of primeval bliss from which man was expelled for eating the apple of knowledge. For a moment, we may regain the pagan innocence of the Golden Age, the inexperienced innocence also associated with preverbal childhood.

Unlike the underlying utopian political ideology of geometric Constructivism, there is no program for progress in Chihuly's work, no apology for luxury, no moralistic reformist diatribe, no progressive agenda. His is an art of the here and now, an incredibly generous and spectacular public art that can delight and amaze, transport and stimulate millions of people. Perhaps because of the anti-idealistic and anti-moralizing quality of his art, Chihuly's admirers often seem desperate to save him from being seen as vulgar and guilty of embracing what modernism discards as impure. Chihuly rejects purity as much as he attacks the traditional hierarchy that divides the arts into major and minor—with the decorative arts at the bottom of the order, because they serve architecture as embellishment.

By freeing glass installations from architecture, making the medium do more than it ever has before, Chihuly effectively negates such distinctions and proclaims the autonomy of glass as a fine-art medium. To save Chihuly from the "sin" of being a purely decorative artist, or worse yet, a mere artisan, writers who would be his apologists stress that he is an original and personally expressive artist not bound by the strictures of the glassblowing tradition. This emphasis on individuality and originality is typical of the Renaissance view of the artist. It dates back to Leonardo da Vinci's creation of a hierarchy of the arts, with painting at the top of the pyramid because the painter is above all an intellectual, a thinker, not a mere craftsman. It is a hierarchy that Chihuly in his anarchic nonconformity has by this time effectively destroyed.

Chihuly's forms and techniques are transgressive and illusionistic, hybrid and impure. They are everything that modernism, especially in its puritanical American version, associates with decadence and immorality. Within this cultural context, there must be something suspect in an art so expansive and direct, lush and extravagant, excessive and provocatively sensual. In other words, Dale Chihuly is the art world's bad boy. He has proved that he does not need the approbation of the high priests of the art world to survive and prosper. And that is what accounts for the unique appeal as well as the charm and seductiveness of his works, qualities that high modernism associates with the vulgarity of kitsch.

His eccentric swelling and swollen forms are as buoyant as balloons; his colors as mouthwatering as candy, as luxurious as sapphires, emeralds, and rubies. High modernism associates such direct delight, unmediated by criticism, with the entertainment values of popular culture. And here is where high modernism is mistaken and fails to understand what Chihuly intends and with brilliance and mastery has accomplished, which is to make an art that is glamorous and enticing without compromising its essential properties and qualities or cynically appealing to the lowest common denominator as an artist such as Jeff Koons does. There is a huge difference between popular culture, which has inspired both great music and art, and the stale, recycled, and reproduced images of mass media or the deliberate sentimentality and nostalgia of kitsch.

Chihuly's work is genuinely popular, as are jazz, rock music, Pop Art, and, above all, the movies. Like the best work in these forms, Chihuly's art does not devolve into purely escapist diversion or mindless entertainment. His work exhibits not only a sufficient degree of self-consciousness but also a high level of discipline, experience, and knowledge, not to mention a direct connection to a historic tradition, and that defines fine art. At the same time, however, it has more in common with a synthetic and collaborative art such as cinema than it does with the discrete, individualistic traditions of painting, sculpture, and architecture. Film at its best is a totalizing, all-encompassing, optically, physically, and emotionally involving experience from which the viewer cannot be distanced because of the degree of personal identification and synesthestic experience.

Given this, it is not surprising that Chihuly has referred to his role in the team production of the art he conceives in drawings and paintings as that of a movie director. A description by Walter Darby Bannard of how the atelier works gives a vivid picture of the collaborative effort: "A Chihuly glassmaking session is like a movie set or a football game. The participants know what they want more or less, but they are not exactly sure how they are going to get there. Ideas spring from Chihuly, from the workers who move around him as they would around a director or a coach, and from the piece itself as it takes shape."

The way his role evolved and the kind of art he makes are a result of Chihuly's personal experience and history. Born in 1941 in Tacoma, Washington, he was the younger son of a butcher, whose profession he celebrated in a work involving images of the cutting process. Coming from such a modest background, he had nothing given to him on a silver platter and had to be practical, ingenious, and hardworking to acquire the means to study, learn, and perfect his craft. Fortunately, he had the energy and discipline necessary to do so.

Chihuly's early life was touched with tragedy, which may explain why his art gradually evolved into a resistant paean to joy as an antidote to giving in to the pain of suffering. When he was fifteen, Chihuly's older brother died in an airplane crash, and the following year his father died. The auto accident that took the sight of his left eye in 1976 explains the pirate's patch he wears, which has become a kind of personal trademark. It also accounts for why he had to change his way of working, to become the director of a team effort rather than an individual glassblower, because his impaired eyesight did not permit him to accurately see the forms being blown.

Throughout his extraordinary life, Dale Chihuly has been able to turn liabilities into assets. His extroverted personality attracts gifted collaborators. From the outset, he has been both teacher and student, working with others, whose contributions he is always careful to acknowledge. Rather than being a victim of provincialism, he drew on his early experiences in the forests and abundant nature in the remote Northwest to provide rich subject matter for his art. In 1961, he began melting and fusing glass in his basement. As Henry Geldzahler, who acquired works by Chihuly for the Metropolitan Museum of Art early in the artist's career, observed, despite its five-thousand-year history, glass became a fine-art medium only in the 1960s, when universities established small glassblowing studios.

For the restless and adventurous Chihuly, whose life seems to imitate the style of a road movie, the 1960s was a decade of learning, traveling, experimenting, and expanding his knowledge of the ancient medium he would transform. In the early sixties, he toured Europe and worked on a kibbutz in Israel, as well as studying interior design and architecture at the University of Washington.

In a weaving class there, he incorporated glass into the warp and woof of tapestry. By doing so, he exhibited knowledge of the theoretical basis of stained color field abstraction, which demanded that surface and support be fused and that the intrinsic material qualities be declared as such. No wonder, then, that color field painter Walter Darby Bannard praised Chihuly for emphasizing in a highly conscious manner the *glassness* of glass.

By now known as an award-winning weaver, Chihuly blew glass for the first time in 1965. He took the following year off from his studies to work as a commercial fisherman in Alaska, to earn money for graduate studies in glass-blowing at the University of Wisconsin, where he earned a master of science degree in 1967. Adding to this technical experience, he continued his studies at the prestigious Rhode Island School of Design, where he earned an M.F.A., became a member of the faculty, and later founded its renowned glass department. At RISD, he met the inspirational and nonconformist sculptor Italo Scanga and made his first large-scale environmental sculptures, incorporating neon and plastic.

By the end of the sixties, Chihuly was beginning to be recognized as a uniquely gifted artist. In 1969, he received both a Tiffany Foundation grant and a Fulbright Fellowship to study in Venice. There he became the first American glassblower to work in Murano at the legendary Venini factory. Back in Providence, Rhode Island, at RISD, he met James Carpenter, a student with whom he began a four-year collaboration, making conceptual and environmental site-specific outdoor works.

One such work, *Dry Ice, Bent Glass and Neon,* was an experiment to see how far molten glass could be stretched. Its theme was the Crystal Palace, the steel-and-glass pavilion in London designed to house the great nineteenth-century international exhibition that launched the Arts and Crafts movement. The later destruction of the Crystal Palace by fiery meltdown is symbolic of the liberation of glass from the tight geometric strictures of the metal girdle needed to keep it in place in a framework and context determined by the needs of architecture. It was a fantasy Chihuly would realize fully in his own revolutionary work.

In 1971, Chihuly returned to his home state of Washington to start the Pilchuck Glass School north of Seattle, where he did his first environmental installation. Later that year, back at RISD, he continued installation work including *Glass Forest #1*, a huge collaborative project using glass, neon, and argon. *Cast Glass Door*, another dramatic installation consisting of parallelograms of blue toned glass arranged in space, was completed at Pilchuck the following year. During this period, Chihuly spent some time in Venice blowing glass at the Venini factory and working on architectural glass projects. At a glass factory near Philadelphia, he created new site-specific works such as *Mitla* (1973). The title refers to a pre-Columbian site near Oaxaca, Mexico, because he glued together sheets of plate glass in a pyramid form that referred back to the architecture of Mesoamerica.

In 1974, he began experimenting with drawing in glass at Pilchuck. Then, in a surprise move, he accepted an invitation to build a glass studio at the Institute of American Indian Art in Santa Fe, New Mexico, to teach Native Americans the ancient craft. In the country outside Santa Fe, he did *Glass Pour,* in which liquid molten glass was poured into the ground to become a cast of the earth's surface when it hardened. The piece had obvious reference to contemporary earthworks and process pieces, as well as to Jackson Pollock's borrowing from the technique of the Navajo sand painters to pour paint onto canvas.

During the mid-1970s, conceptual installations continued to occupy Chihuly's attention even as he pursued learning more about glass and its properties as a medium. At Artpark in Lewiston, New York, in 1975, he set transparent colored glass panes precariously on rock ledges in the shadows of a nearby river. That year he also received a National Endowment for the Arts grant, which permitted him to develop the work he had begun in Santa Fe. He had used the inspiration of Navajo blanket weaving to create glass cylinders decorated with woven-patch design patterns. In these, he laid out shards and threads of colored glass on a flat surface and then rolled a molten glass cylinder over them, fusing them into its surface. The result was a hybrid, a glass object that suggested the texture of woven blankets.

In the summer of 1977, Native American art once more inspired an important series of works. The *Navajo Blanket Cylinders* led to the series of *Pilchuck Baskets,* influenced by Northwest Coast Indian baskets. Chihuly recalls, "The *Baskets* turned out to be one of the best ideas I have ever had. I had seen some beautiful Indian baskets at the Washington State Historical Society, and I was struck by the grace of the slumped, sagging forms. I wanted to capture this grace in glass. The breakthrough for me was recognizing that heat was the tool to be used with gravity to make these forms . . . sagging under their own weight."

Like many artists with roots in the sixties, Chihuly works in series and uses permutations to add variety. The step from hard to soft cylinders was an obvious one to take next. The collapsed cylinders of the *Pilchuck Baskets* parallel Eva Hesse's work in fiberglass. They are vulnerable and humanized forms. The *Pilchuck Baskets* were exhibited at the Renwick Gallery in Washington, D.C., in 1978. They were the last works Chihuly would make by himself. That year he dislocated his shoulder and could no longer be the gaffer, who holds the long pipe through which the glass is blown into a hollow shape. In 1980, Chihuly began the extended series of *Seaforms,* which brought a new dimension of complexity and creativity to his growing repertoire. He also made large-scale, acid-etched, handblown stained-glass windows for the Shaare Emeth Synagogue in St. Louis, his last conventionally armatured works.

In the *Seaforms,* Chihuly's attraction to bizarre candy-cane swirling patterns begins to take over and introduce a baroque and expansive element to the work. The embedded glass wraps expand in ripples suggesting a shell or flower that could be indefinitely distended. The object loses its sense as a vessel and begins to spread and enlarge into swelling open surfaces, rather than the closed contained vessels associated with traditional glass works.

In 1981, Chihuly began the *Macchia* series. *Macchia* is the Italian word for spot, and the works were enlivened by brilliant patches of color pressed or laid into glass in an Impressionist fashion. As the series of *Macchia* developed, the forms grew larger and more colorful, as well as more elaborate and extended.

In 1986 he began the extended series known as the *Persians,* because of the richly patterned decorative effects reminiscent of Persian carpets and manuscripts. These were eccentrically shaped objects encrusted with color, which he thought of as excavated ancient treasures. The series was shown at the Musée des Arts Décoratifs, at the Louvre in Paris, adding luster to Chihuly's growing European reputation. At first, the *Persians* involved the contrast between two colors and between open and closed forms. They were striped and stippled with color as rich and intense as that of Fabergé eggs, whose luxuriousness they echoed.

Important commissions, such as the 1987 *Rainbow Room Frieze* at Rockefeller Center, followed. With growing confidence and experience as well as expertise and skill, Chihuly returned to Murano again in 1988. In a blow at his new VandeKamp hotshop he began the series of *Venetians* with master glassblower Lino Tagliapietra. The *Venetians* were originally inspired by a private collection of exquisite Venetian art deco vases. The series was continued into the following year when Chihuly collaborated with Pino Signoretto, who enlivened the pieces by adding *putti* and other figurative and filigree elements to the *Venetians.*

The success of these and other works gave Chihuly the means to purchase and renovate the Pocock Building—known to one and all as The Boathouse—on Lake Union, realizing his lifelong dream of having a studio on the water in Seattle. The work at The Boathouse is difficult and demanding, and Chihuly is up at 5:00 A.M. to oversee his state-of-the-art glassblowing facility. There any fantasy can be realized.

Transformations began to occur with the placement of all of Chihuly's pieces. The first *Persian* groups were removed from pedestals and placed on shelves. Then came wall pieces. In later versions of the *Persians,* the forms became room-size installations. David Bourdon saw these as flamboyant corsages with "ornate edges all but alive with potential movement." Chihuly has said that he is as interested in the way his art works in a space as in the art itself. In 1988, an installation at Chancellor Park in La Jolla combined shelf groupings with wall-mounted pieces.

Gradually the smaller pieces disappeared, and the groupings became more and more expansive and fantastical. In a 1992 wall-collage installation at Union Bank Center in Seattle, the original elements were enlarged, hybridized, and permuted as if they were evolving and growing like living organisms. The *Persians* had first moved to the floor for a 1991 Kyoto, Japan, installation and then extended to the windows and a ceiling for Chihuly's one-man exhibition at the Seattle Art Museum in 1992. Eventually, that same year, the *Persians* were transformed into site-specific window collages, sixteen by sixteen feet in size, for the Little Caesar's corporate world headquarters in Detroit.

The move from the object to the environment was inevitable for Chihuly, given his early experiments in site-specific installations. The tension of the contradiction between the fragile material and the exigencies of the public project became a dramatic encounter. His glass installations began to have a life of their own, like radiating tropical foliage or exotic flowers. Chihuly made dizzying varieties of *Persians*. Gradually they became room-size installations. Their shaded and expansive lips suggested vulval and erotic shell forms enhanced by the psychedelic rippling effects implicit in Murano techniques of striation. The 1994 window piece in Tacoma's Union Station, titled *Monarch Window,* acknowledges this inspiration.

In his uninterrupted creativity, Chihuly seems completely unself-conscious, permitting creation to flow with Dionysian abandon. The later environments make us feel we are lost in the repetitive elements. The psychedelic perceptual overload induces the hypnotic delirium of Persian and Islamic art. The butterfly wing striations become persistent repeated patterns like the tiles in the Turkish mosque of Hagia Sofia. In 1995, the *Persians* grew into an overhead pergola, as if the carpet had been decontextualized to become a ceiling. A cross between a chandelier and an Islamic carved ceiling decoration, the work is wildly extravagant and disorienting.

Matisse, of course, was inspired by the lush sensual decorativeness of Persian miniatures, but his wish to return to the world of *luxe, calme, and volupté* was doomed by the modernist consciousness that paradise was forever lost, doomed by the industrialism that is only now beginning to challenge the far woods of the American Northwest. Thus, Manet's *Luncheon on the Grass* is a picture not of an innocent picnic but of an already lost paradise. The men in business suits are uncomfortably and self-consciously aware that the naked ladies are a momentary diversion, not part of a timeless ride to the island of Cythera, where pleasure is permanent.

We are reminded in Chihuly's installations, and especially in the overhead *Chandeliers,* of both the stalactites and stalagmites of natural caves, as well as of the dazzling decorated ceilings of the Moorish Alhambra. In Western art, only medieval stained glass comes close to the totalizing effect of Mozarabic and Islamic decorations. The decorative effects of Islamic art, which break up light and space on ceiling, domes, and corners and use tile and plaster to create totally encompassing physical environments, are clearly the inspiration for the *Persians*.

Because of the hybridized and synthesized quality as well as the totalizing effect of his art, it is a mistake to see Chihuly as a continuation of the tradition of French or American art nouveau glass. Actually, he is the opposite of Louis Comfort Tiffany, who made glass in the medieval tradition enclosed in a metal armature, or even for that matter of Frank Lloyd Wright, whose glass pieces were exclusively decorative additions to his architecture. Both used glass in flat planes. The small-scale domestic objects produced by the Arts and Crafts movement were in fact quite the contrary of Chihuly's extravagant spectacles and theatrical pageants. In the end, his work has little to do with the history of glass, everything to do with the crisis in avant-garde art after the death of Jackson Pollock.

We have remarked that the modernist emphasis on the process of making was one of Chihuly's initial preoccupations. Chihuly, however, takes the intrinsic properties of glass—its change of state from hot liquid to cold solid, its molten liquidity and its fragility that normally require it to be small in scale, and its history as a useful vessel—and subverts them. The molten and liquid character of glass is preserved in the forms he creates, which are not the perfect molds of vessels but rather records of what glass has undergone in its making.
The unpredictable, distorted, and asymmetrically irregular forms are a reaction of the material to the conditions of its production. When the spontaneous extrusion is solidified, it becomes like the action painter's brushstroke, caught

in media res. The cooling and hardening into form parallel the process by means of which the liquidity of the paint dries on the canvas, fixing gesture into permanent form.

The improvisation that creates these distended and hybrid forms, stretching glass to its physical and formal limits as well, requires quick reflexes and perfect timing. The spontaneous effects involve a high level of risk. This means that, as in Pollock's poured paintings, mistakes result in lost works, which cannot be retrieved through correction. Such a process communicates a sense of freshness and instantaneous creation that the contemporary sensibility, rooted in experiences of speed, appears to require.

Chihuly's glass works bear a curious relationship to the crisis in painting that Pollock's allover paintings provoked. Pollock's wish to render the ground transparent so that the image appeared to hover in space eventually led him to paint on glass. Pollock's use of aluminum paint and glass shards in his paintings (which dramatized and emphasized the literal qualities of reflective surfaces) ultimately led artists such as Donald Judd and Larry Bell to abandon painting in favor of three-dimensional objects in which color, form, and material were married as they are in Chihuly's pieces.

The path to a new kind of public art that addresses viewers directly without critical intervention and outside the museum context begins with earthworks, which got art out of the museums into the landscape, and with Pop Art, which spoke in the language of the people. Pop Art avoided elitist art theory, a mannerist activity embraced by conceptual art that aspired to the approbation of the academy to confer prestige and status. Like the best public artists, Chihuly has a healthy disdain for the arcane meandering of art theory and its pretentious "discourse" that excludes the uninitiated. His attitude is reminiscent of that of the sixteenth-century Spanish artist Diego de Hollanda, who returned from Italy to describe the obscurity of mannerist art theory as an activity that "quebrantan las cabezas"—gives you a headache.

The failure of most public art is that it speaks in a subjective and elitist language the public does not understand and to which, as a consequence, it is overtly hostile. Chihuly's art shares the most basic concerns of abstraction—

color, light, form, and space. However, its subliminal references to shells, coral and crystal formations, butterflies, birds, and undersea marine life make it more accessible to the public than abstraction.

The inclusive relationship of Chihuly's art to historical style and form may well identify it with postmodernism, as Donald Kuspit persuasively argues. The central issue of postmodernism is neither appropriation nor reproduction but an attitude toward styles that is transhistorical as well as transcultural. Certainly its excess and extravagance define it as aggressively post-minimalist. Against the severe, geometric, closed gestalt volumes of minimal art, Chihuly pits the open forms and transparencies of glass blown into isomorphic shapes and liquid patterns. Gorgeousness is involved in the gold and silver iridescence and the luxurious ornamentation of the *Venetians*.

As several critics have pointed out, however, the exotic forms sometimes portend danger; the strangeness suggests the uncanny or the perverse. Chihuly's forms pushed to their most bizarre extremes remind us of the overripe lushness of the vegetation in the opening scene of David Lynch's *Blue Velvet*, because their color is artificial rather than natural and their size is colossal. The large-scale *Macchia*, like unnatural giant flowers, are as artificial and oversized as American agricultural produce when they are scattered across lawns.

The gorgeousness and luxurious ornamentation of the *Venetians* can go so far as to be over the top. According to Jack Cowart, "One cannot enjoy his opulent *Seaform* shells of color, bulbous *Chandeliers* or exquisite extrusions and tendrils without a subliminal recollection of a floating world of stinging nettles, poisonous Portuguese men-of-war and other otherworldly dangers." The exaggerated voluptuousness of these forms may become deadly and turn them into repulsive Flowers of Evil.

Despite his directorial role, Chihuly has a one-to-one relationship with what he creates. These are his forms, created by him in drawings and paintings and then translated into glass by the team he oversees. Unlike Tiffany, Gallé, and Lalique, the names associated with the art nouveau glass produced by the craft revival movement in the nineteenth century, Chihuly does not use standardized molds that permit reproduction. His creations depend on spontaneity

and on-the-spot decisions. They are created with the freedom to improvise of Surrealist automatic drawings and are also perverse and precarious, given the way glass is blown and takes on its permanent shape, changing from molten liquid into hard, transparent substance. His wildly imaginative assemblages are not dysfunctional objects, they are nonfunctional—in other words, useless. And this is precisely why they are art, not craft.

Henry Geldzahler was right to see Chihuly's work as distinctively "American in its vulgarity, its brazenness, and its fearlessness to move farther out west even if there is no further west to move to." Chihuly's modernism expresses itself not as hostility but as perverse subversion. His strategies of subversion are as brilliant as his ability to keep pace in a parallel way with the essential changes in fine art, while rejecting the narrow academic theoretical concerns that alienate the broad public. His is the bravura of the virtuoso, the rare talent of the prodigy.

Chihuly is constantly searching for new challenges. In 1993, he received an important commission to do the sets for the Debussy opera *Pelléas and Mélisande,* to be performed in Seattle. The project became an impressionistic installation of rippling fabric sheets appropriate to Debussy's score. In 1996, the tour de force *Chihuly Over Venice* installation of weighty *Chandeliers* suspended at various sites throughout the canal-dotted city was a celebration of unprecedented daring and accomplishment. Kuspit describes the huge celebratory installation as a "grand recapitulative climax of his works . . . a self-apotheosis, a Venetian orgasm."

Chihuly seems bedeviled by a drive to push both his material and himself to extremes. One project involves four colossal sculptures for the Atlantis Resort on Paradise Island in the Bahamas. The *Crystal Gate,* a twenty-foot-high glass tower that defies gravity, consists of more than three thousand handblown crystals magically fused together. The *Temple of the Sun,* made of brilliant hot yellow, orange, and red elements, forms one side. It is flanked by the *Temple of the Moon,* which is colored cobalt blue and opalescent white. Nearby hangs the *Atlantis Chandelier,* an immense glass assemblage of writhing tentacles reminiscent of the jellyfish and sea anemones that live in the waters of the Caribbean below.

Walter Darby Bannard had it right when he described Chihuly's achievement: "Like most good art objects, Chihuly's works are often liked or disliked for the wrong reasons. So take them for what they are; take them as glass. This is glass that has had things done to it no other glass has, glass made on its own terms as viscous liquid which likes to be blown out, attenuated, pressed, slumped, stretched, twisted, perforated, laden with color, fused, and melted. Chihuly has mastered glass by yielding to it, by discovering and accepting what it is rather than deciding what it should be."

Unique in that he transcends the narrowness of the avant-garde without totally ignoring where it is going and where it has been, Dale Chihuly speaks directly to people in a vernacular they understand without interpretation. Yet his work is neither simplistic nor condescending. Its aesthetic sophistication equal to its technical mastery, his work stands as an example of art that does not sacrifice quality for popularity.

The Public Voice by Dale Lanzone

"The eye sees only what the mind
is prepared to comprehend."
Henri Bergson

Historically, changes in social, political, and religious beliefs have resulted in parallel changes in the production of public art. These changes can be temporal (as from one decade to the next) or geographic (community to community, city to city, state to state, country to country). Ethnic and religious groups may simultaneously occupy the same geographic territory, for example, yet have significantly different belief systems, values, and cultural production.

The dramatic shifts and changes in the public presentation of art from its Neolithic beginnings to the present, and the constant struggle to invent new modes of cultural production, have attracted our attention and informed us in surprising and often unpredictable ways. The "allowed" and "prohibited" meanings that are directly or indirectly expressed through a public work of art form a complex composition of ideas incorporating dreams, ambitions, myths, and fears—the many nuances of the objective and subjective self as a public entity. Works of art are necessarily encoded with the intelligence, vision, and resonating will of the dominant influences of their time.

Emerging from the Enlightenment, the modern world struggled to be free from the vestiges of nineteenth-century social and cultural norms. This struggle was active and highly critical in its approach to history. By the late eighteenth century, the forces of democratic and social idealism were revolutionizing European and American political, social, and economic life. This new, overtly critical activist movement enabled new modes of cultural expression challenging the hegemony of long-held European social and cultural traditions defined by orthodoxy and protectionism. Through the ascendancy of democratic modes of thinking, critical activism in the arts and sciences became institutionalized to the degree that the practice of freedom and those conditions enabling critical activism became one and the same.

The social and cultural practice of making art and placing it in public places has from America's colonial past to the present been a challenging and often controversial enterprise. During the colonial period, figurative monuments that commemorated the deeds of British military heroes and celebrated the power and authority of the monarchy were the order of the day. Communities, associations, and important individuals commissioning public monuments or commemorative sculpture looked to England for sculptors. The colonies were far too young and raw culturally and economically to support such a discrete artisan practice. As evinced by the vandalization and eventual removal of English artist Joseph Wilton's sculpture of King George III by New York City colonists during the American Revolution, commemorative monuments signifying British power and authority were ultimately rejected by the American colonists.

Following the American Revolution, the new republic embarked upon its own public art enterprise in much the same way and for similar purposes as had the British. With few exceptions—such as the allegorical sculptures of Comedy and Tragedy (1808) by William Rush that adorn Philadelphia's Chestnut Street Theatre—this period in American history produced monuments and statues by first-generation professional American sculptors such as Rush, Horatio Greenough, and Hiram Powers that commemorated Revolutionary military accomplishments and honored national heroes. Inspired by the dignity and grace of neoclassicism, sculptures of this period were held in high esteem by the public. Many of these works were the focal points for special honors and tributes during annual foundation celebrations and were used as scenographic backdrops for grand public events. This was the beginning of a golden age for public art in America.

Through the energetic development of abundant natural resources and a political and social commitment to industrialization, nation-building intensified and a public art followed that reflected the character and ardor of America's new vision of Manifest Destiny. In 1864, sculpture as a means of expressing American values and vision found formal public support from the U.S. Congress with the passage of legislation introduced by Justin Smith Morrill of Strafford, Vermont, to create a National Hall of Statuary in the former chambers of the U.S. House of Representatives. Such official endorsement of sculpture led to the increased production of works of public art celebrating the aggressive social, economic, and political ideals and practices of nation-building. Public art became a significant means through which the nation could define and honor its belief in itself, both for the sake of its own identity and before a curious and watchful Europe.

The social, economic, and political ideals embodied in the concept of Manifest Destiny inspired a broad range of neoclassical, Beaux Arts, and new American naturalist works of public art. Works by such sculptors as Augustus Saint-Gaudens, Daniel Chester French, and Gertrude Whitney, all of whom produced statues, memorials, and architectural arts, populated American parks, plazas, halls of business, places of worship, government buildings, and private homes (some of which later became public museums).

This aggressive support for art in public places culminated with the presentation of the extraordinary national expositions that began in Chicago in 1893 and continued in Buffalo in 1901, St. Louis in 1904, and San Francisco in 1915. These exhibitions created grandiose venues for the installation of art in public places and grand thematic opportunities for artists to consider and interpret modern subjects such as energy, evolution, and race at a scale of production that has not been matched in this century. Fueled by the resonance of commonly understood figurative sculptural narratives, works of art created during this time continue to attract support and interest from the general public to this day and are often looked upon by public decision makers as the standard for greatness in American public art. Public works of art of this period idealized and affirmed the officially supported social, economic, and political doctrines of the time, thereby gaining broad-based public acceptance and support.

Following the First World War, the booming American industrial and capital markets led to an unprecedented growth in industrial and urban development. High-rise buildings and massive urban complexes reshaped the cityscape, and the new captains of industry and finance began building palaces of commerce to rival the great palaces of Europe. The streamlined, modernized sculpture of artists such as Gaston Lachaise, Paul Manship, and Elie Nadelman gained great favor in this new, energetic environment. The harsh social and economic realities of the Great Depression were still a decade away, and the highly stylized motifs of this new modern work were publicly acceptable in part because the work continued the trend in public art of affirming acceptable (even traditional) social and cultural ideals.

The Great Depression of 1929 gave voice to a new form of public art that began shortly before the first decade of the new century, with social realist sculptures by Abastenia St. Leger Eberle, Mahonri M. Young, Harry Wickey, and Bessie Potter Vonnoh. These artists depicted nonidealized, common activities and images of the common moments and circumstances of American life. This new social realism found no public patronage until the conditions of the Great Depression forced the emergence of a new populist art, expressing themes of economic, social, and political realism and bringing with it the emergence of a new voice—social criticism. The ideals of this new form celebrated the strength, trials, and tribulations of the common man and woman as the genuine bedrock of American life and values. The 1930s were a critical time in the development of an American artistic vocabulary and agenda bound to ideals of social, cultural, and racial equity. Of the numerous initiatives advanced by President Franklin D. Roosevelt to combat the nation's economic collapse, a series of programs managed through the successive Civil Works, Works Progress, and Work Projects Administrations created innovative opportunities for American artists to create works of art. Public sculptures, murals, easel paintings, photographs, and works of graphic art created under the auspices of these new "socially progressive" programs were placed in both permanent and temporary sites. They toured the nation's art centers, and in some cases they formed the basis for museum collections around the country. These publicly funded programs resulted in the largest public art enterprise in American history.

The last of the major Depression-era federal funding initiatives for support of the arts, the Works Projects Administration, was abolished in June 1943 following America's entry into World War II. Following the Second World War and the resultant destruction of Europe's industrial base, America's productive forces were unchallenged. America was a fully industrialized nation standing on much stronger footing than the war-ravaged European nations, whose industrial bases had to be rebuilt and modernized. The American drive to create a new, modern world that challenged and swept aside the institutions and values of the nineteenth and early twentieth centuries inspired the public to accept and even marvel at new forms and functions in architecture, transportation, mass communications systems, and entertainment. America's break from the past was purposeful and willful, and "newness" and modernity defined a category of cultural values that supported the consumption/production cycle necessary to sustain rapid economic growth and development. The words "new" and "modern" were used to suggest a world where the problems of the past had no future. In this same mode, the previous traditions and imperatives for public art that communicated social purposes and values were eschewed in favor of independent, forward-thinking expressions of bold, personal visions.

At its core, modernism is a critical enterprise given to both defining and solving problems. Beginning with the Enlightenment, it was assumed that through the objective application of technique and process, a solution could be devised for every problem. Through the application of intellect, hard work, and diligence, the problems of the past could be swept away and replaced by objective rational humanism. Modernism placed value on critically inspired formal structures, structures that devalued and often despised the social and cultural orthodoxies of the premodernist world.

Modernism in public art celebrated the independence of the inventive individual and romanticized willful creativity. New, modern works of art rapidly became signifiers of a community's or company's *modern* character, just as the artist became both an icon and an iconoclast, hero and antihero. Artists came to be viewed as courageous creators forging the conditions and terms of the new world—a world in which anything and everything was possible. Artists such as Alexander Calder, Jacques Lipchitz, Seymour Lipton, Louise Nevelson, Barnett Newman, Isamu Noguchi, and David Smith defined the terms of the new public art with their self-contained forms, embracing abstraction as a symbol for artistic "newness" apart from tradition and academicism. Concepts in modernism were expanded by such artists as Carl Andre, Larry Bell, Ronald Bladen, Dale Chihuly, Walter De Maria, Mark di Suvero, Dan Flavin, Nancy Graves, Robert Grosvenor, Michael Heizer, Ellsworth Kelly, Sol LeWitt, Robert Morris, Bruce Nauman, Claes Oldenburg, George Segal, Richard Serra, Tony Smith, Robert Smithson, and Keith Sonnier to encompass a range of individual interests and modes of expression as broad as phenomenal experience would allow.

Modernist theory and practice in public art of the 1950s through the late 1970s placed requirements of truth and integrity upon the production of works of art, directly contradicting the traditional public art modes of figurative representation and narrative idealism. A modernist sculpture's meaning was predicated upon the concrete experience of the material object, removed from the burden of expressing content or subject. A work of art could be a wholly personal experience whose "meaning" would be the same as the viewer's response to seeing and experiencing the work of art itself. Although on the surface this seems simple enough to digest, for a public long accustomed to experiencing works of art with clear, idealized sociopolitical content, such modernist object-based and non-narrative forms left viewers without the historical underpinnings to help them understand or know the work. The greatest and most creative achievements in modernist public sculpture were often the most misunderstood and maligned.

After fifty years of modernist dominance, decision makers grew suspicious of the modernist promise and weary of the pursuit of grand formal solutions to social, political, and economic problems. Beginning in the mid-1980s, both the general public and the decision makers began forcefully demanding a new iteration of "modern" art, requiring the reintegration of public art and public purpose.

We now live in an age of mass "realpolitik." Groups, organizations, even private individuals, regardless of their interests, can through the tenacious application of well-orchestrated criticism dramatically affect the course and outcome of public decision making. Our culture resonates with unpredictability, which has resulted in surprising new forms of social and political anxiety—public officials have become fearfully nervous and apprehensive in their decision making.

In today's poly-cultural, socially unaligned America, criticism has become the common mode of public discourse. Public activities and enterprises are as a matter of course critically deconstructed and repackaged as news or news entertainment by the broadcast and print media. With the recognition and acceptance that public projects automatically attract critical interest, public decision makers hesitate to support activities that are not approved by politically meaningful constituencies. Public decision makers view art as a risky investment for their political support, whereas criticizing the arts has proved to be universally politically advantageous.

The presentation of art for public purposes by public officials using public funds is a highly sensitive operation. Notwithstanding the inclusiveness of contemporary public art decision making, there are almost always forceful interests opposing public art with great conviction and intense moral indignation. Public art always carries with it the potential for political embarrassment; as such, decision makers search for guaranteed positive outcomes to their public art decisions. In response to this political vulnerability, officials are protective to the degree that selected works of art must predictably conform to the cultural and social standards of the recipient community and meet very specific publicly defined criteria—the public expectations for which are no surprises and a positive outcome.

To be consistently successful within this administratively complex and politically sensitive environment, the artist must have at his or her disposal an ever-expanding array of highly refined skills and abilities. Today's public decision makers require evidence of past positive performance: How many public projects has the artist completed? Have the artist's past public works received an overall positive response? Is the artist's creative process flexible? Does the artist present and work well with the public? Does the artist have the appropriate management and technical resources to bring a project to a successful conclusion? Is the artist an asset in terms of conflict resolution?

Artists such as Vito Acconci, Alice Aycock, Jonathan Borofsky, James Carpenter, Dale Chihuly, Houston Conwill, Mark di Suvero, Sam Gilliam, Richard Hass, Larry Kirkland, Maya Lin, Claes Oldenburg, Dennis Oppenheim, Tom Otterness, Beverly Pepper, Dorthea Rockburne, Jim Sanborn, Martha Schwartz, and Ned Smyth have in the past fifteen years successfully completed multiple public art projects in all geographic regions of the United States. Although the work of each of these artists is uniquely different in terms of content, medium, and style, what is similar is the overwhelming evidence of past positive performance in terms of both technical production and public response.

Each of the many projects completed by these artists has embedded purposes that service or engage the public in multifaceted ways—from the often humorous and challenging architectural environments of Vito Acconci to the highly tactile, visually invigorating glass sculptures of Dale Chihuly to the landmark scale of Jonathan Borofsky's and Mark di Suvero's work. All of these artists have been consistently competitive within the public art arena. The range of art represented in the work of these artists demonstrates an ever-increasing public interest and appetite for tactile experience, narrative and symbolic communication, and humor. As they have historically, public decision makers will continue to embrace art that elevates and refreshes the common moment of experience with a kernel of awe and wonder—some small magic that transforms the everyday eye and mind through the efforts and vision of another. Art that performs this function will receive encore after encore after encore in this public art medium—the most democratically expressive form of cultural production.

33 Projects

1

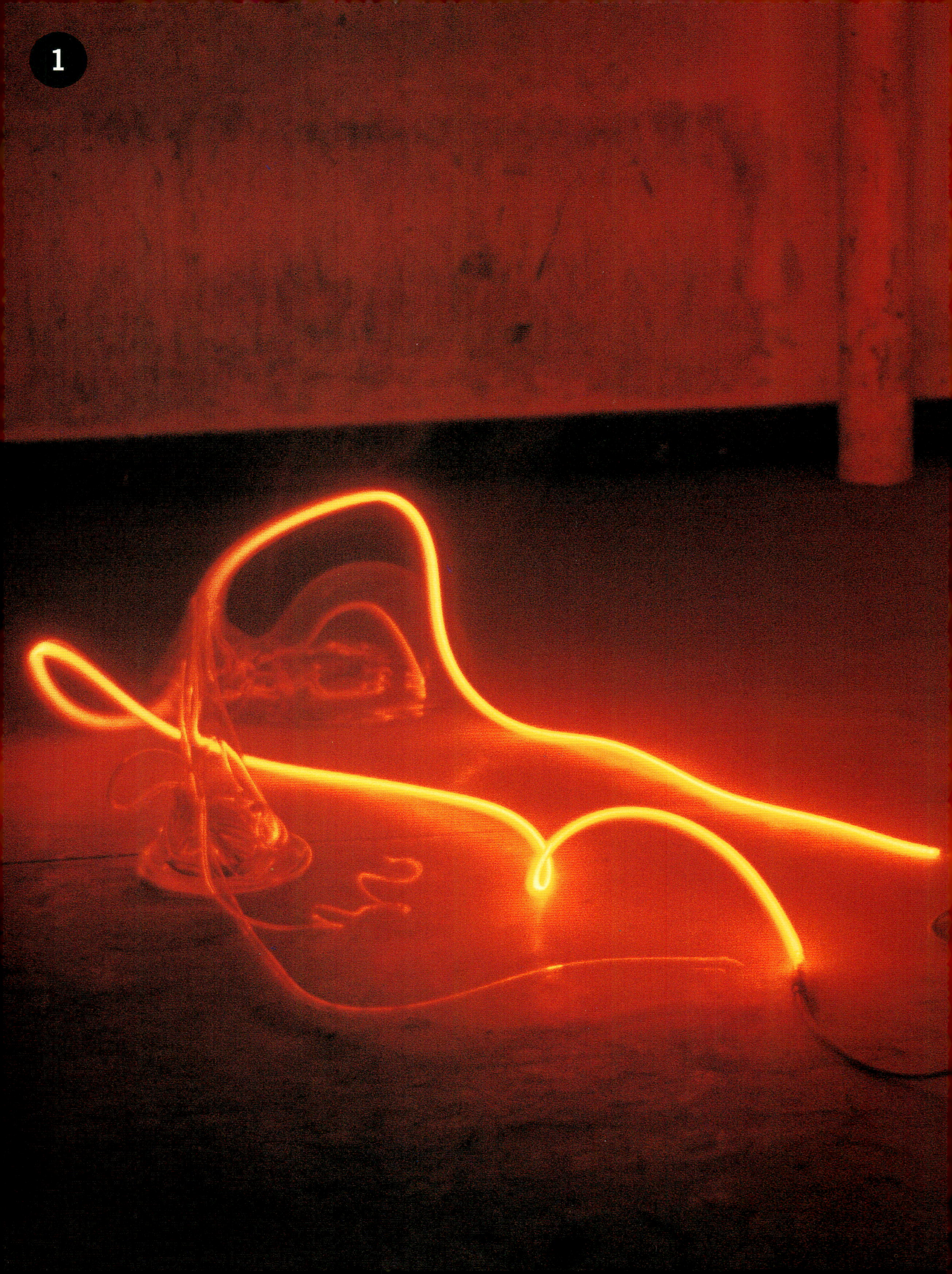

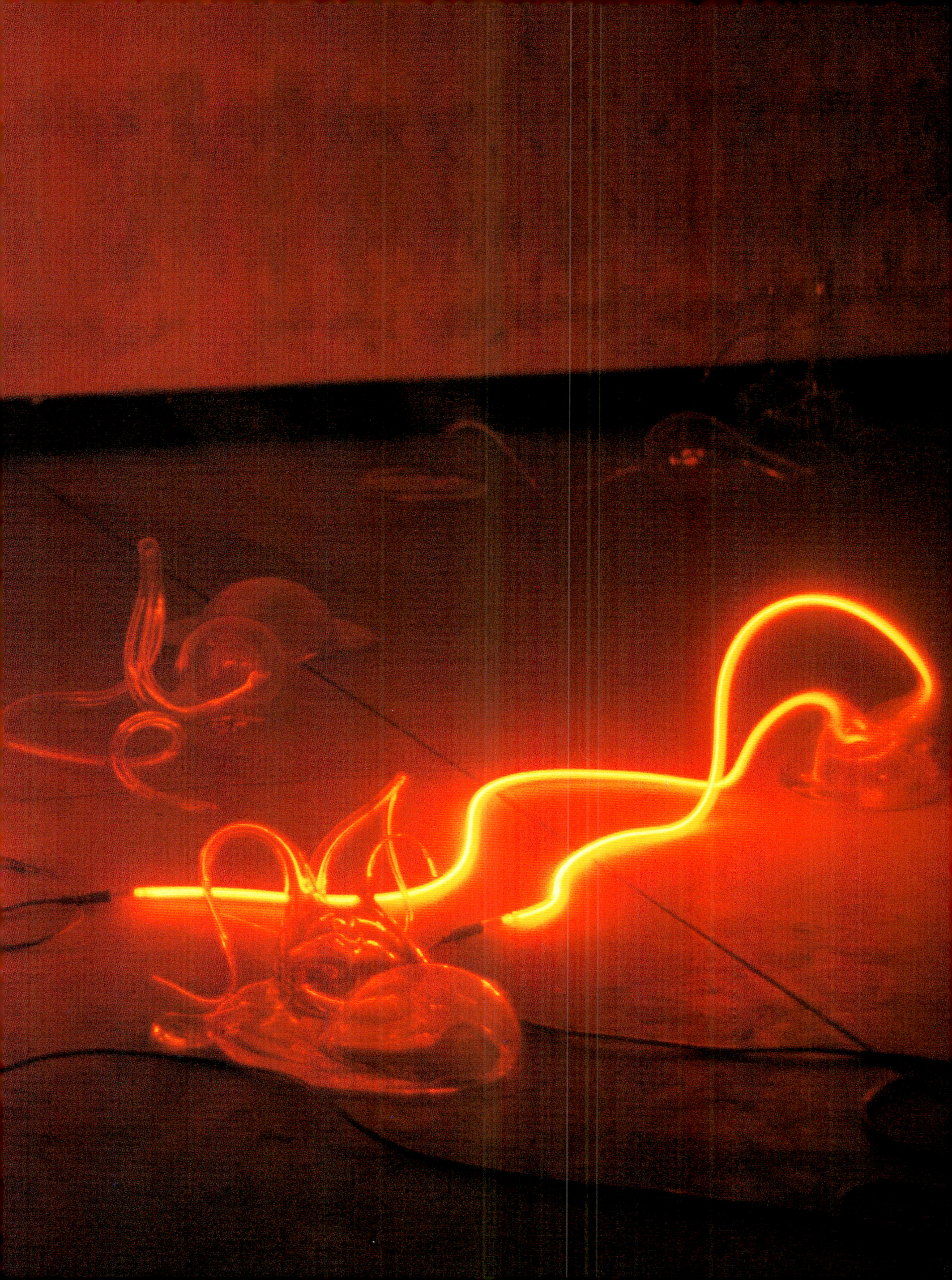

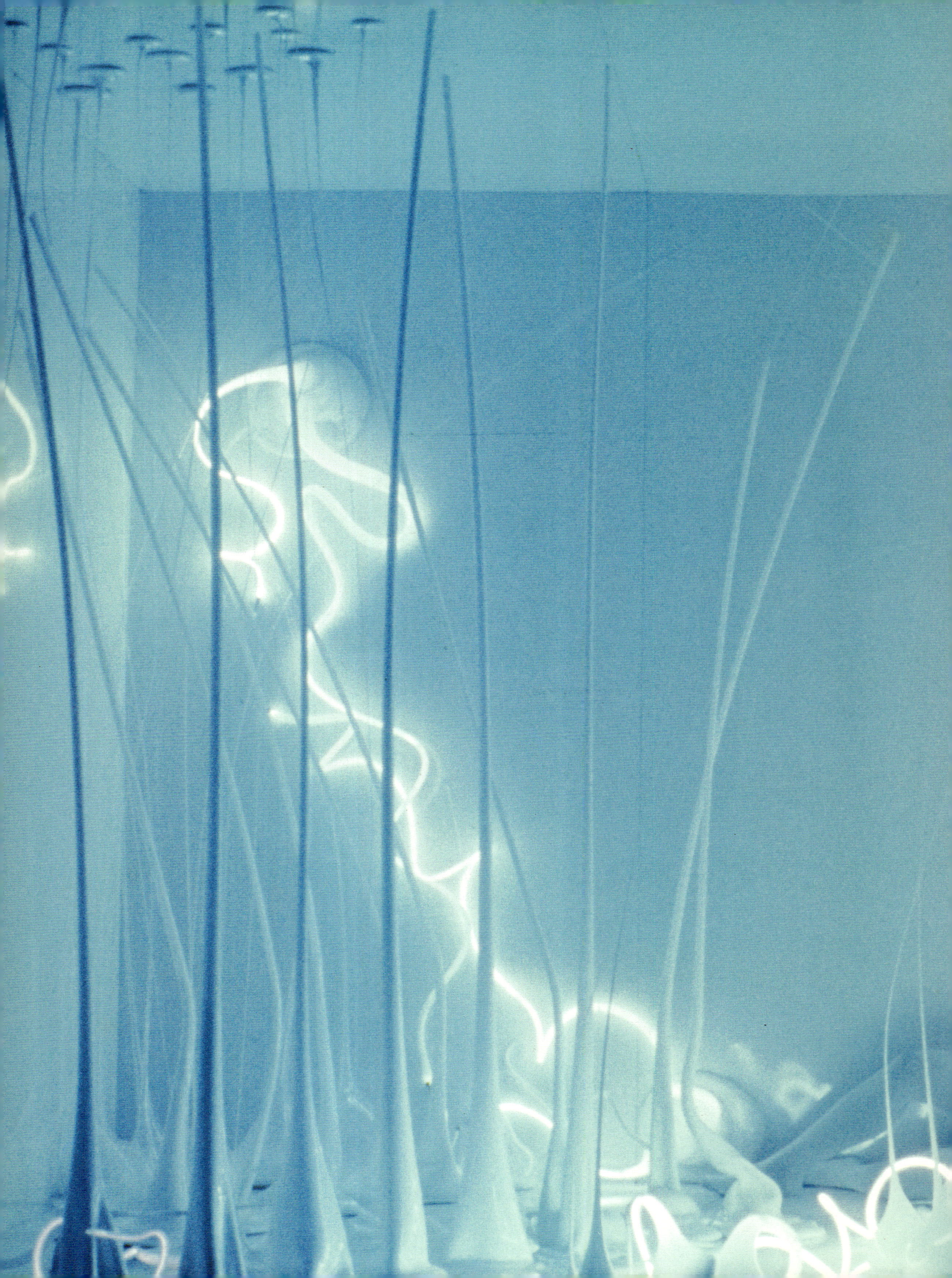

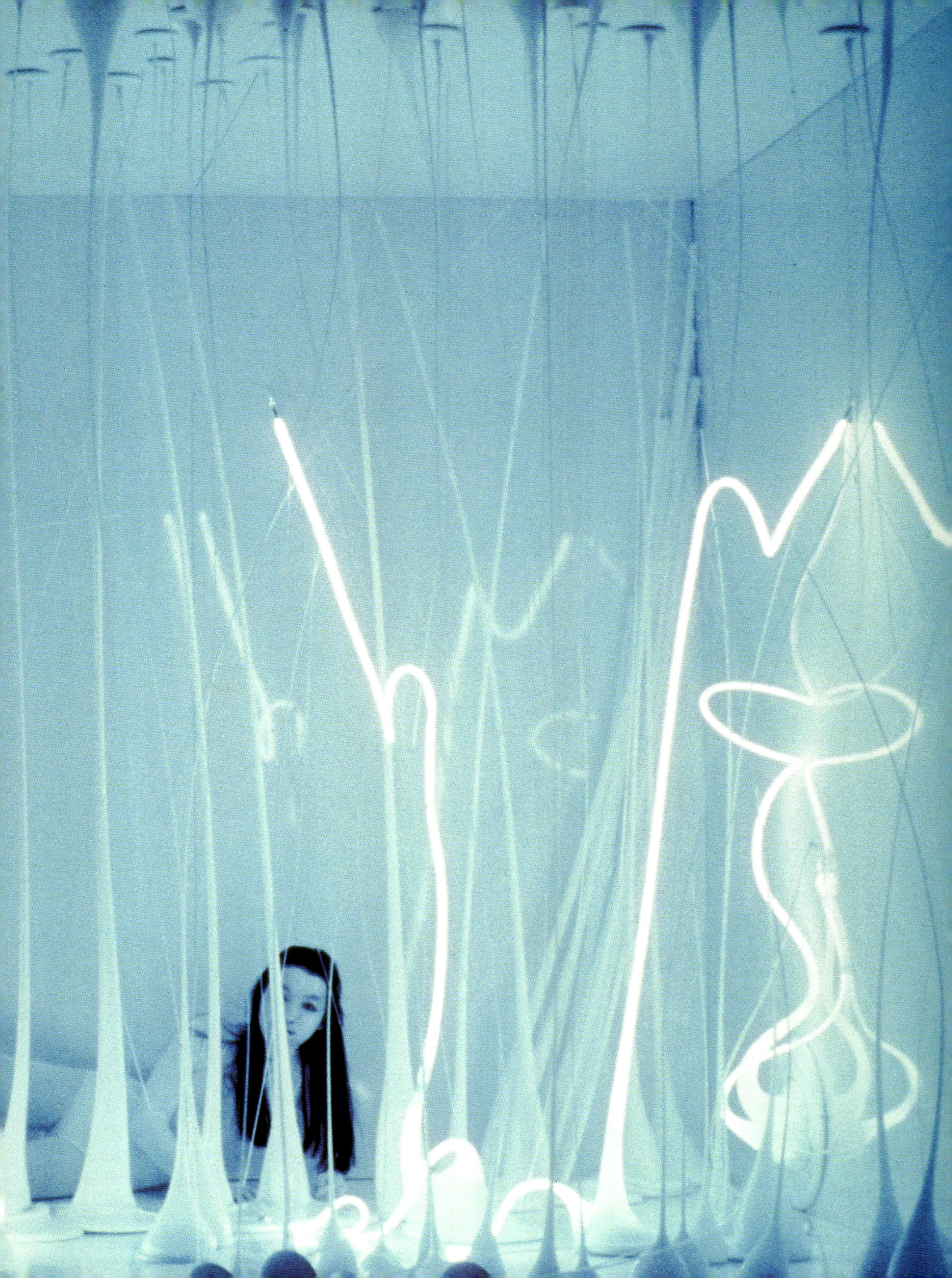

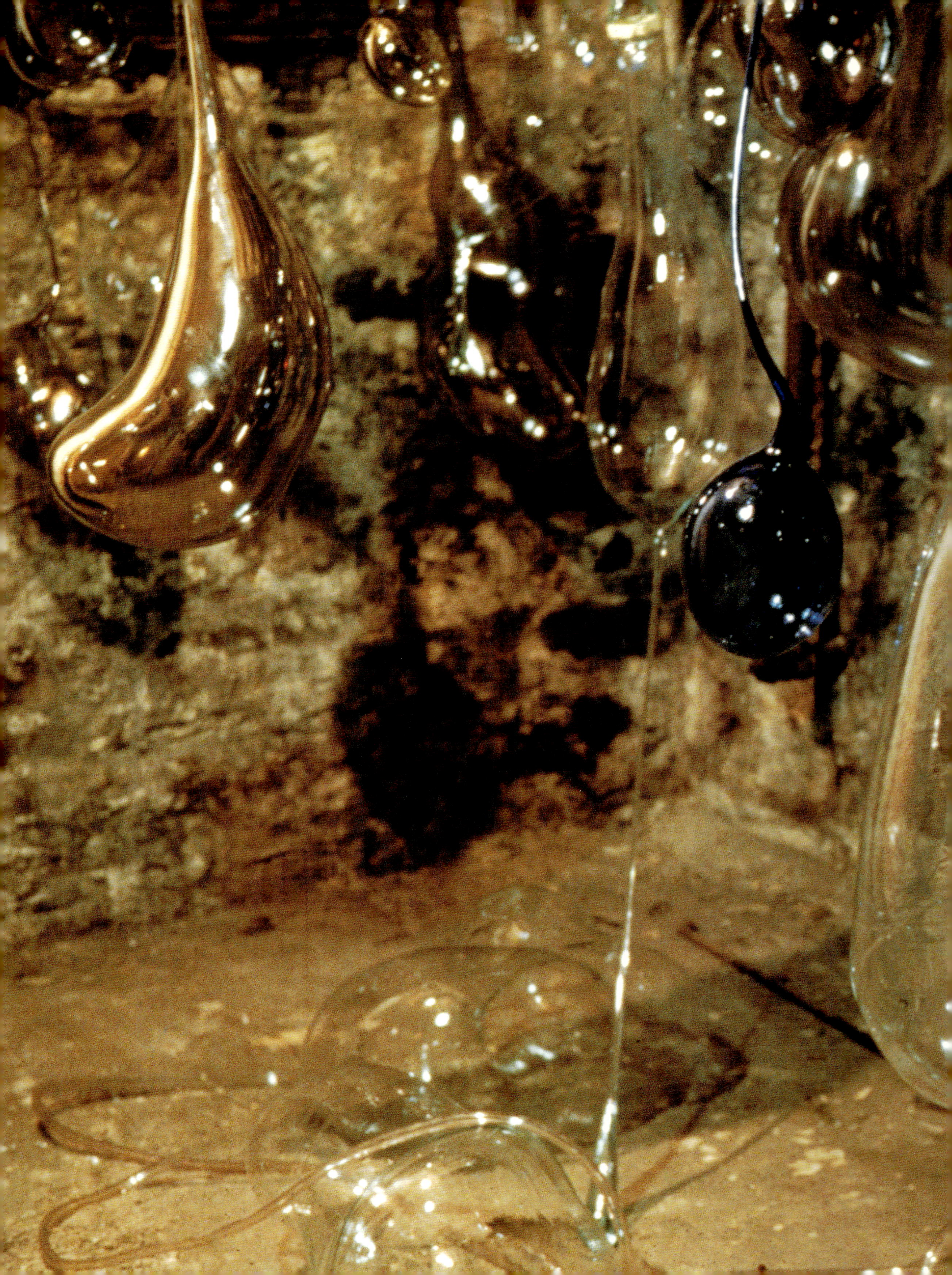

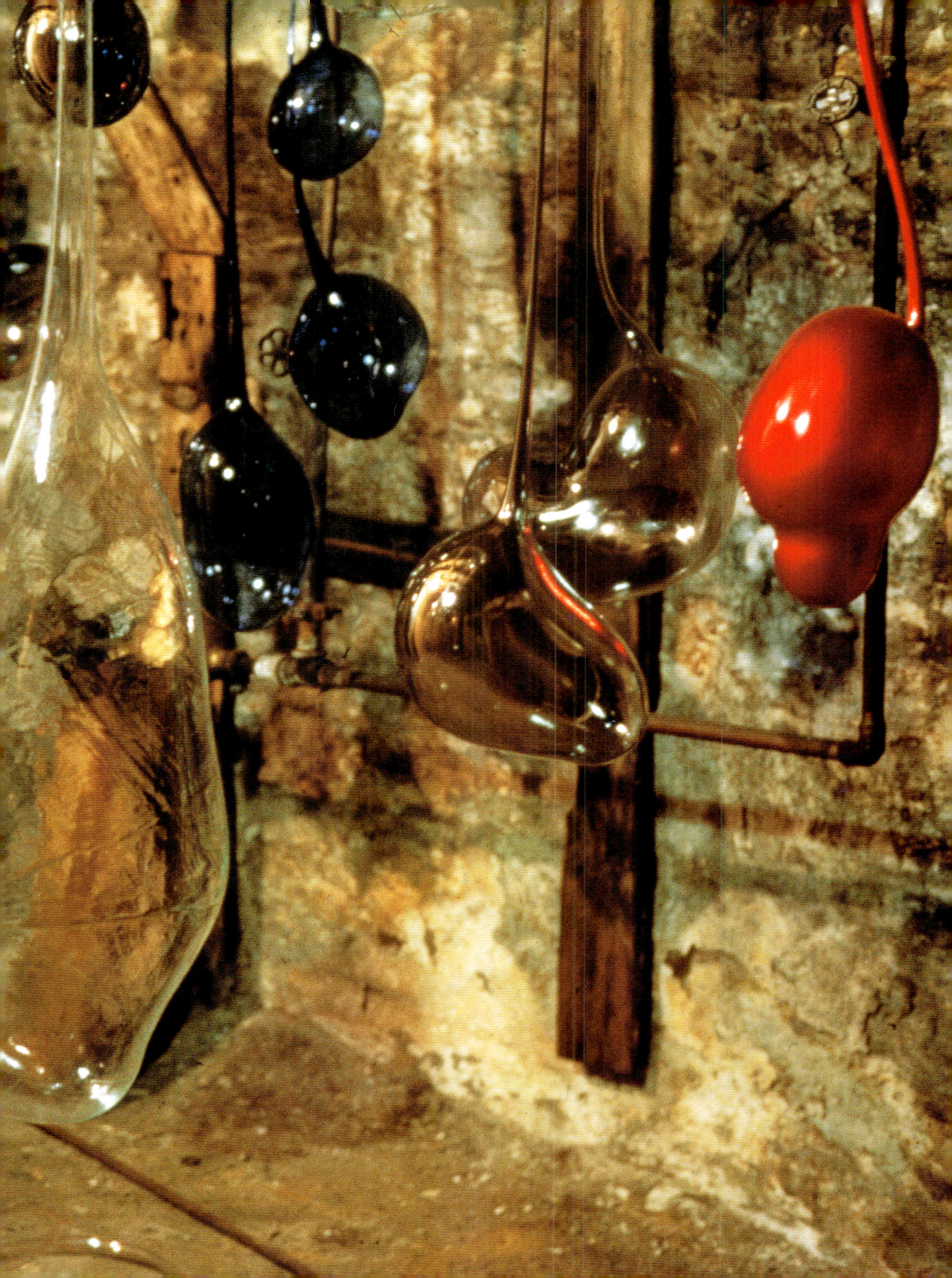

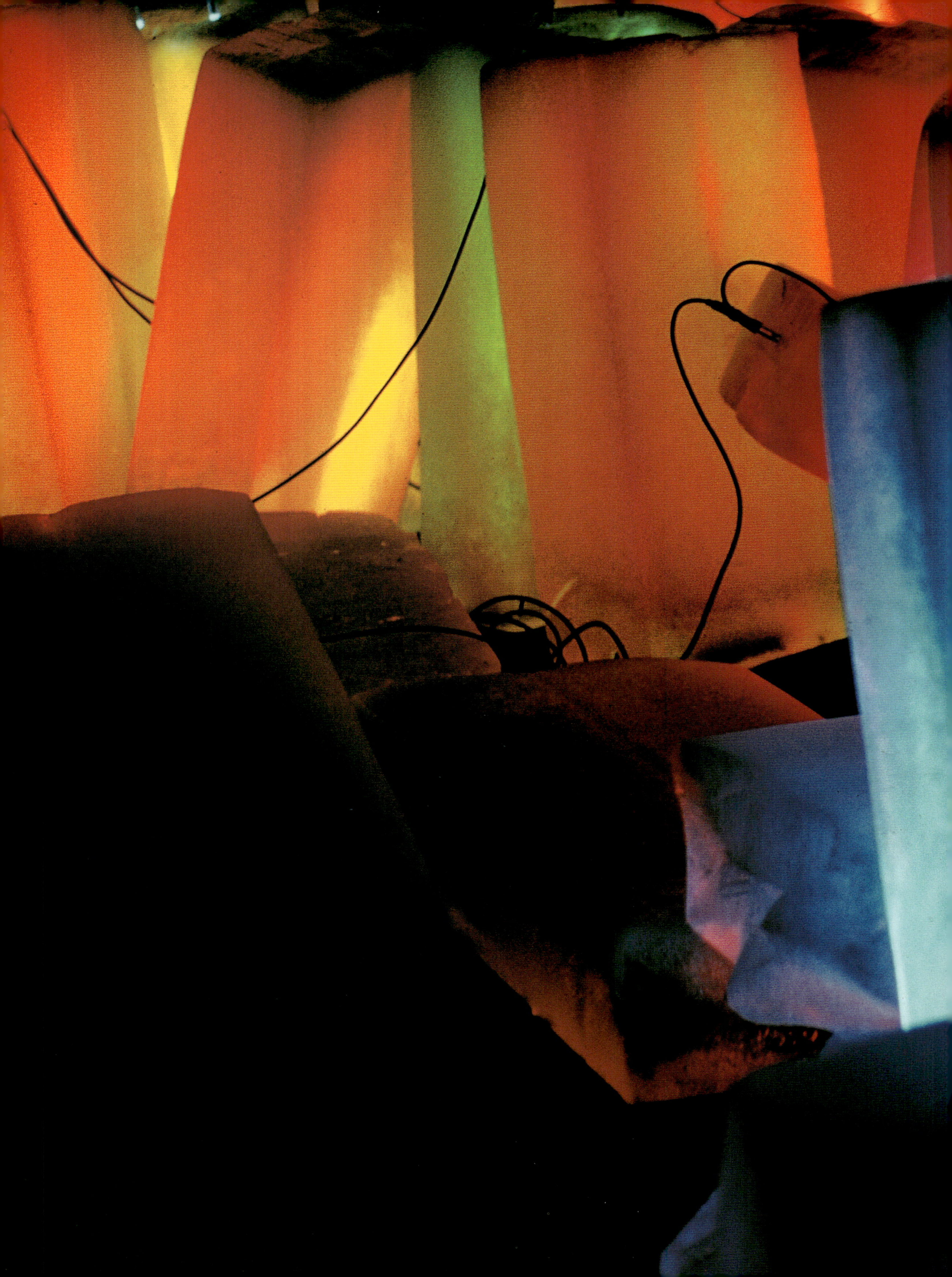

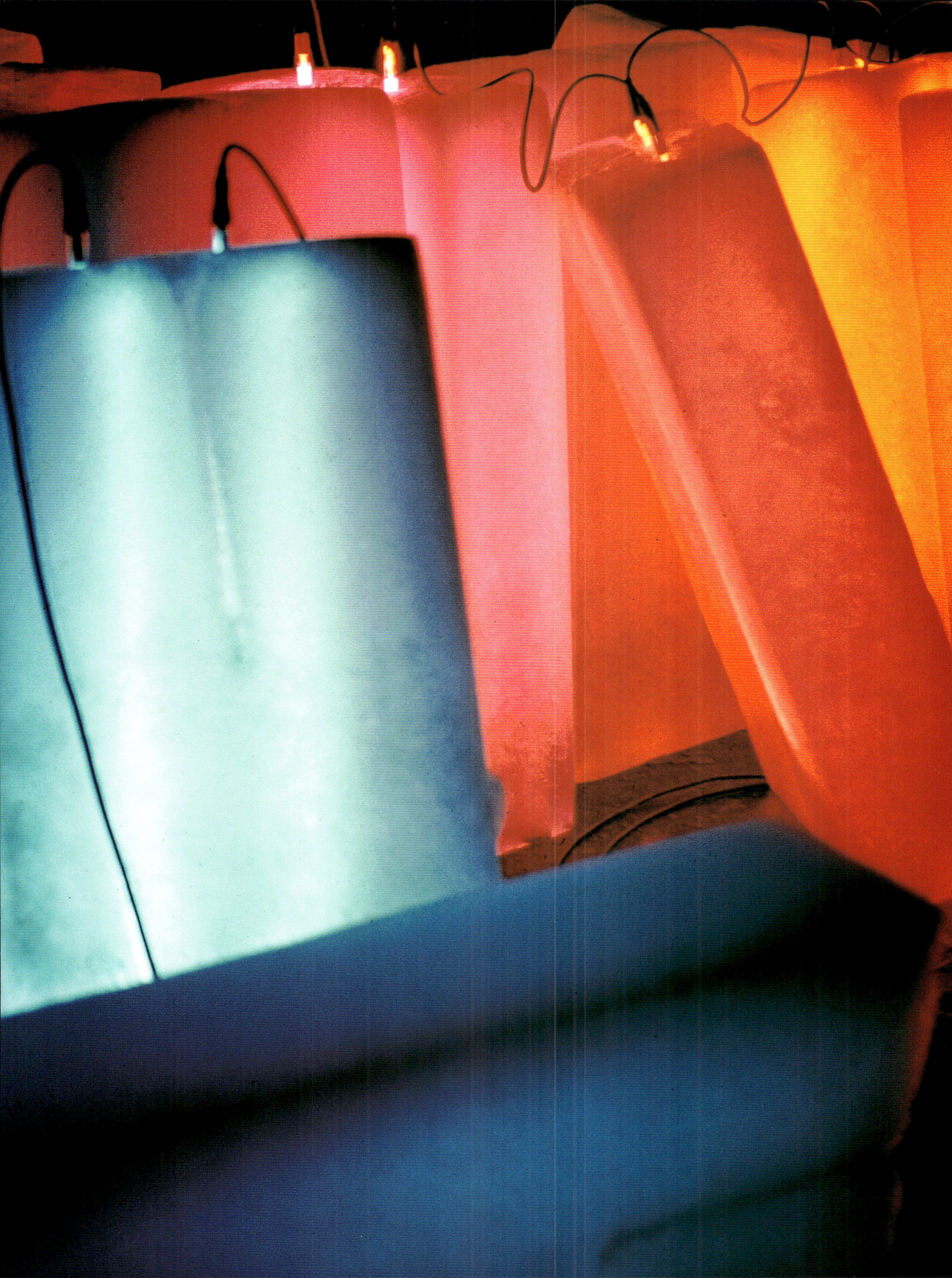

2

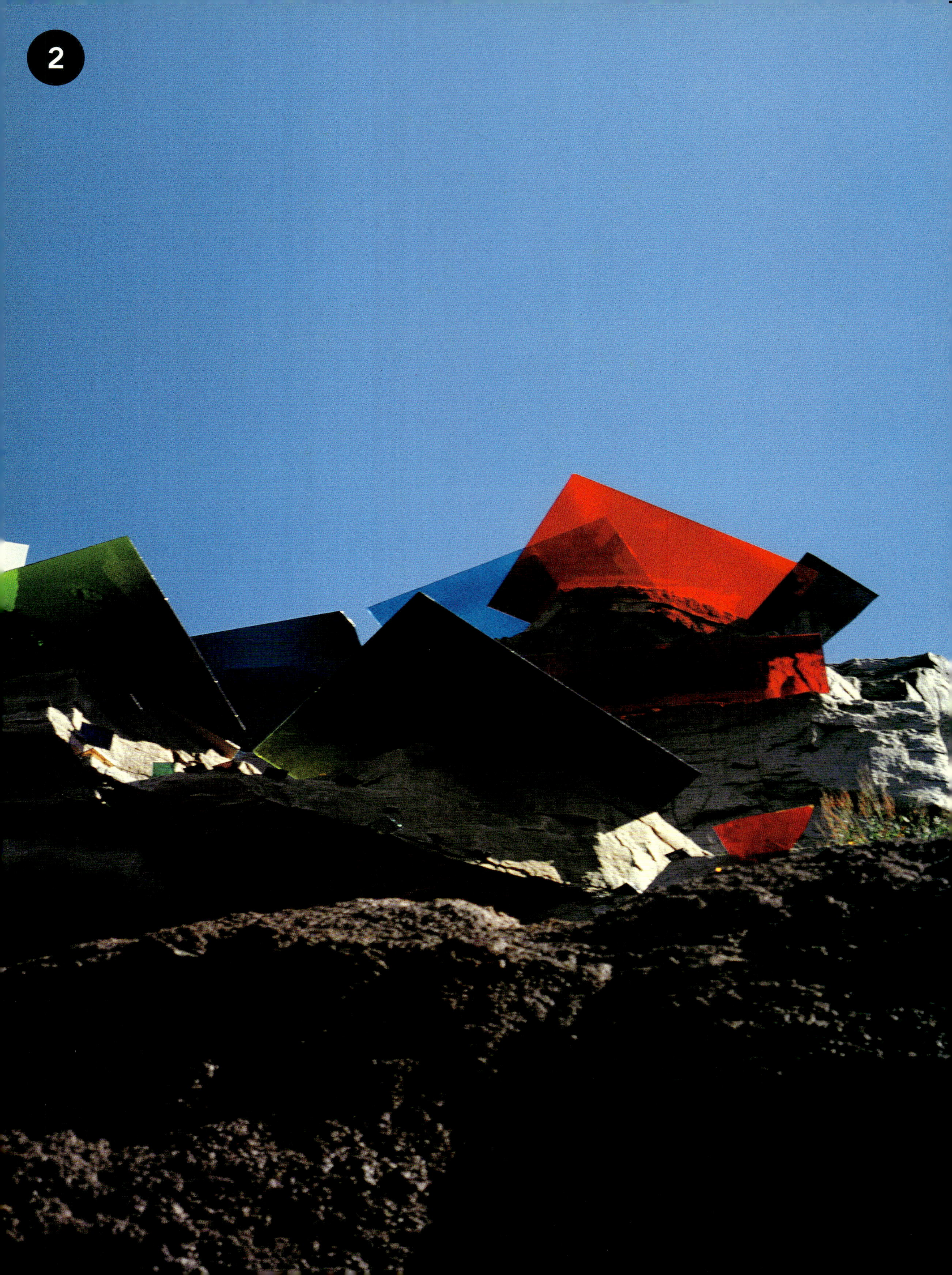

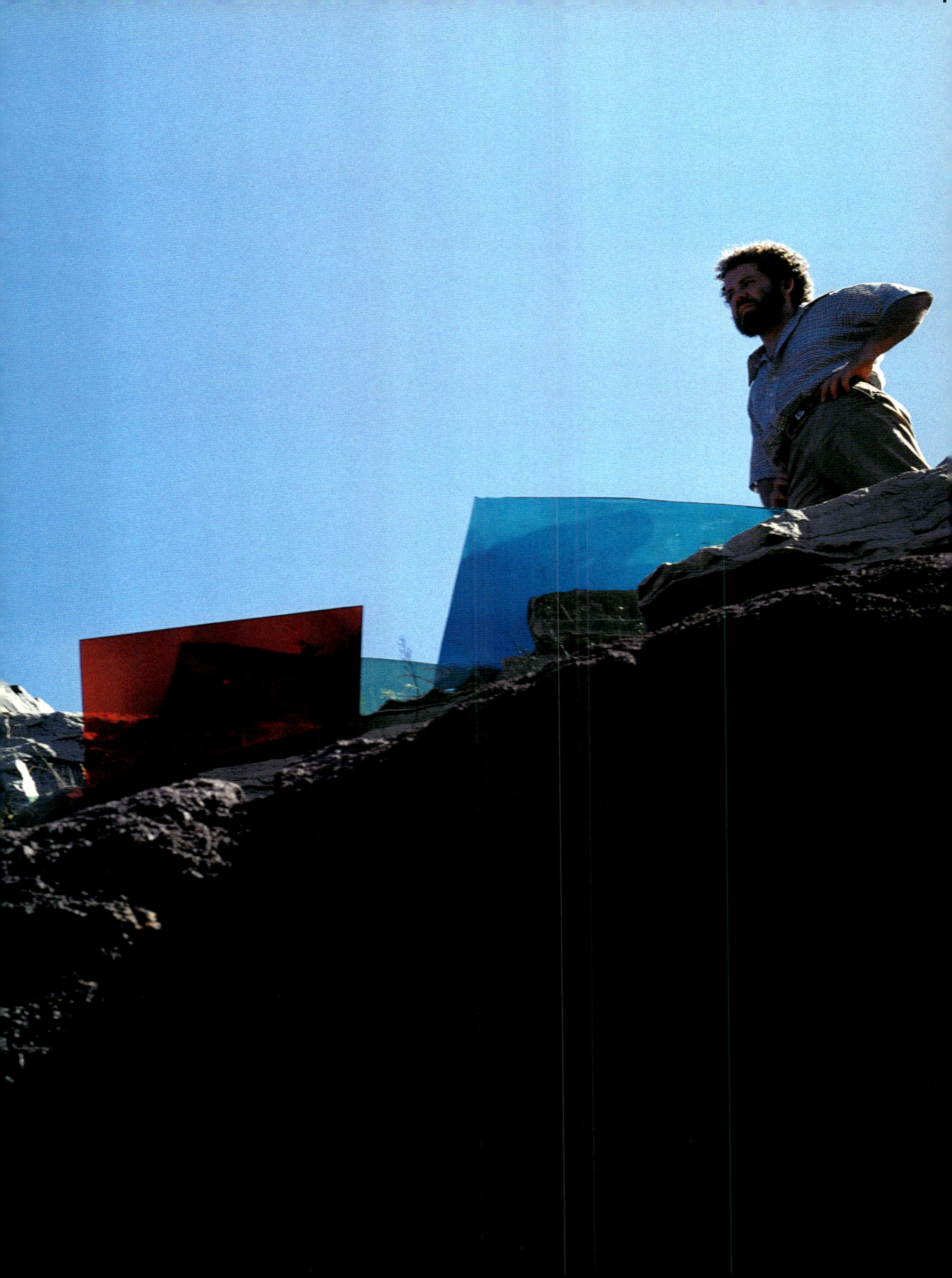

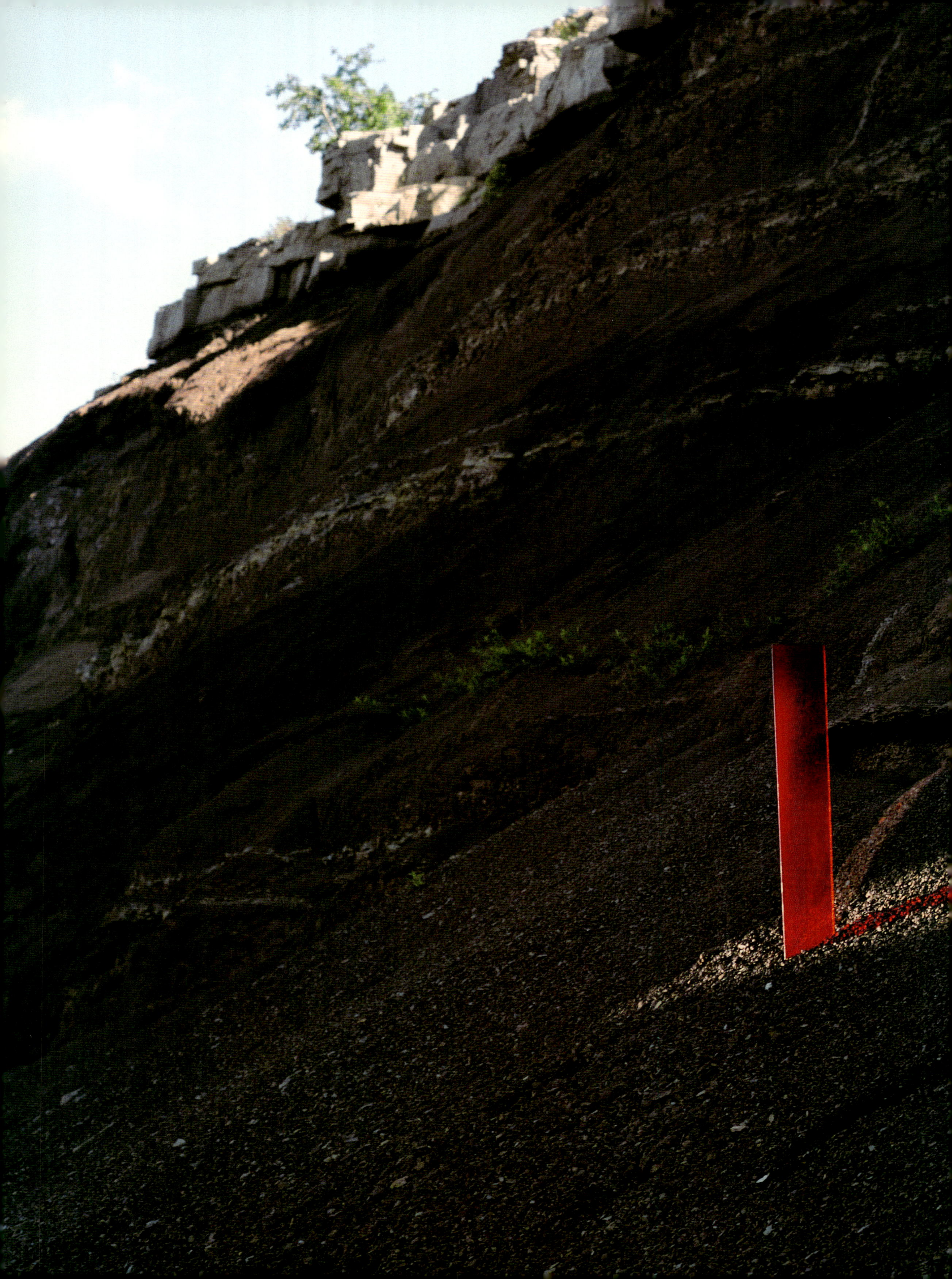

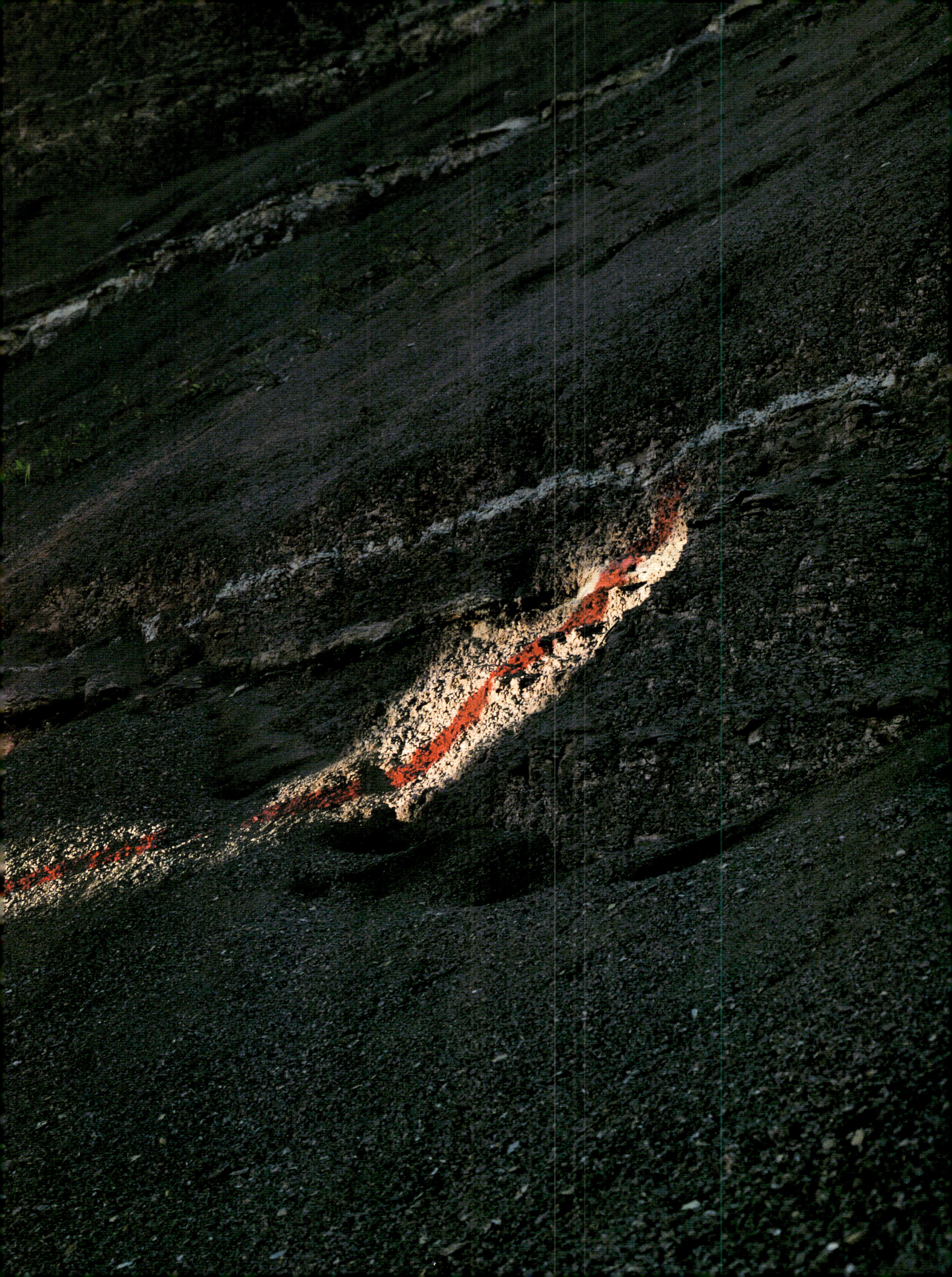

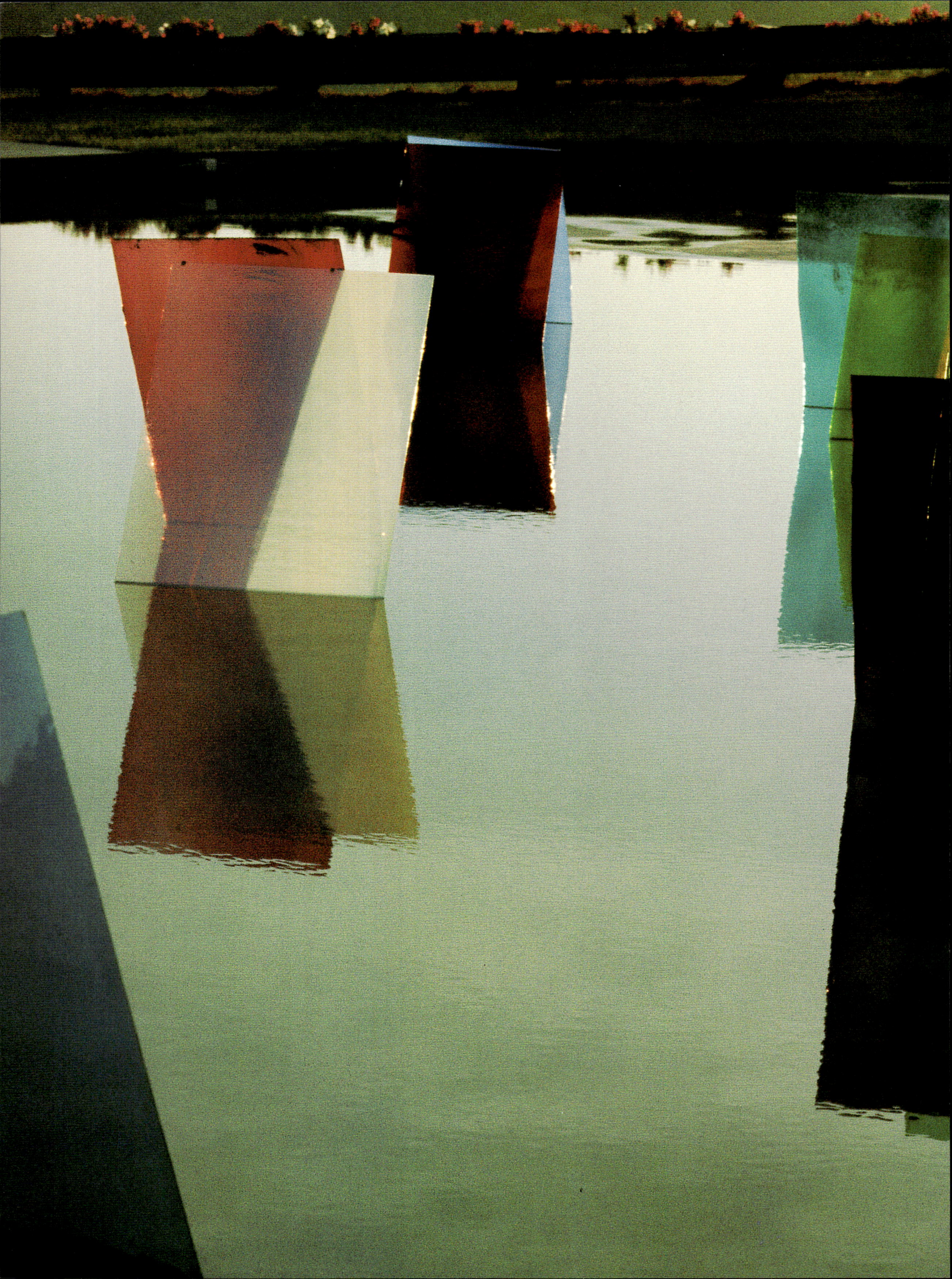

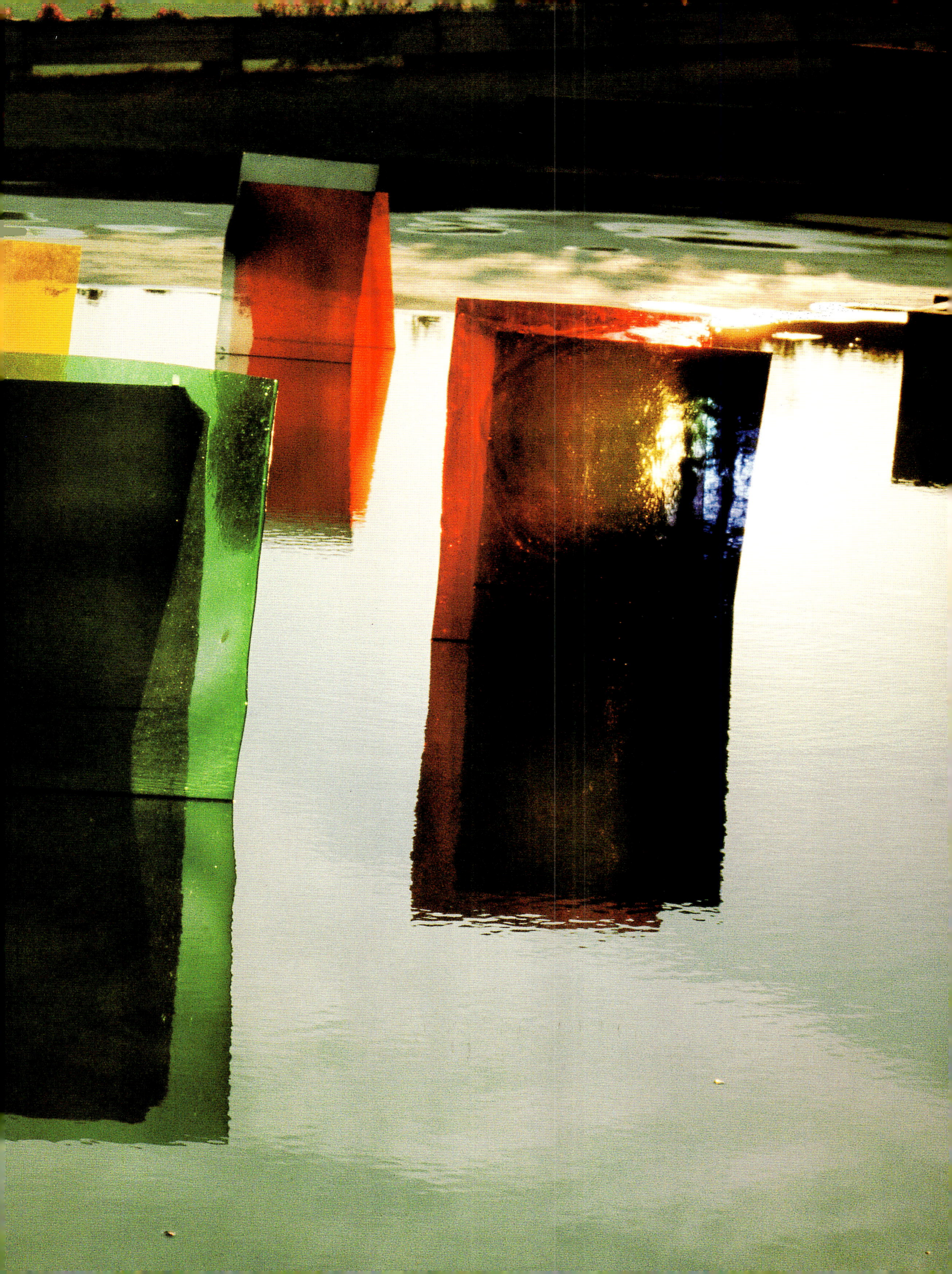

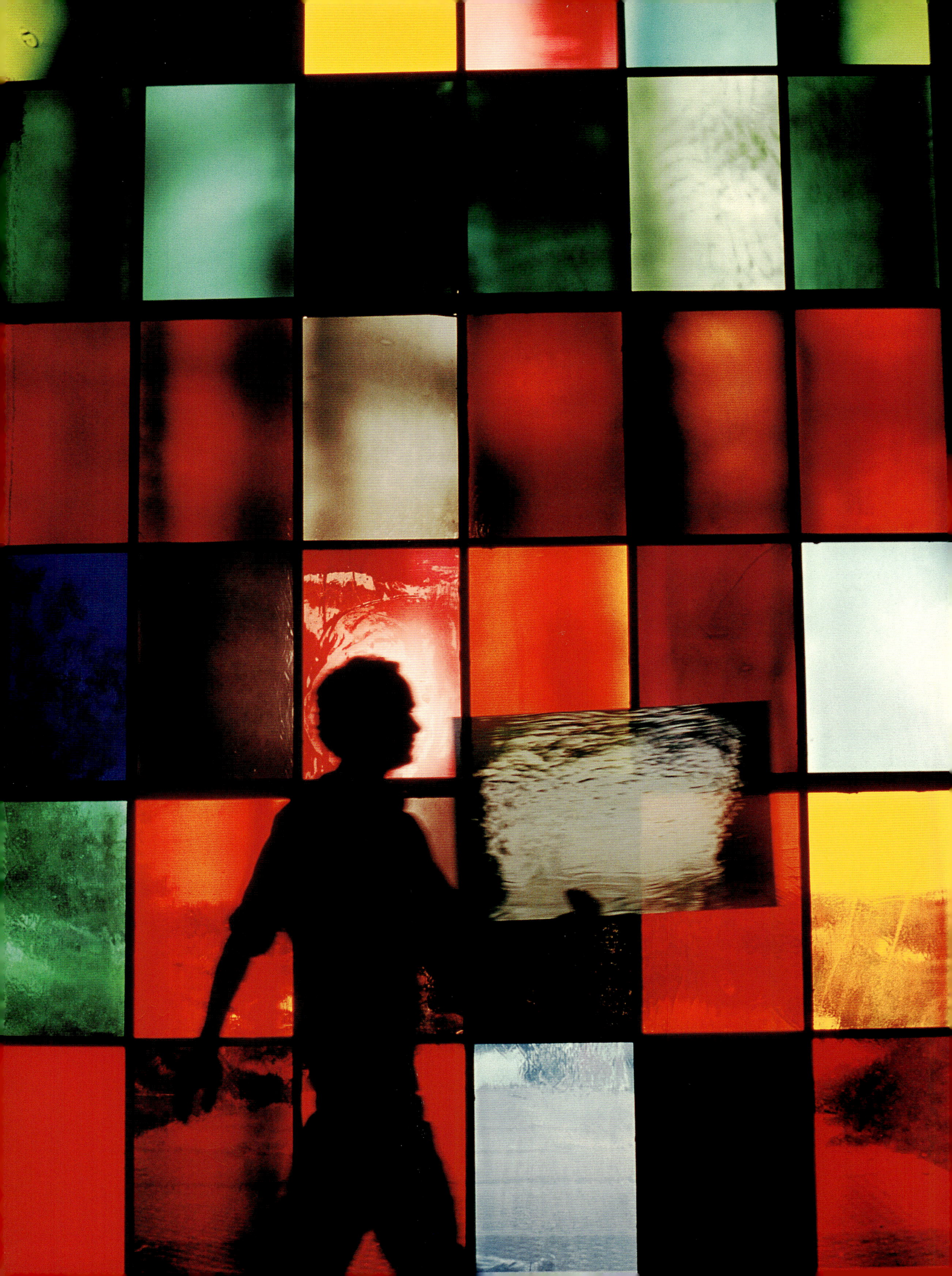

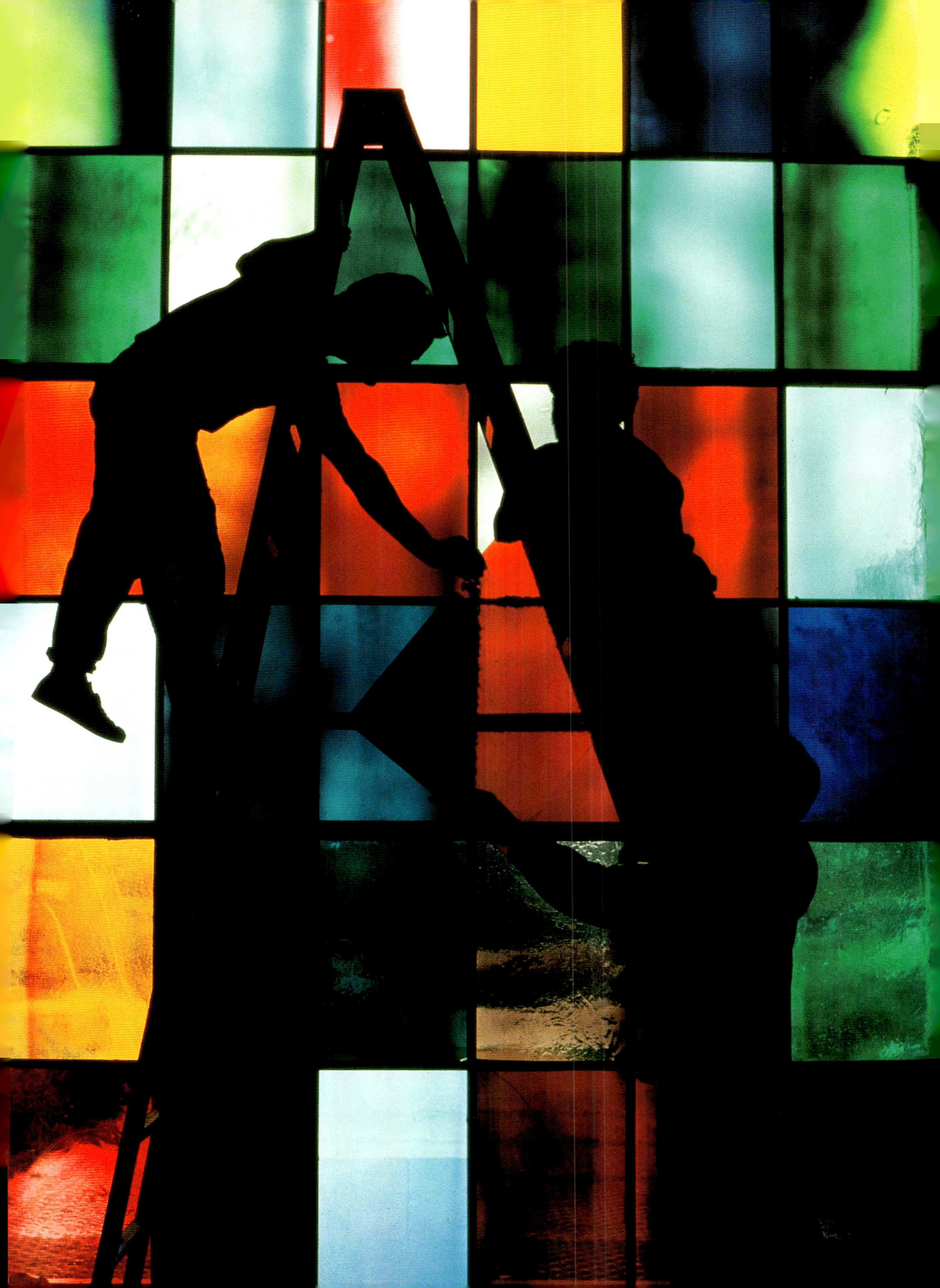

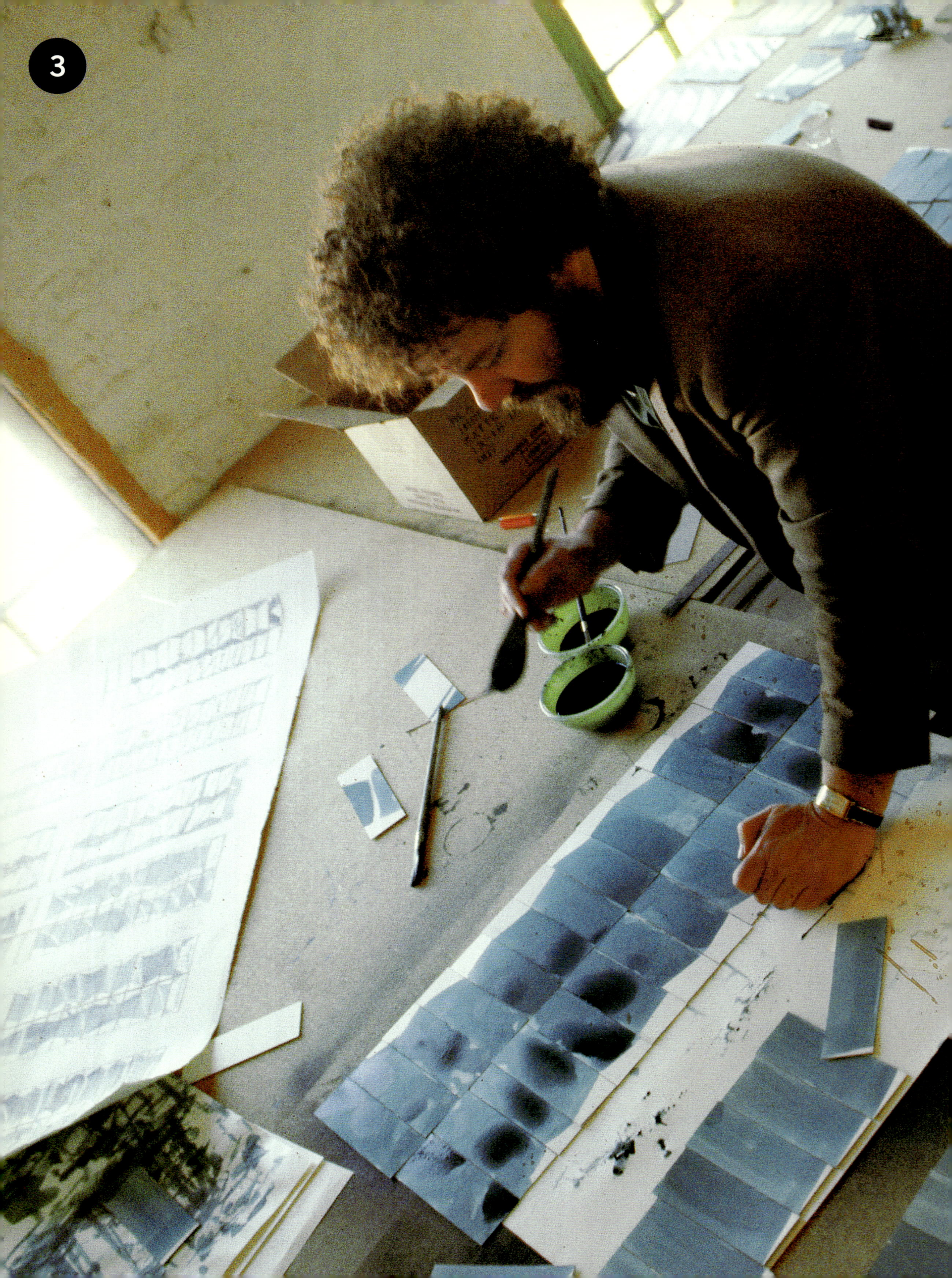

3

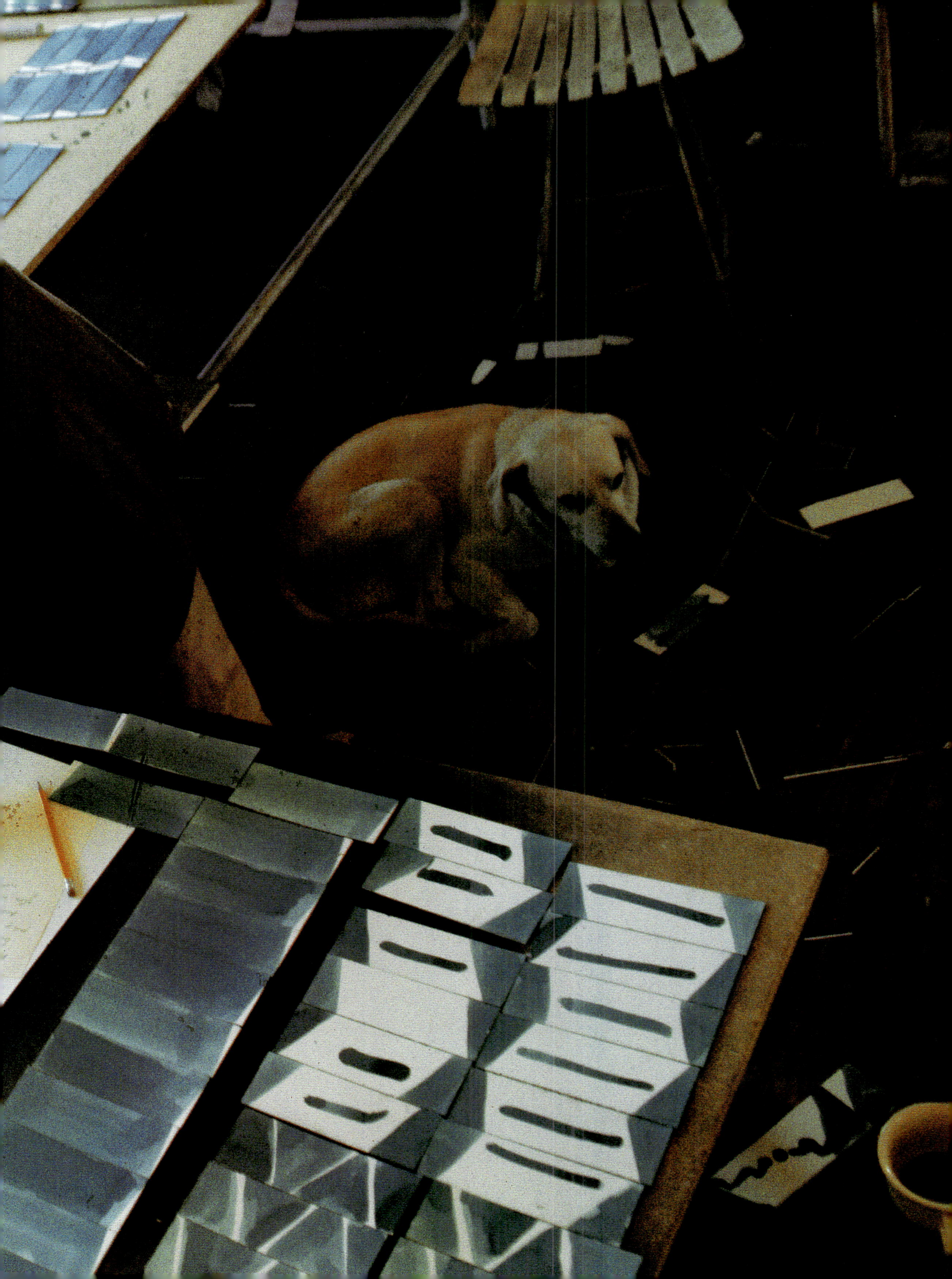

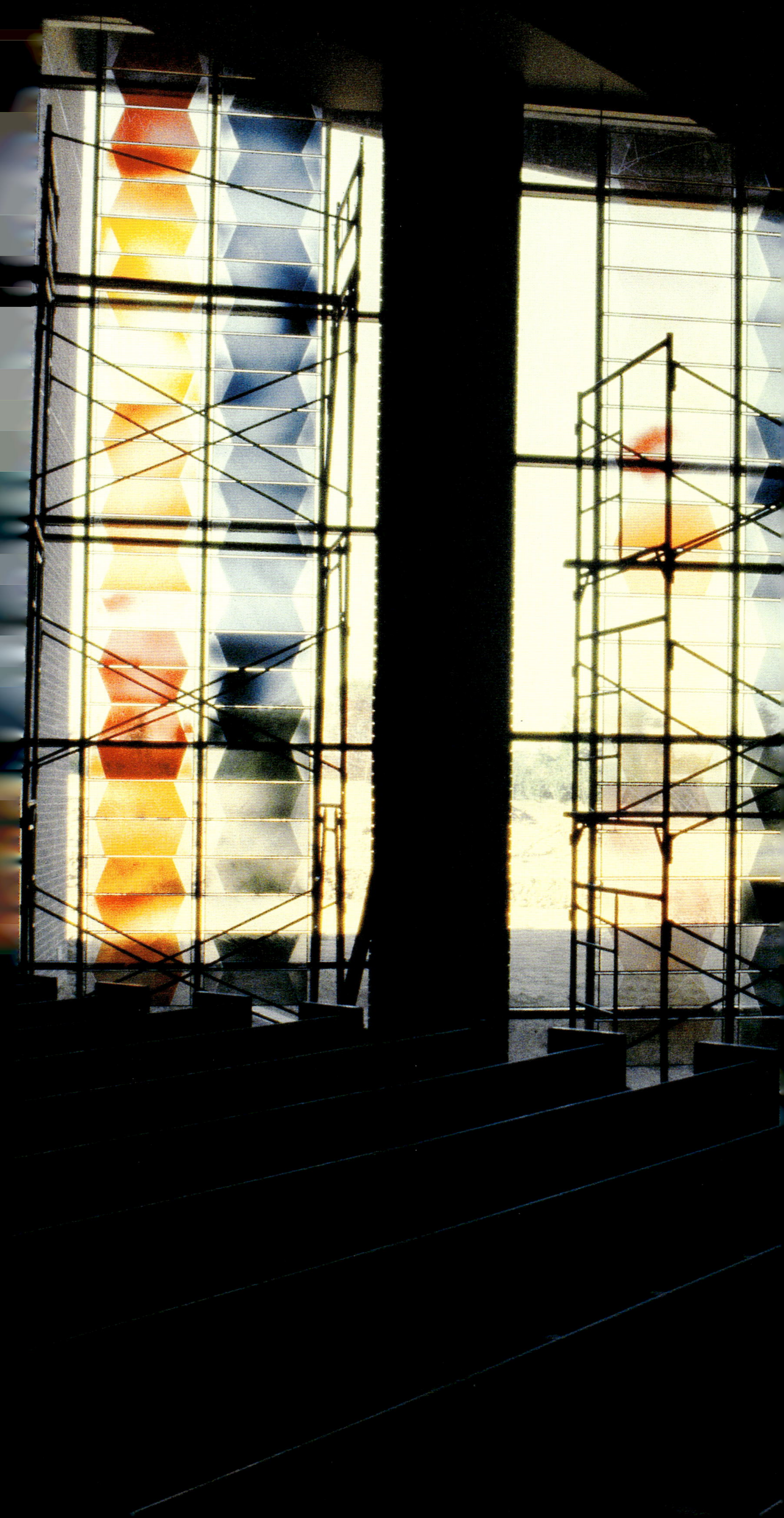

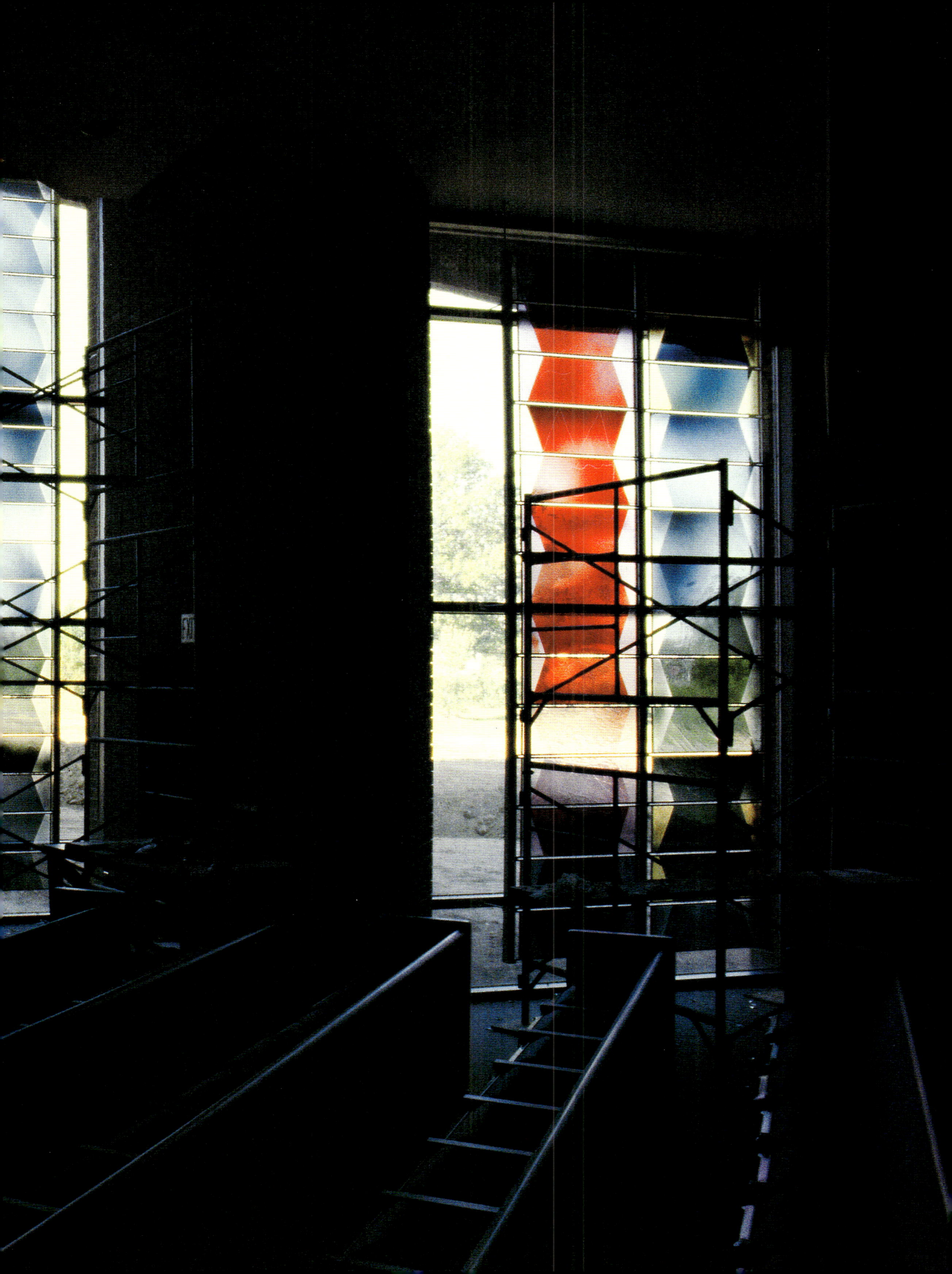

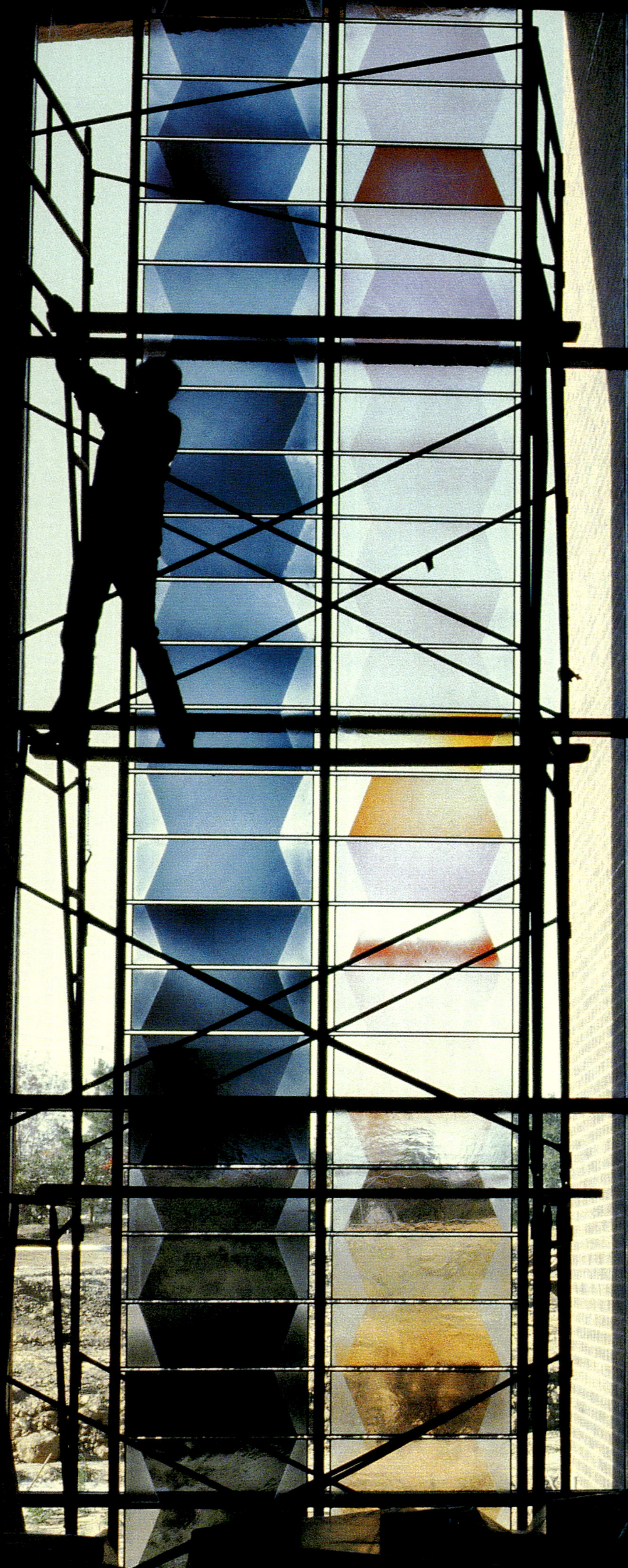

4

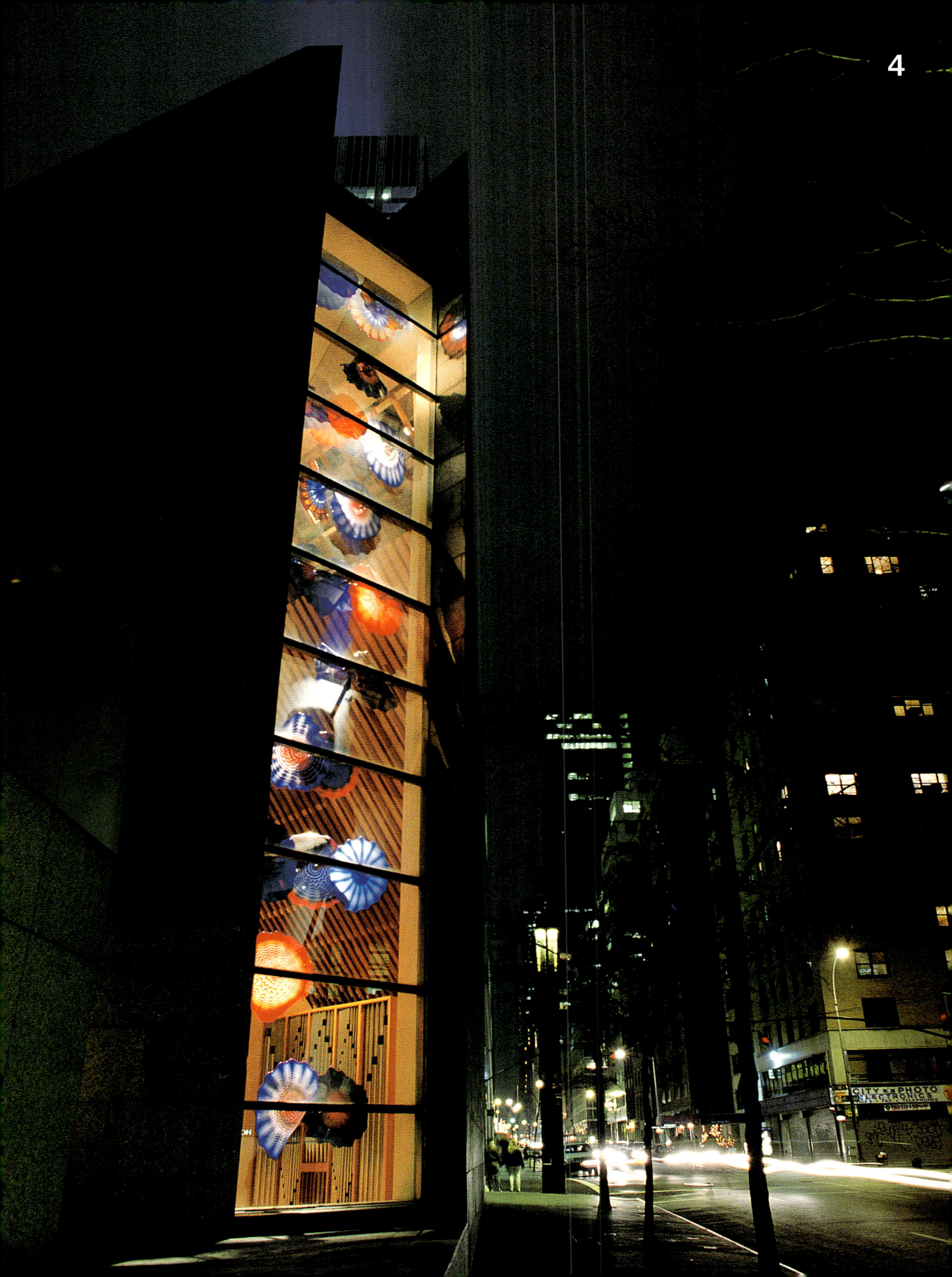

5

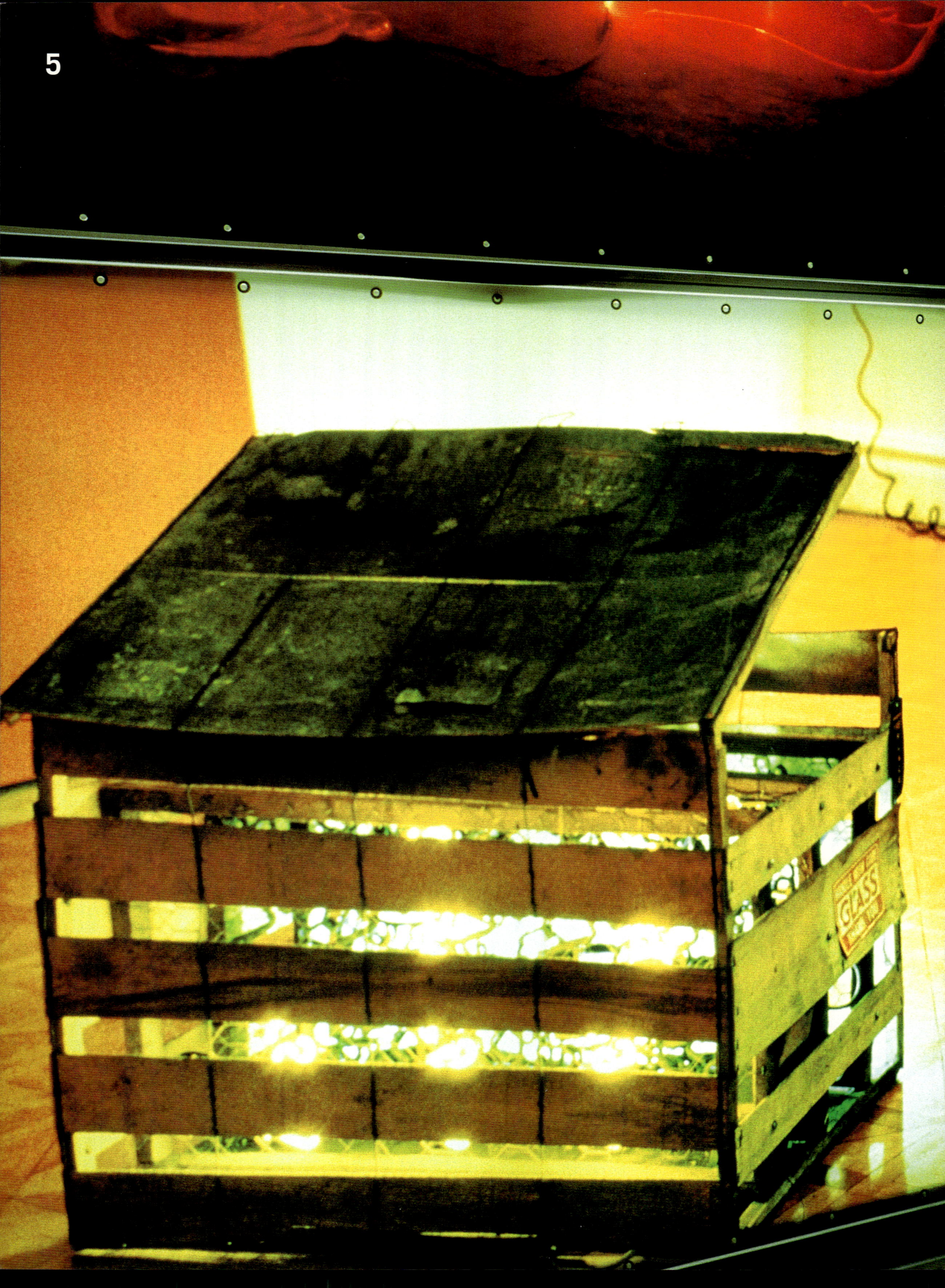

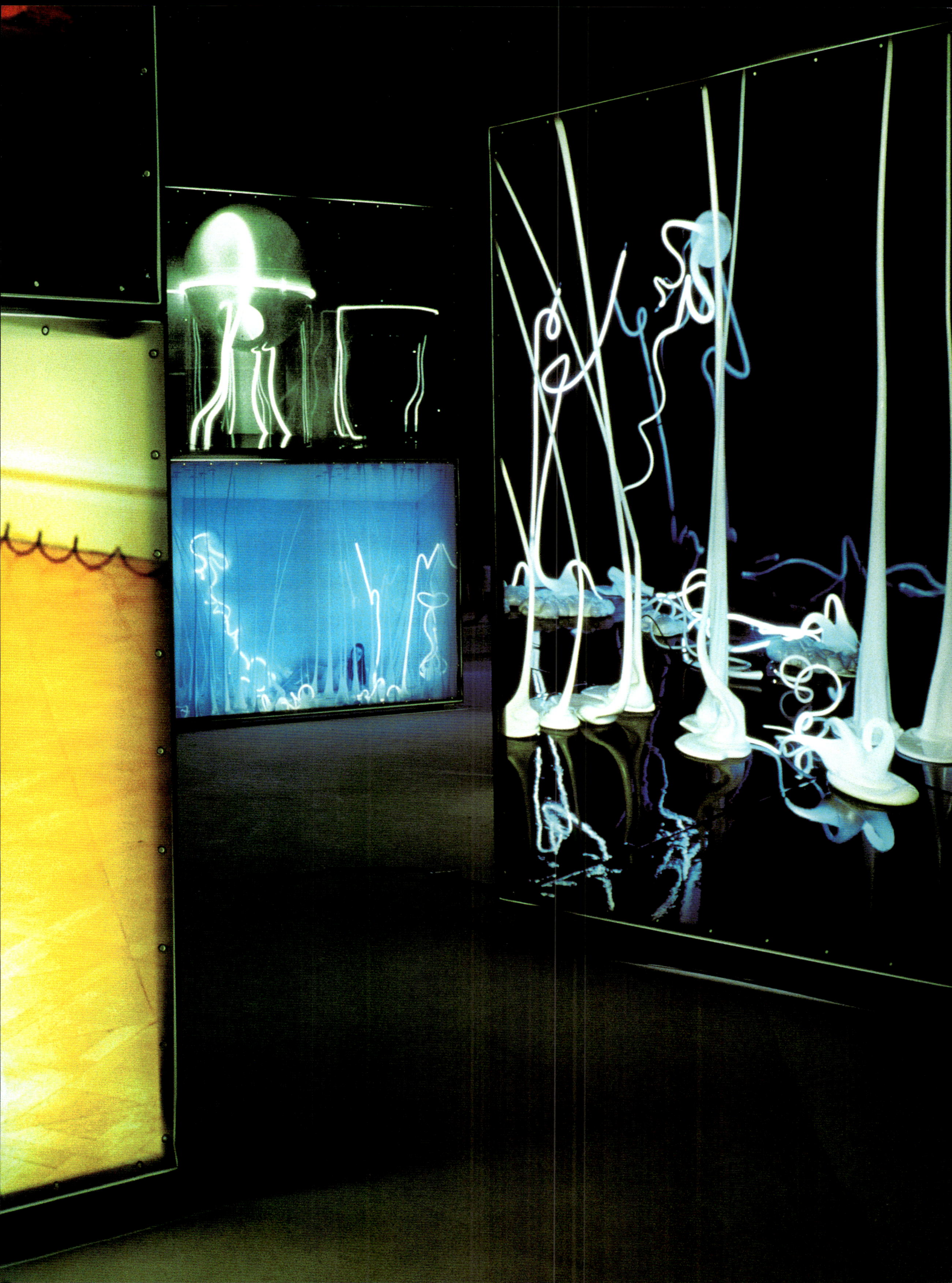

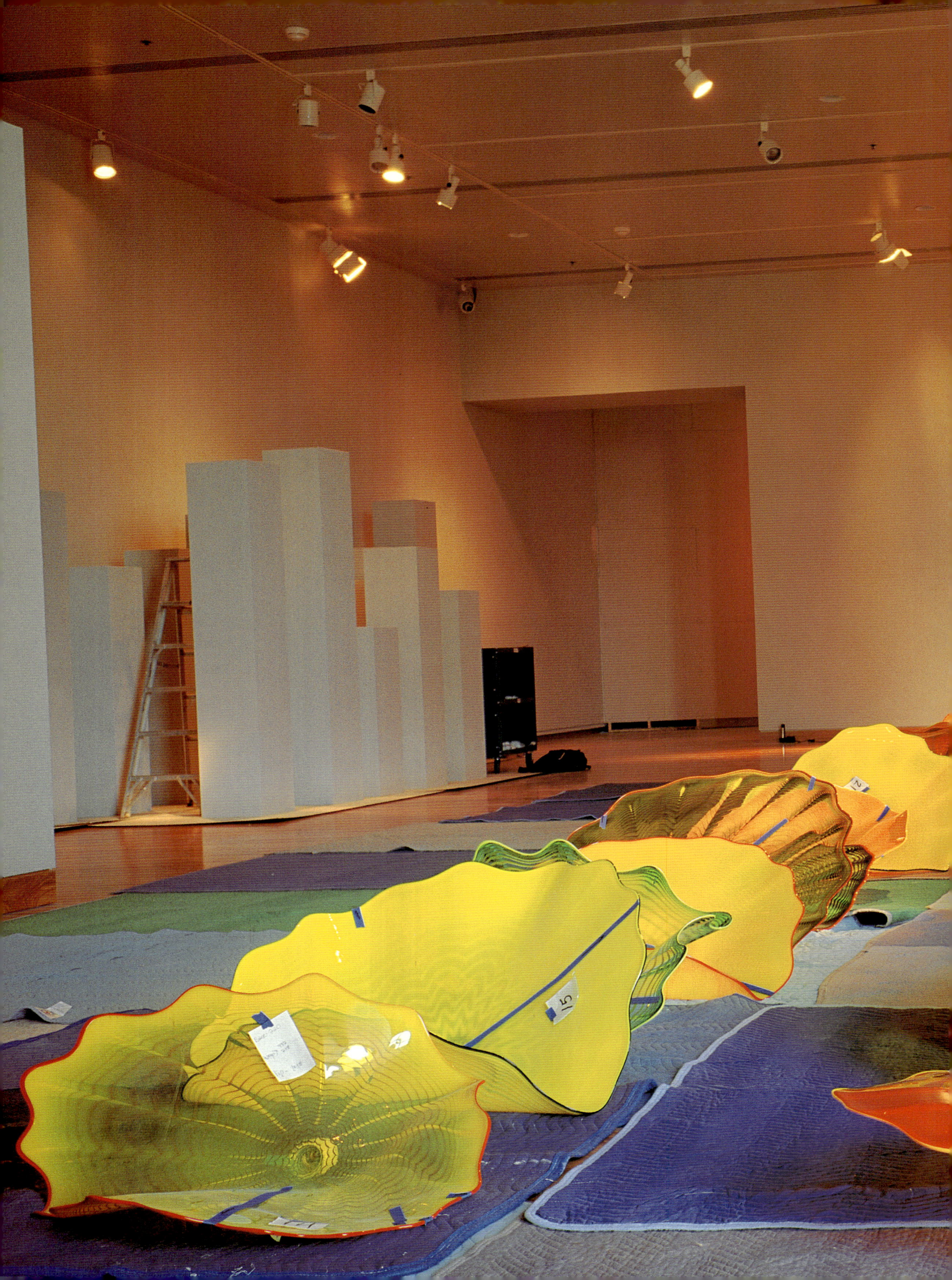
15

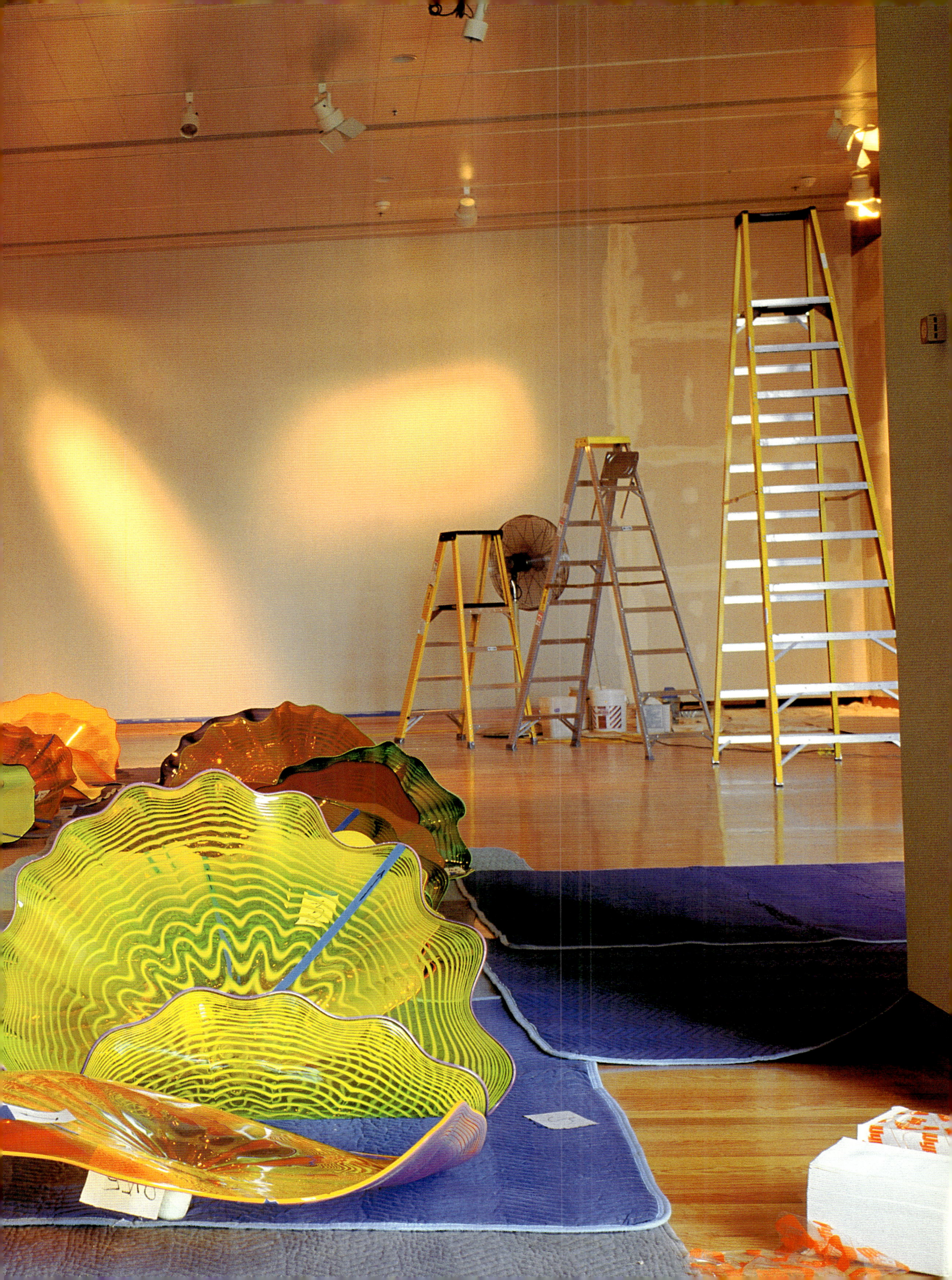

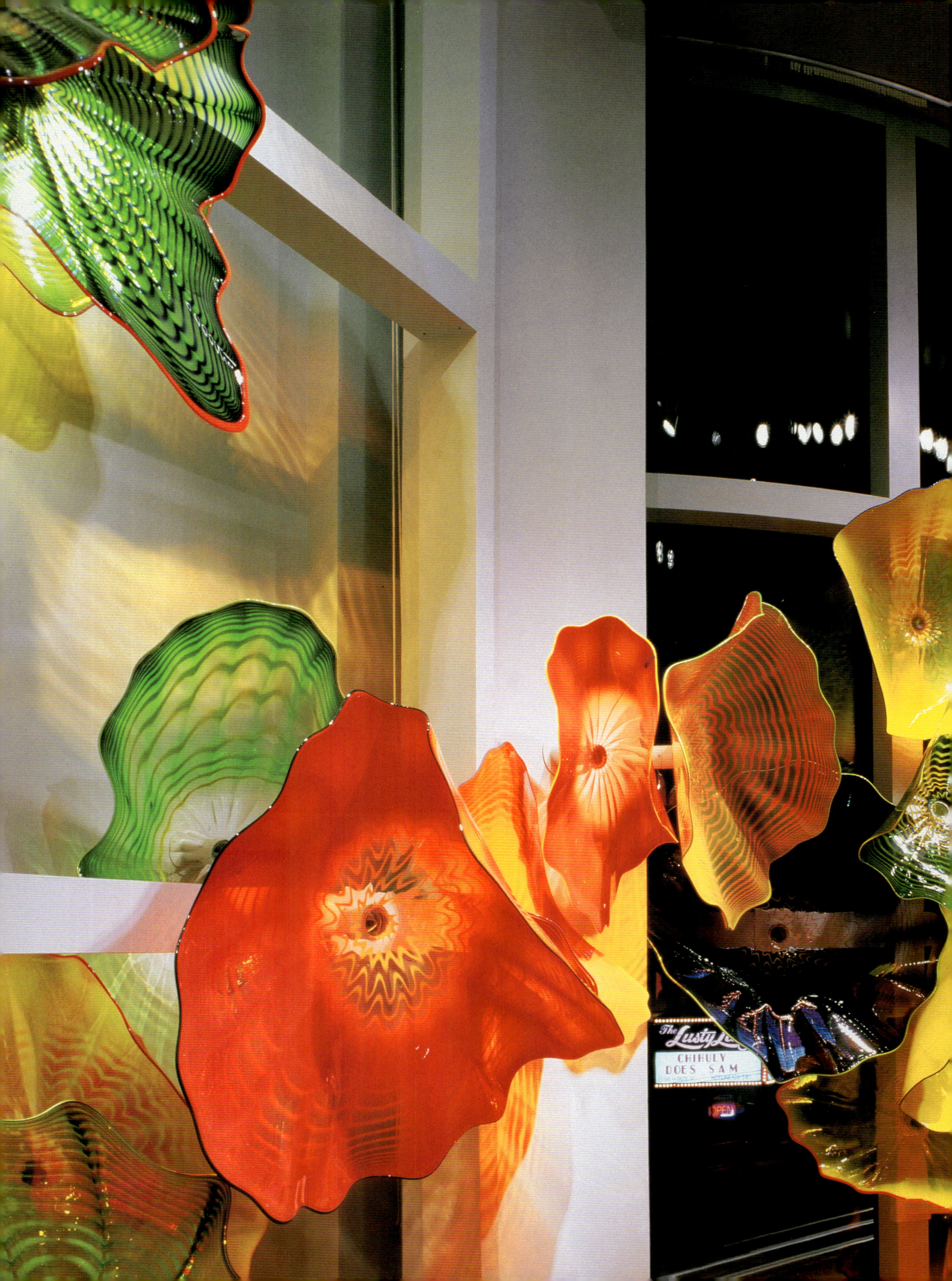

The Lusty
CHIHULY
DOES SAM
OPEN

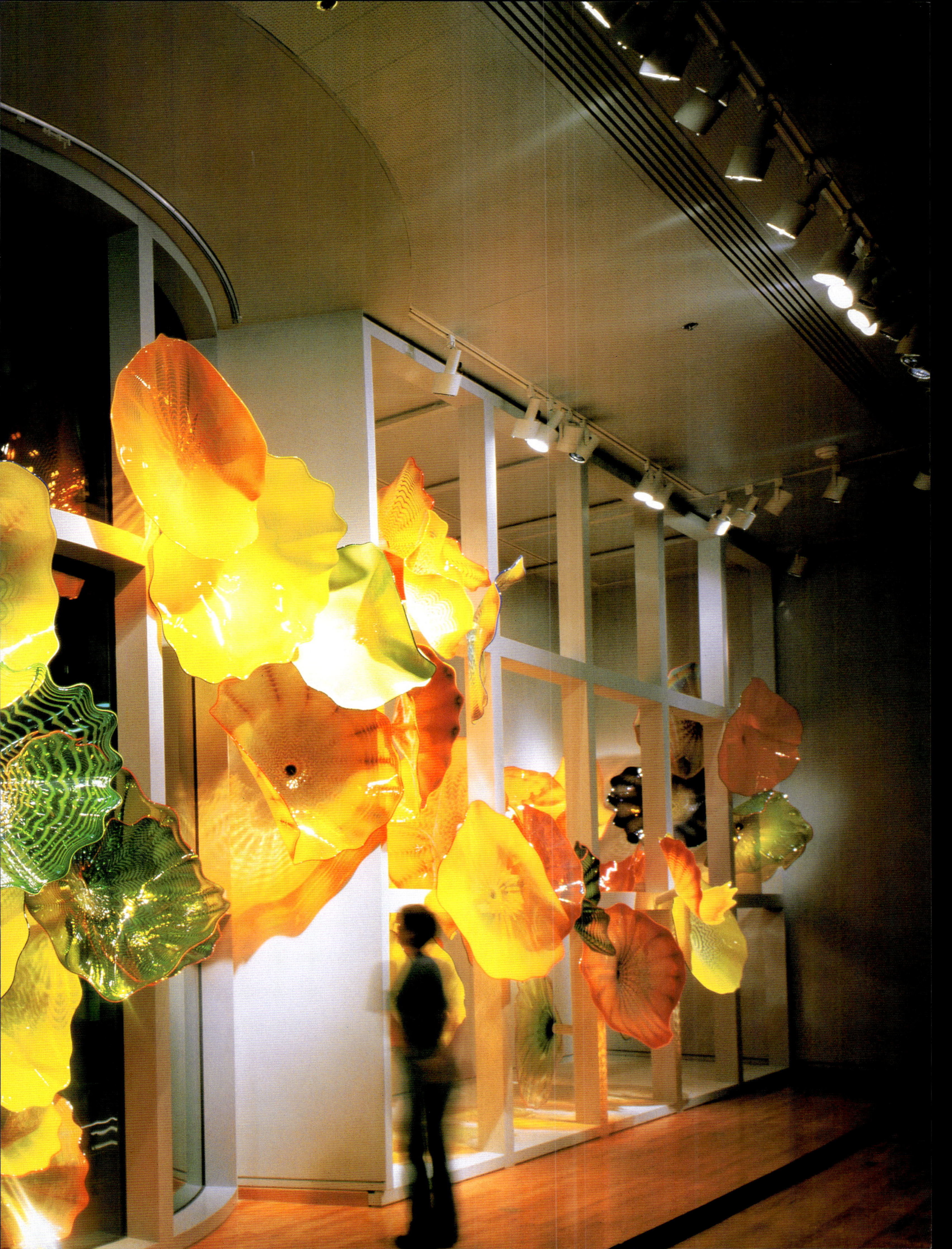

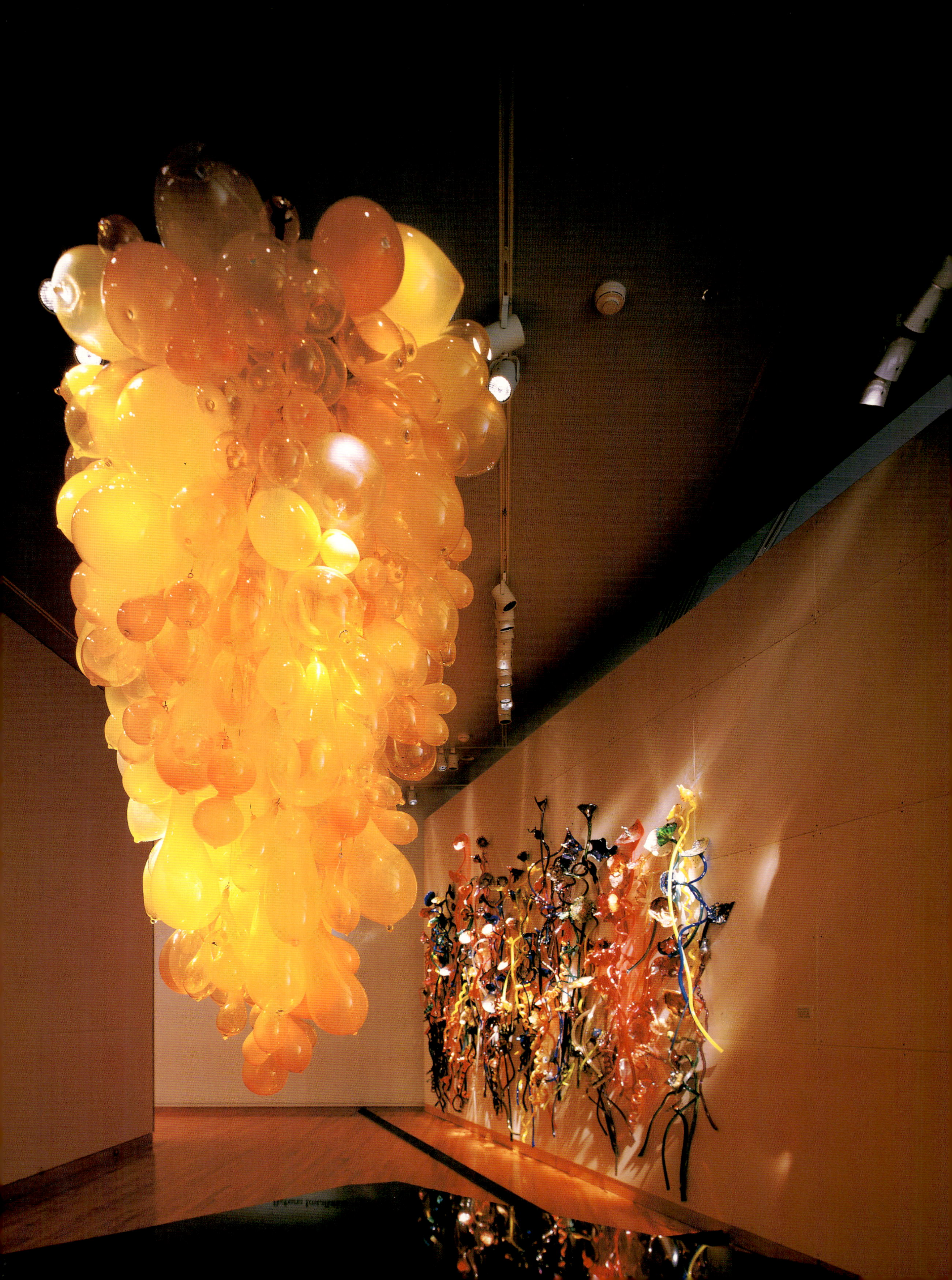

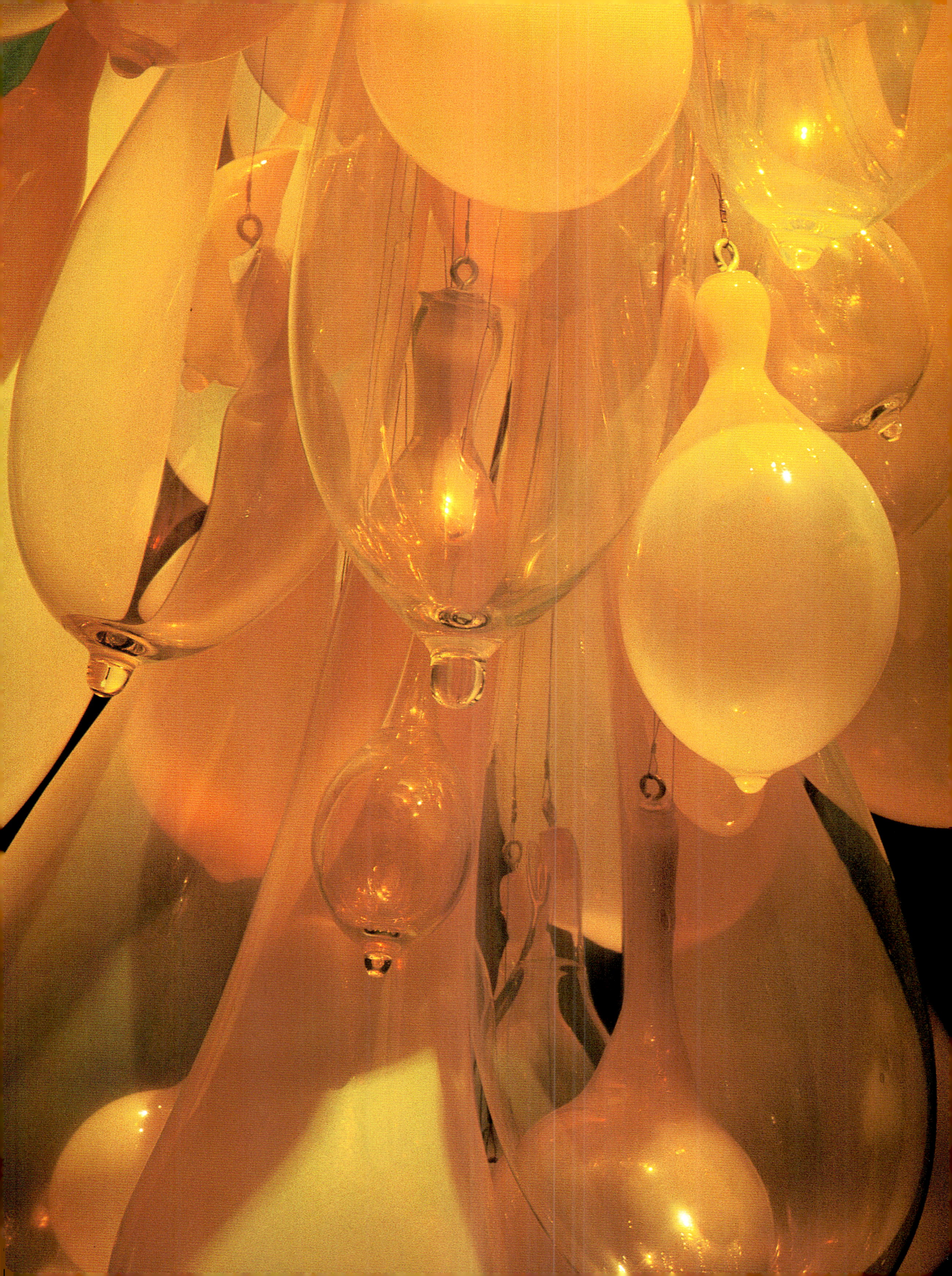

6

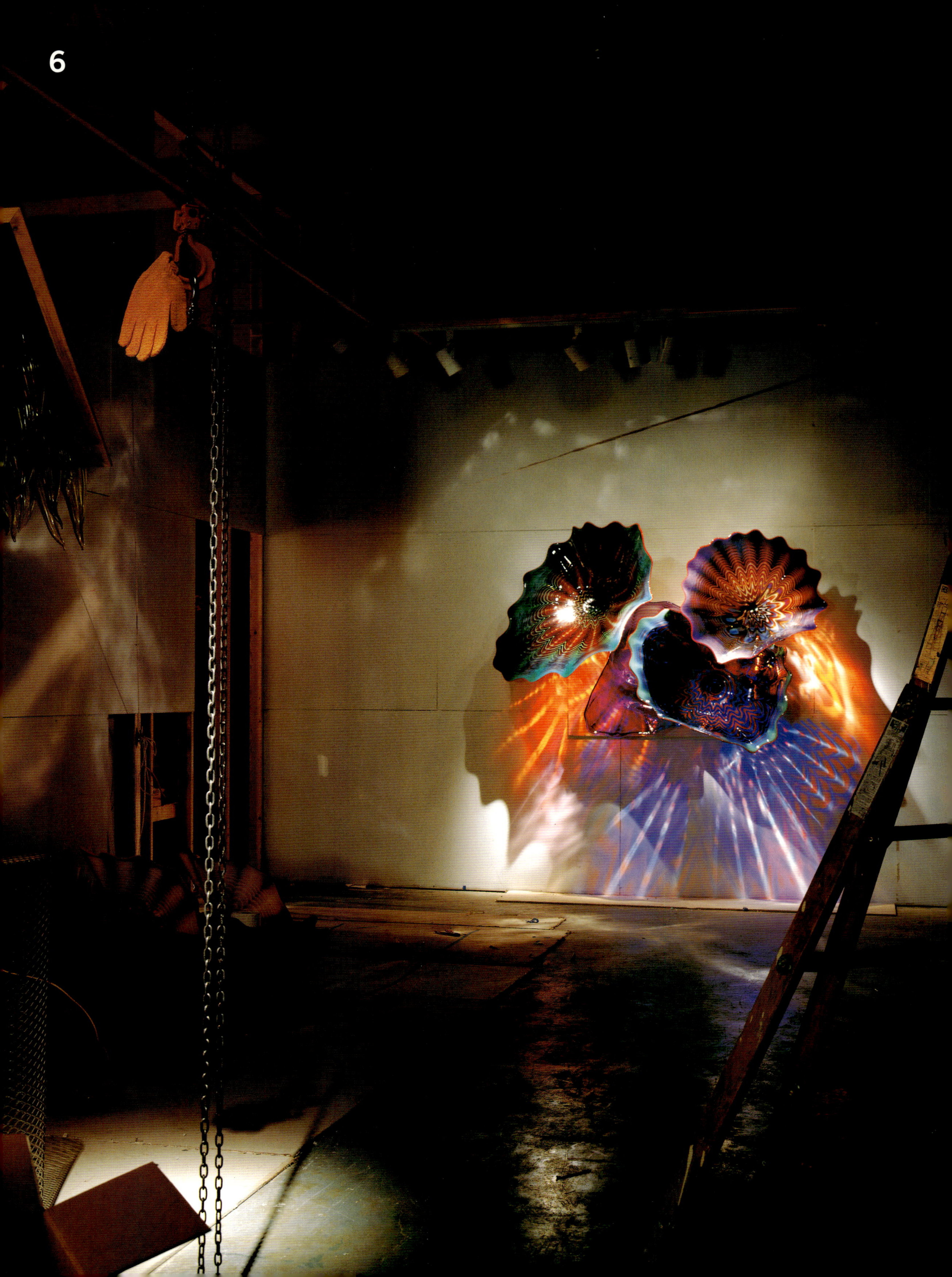

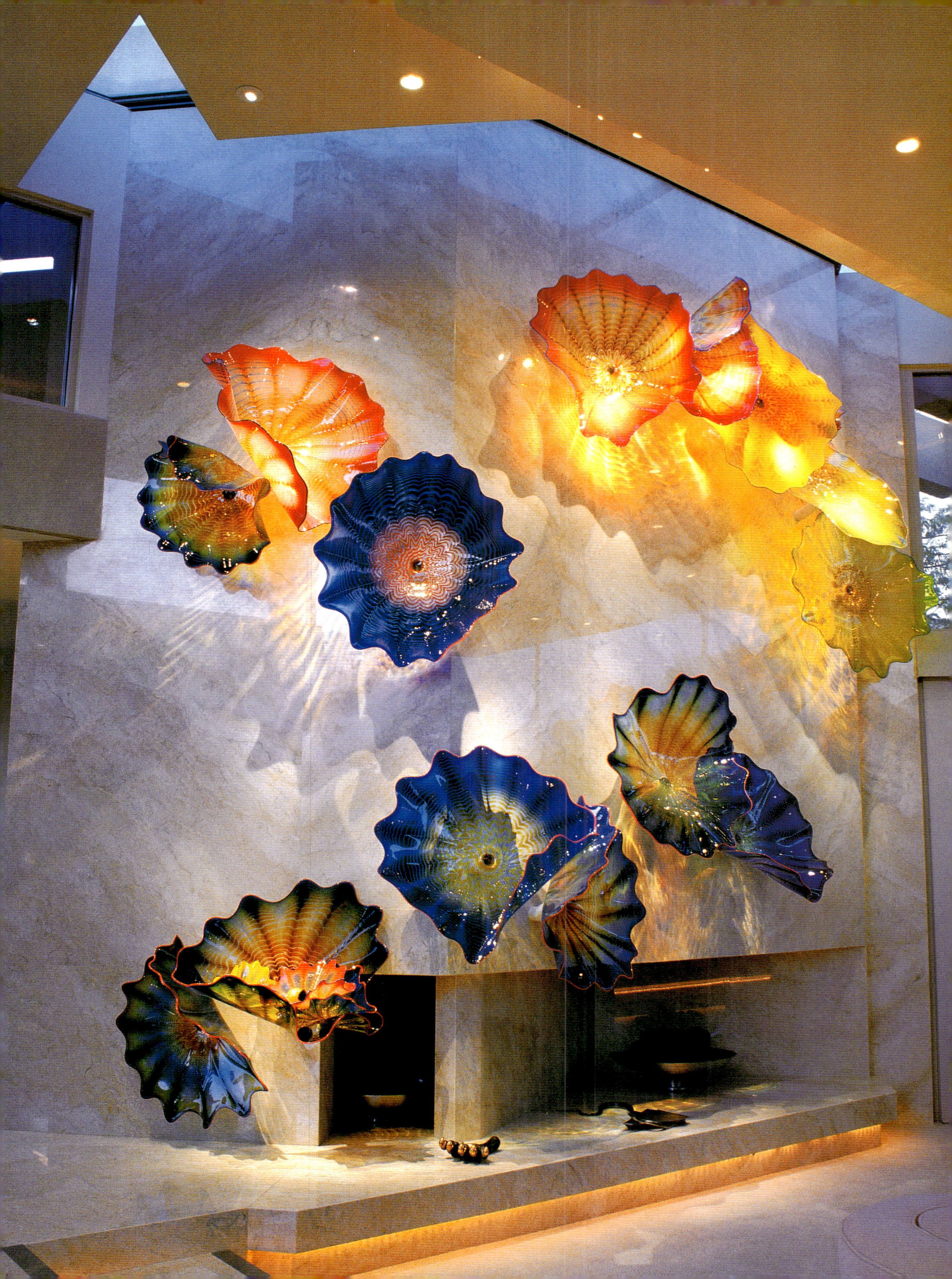

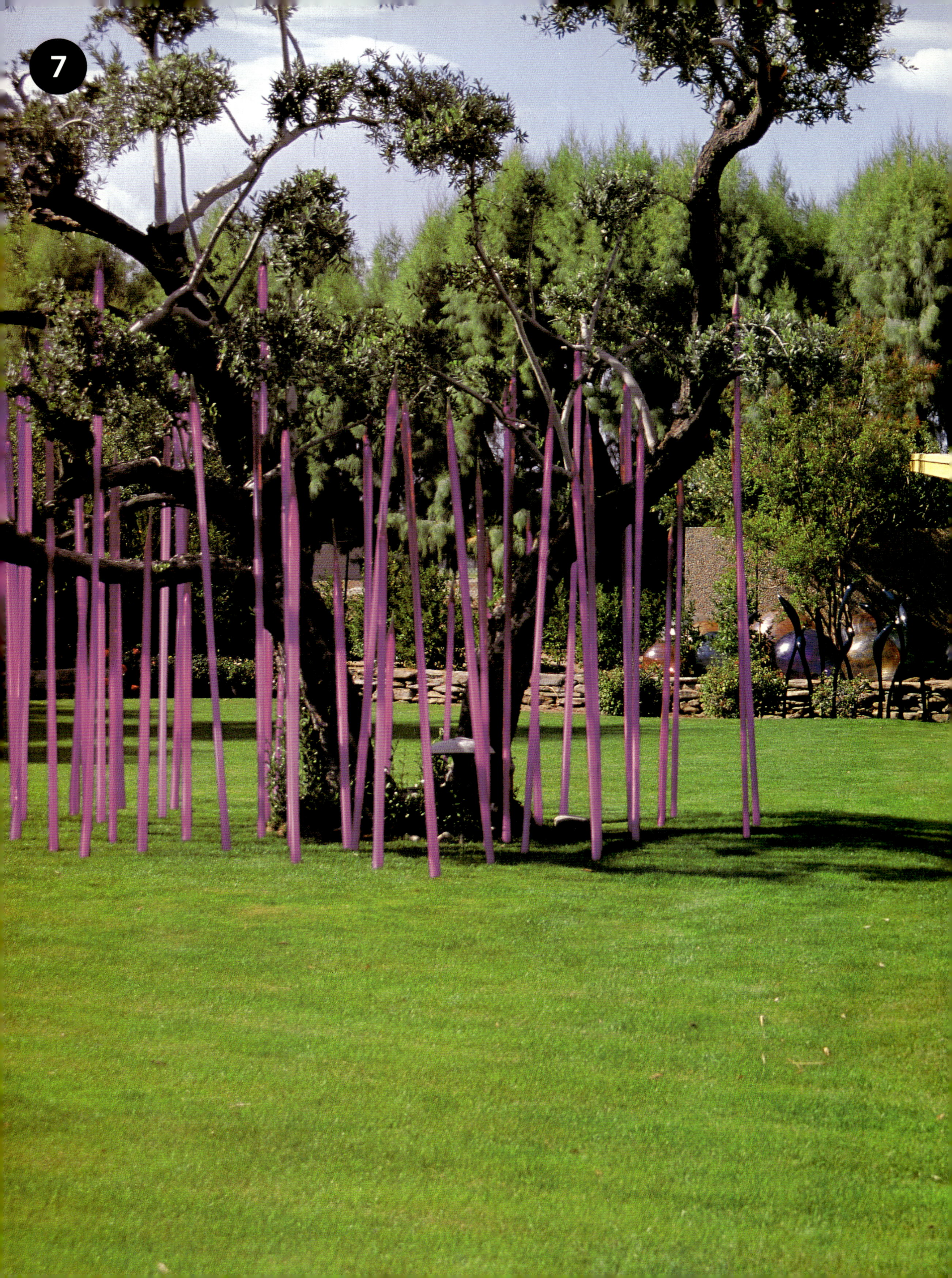

7

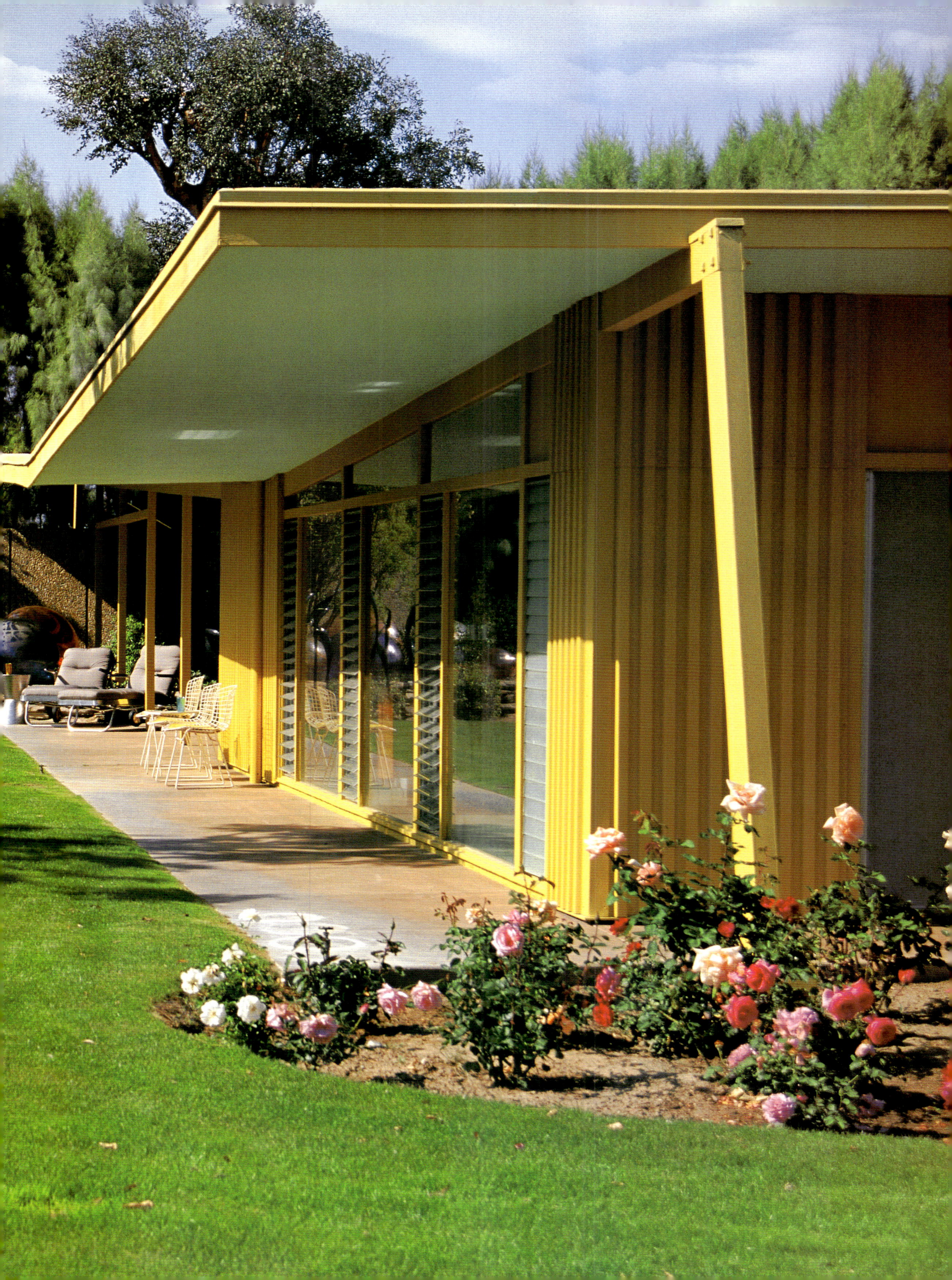

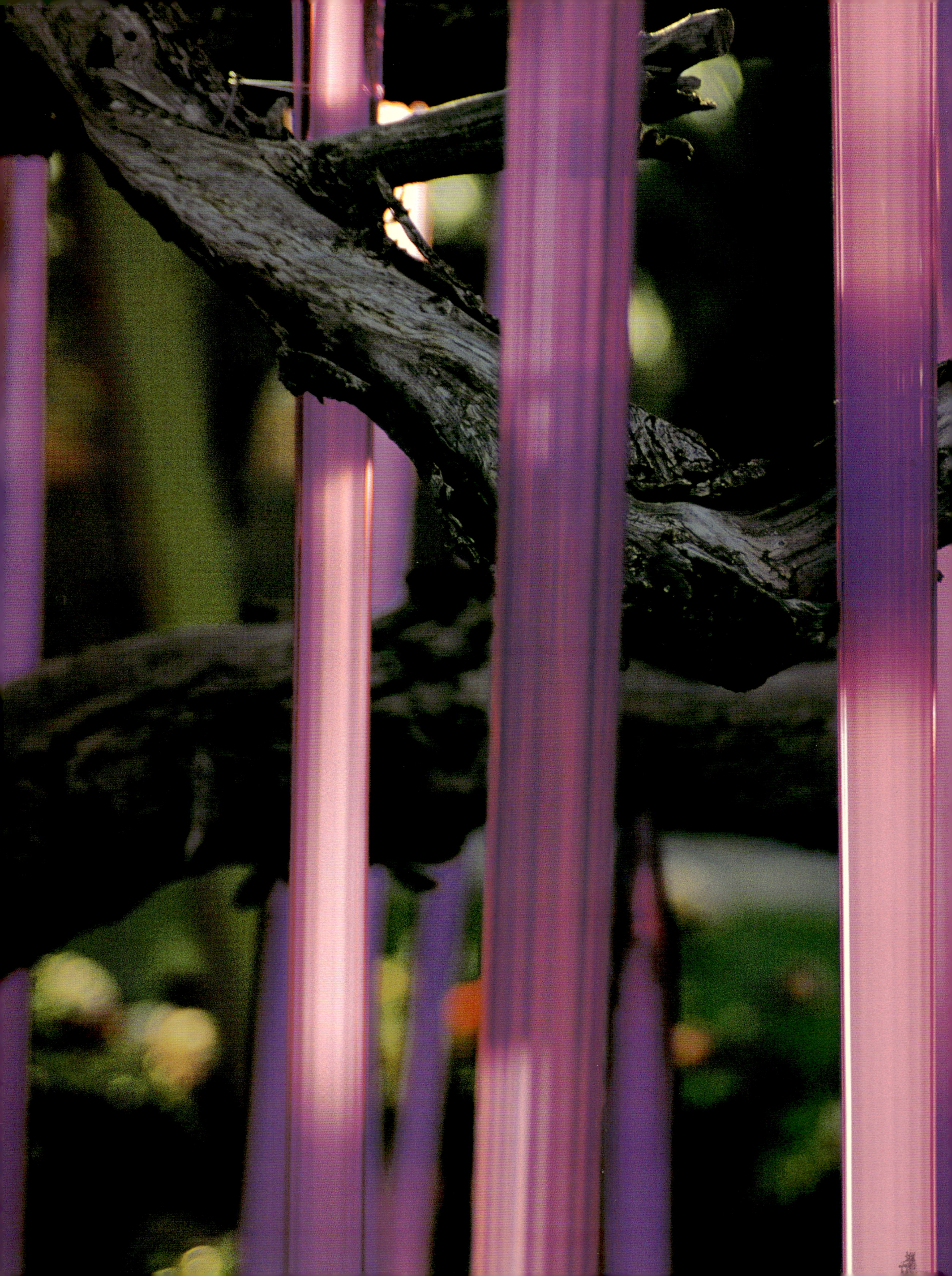

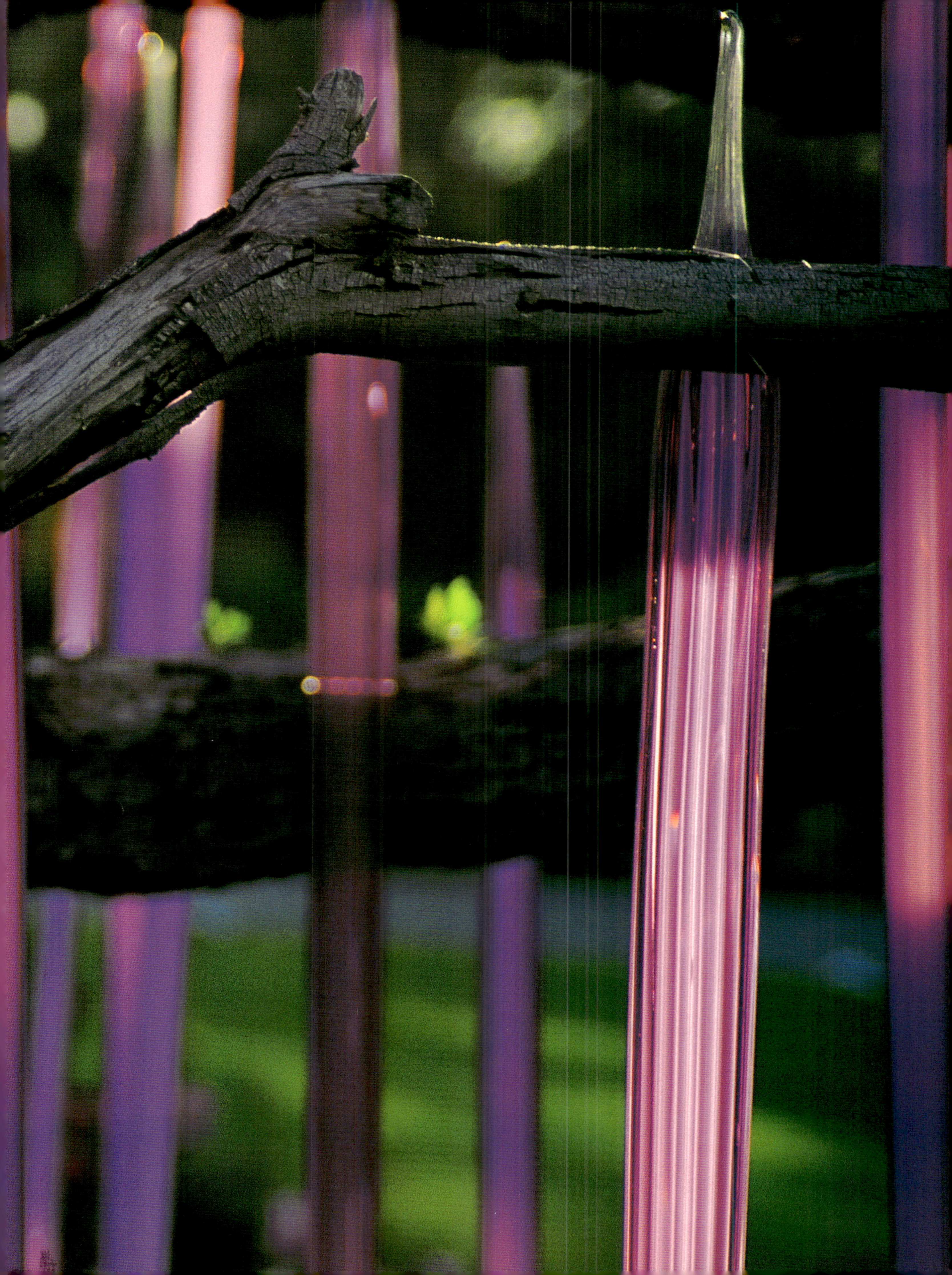

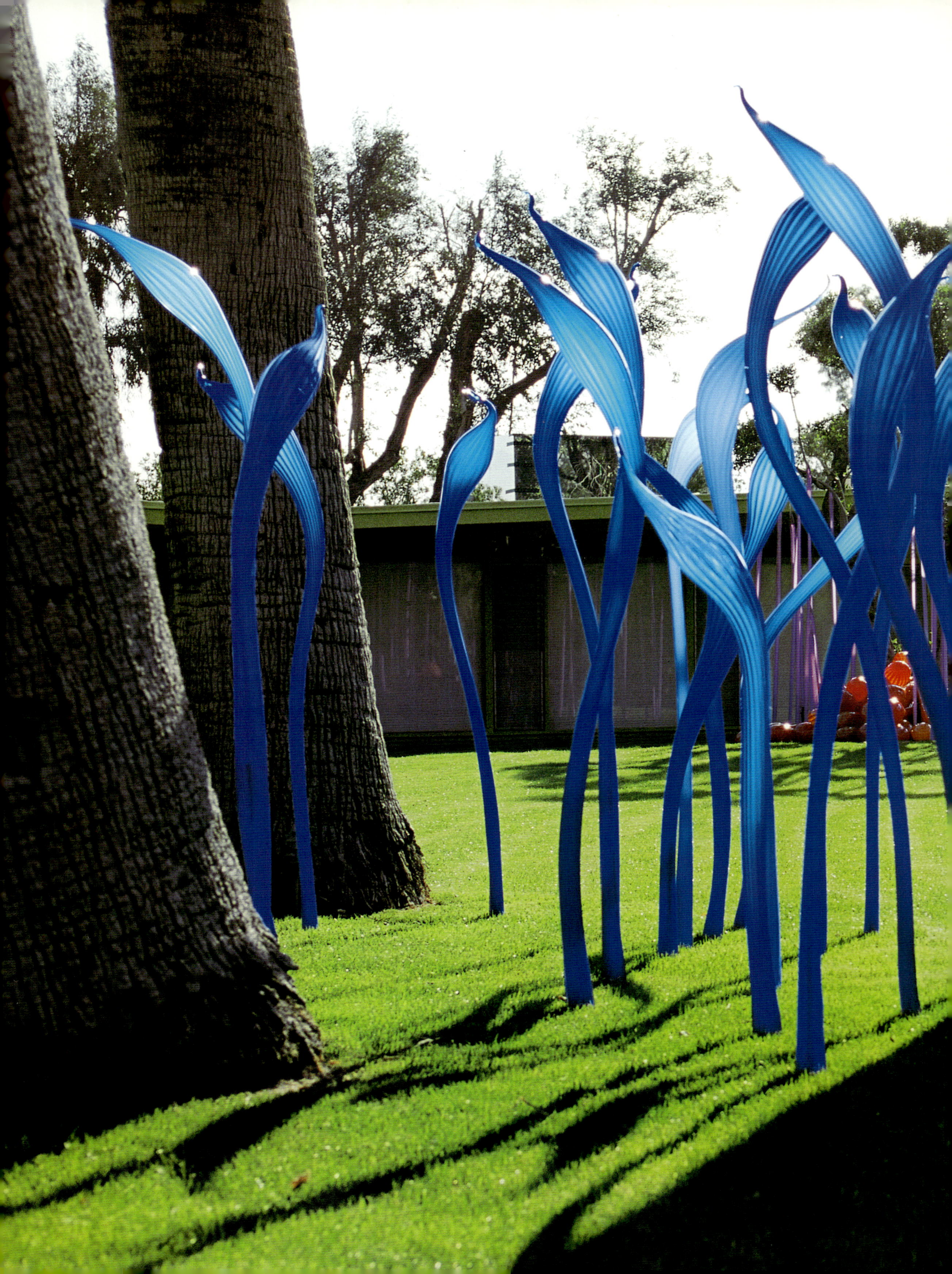

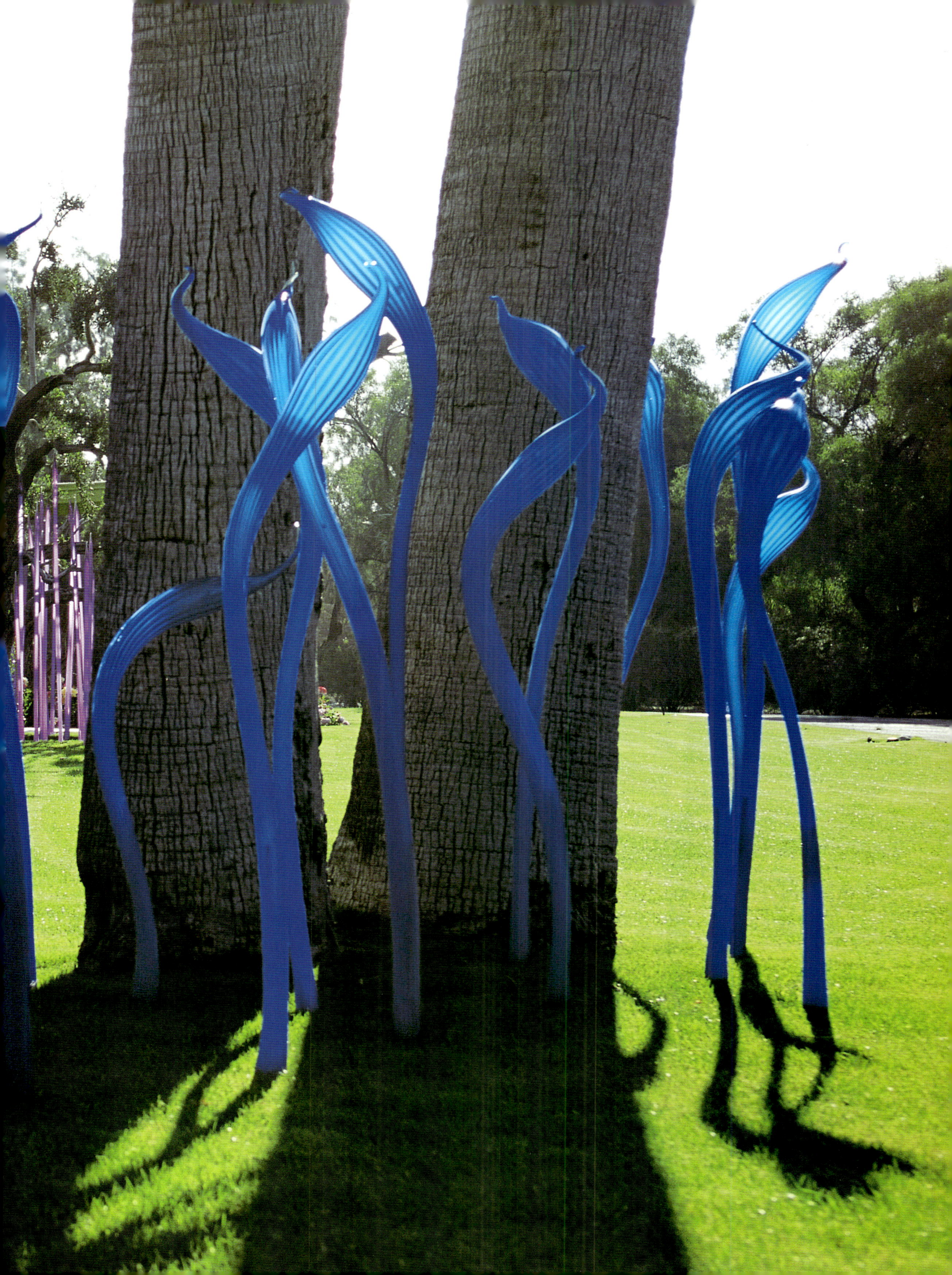

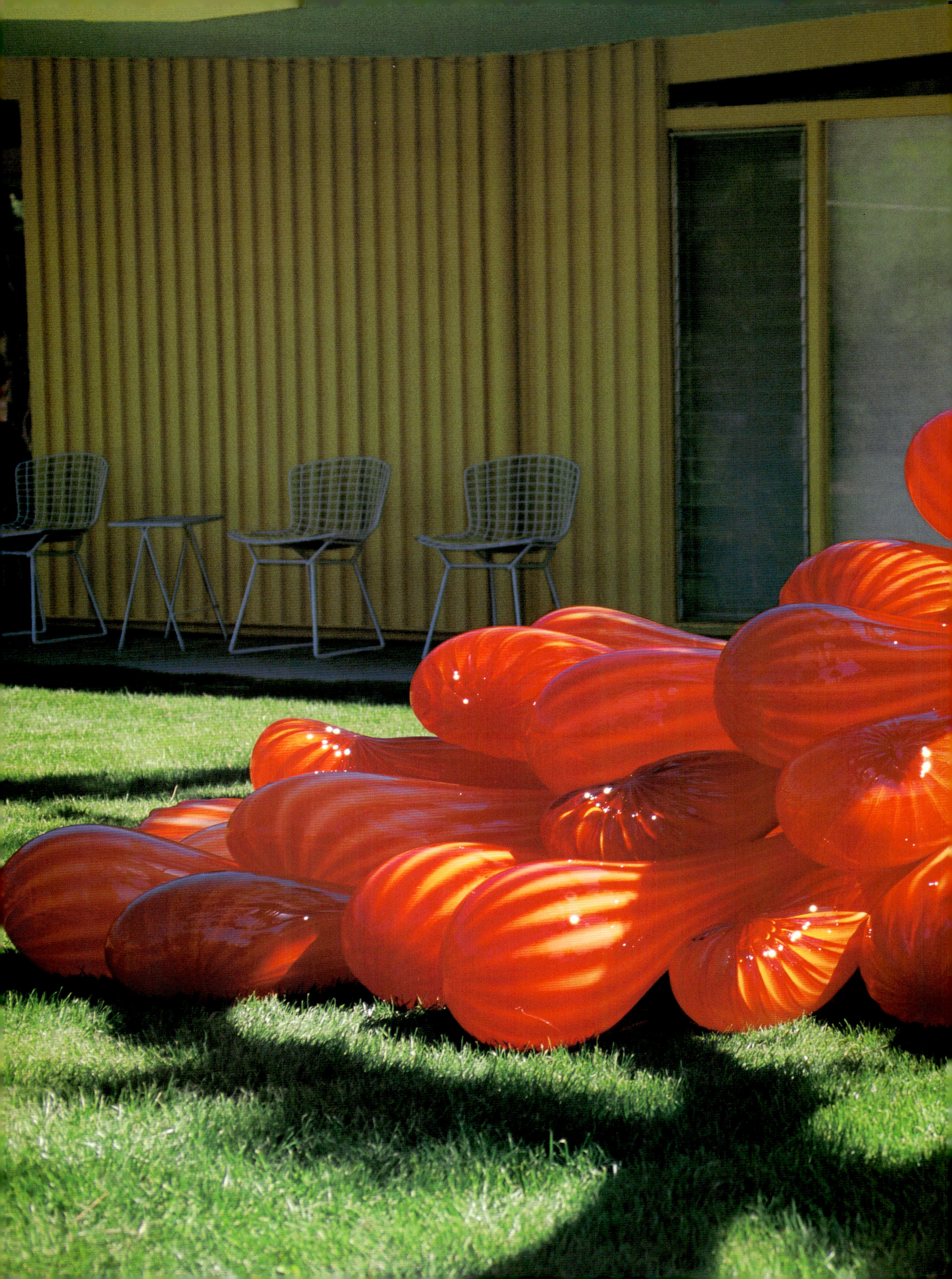

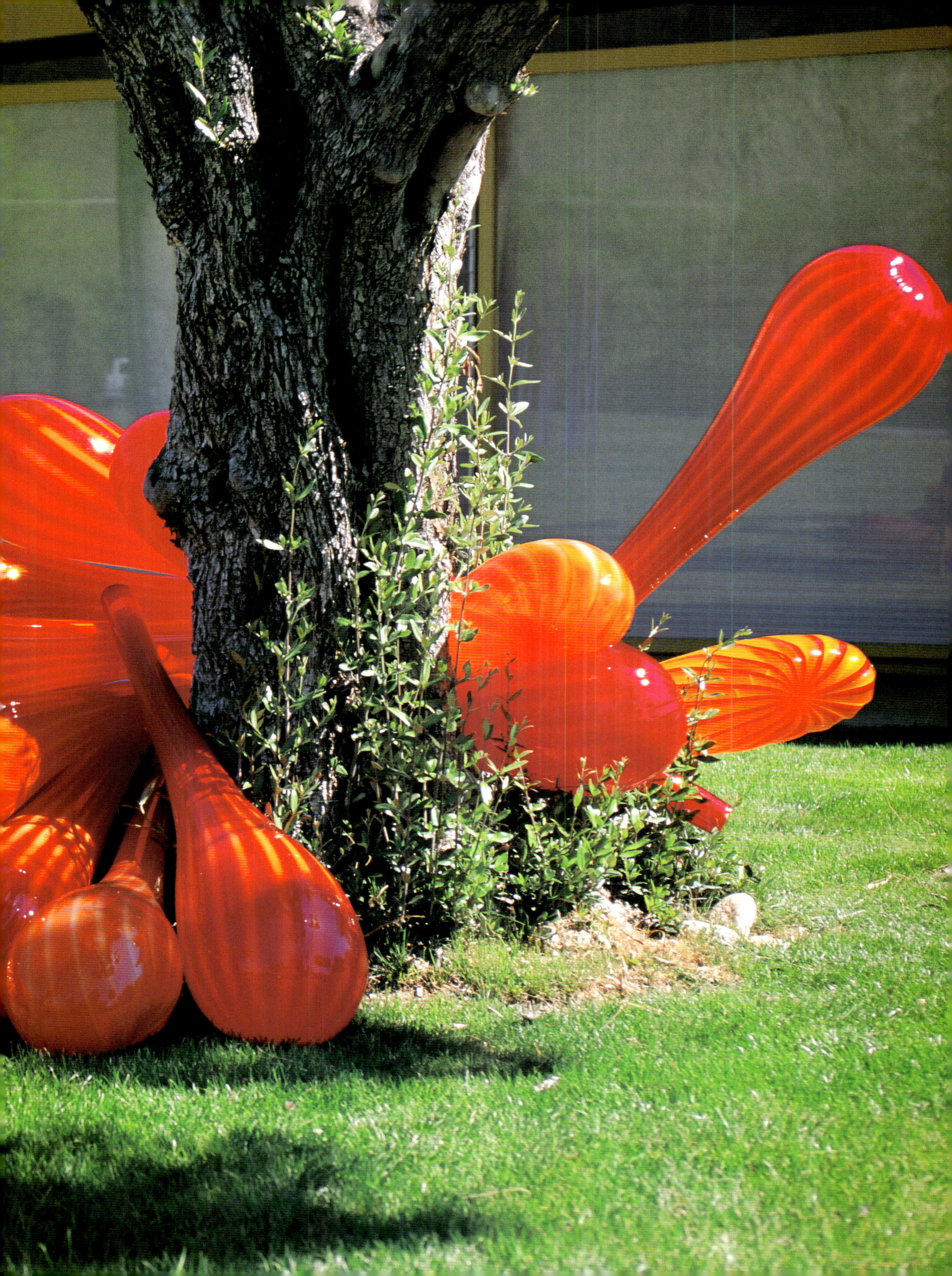

8

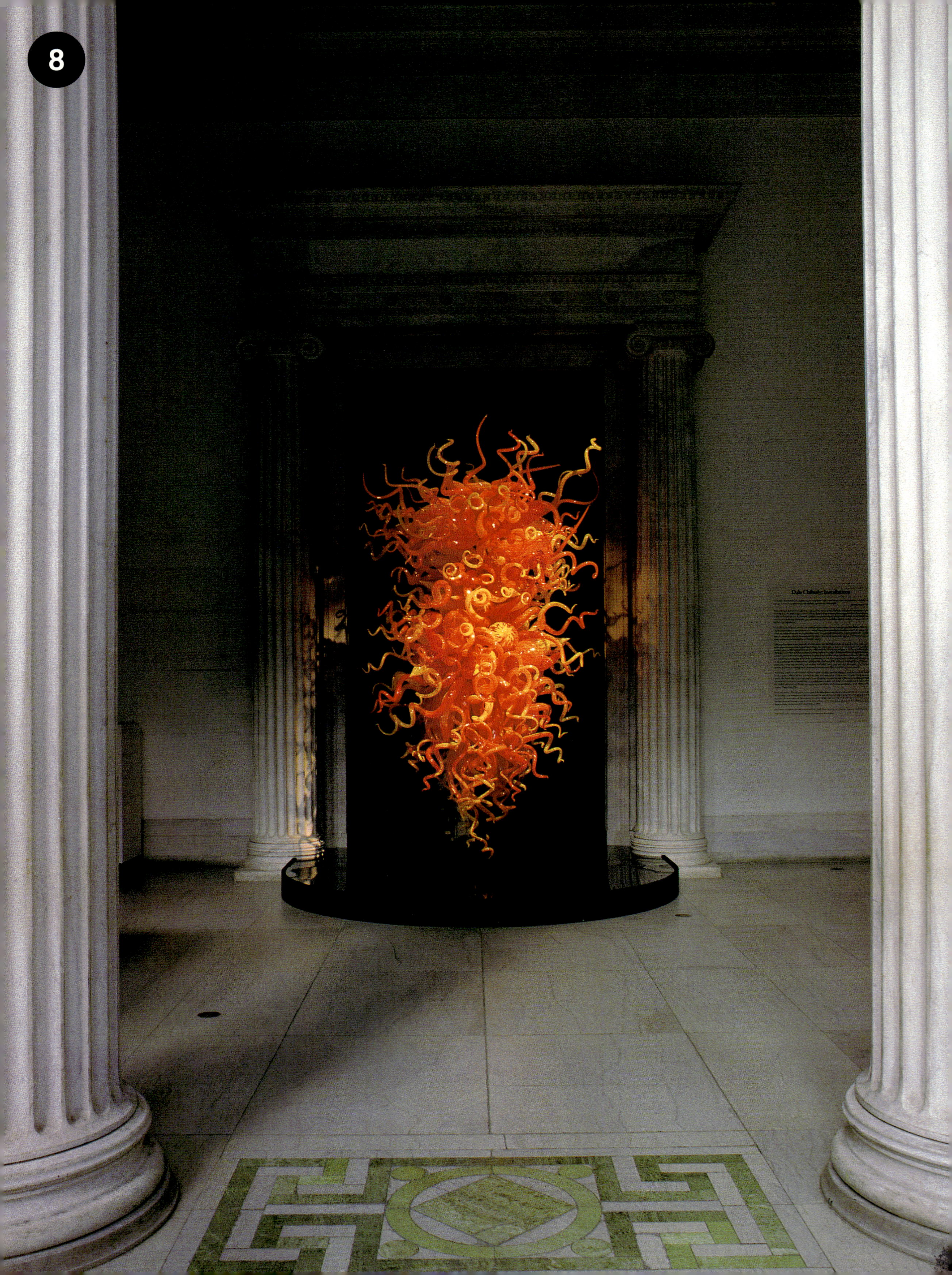

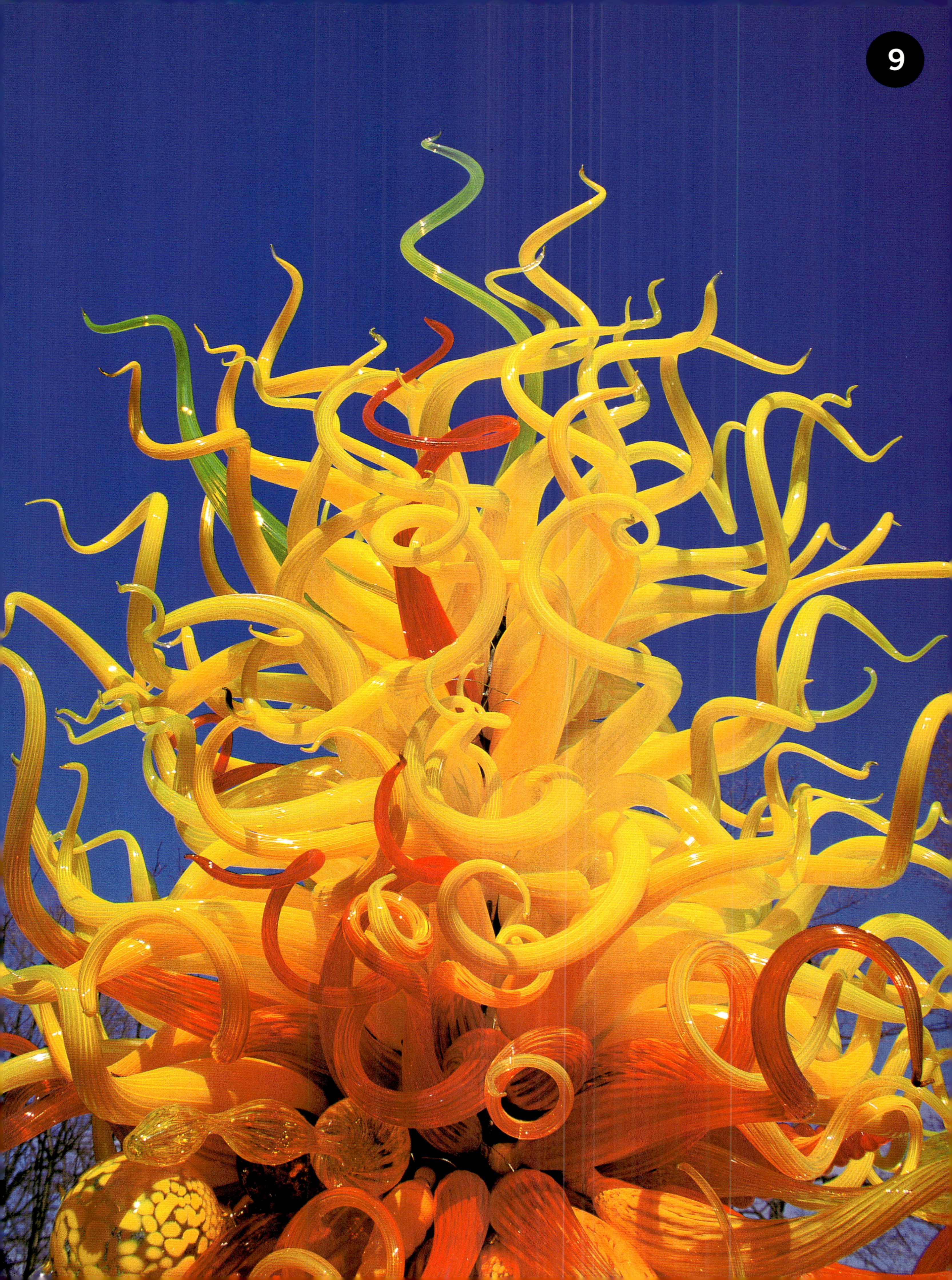

9

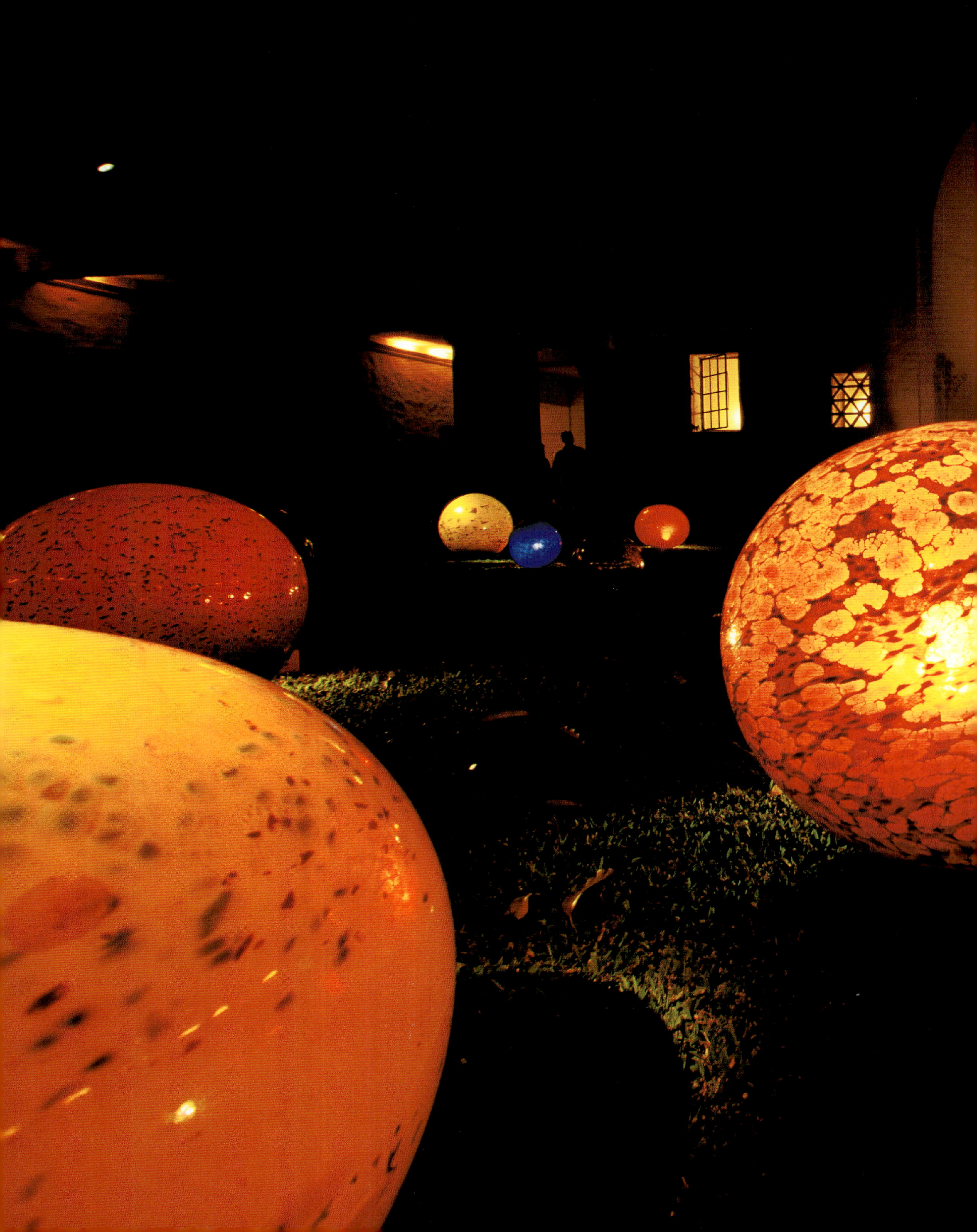

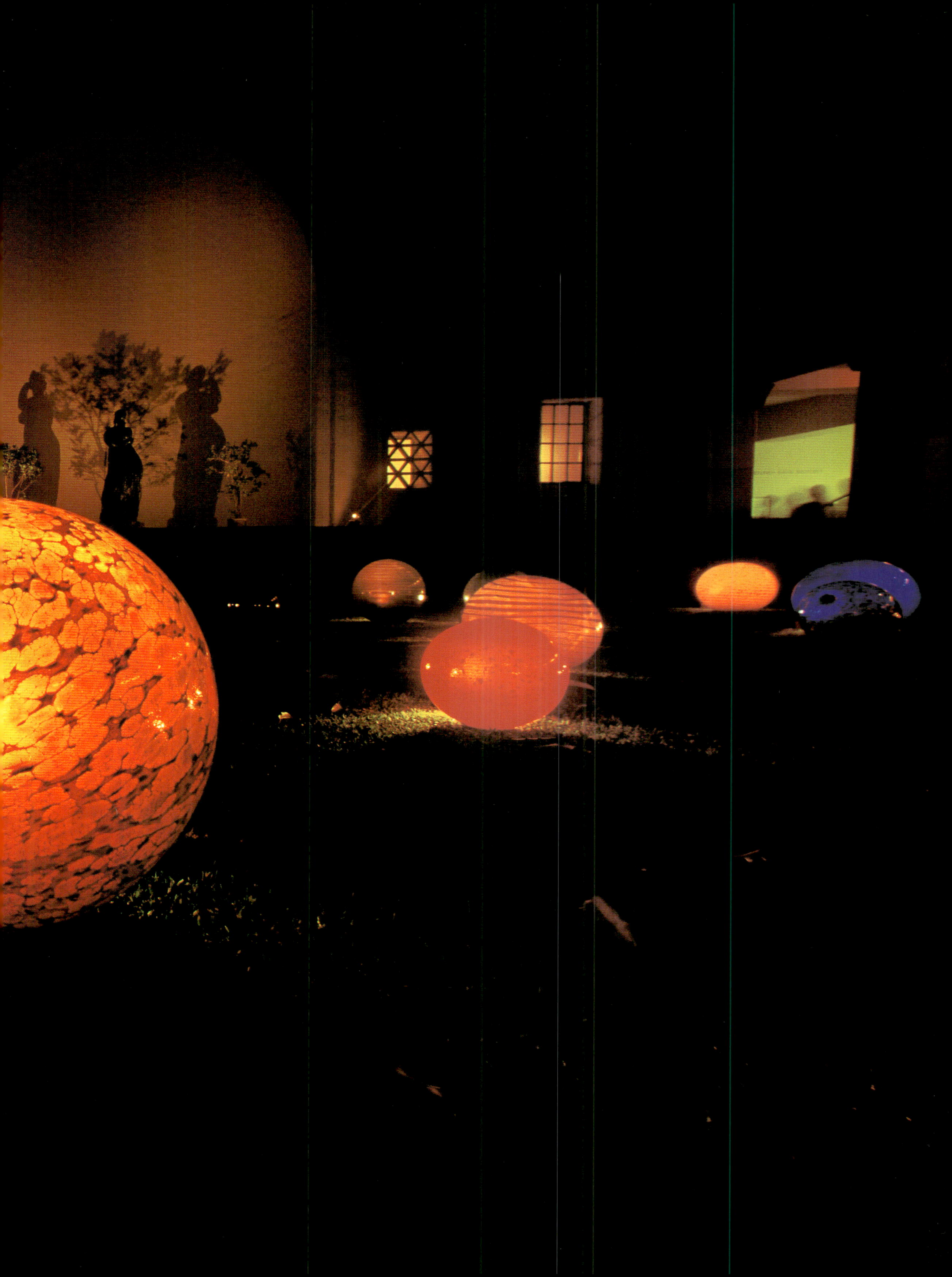

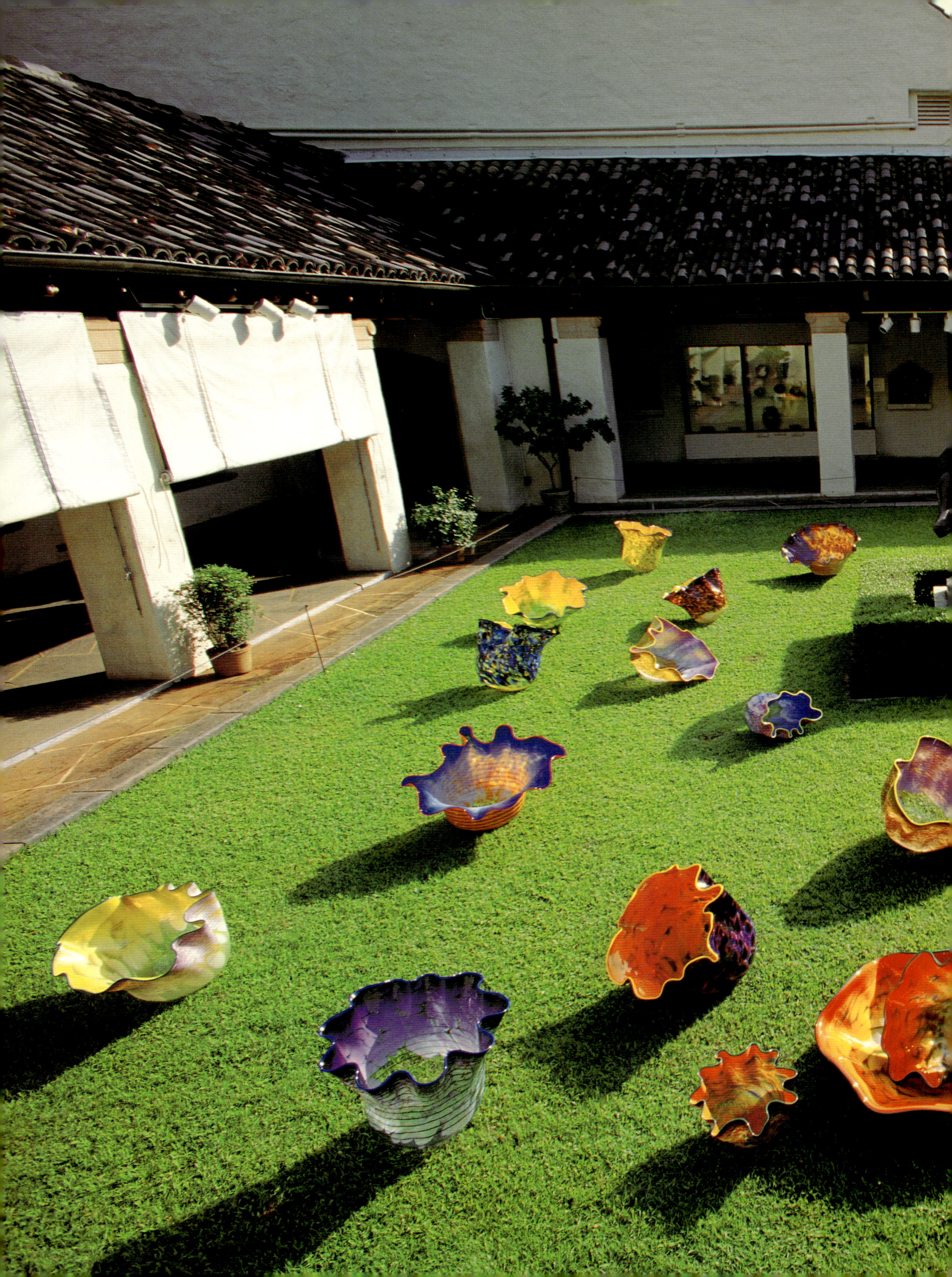

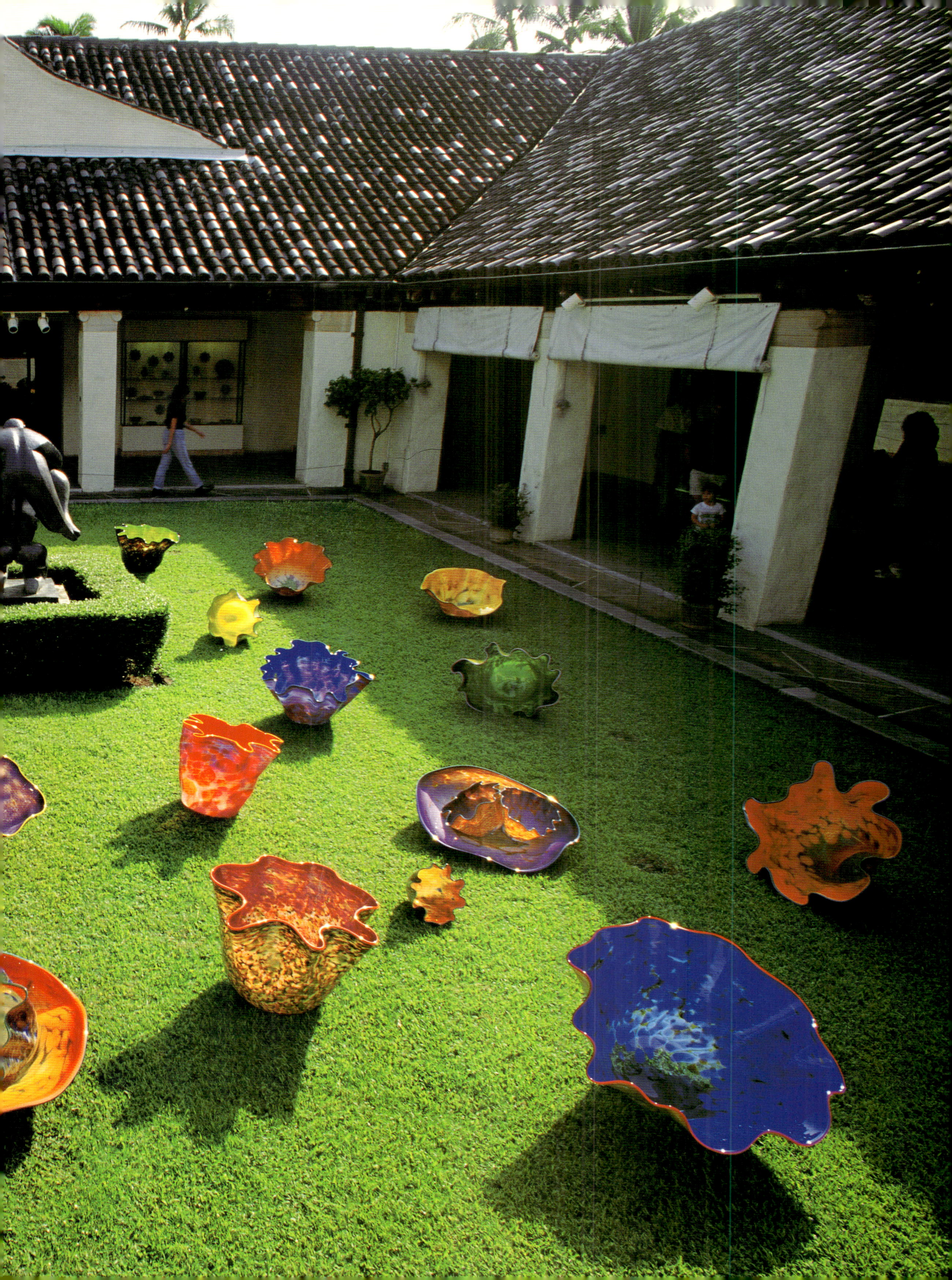

11

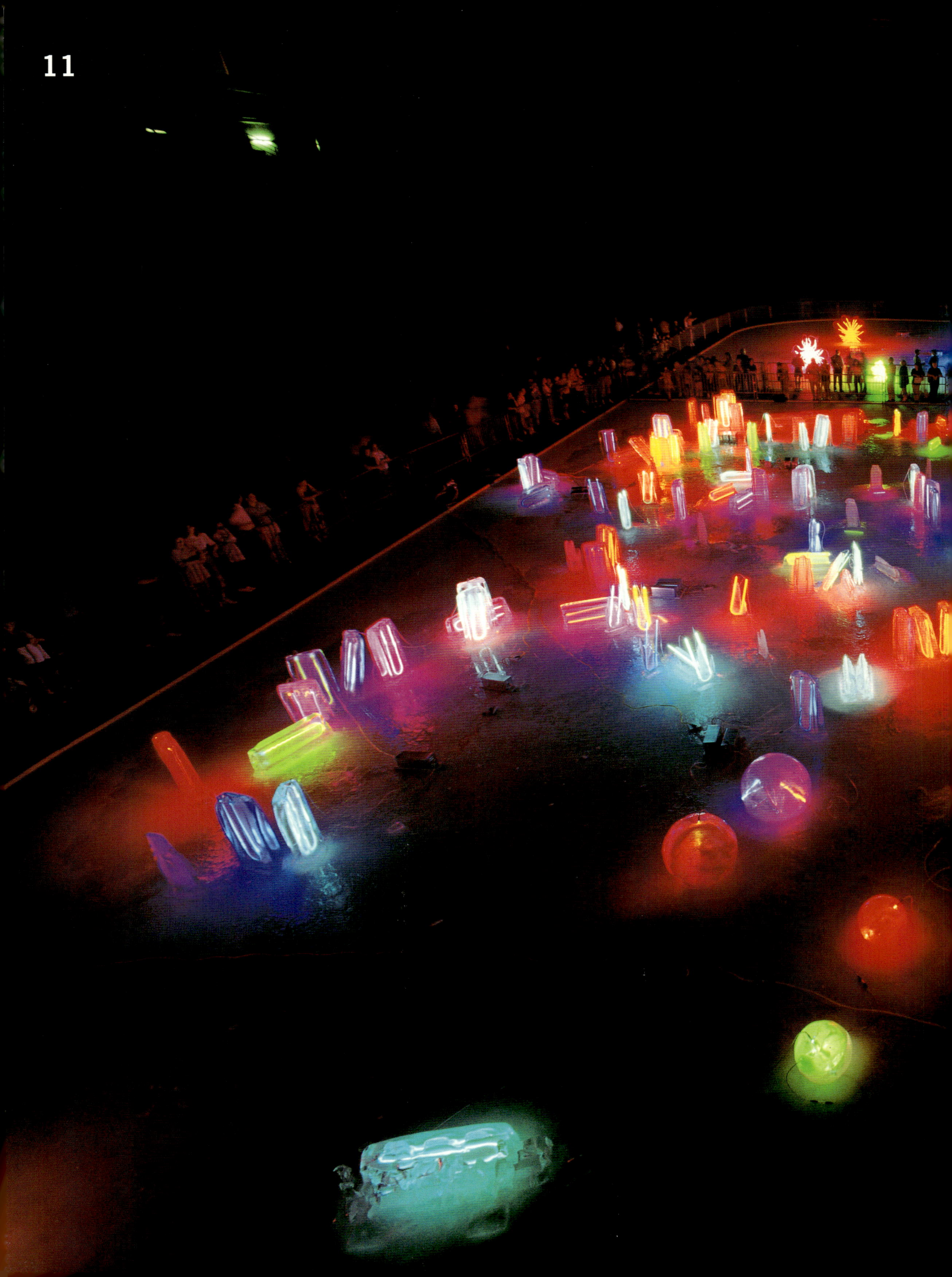

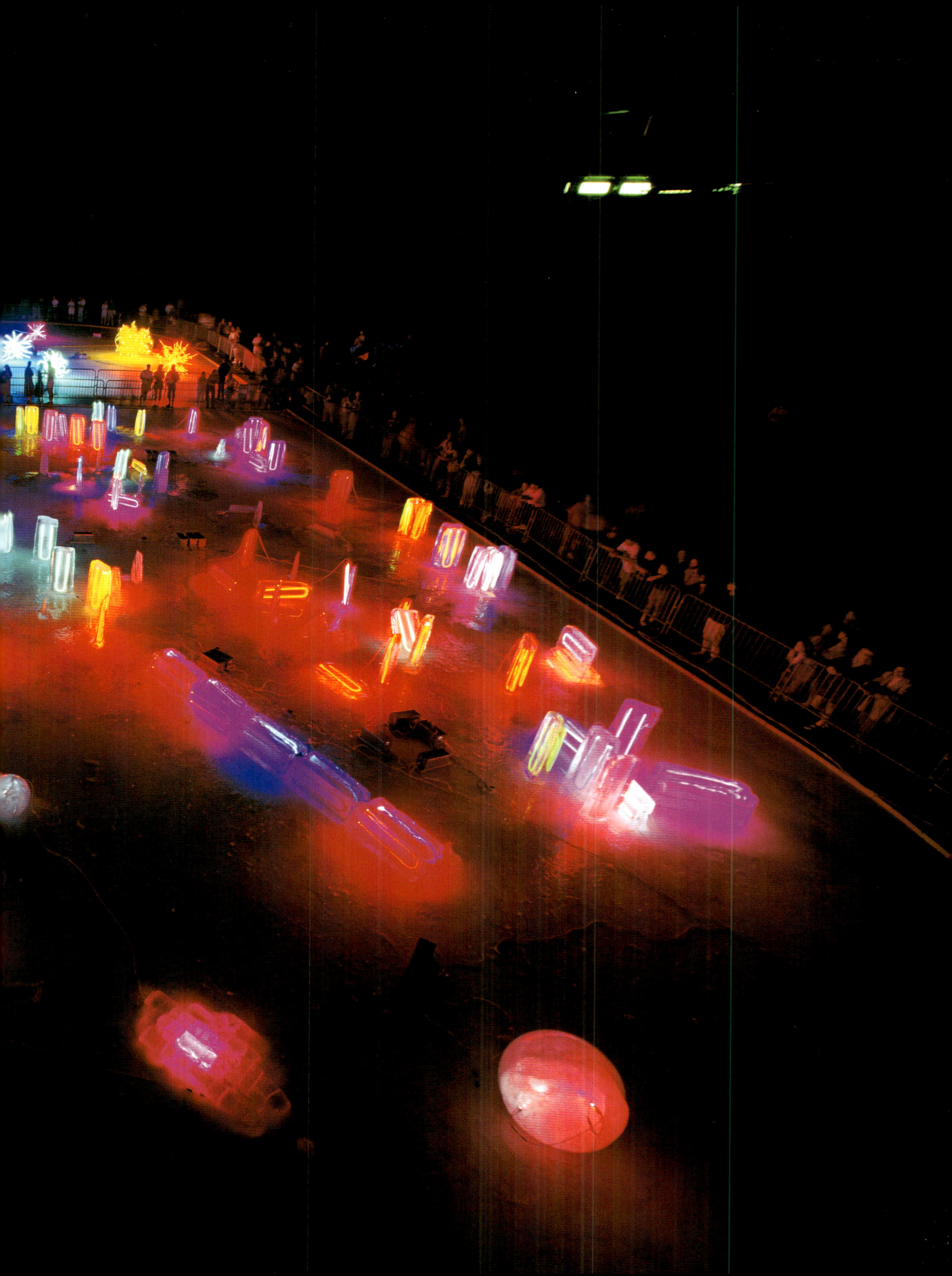

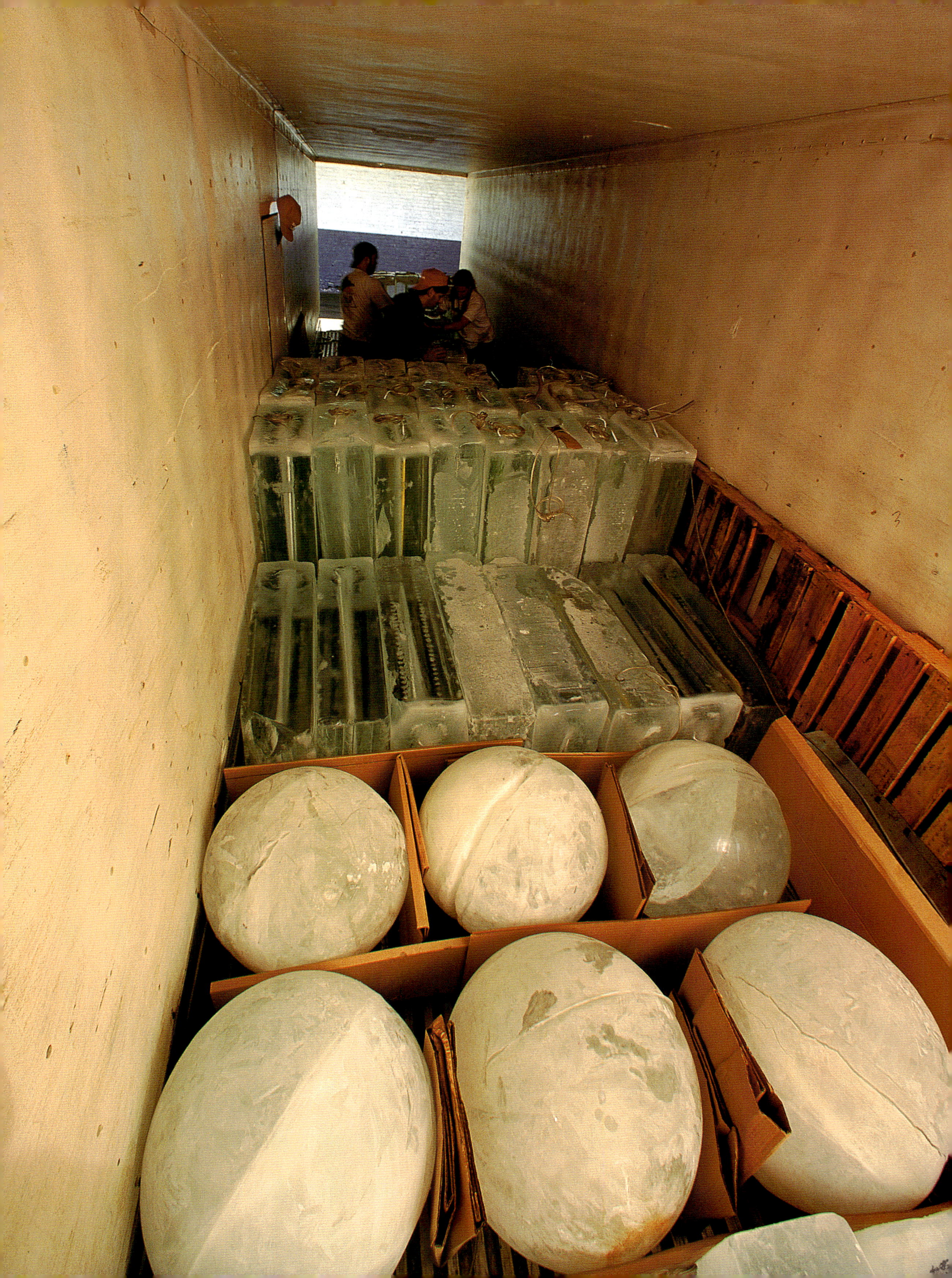

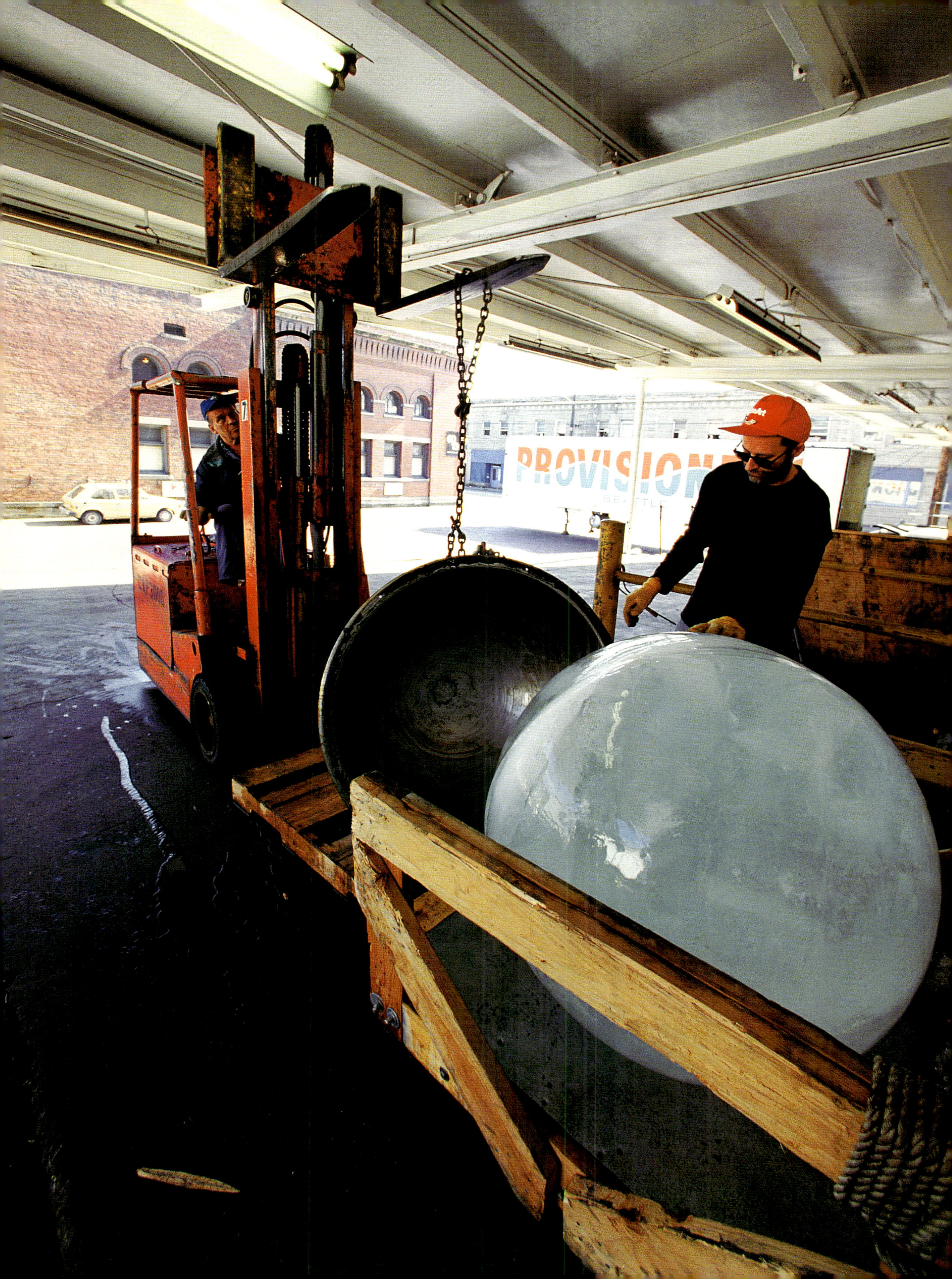
PROVISION

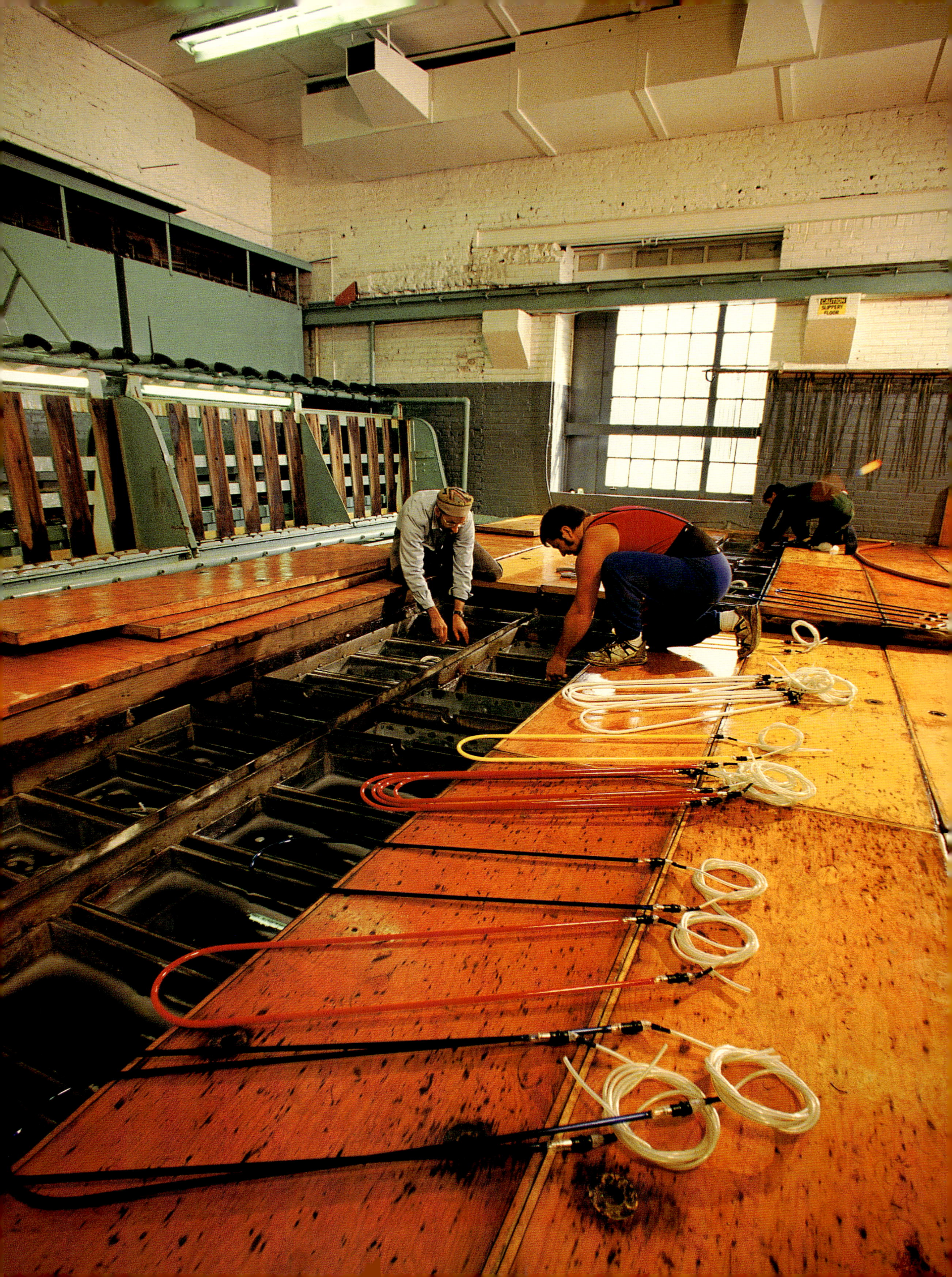
CAUTION
SLIPPERY
FLOOR

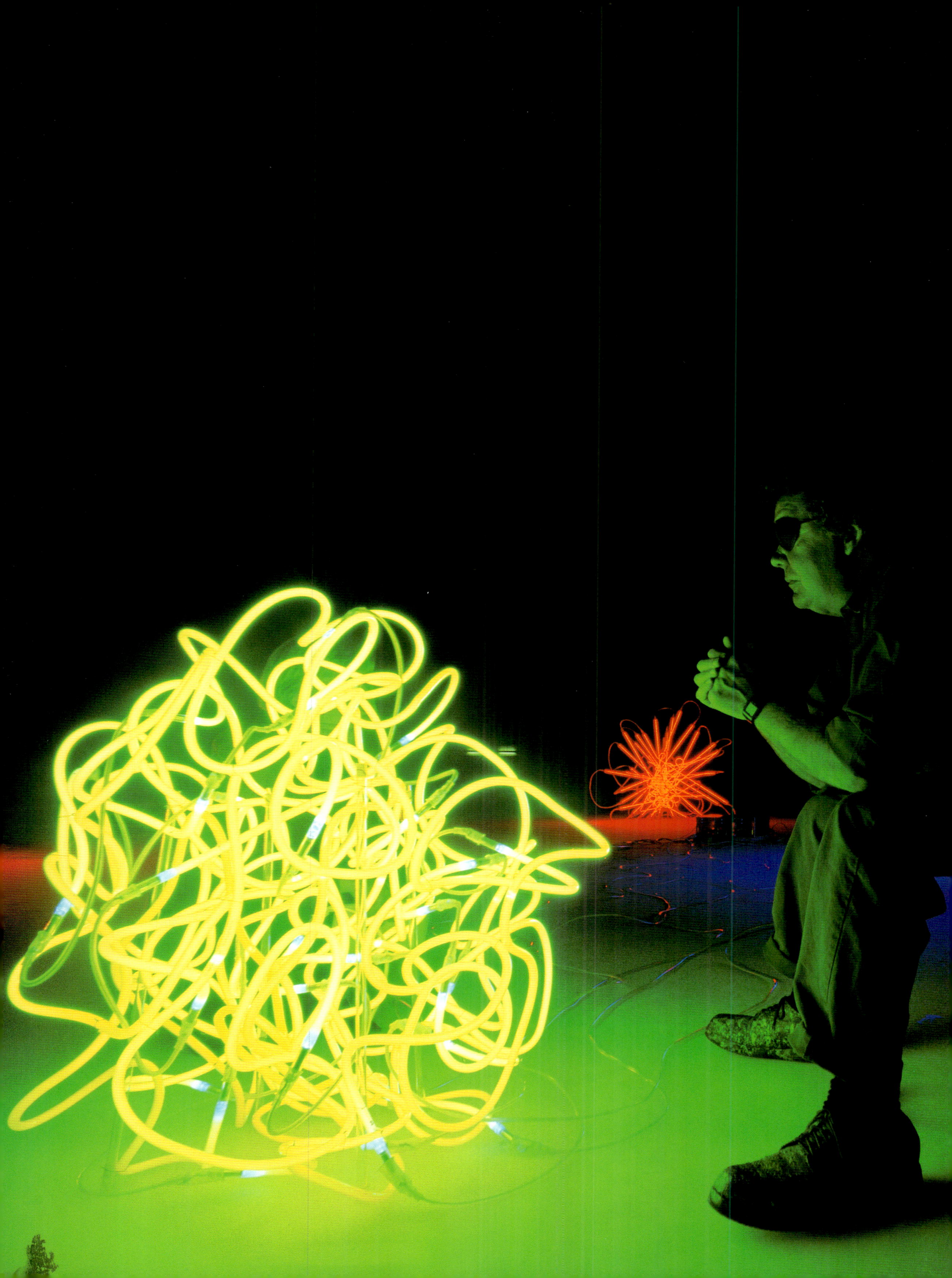

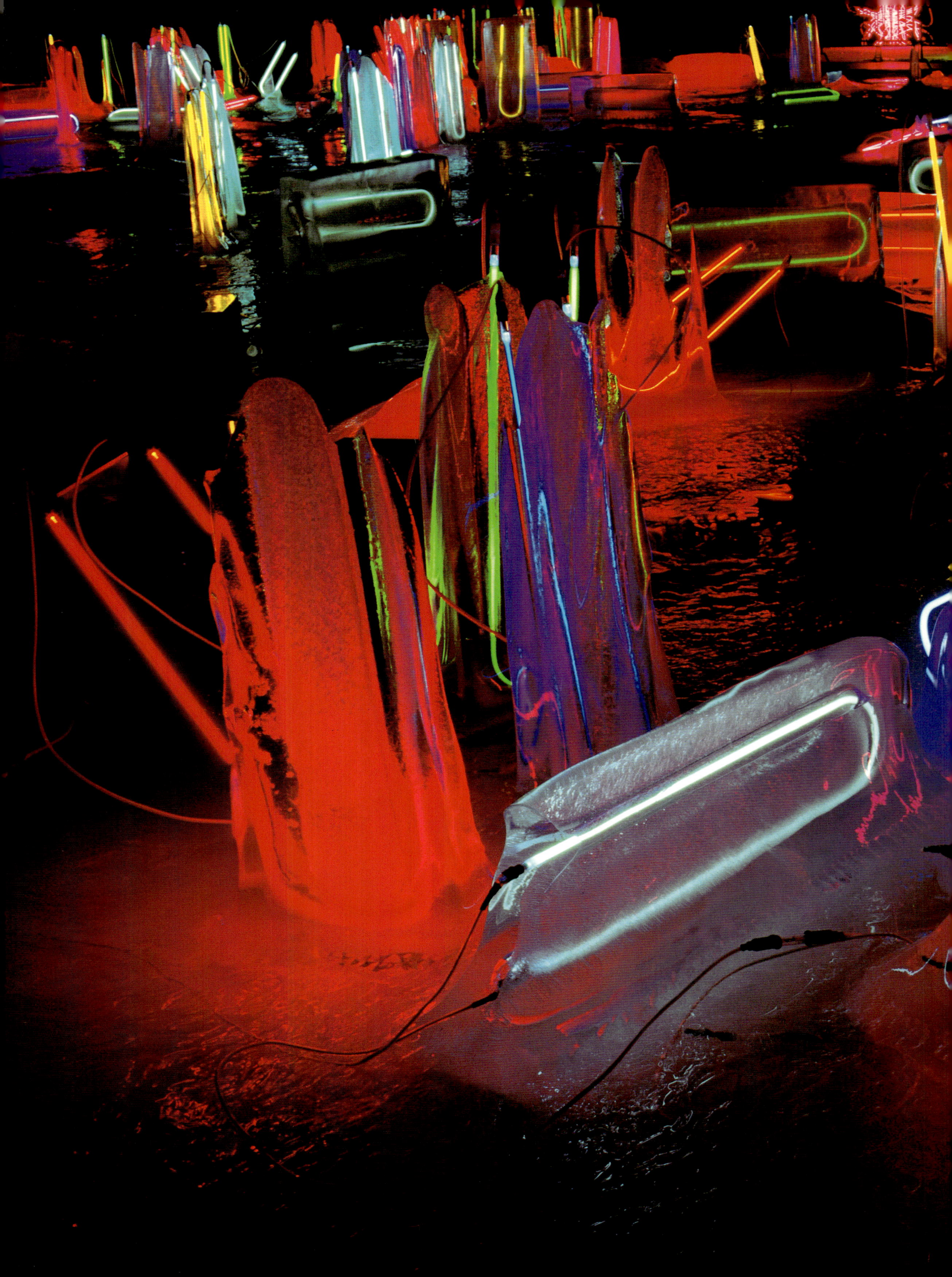

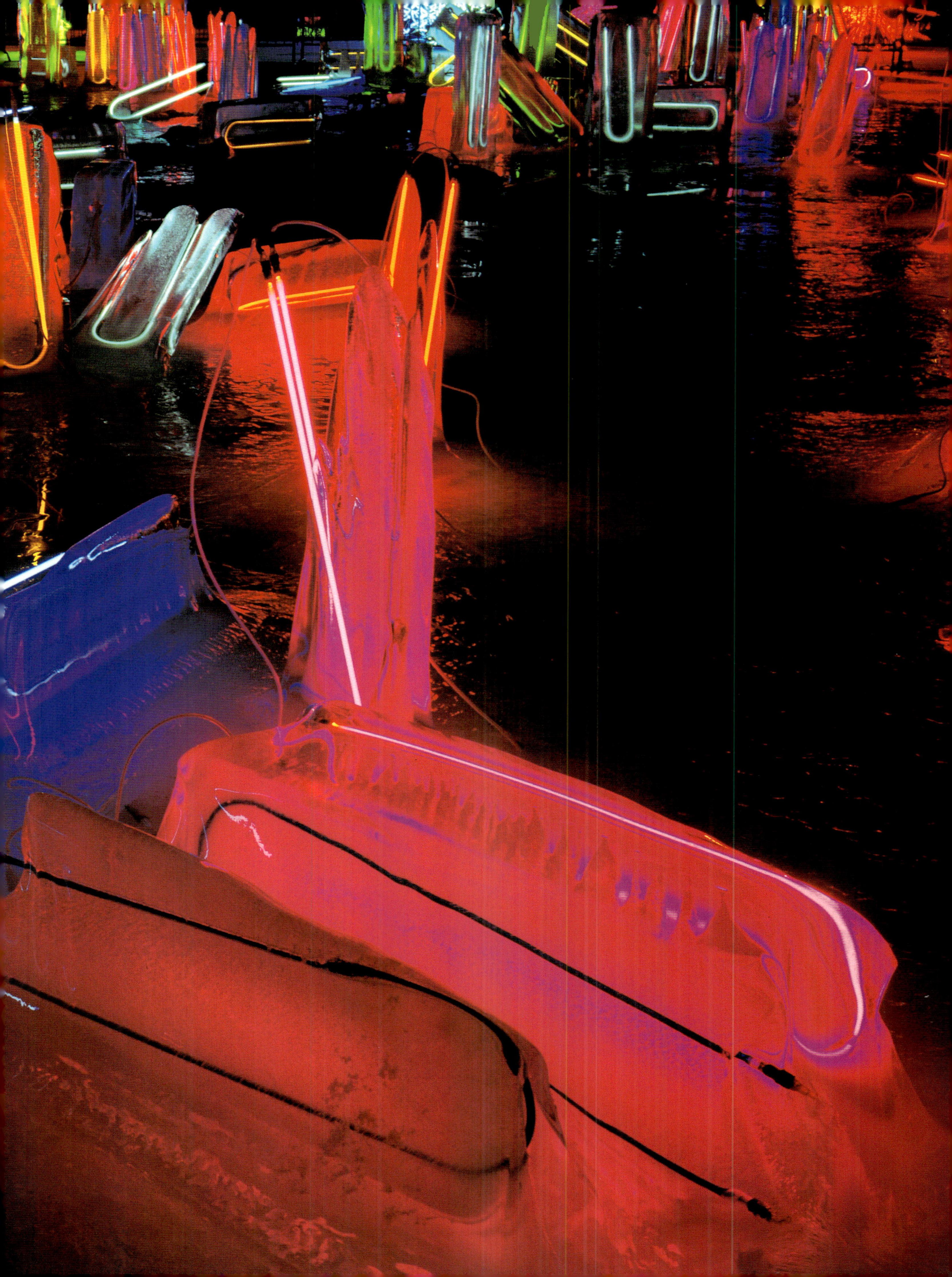

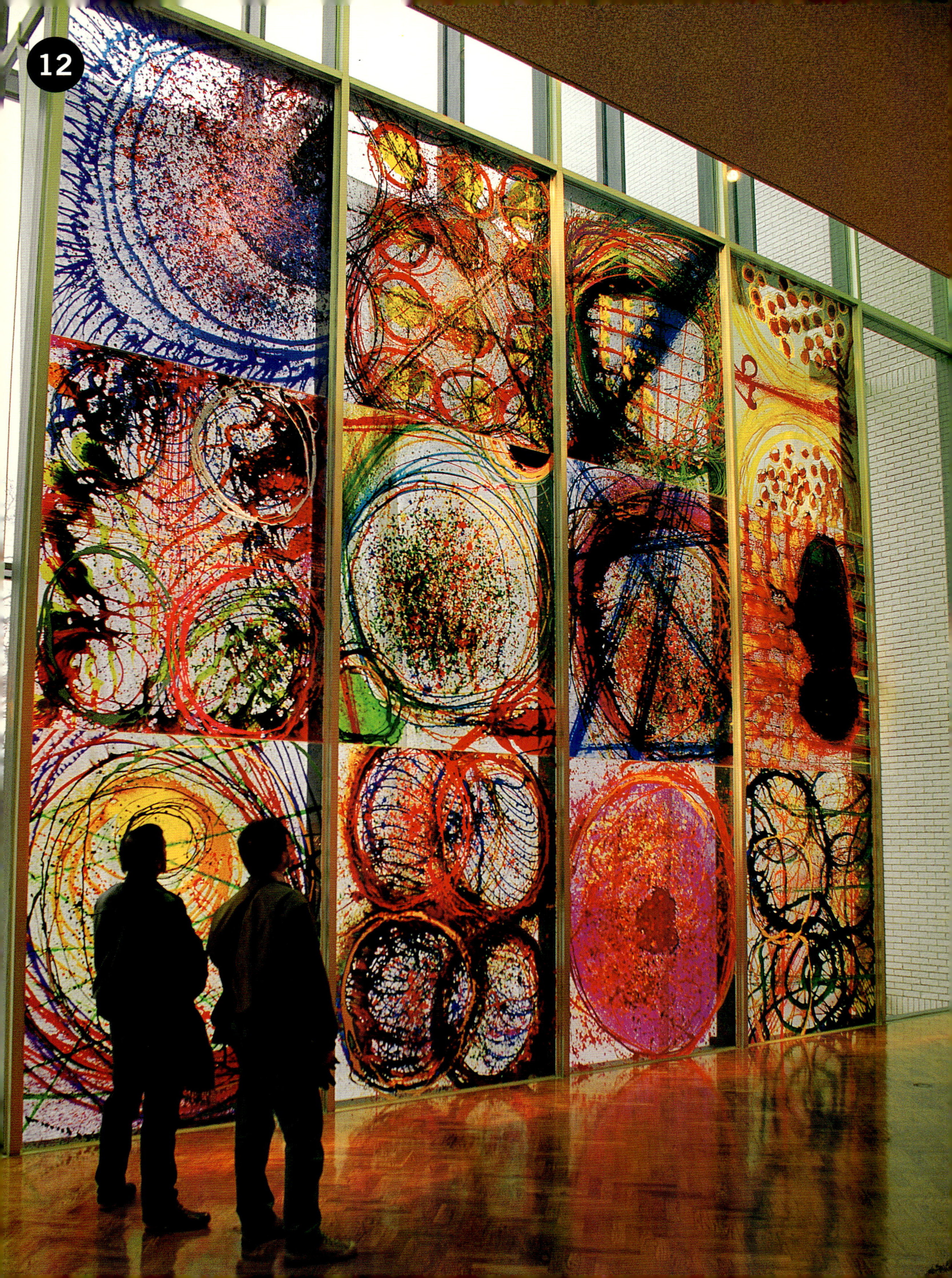
12

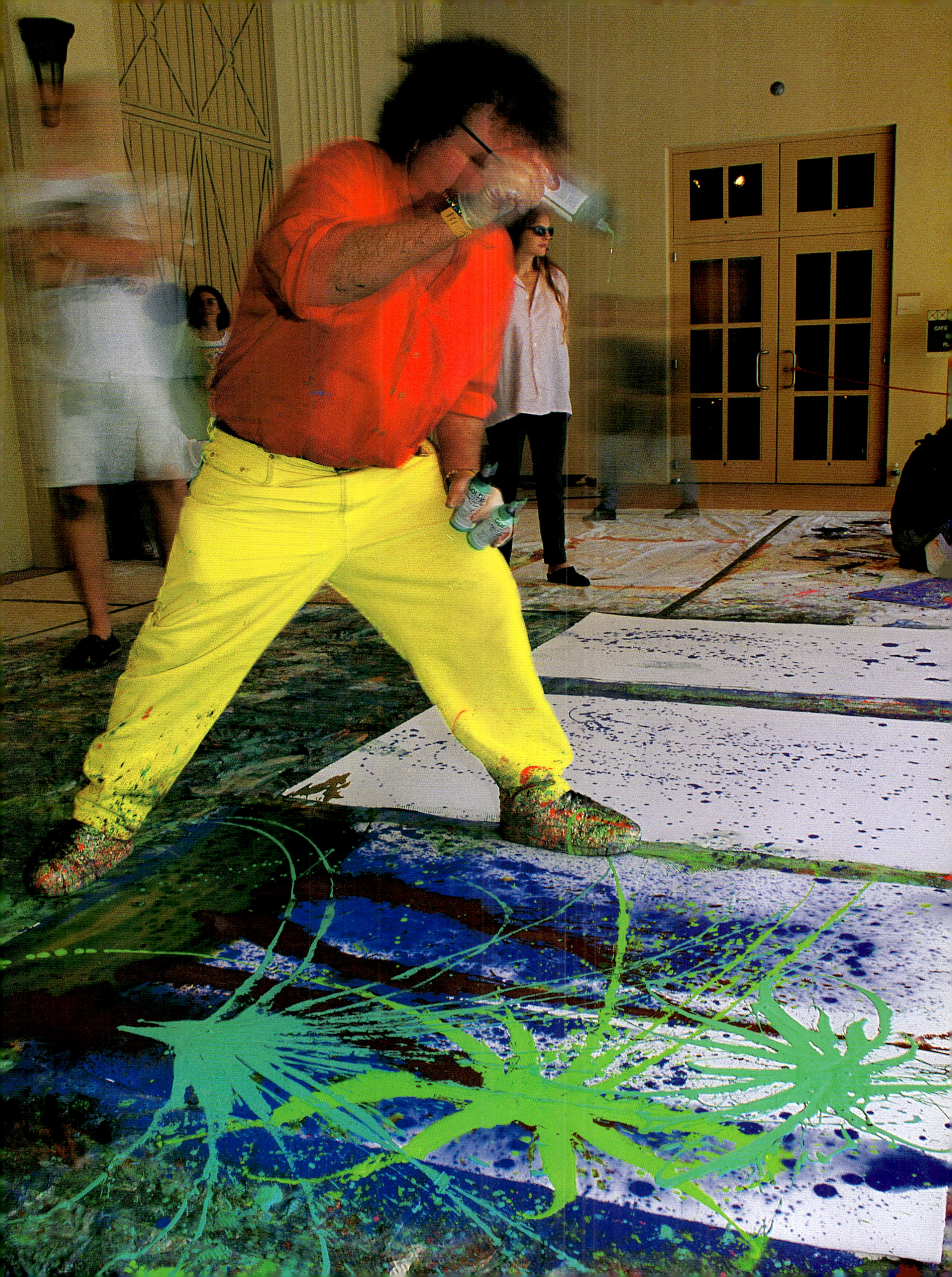

13

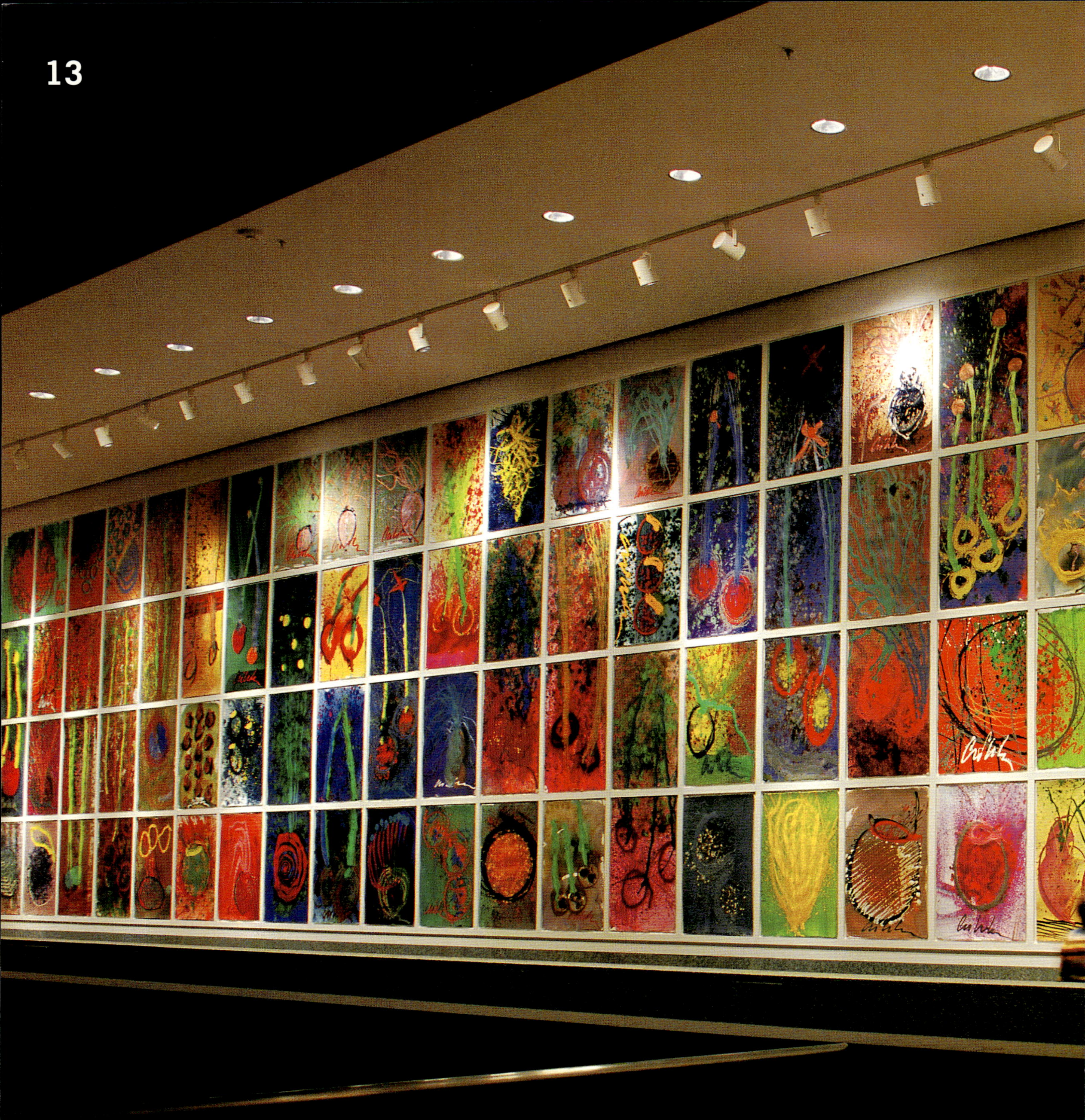

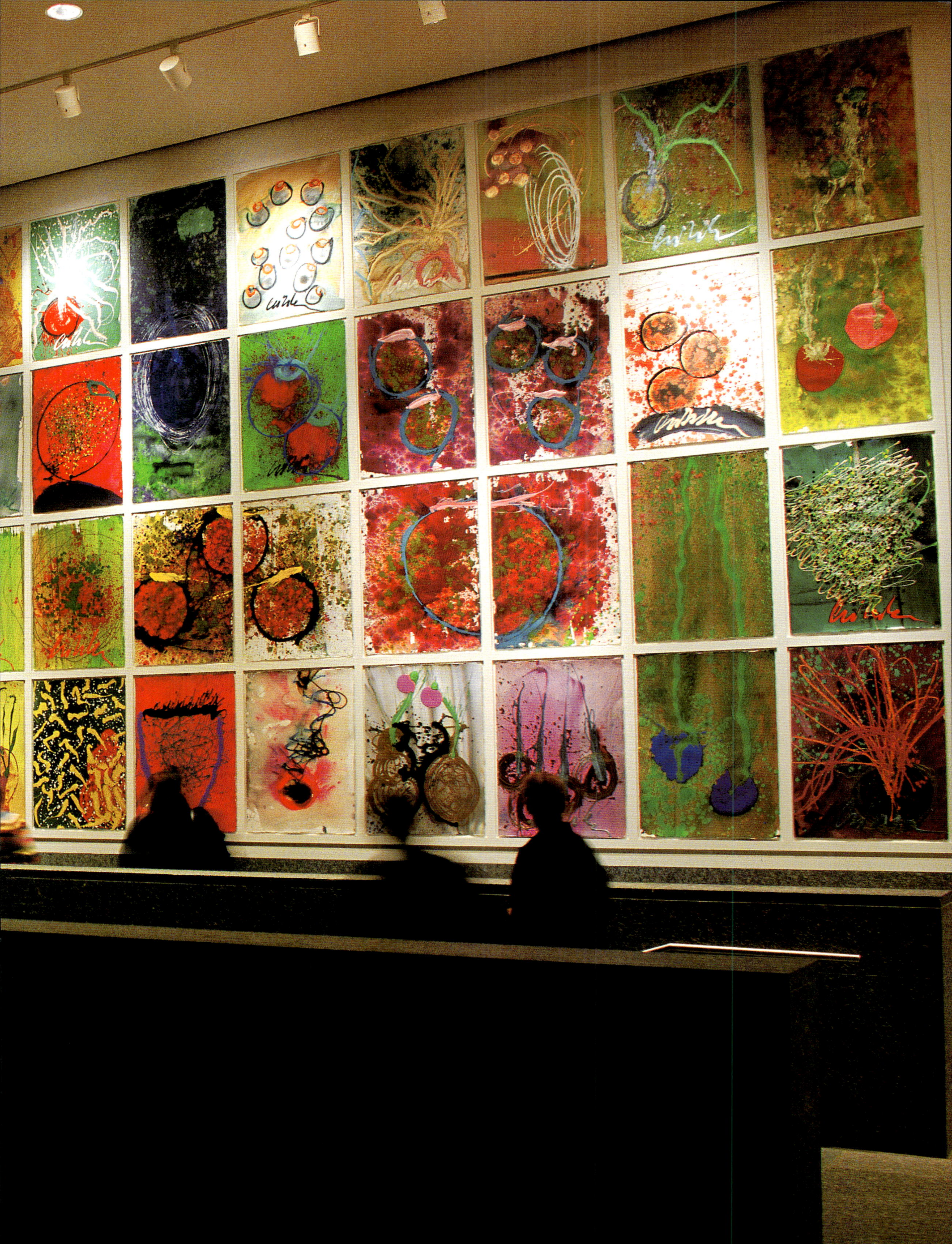

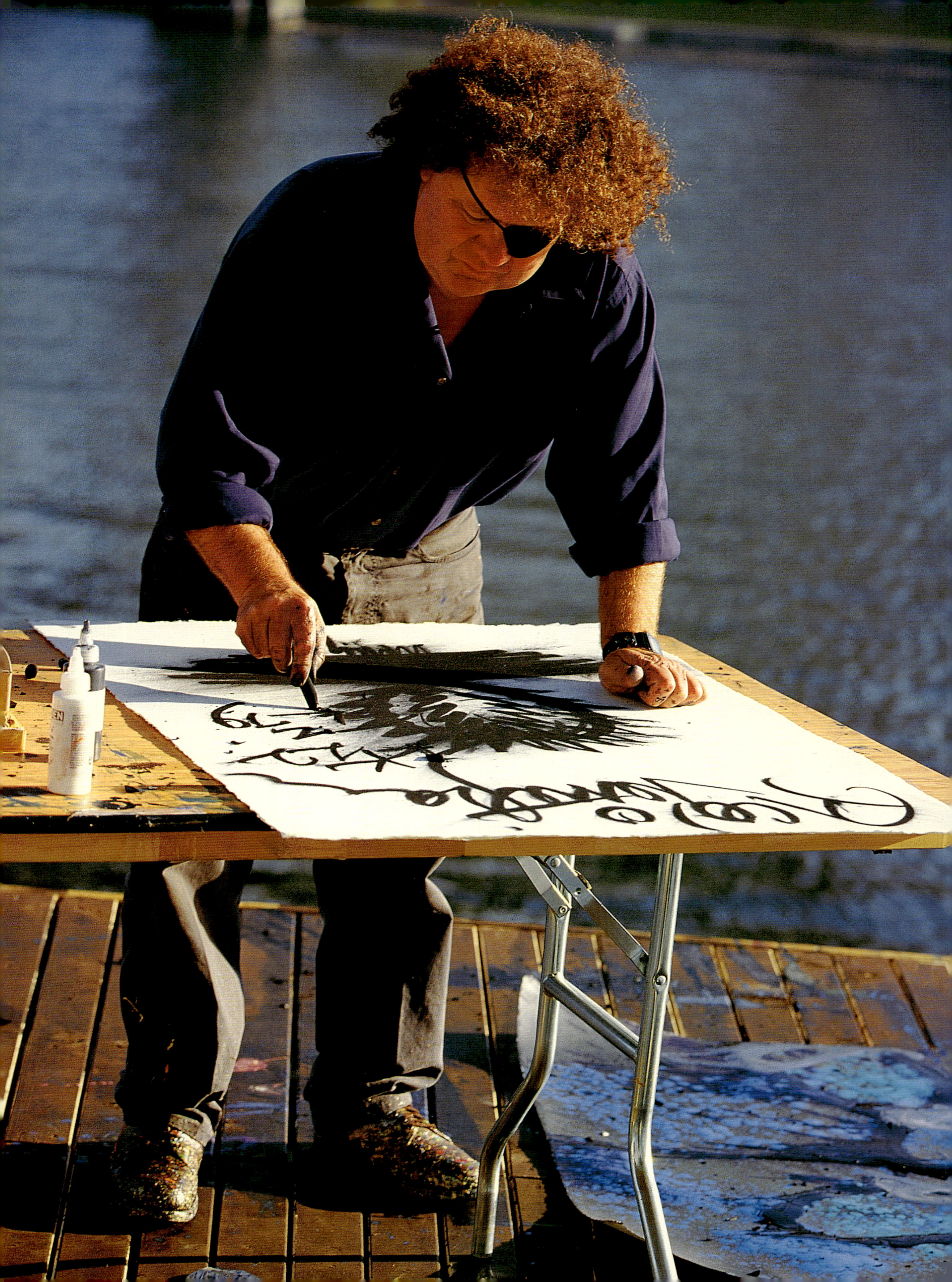

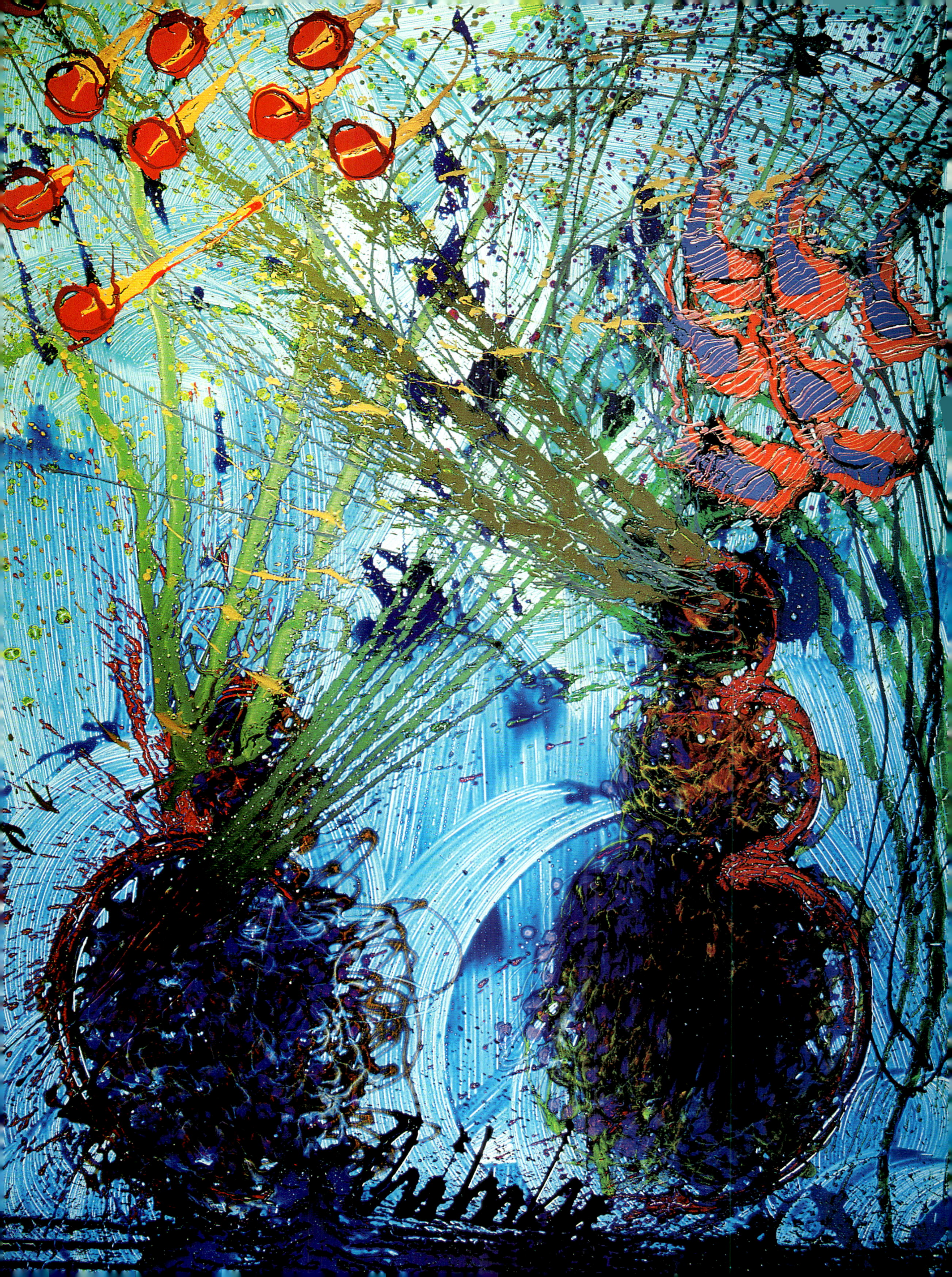

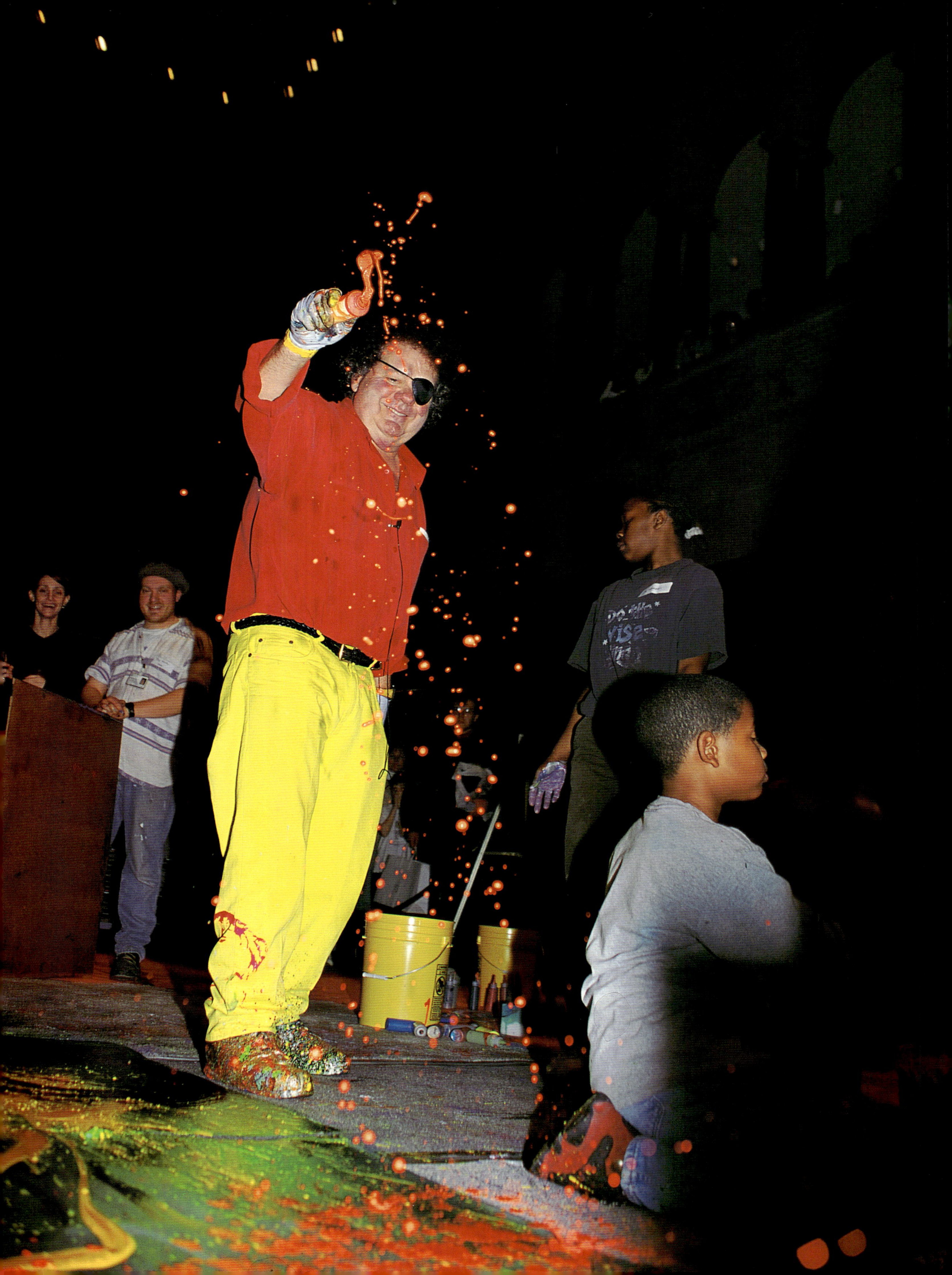

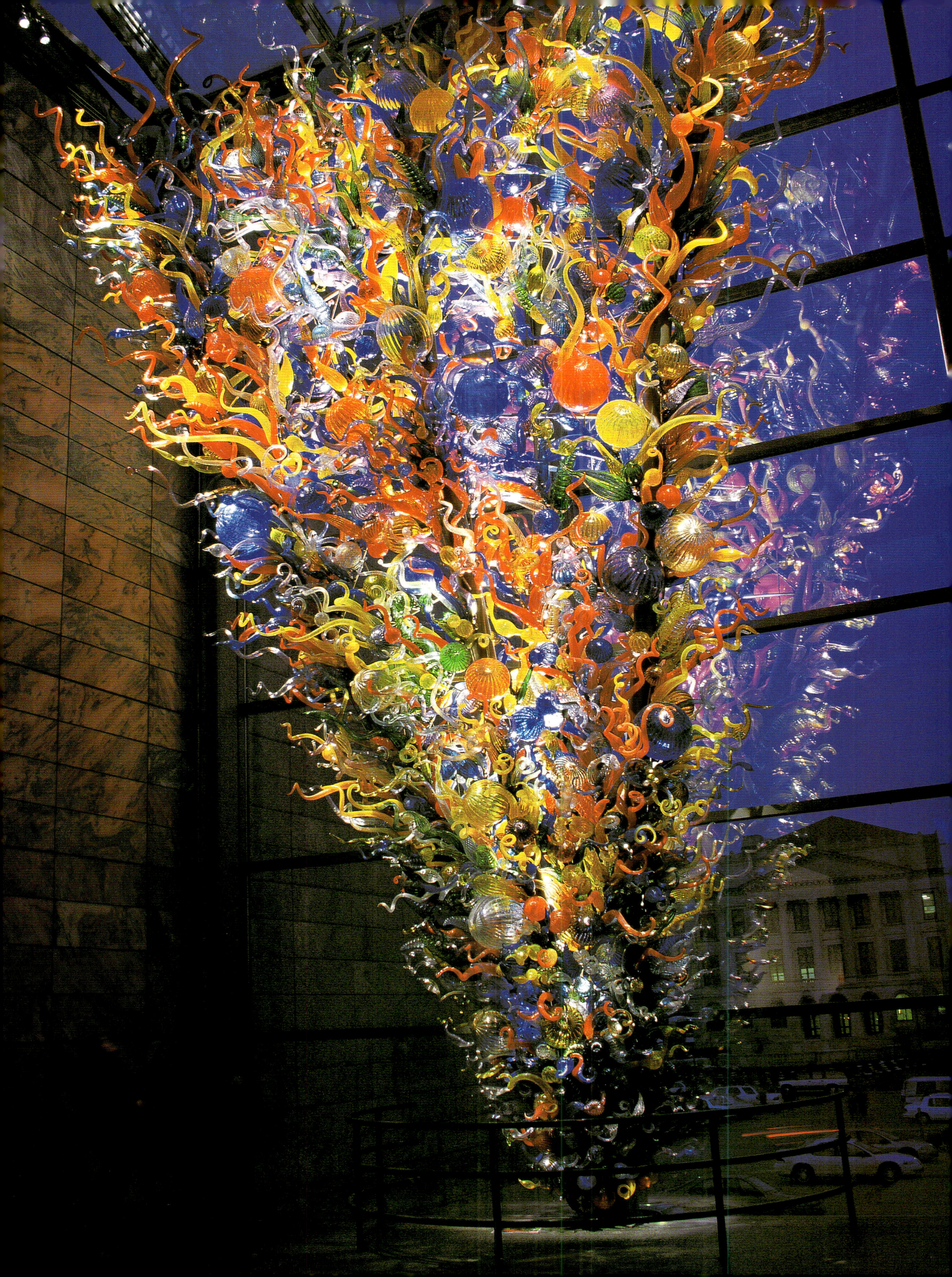

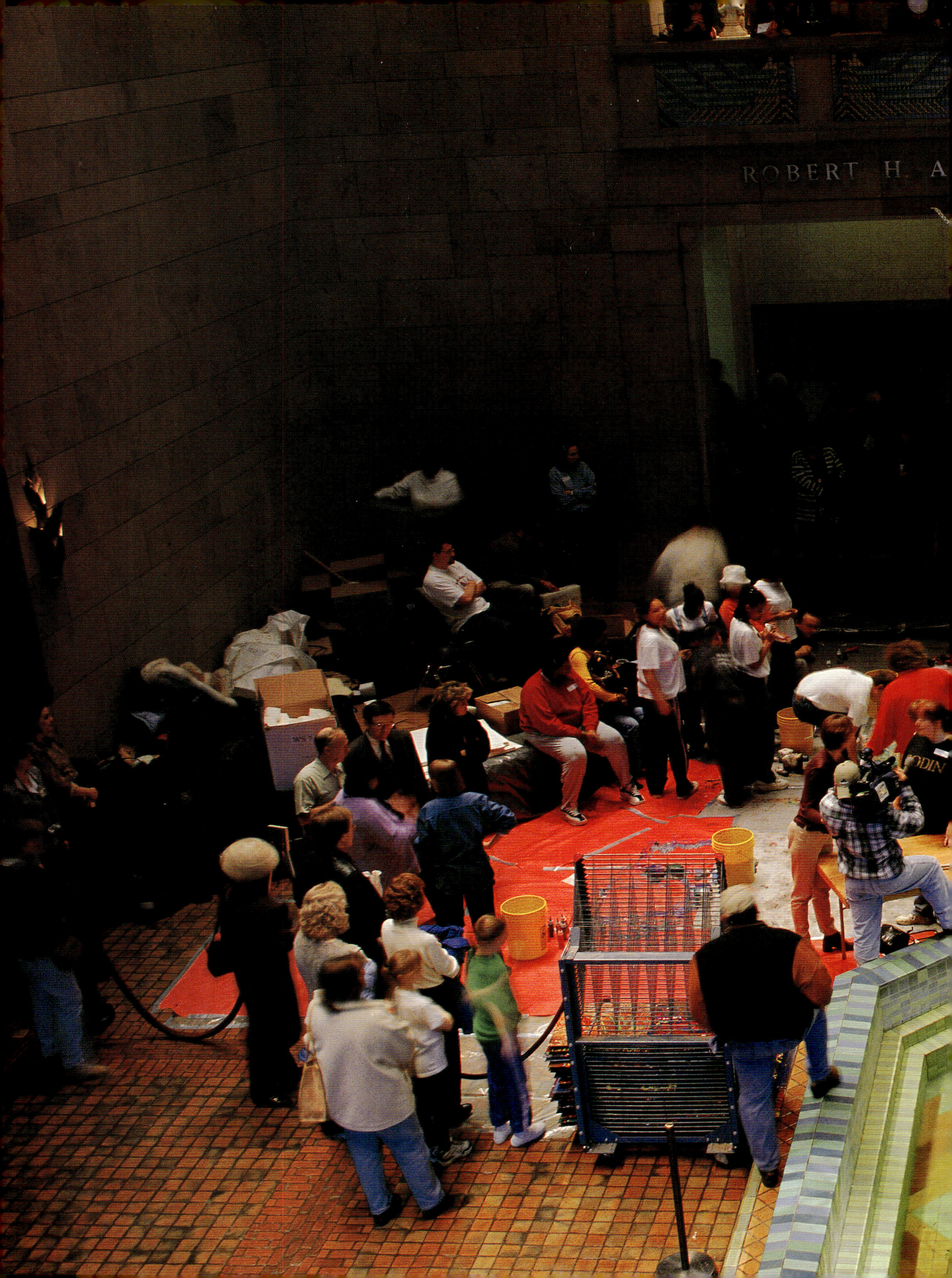
ROBERT H. A

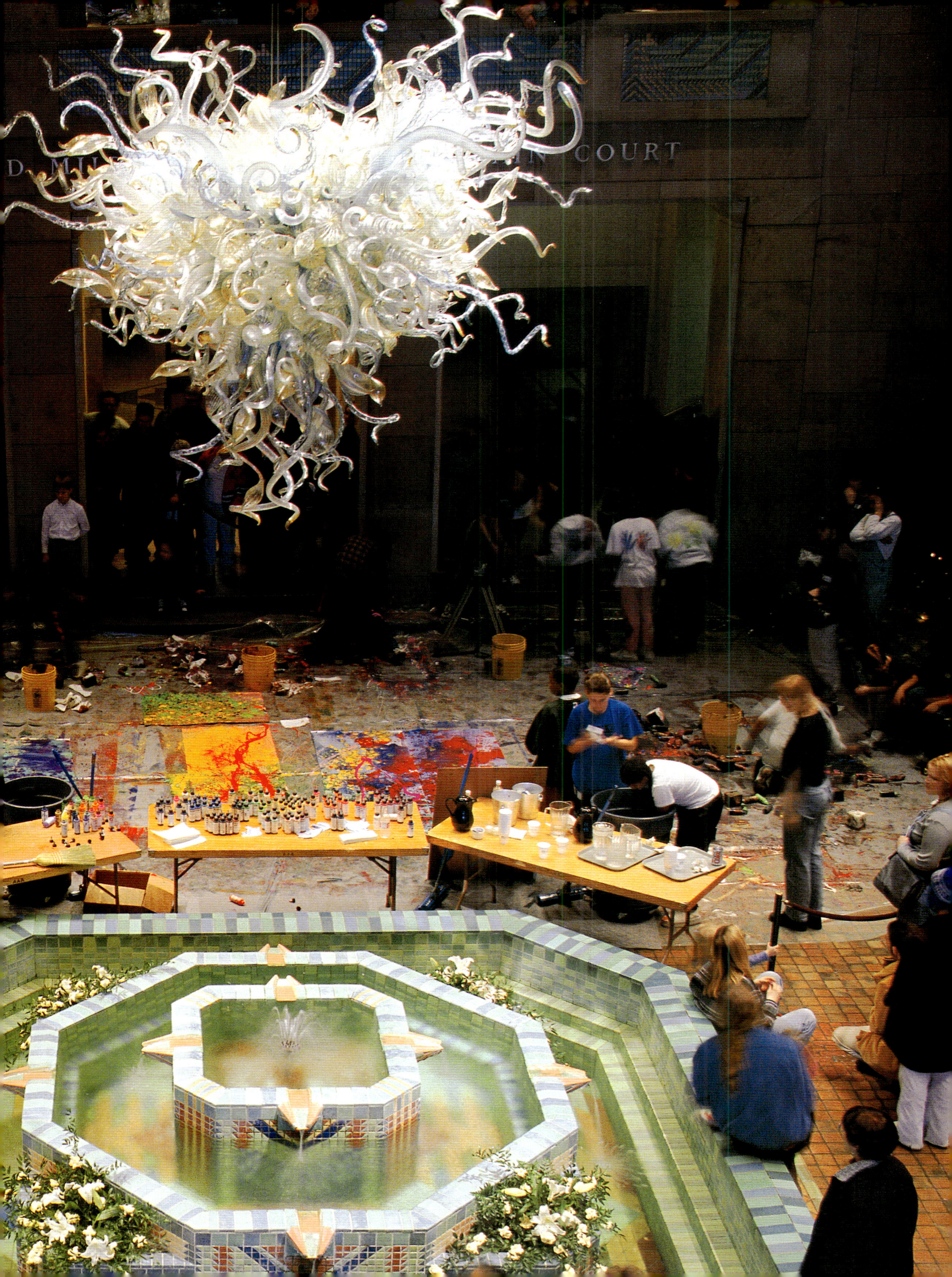
COURT

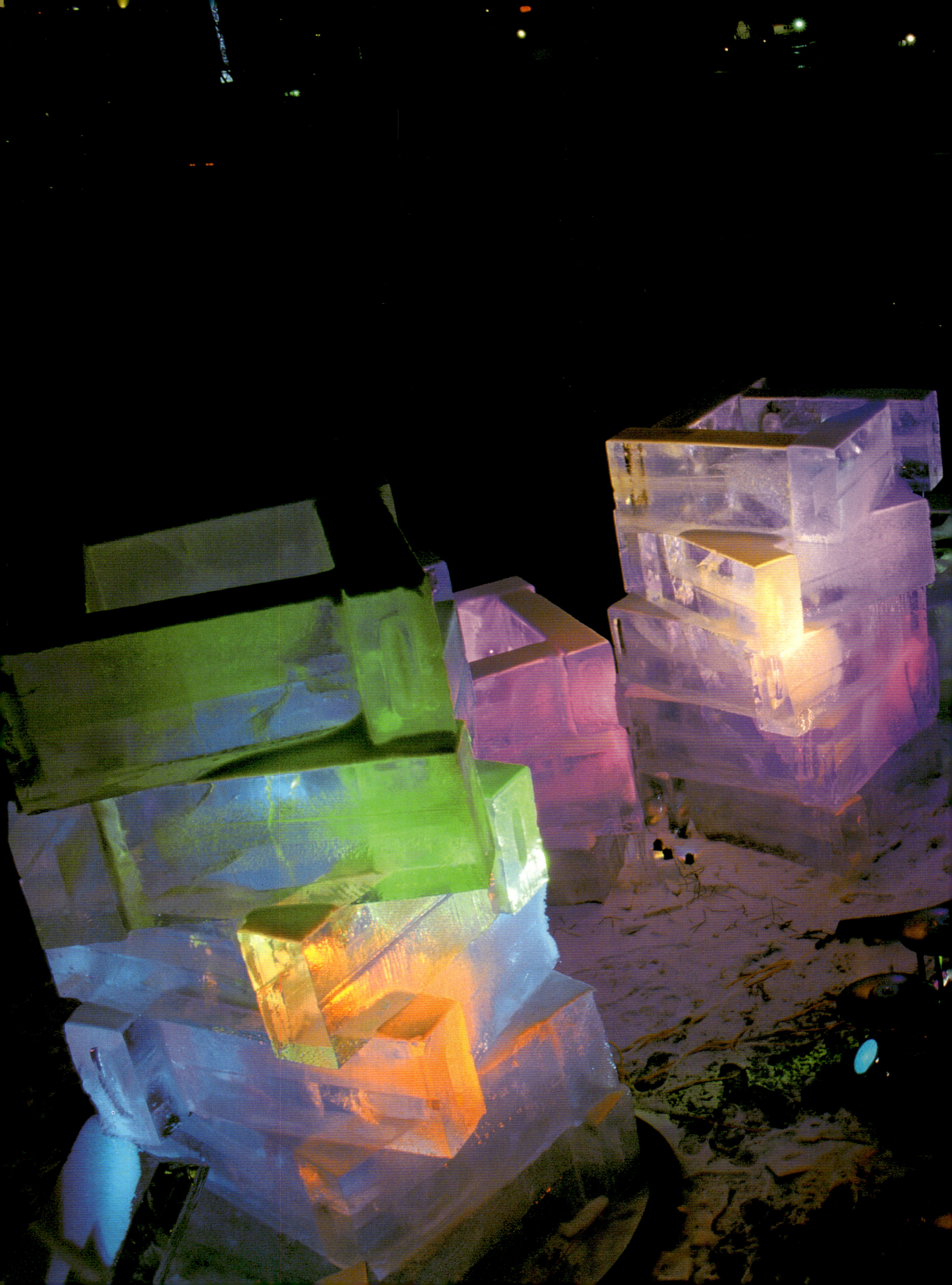

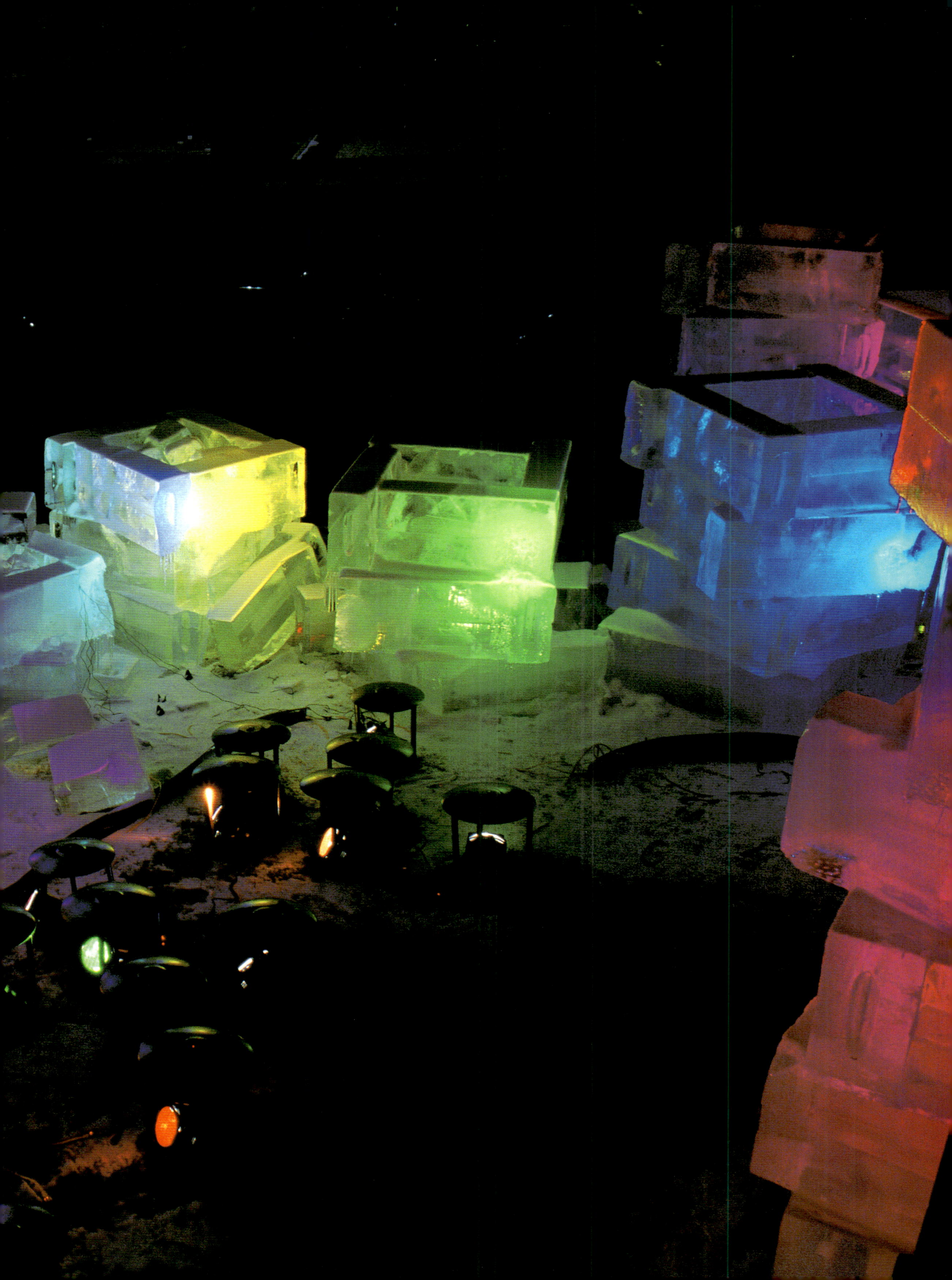

14

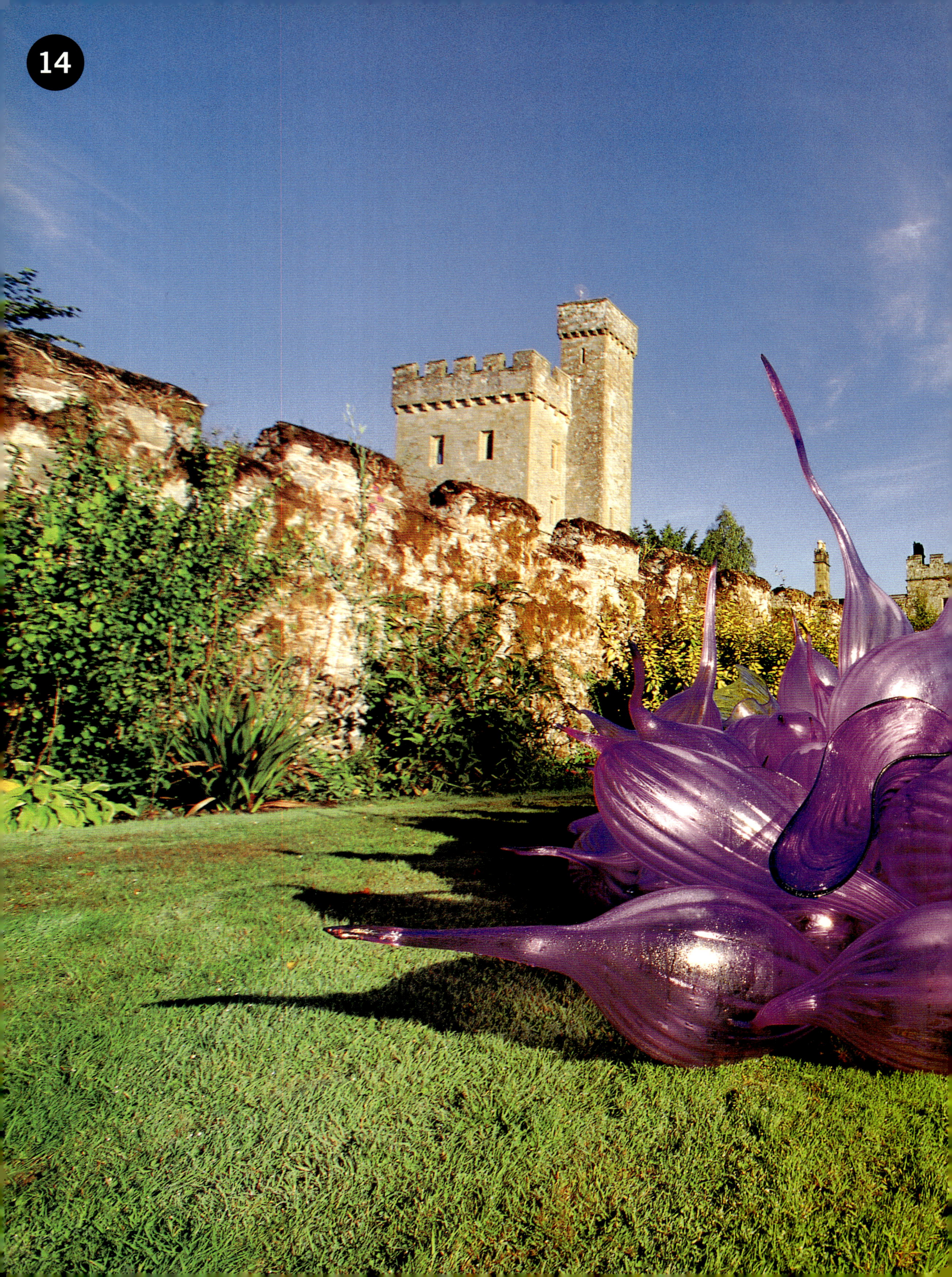

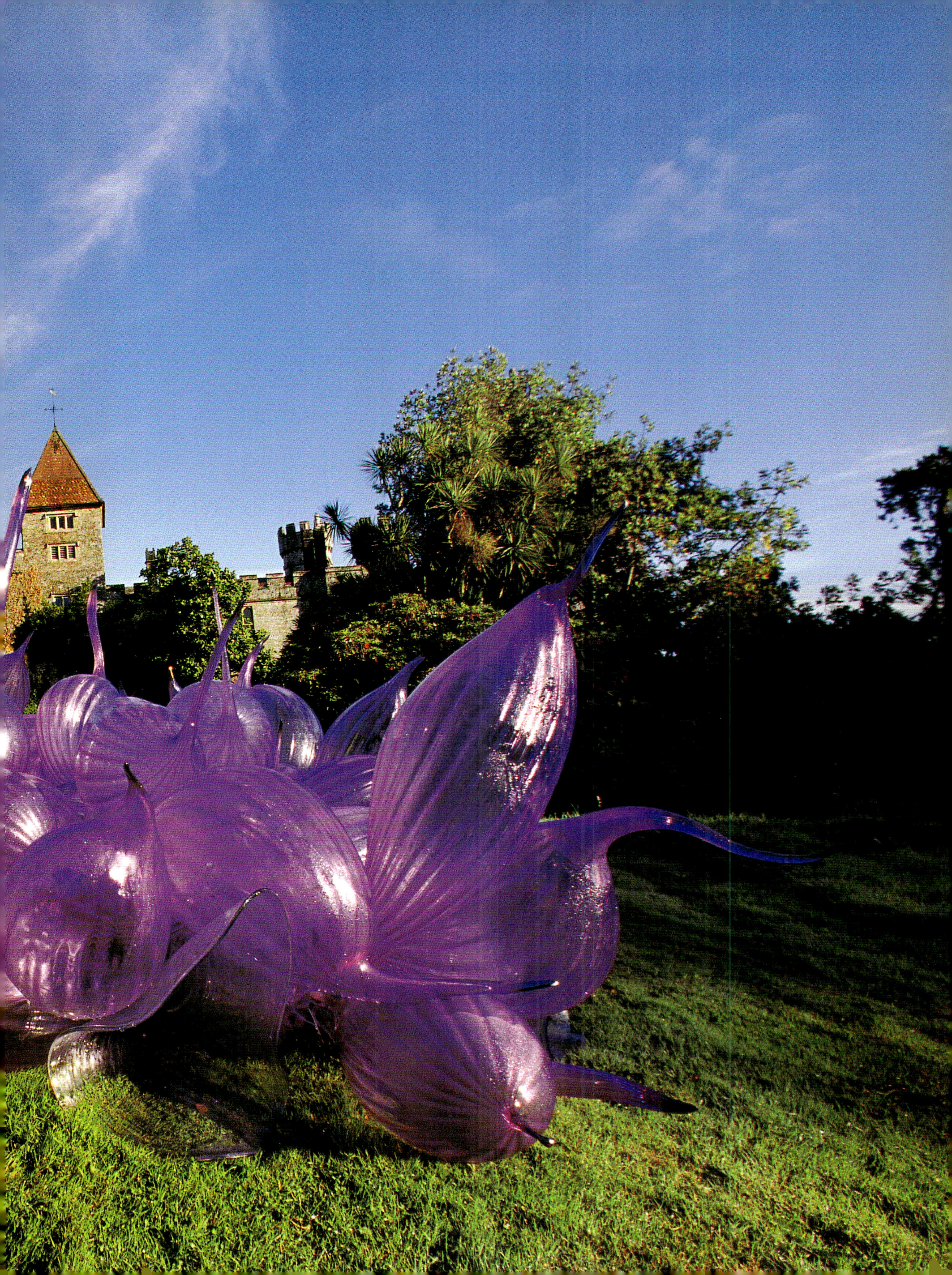

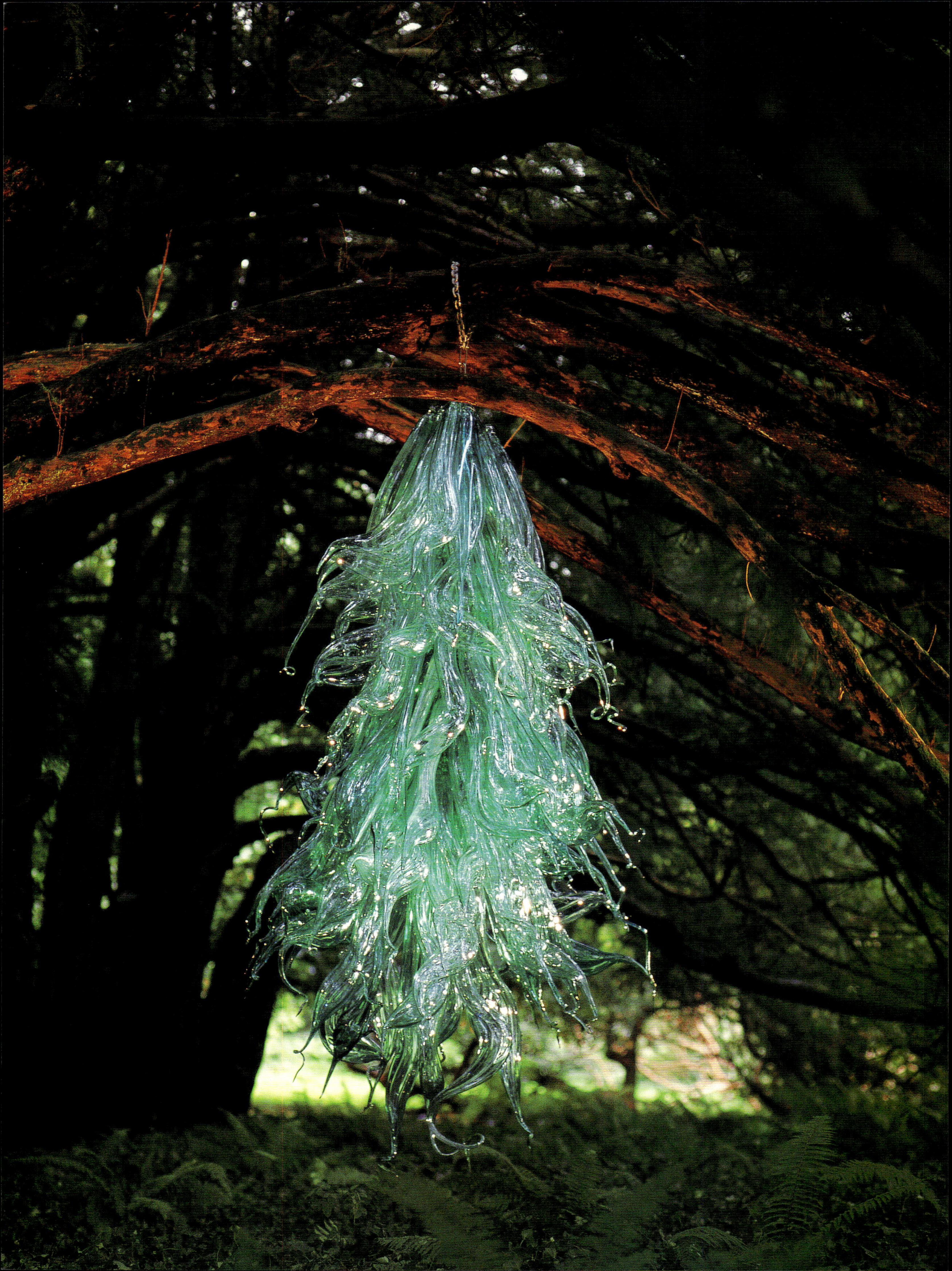

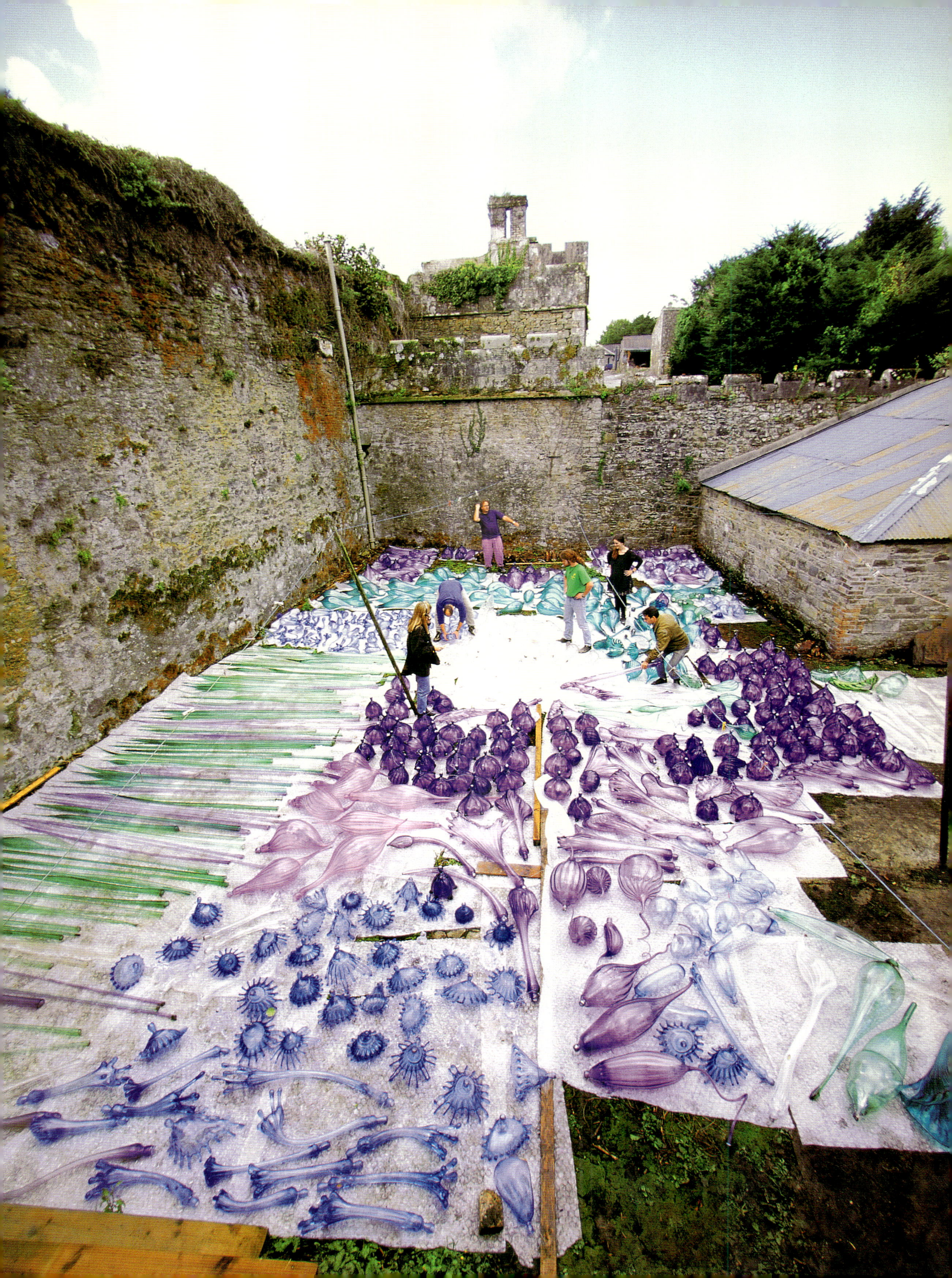

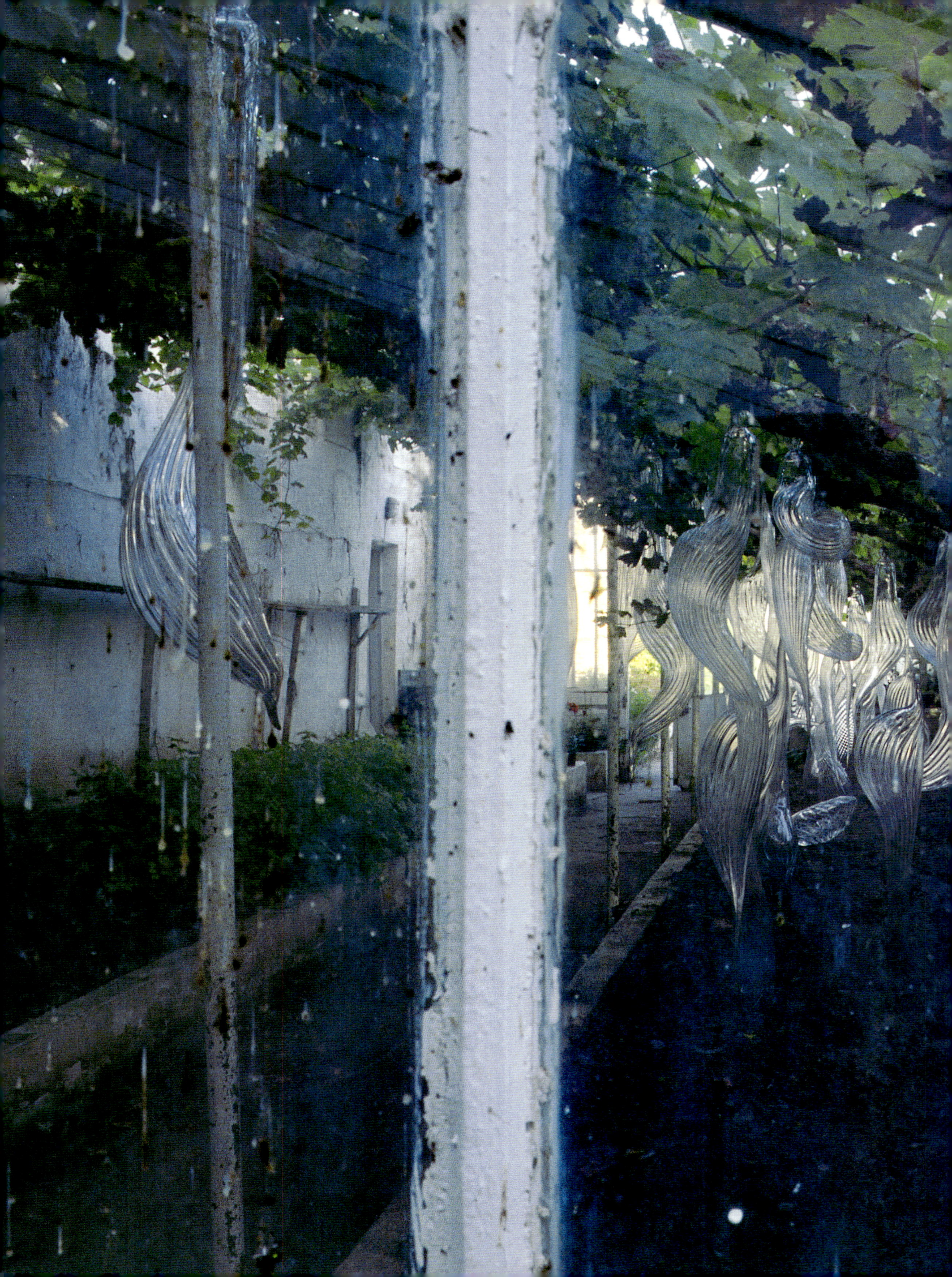

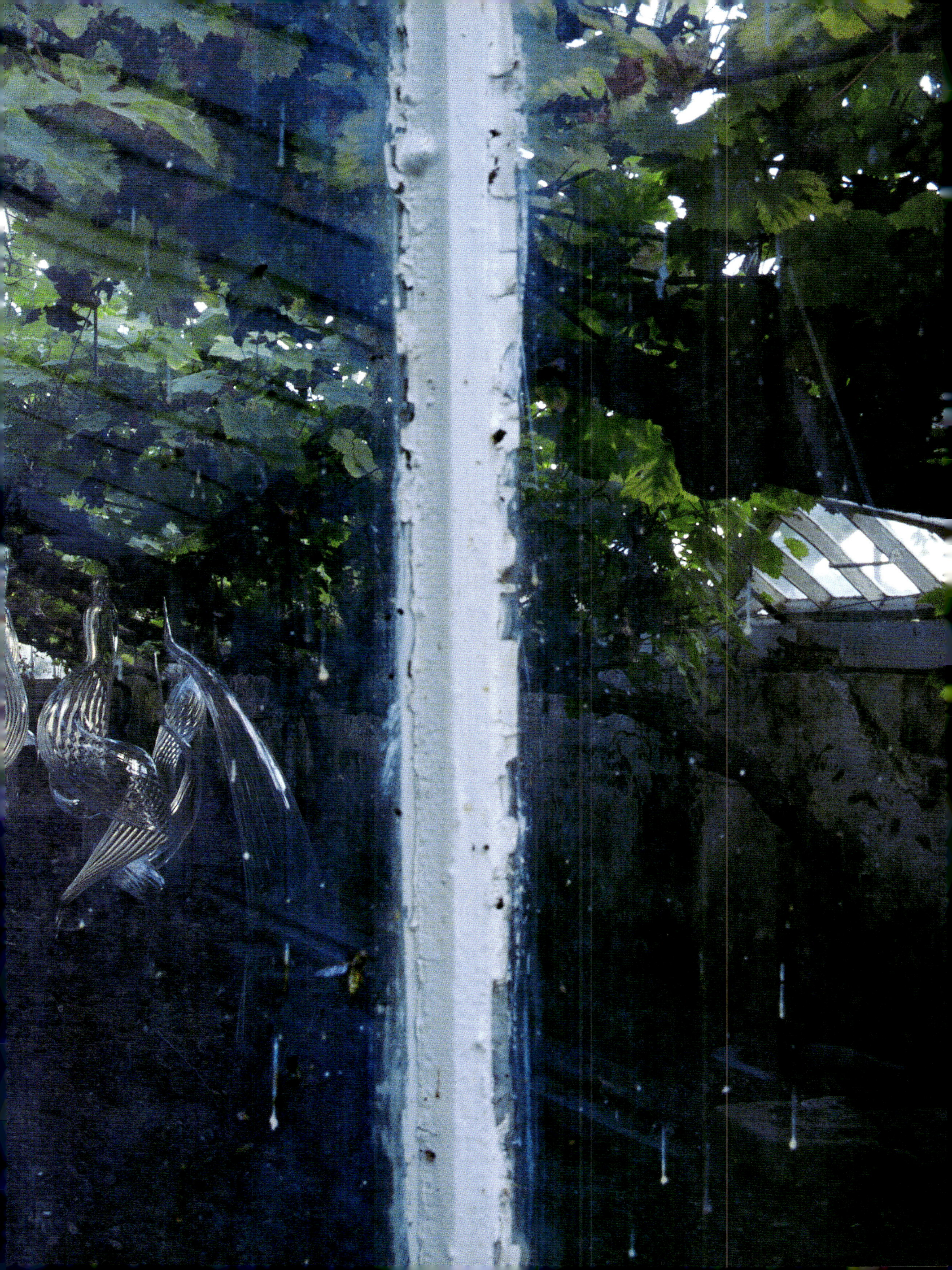

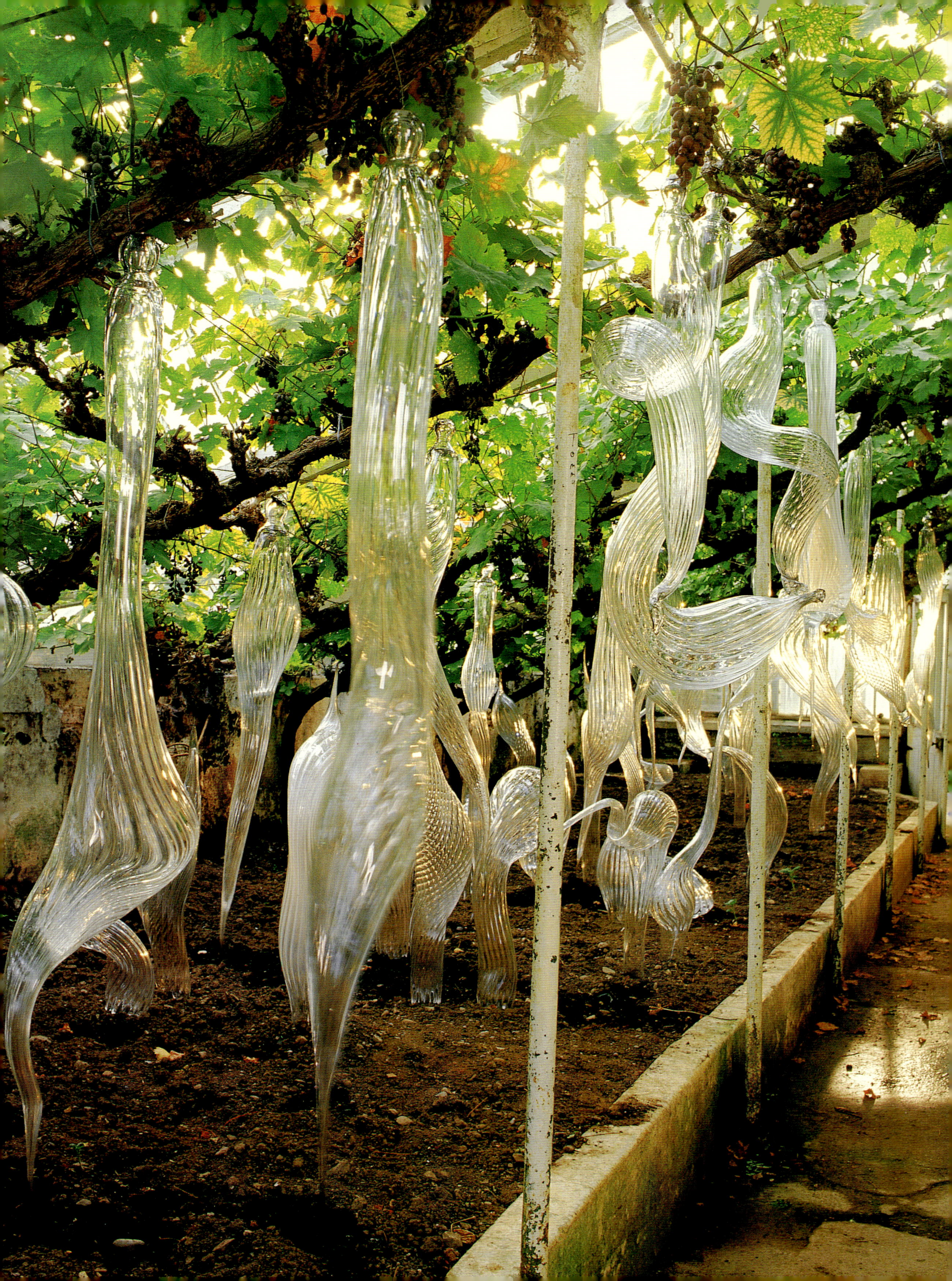

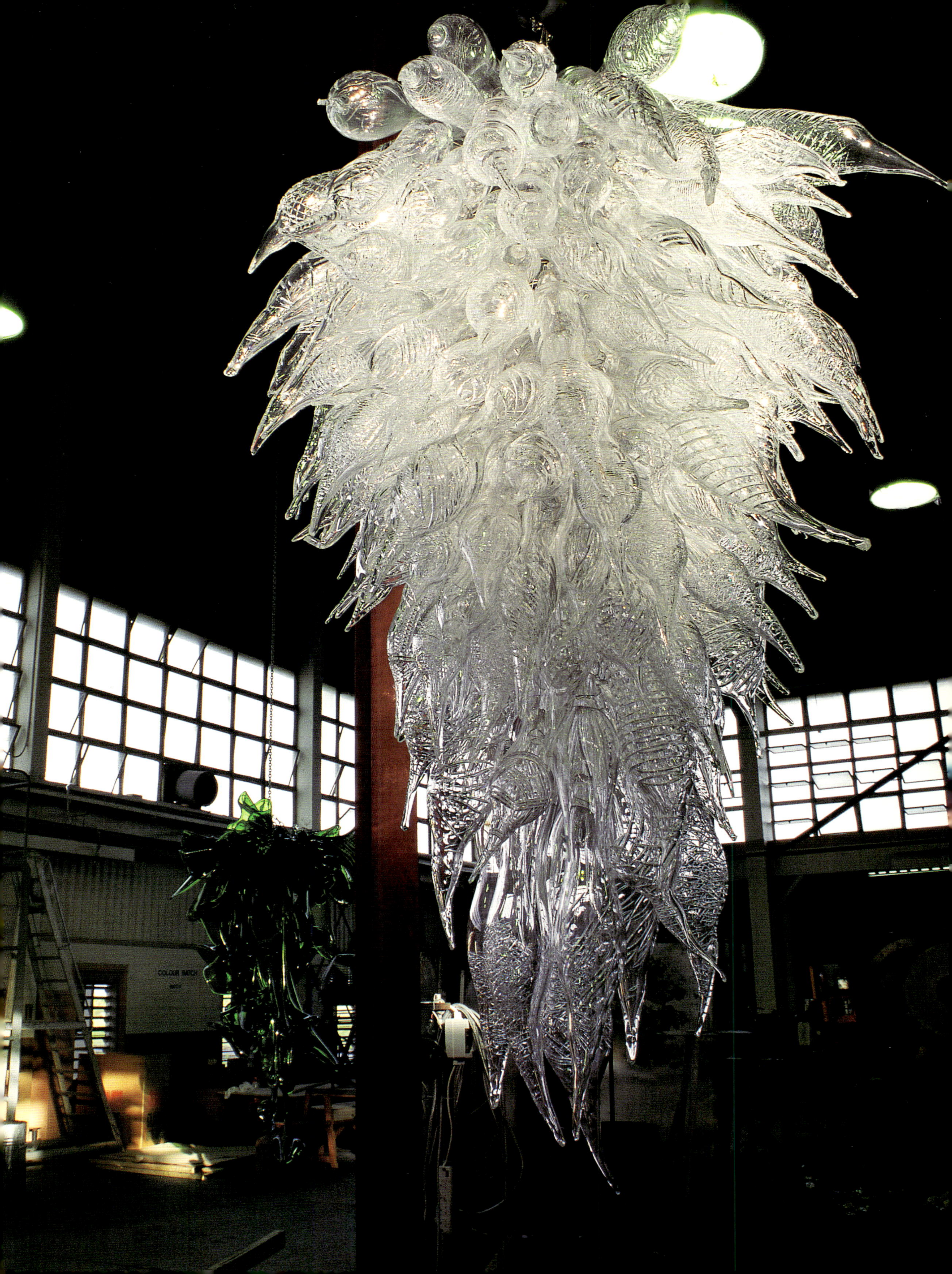
COLOUR BATCH

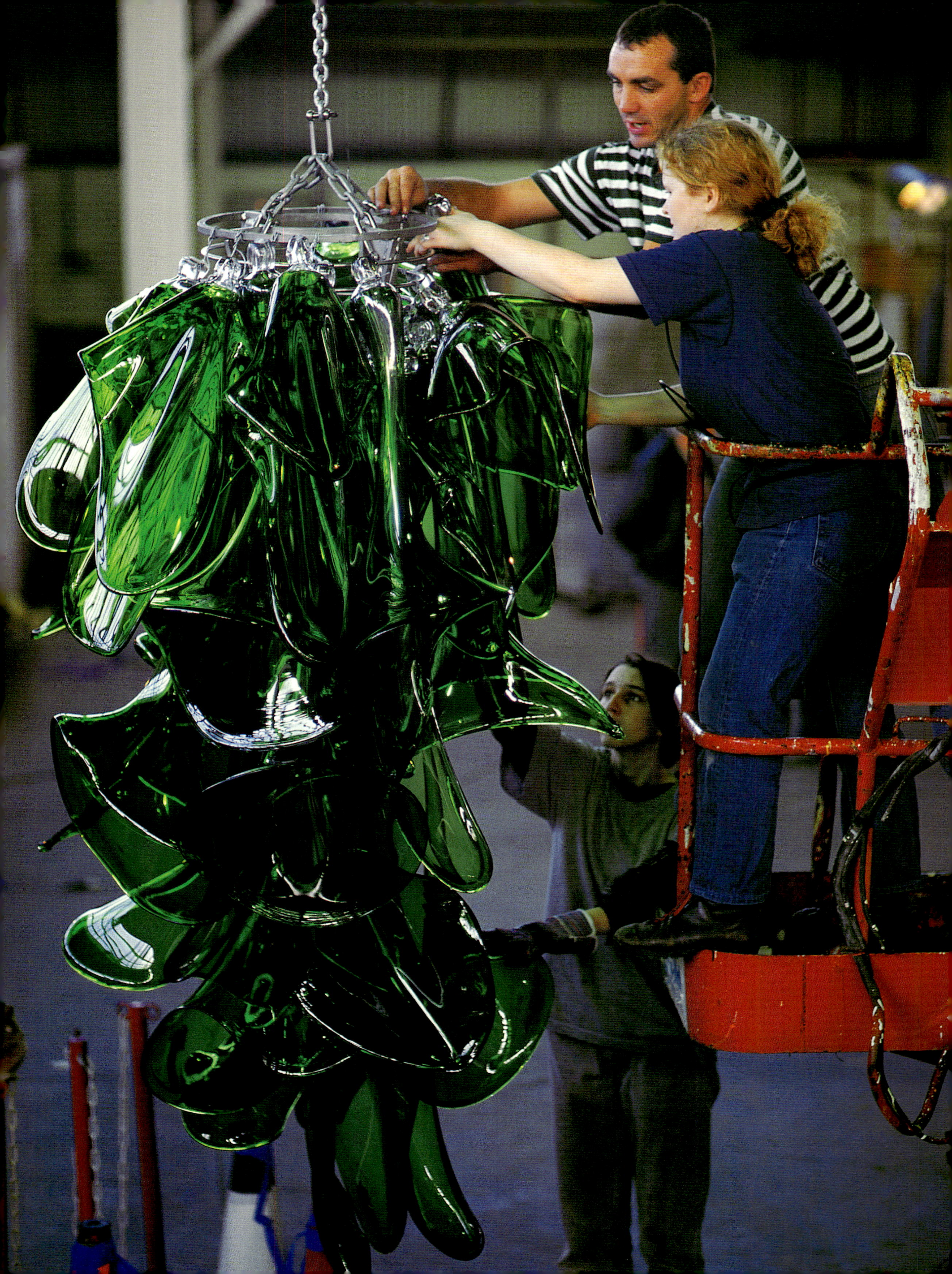

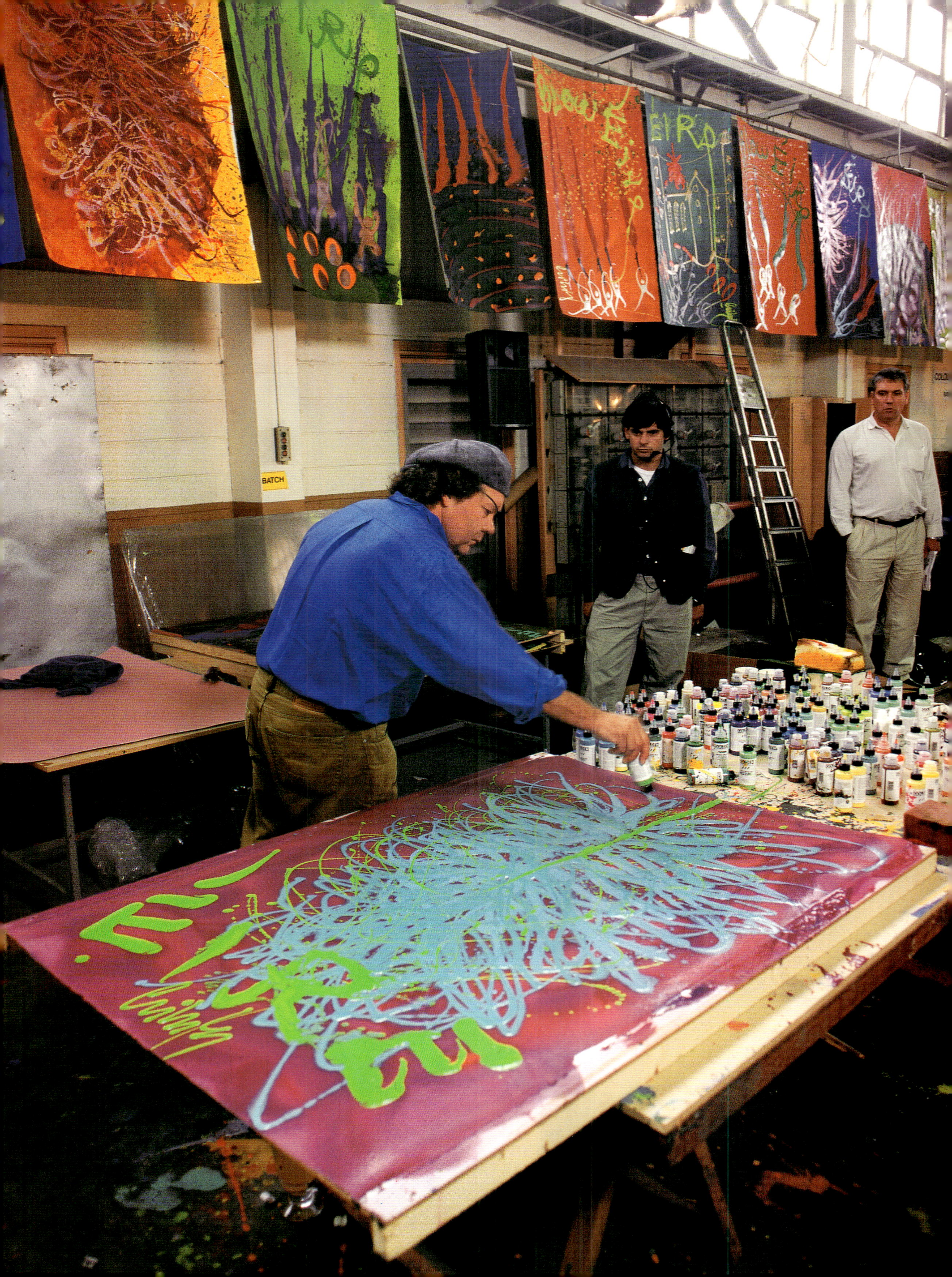
BATCH

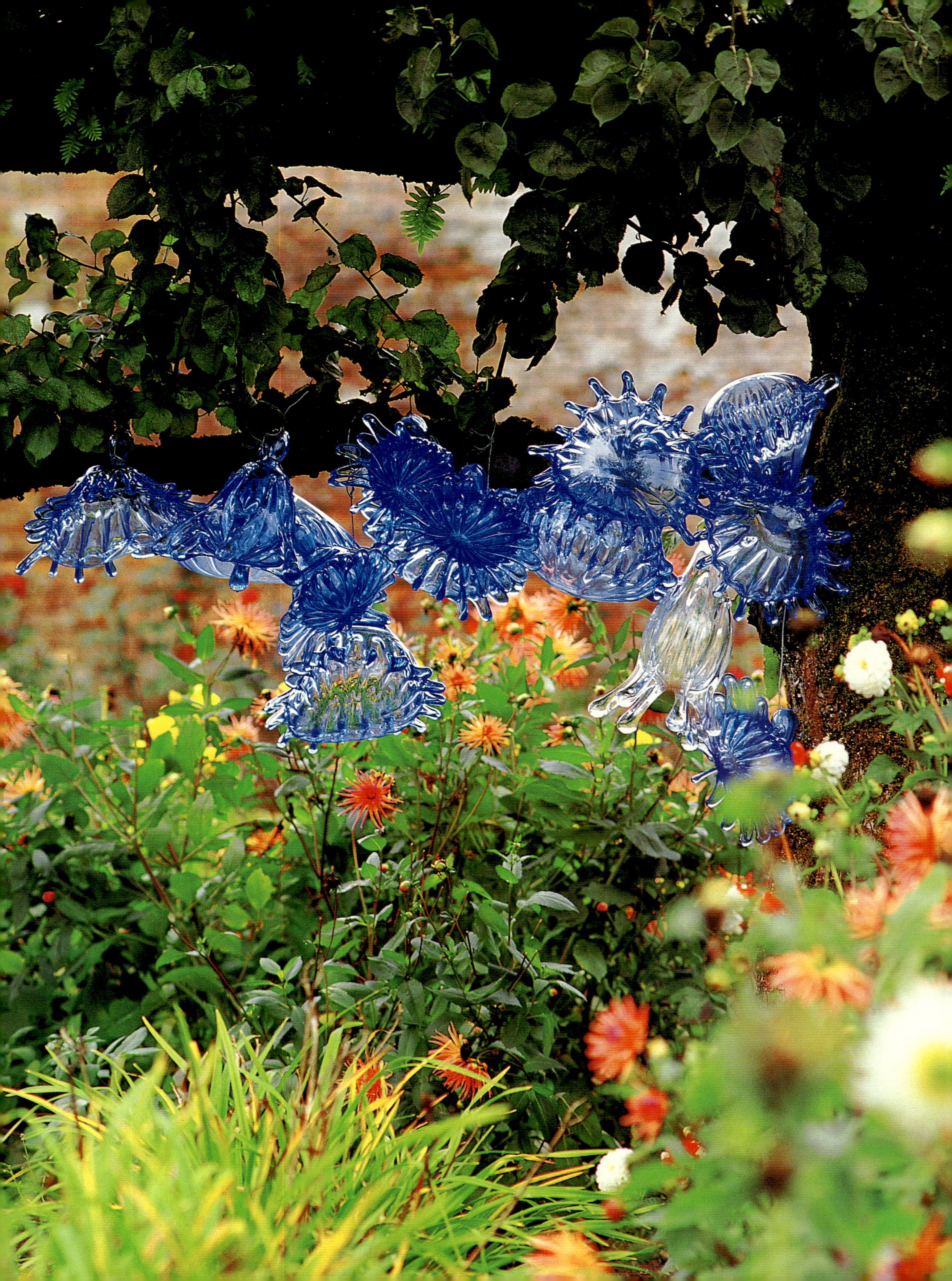

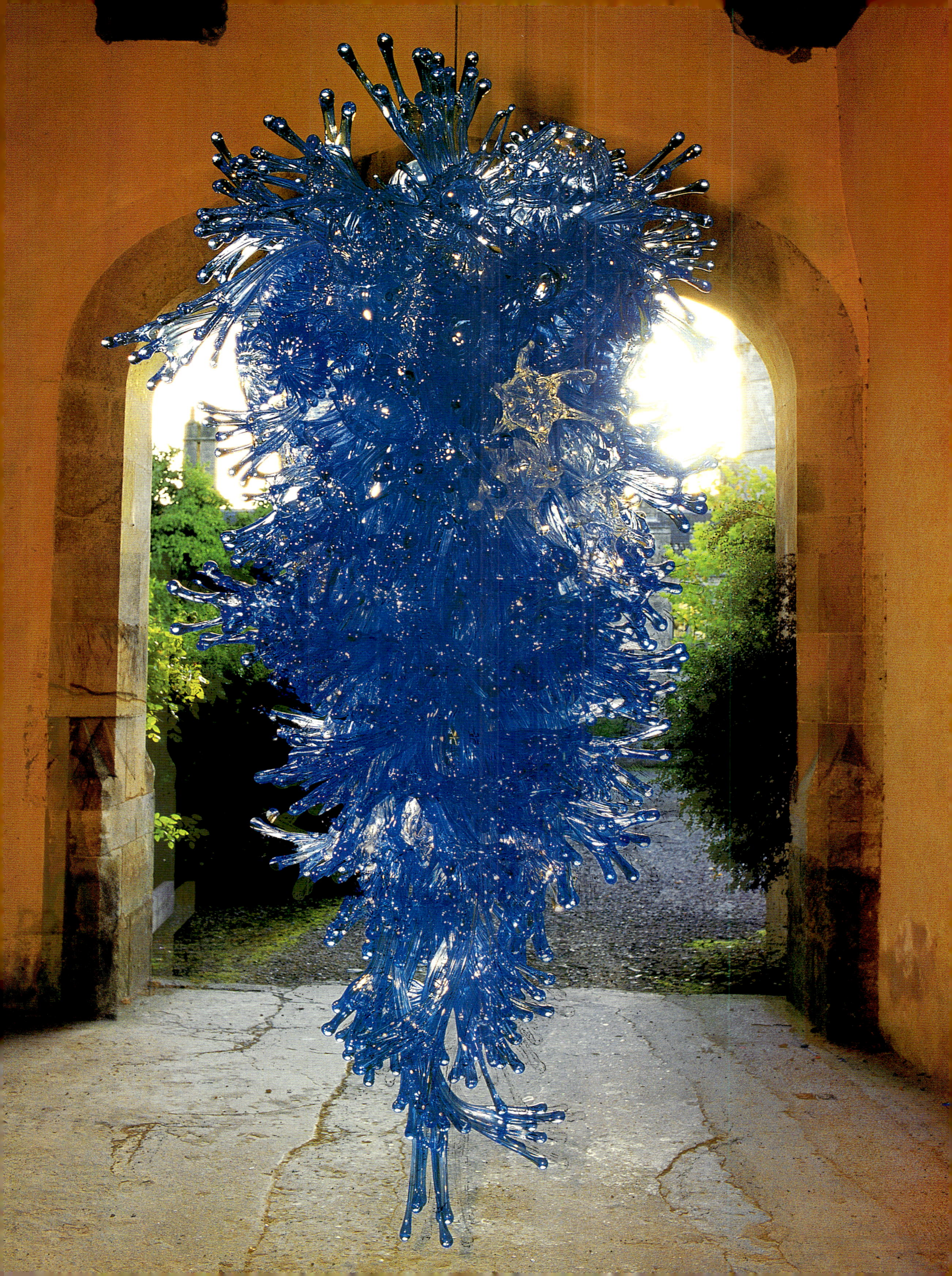

15

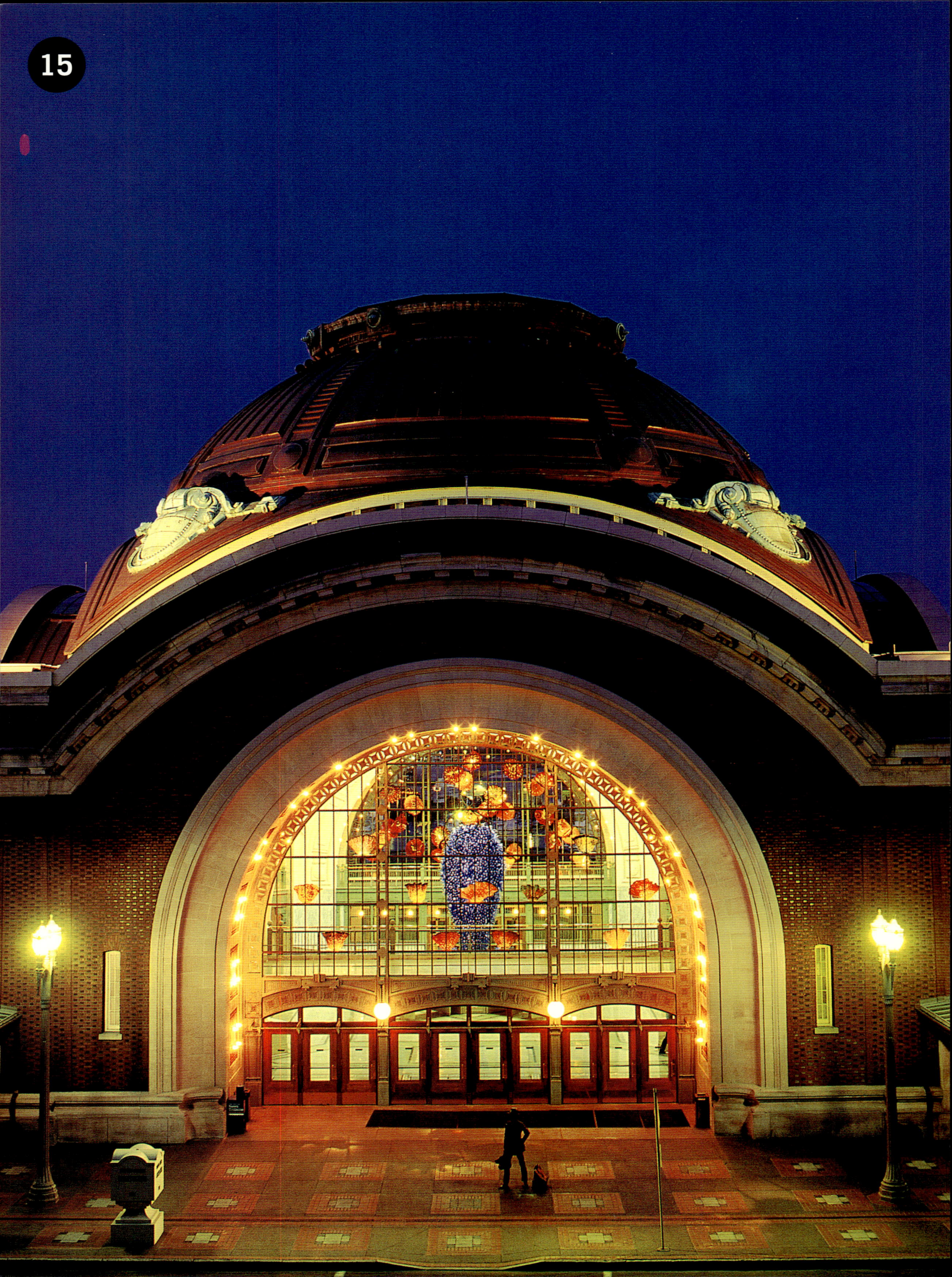

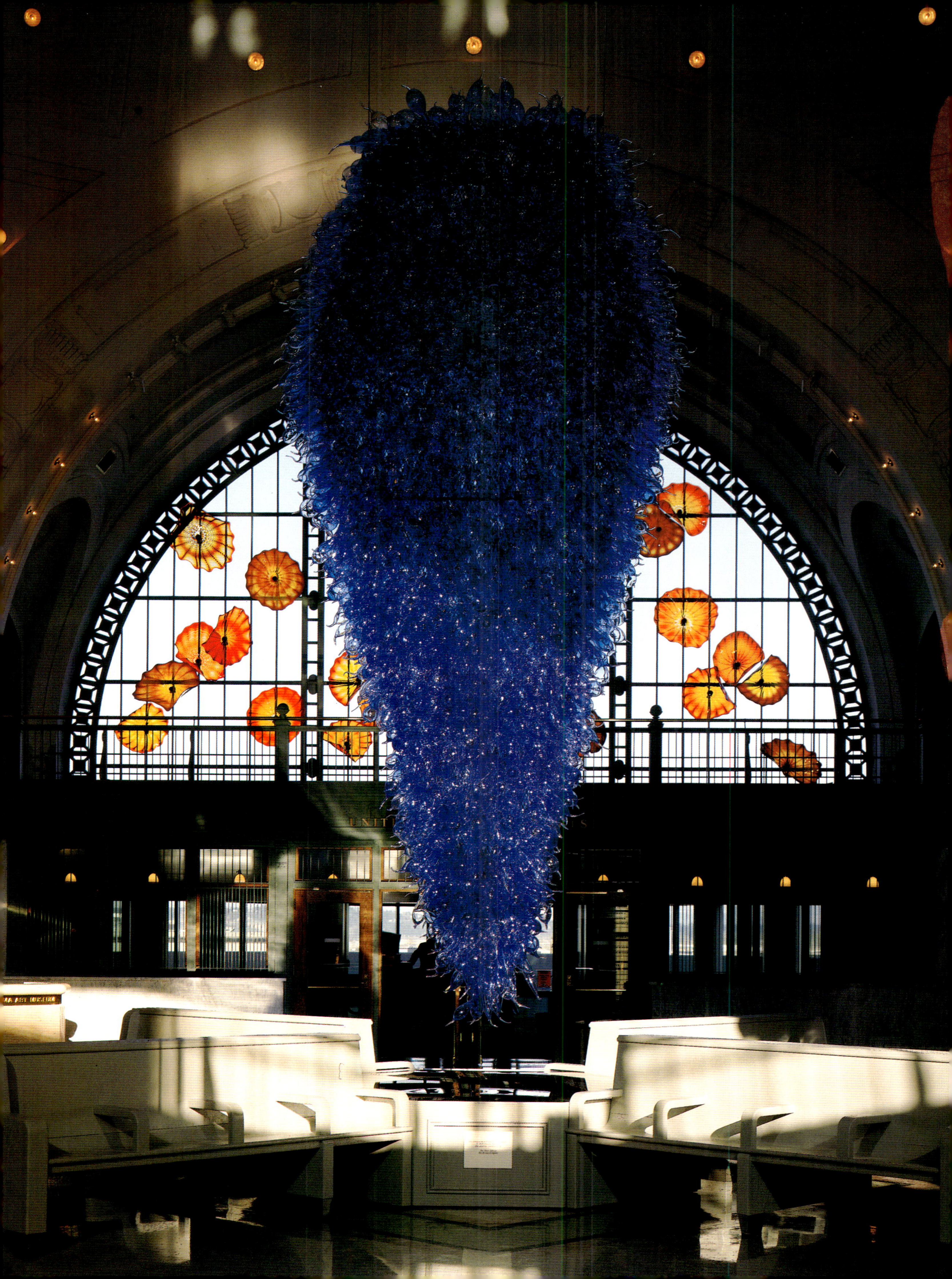

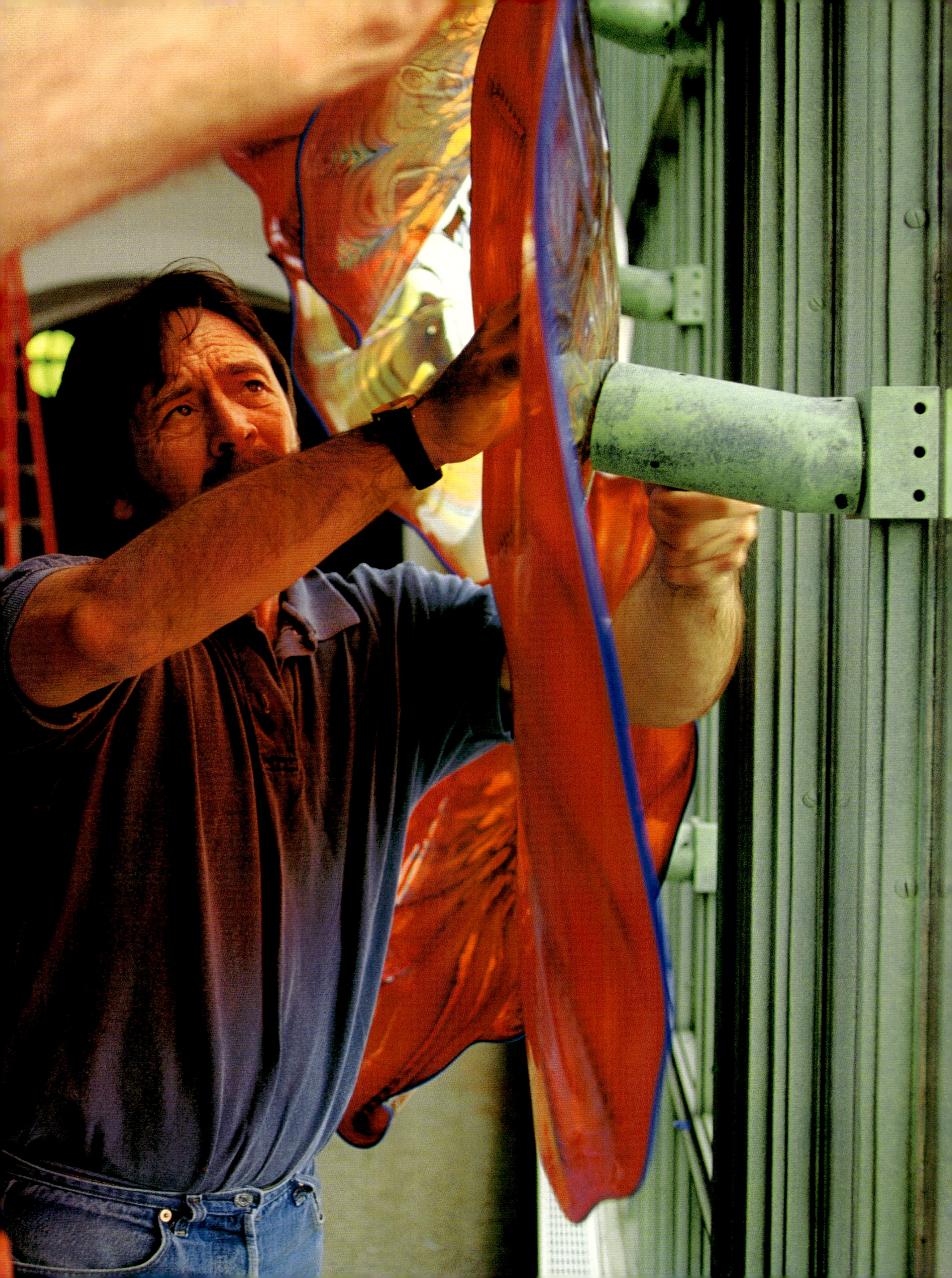

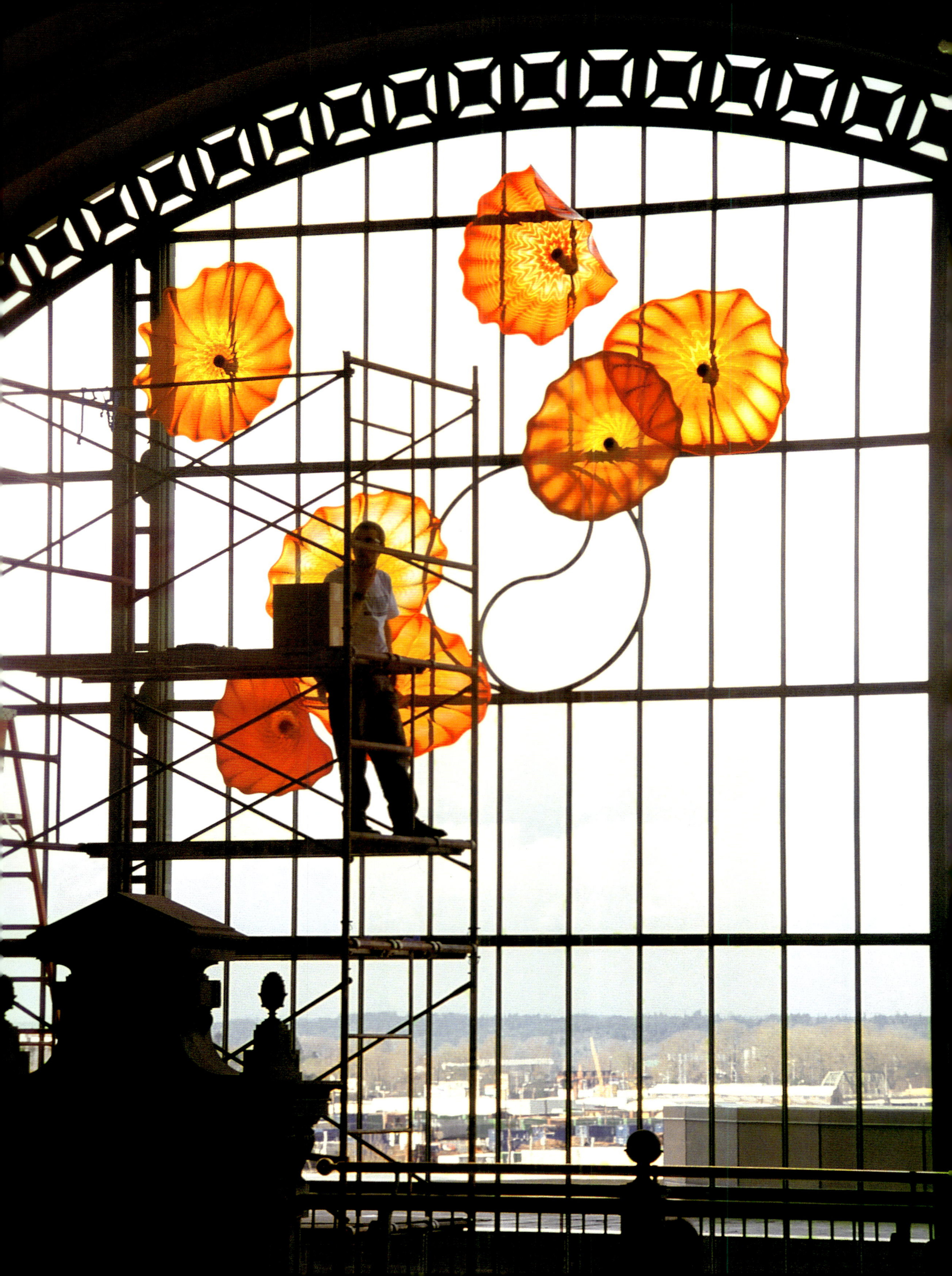

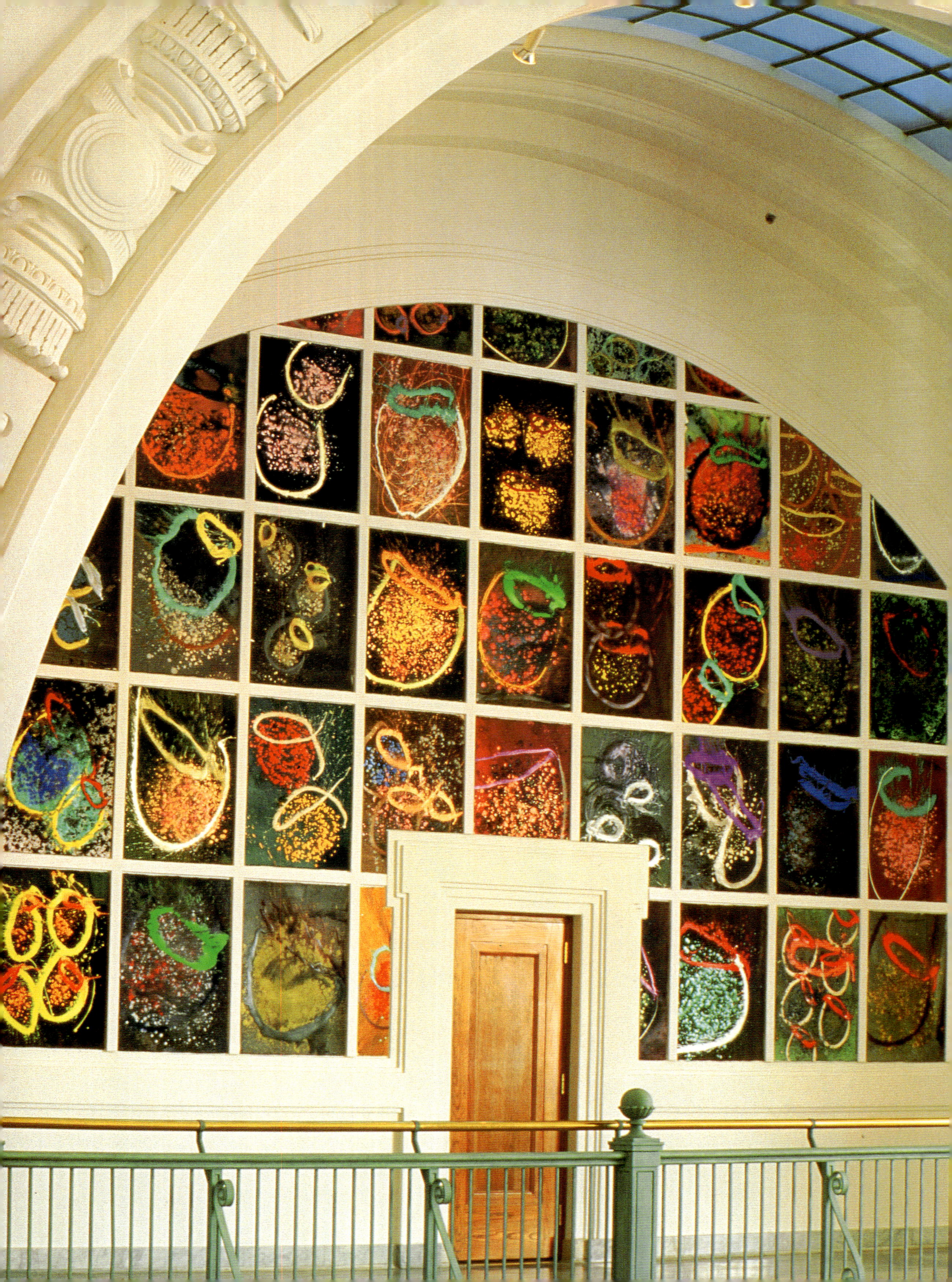

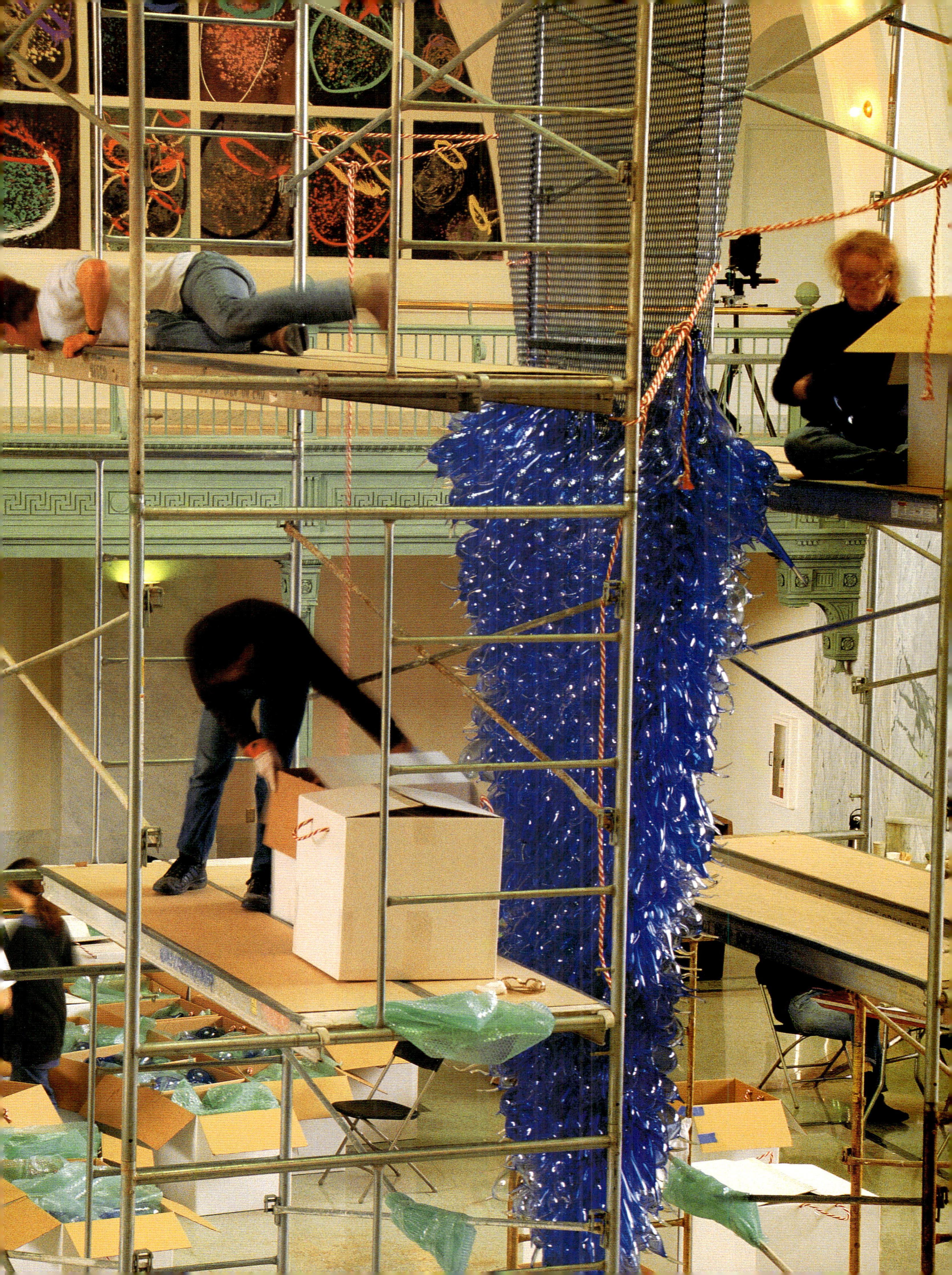

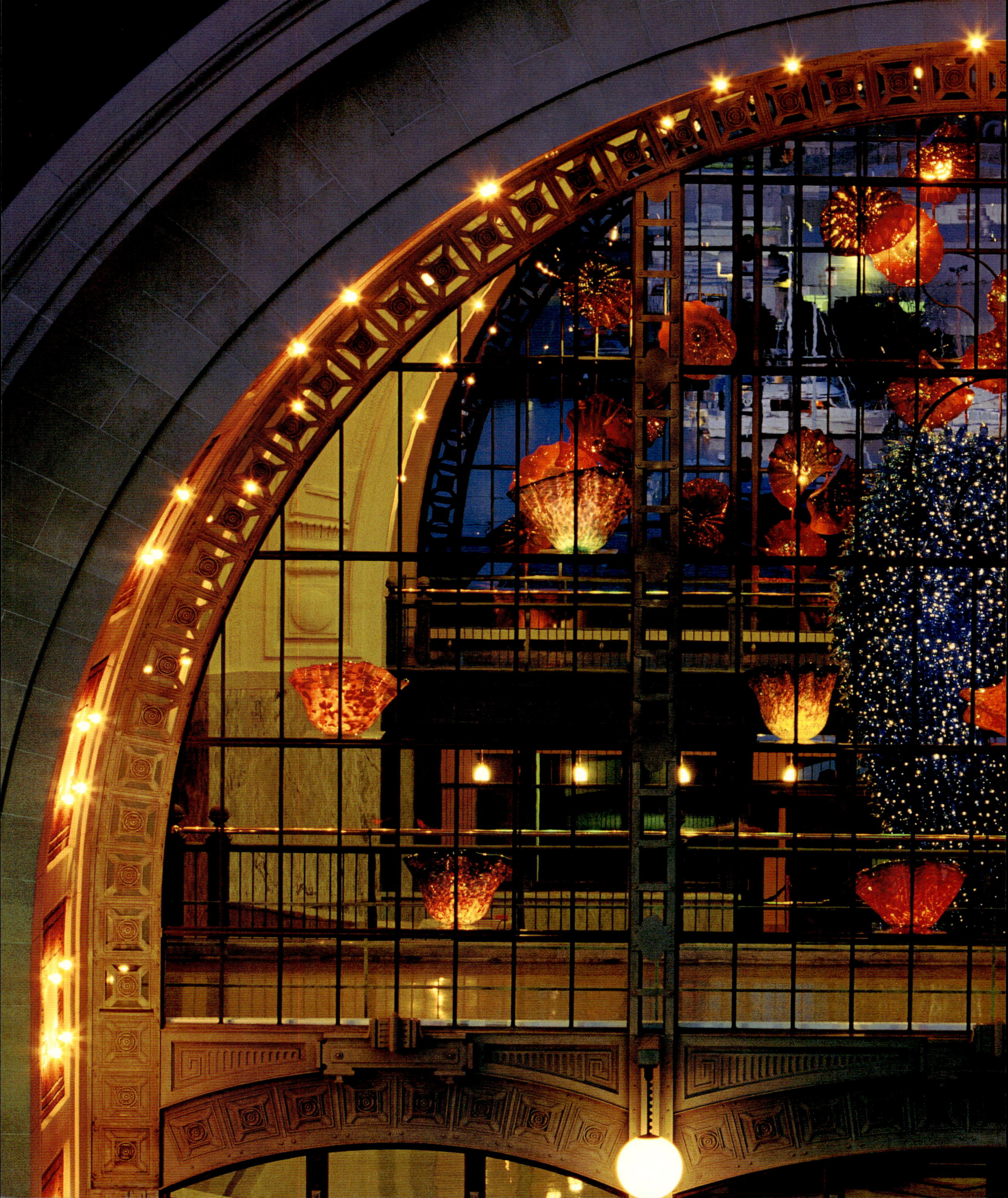

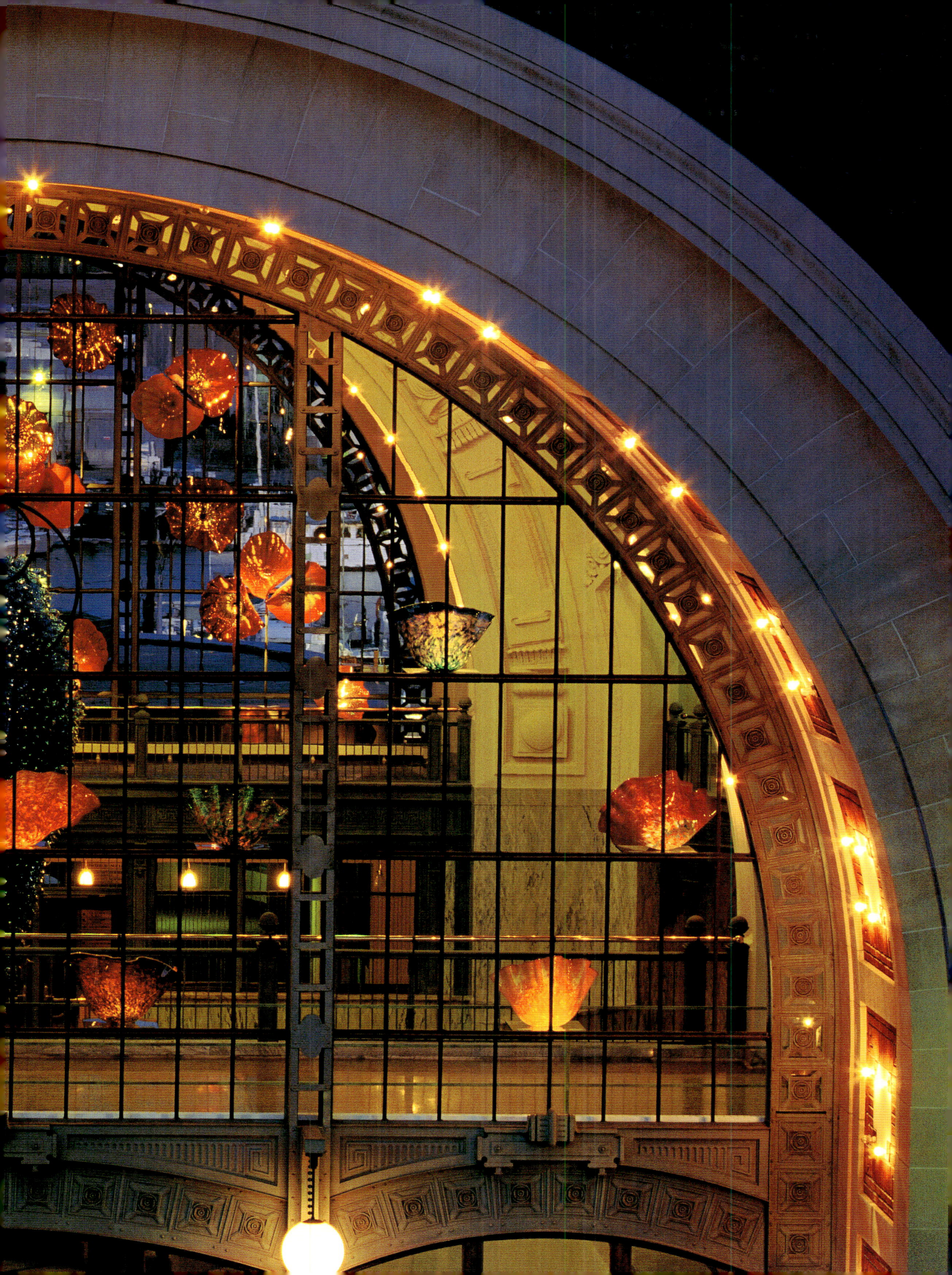

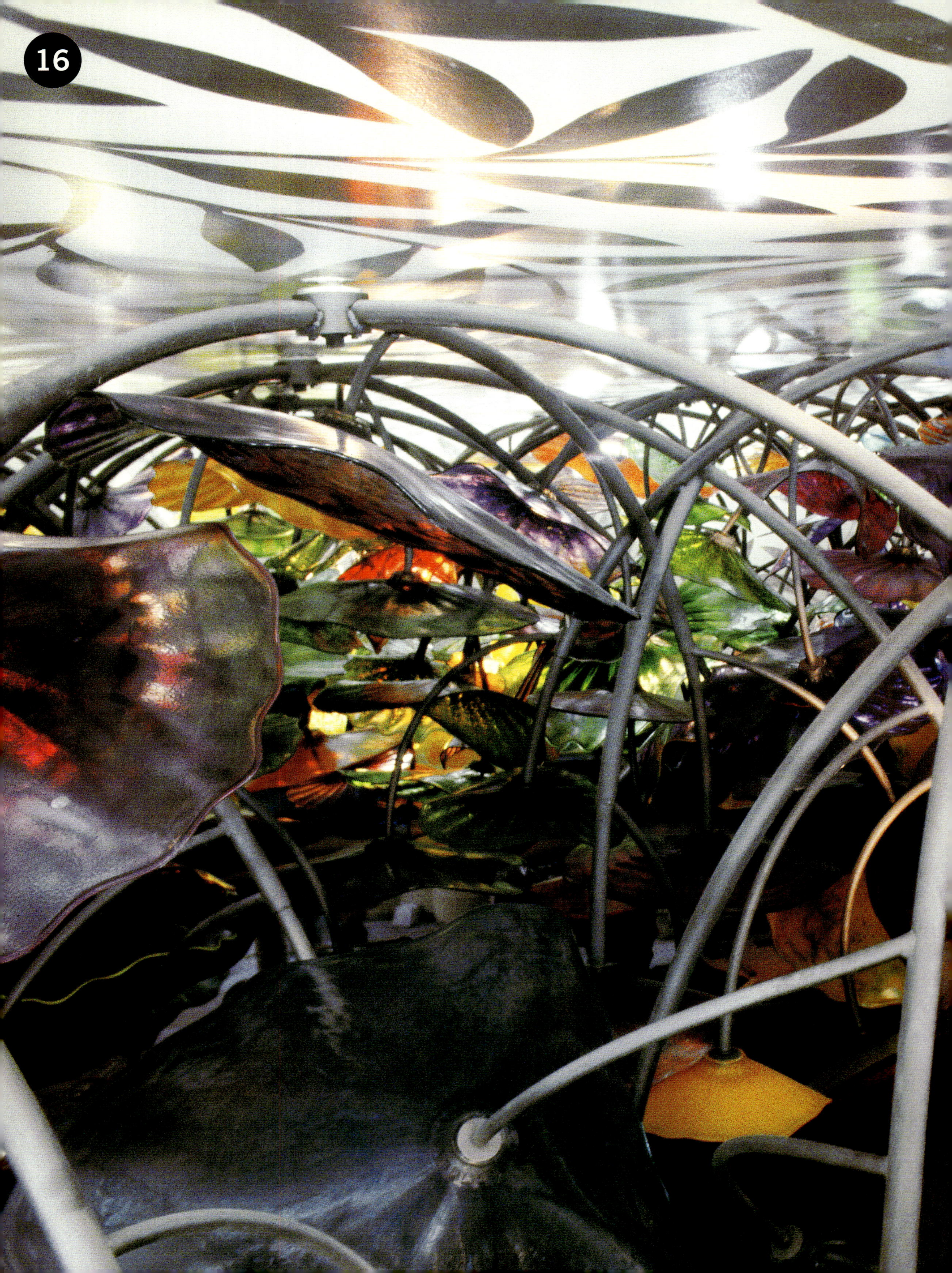
16

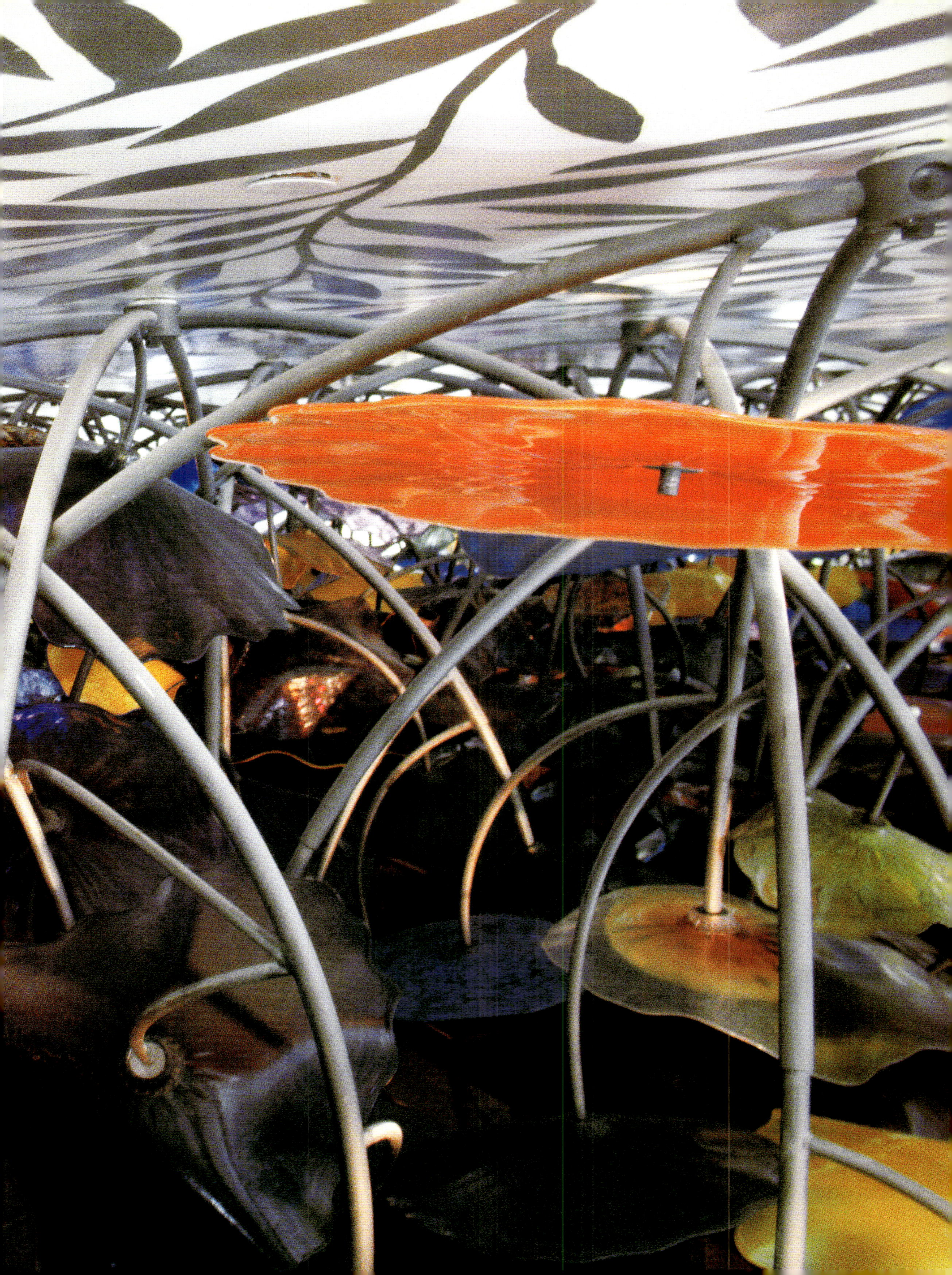

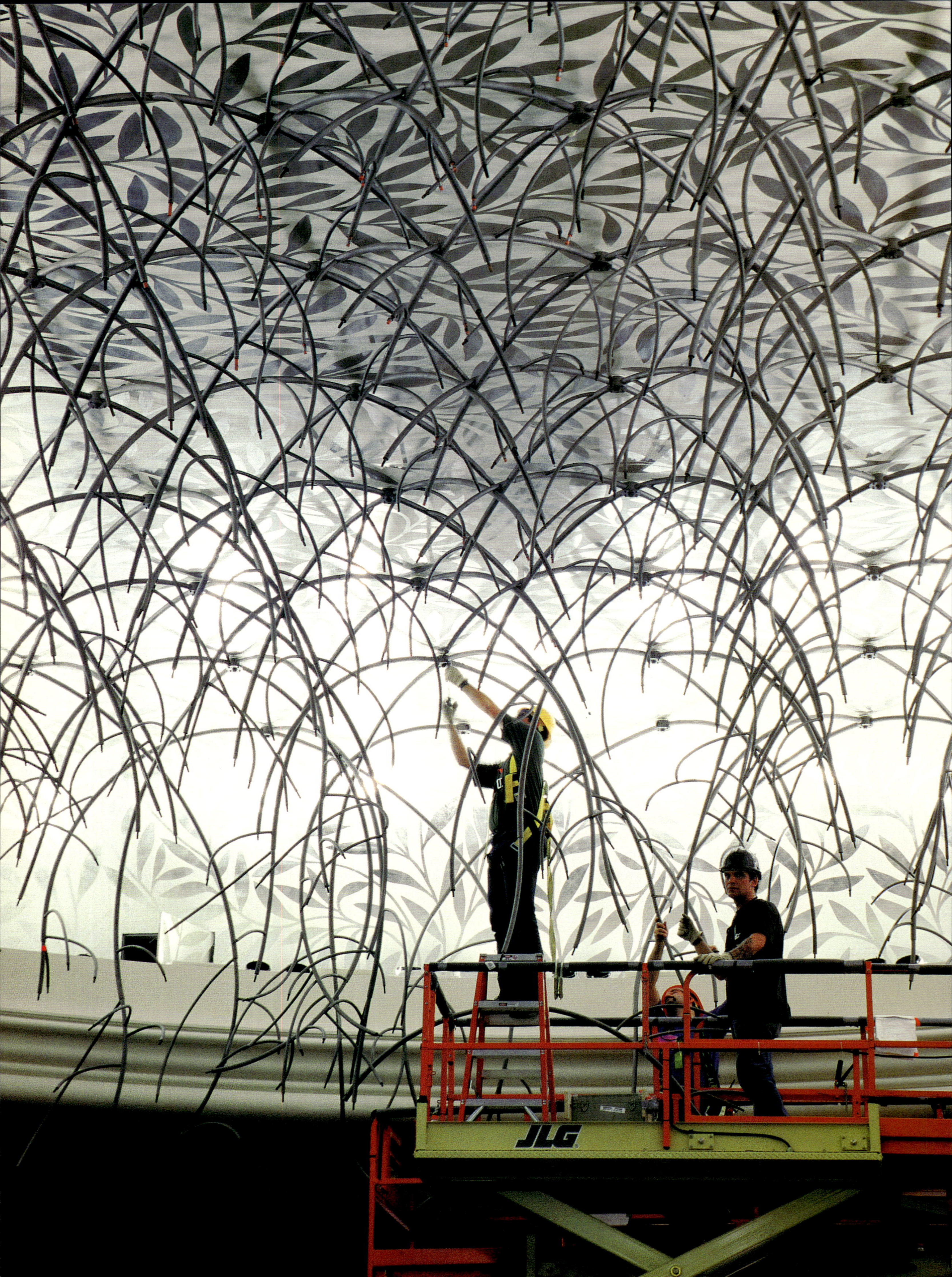
JLG

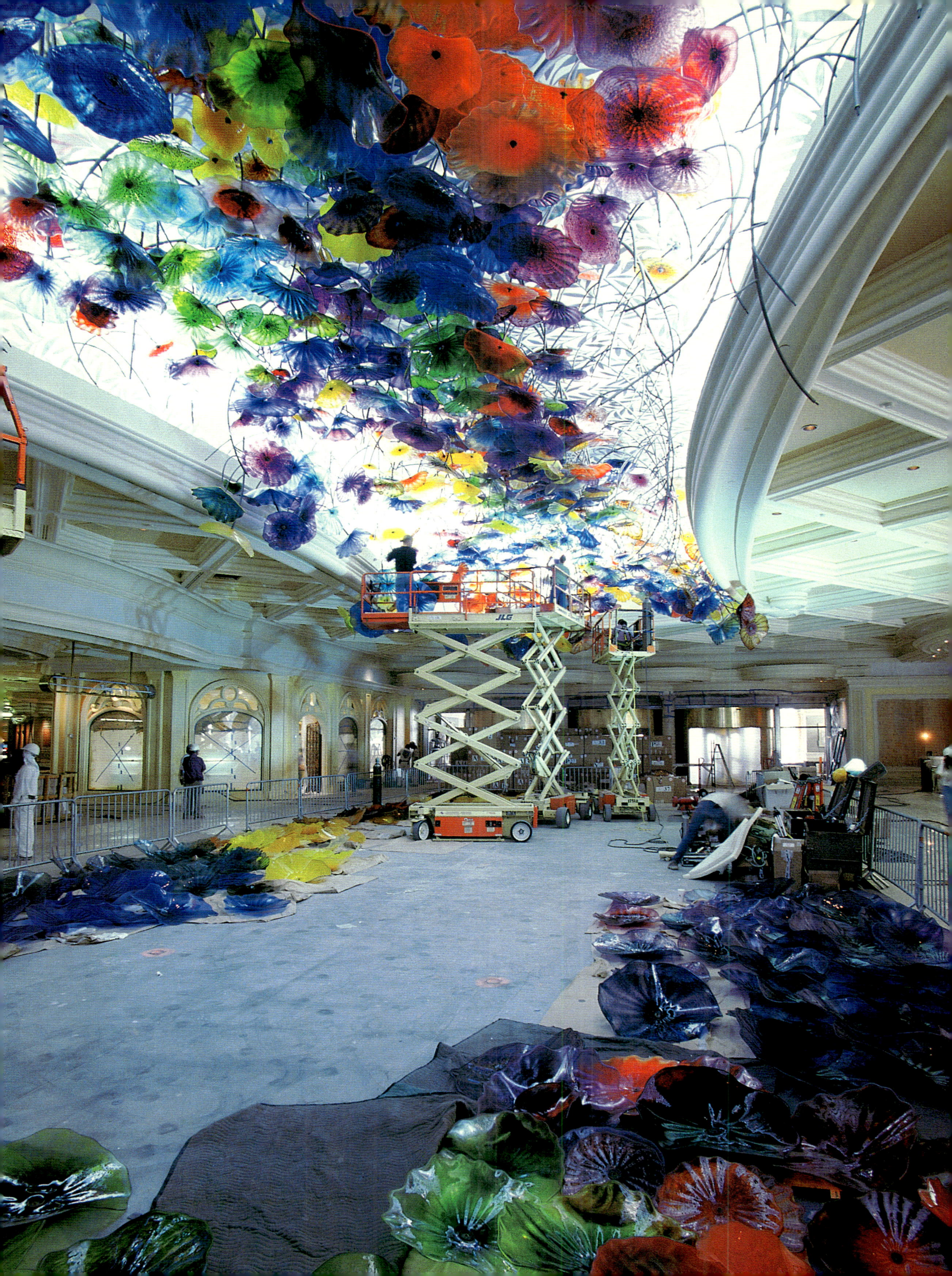

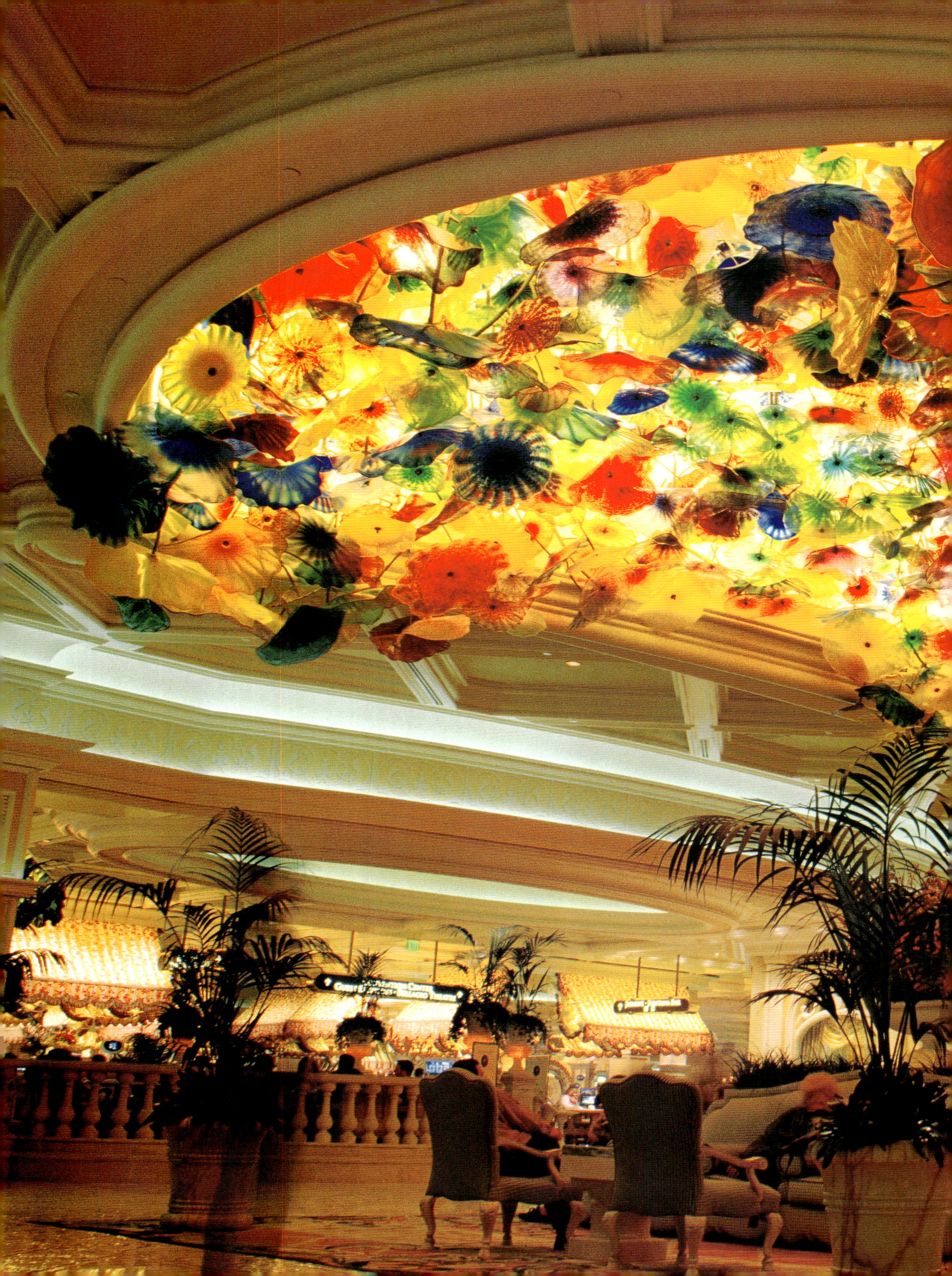

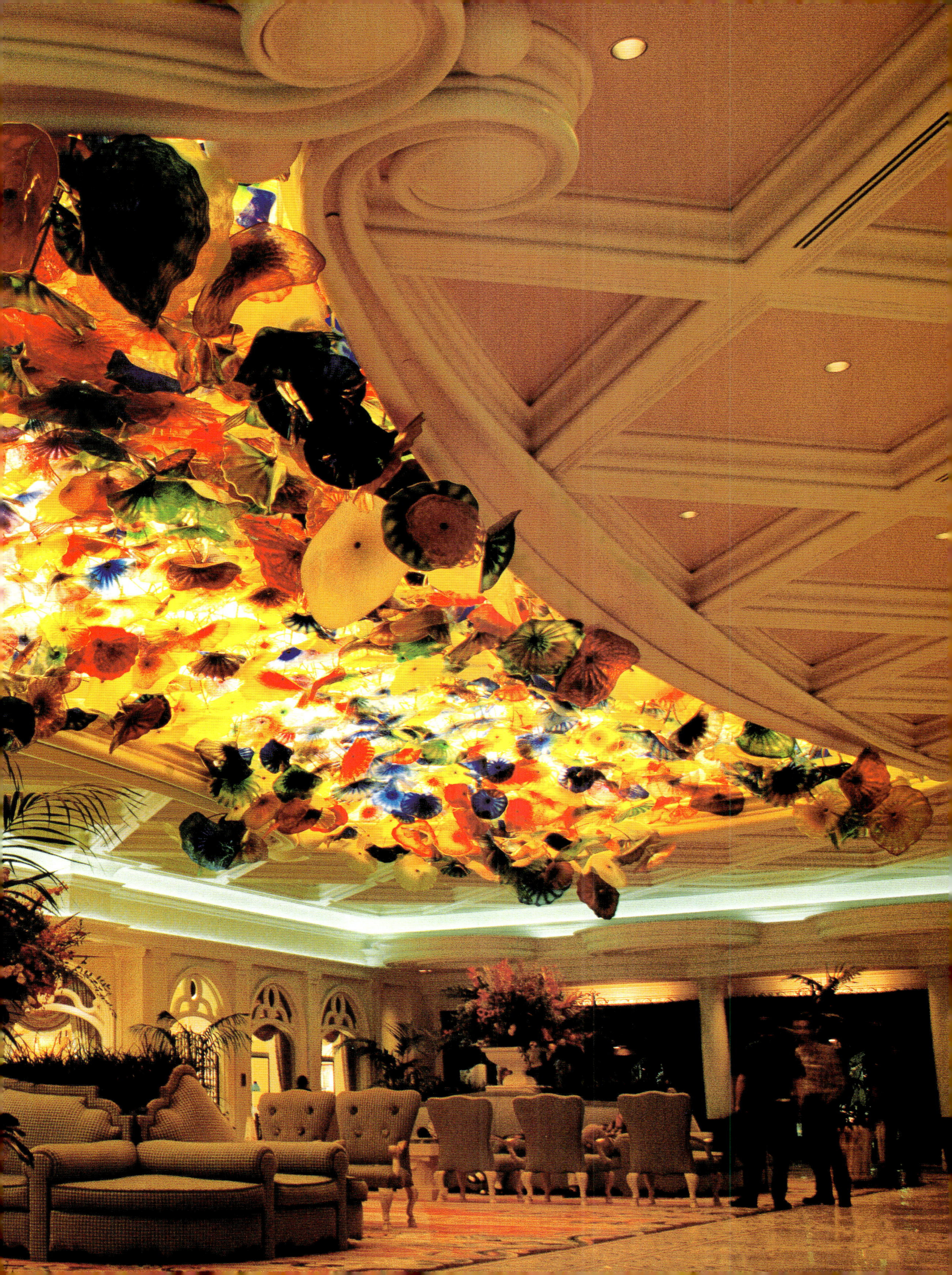

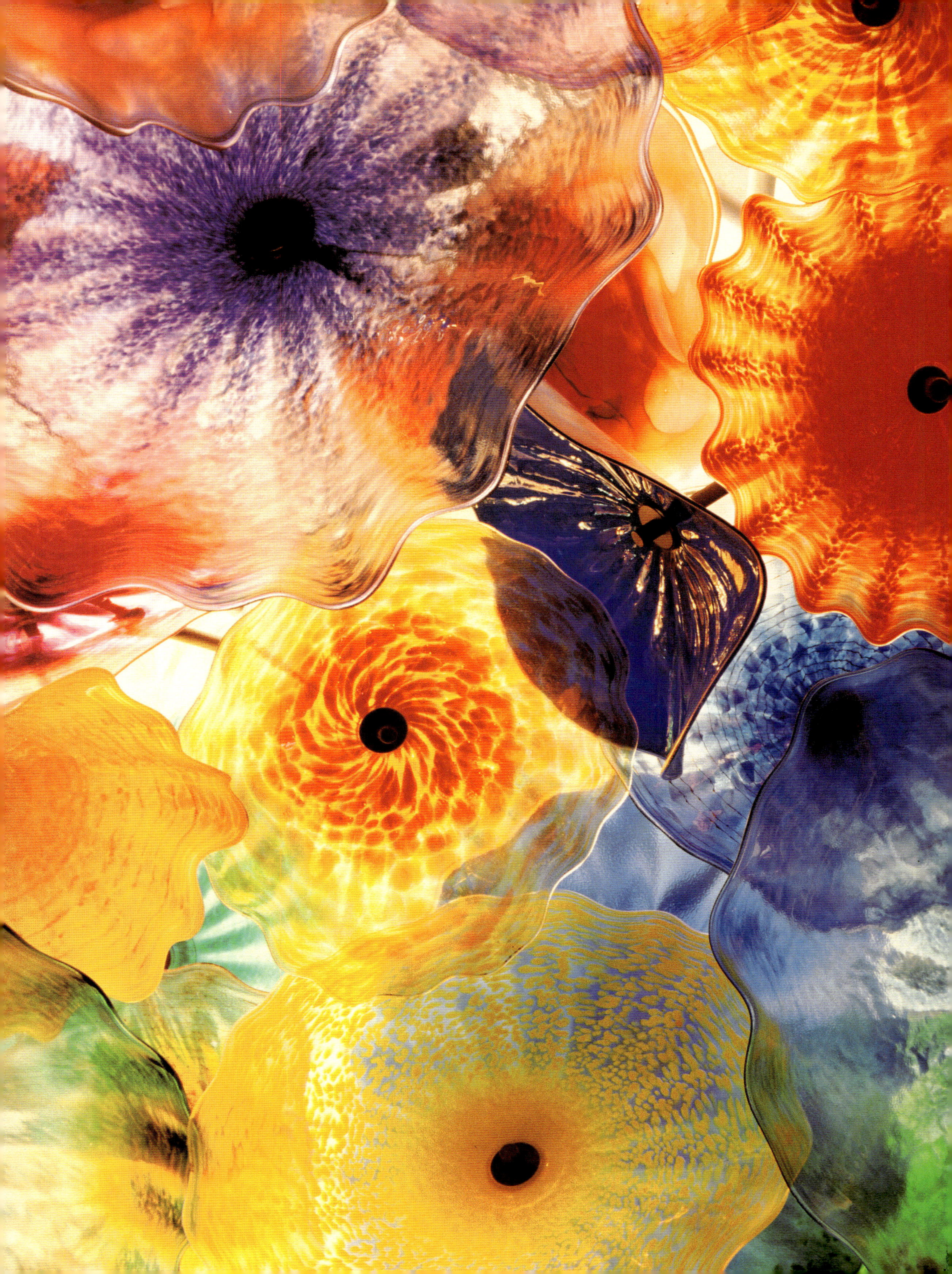

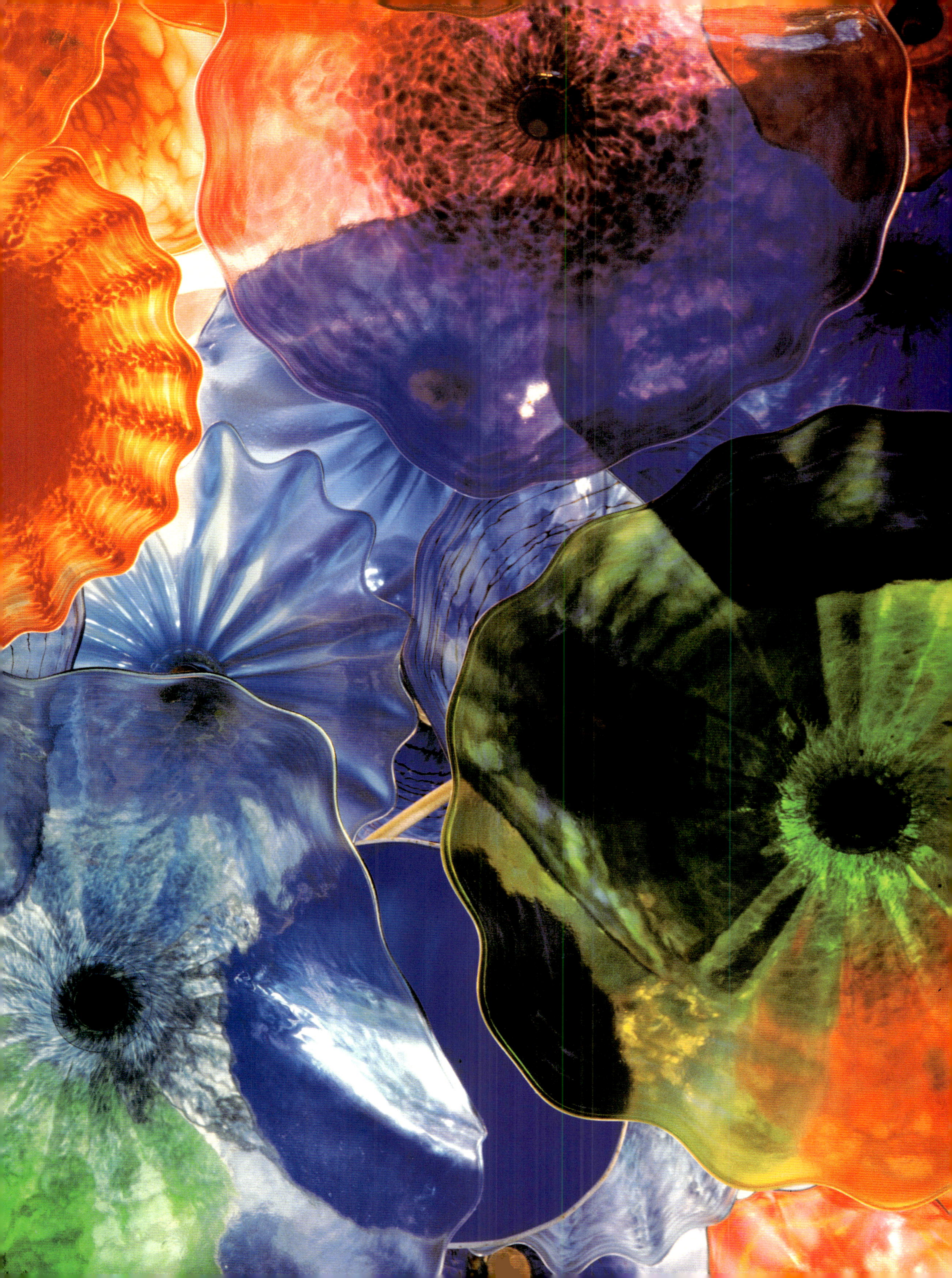

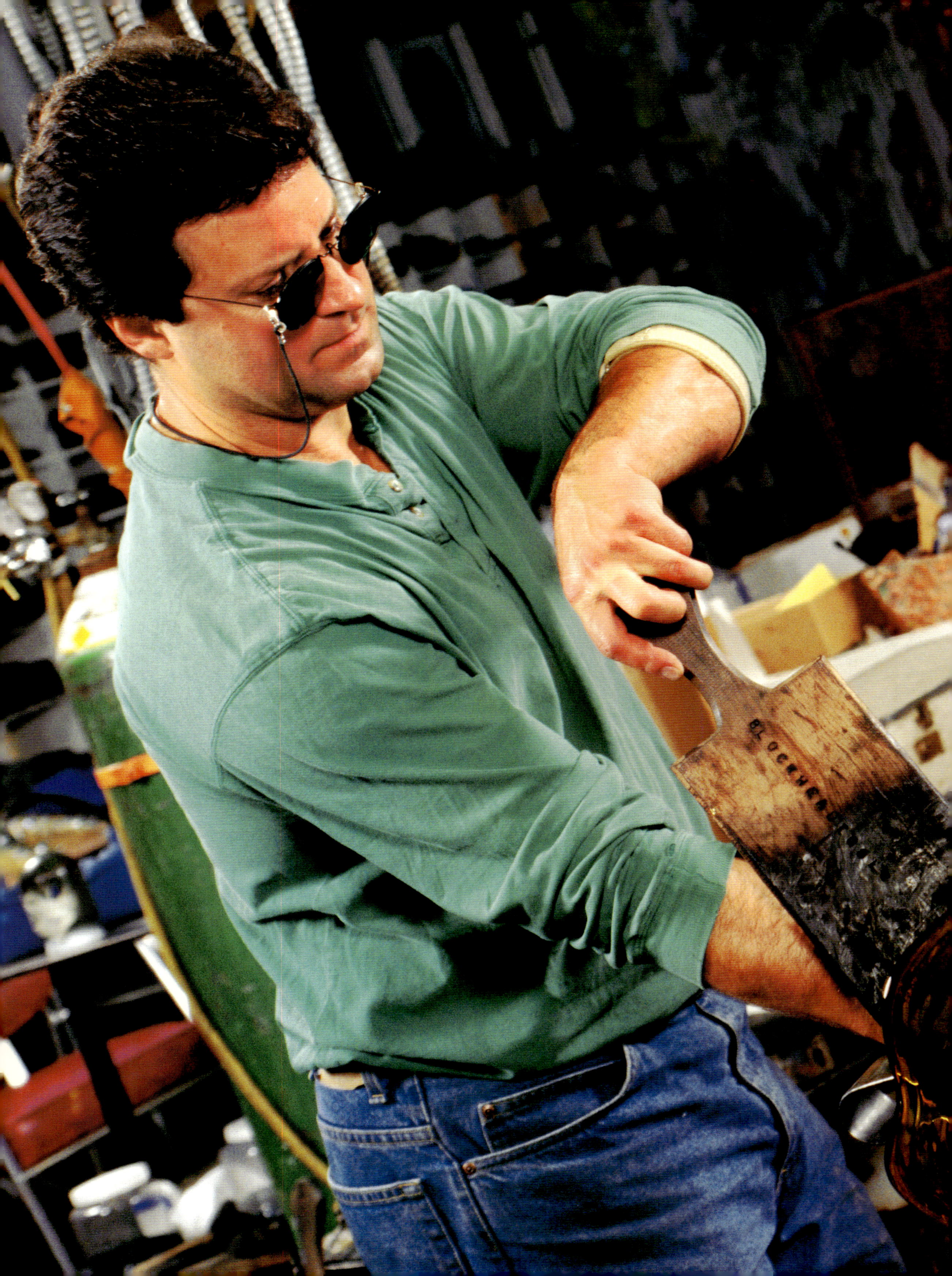

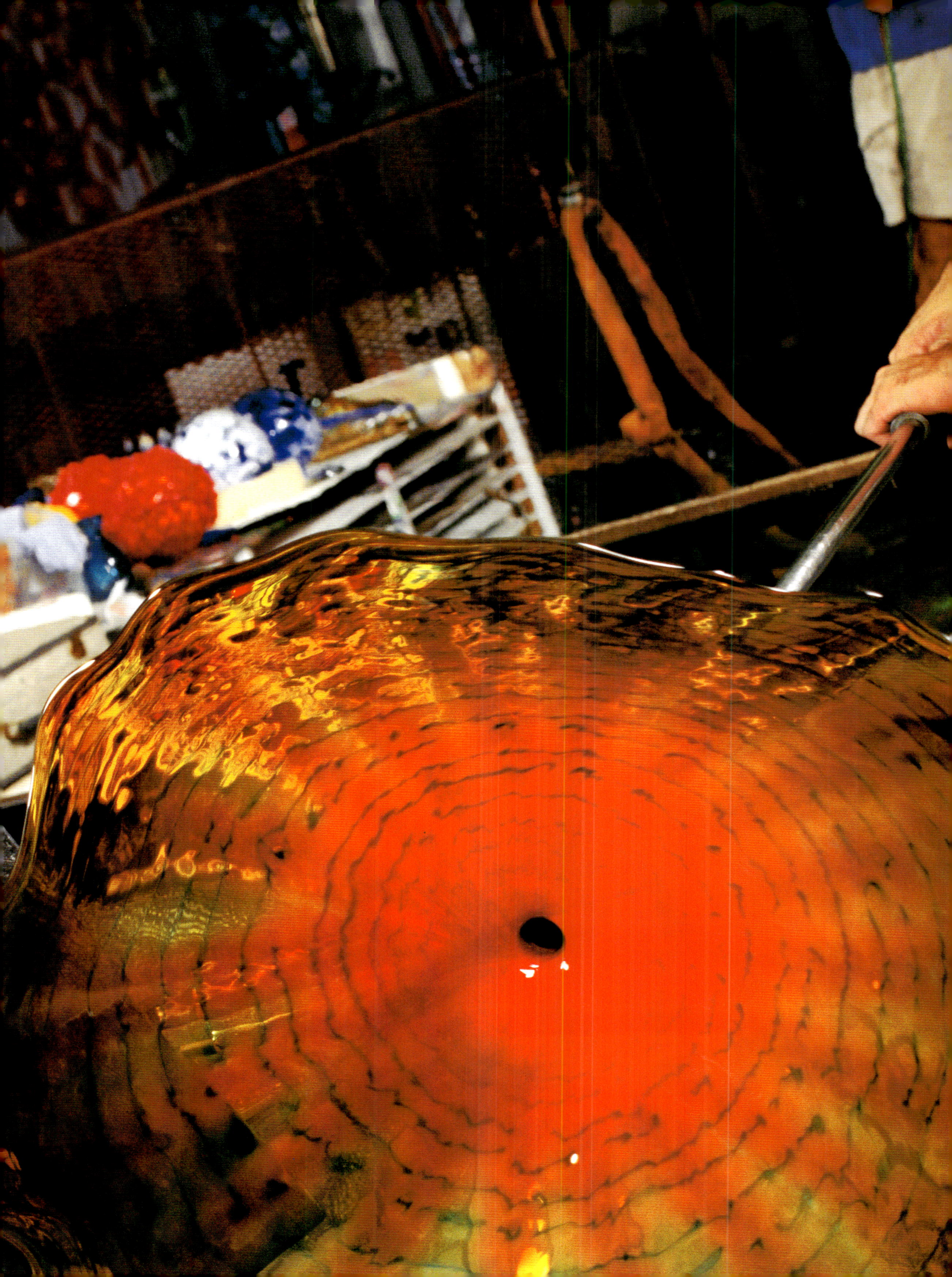

17

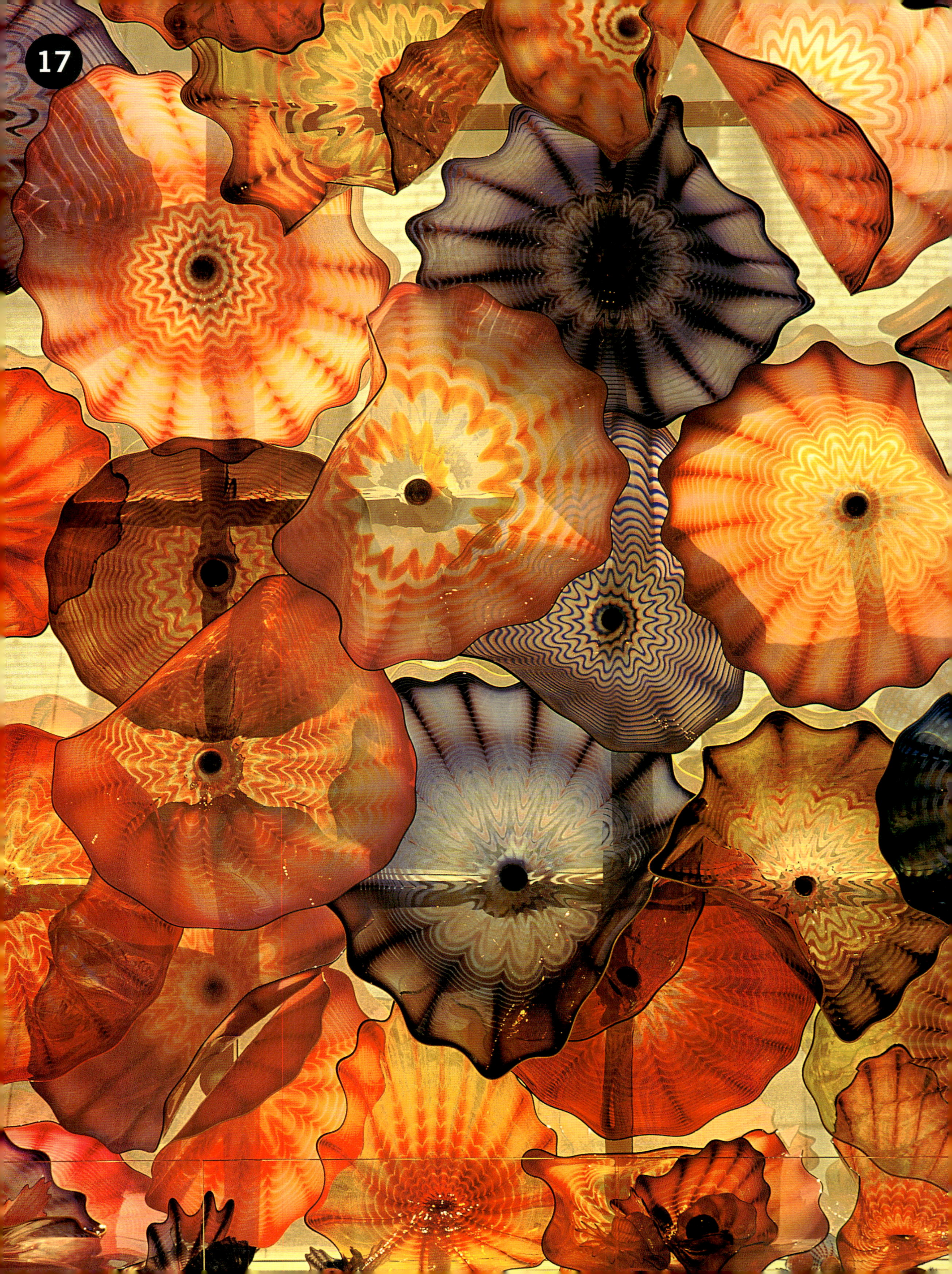

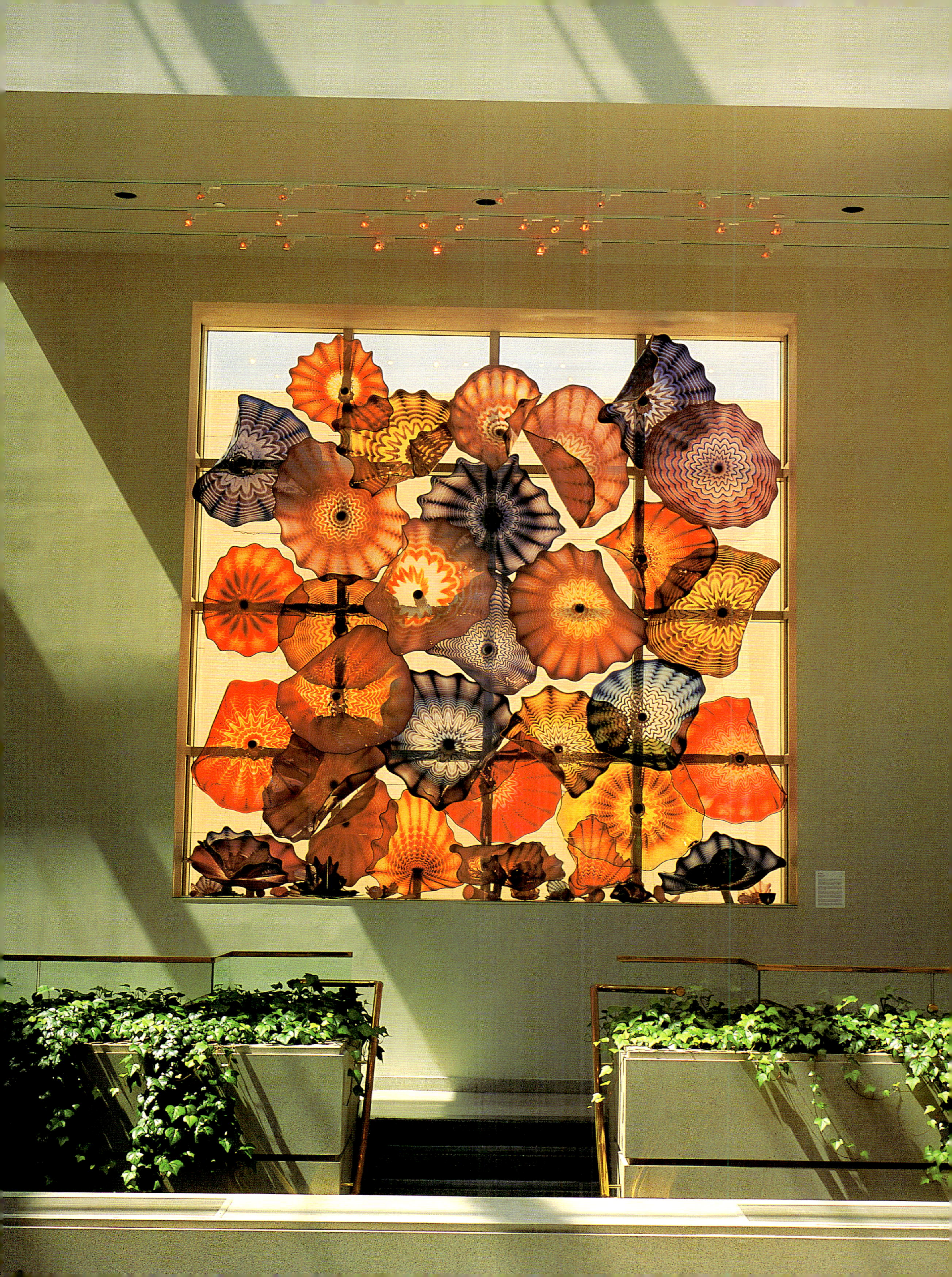

18

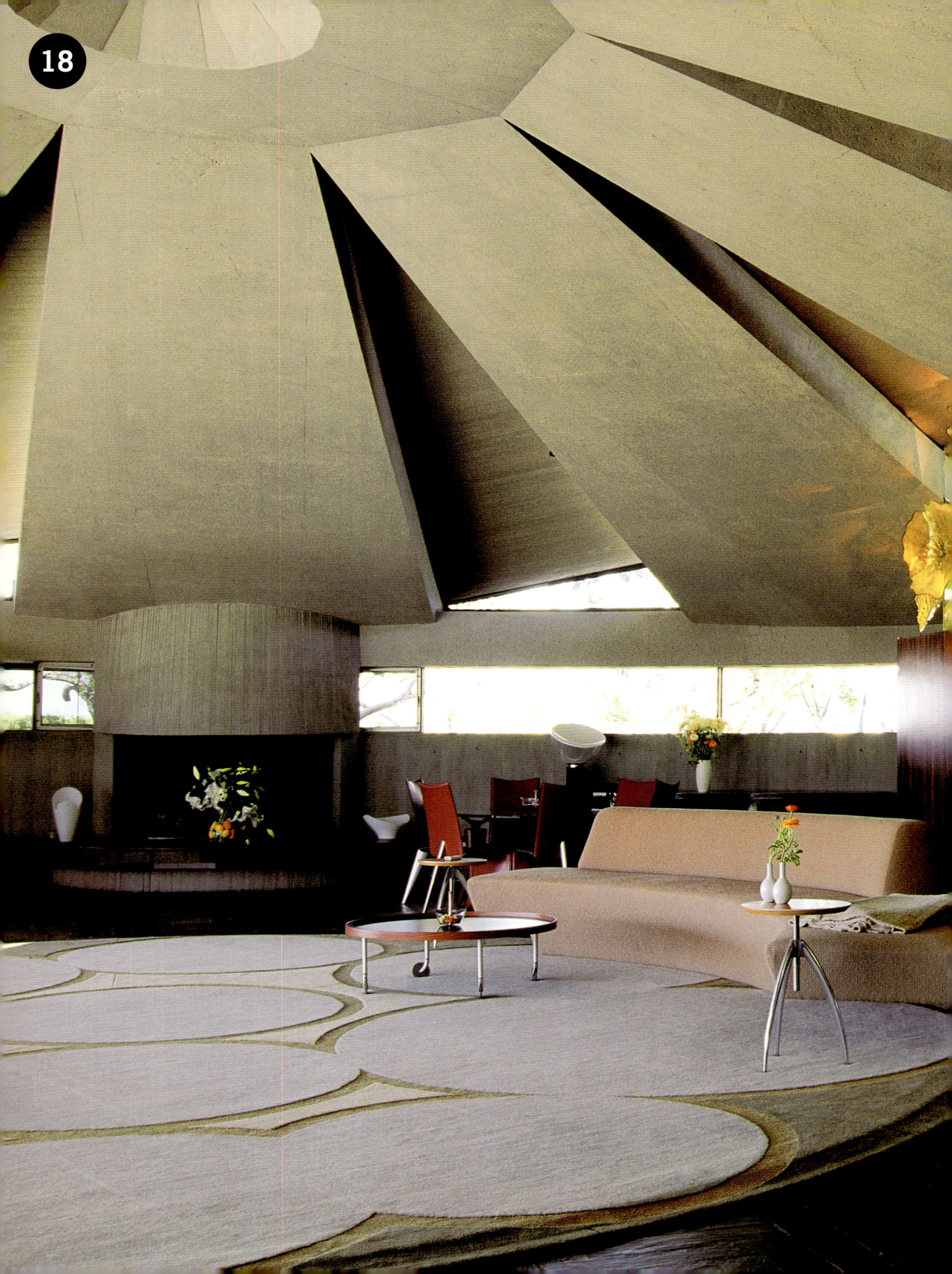

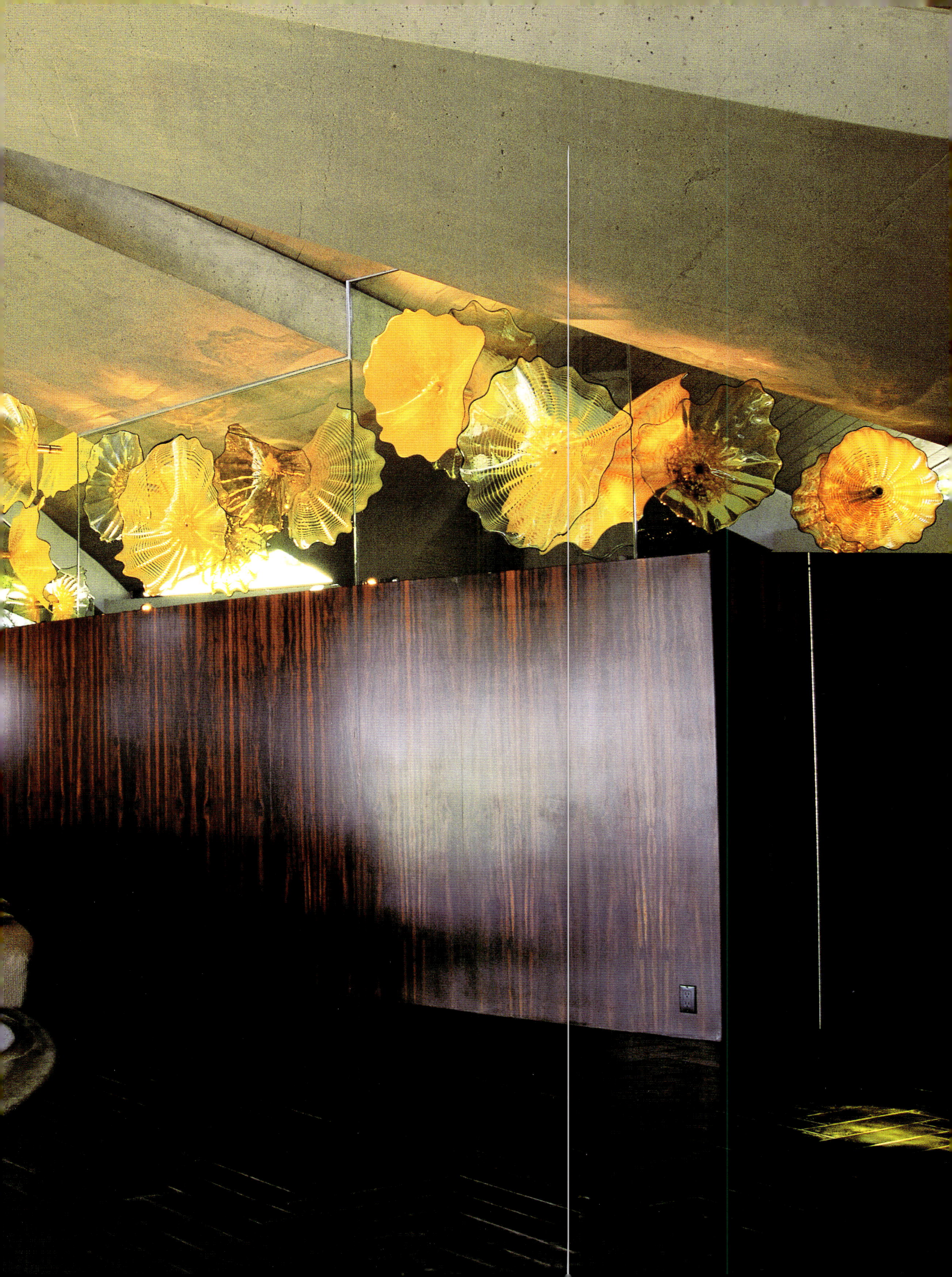

19

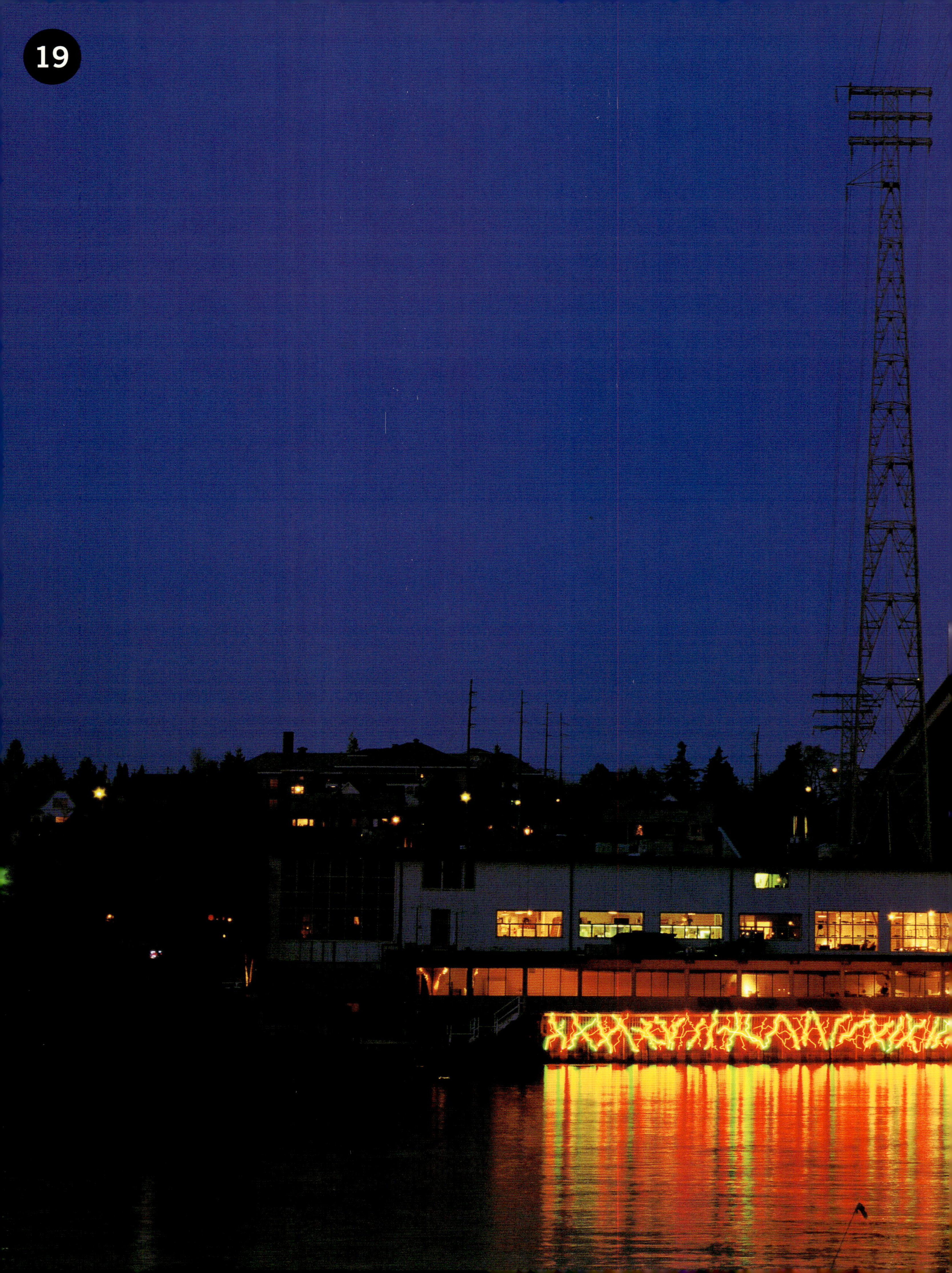

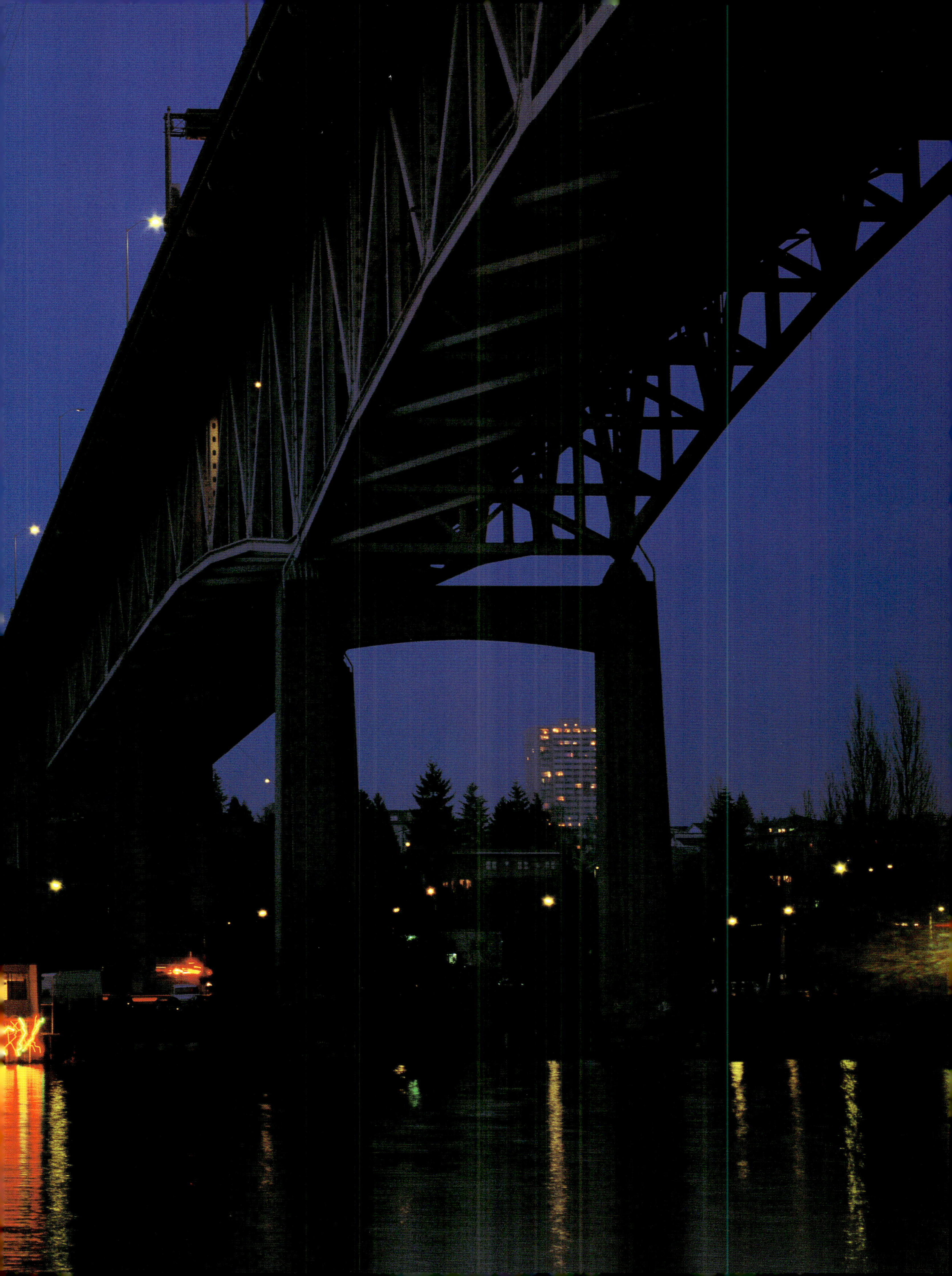

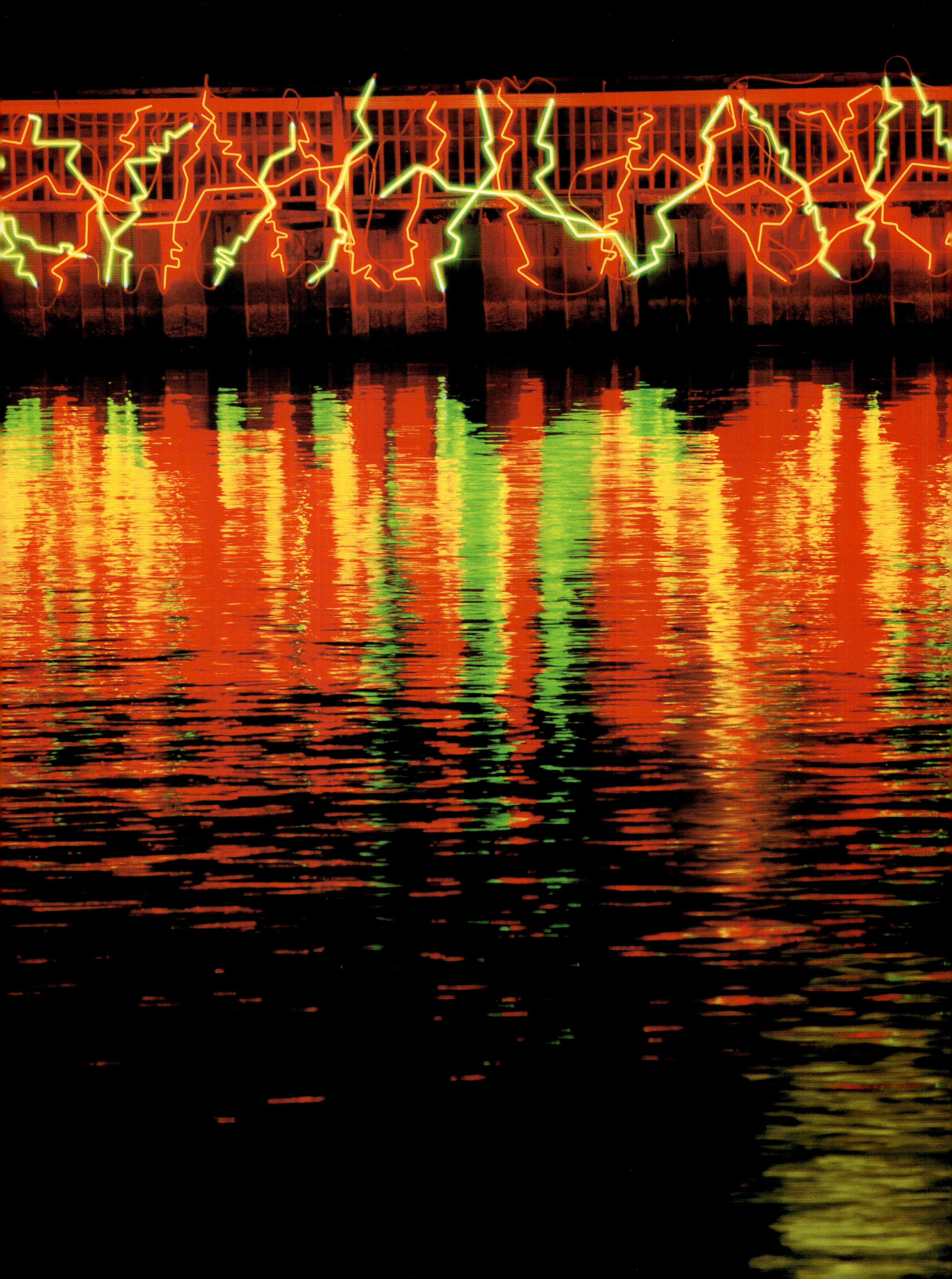

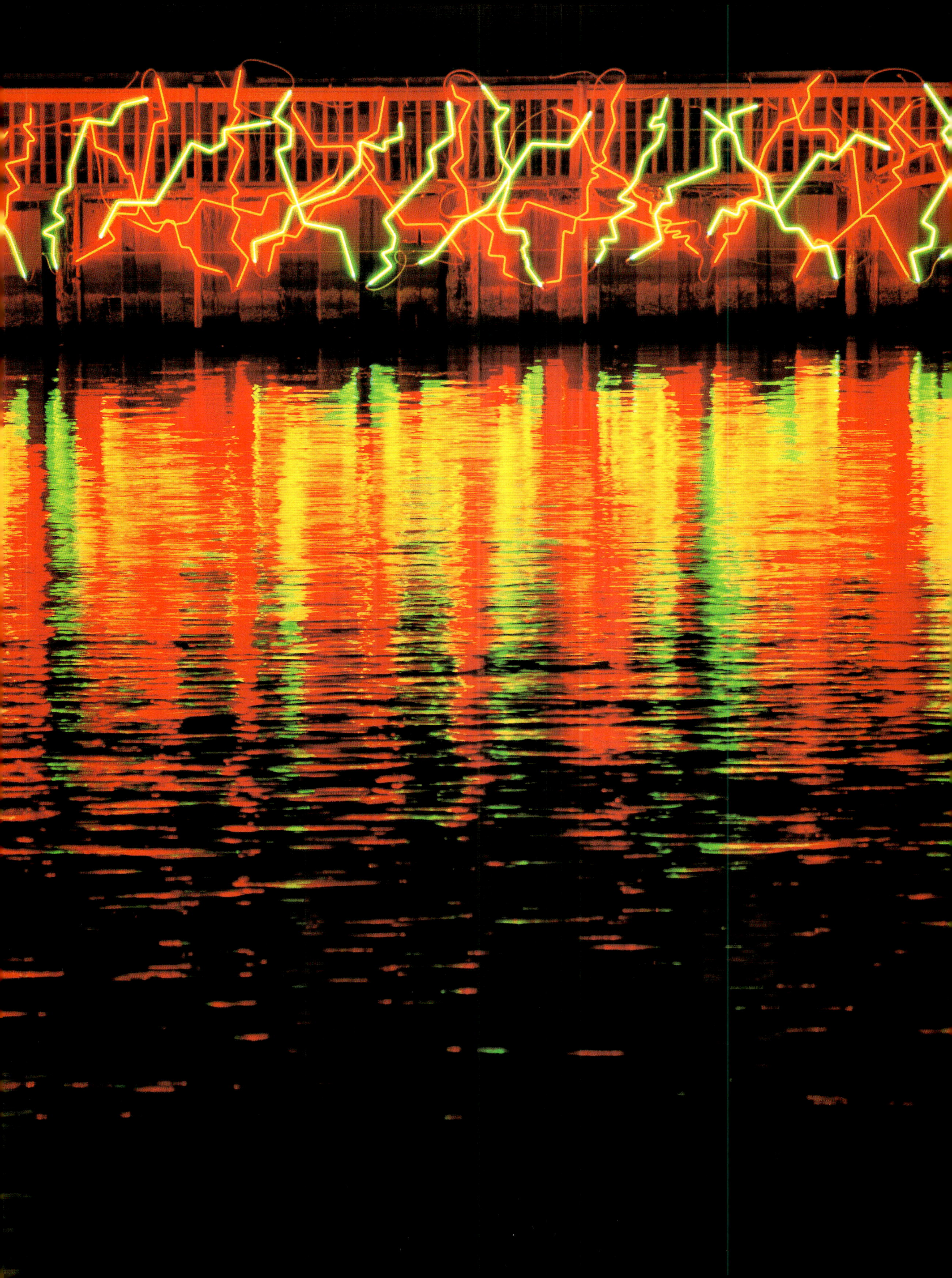

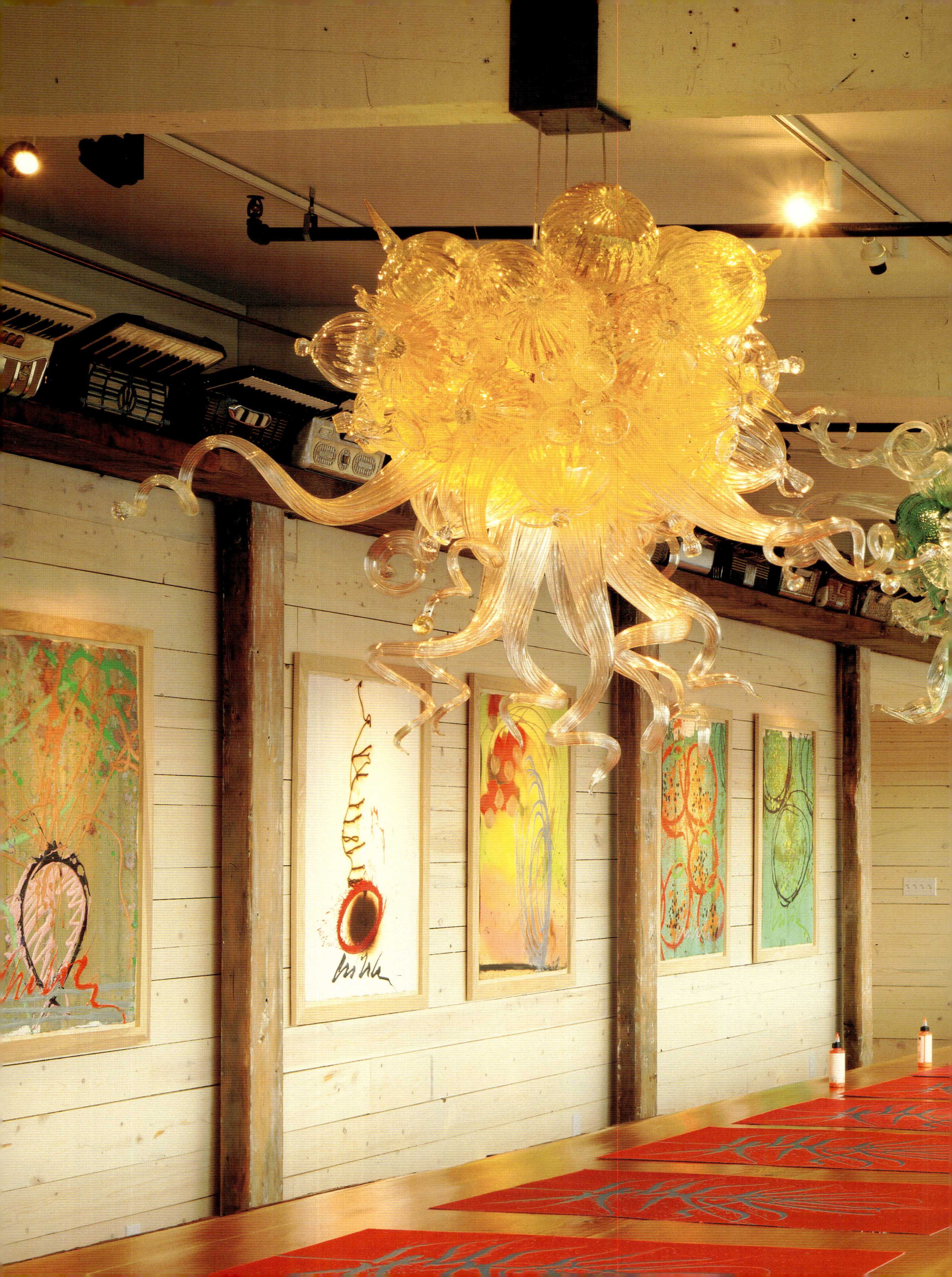

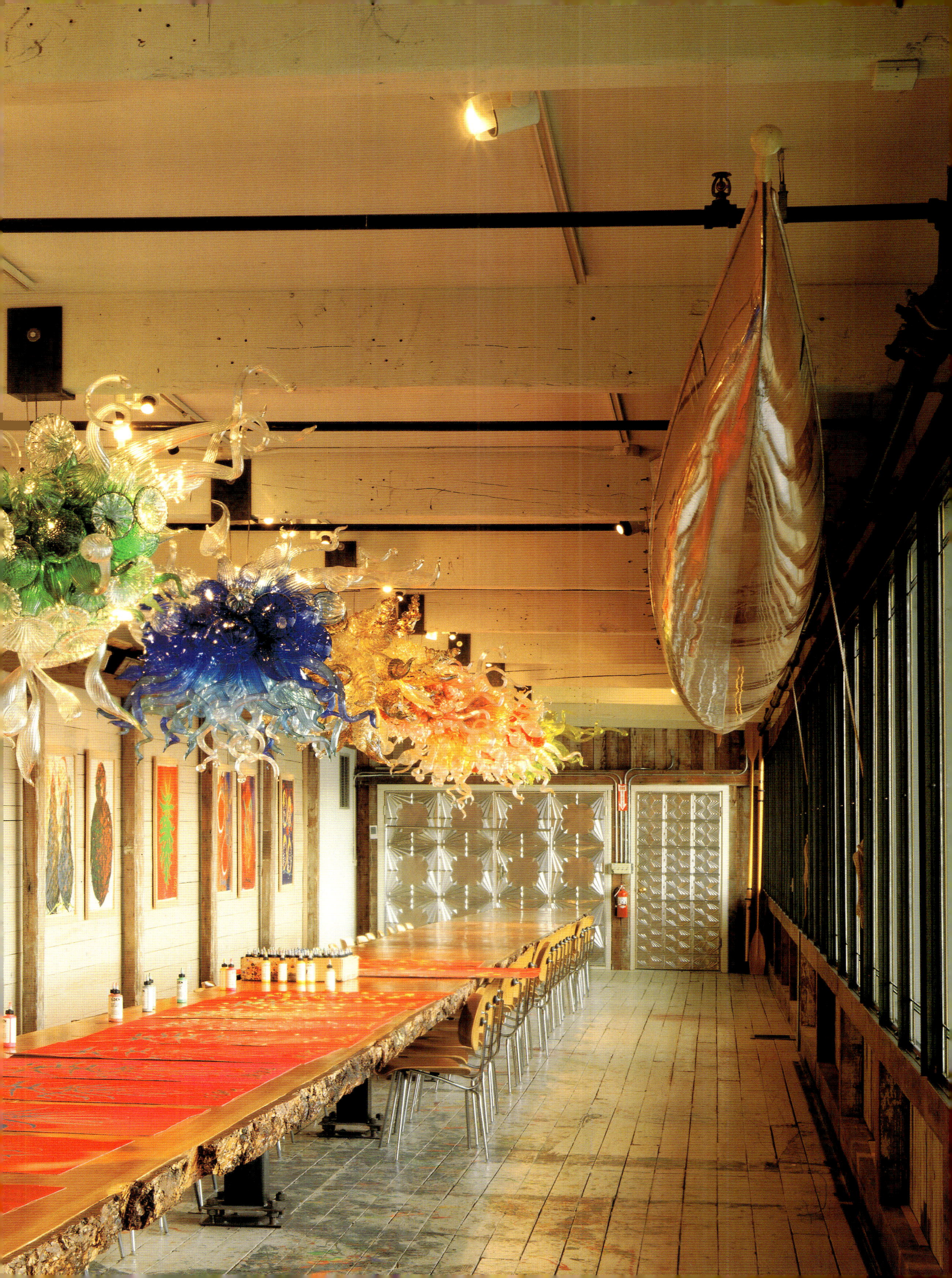

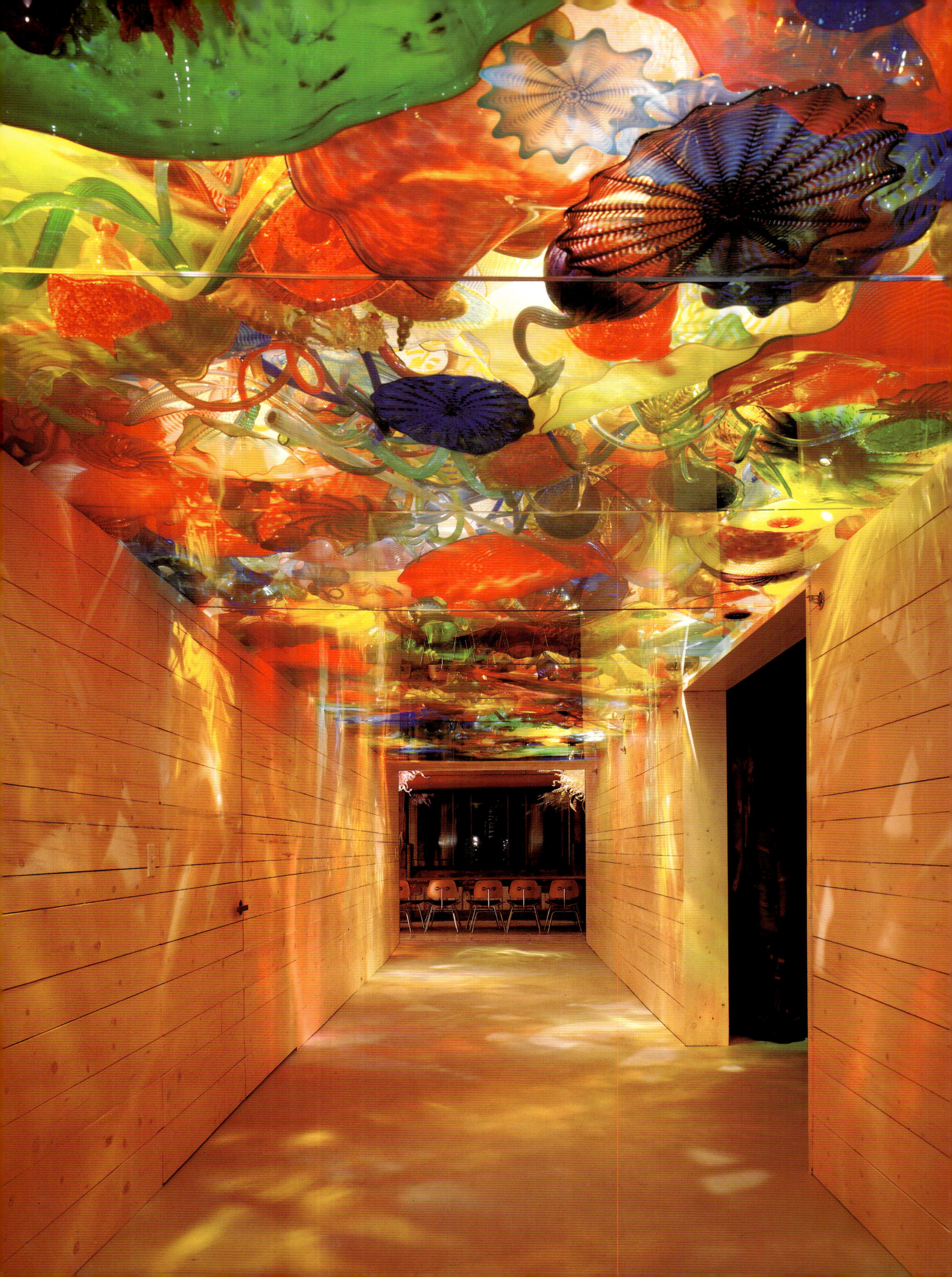

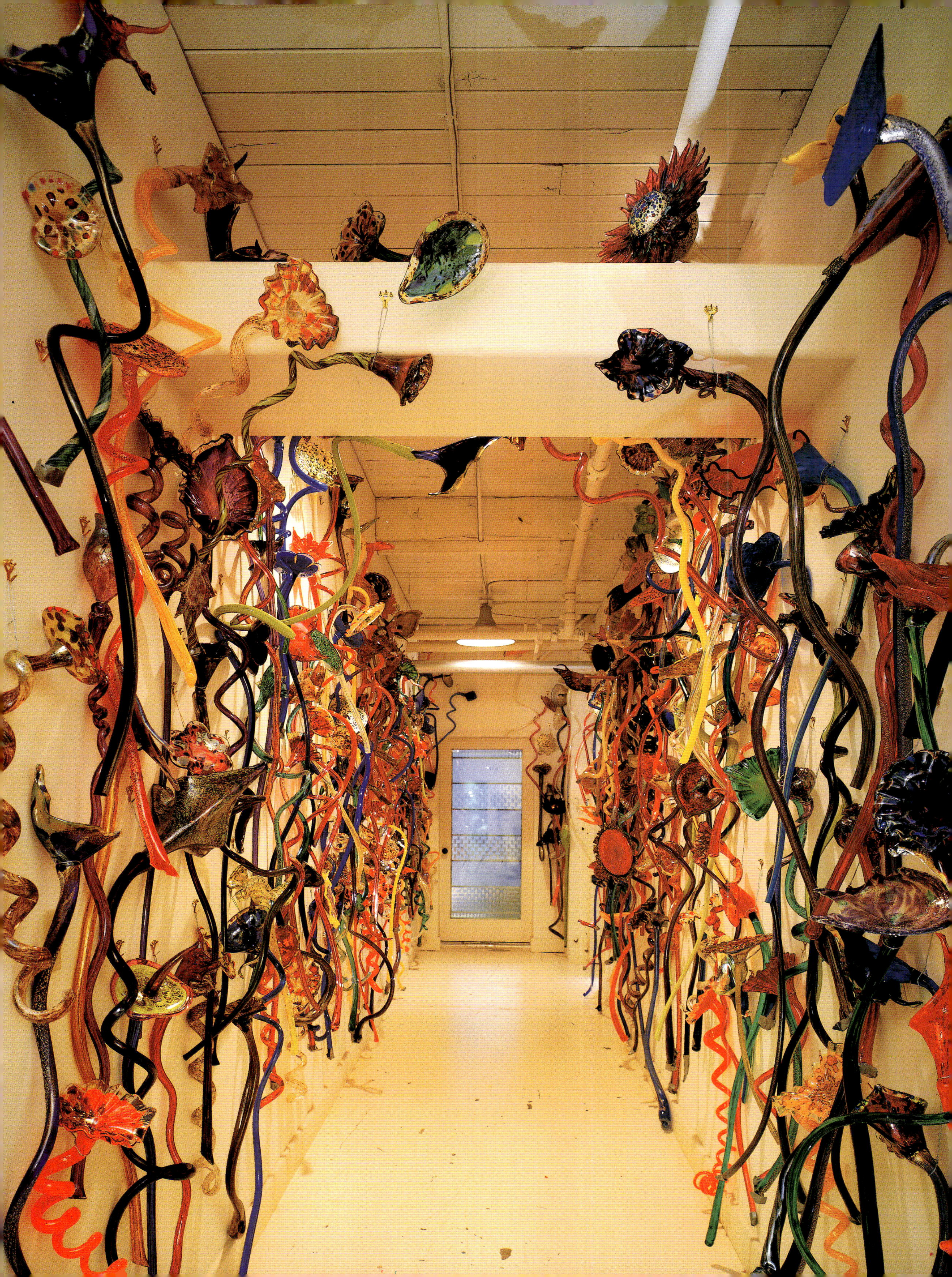

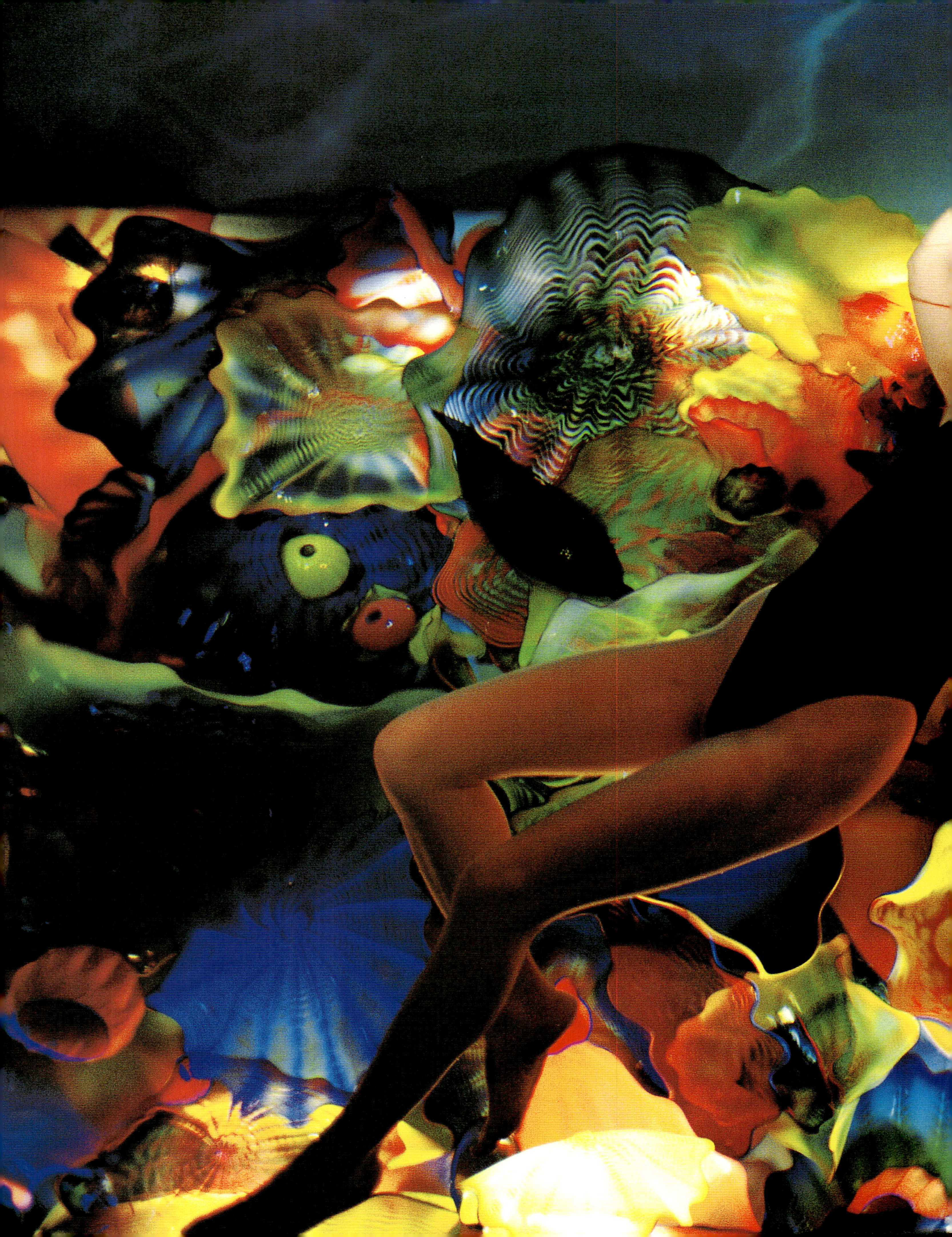

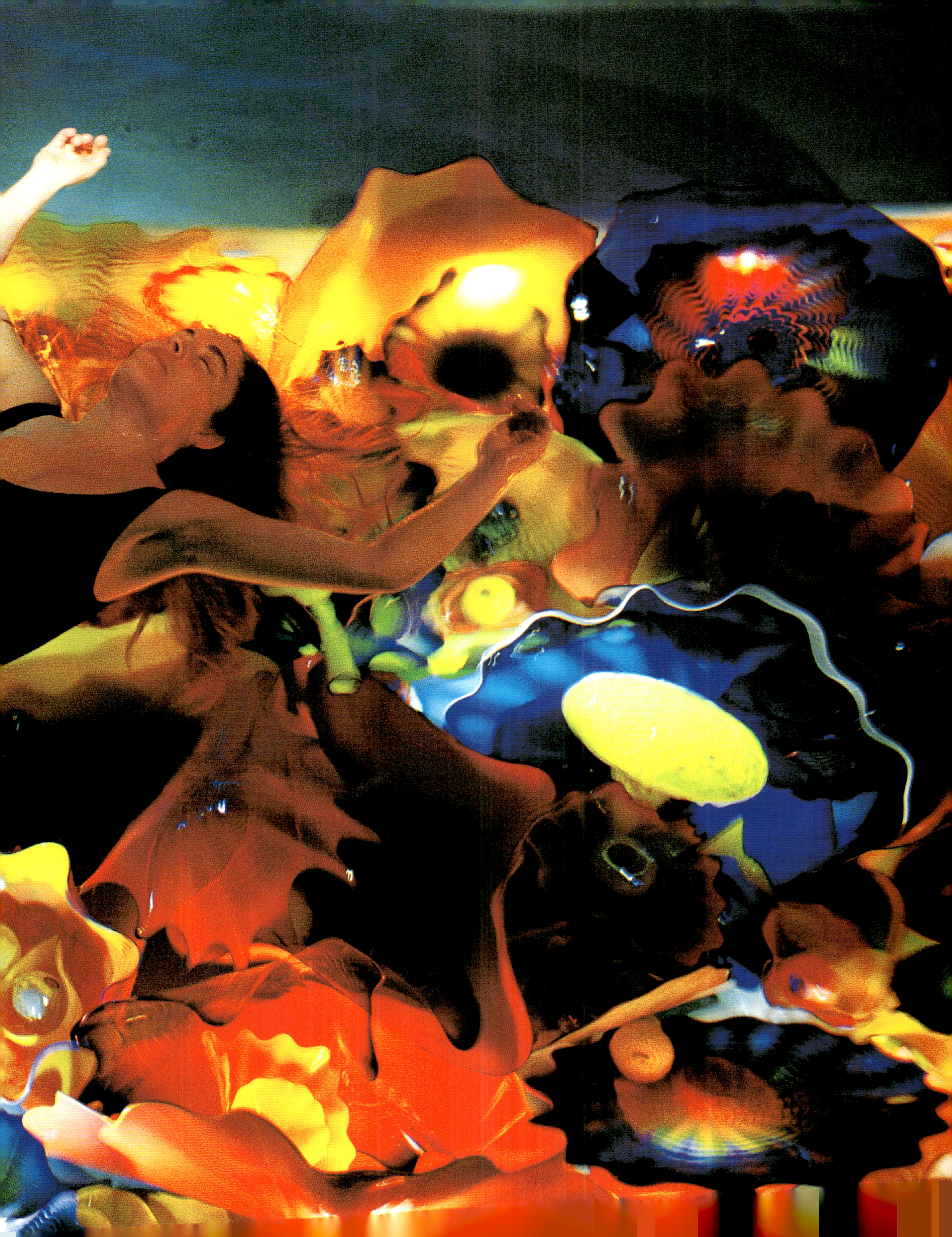

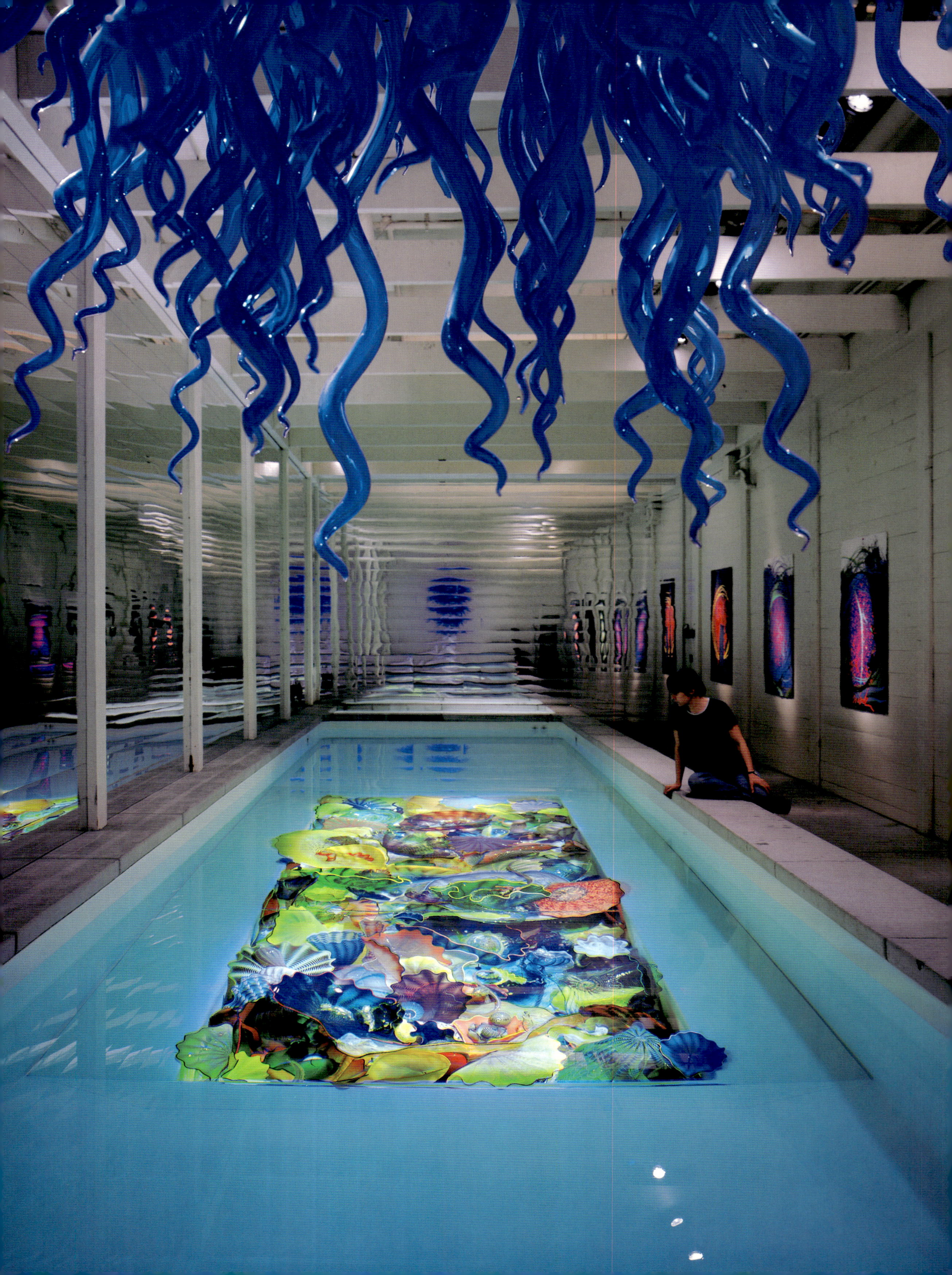

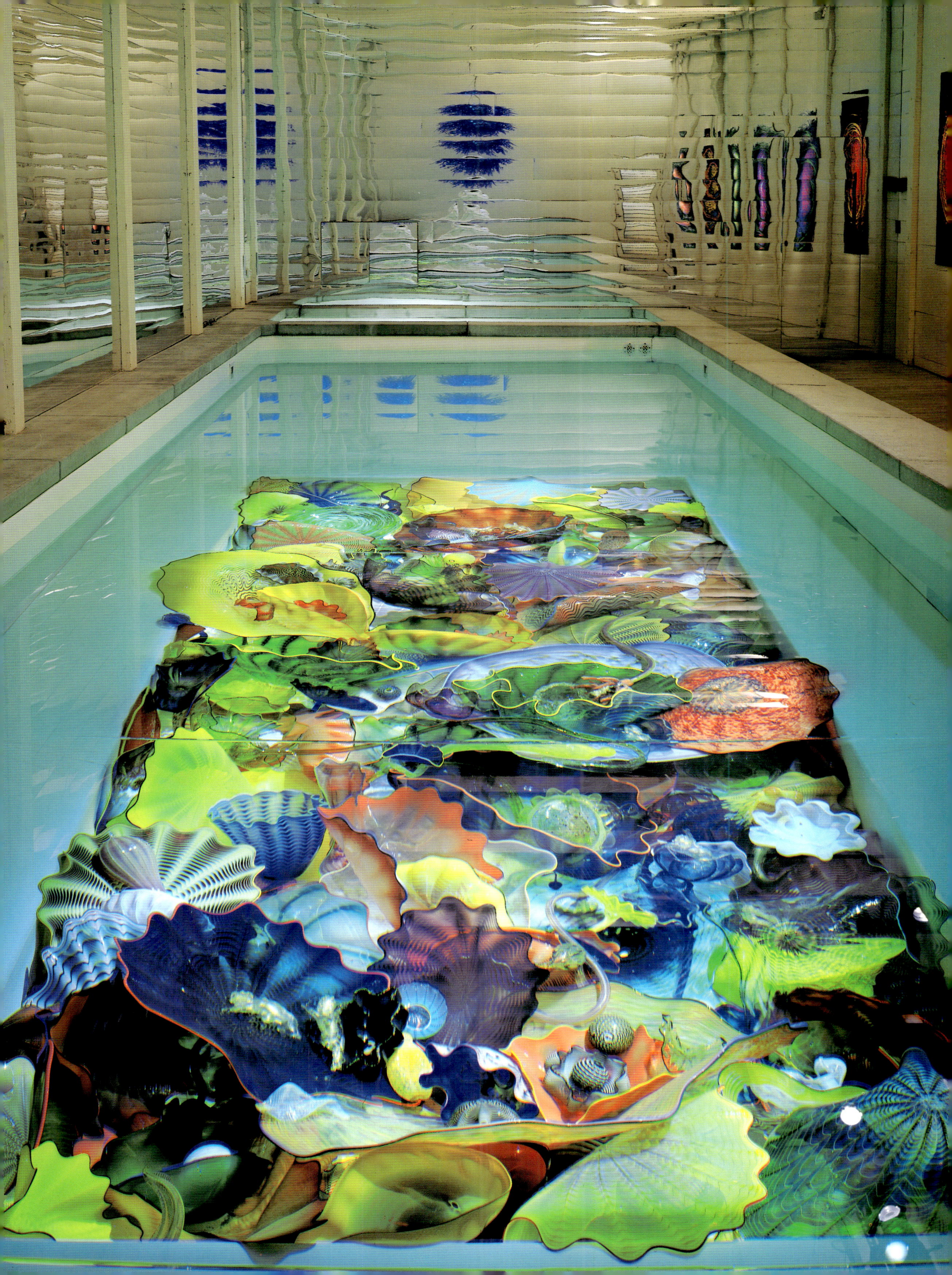

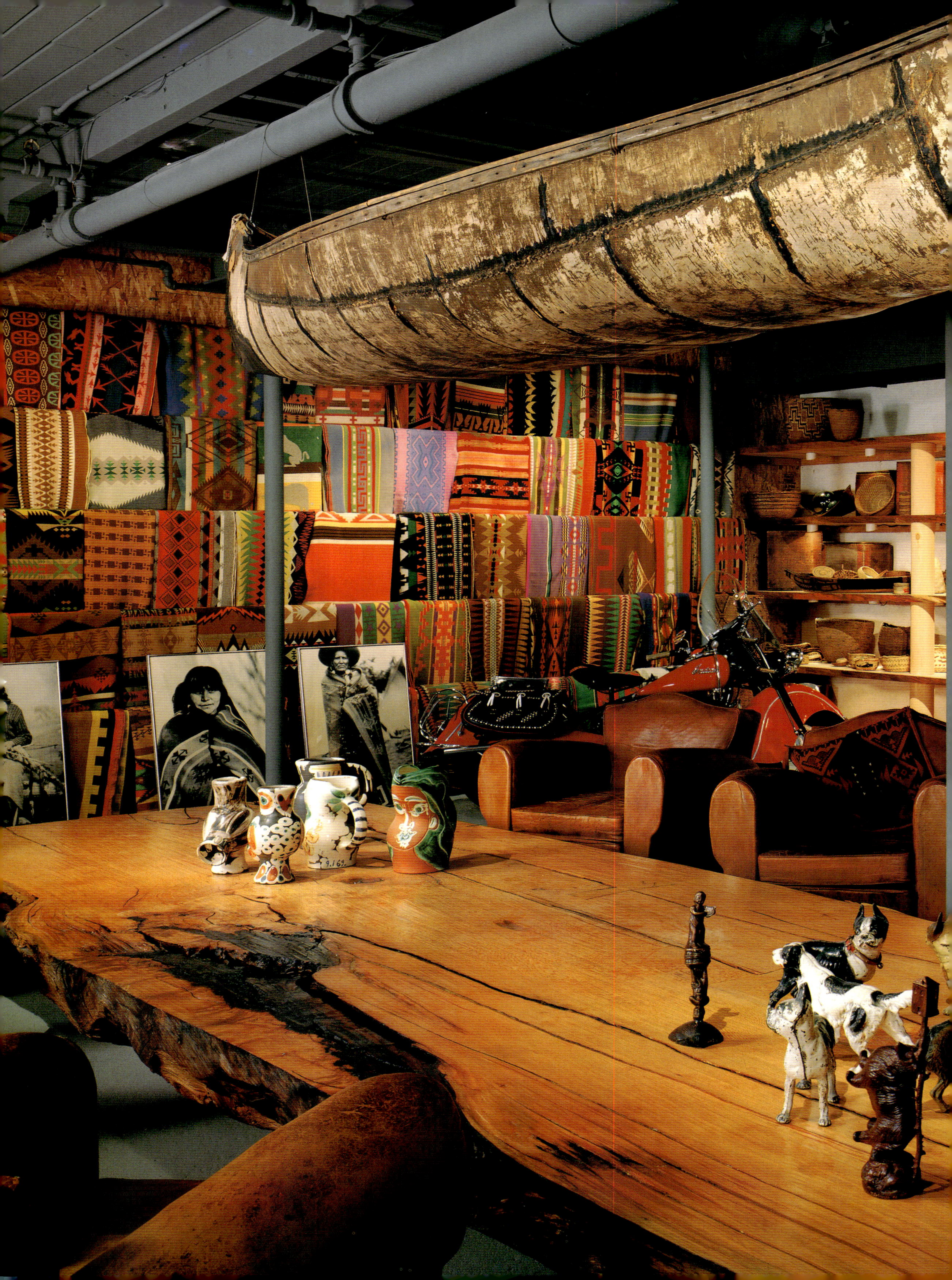

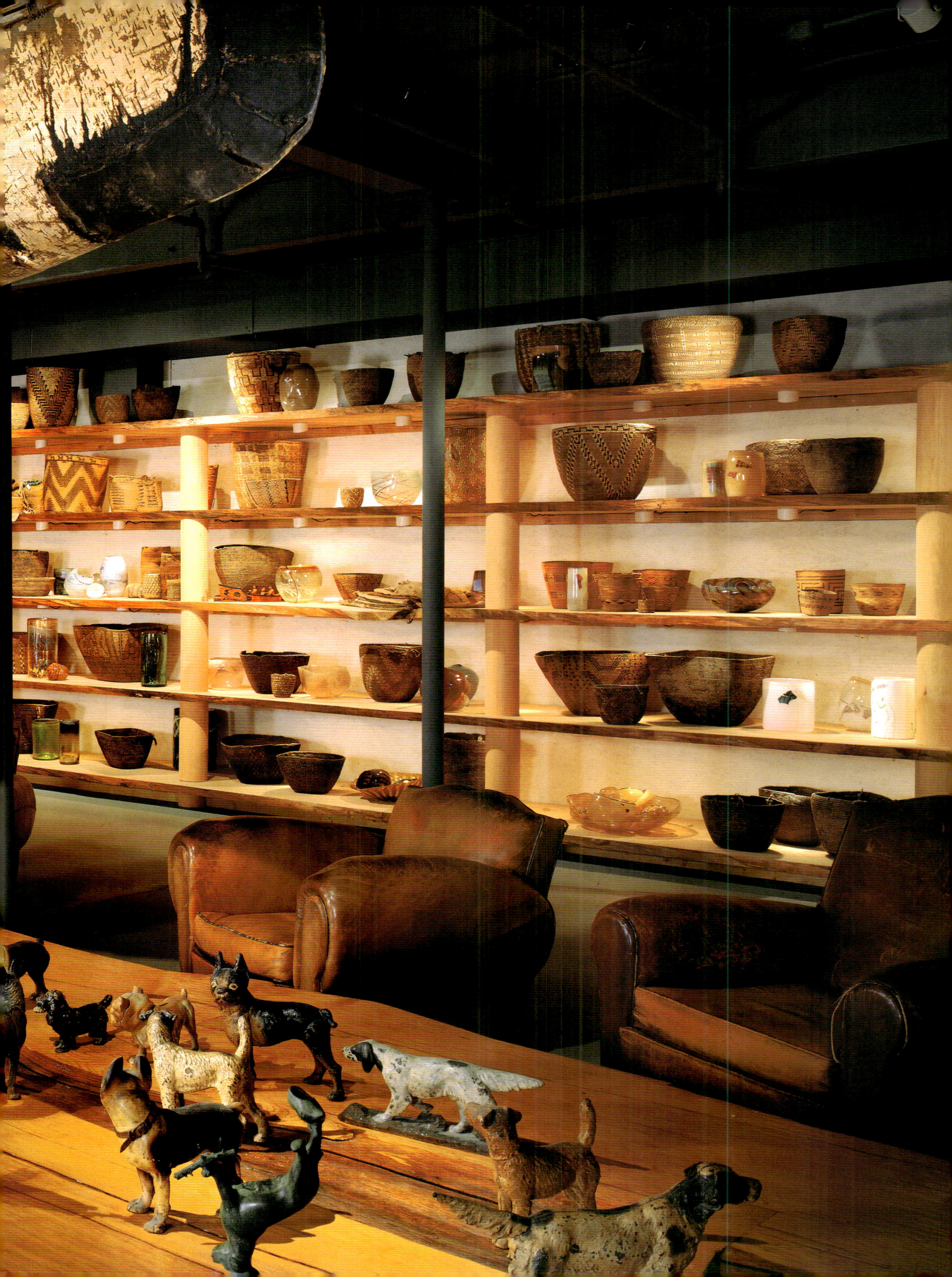

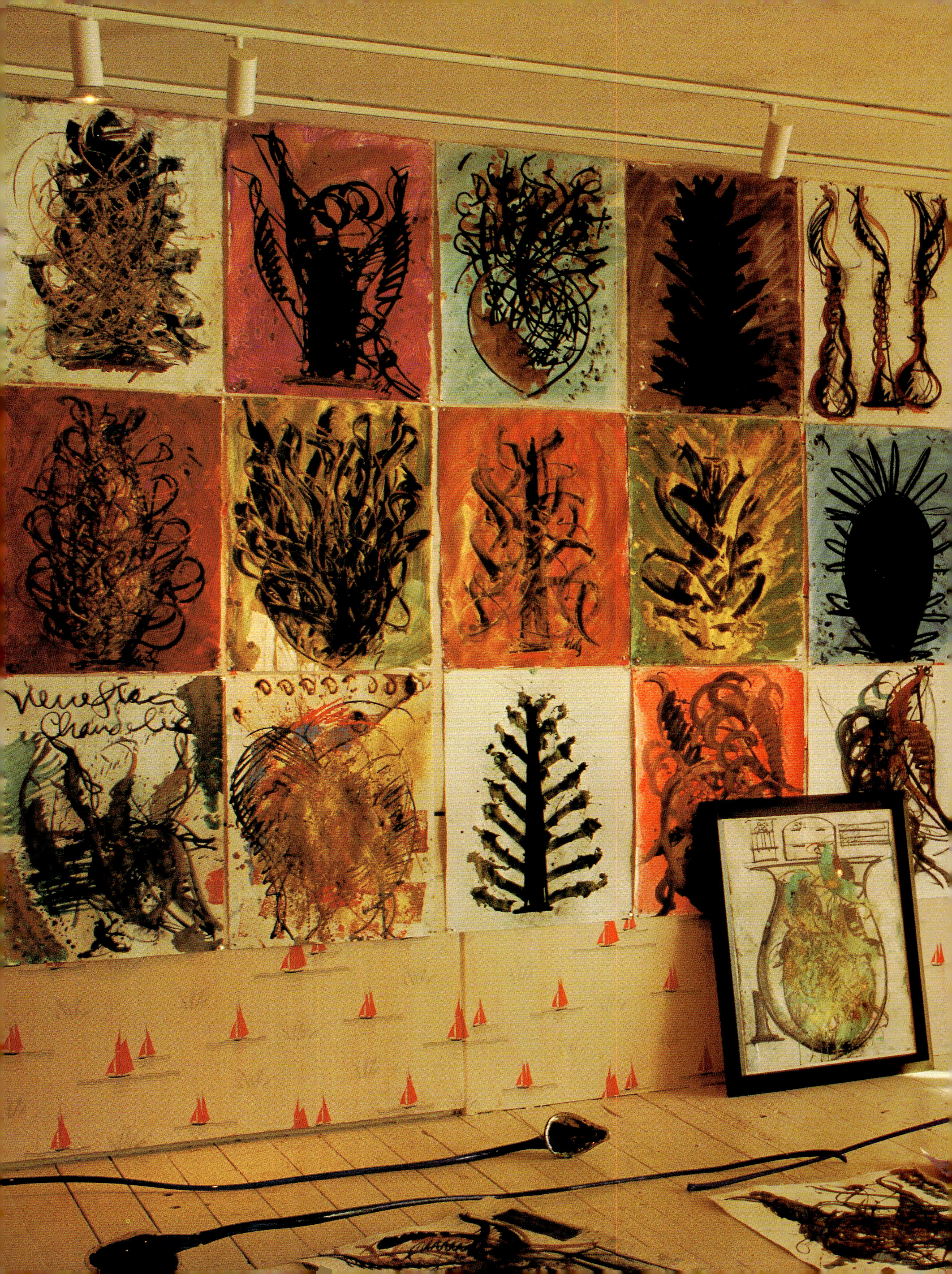

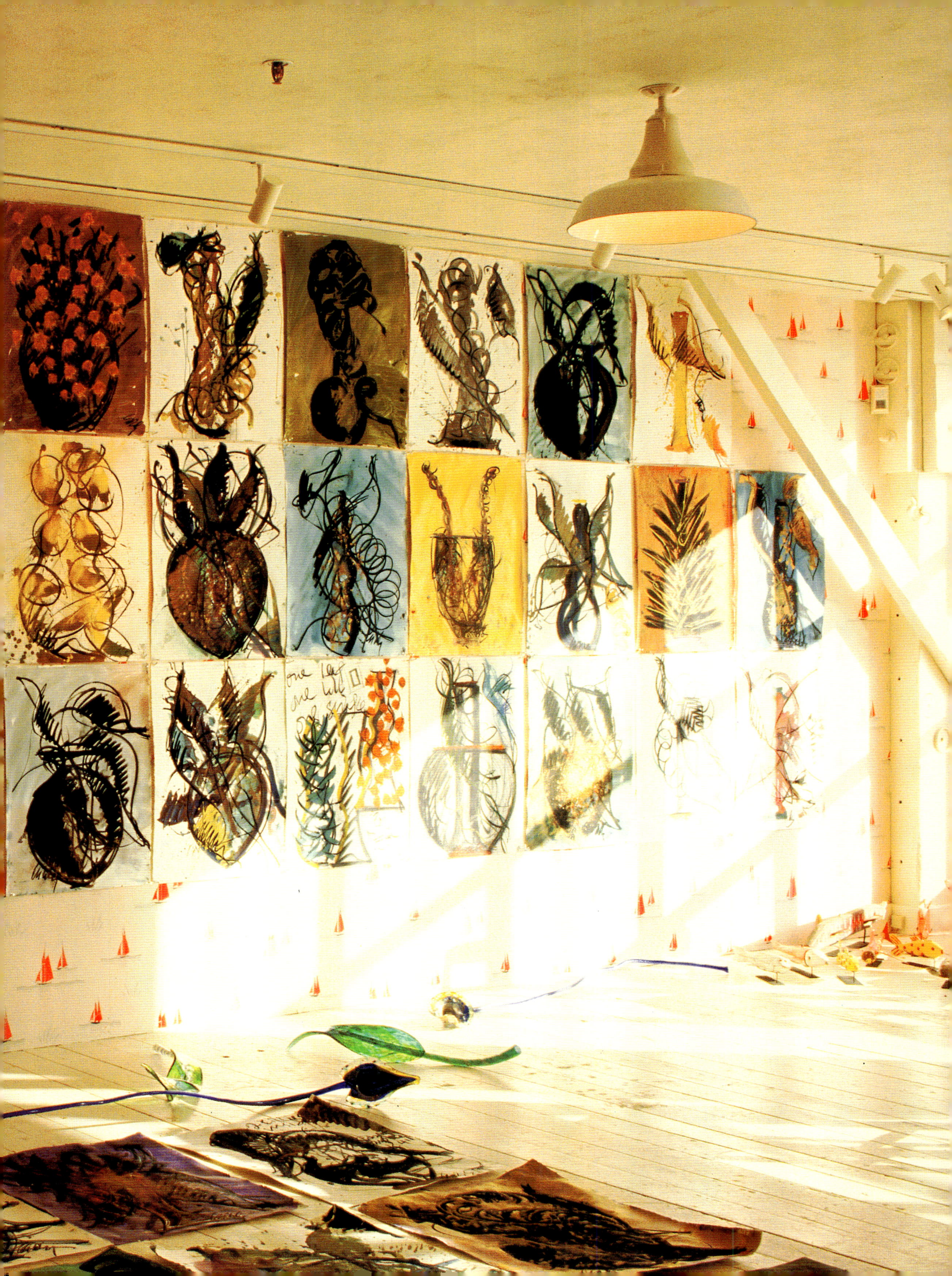

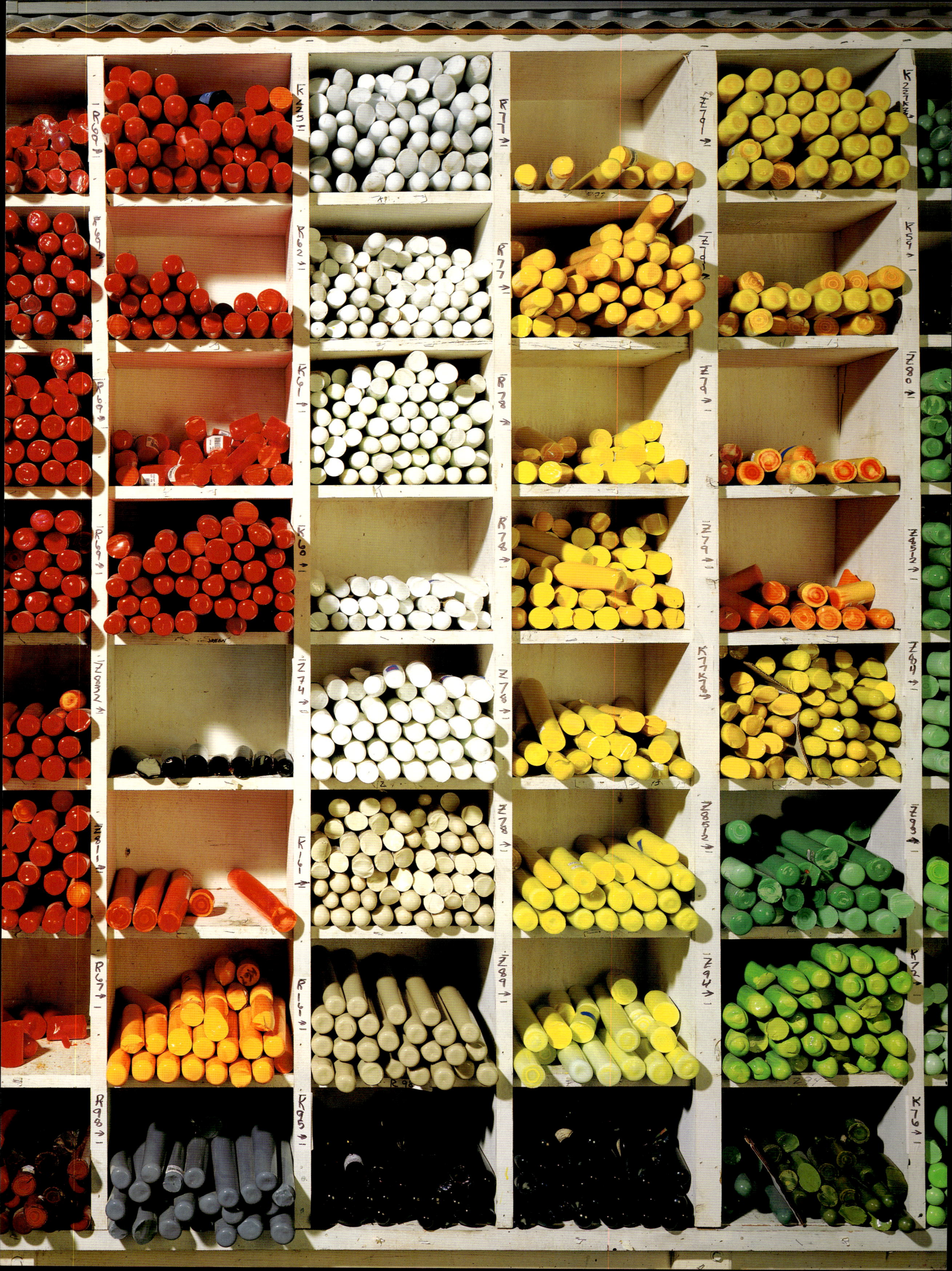

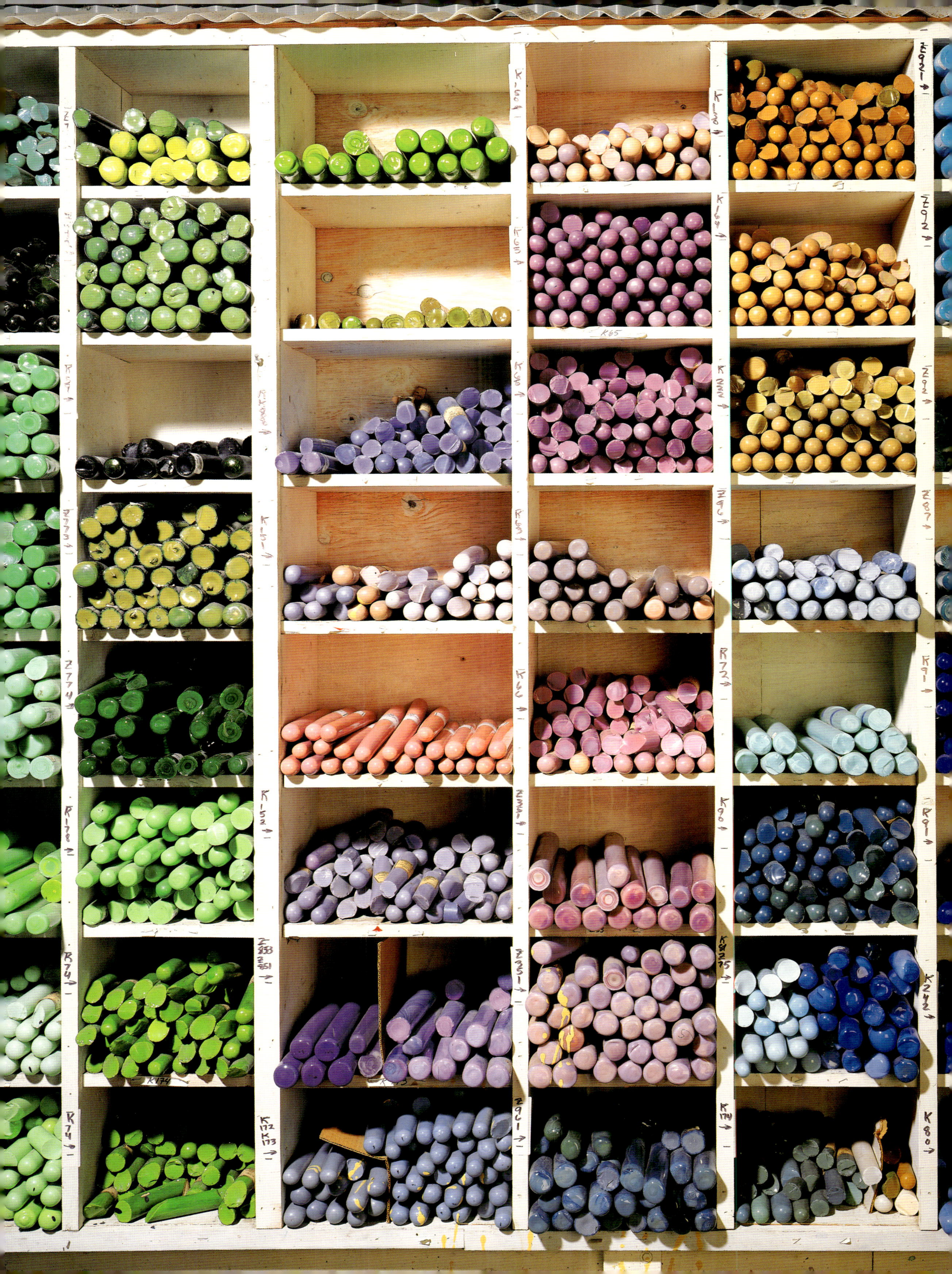

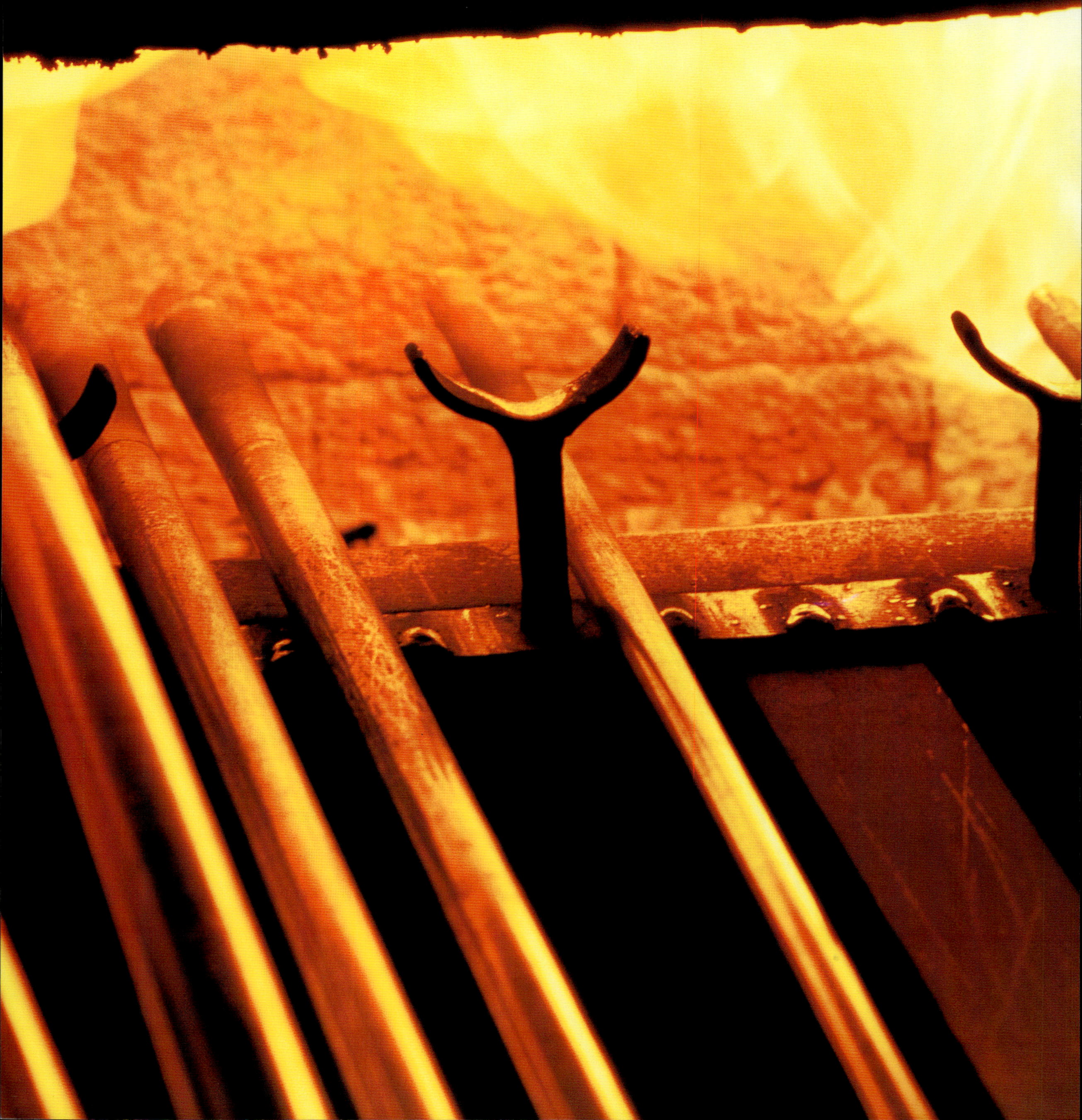

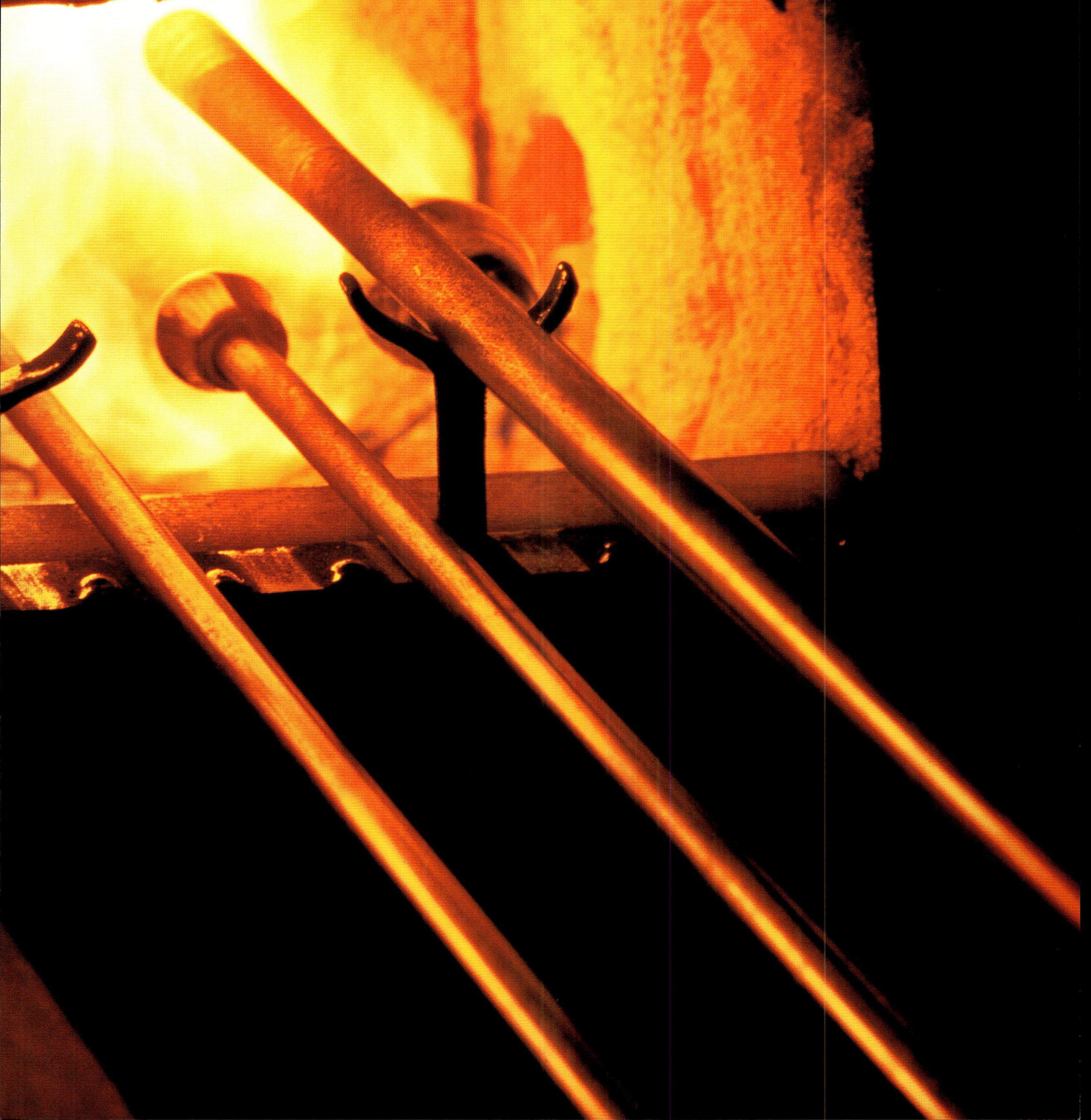

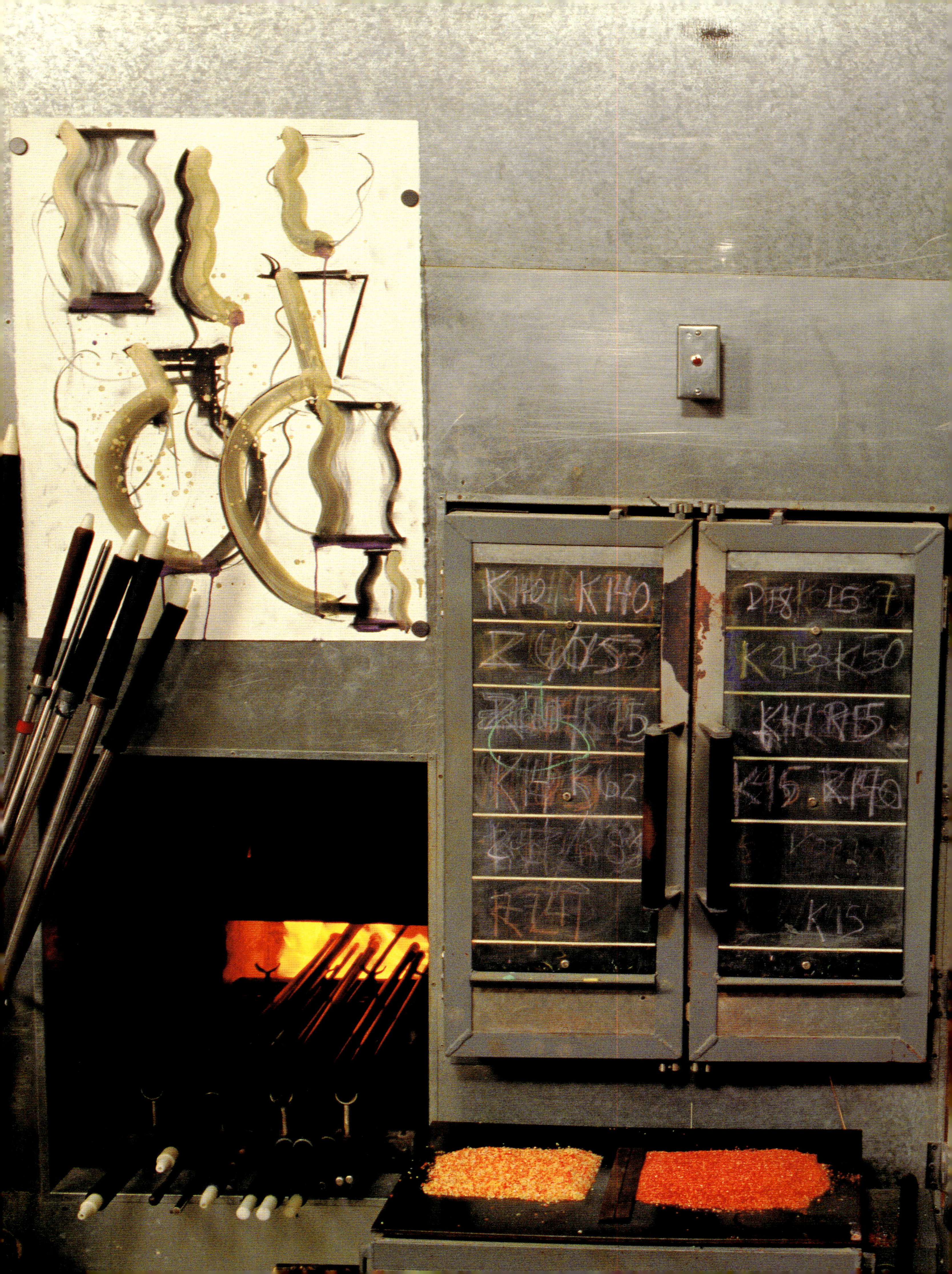

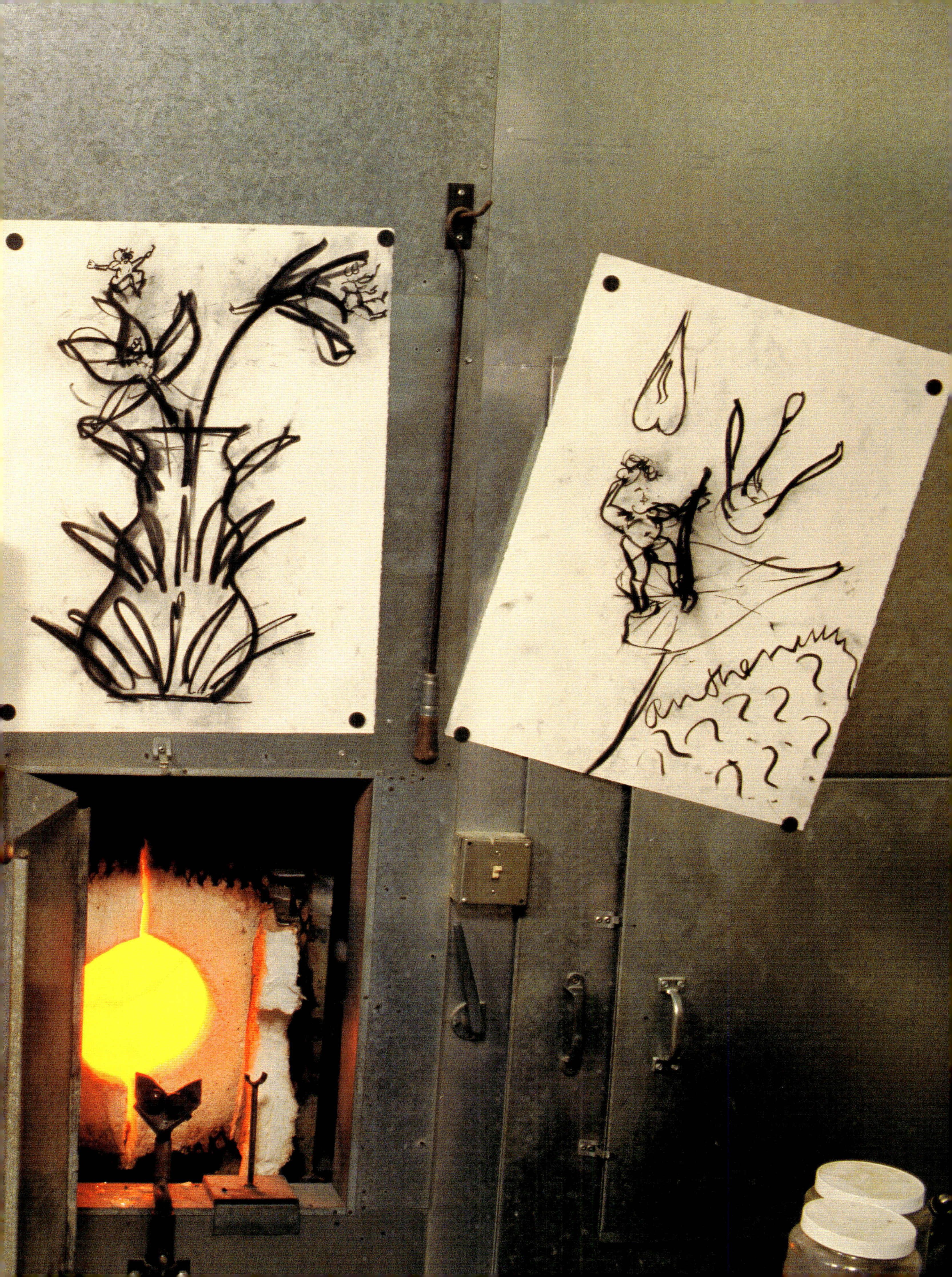

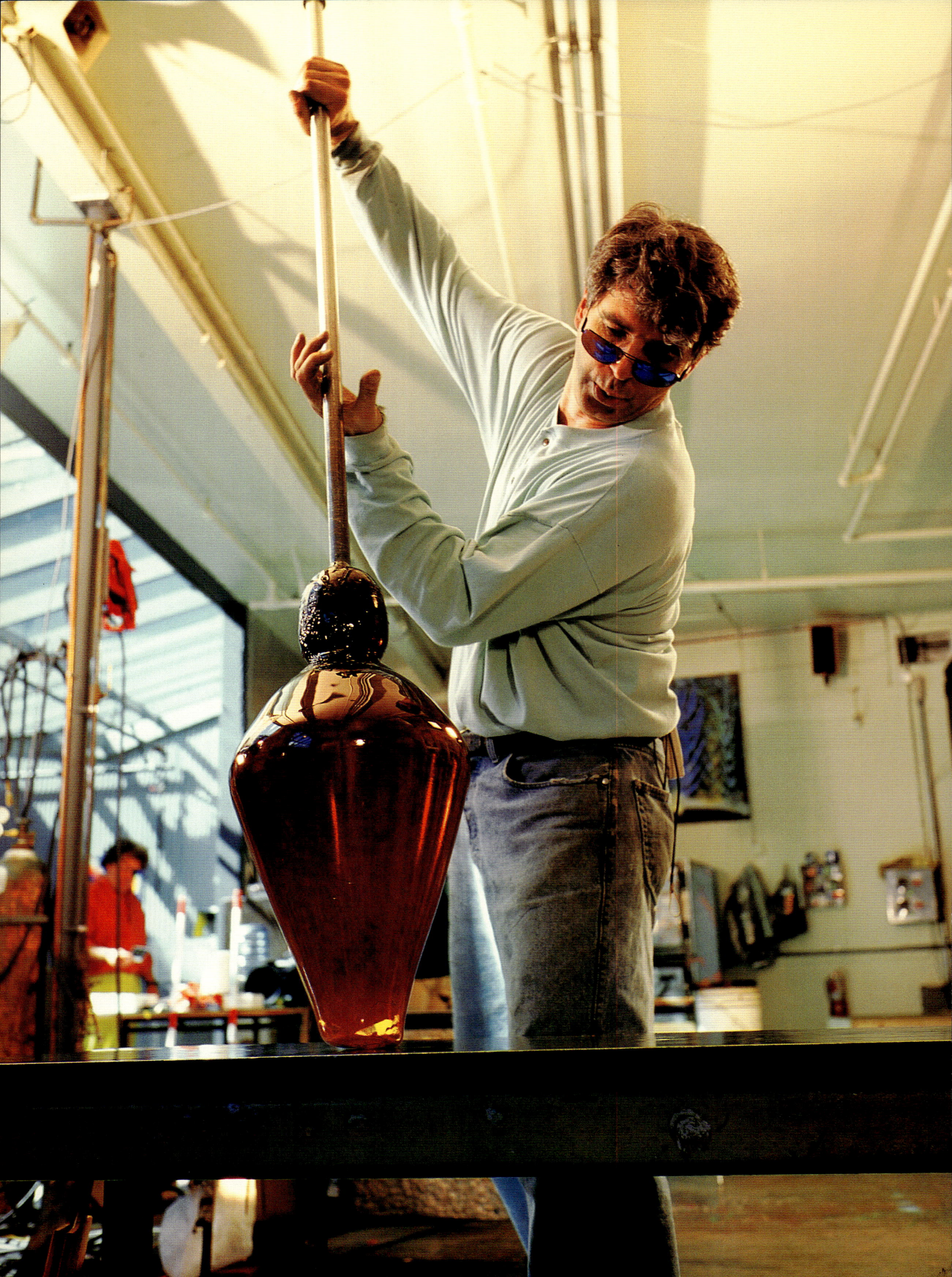

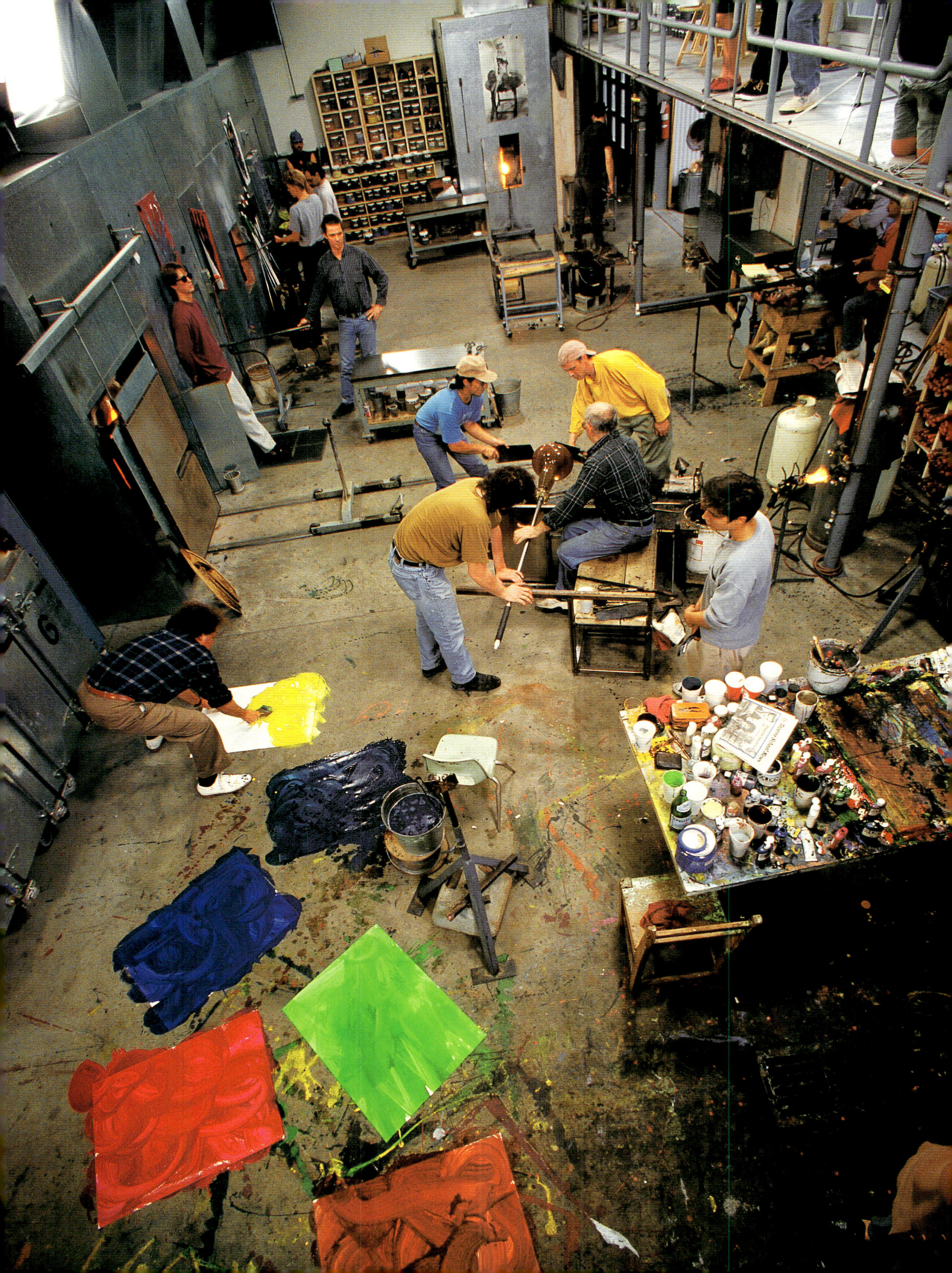

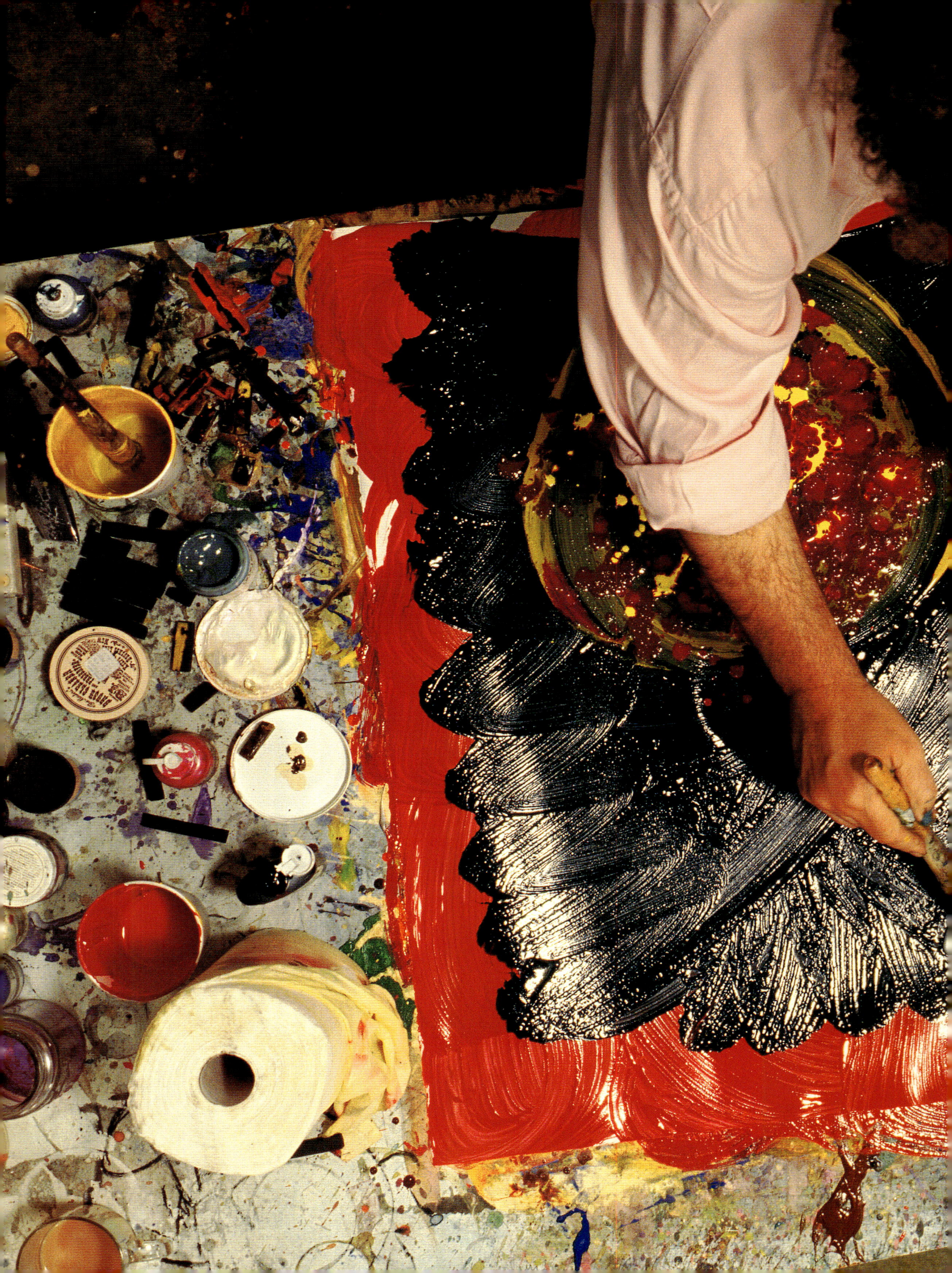

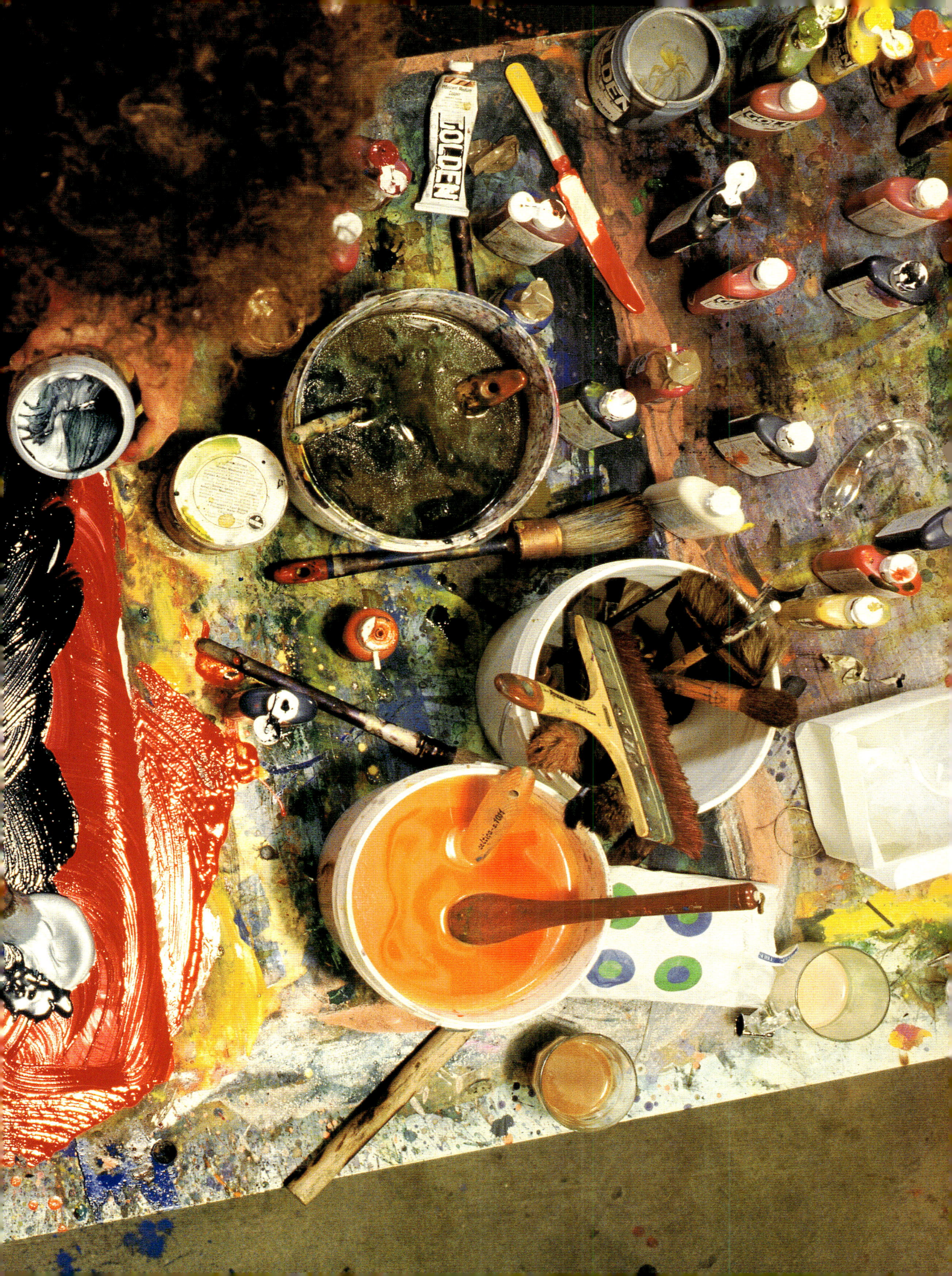
GOLDEN

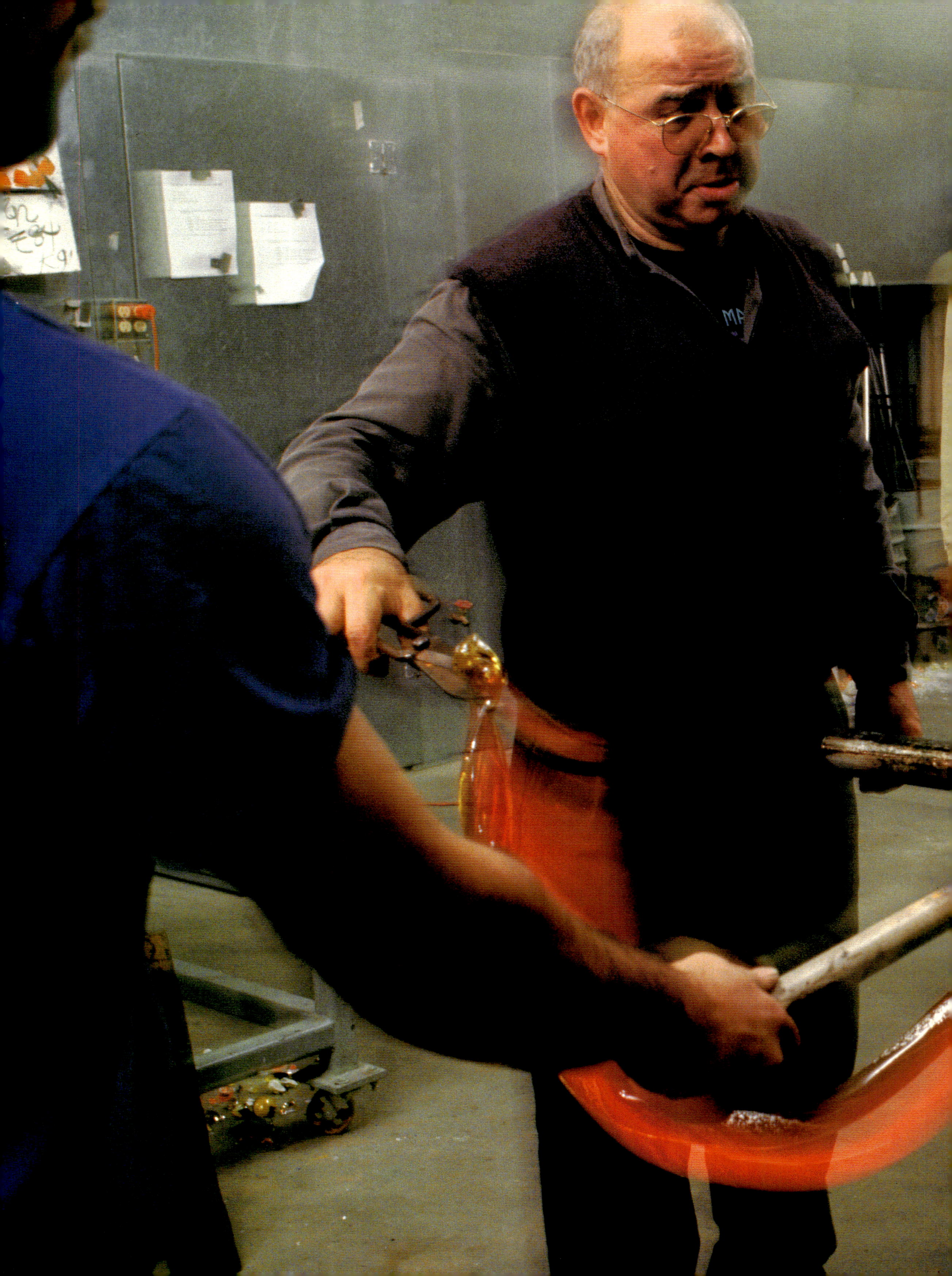

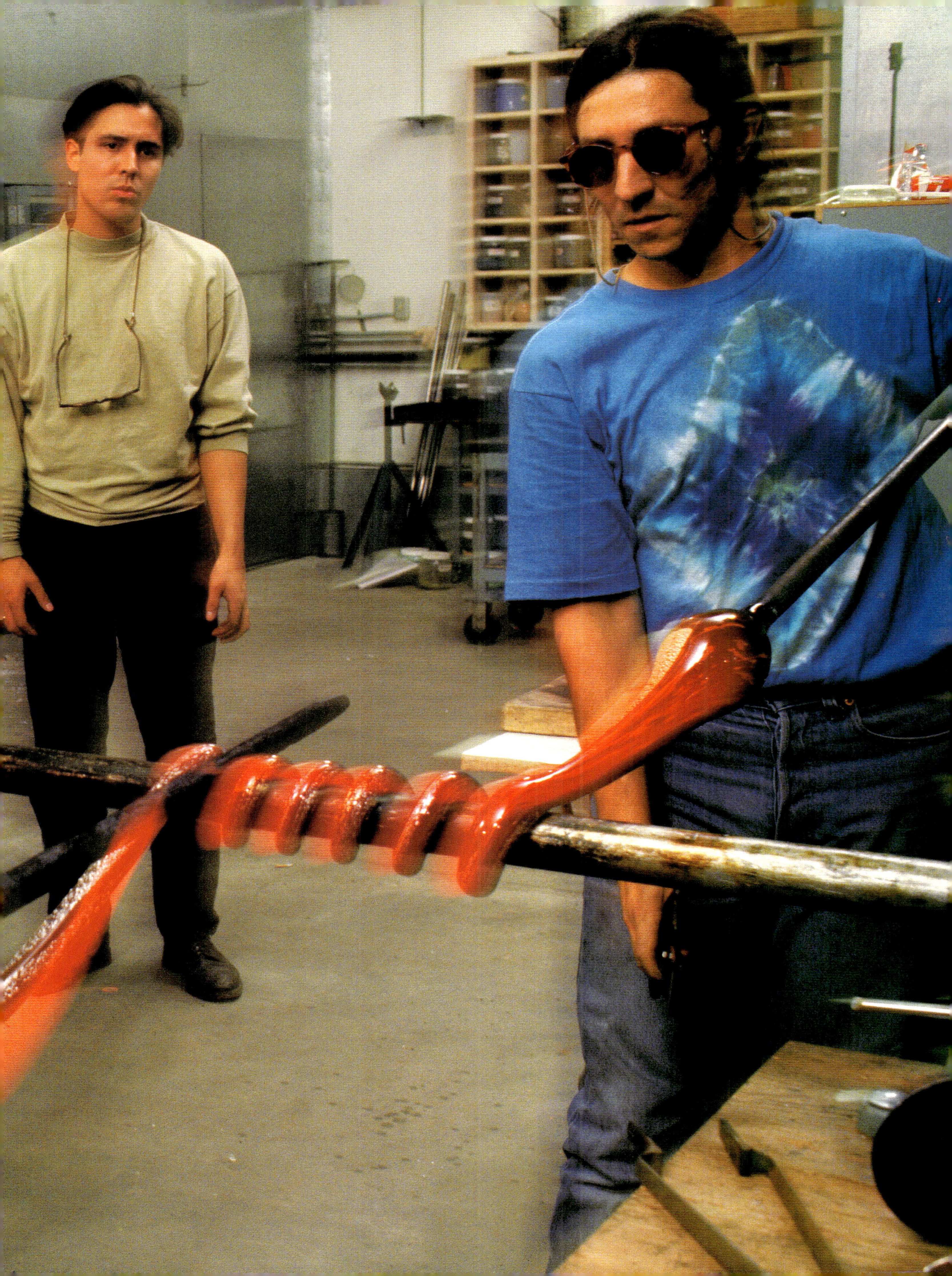

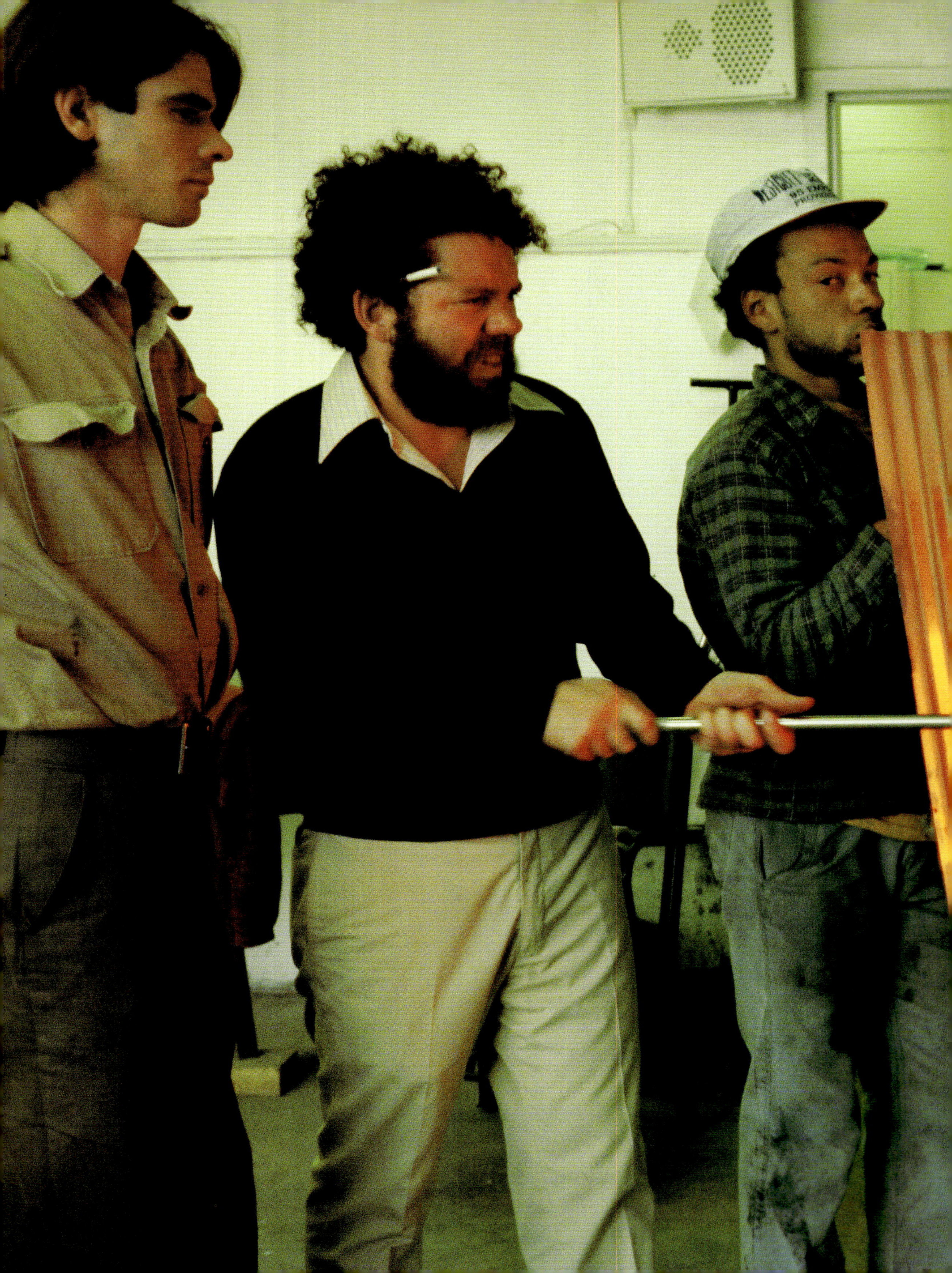

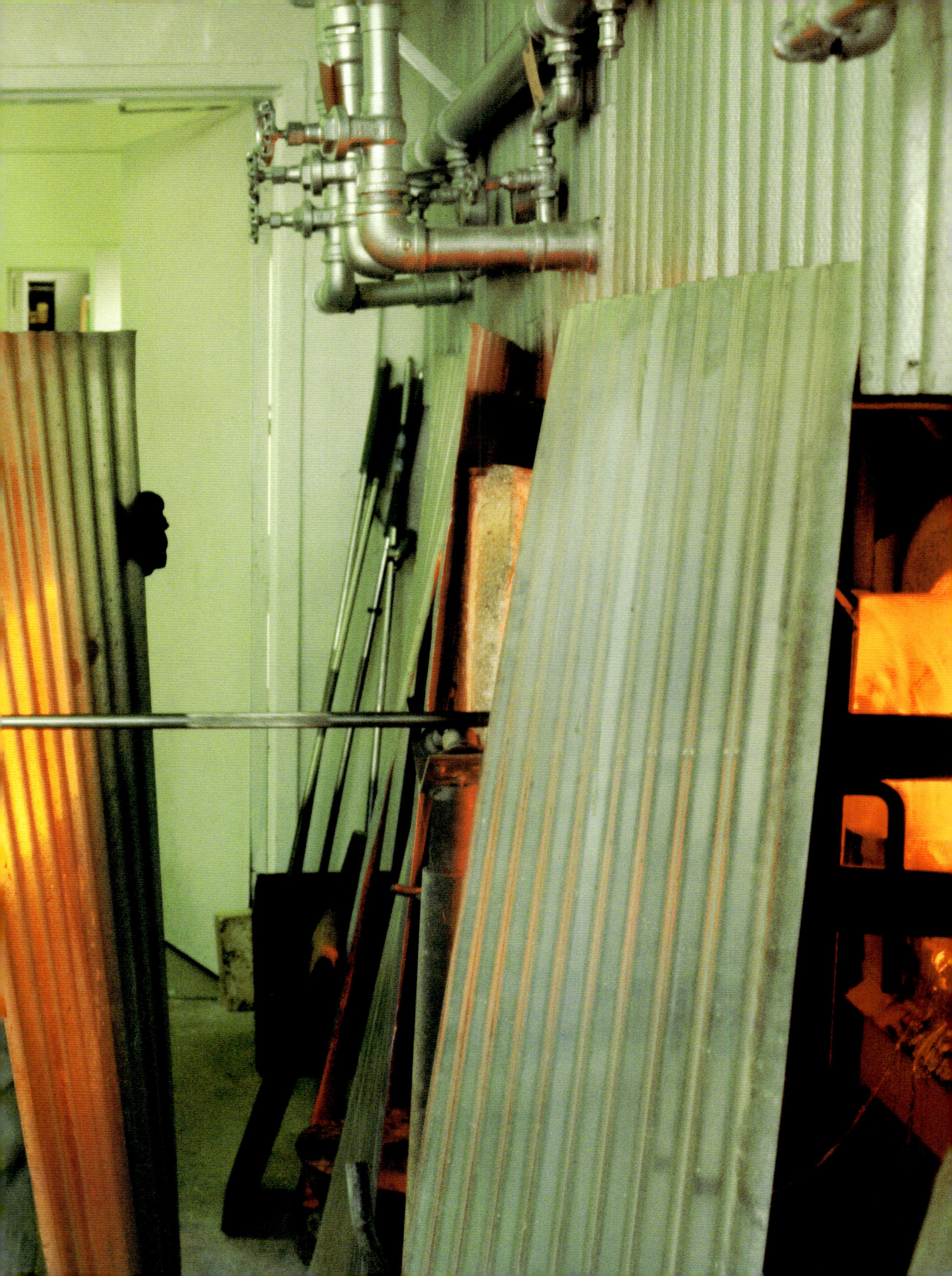

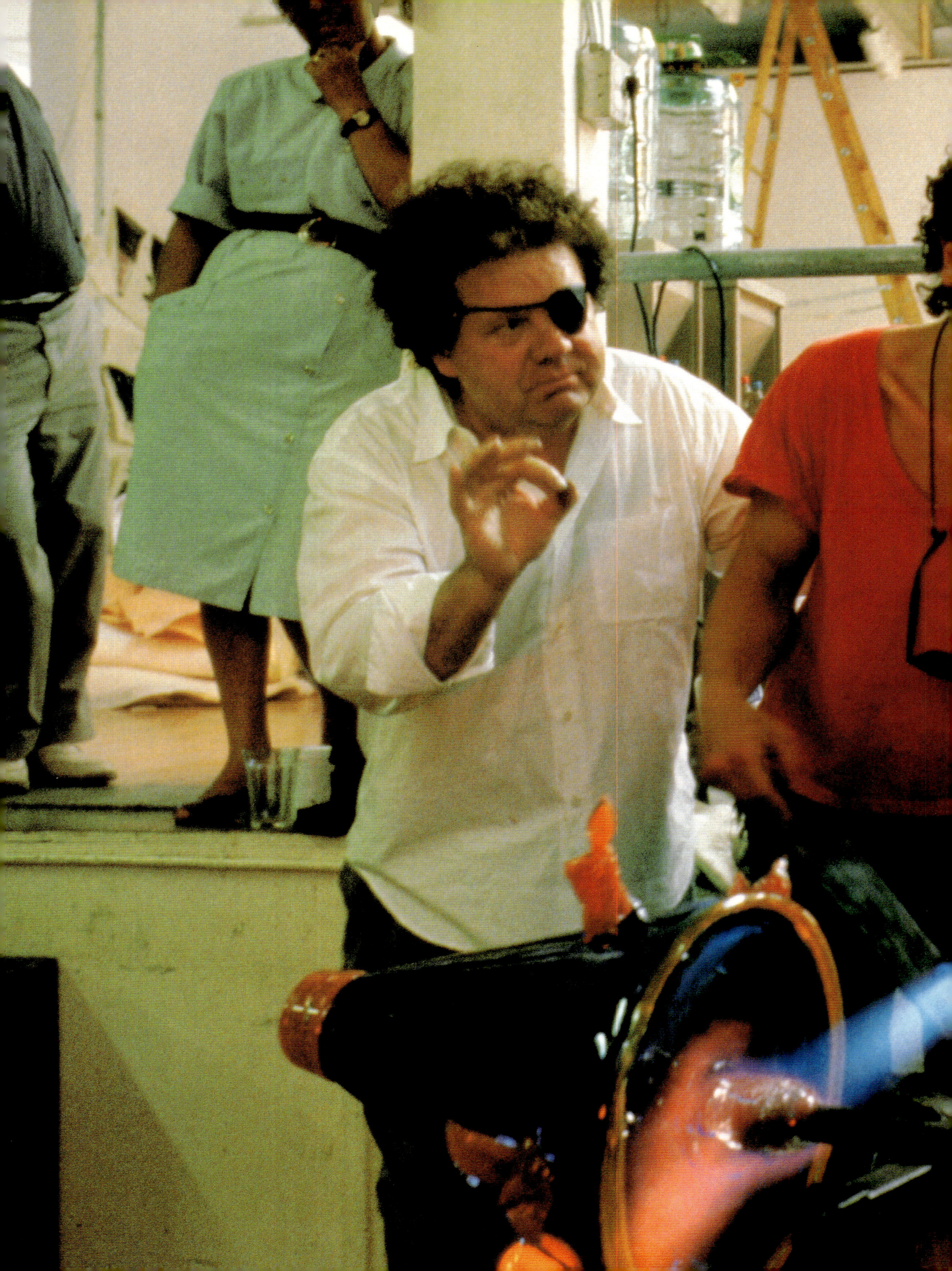

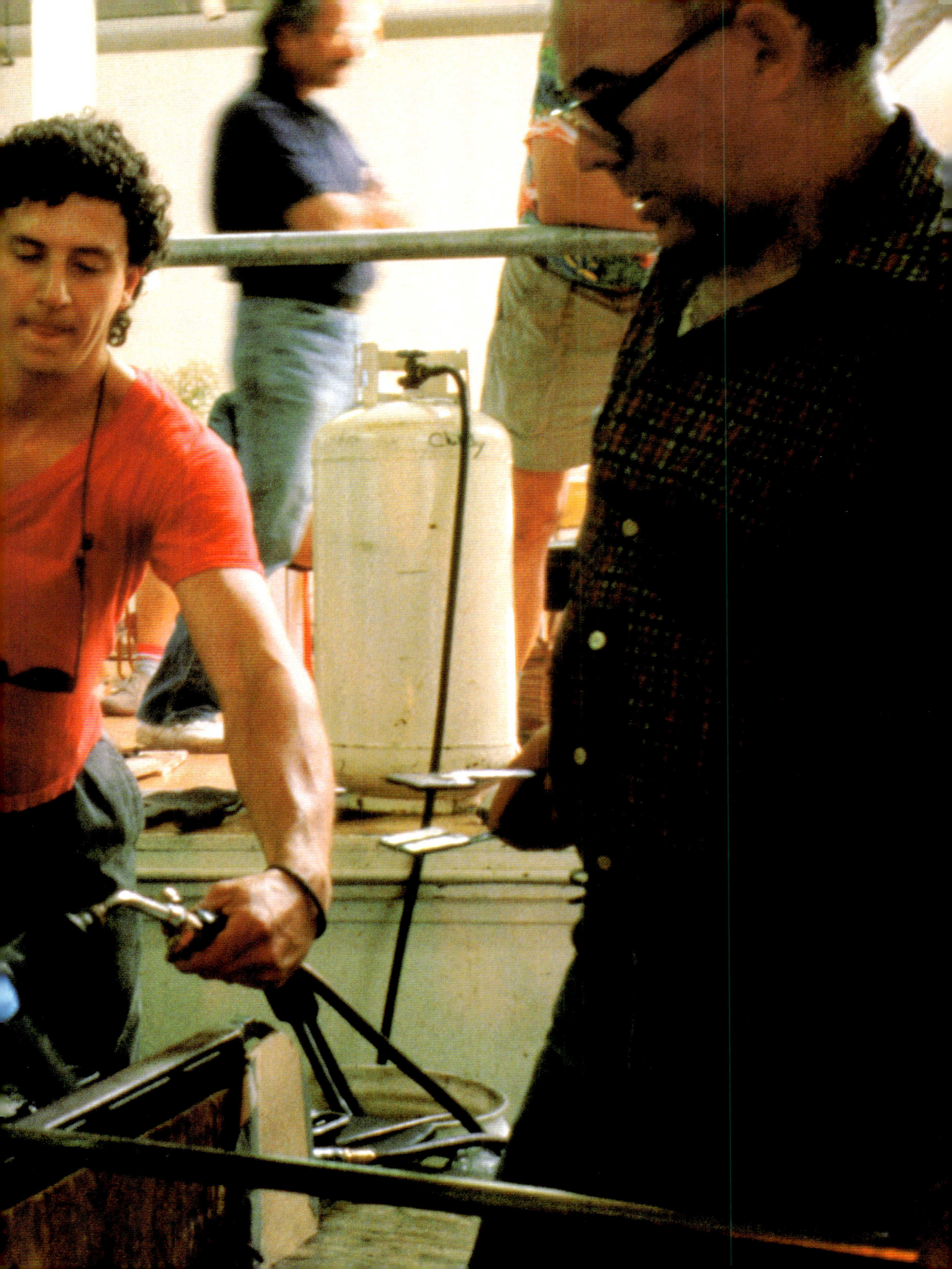

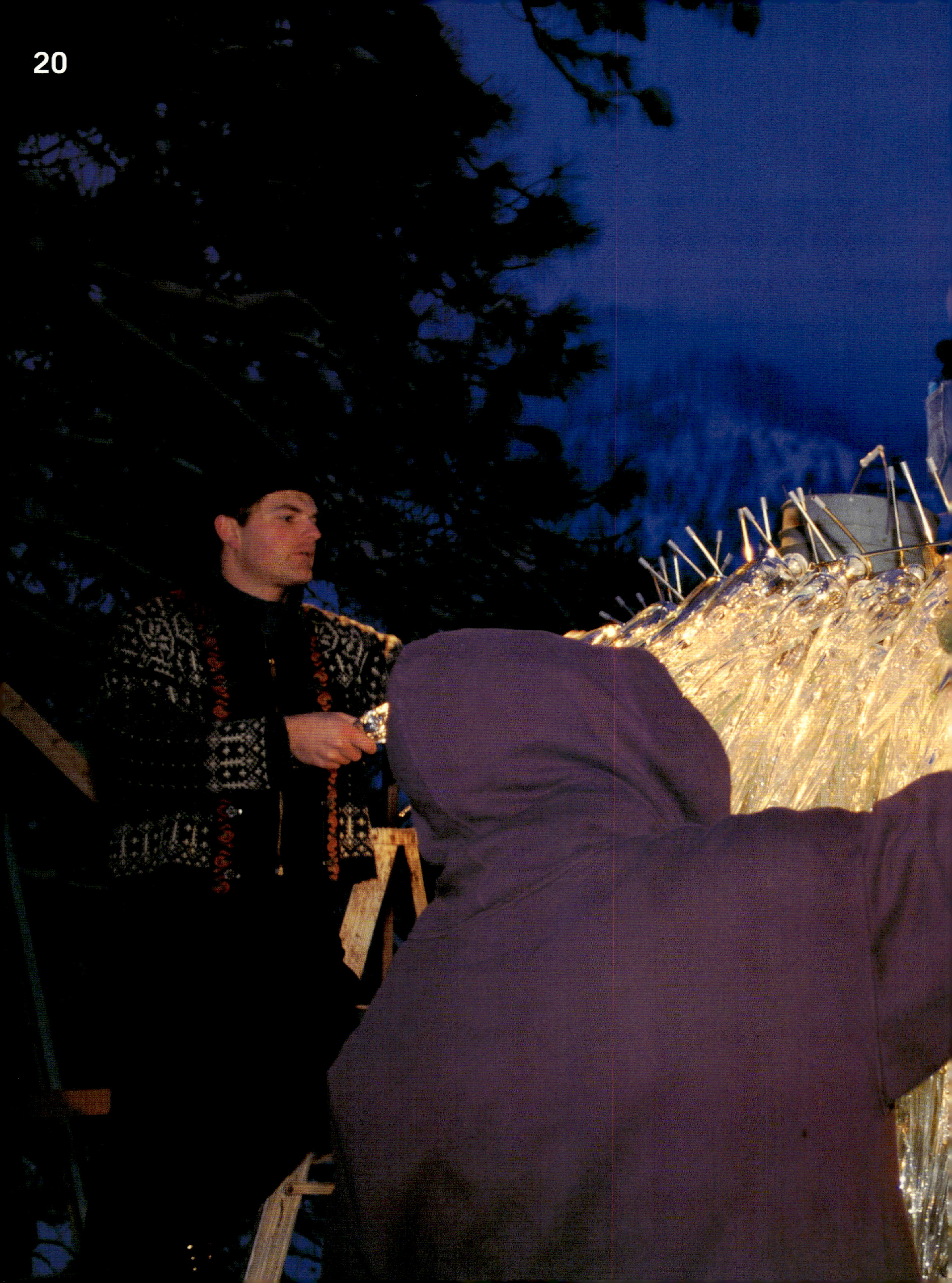

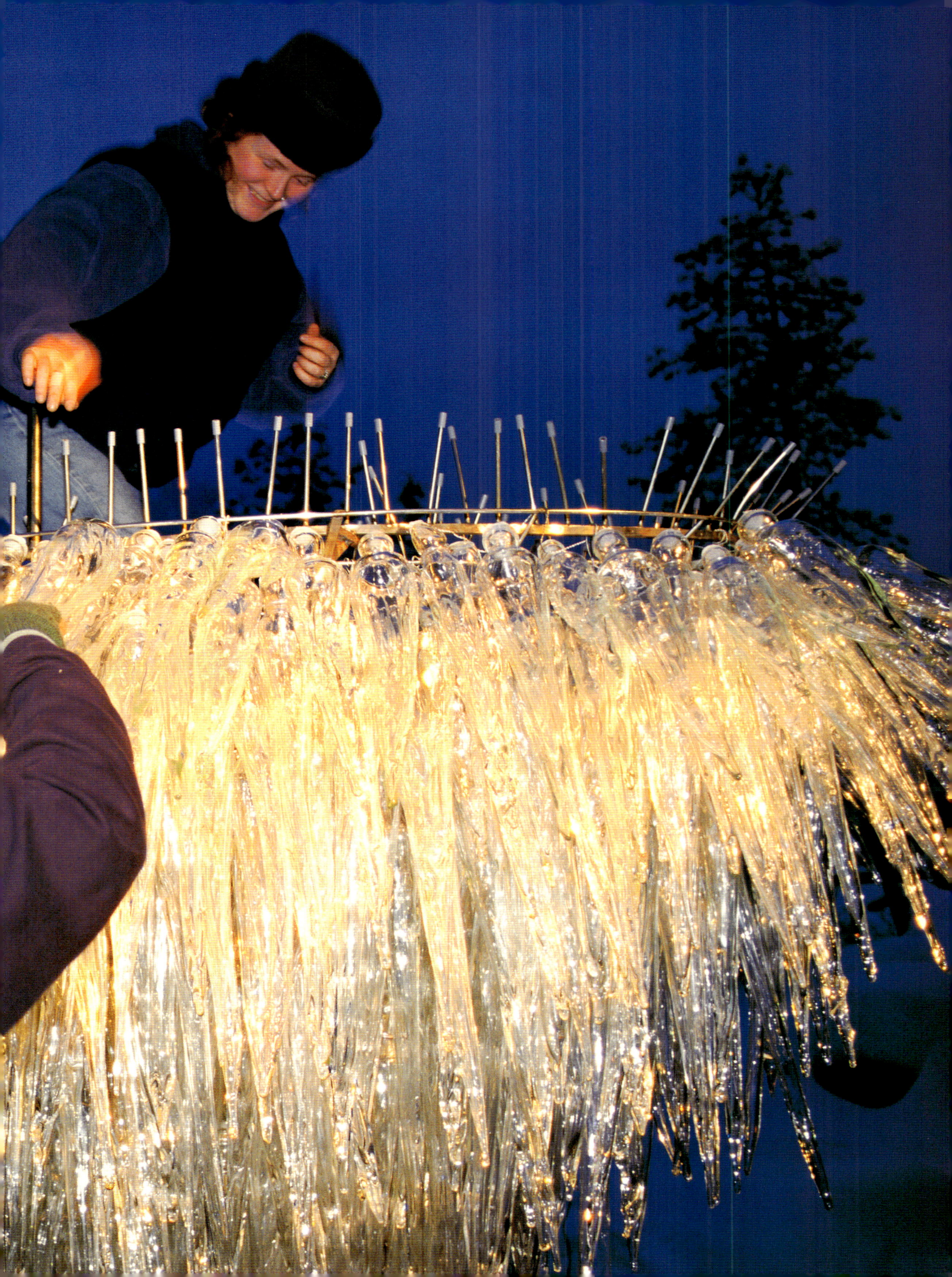

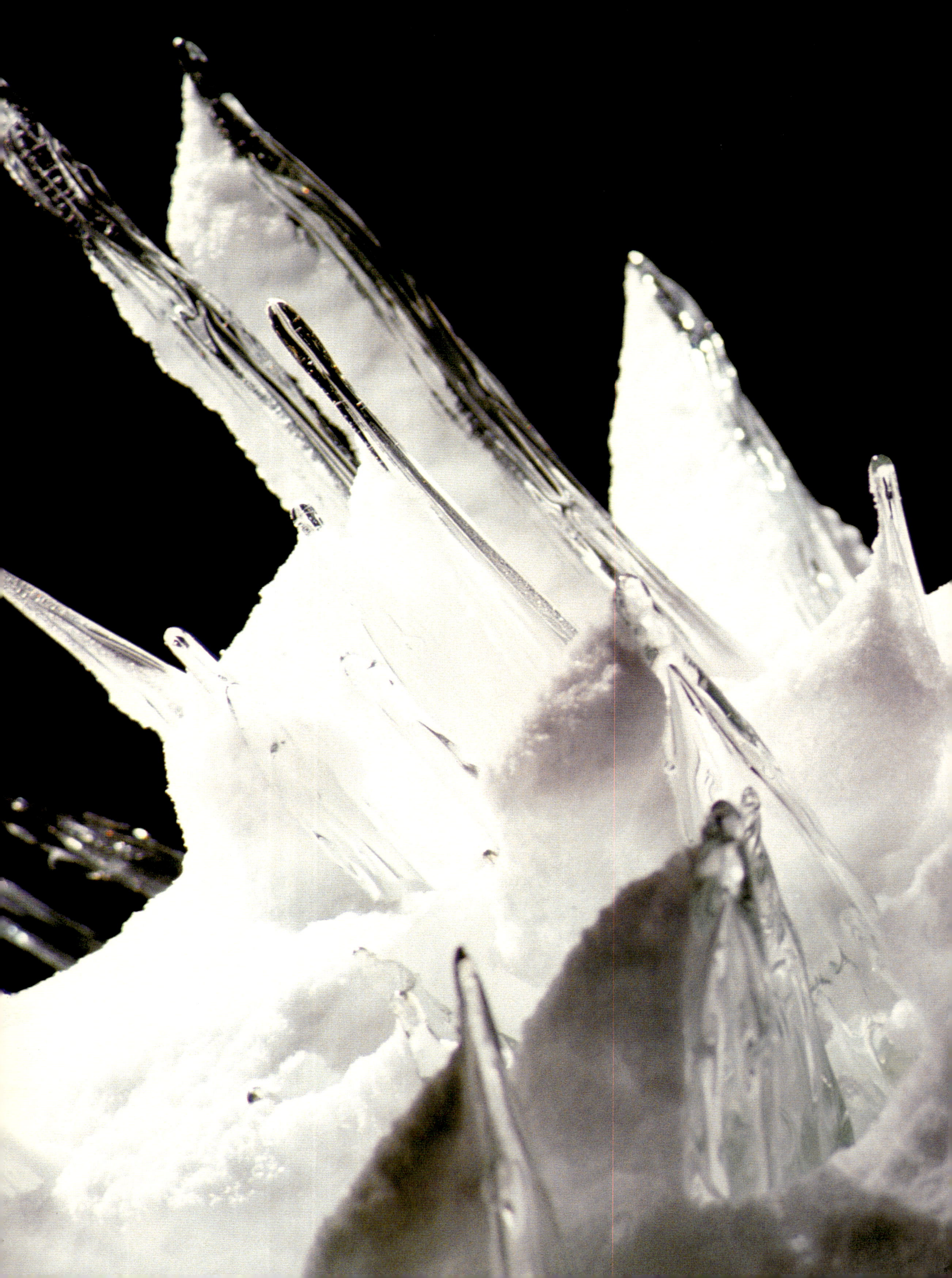

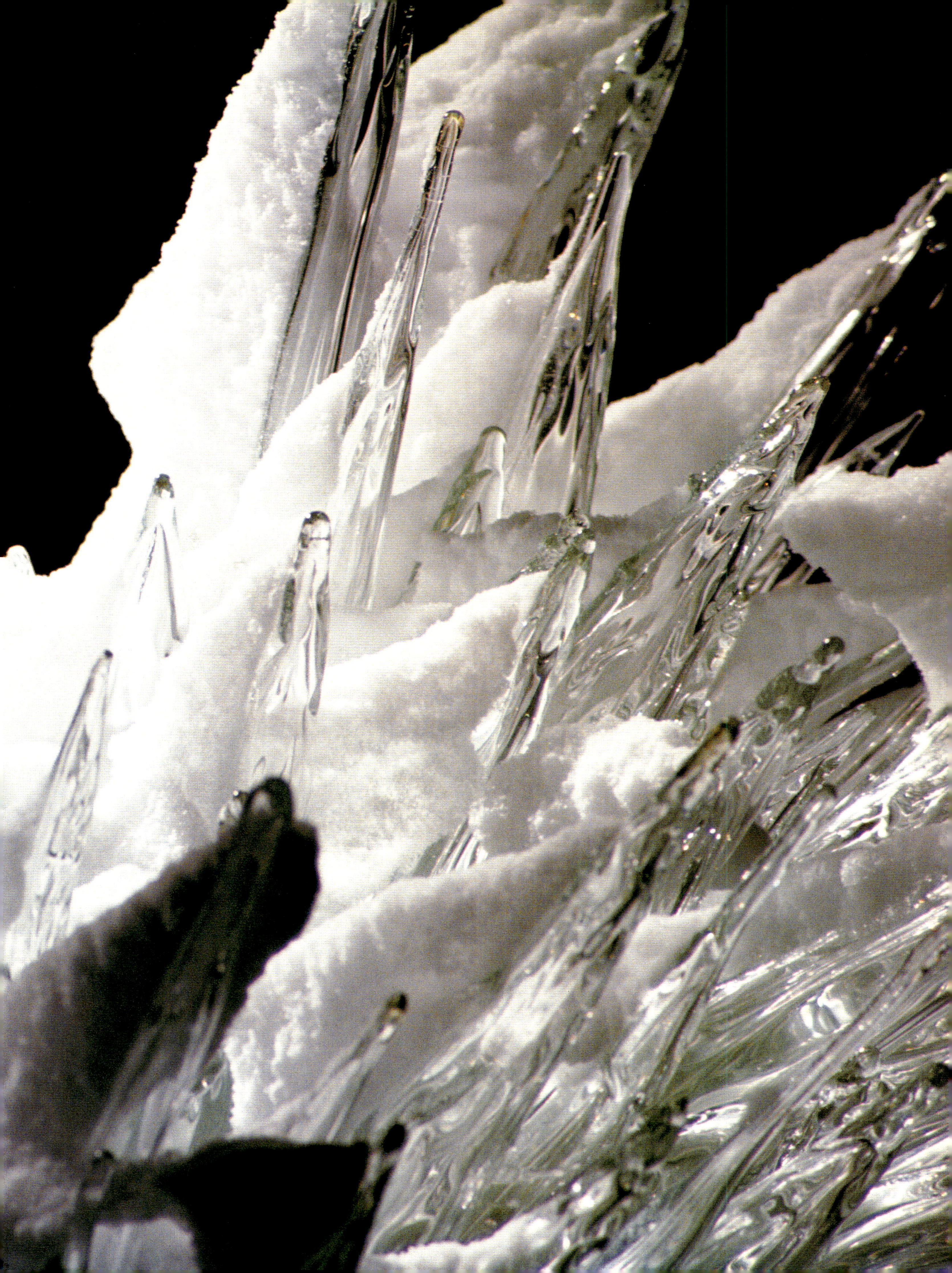

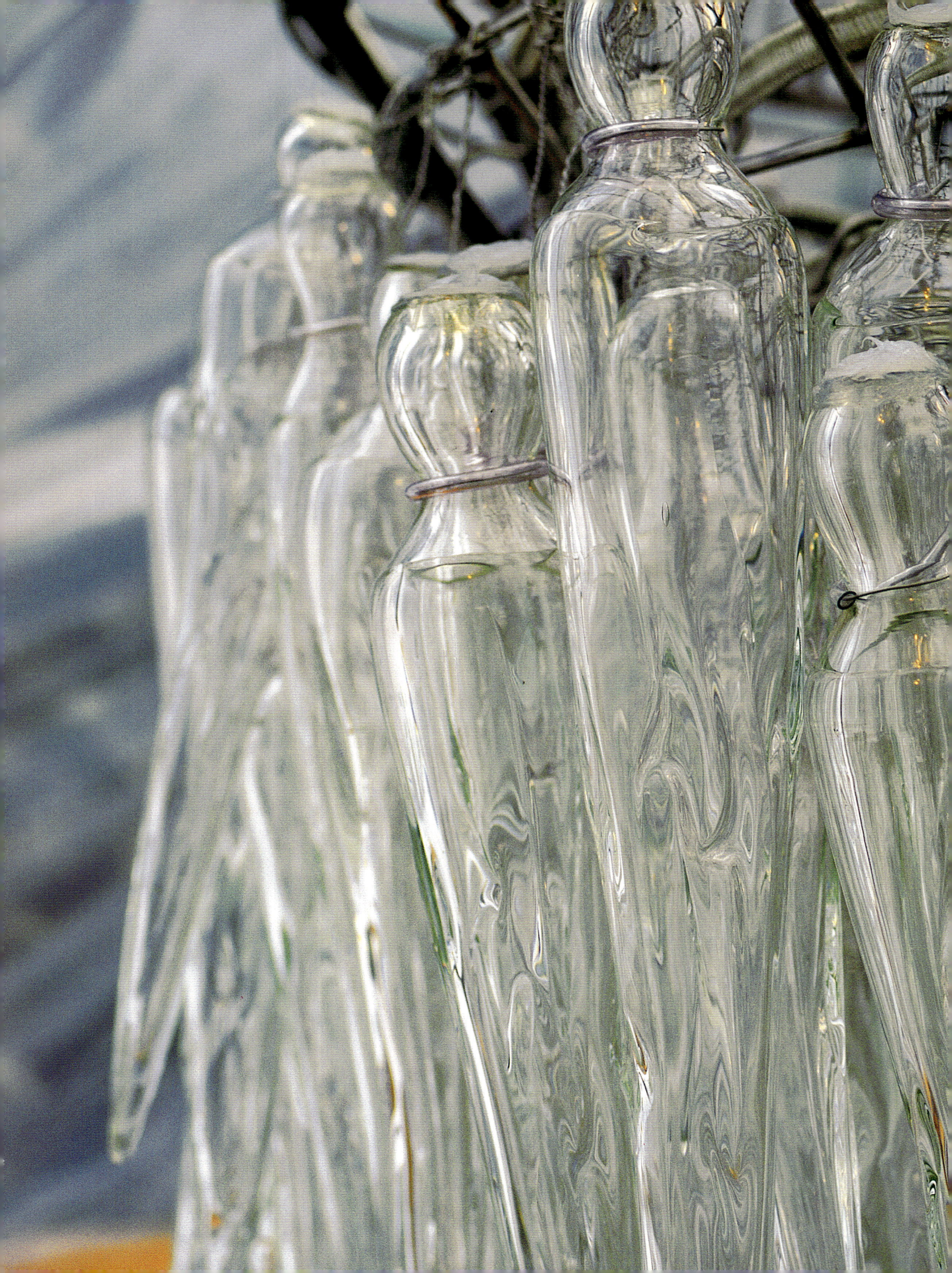

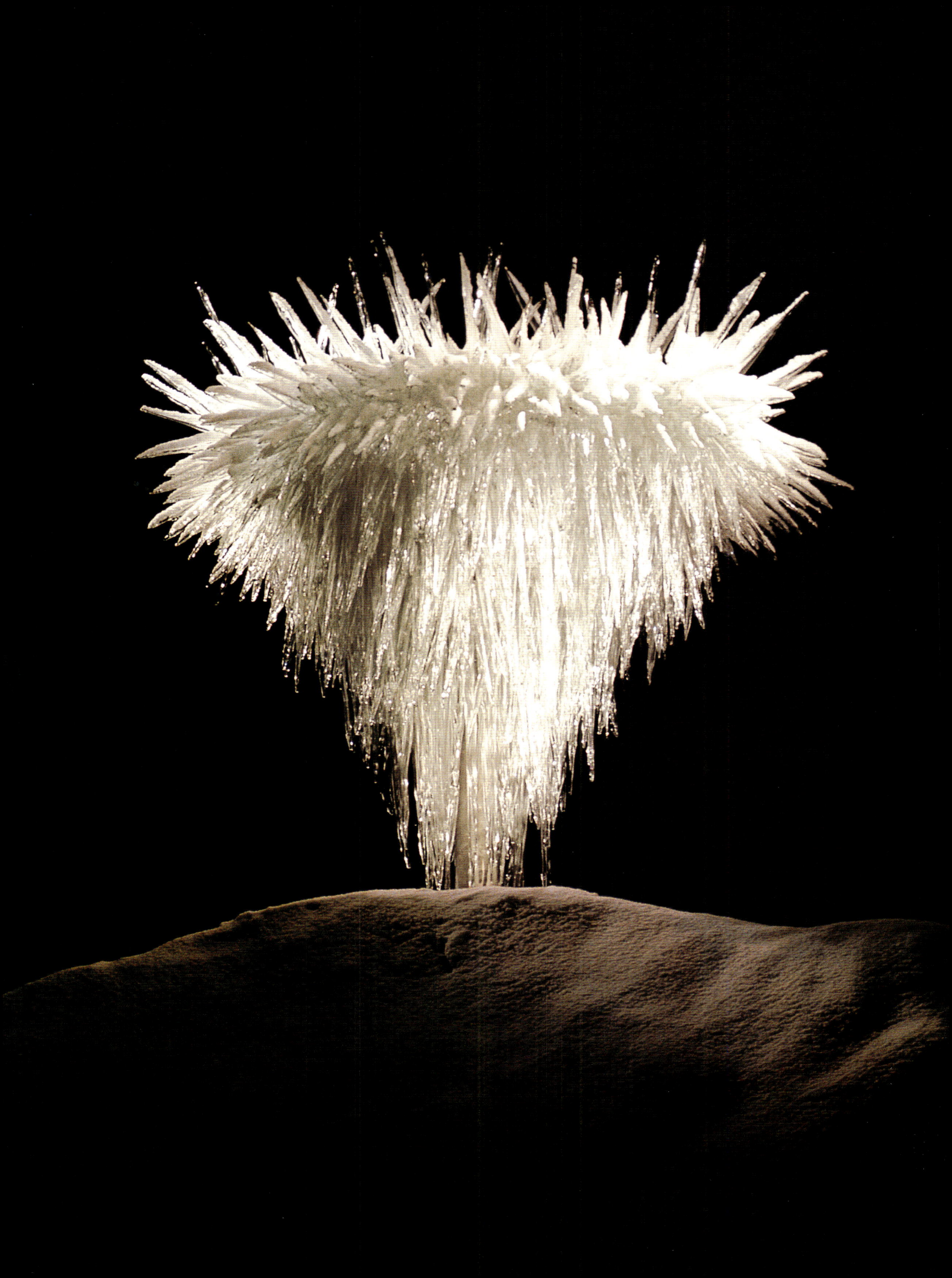

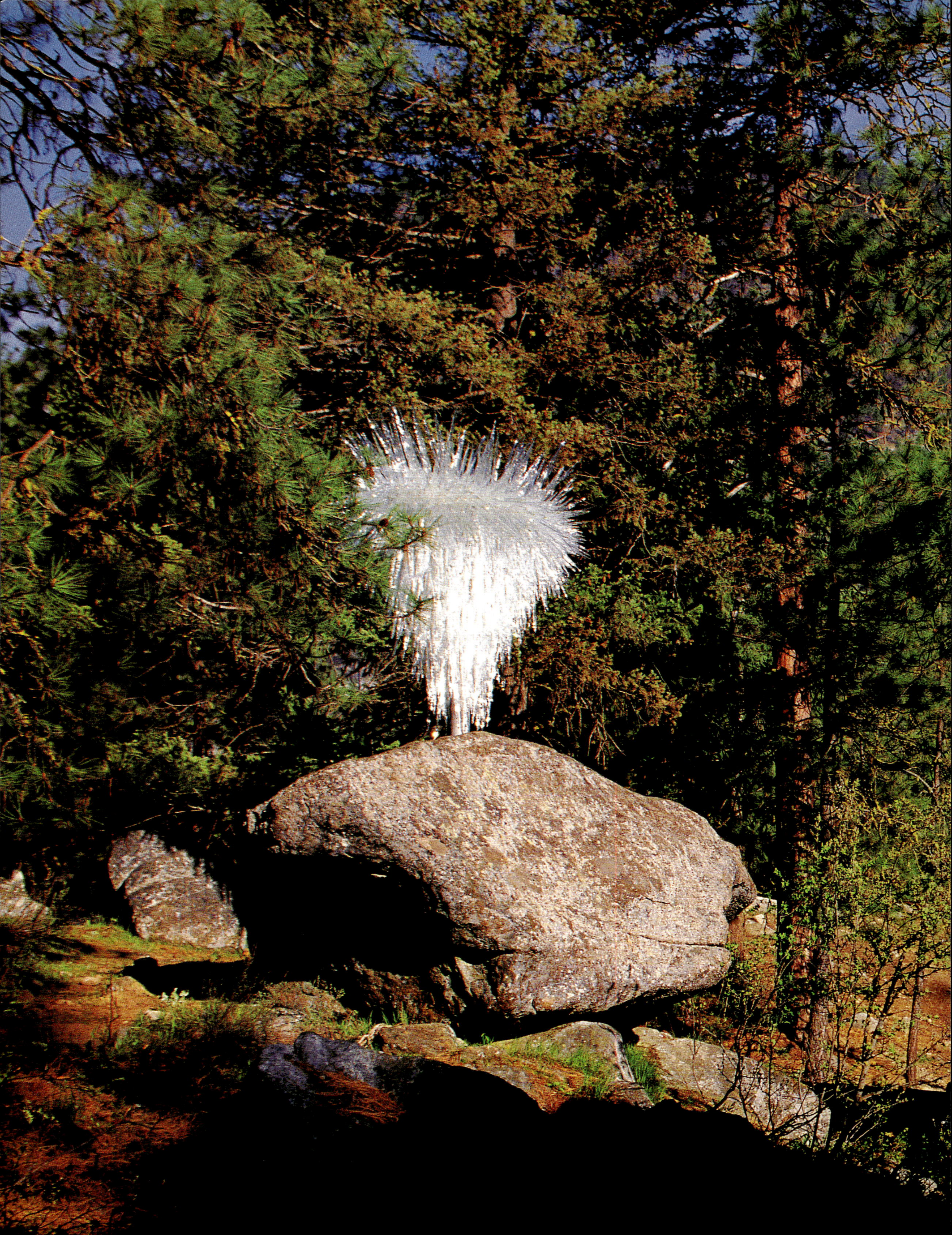

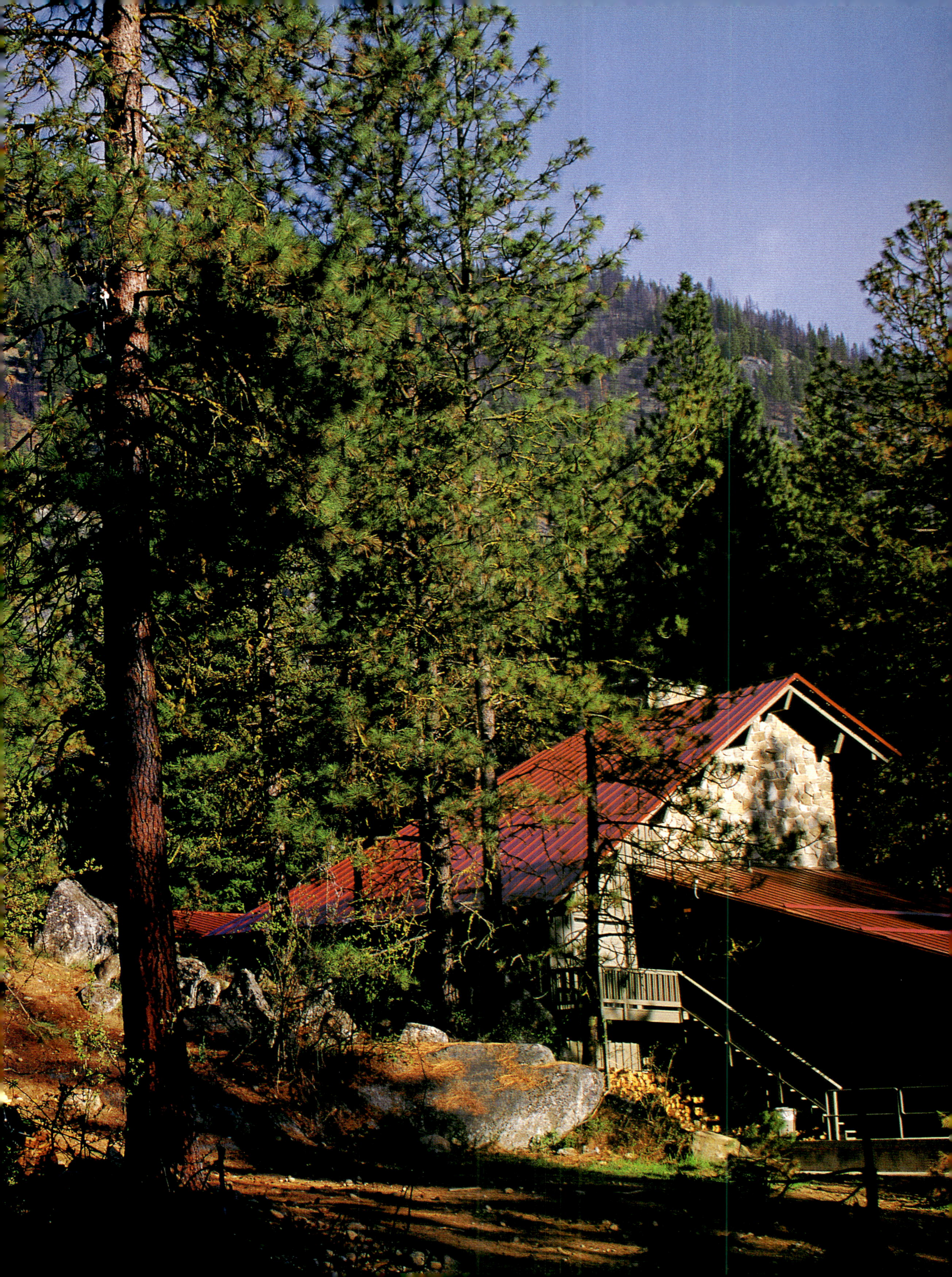

21

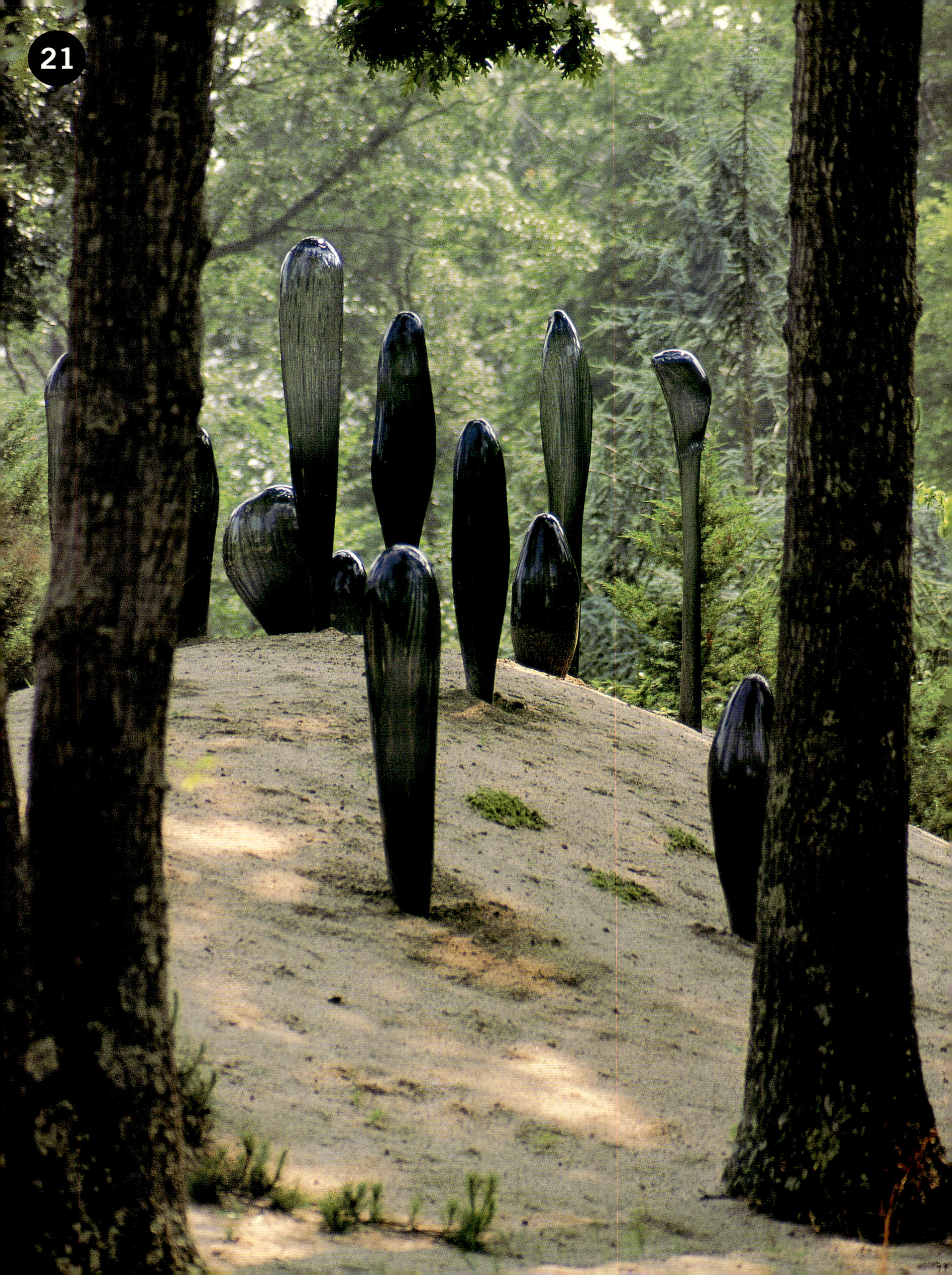

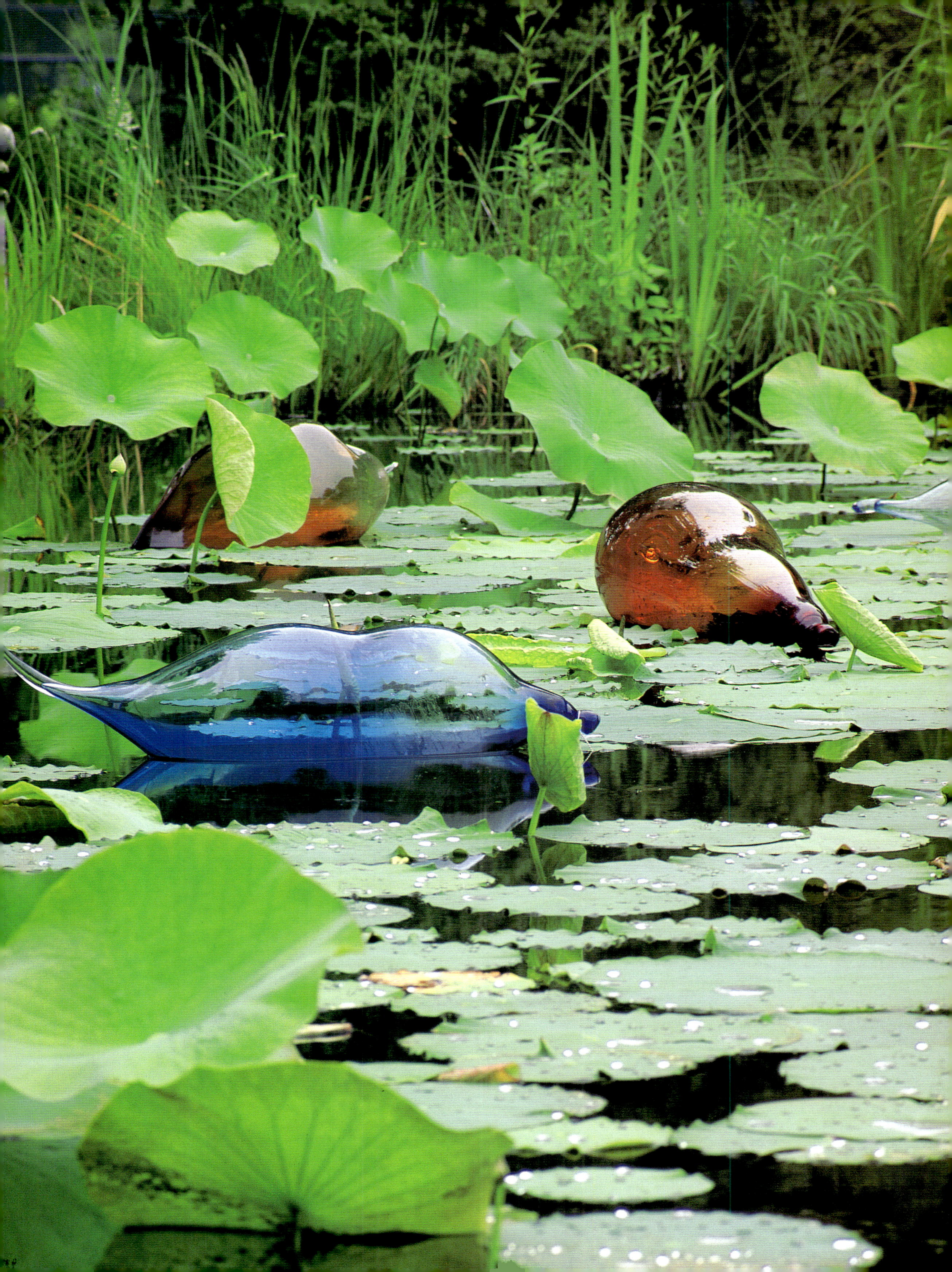

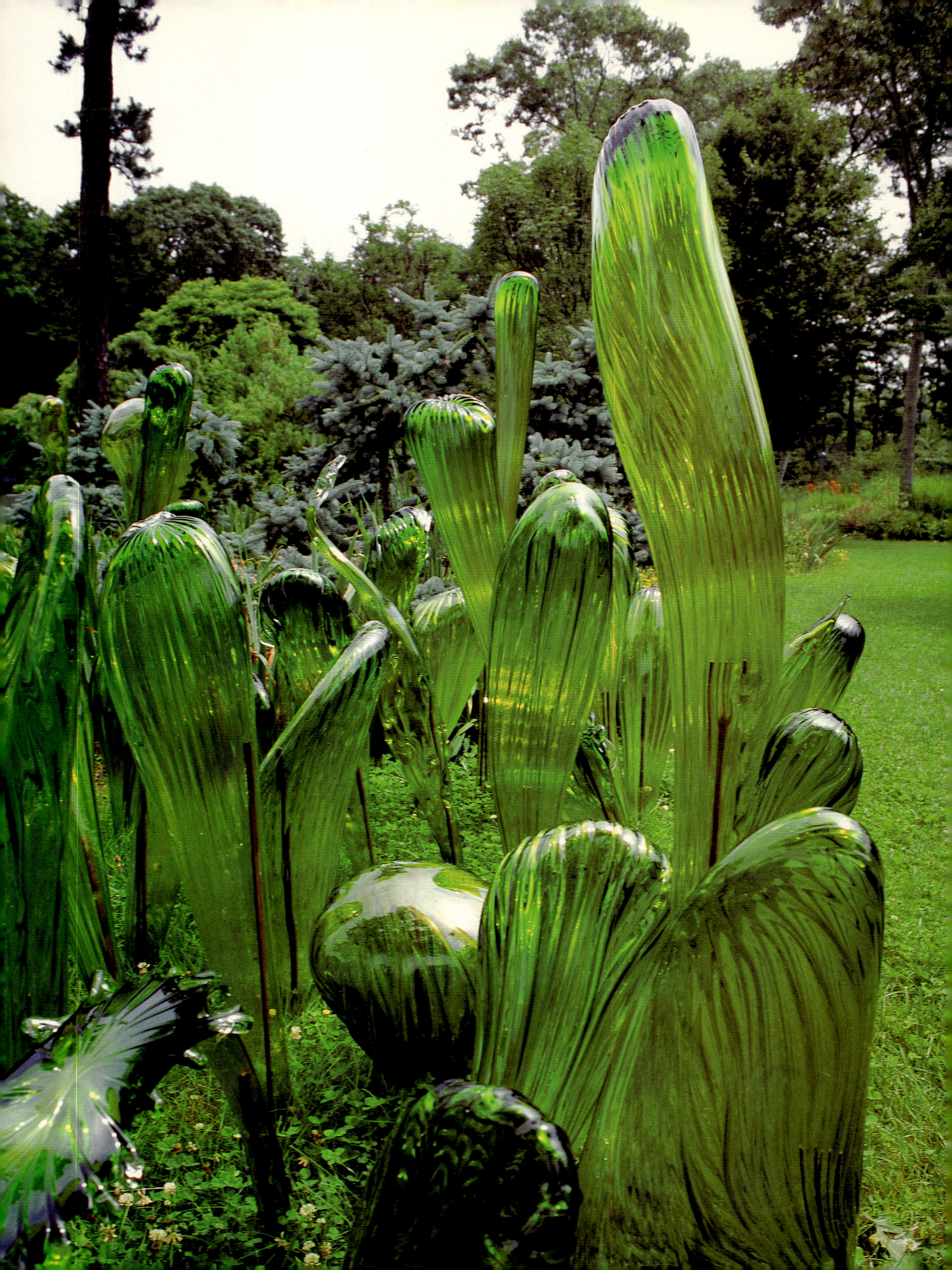

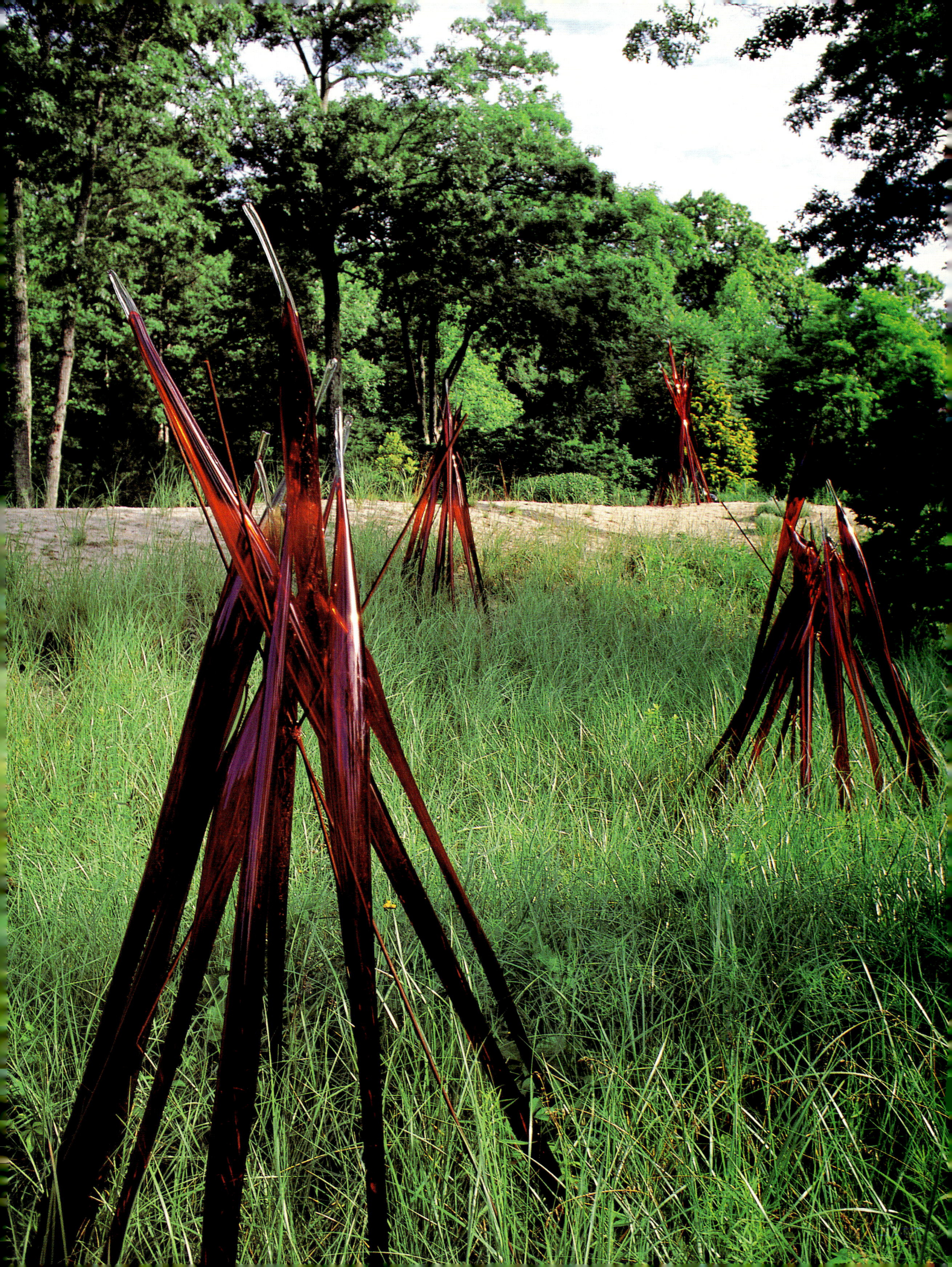

22

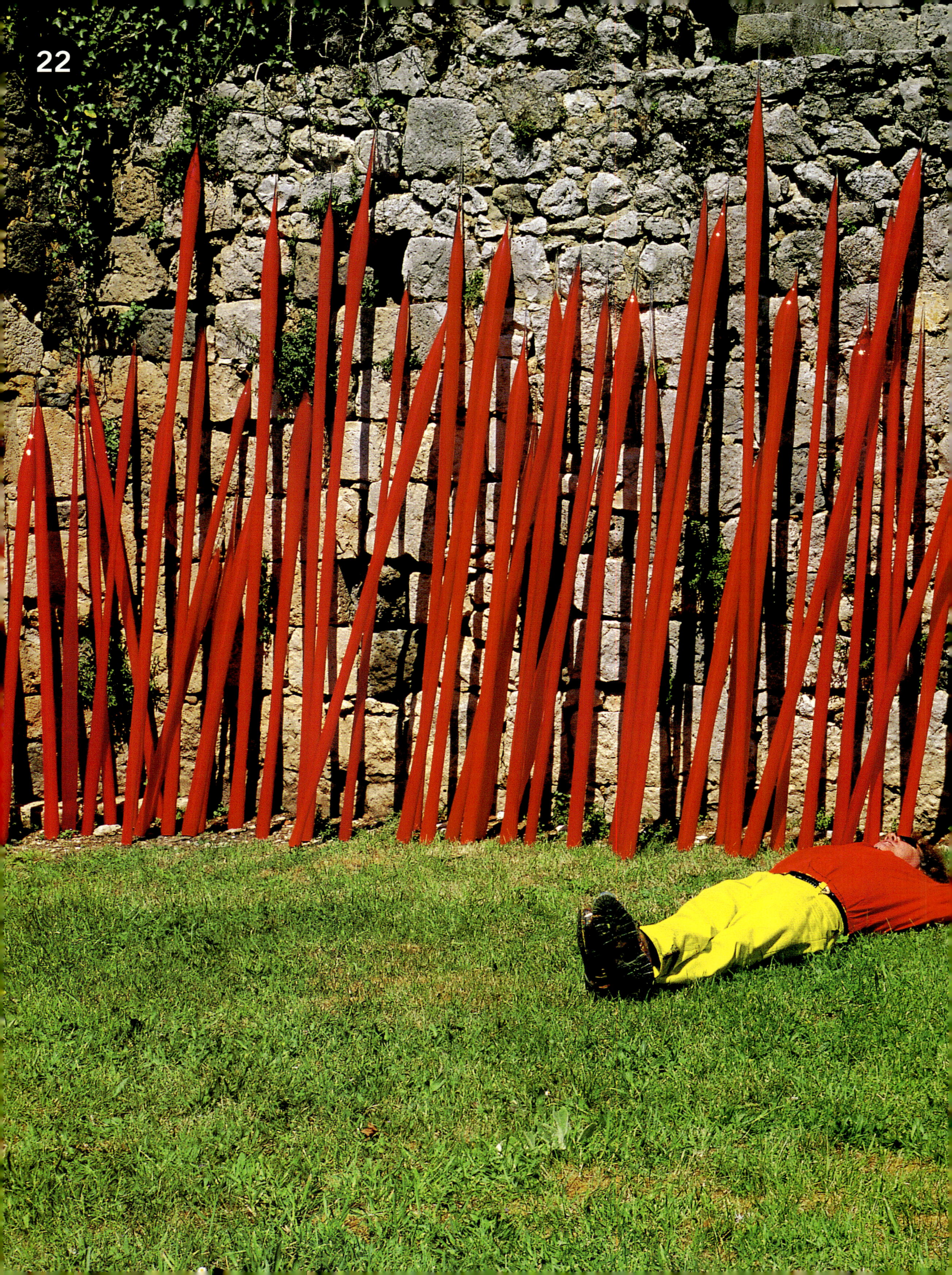

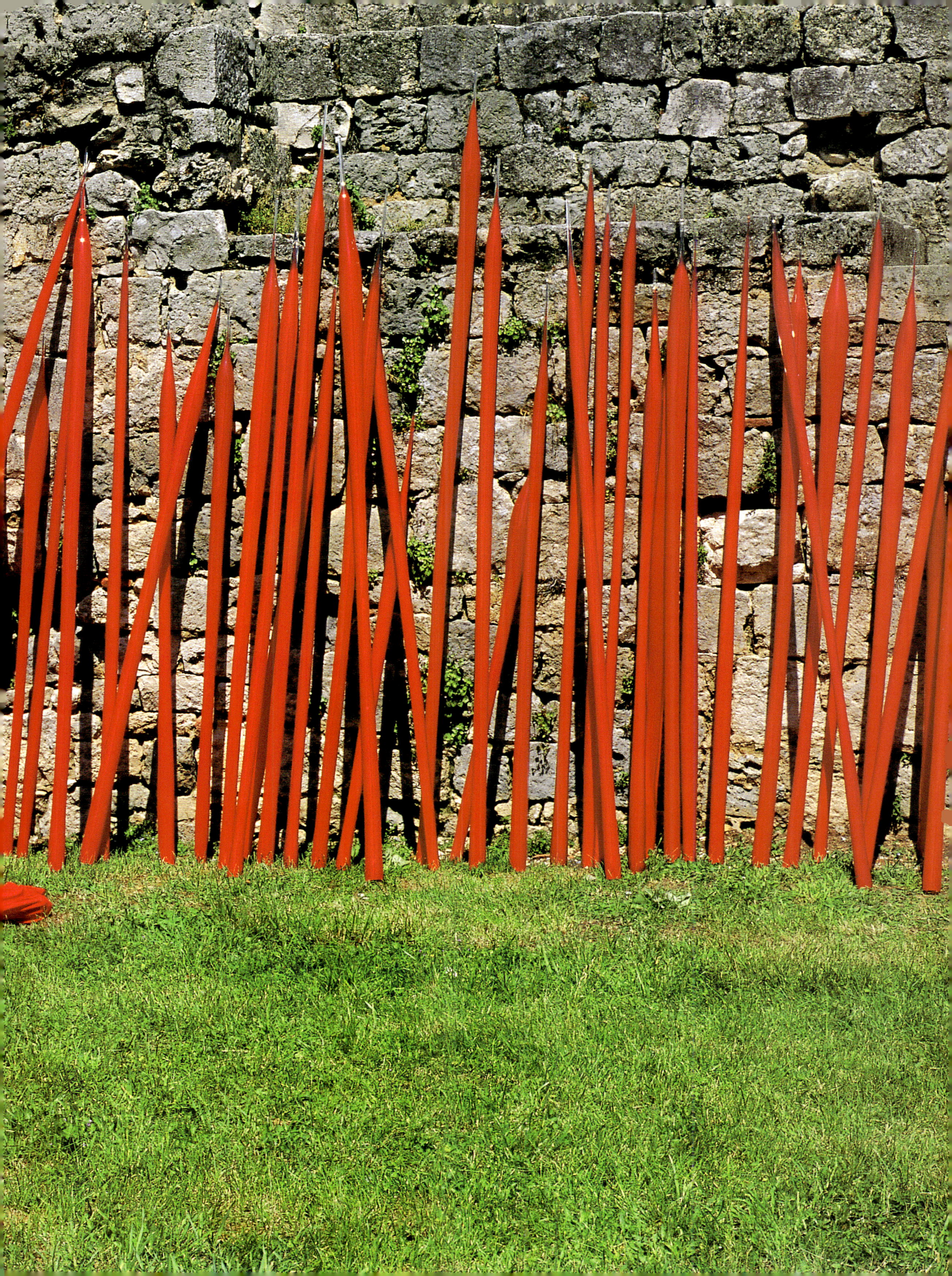

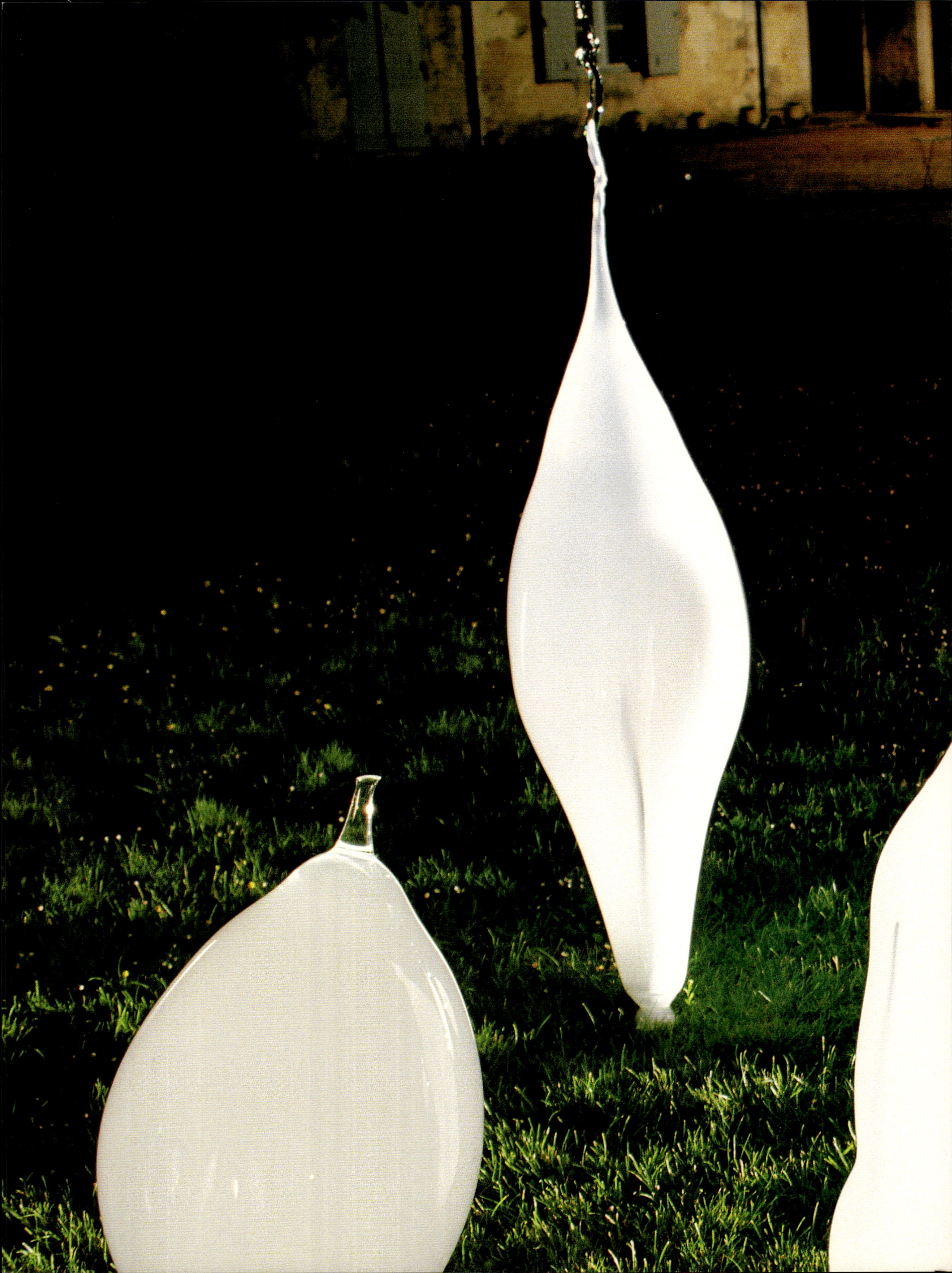

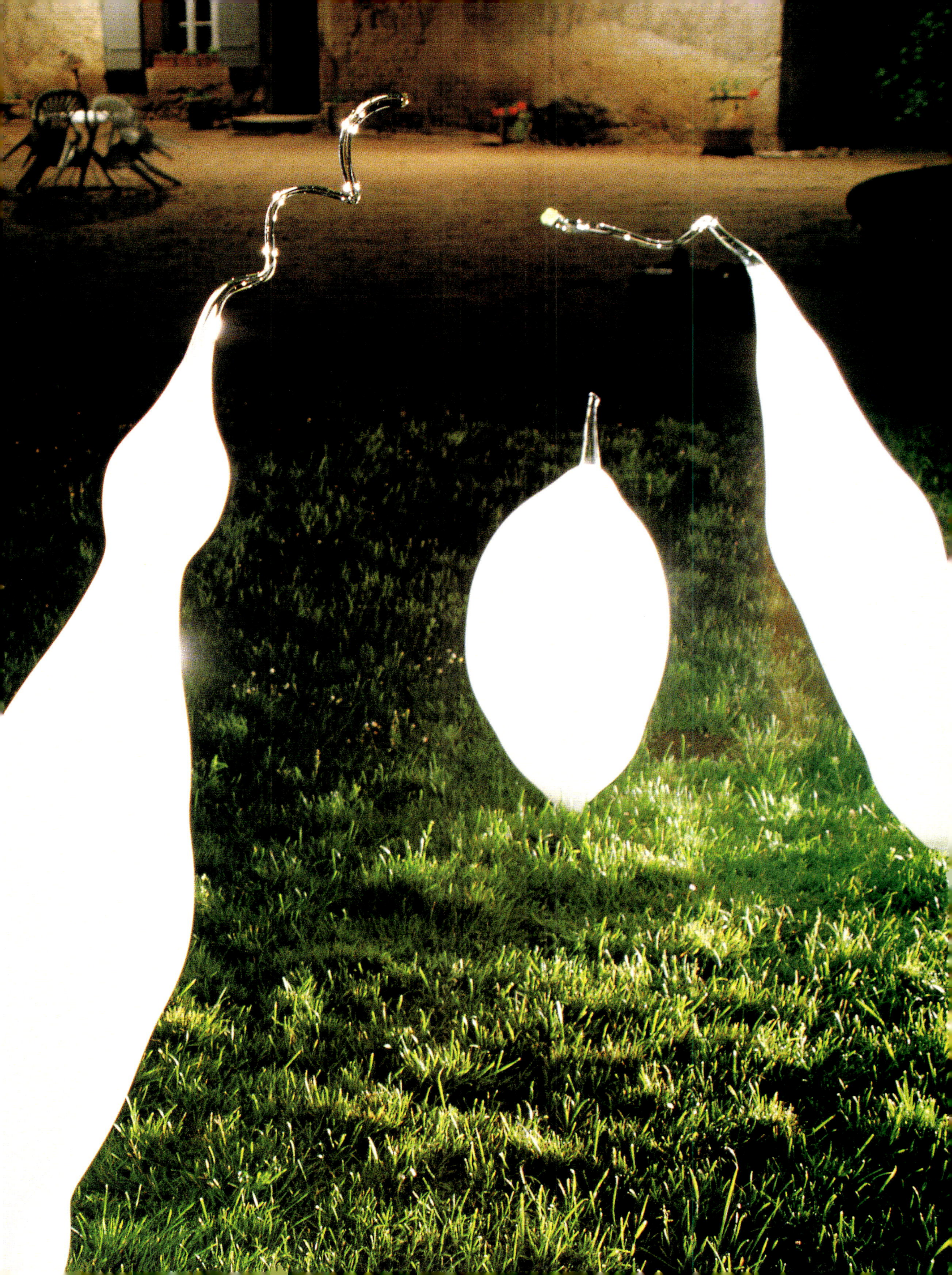

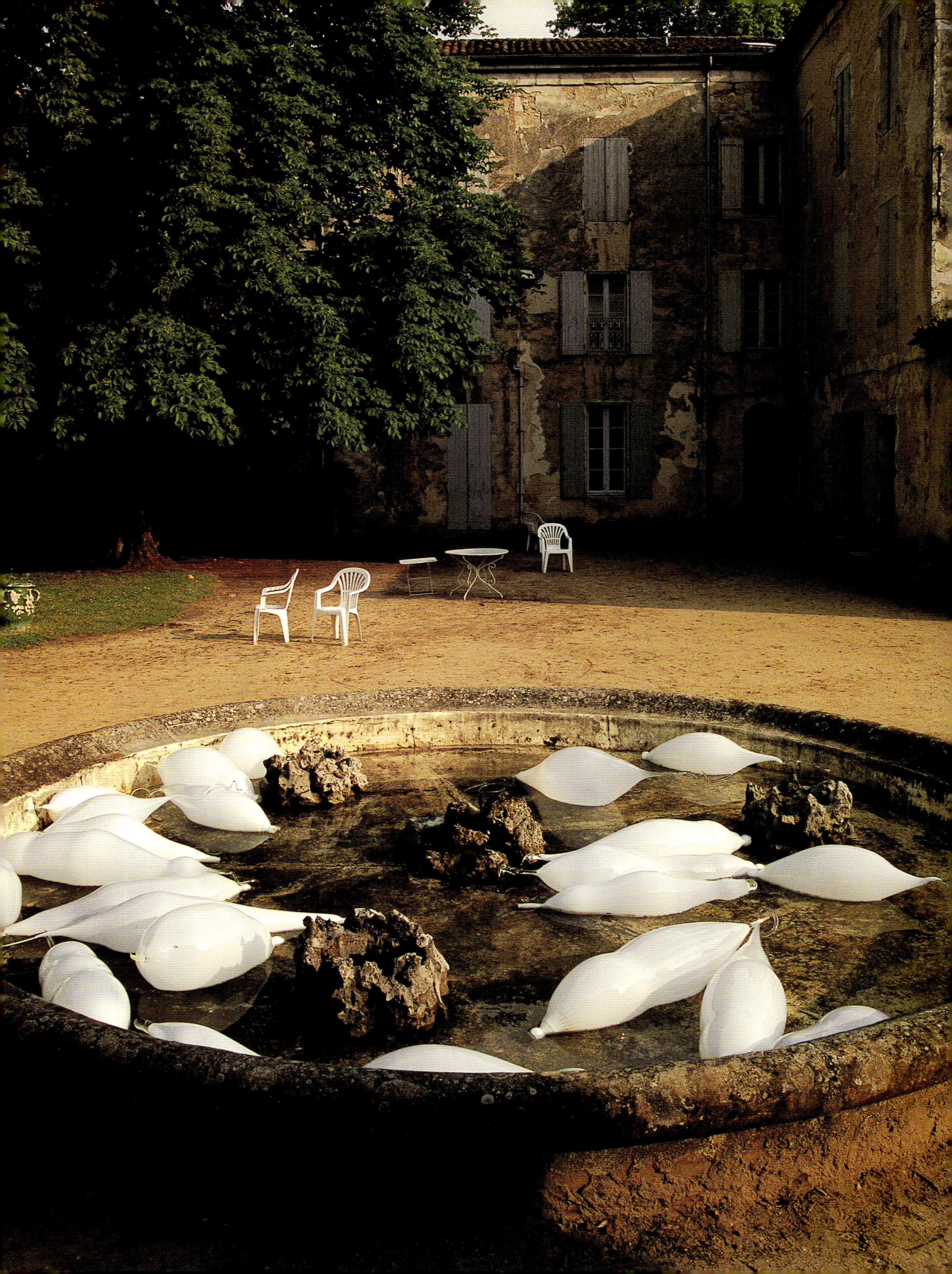

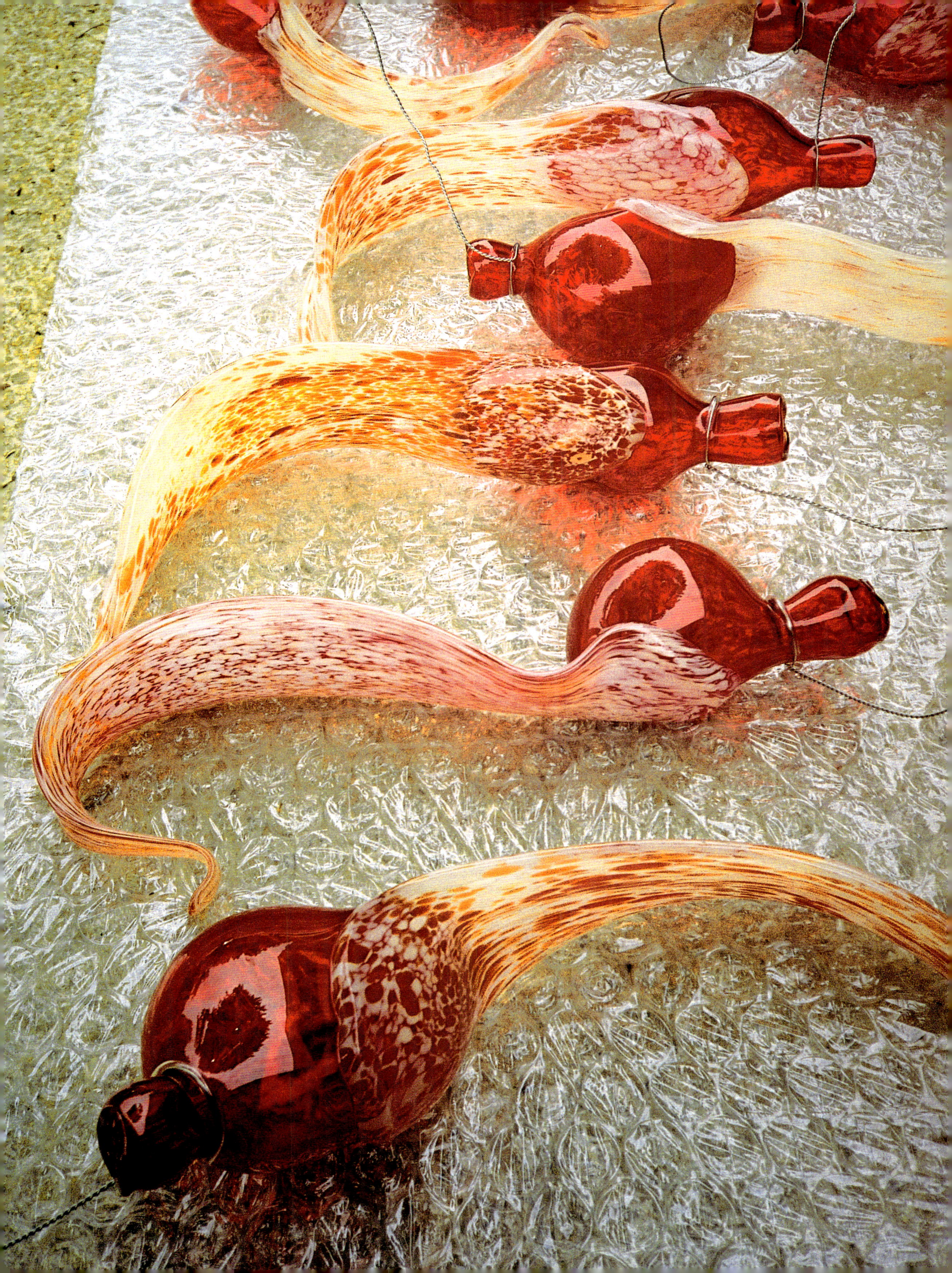

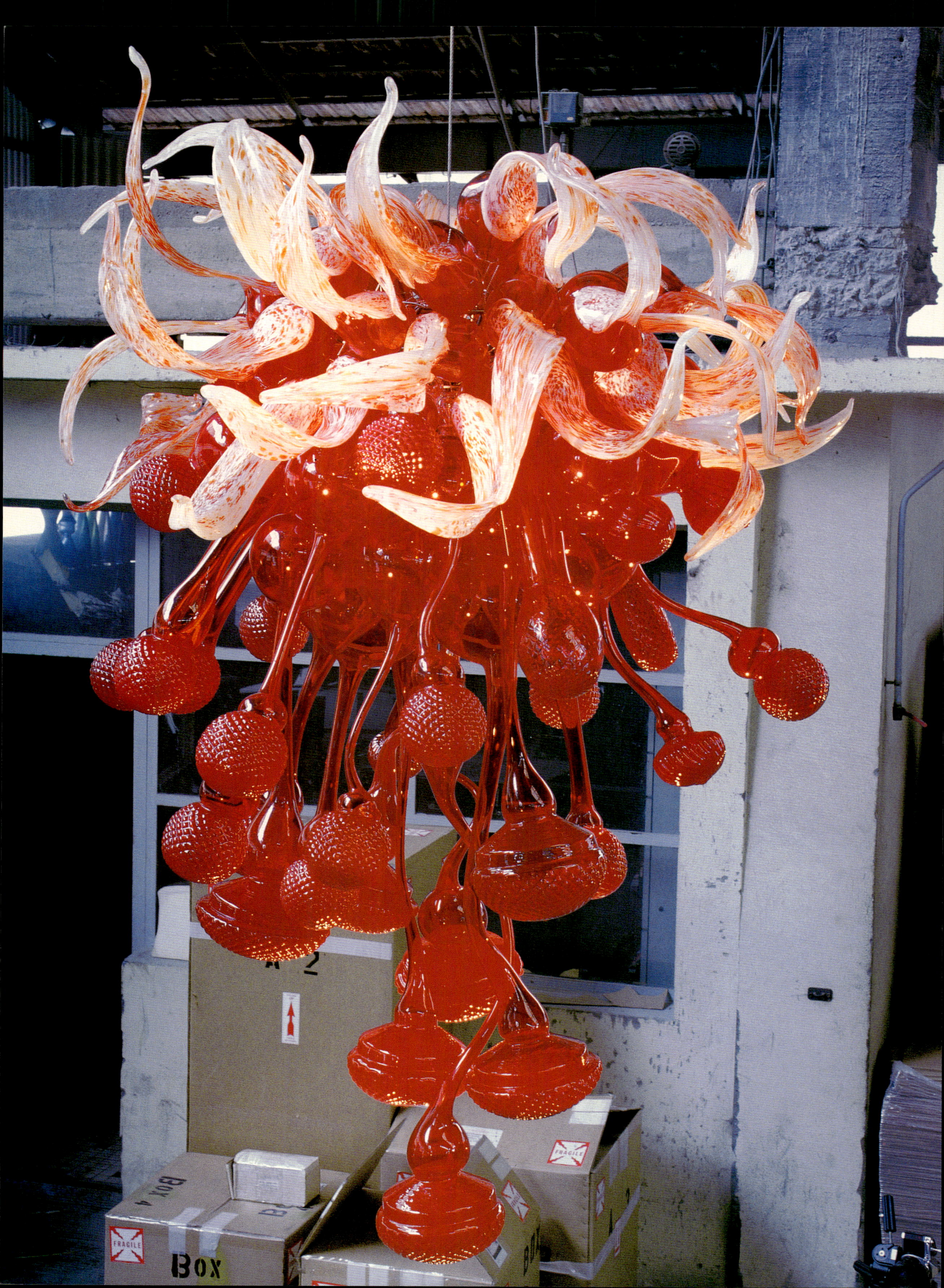
A 2
FRAGILE
Box

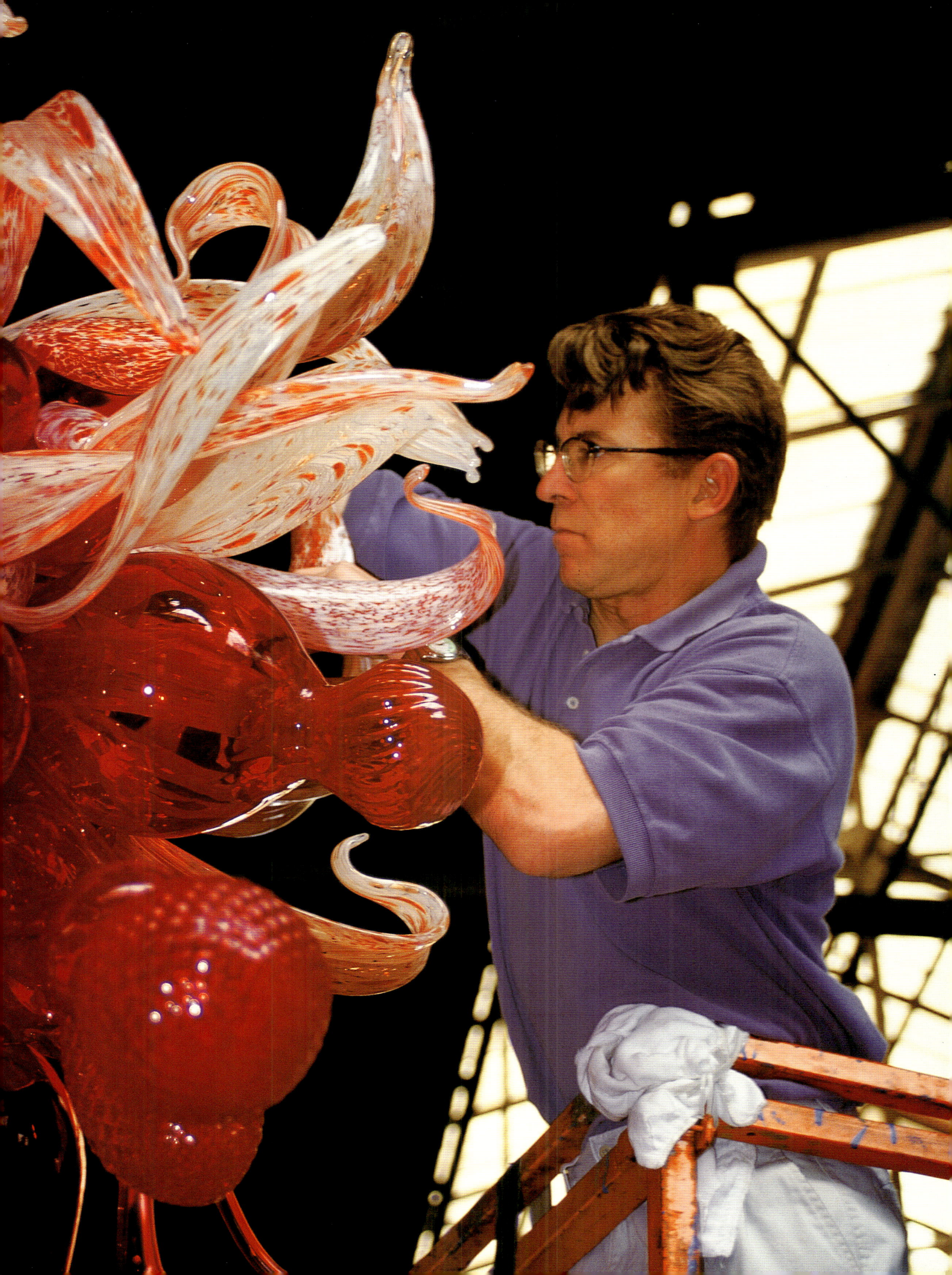

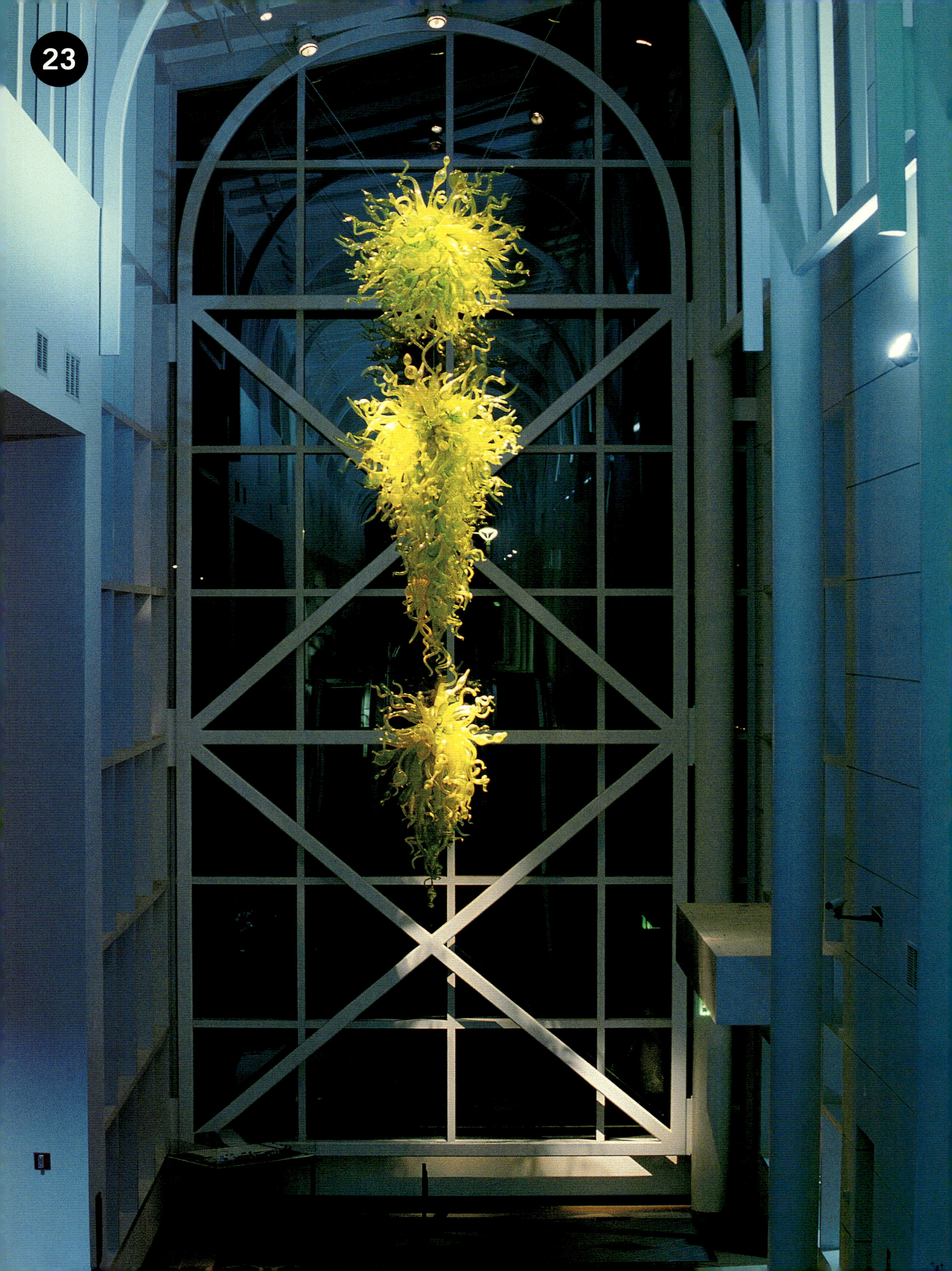

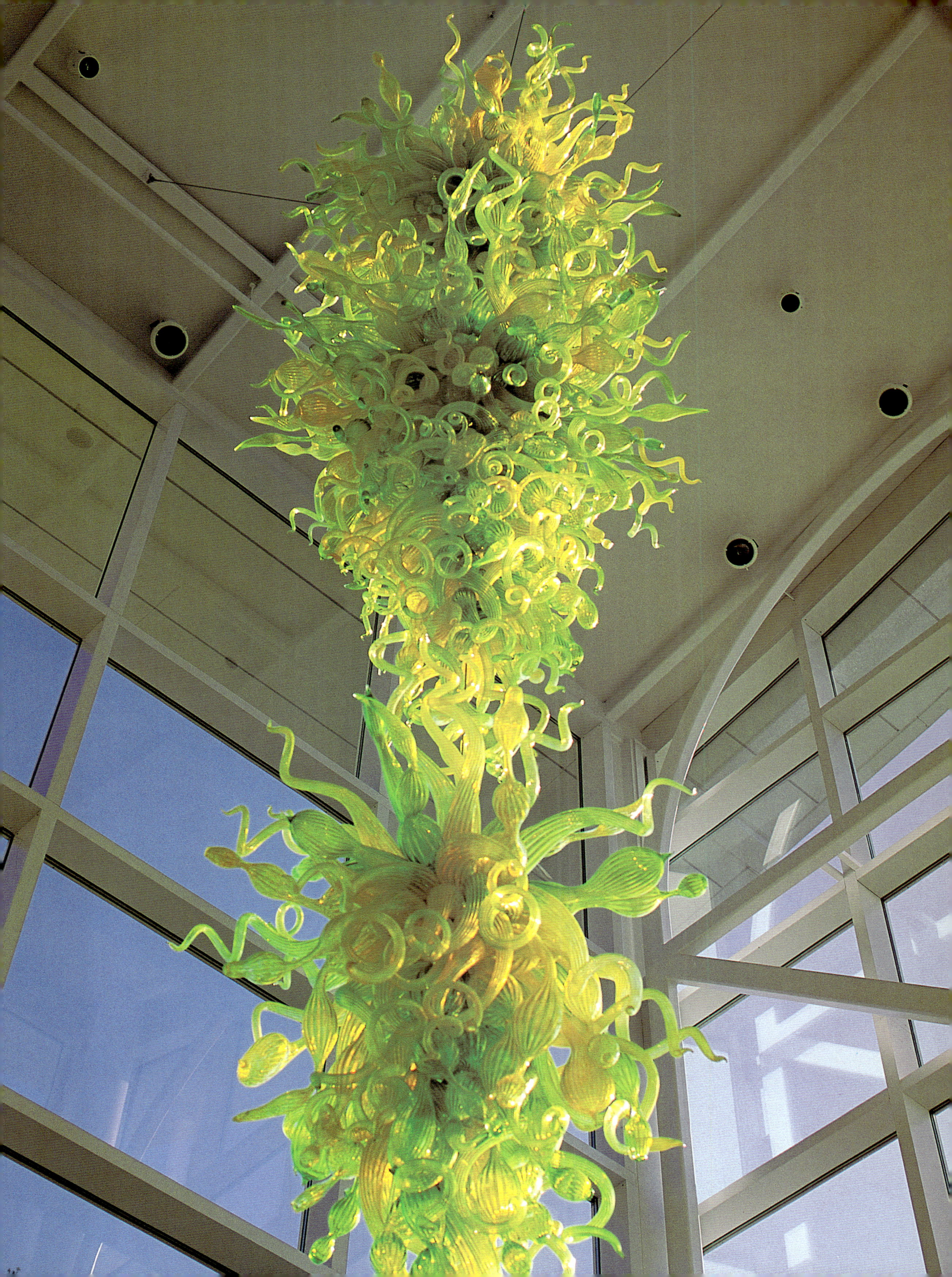

24

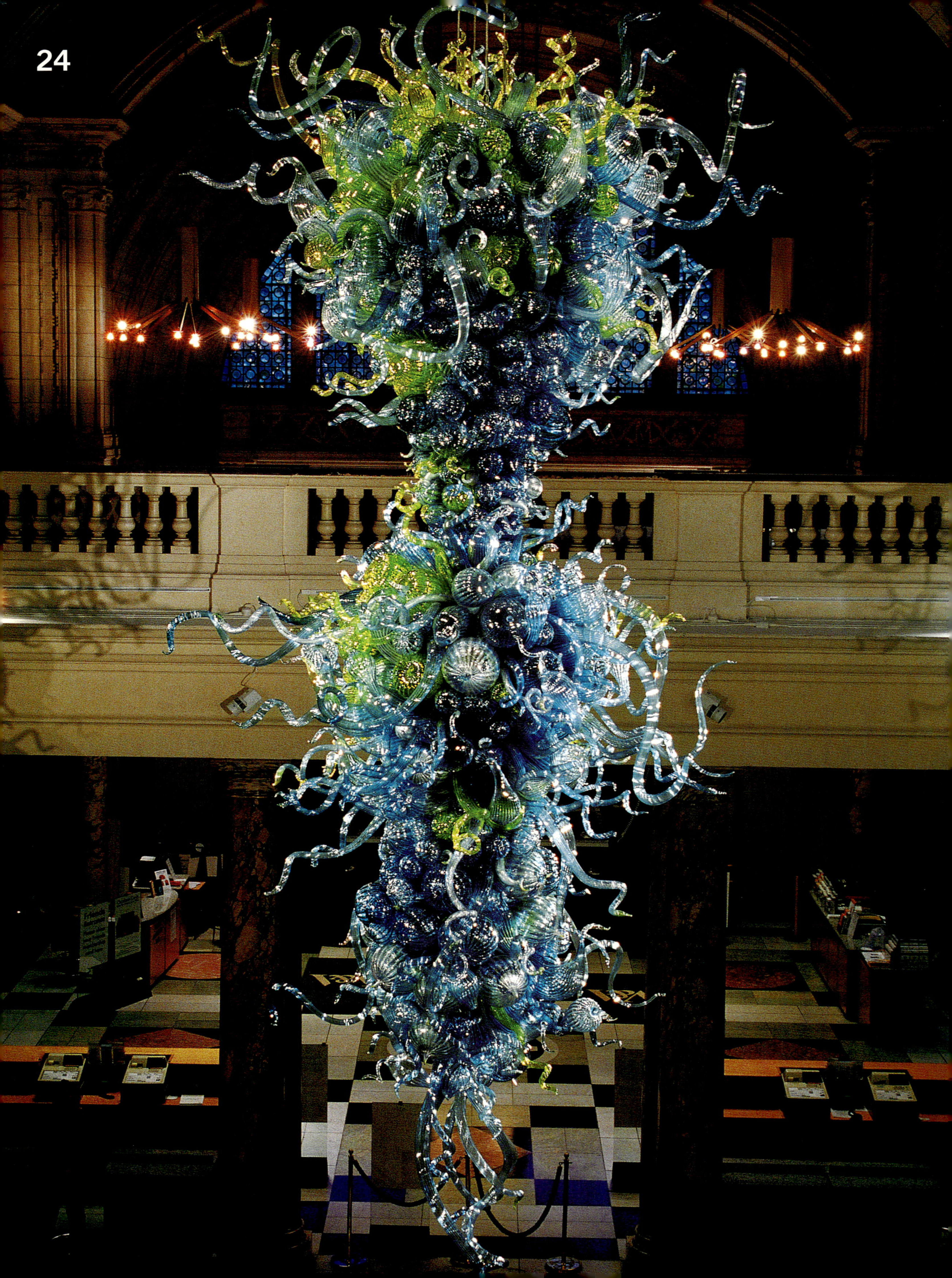

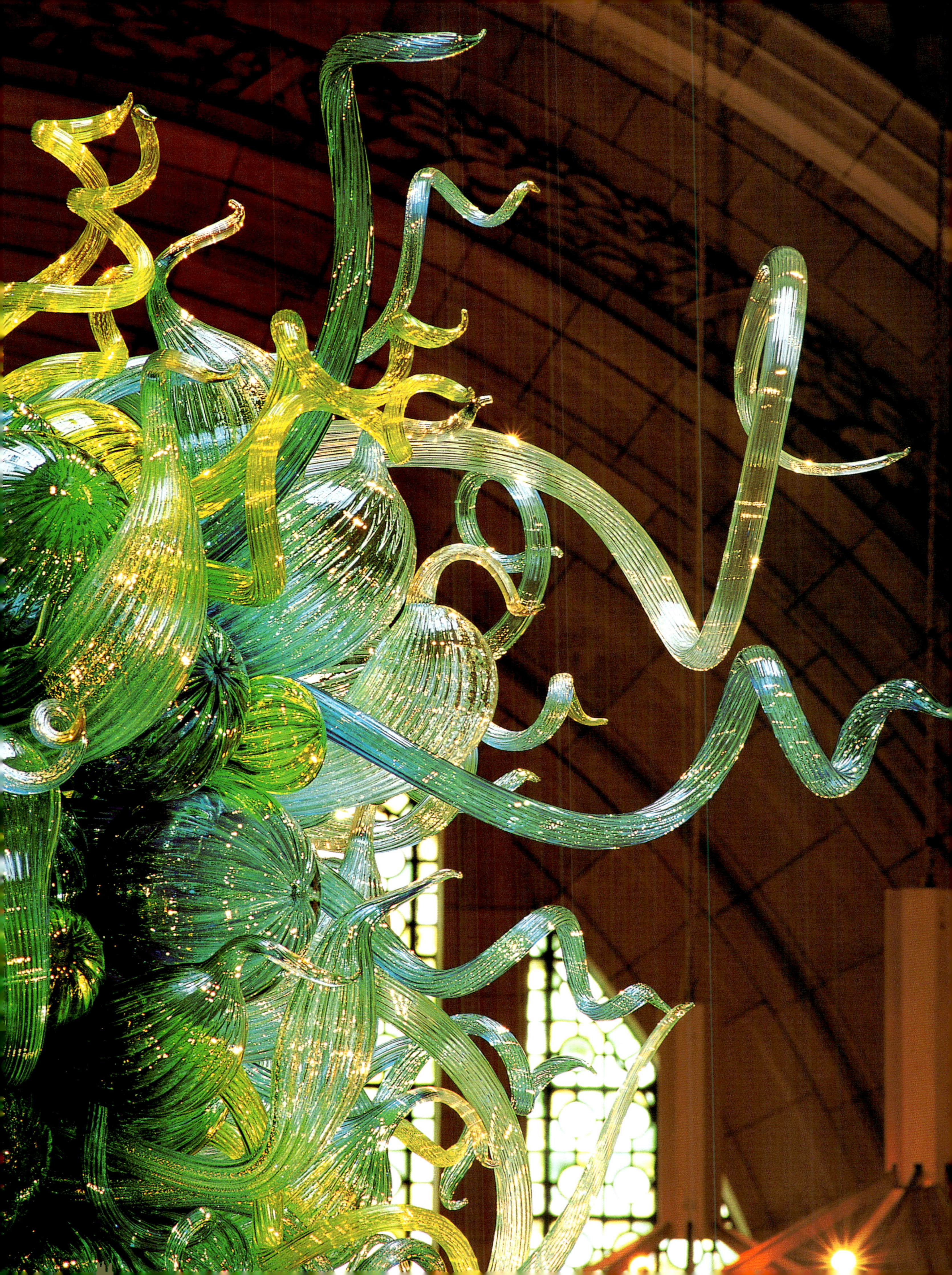

25

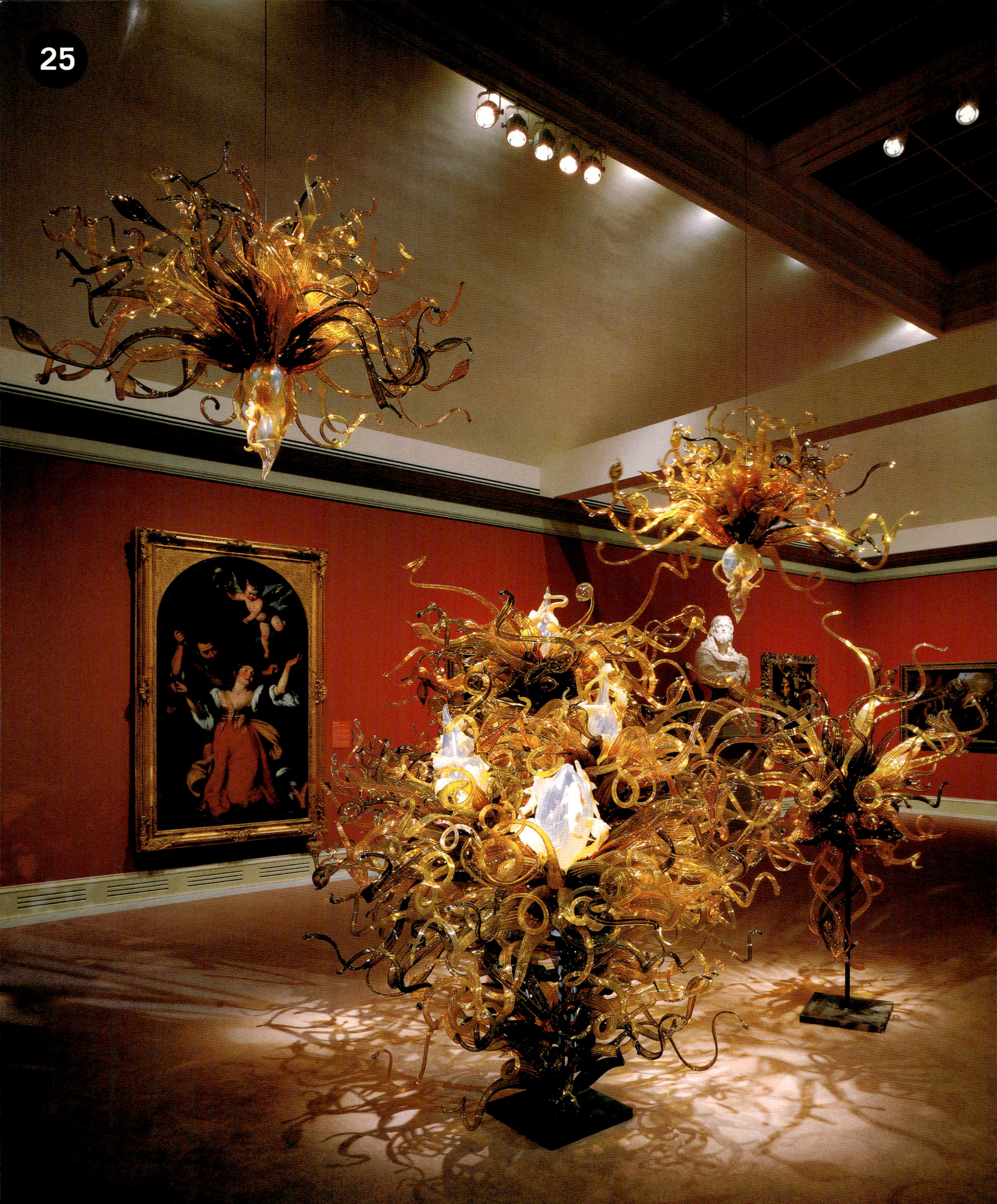

26

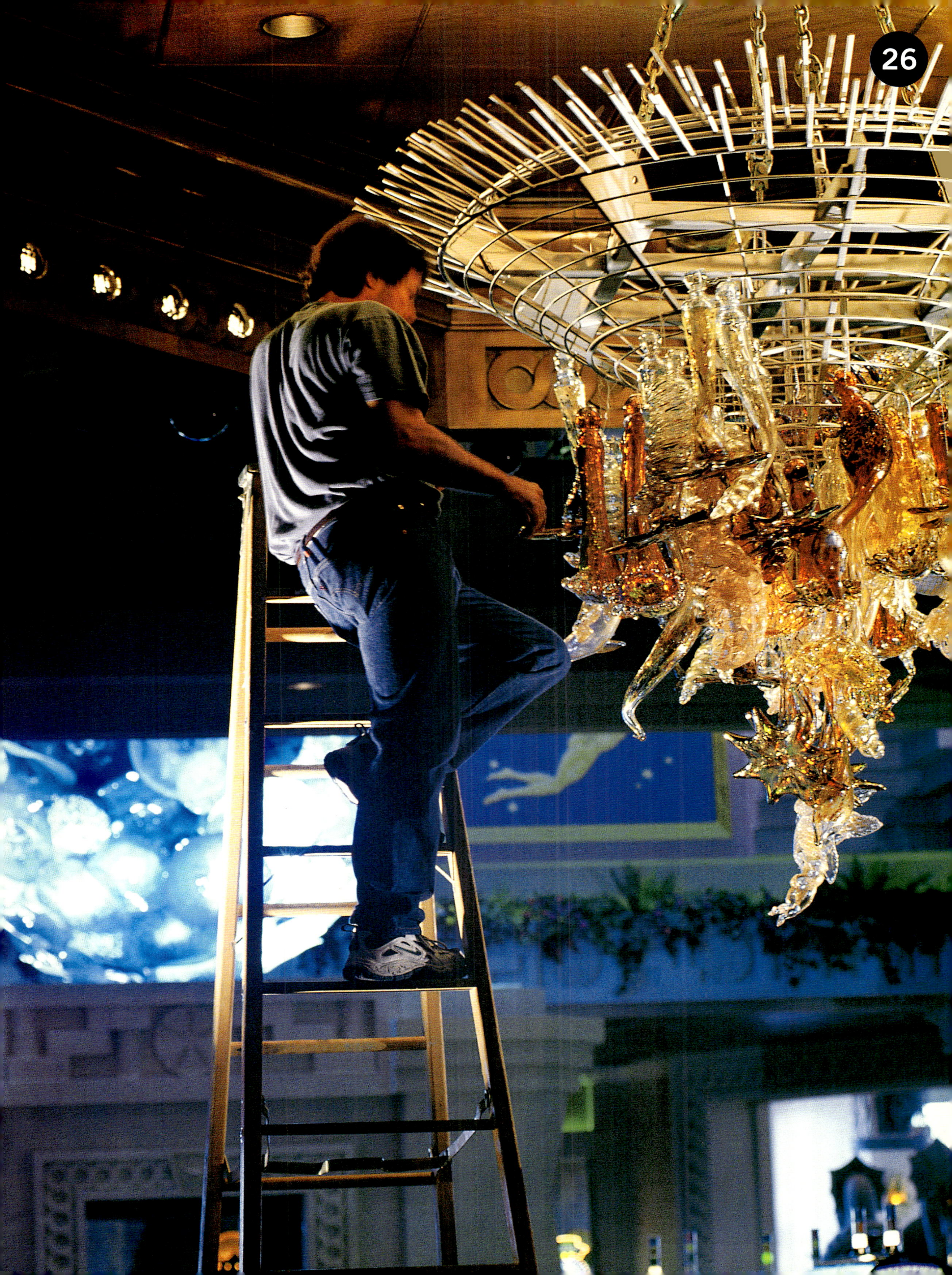

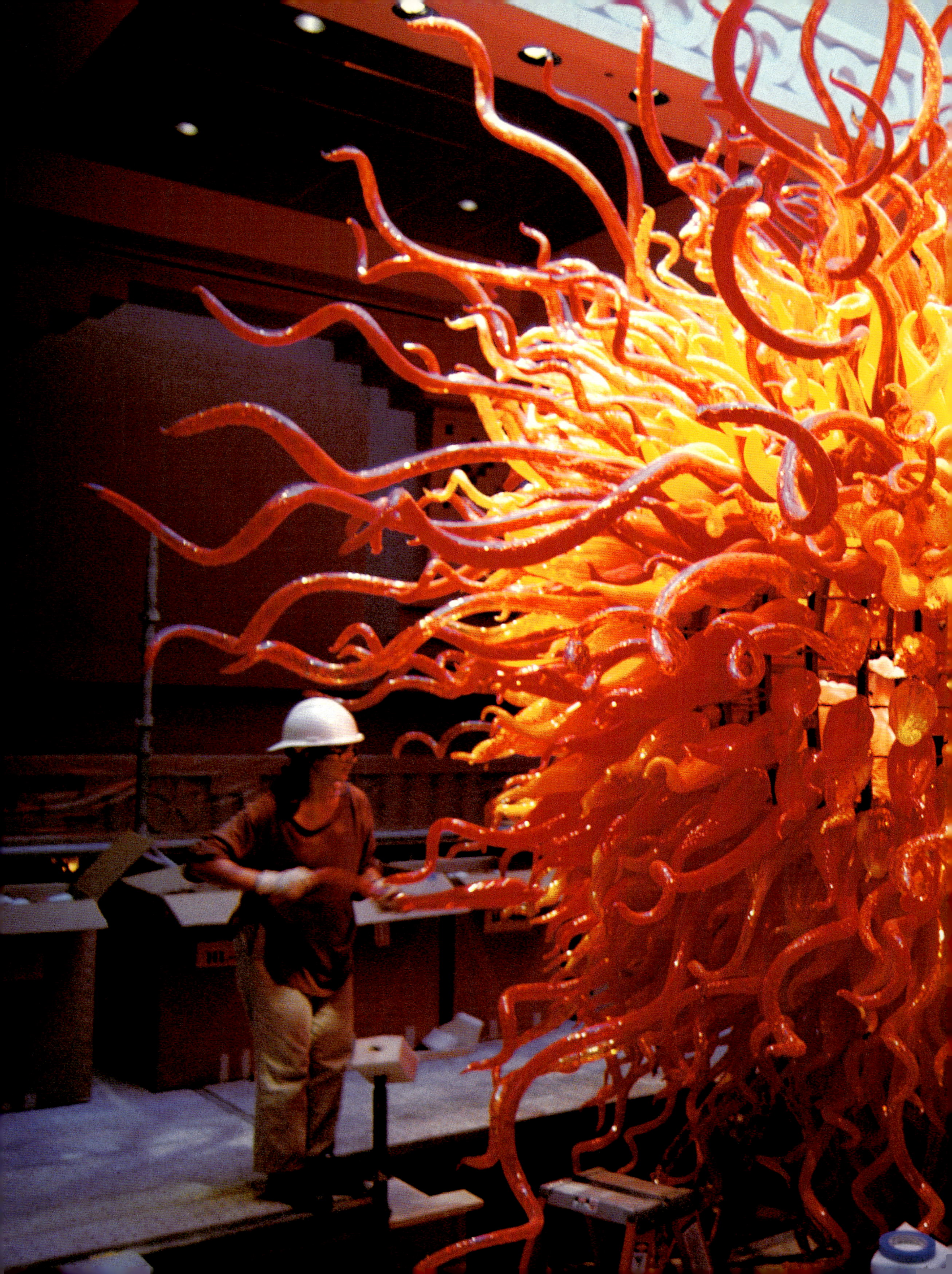

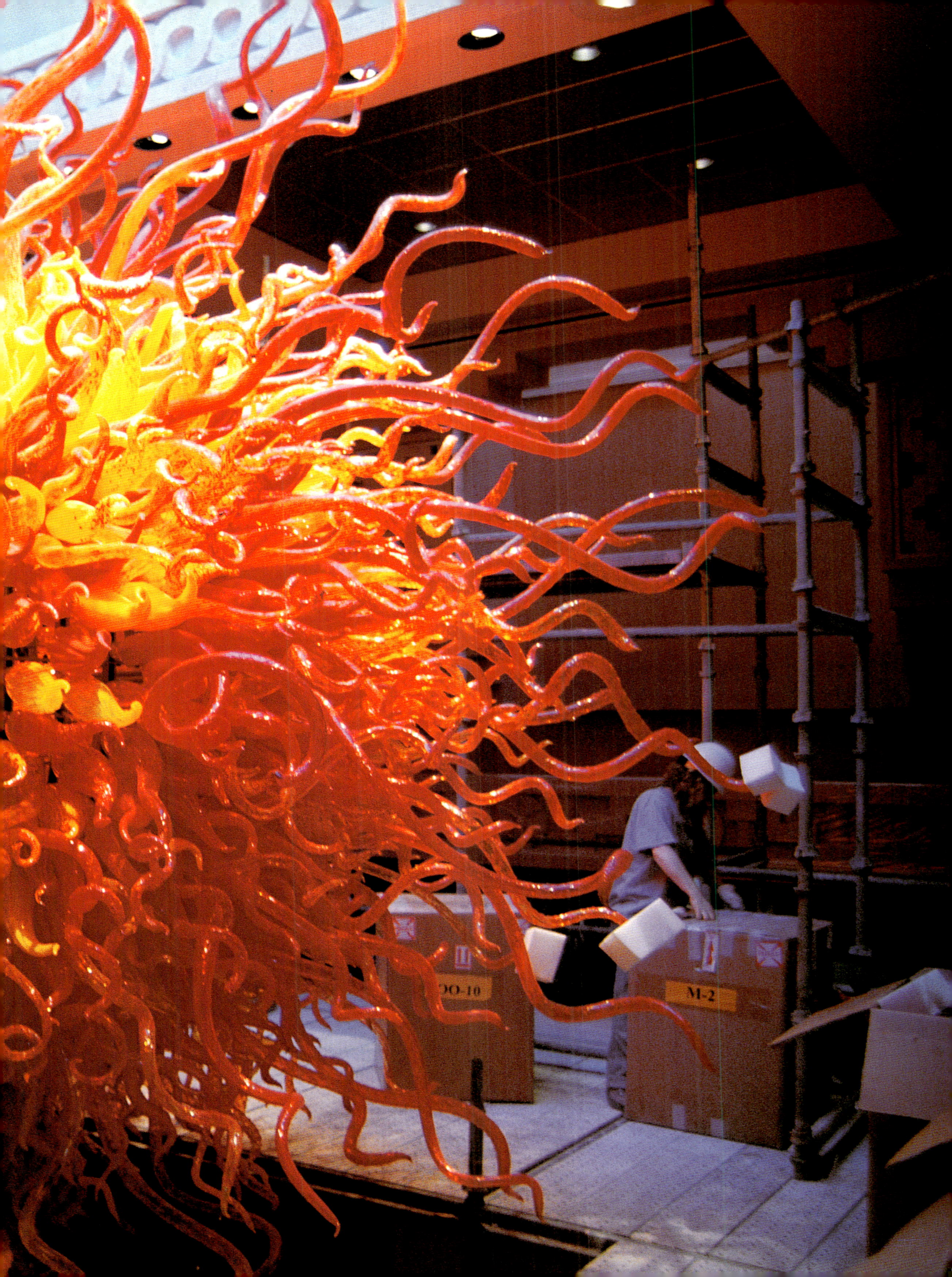
M-2

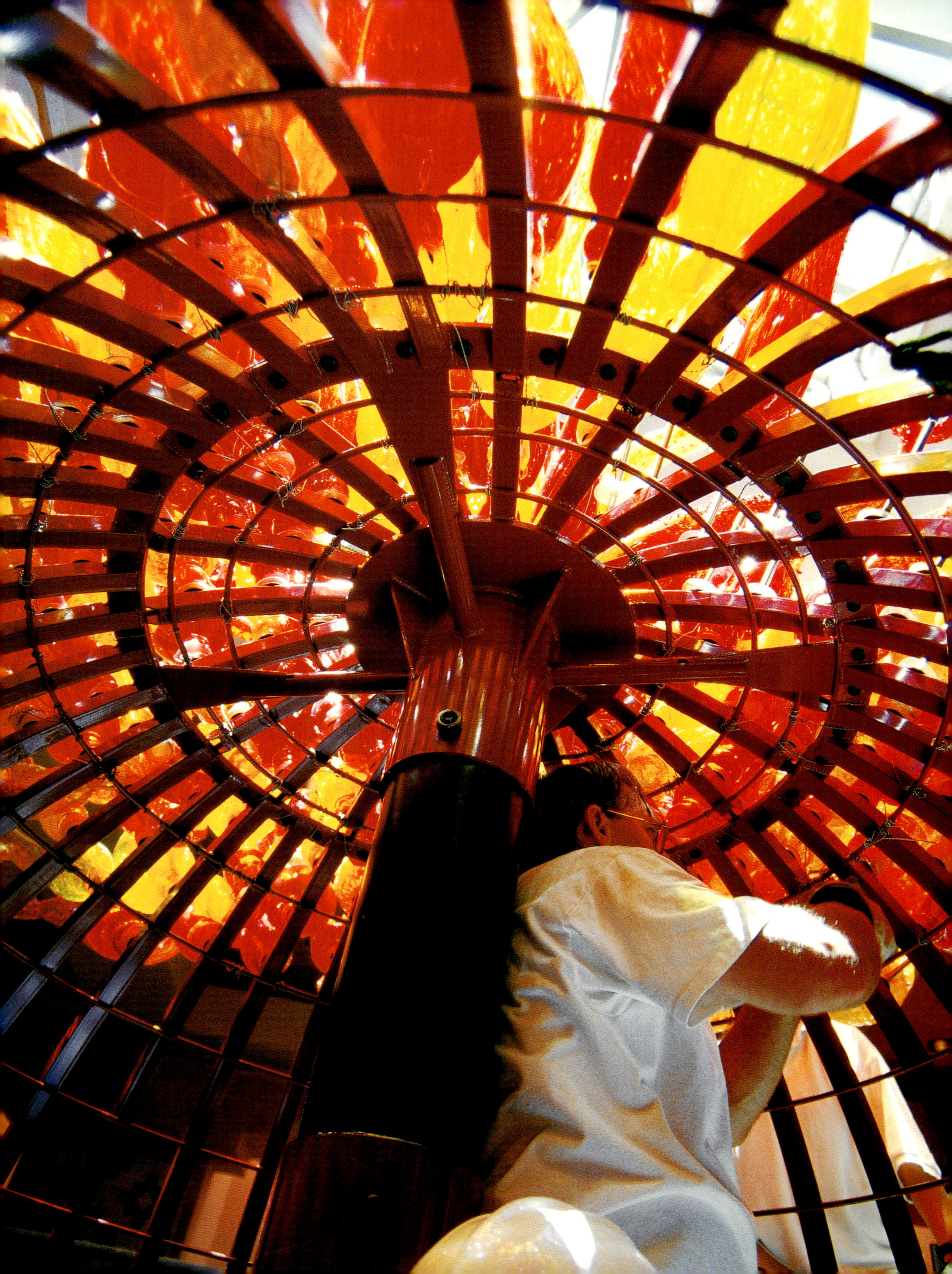

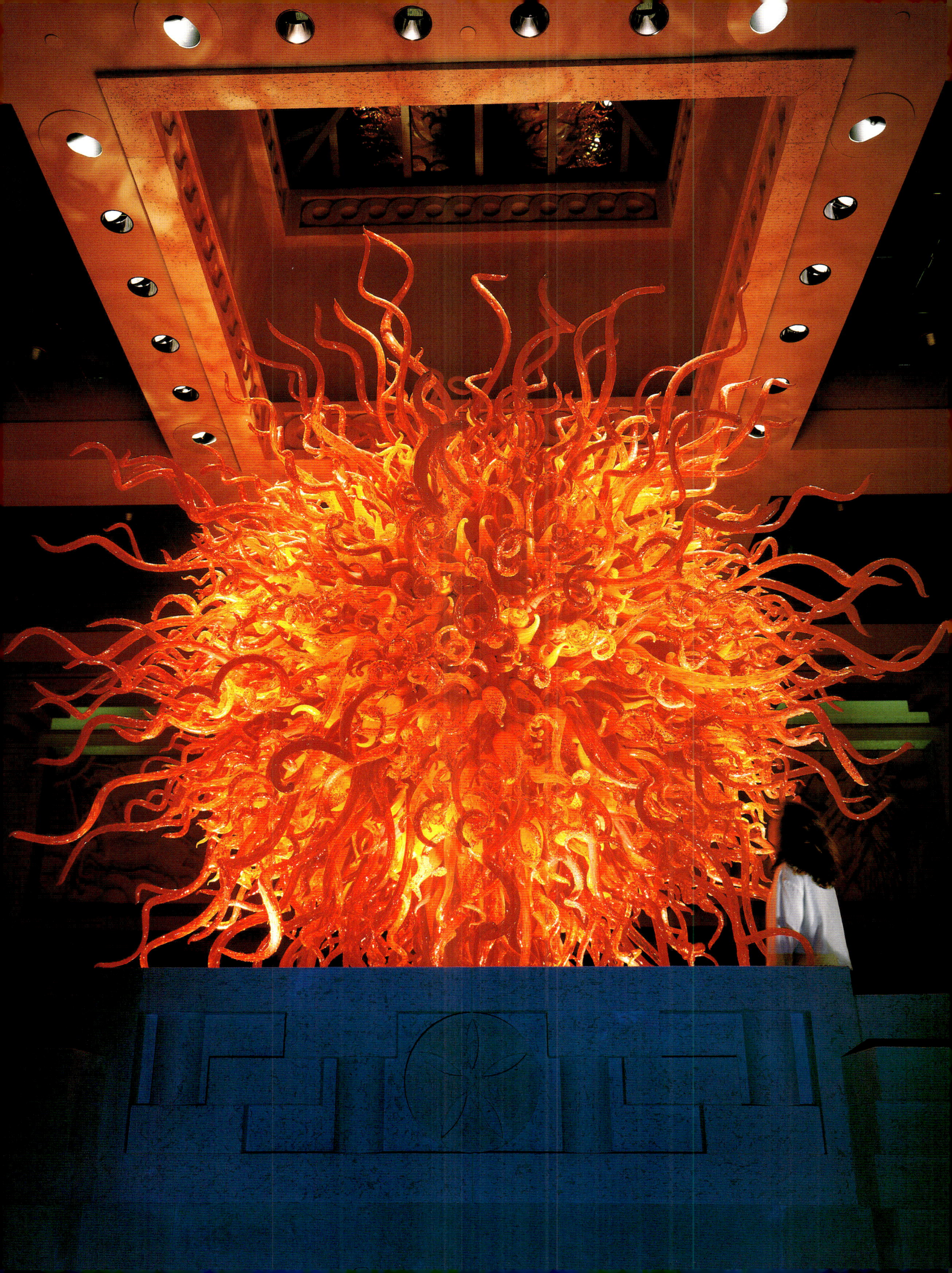

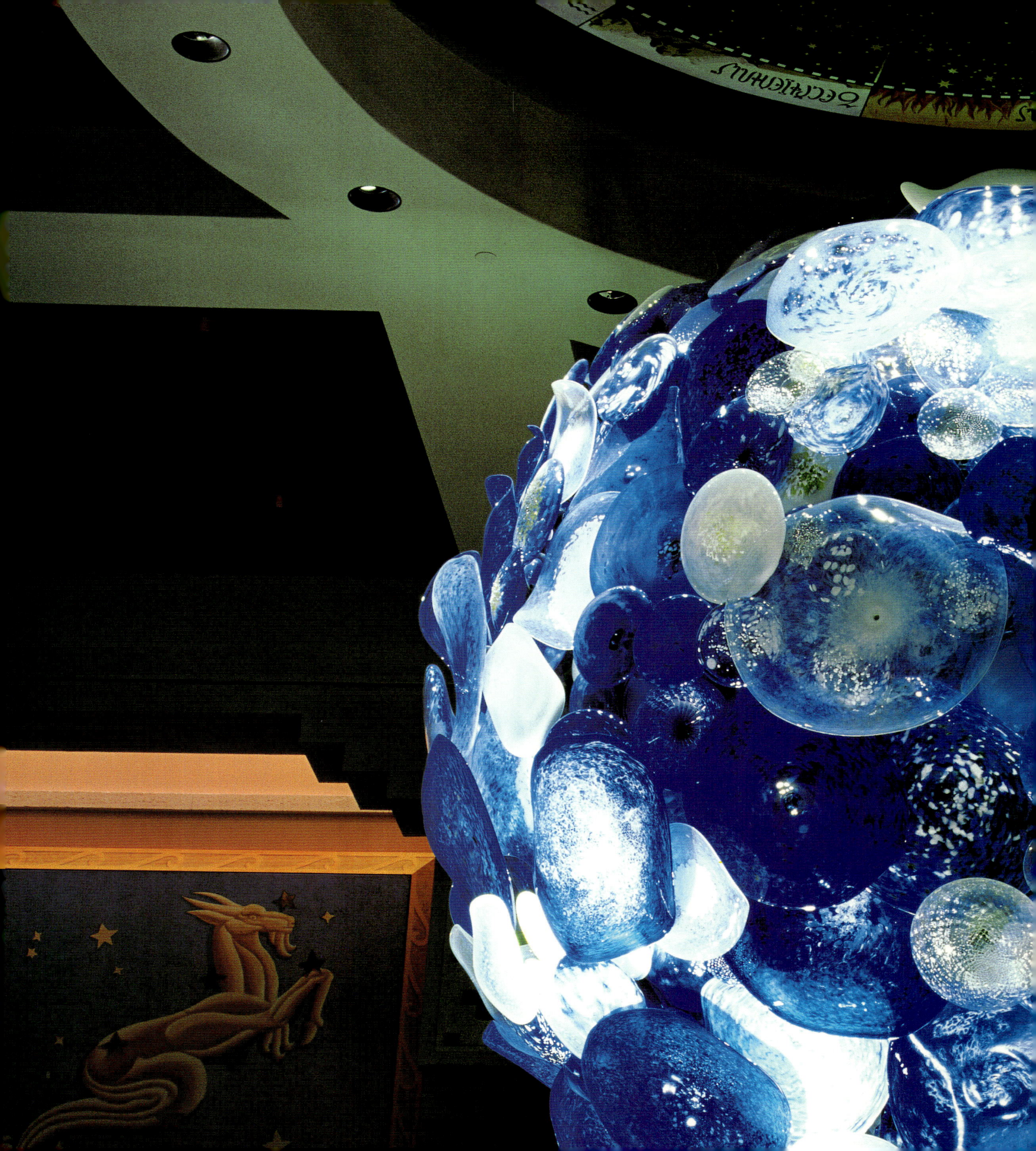

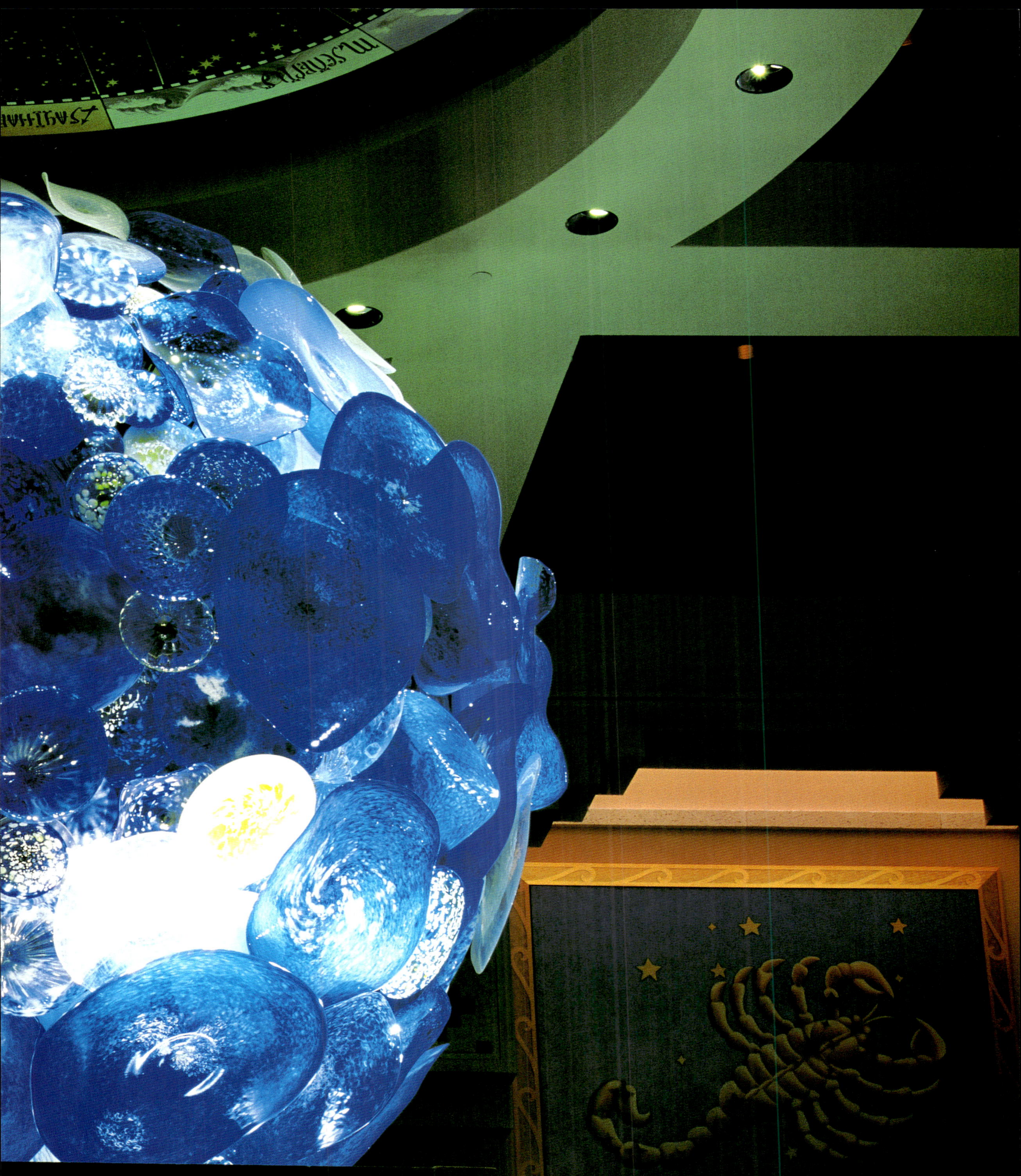

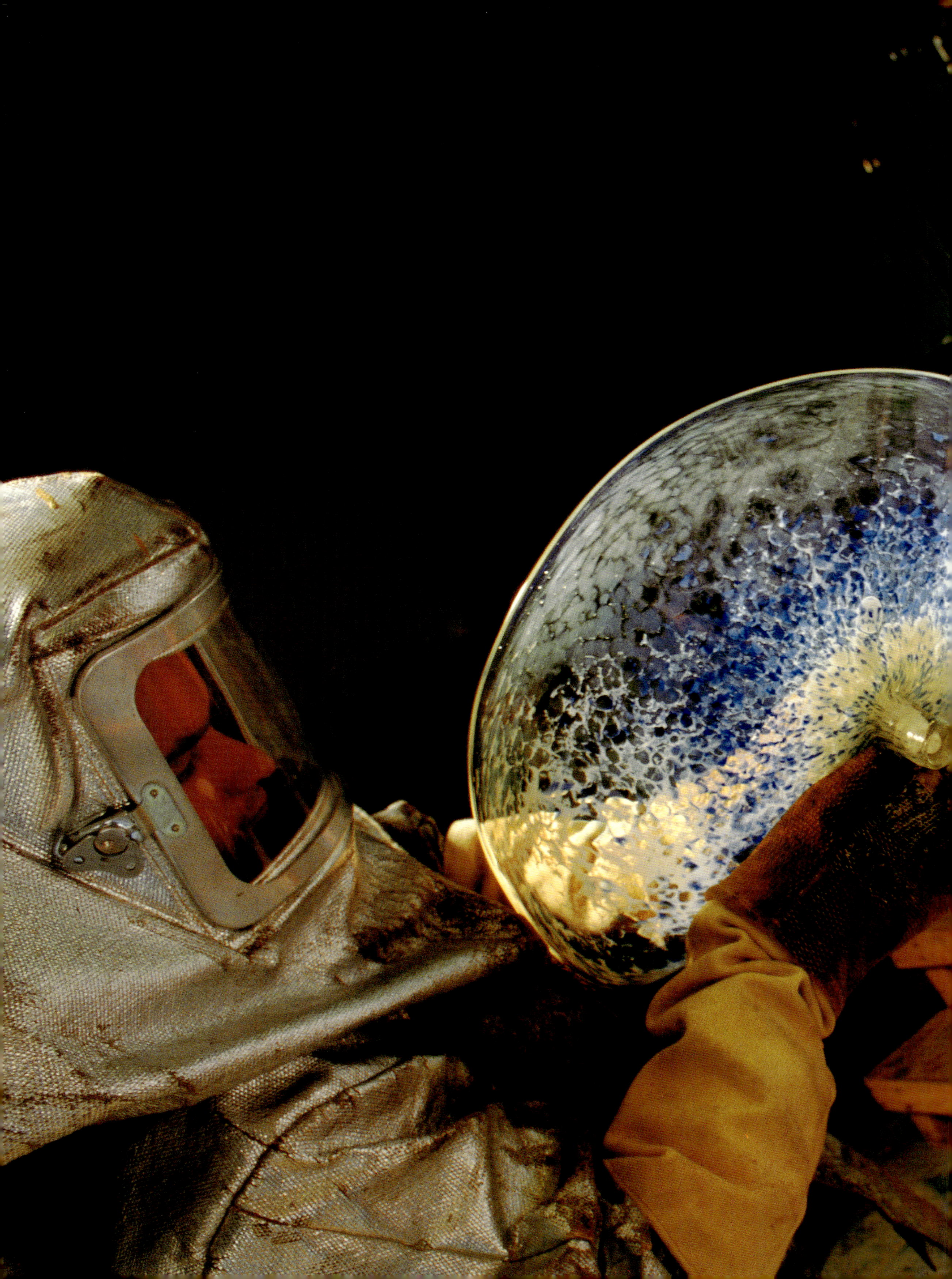

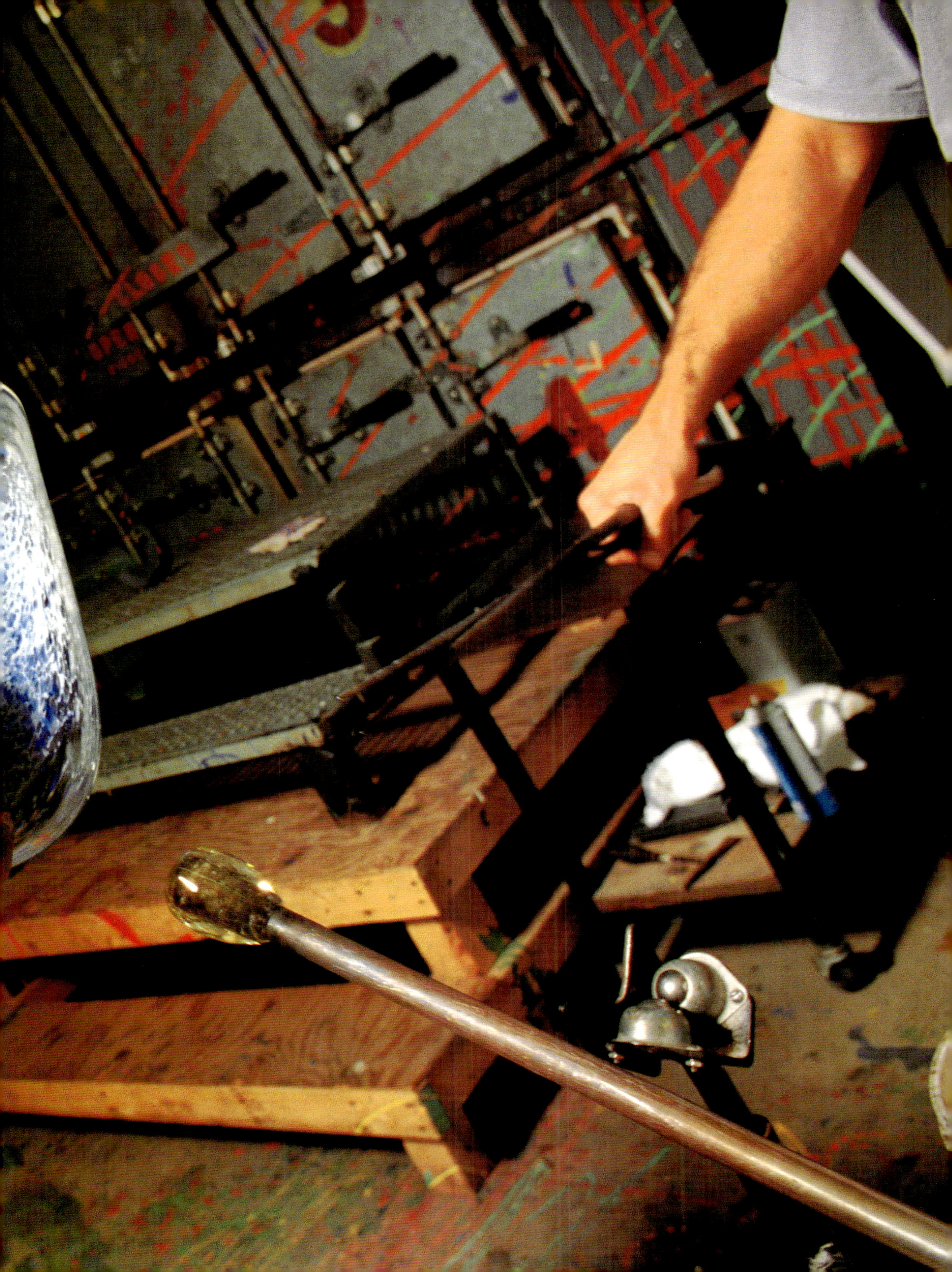

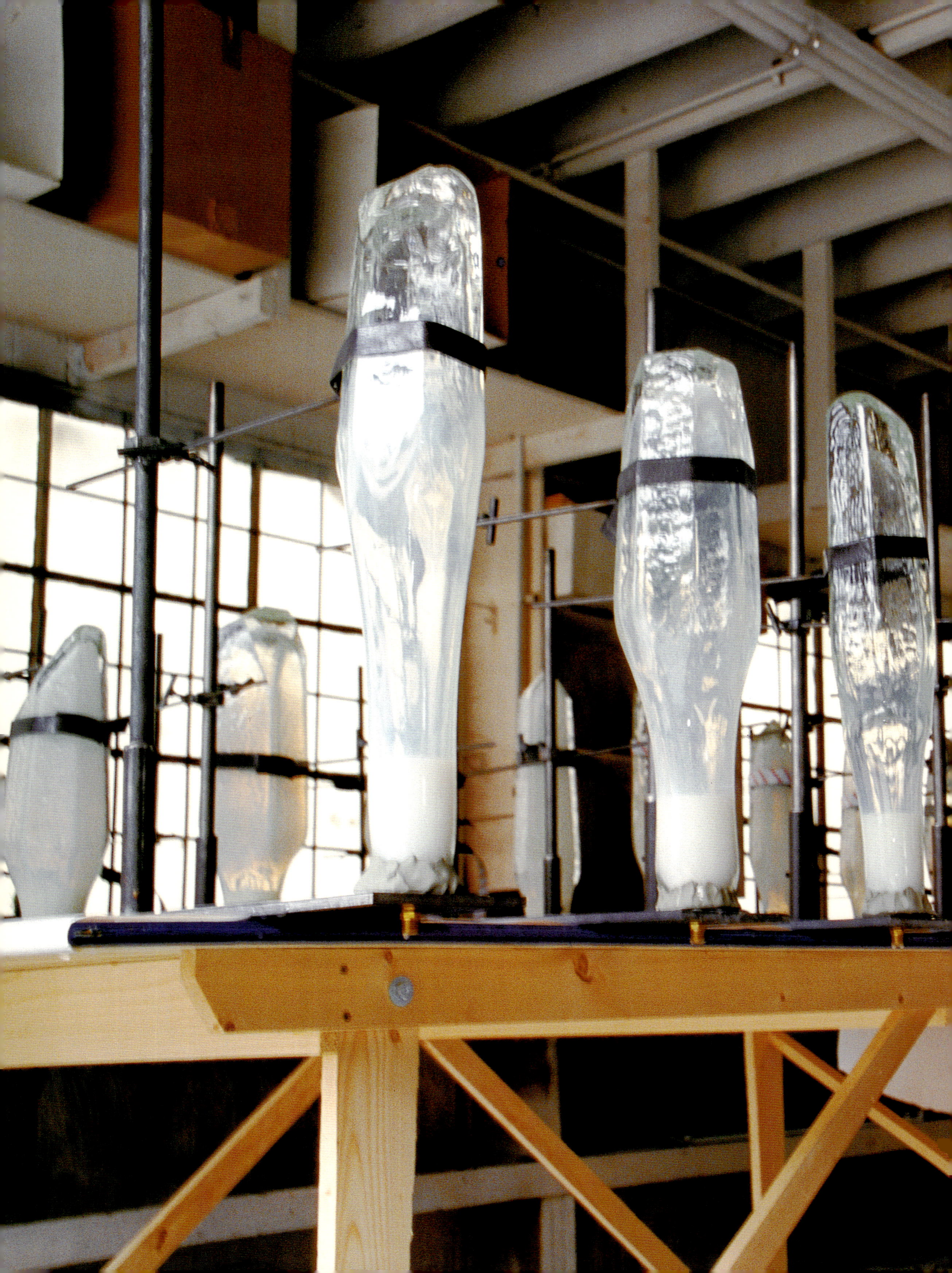

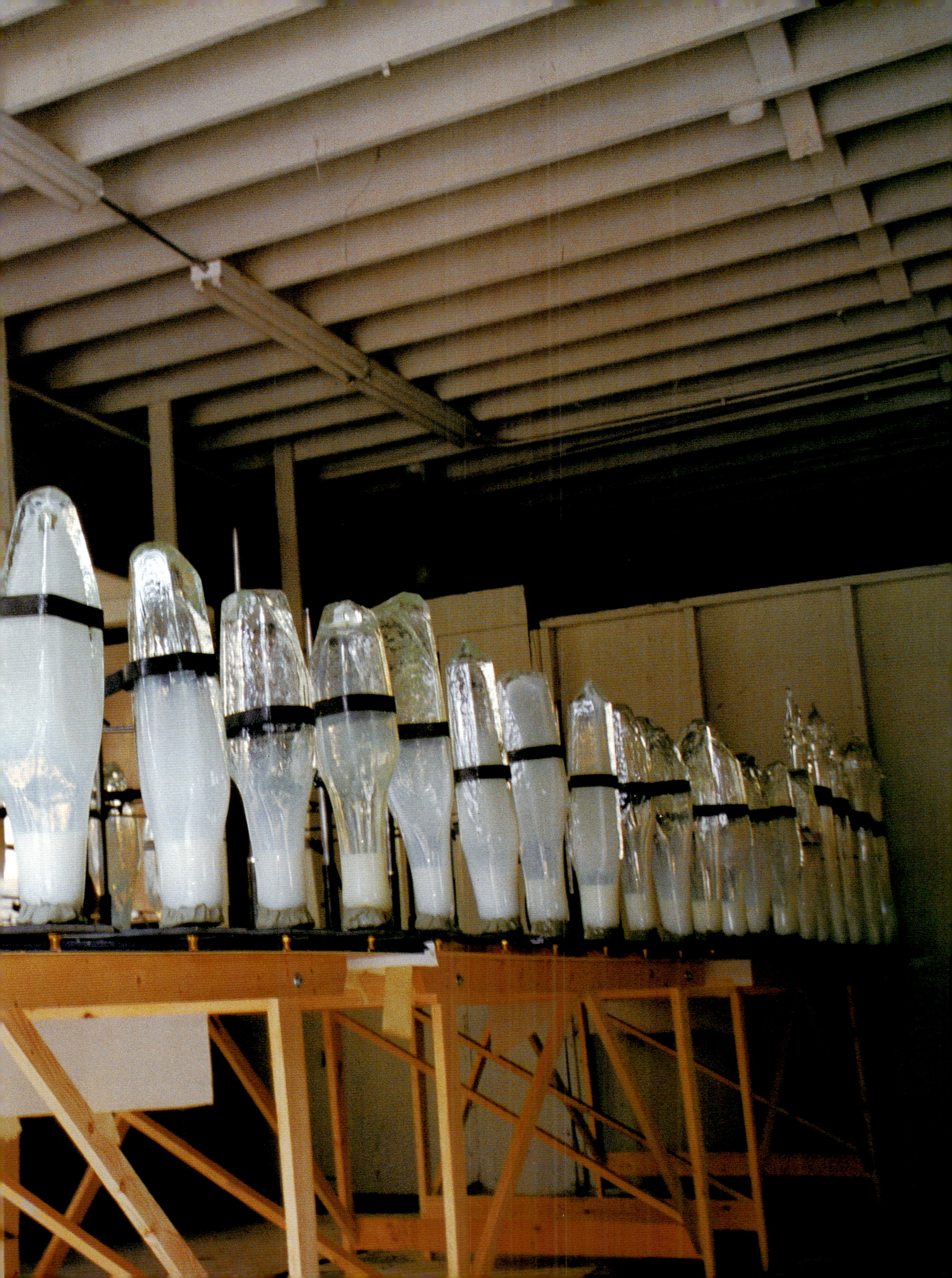

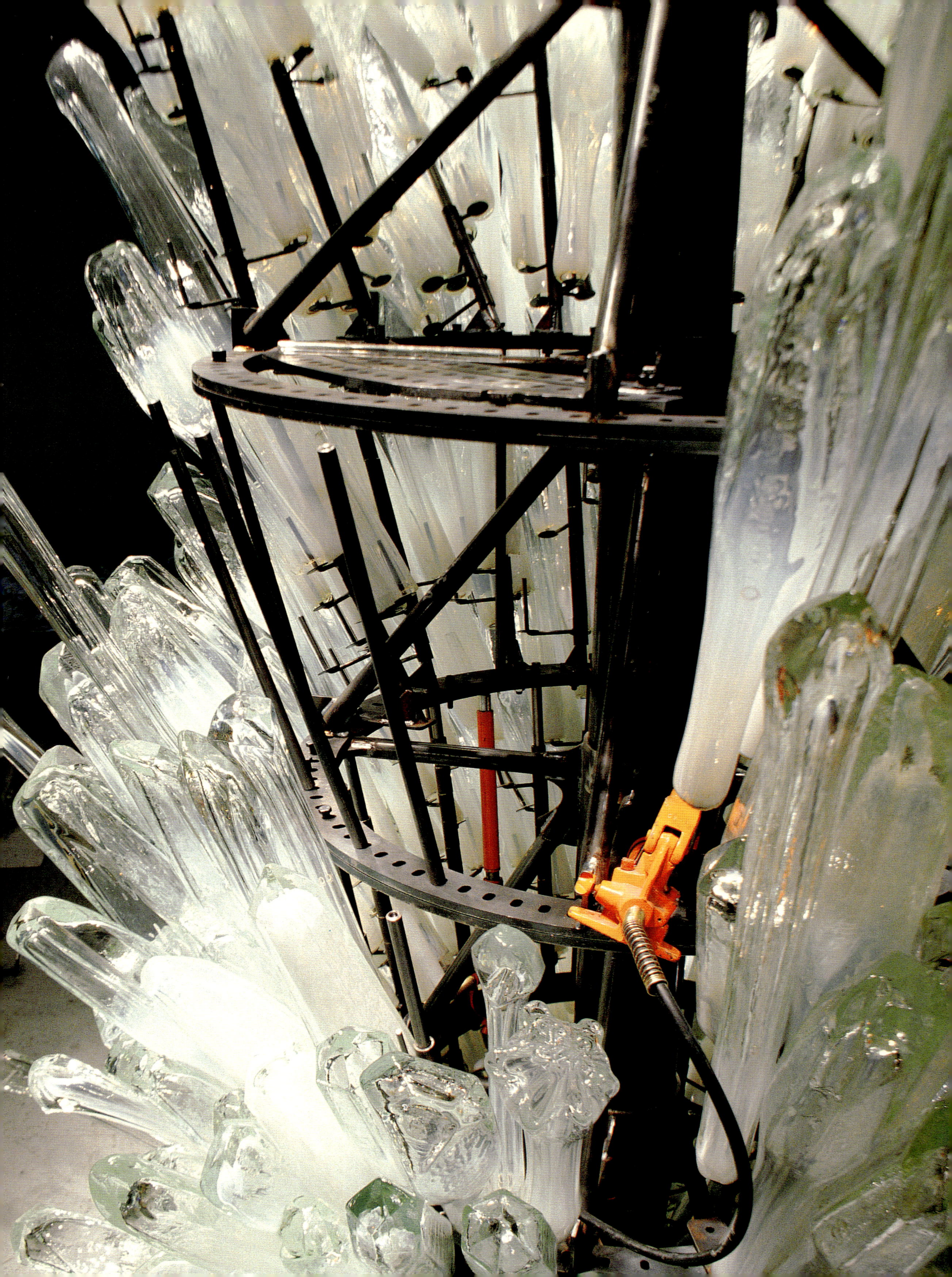

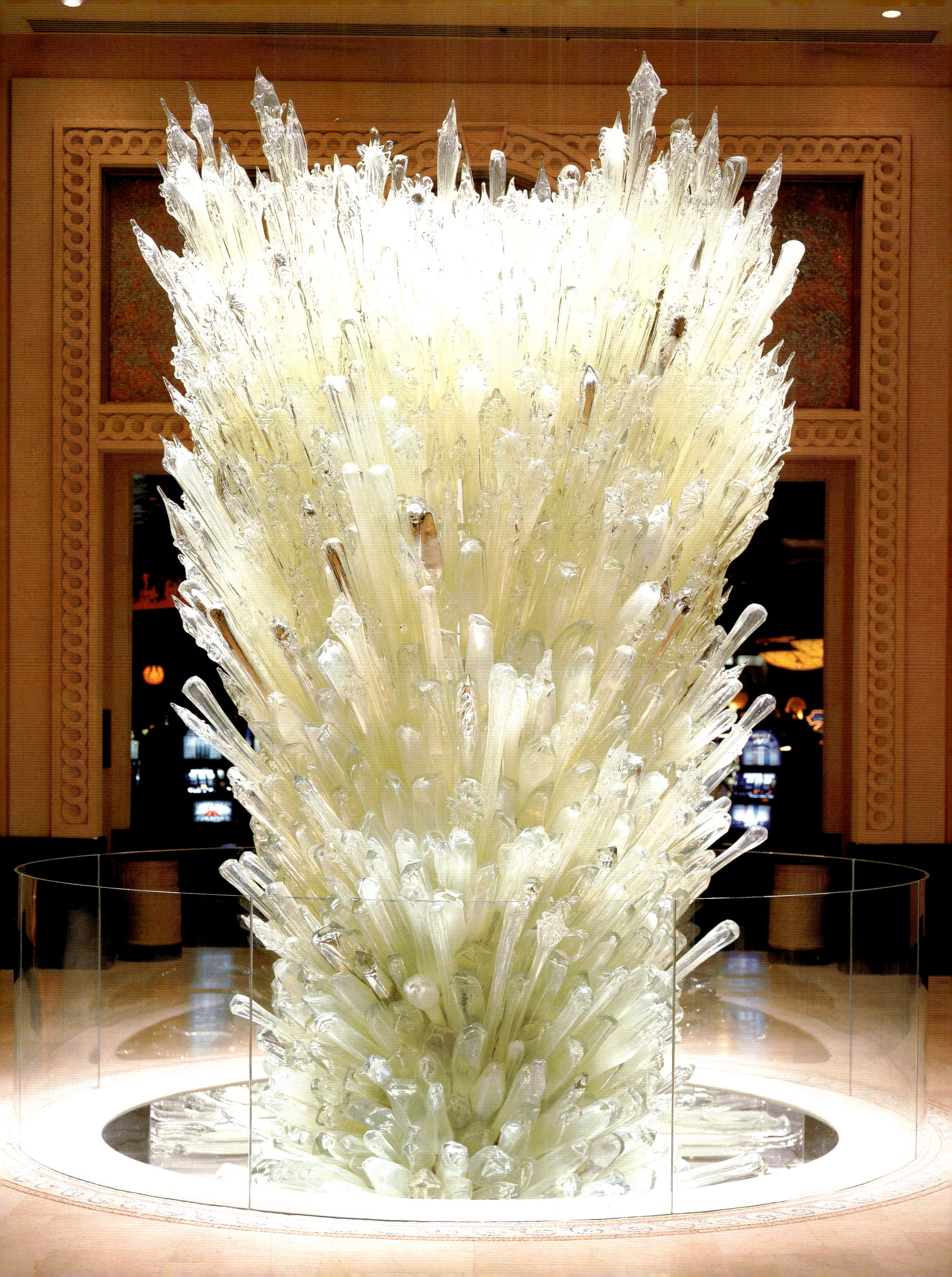

27

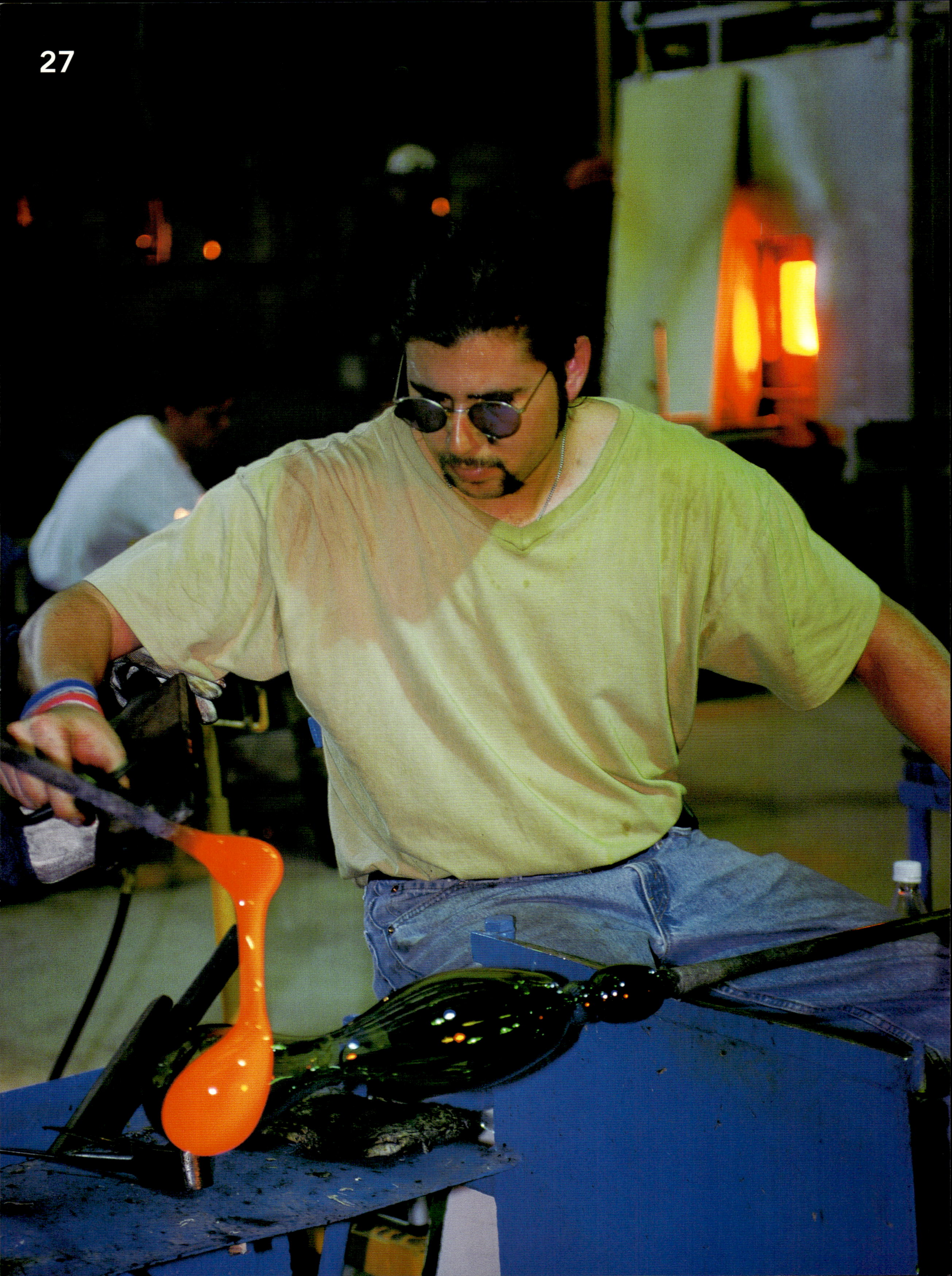

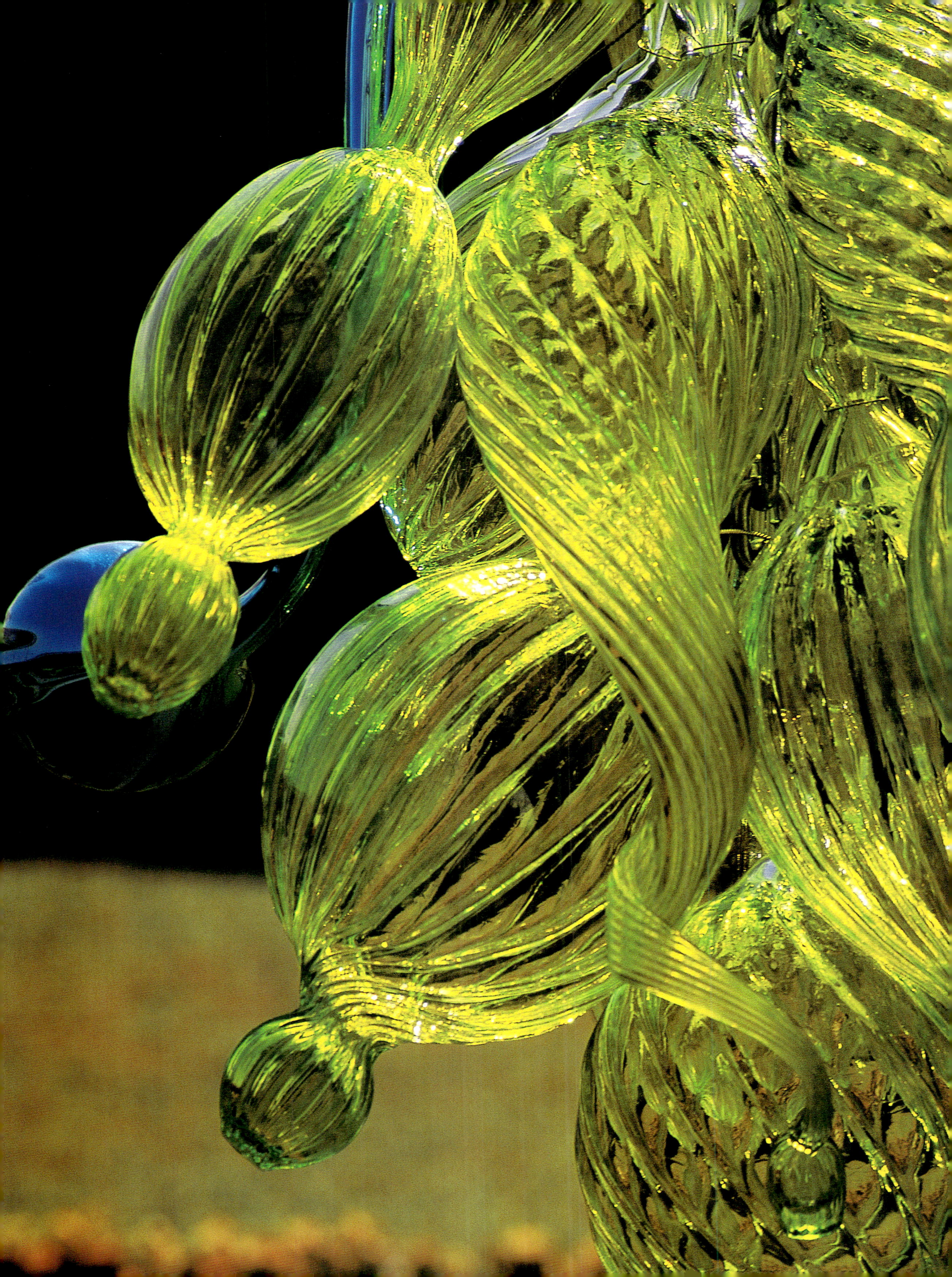

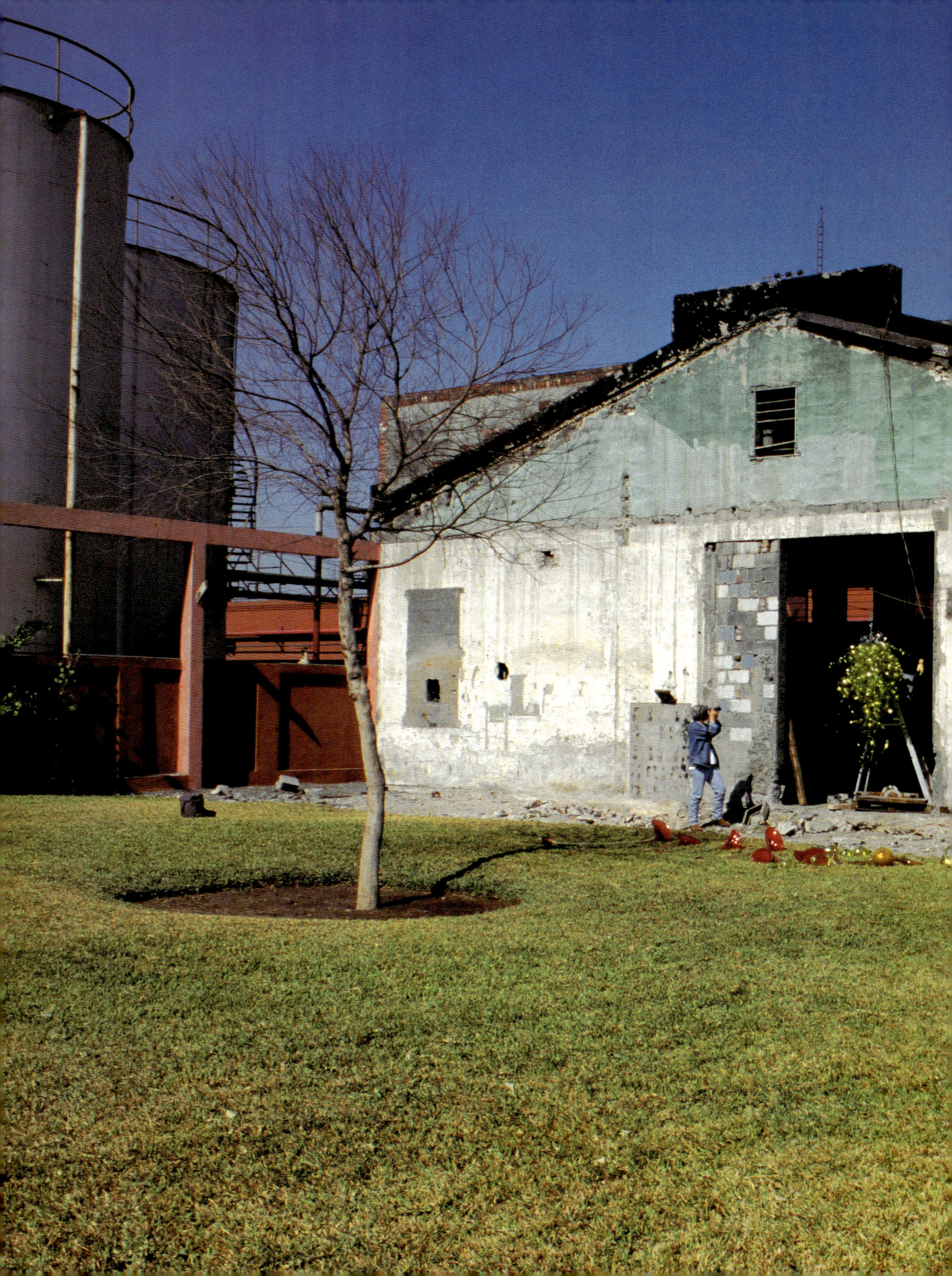

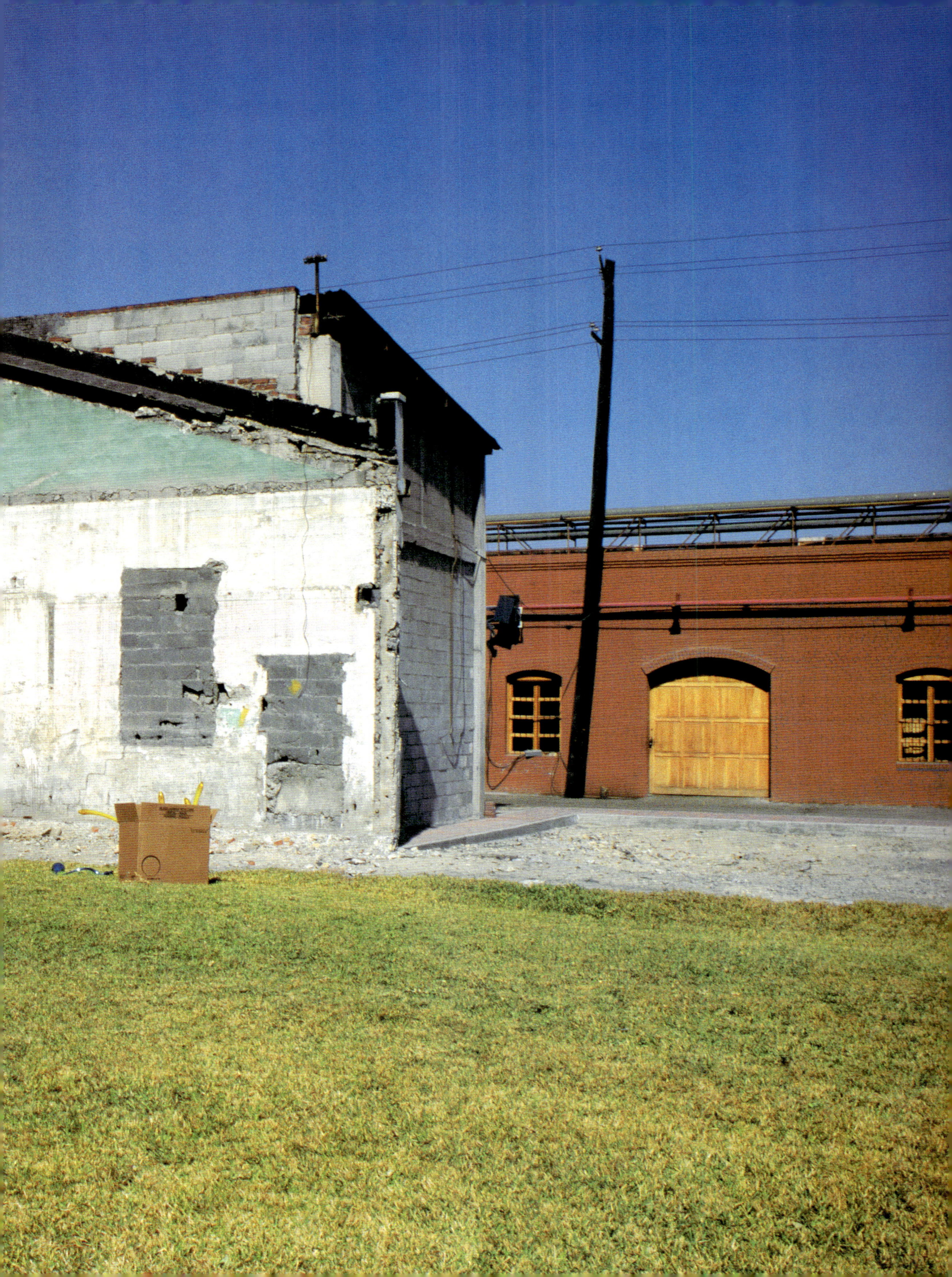

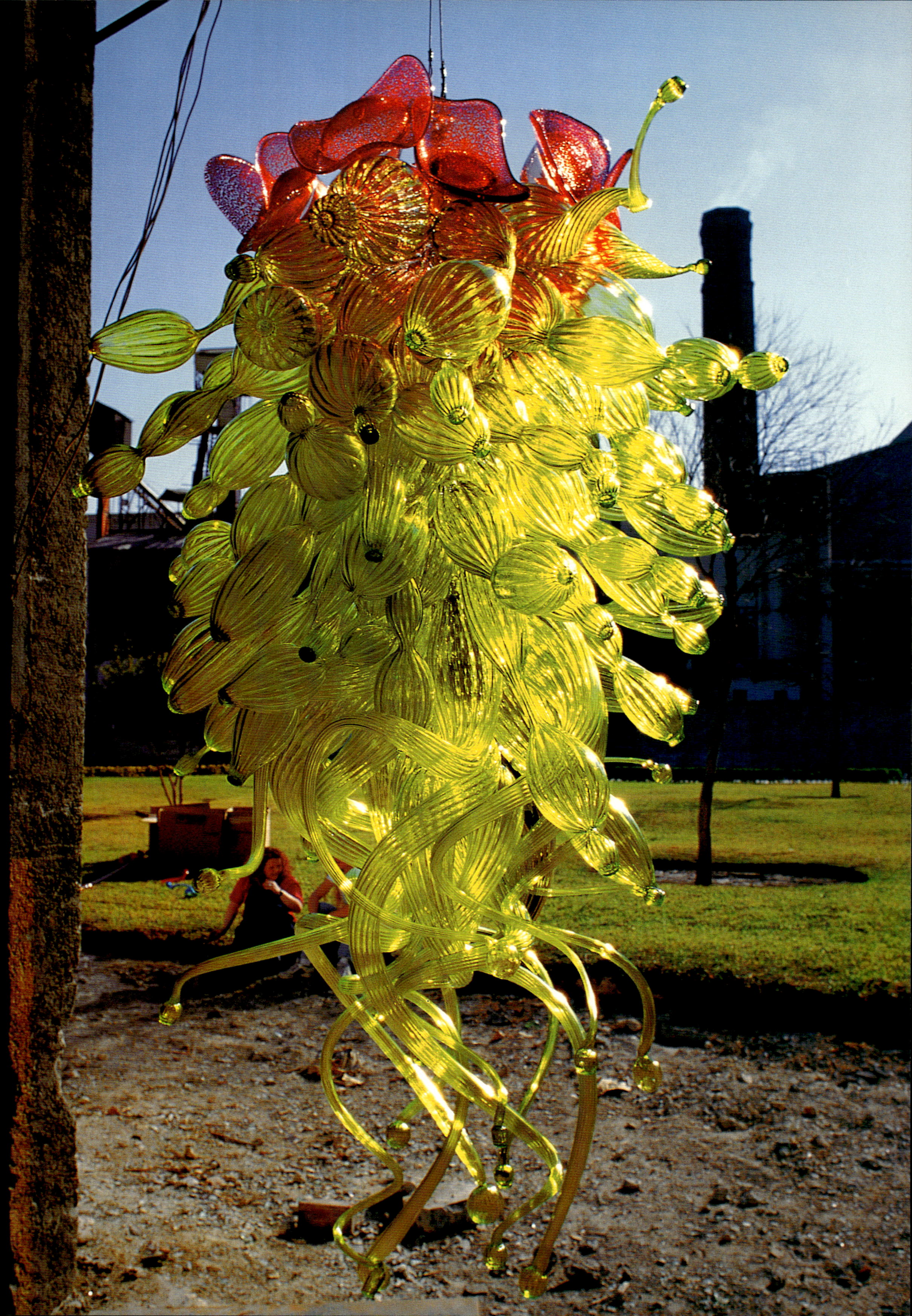

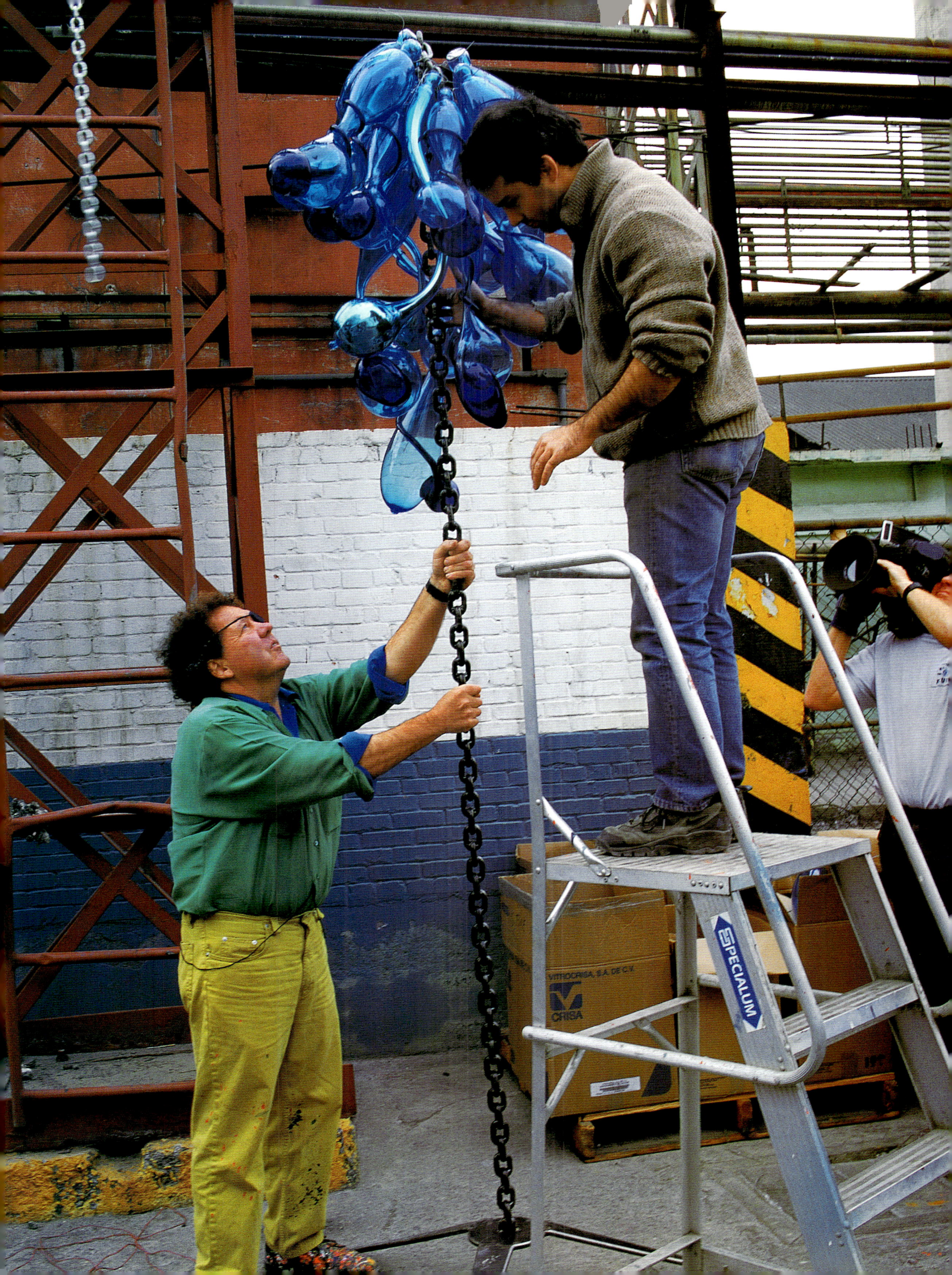
VITROCRISA, S.A. DE C.V.
CRISA
SPECIALUM

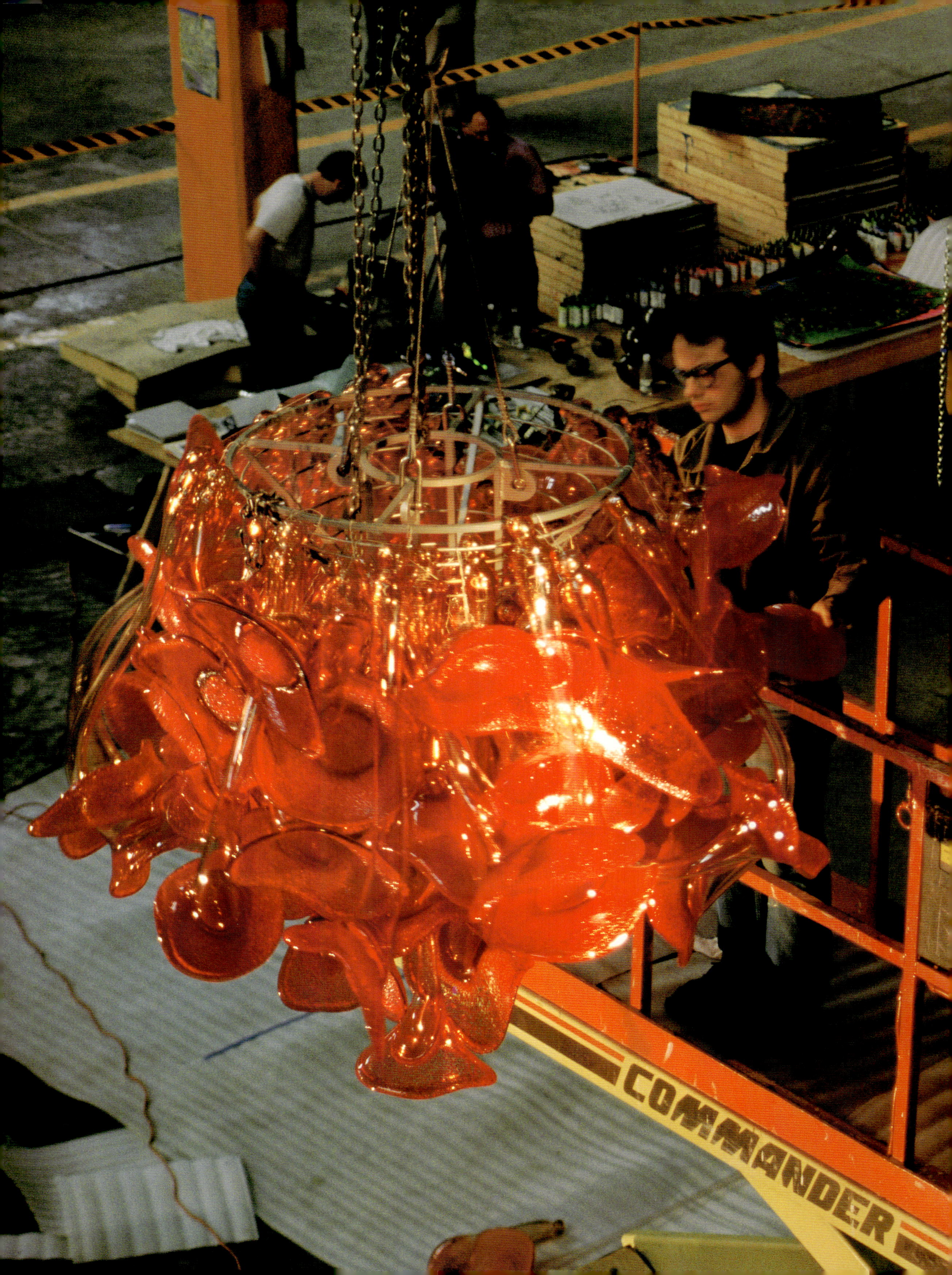
COMMANDER

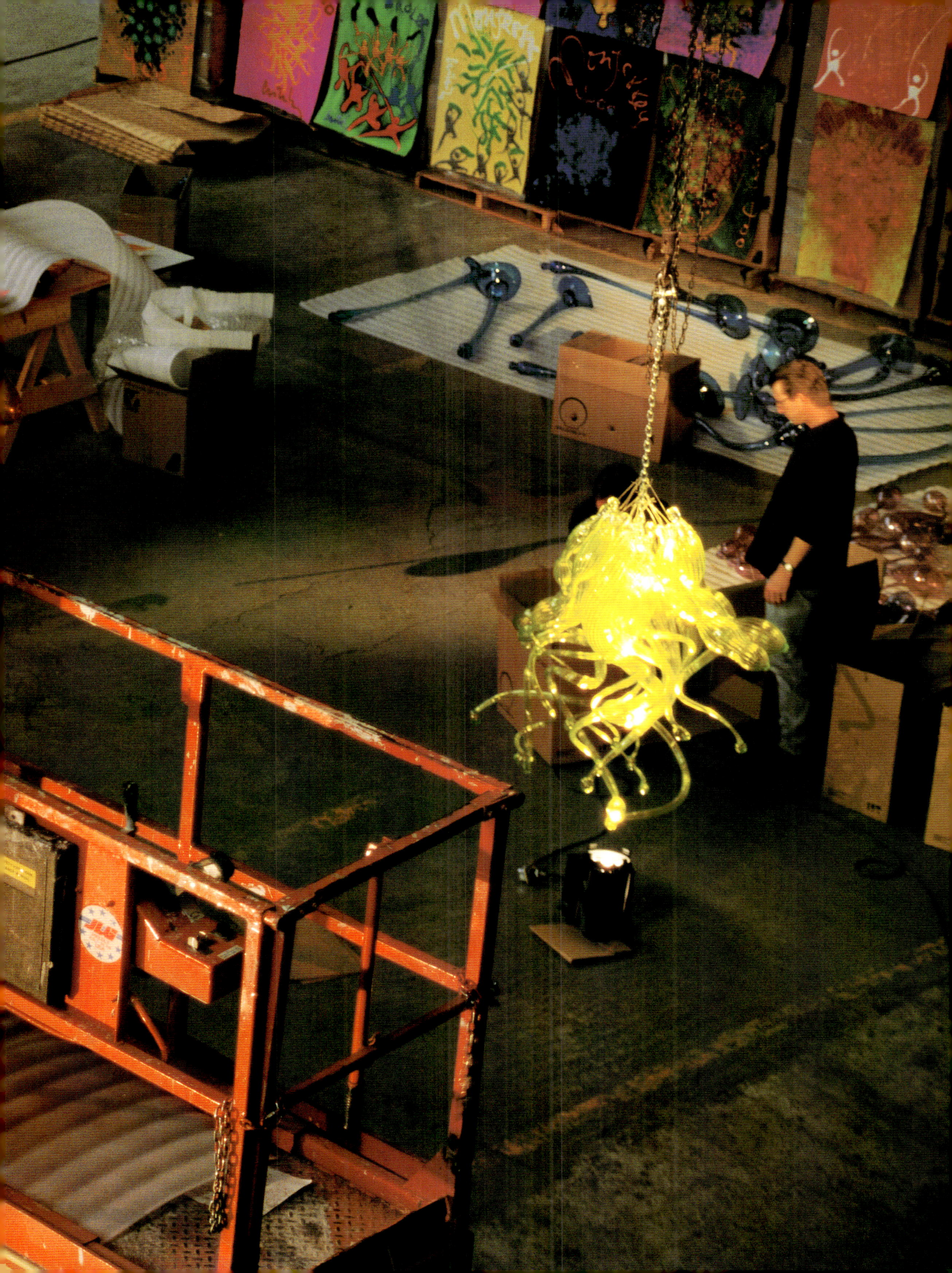

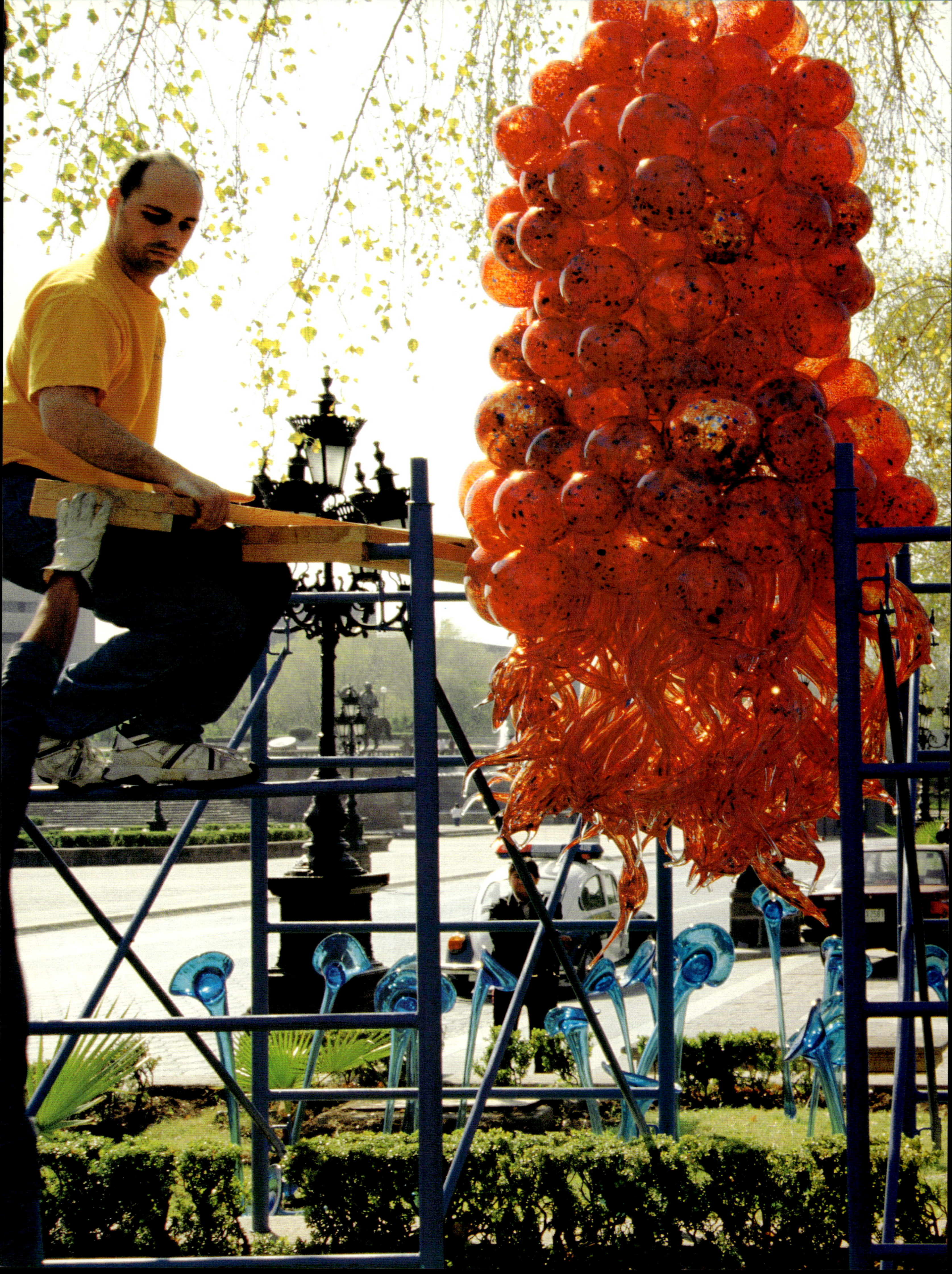

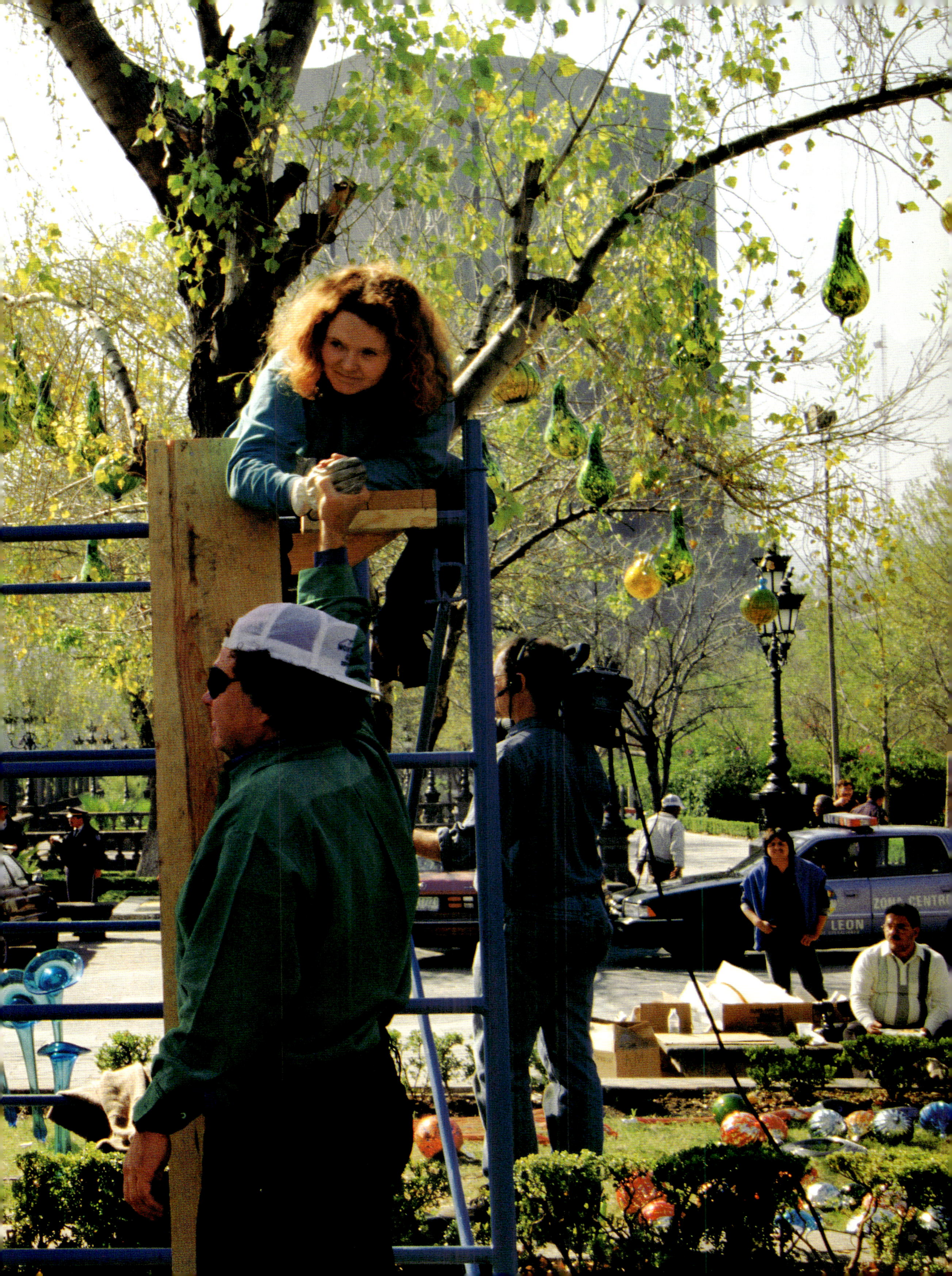
LEON

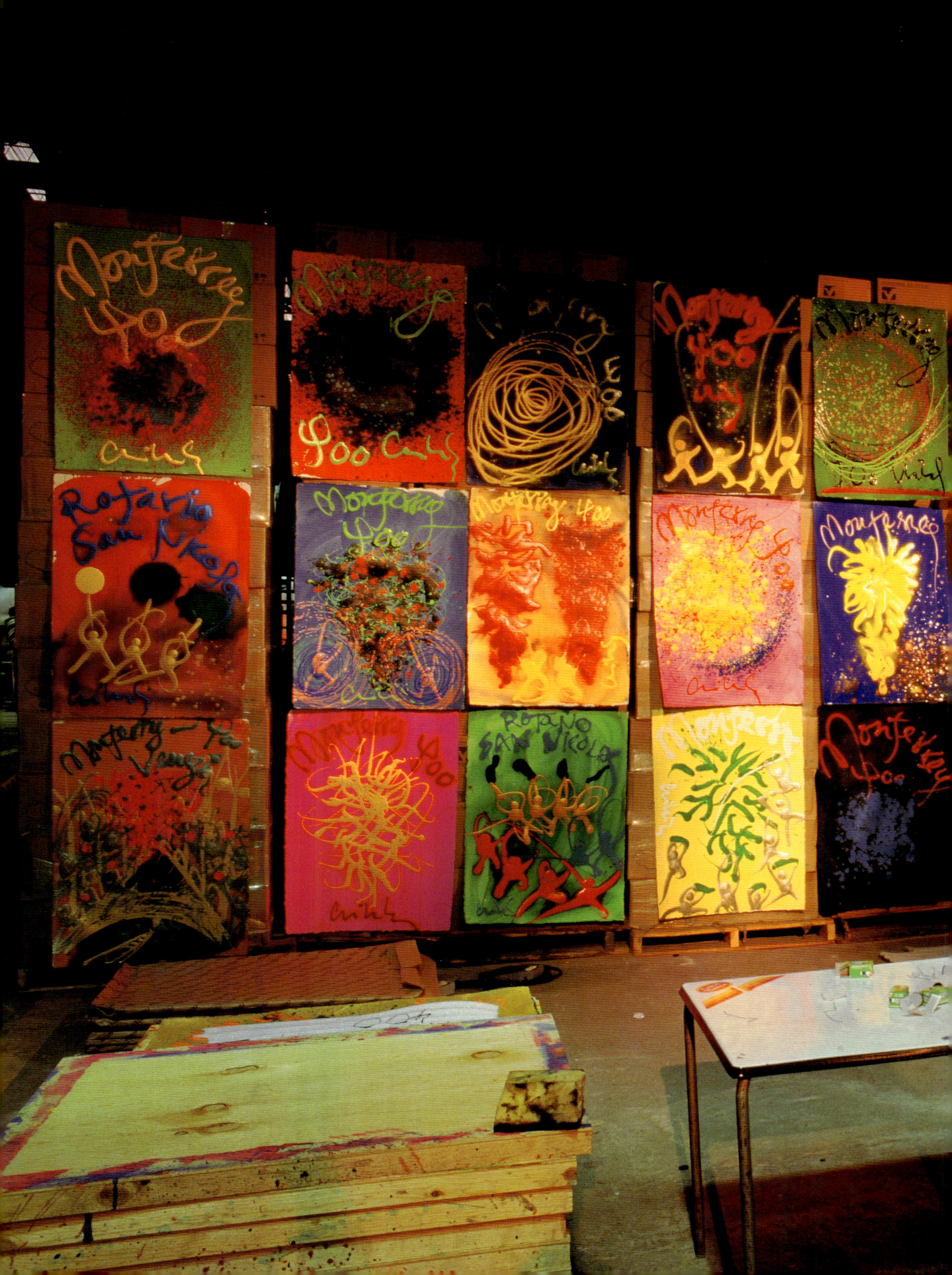

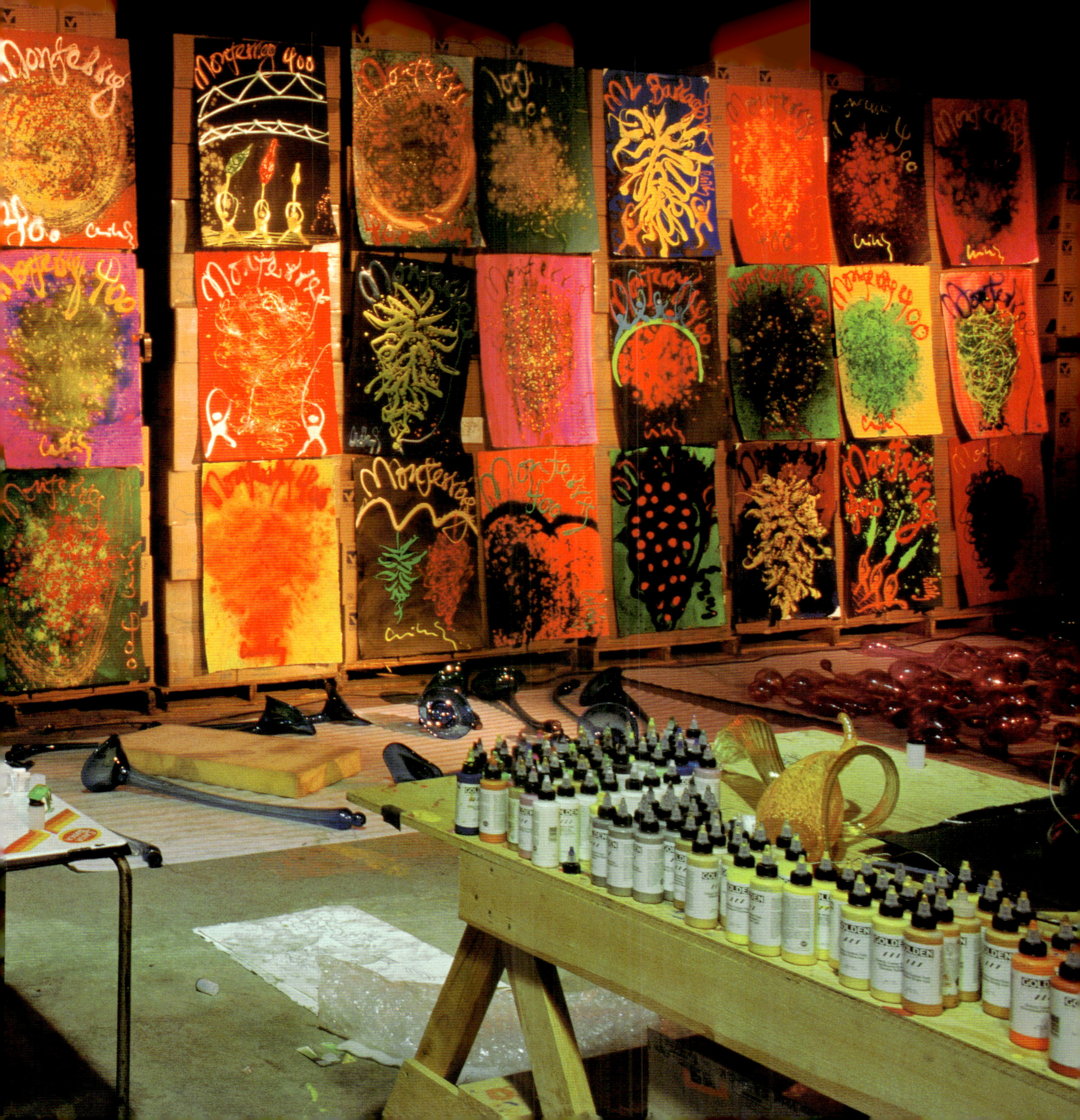
GOLDEN

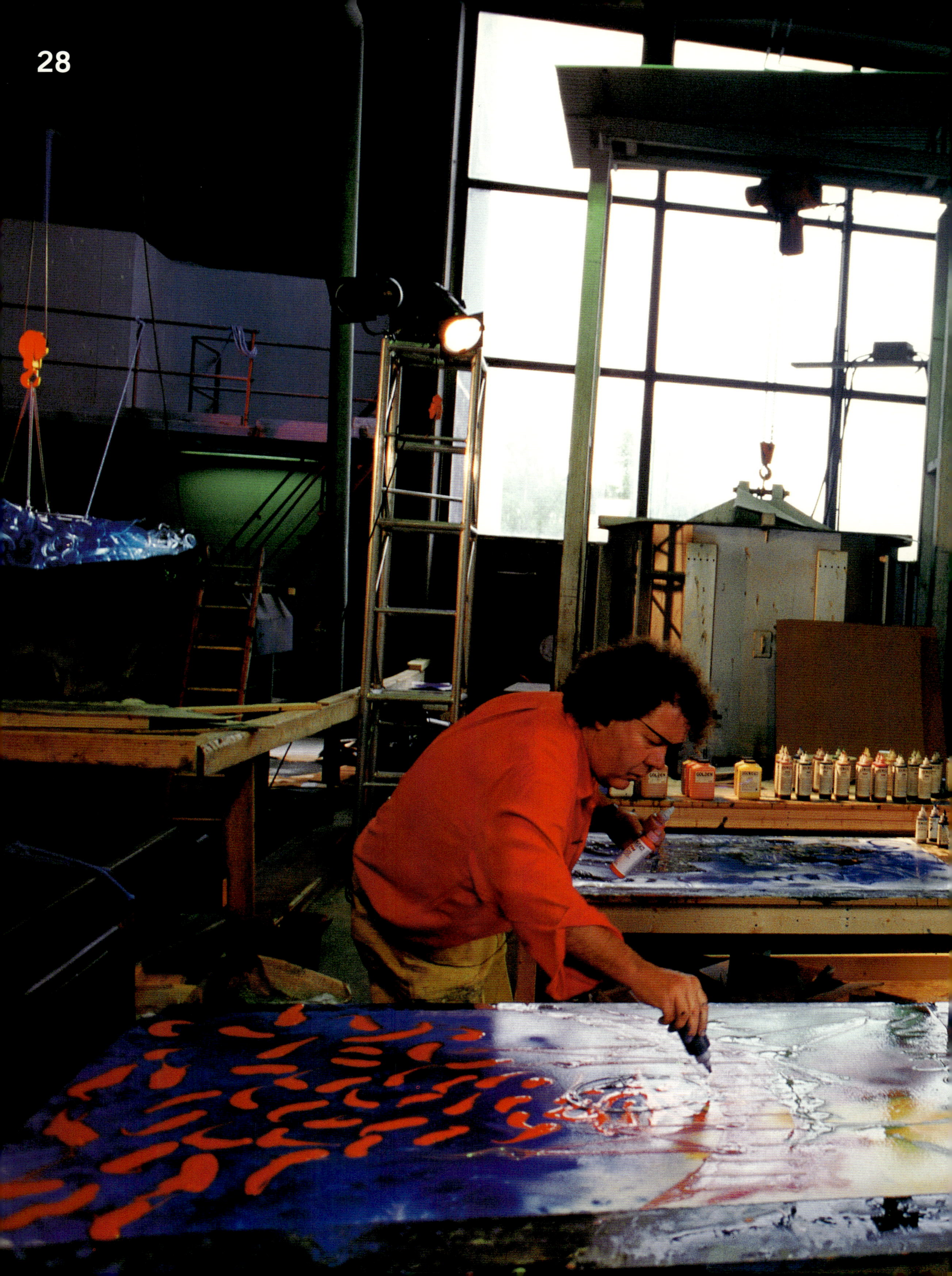

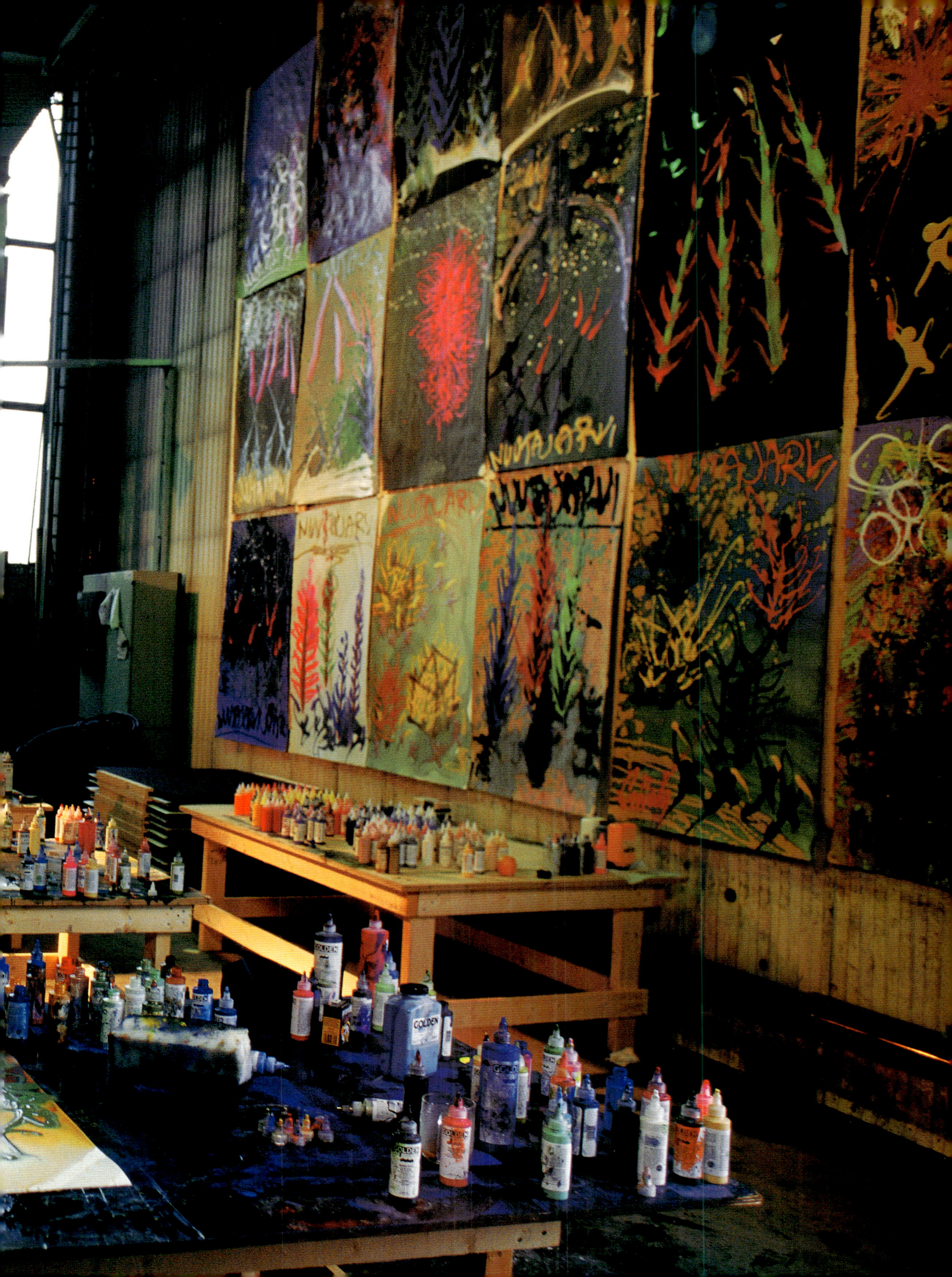

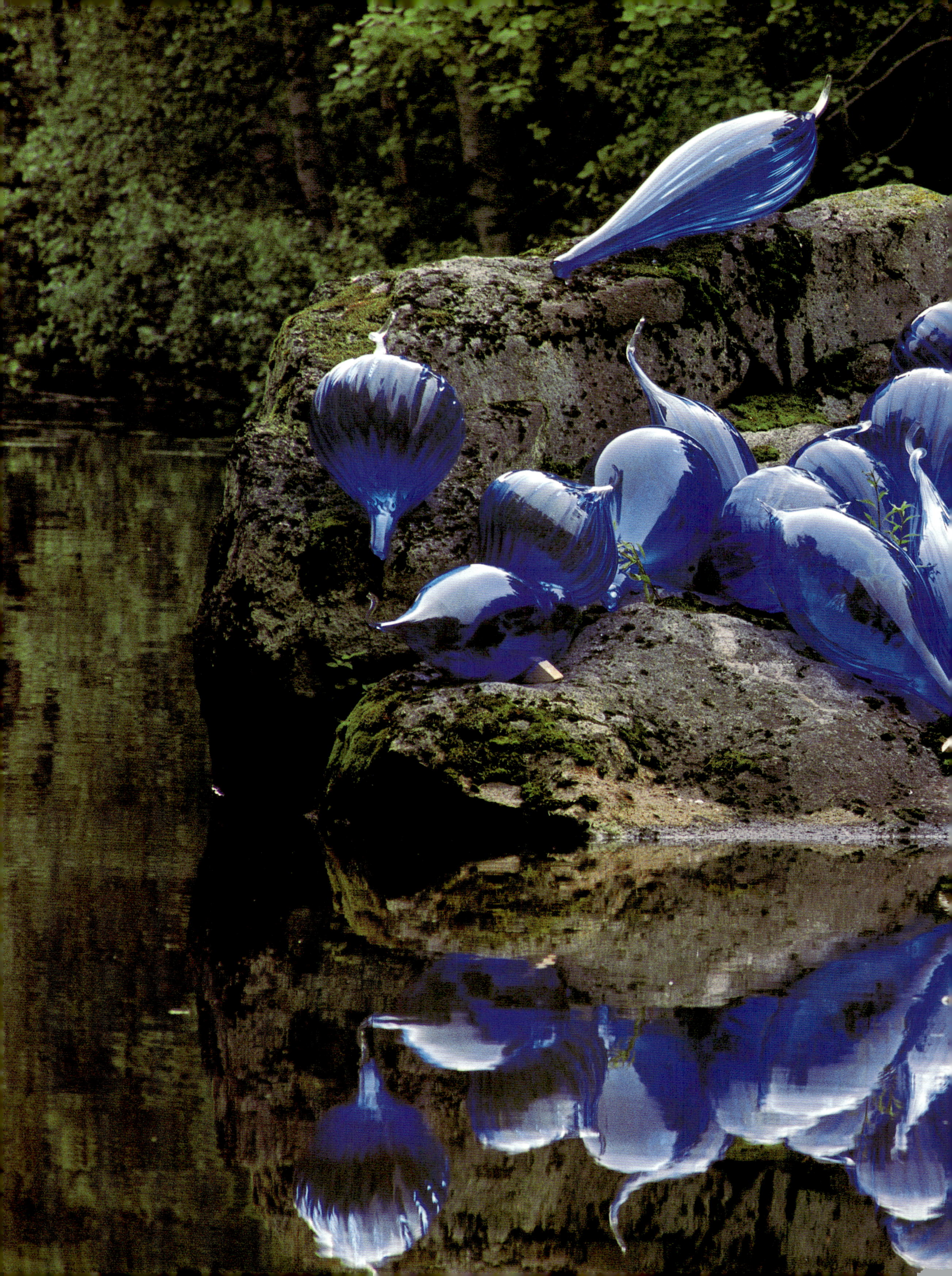

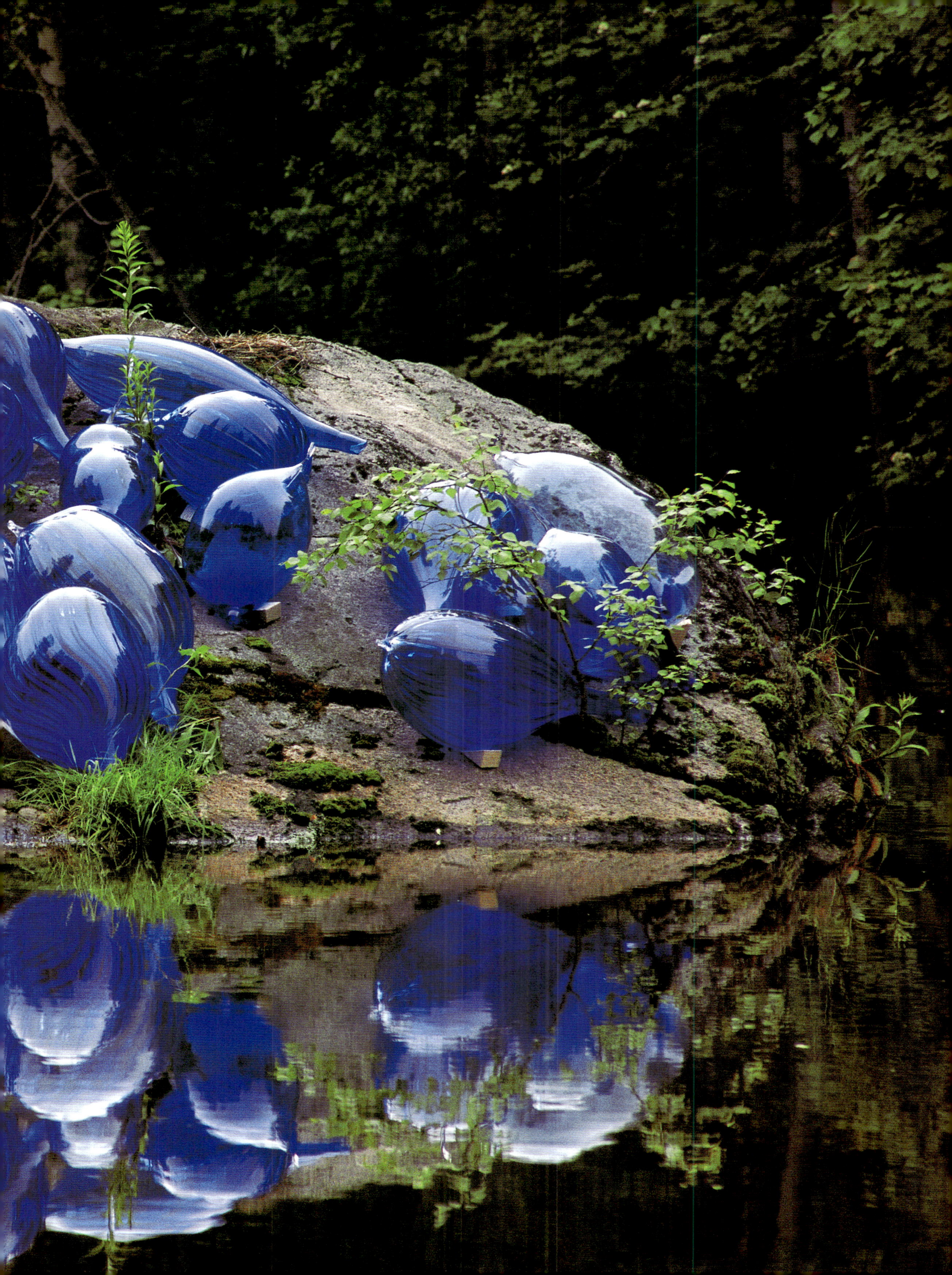

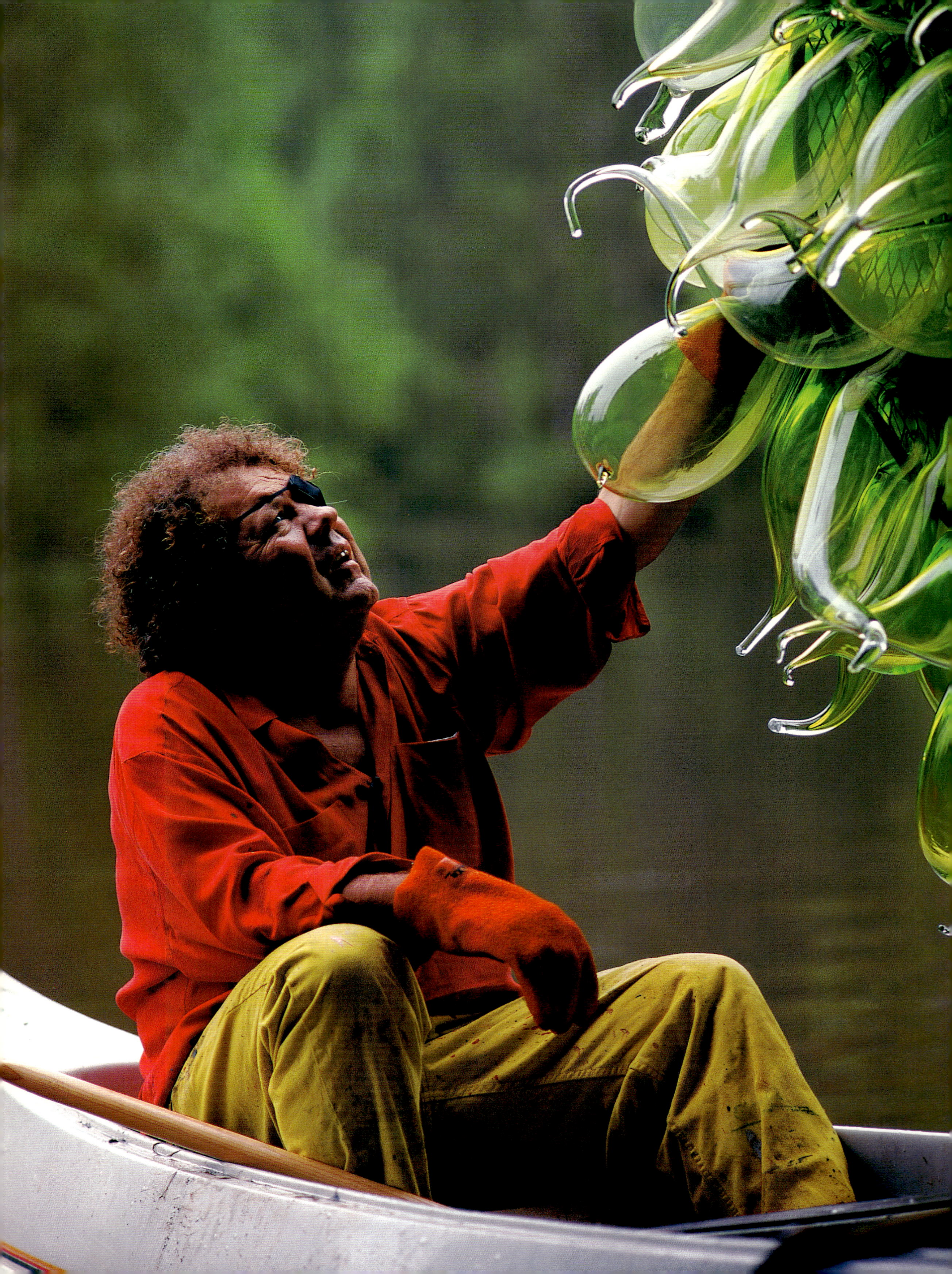

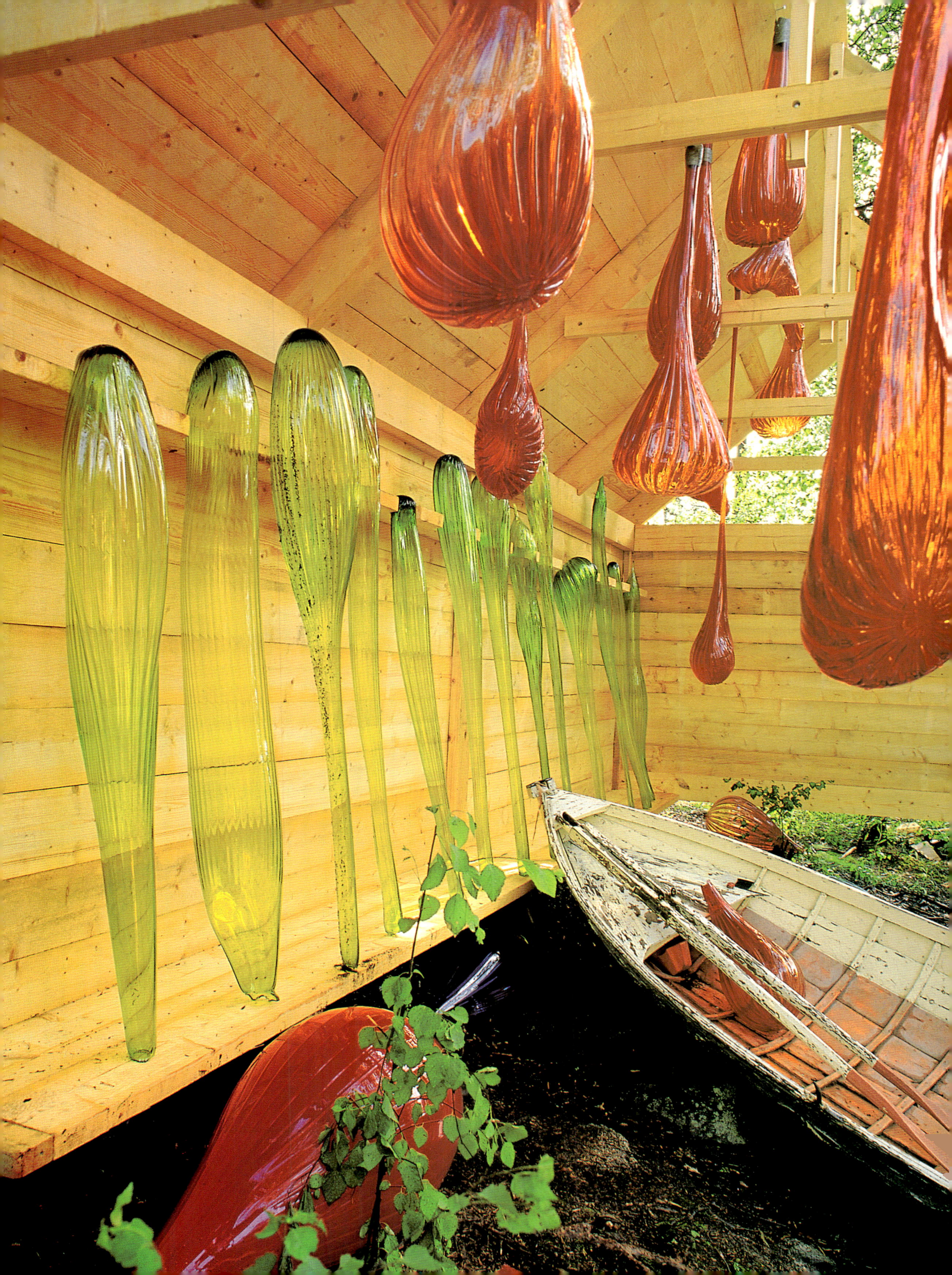

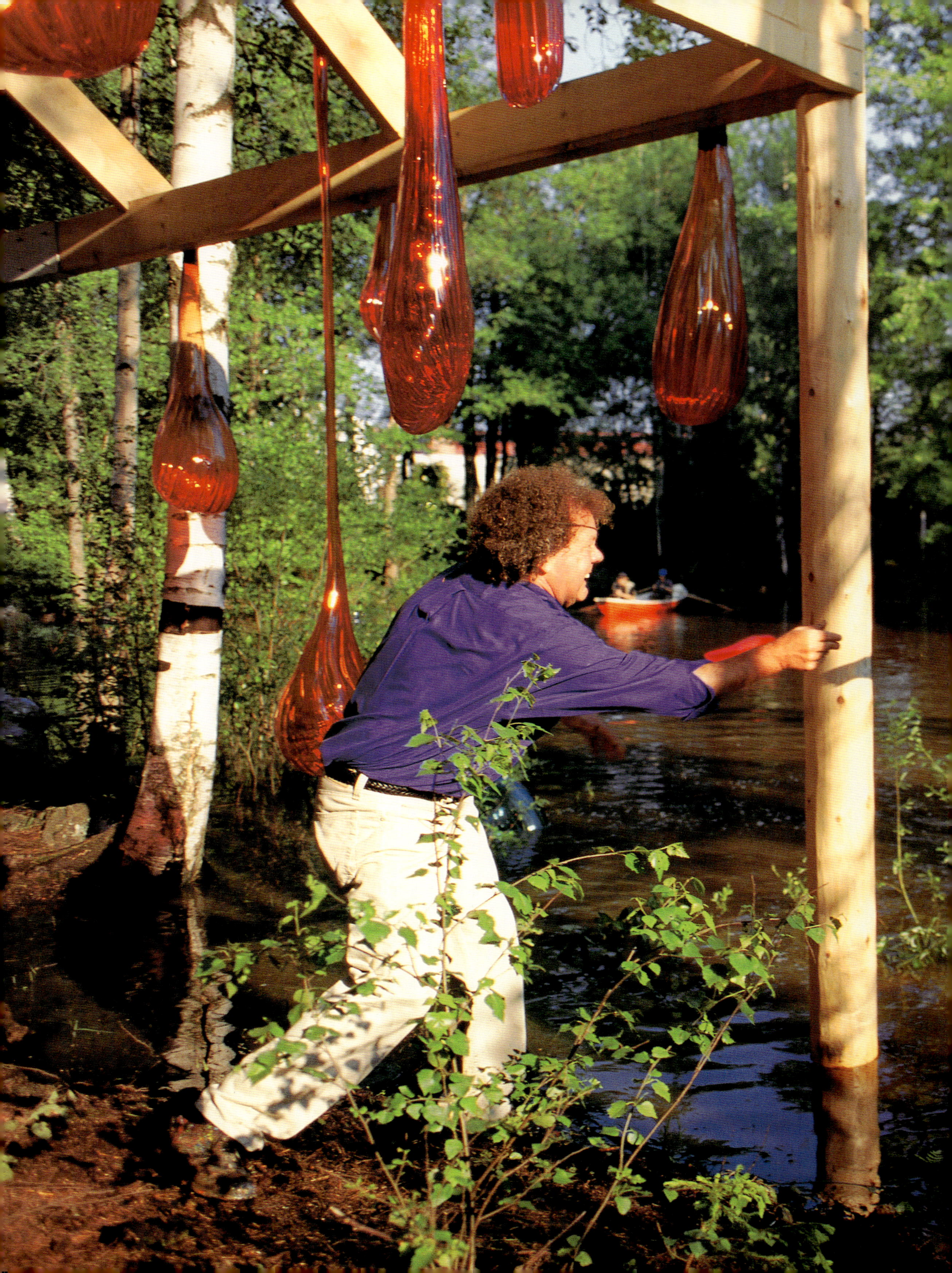

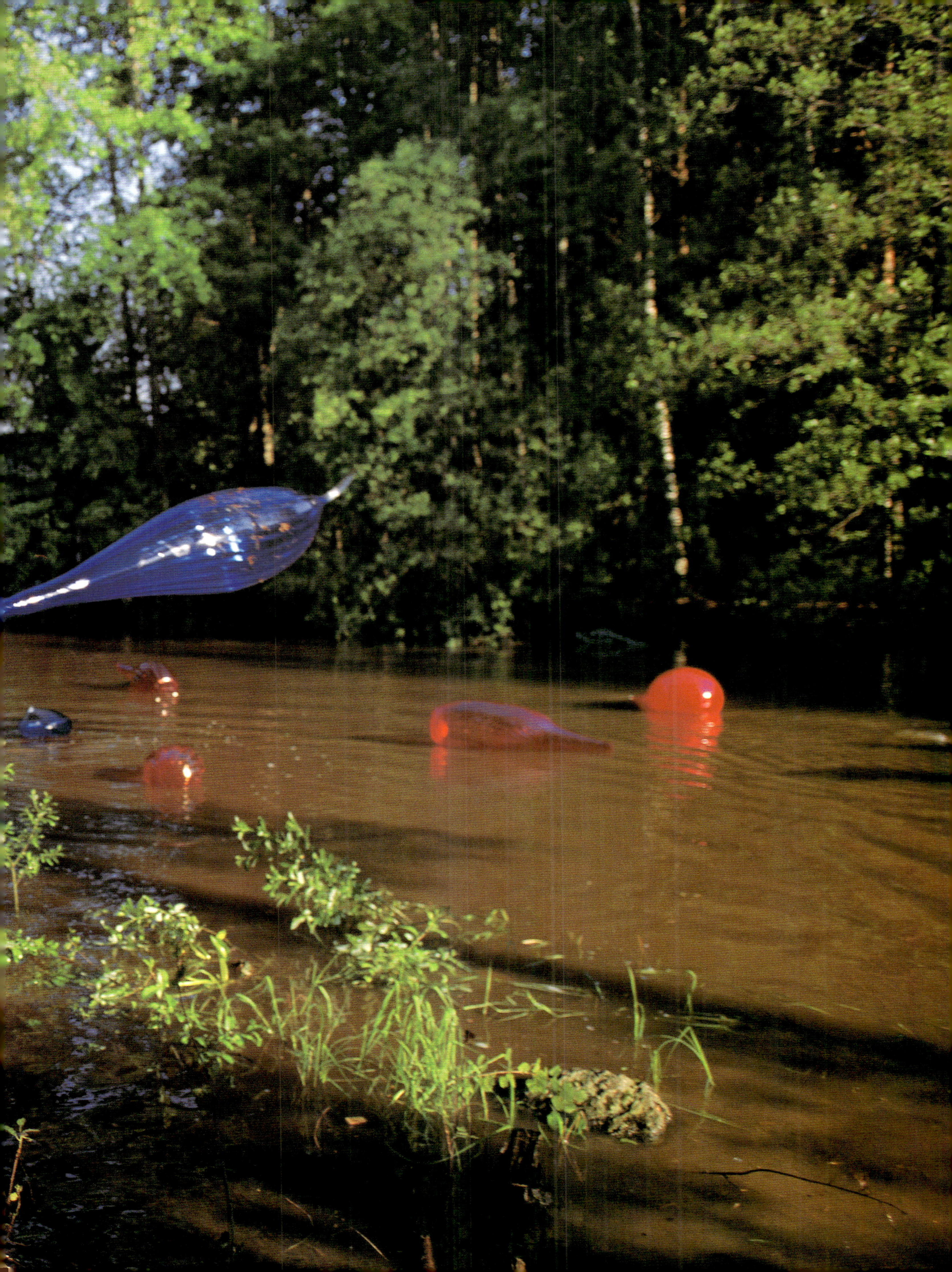

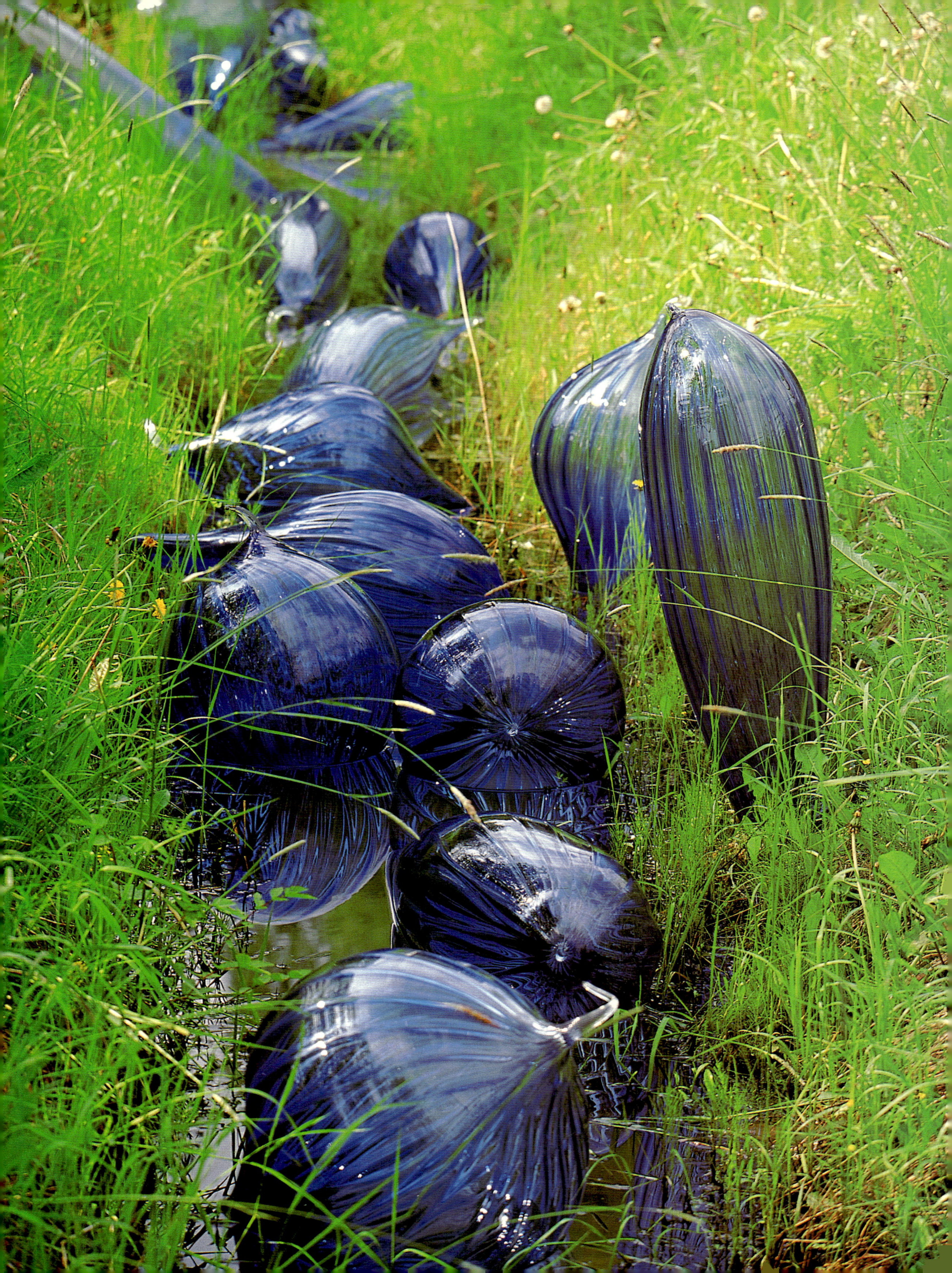

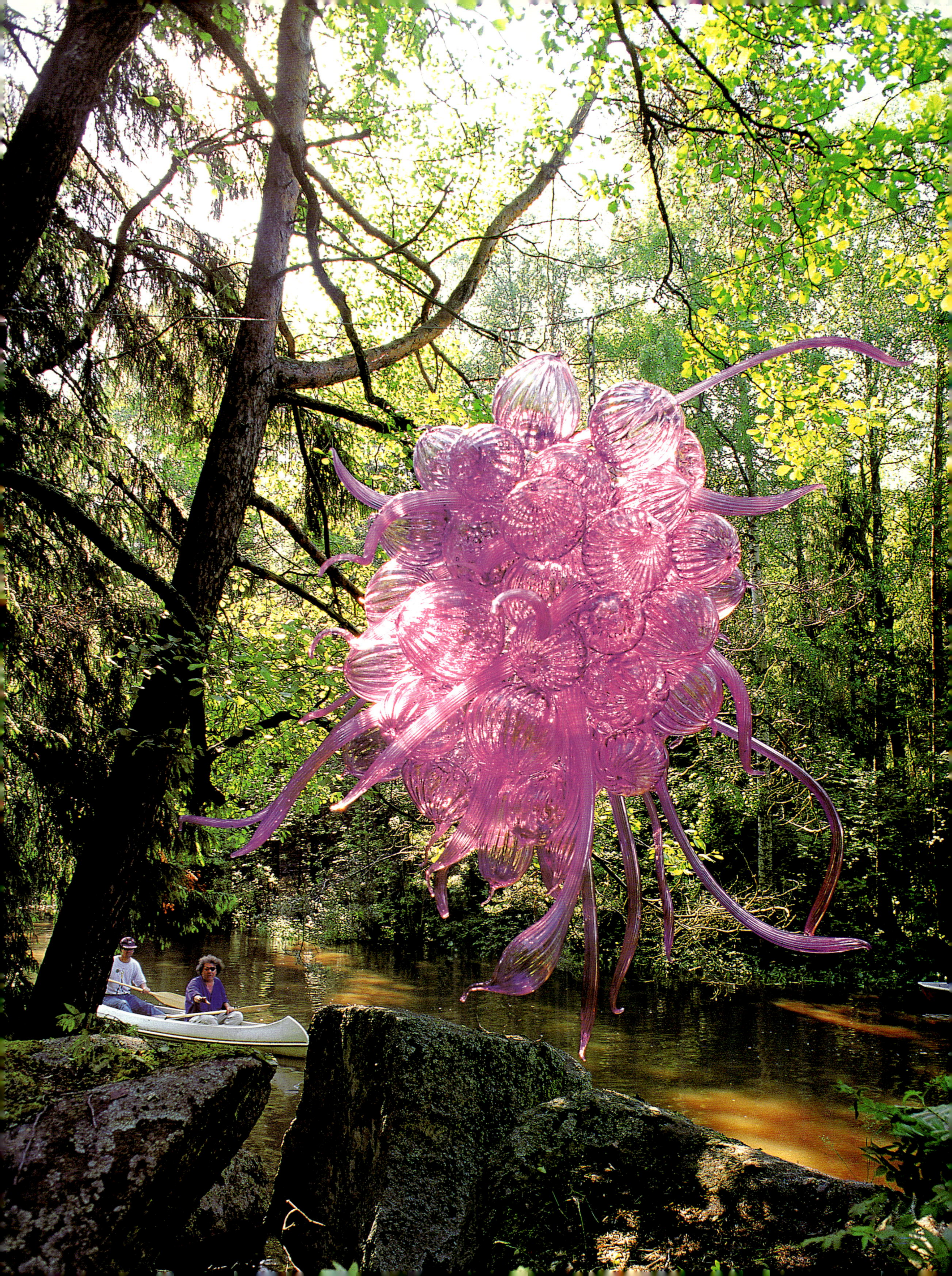

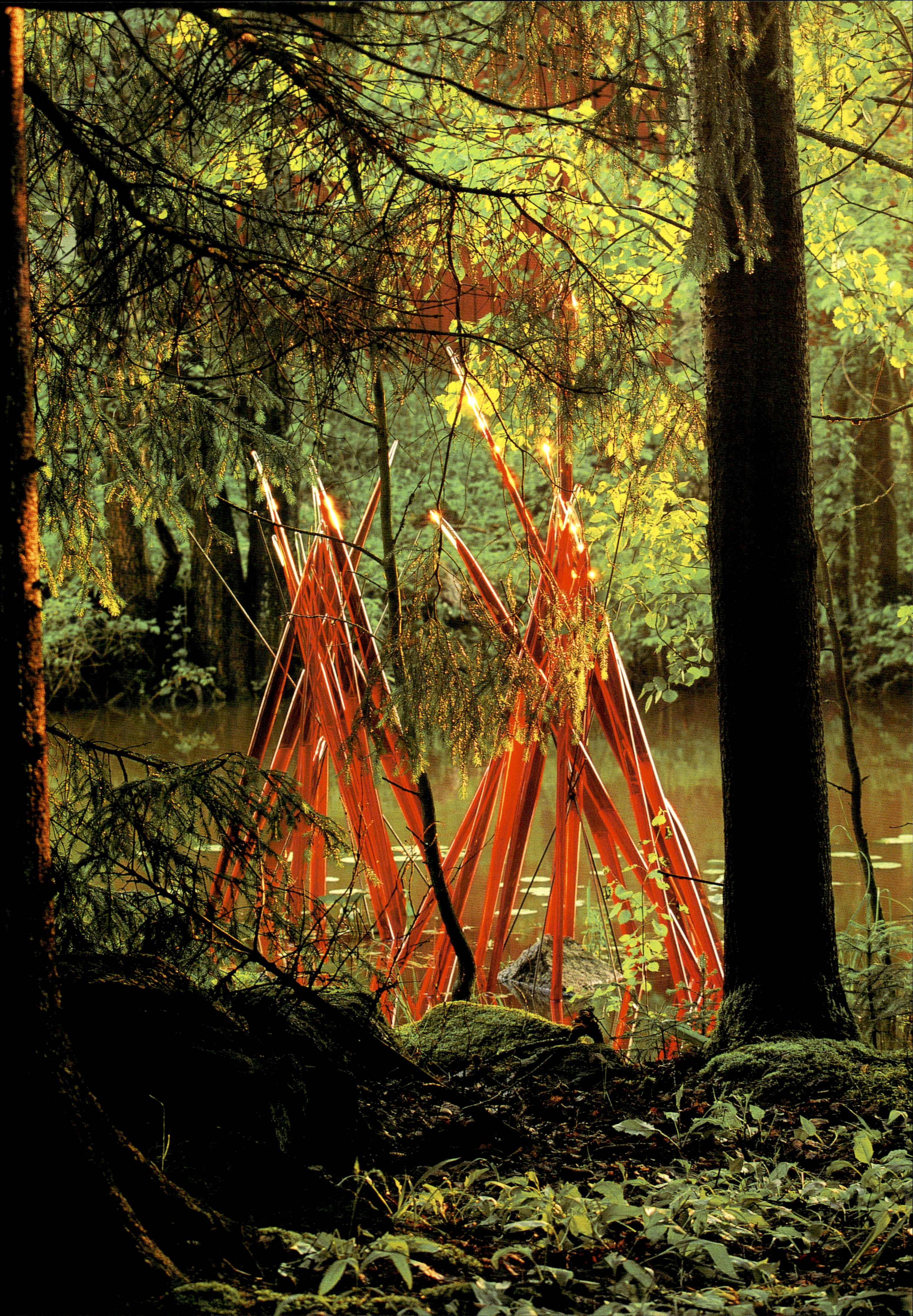

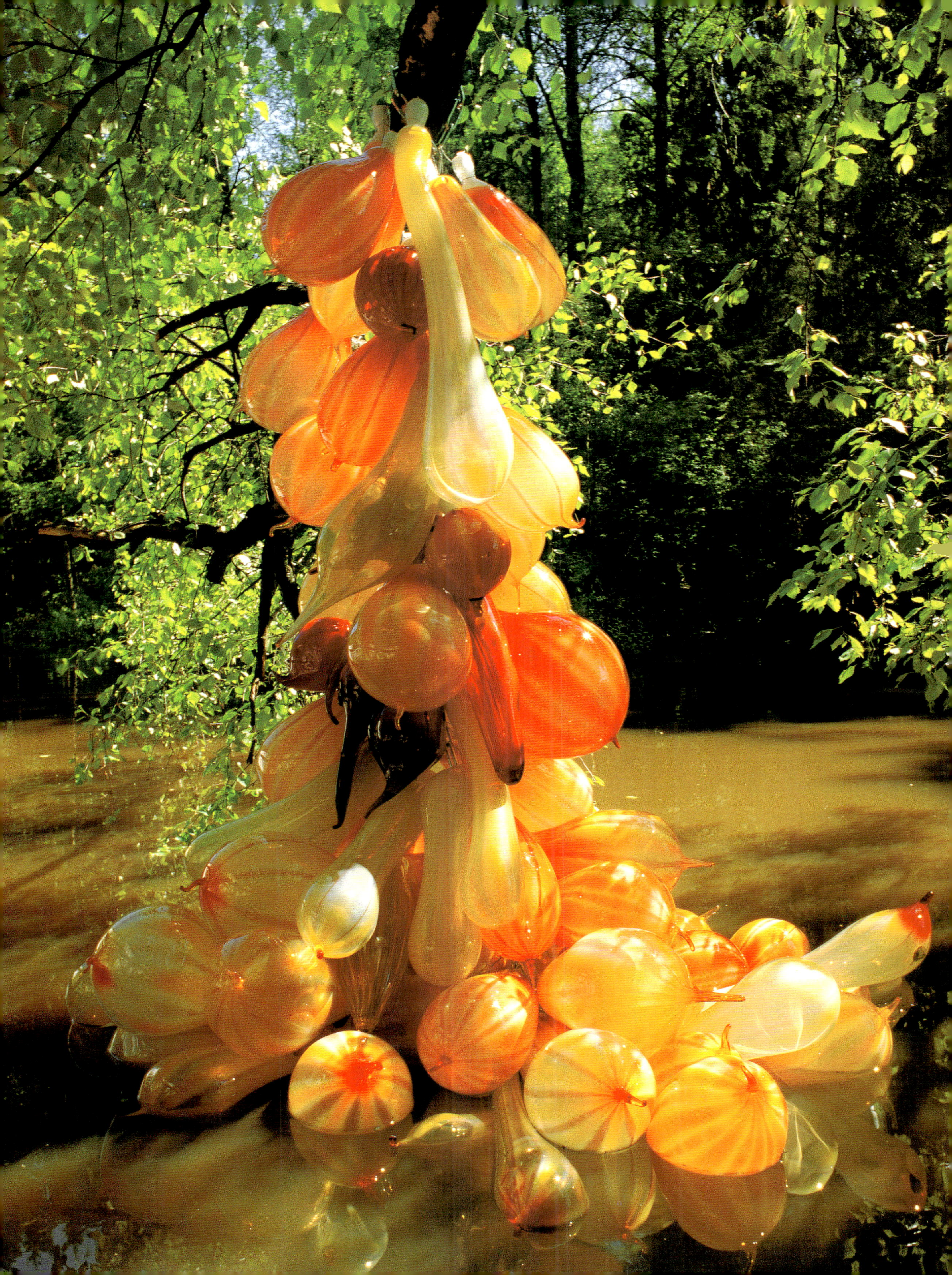

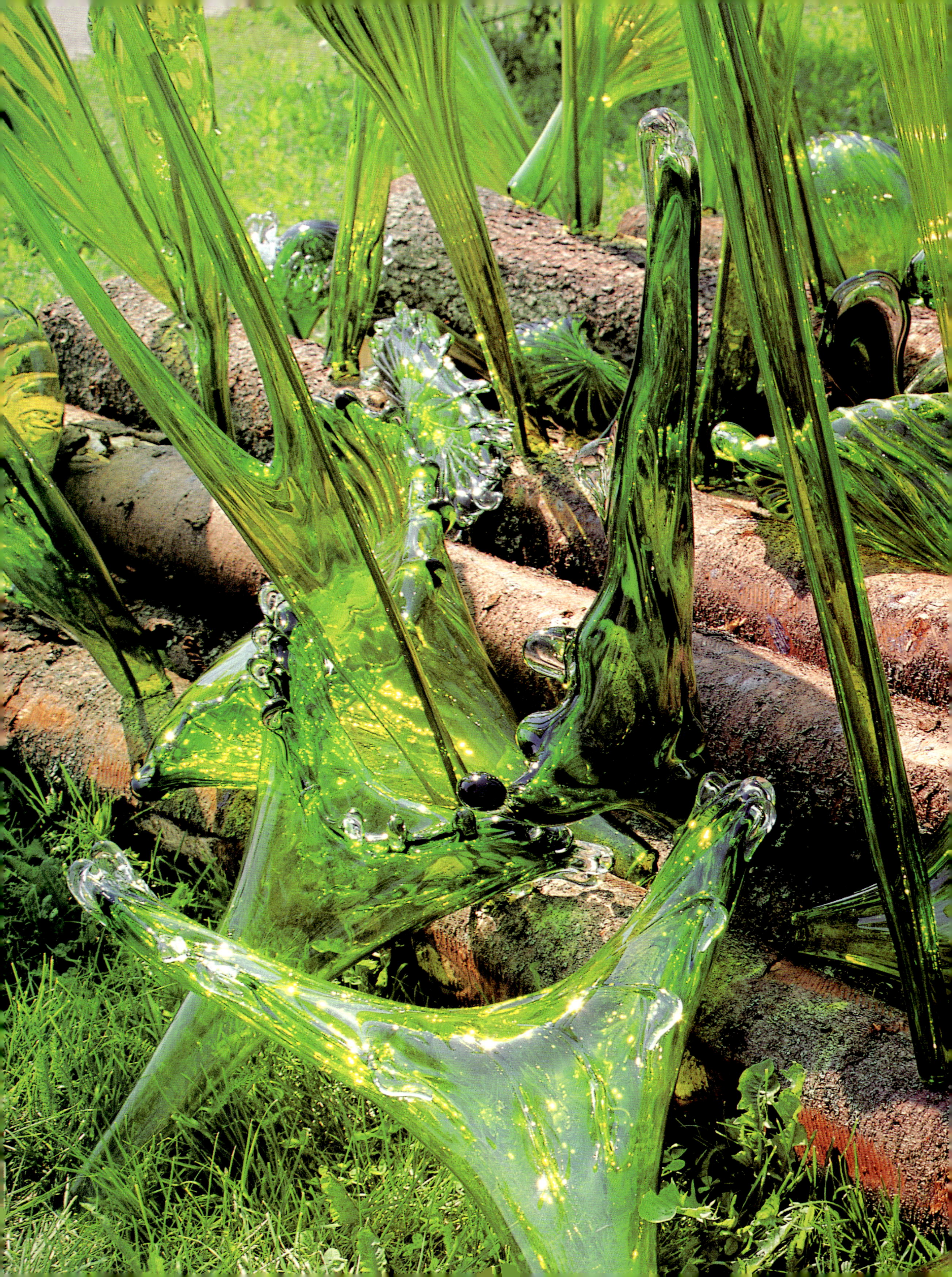

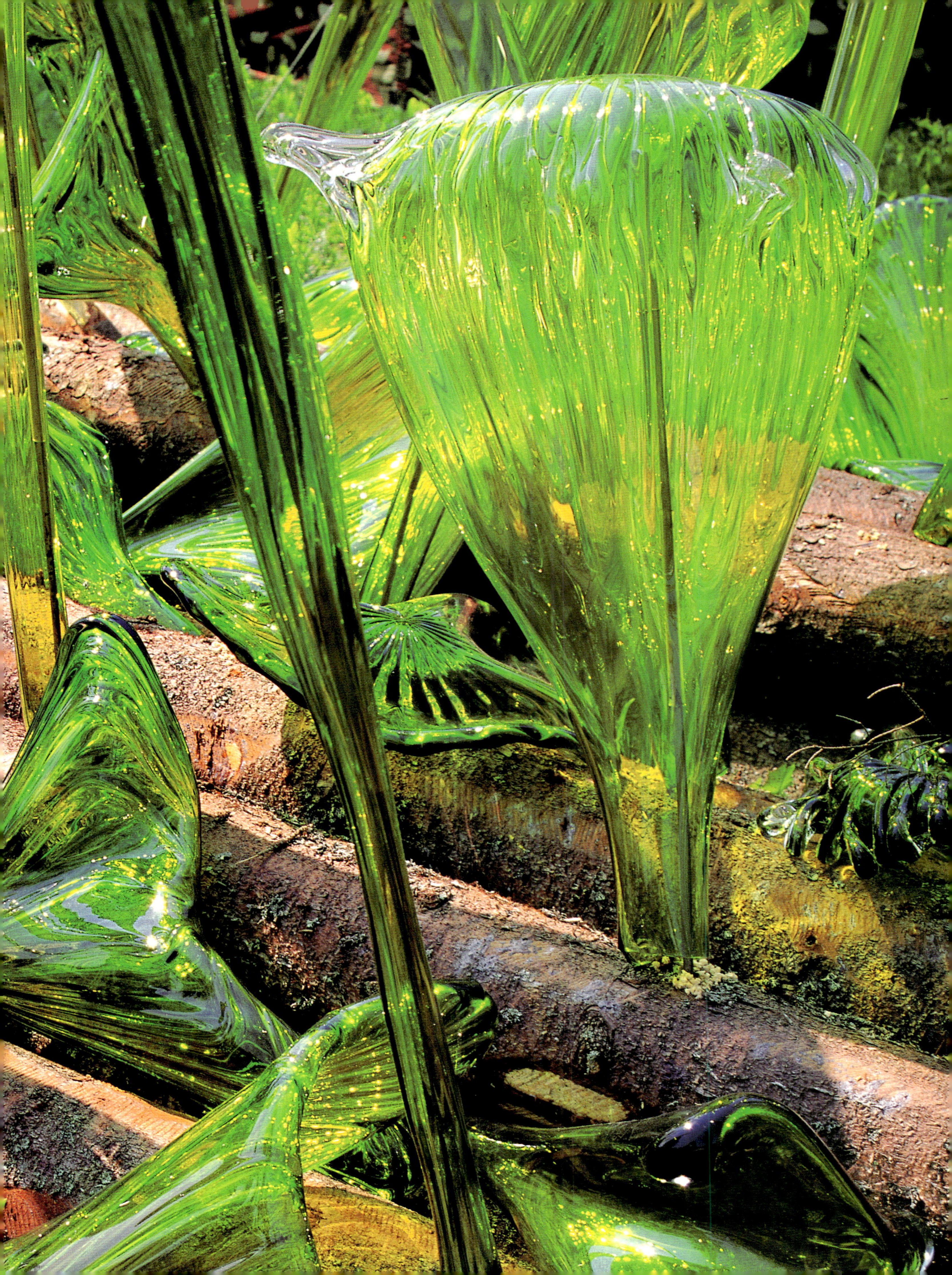

29

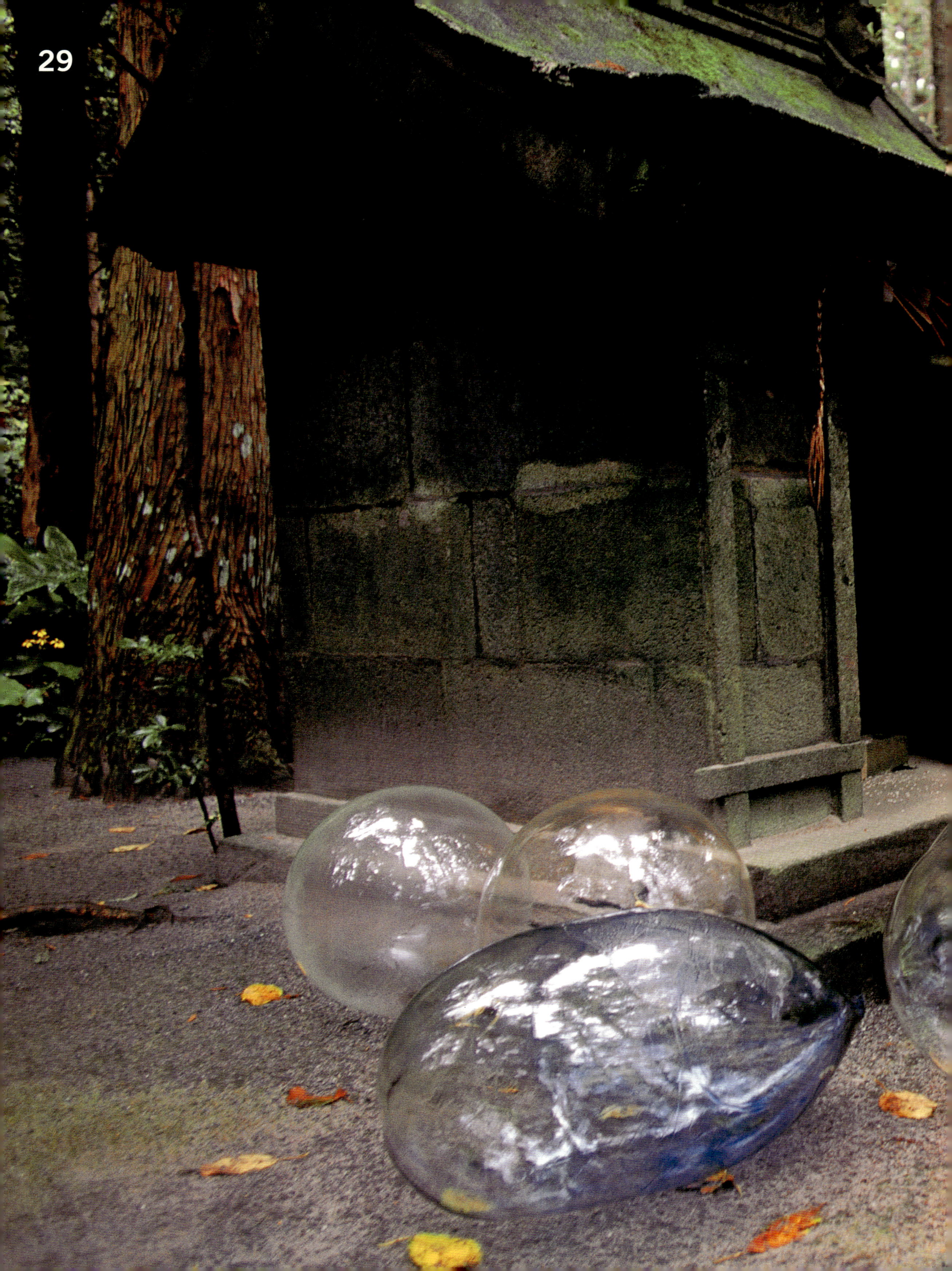

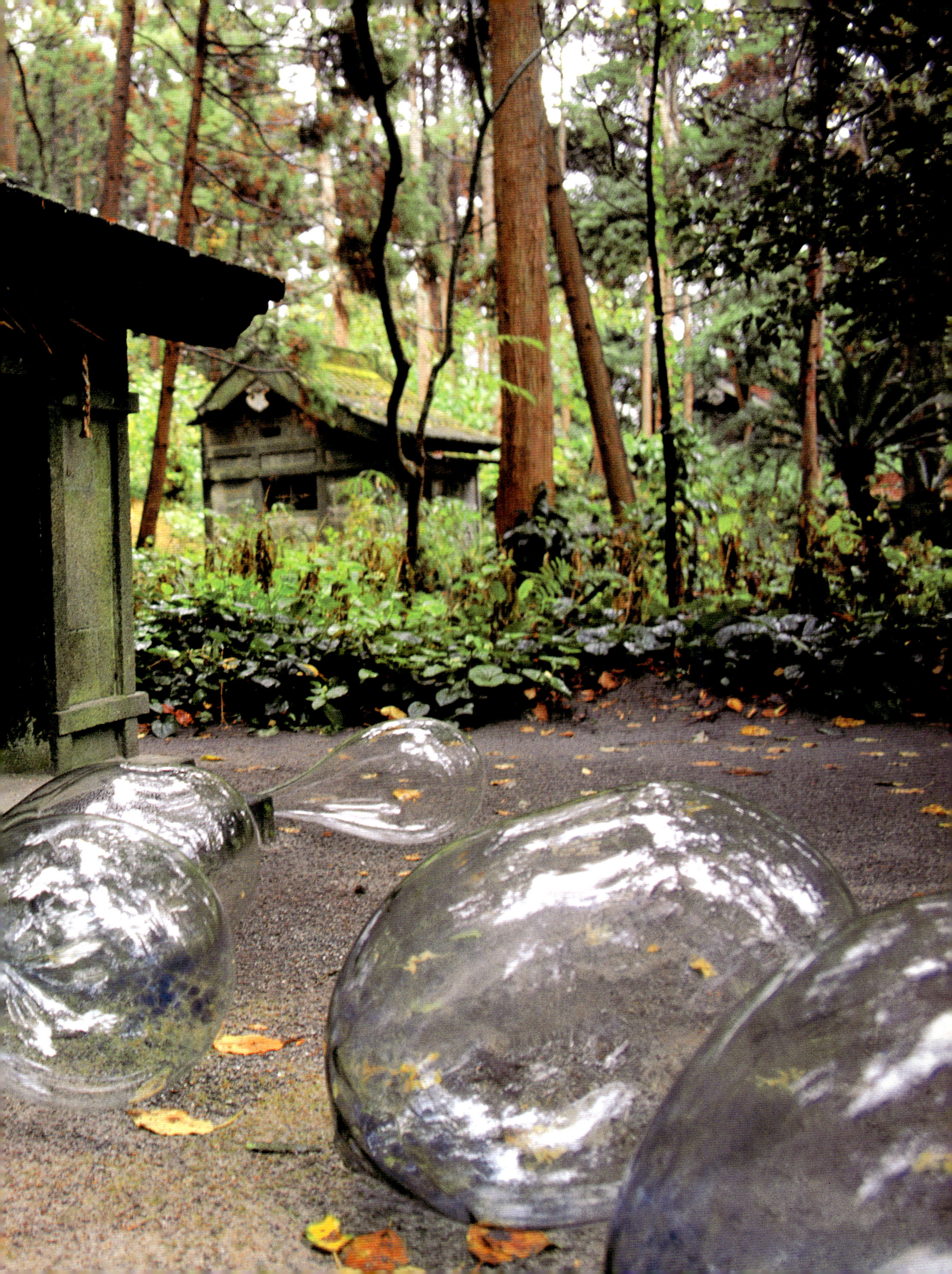

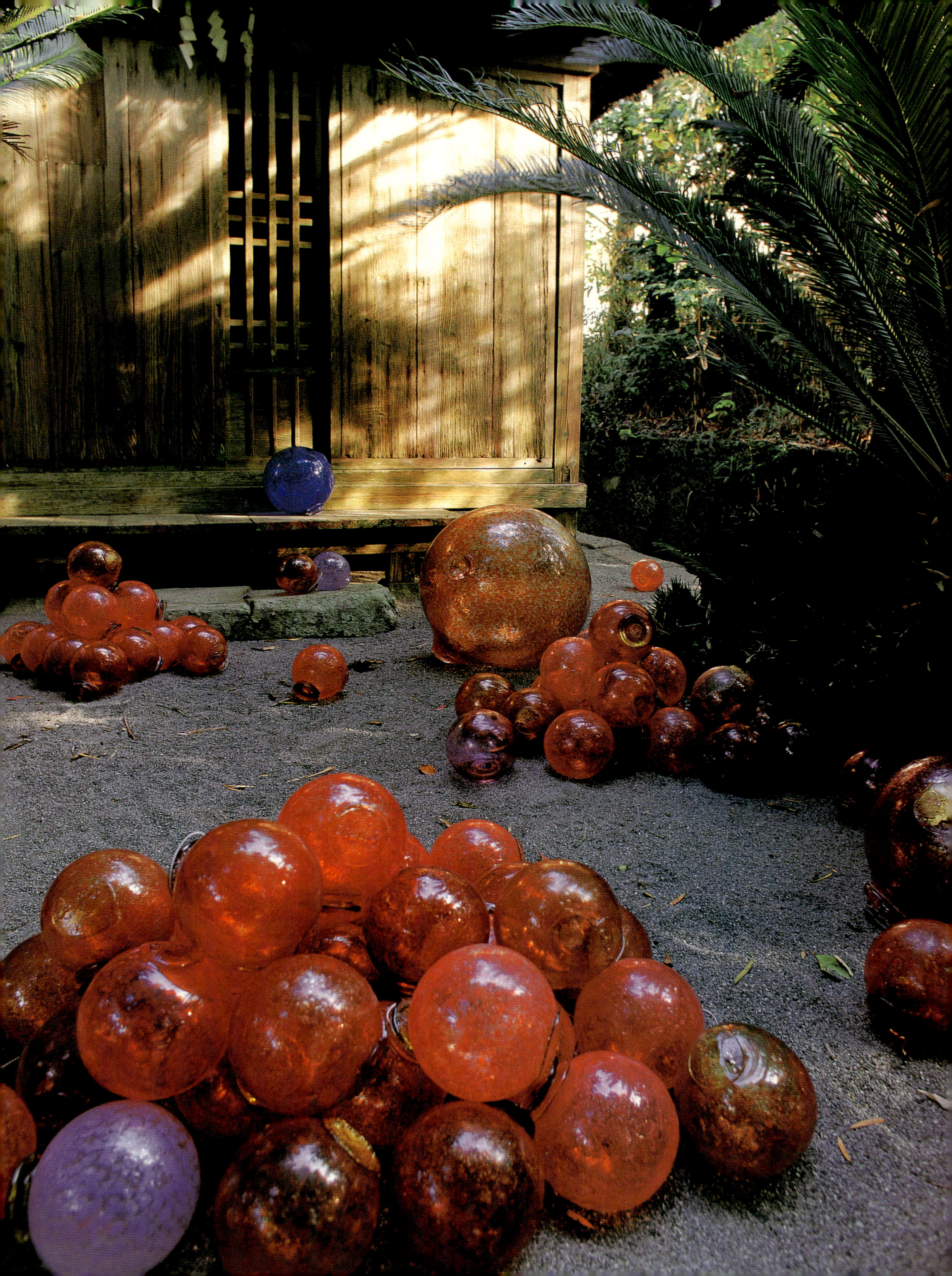

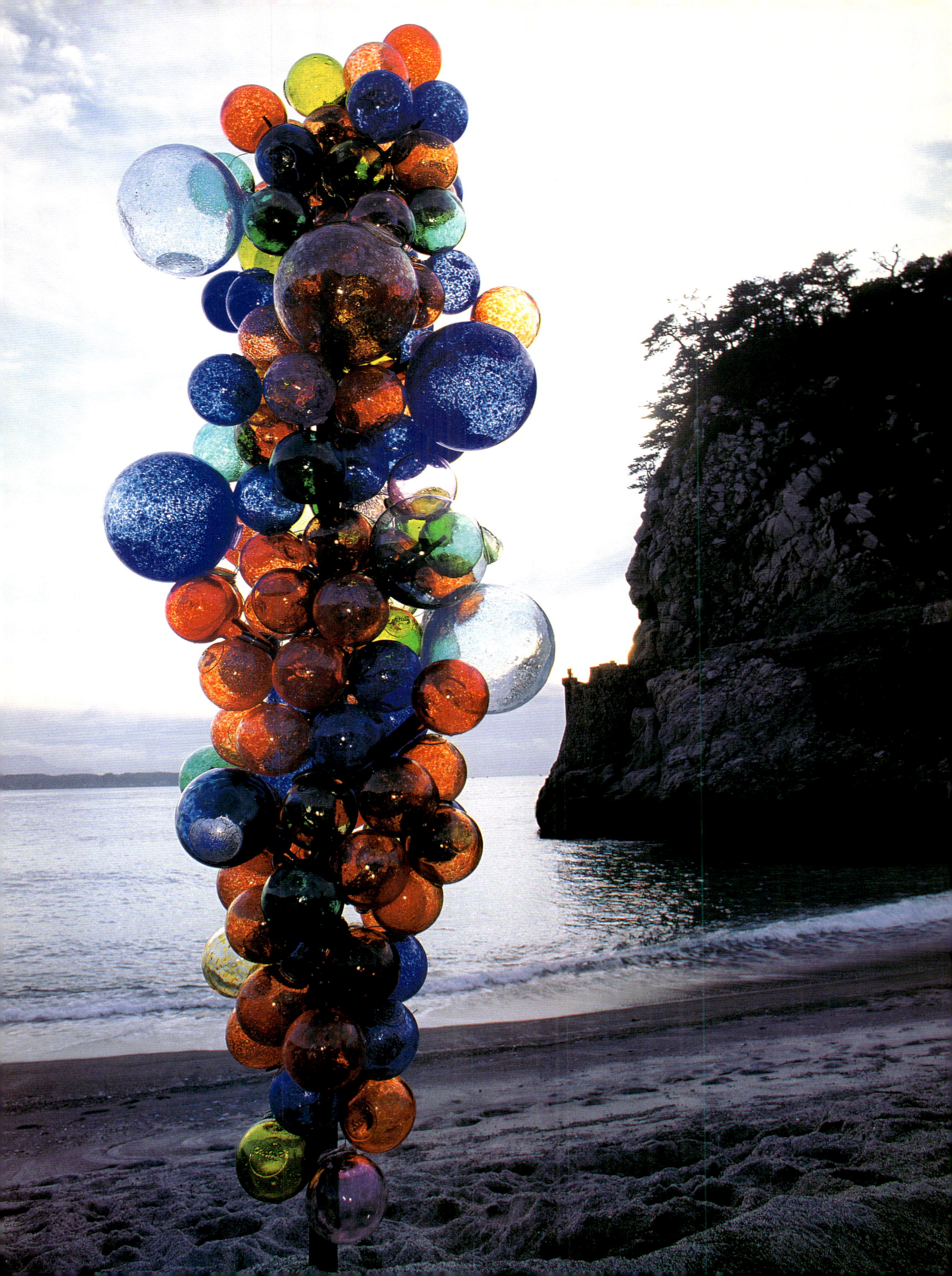

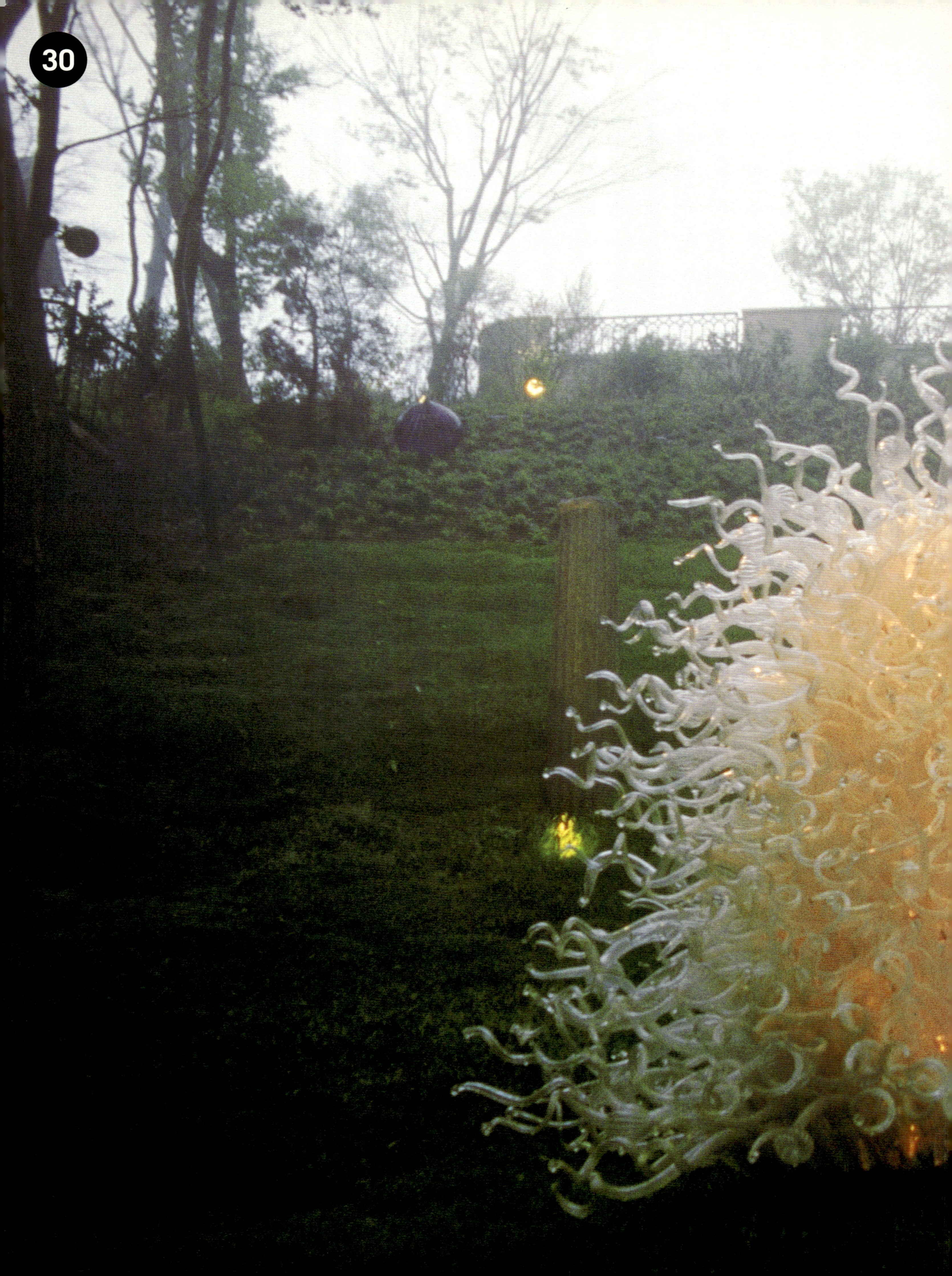

30

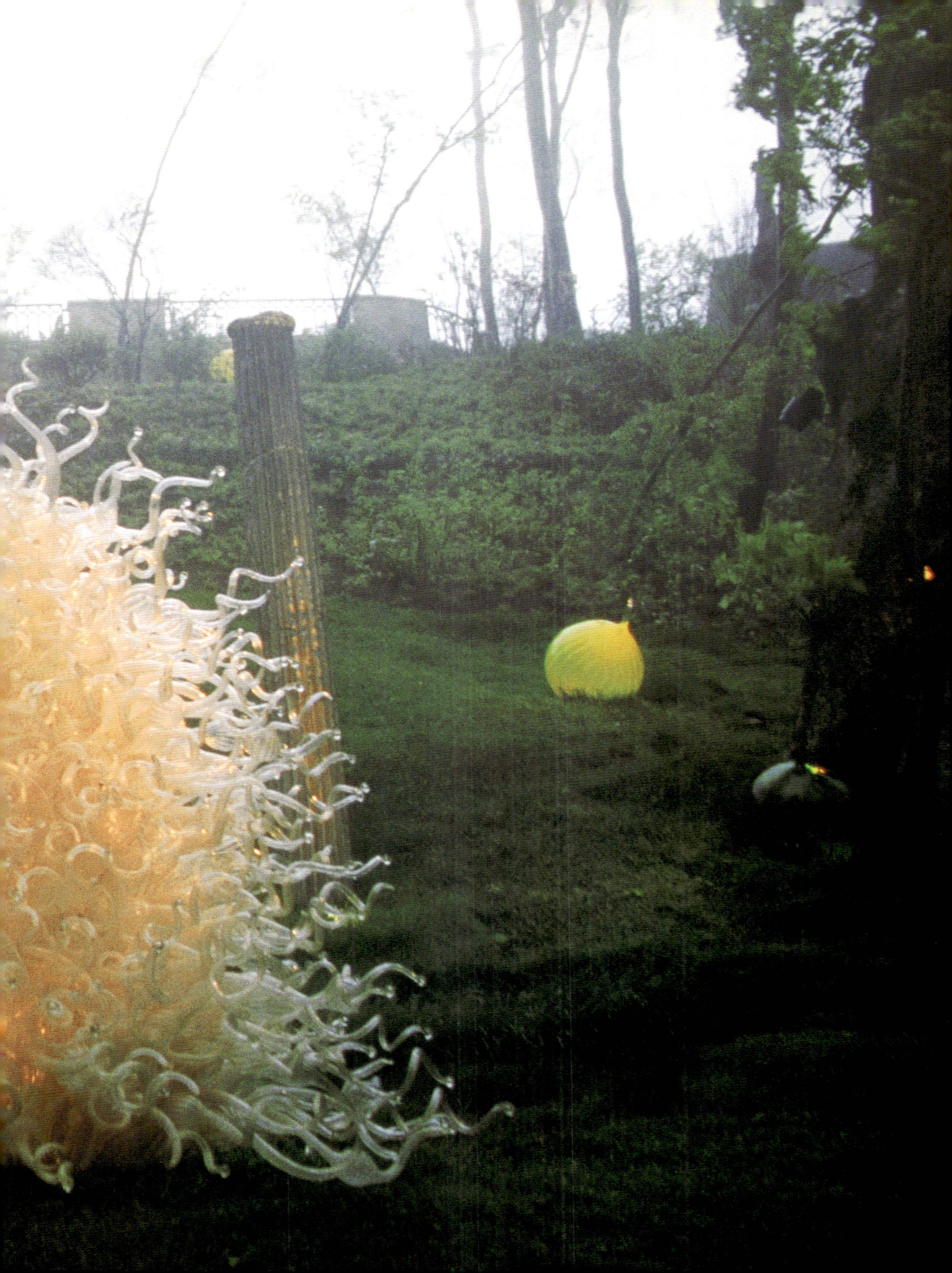

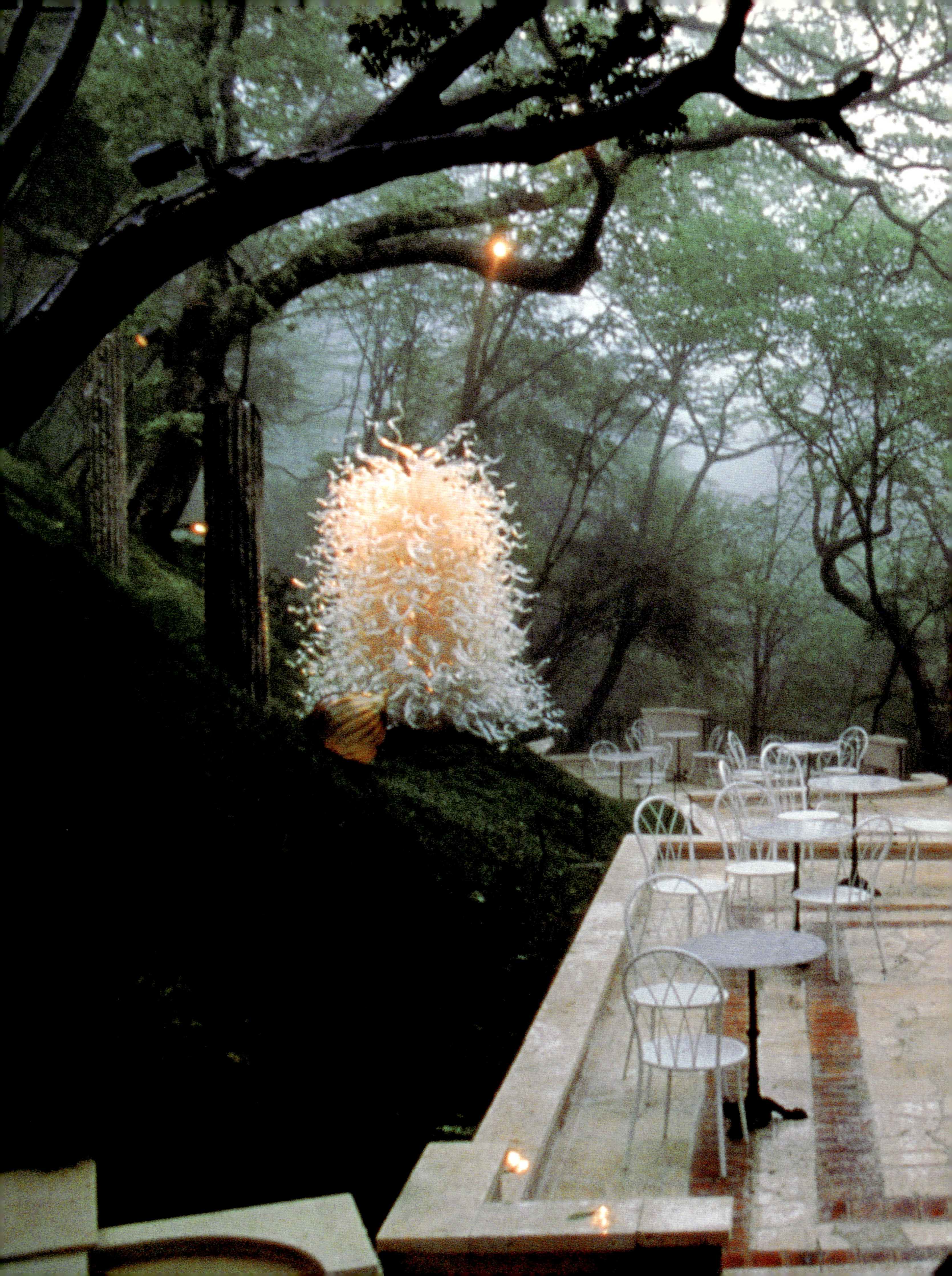

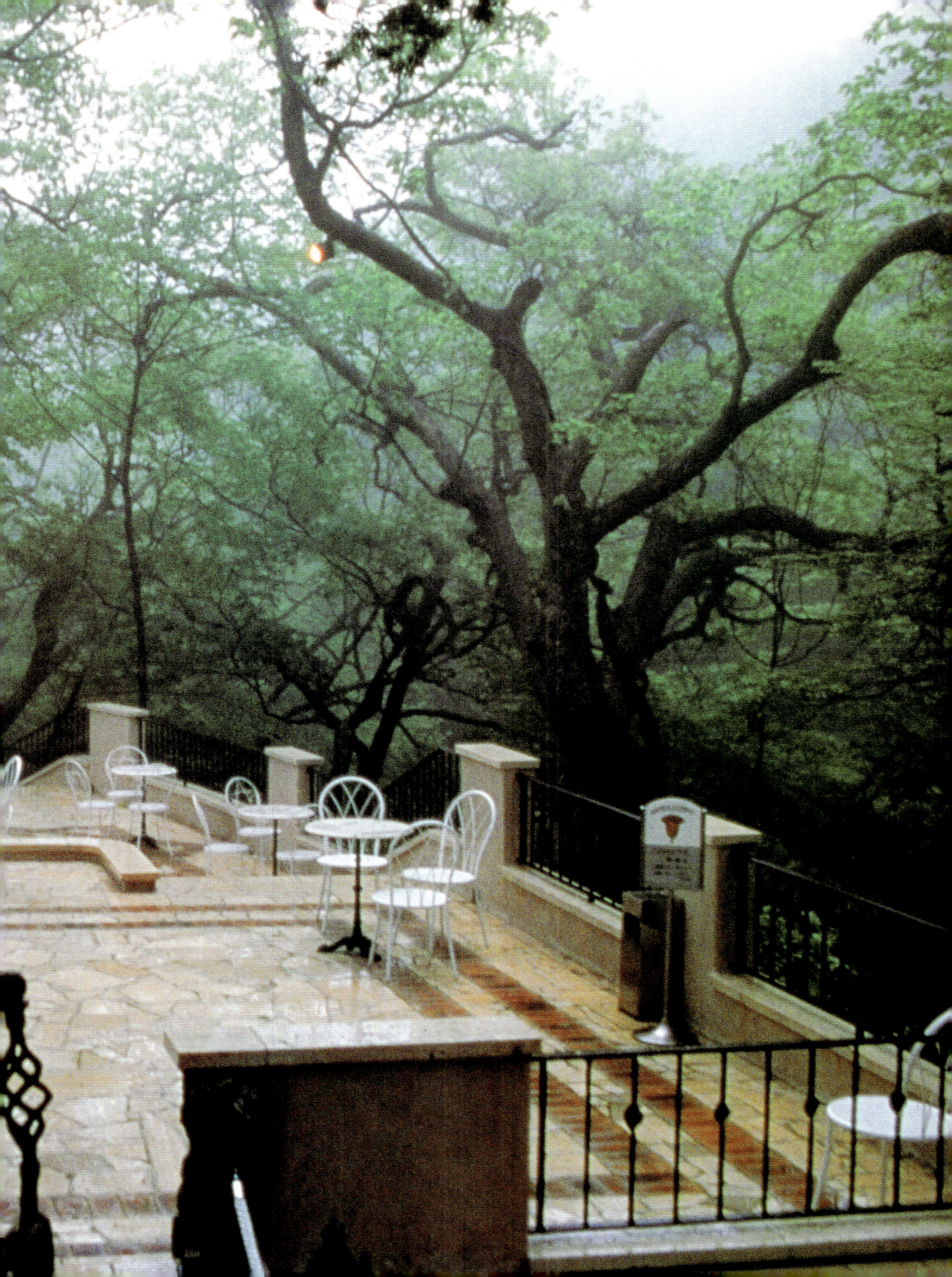

31

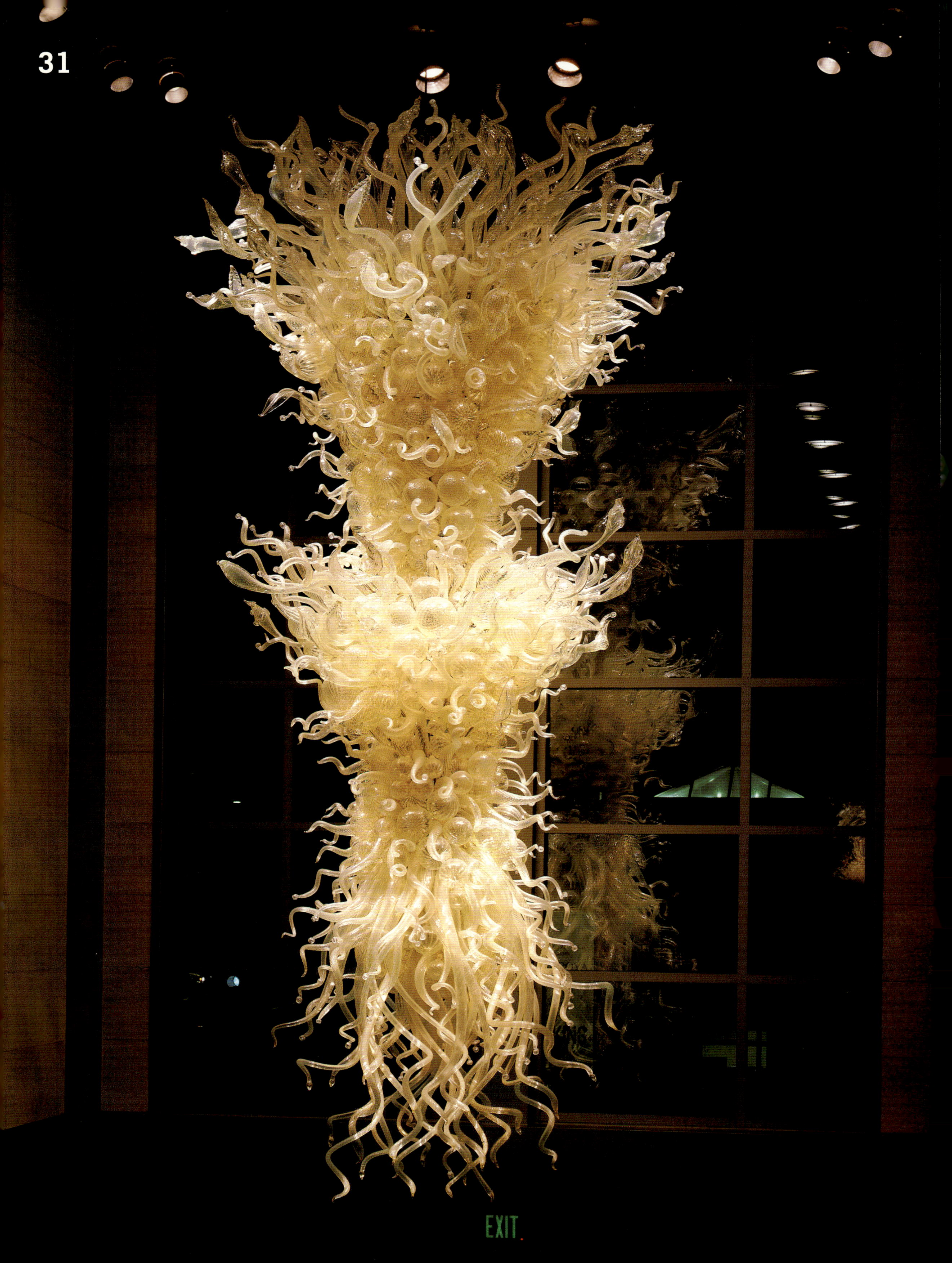

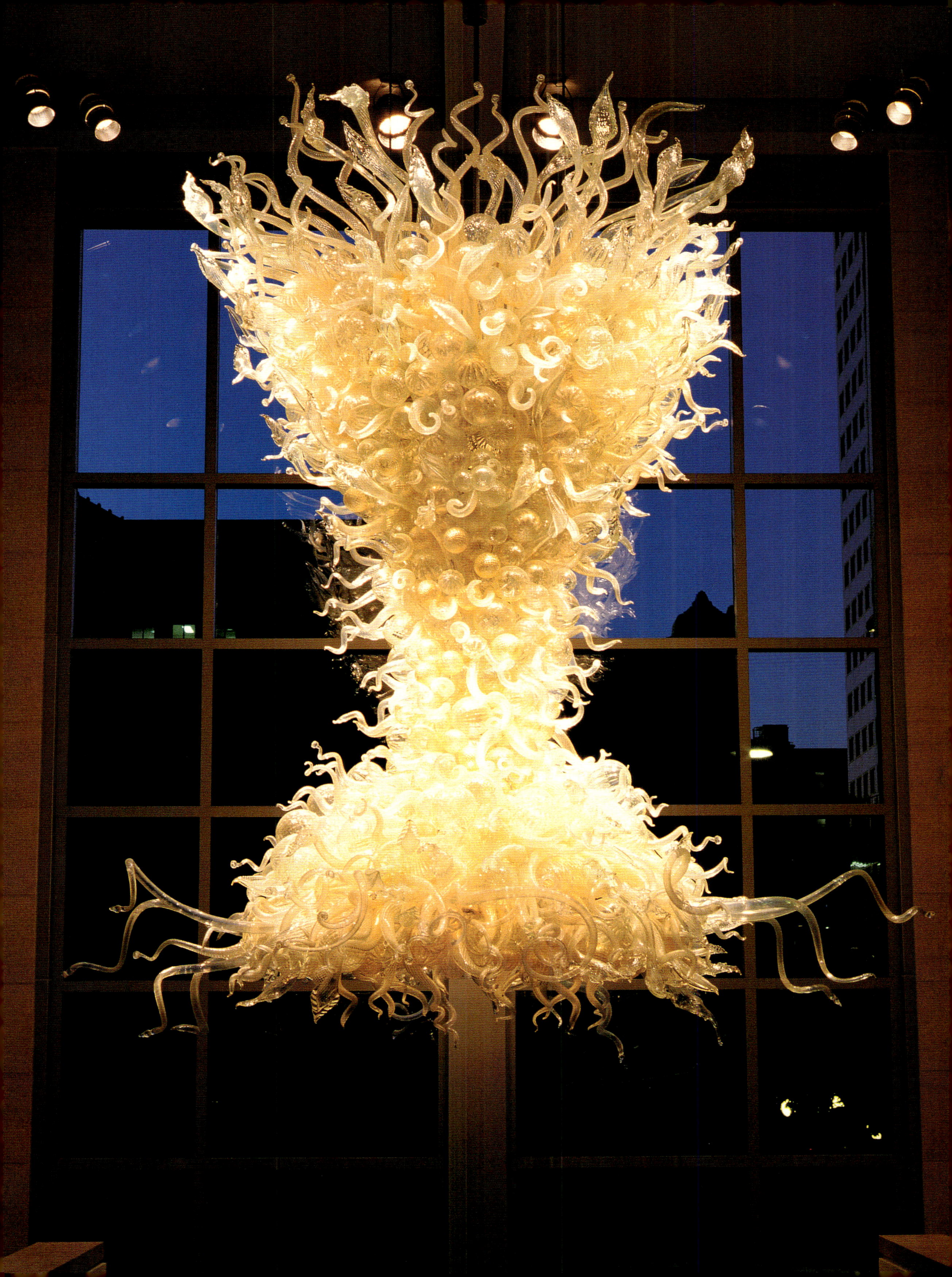

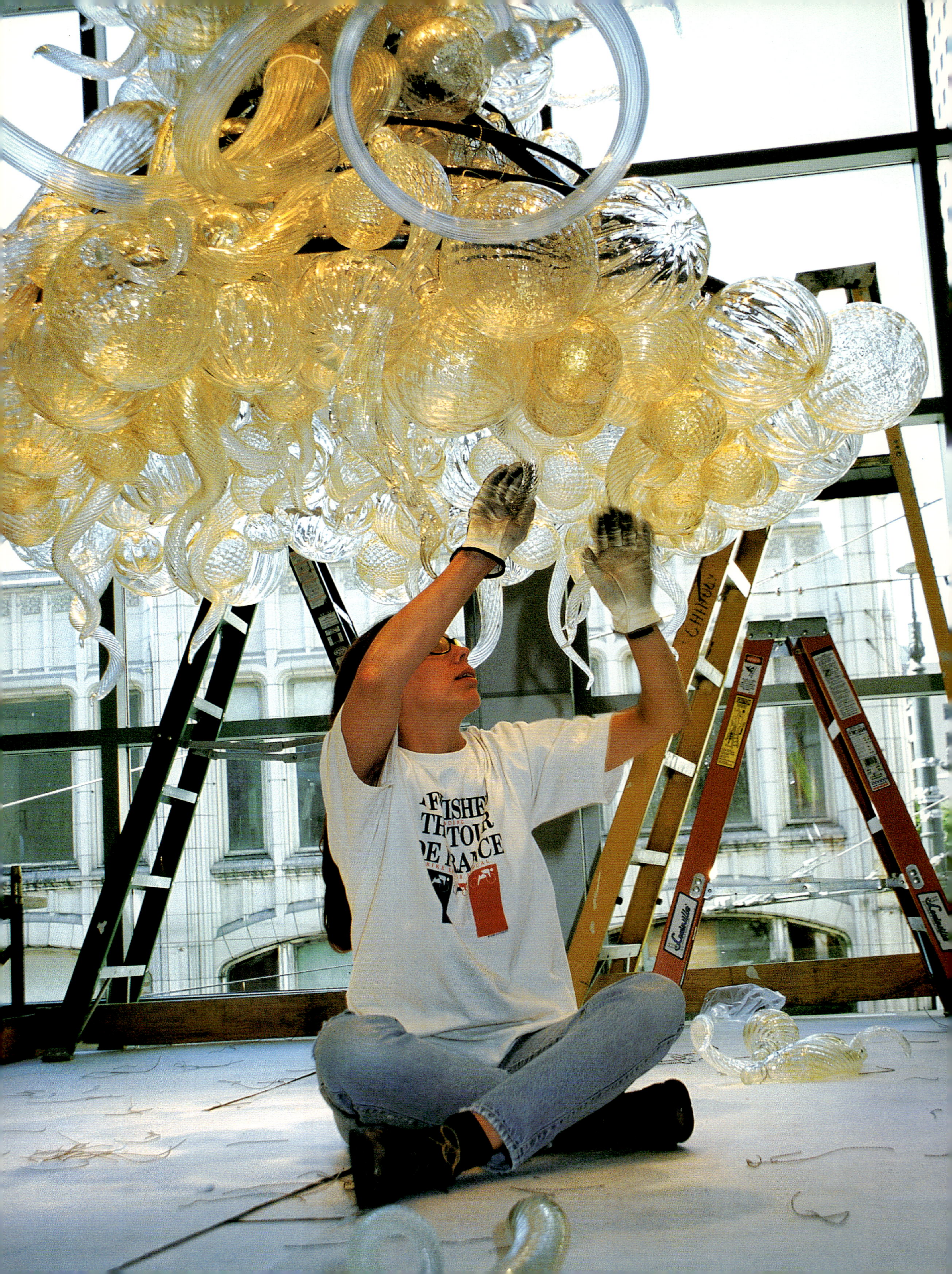

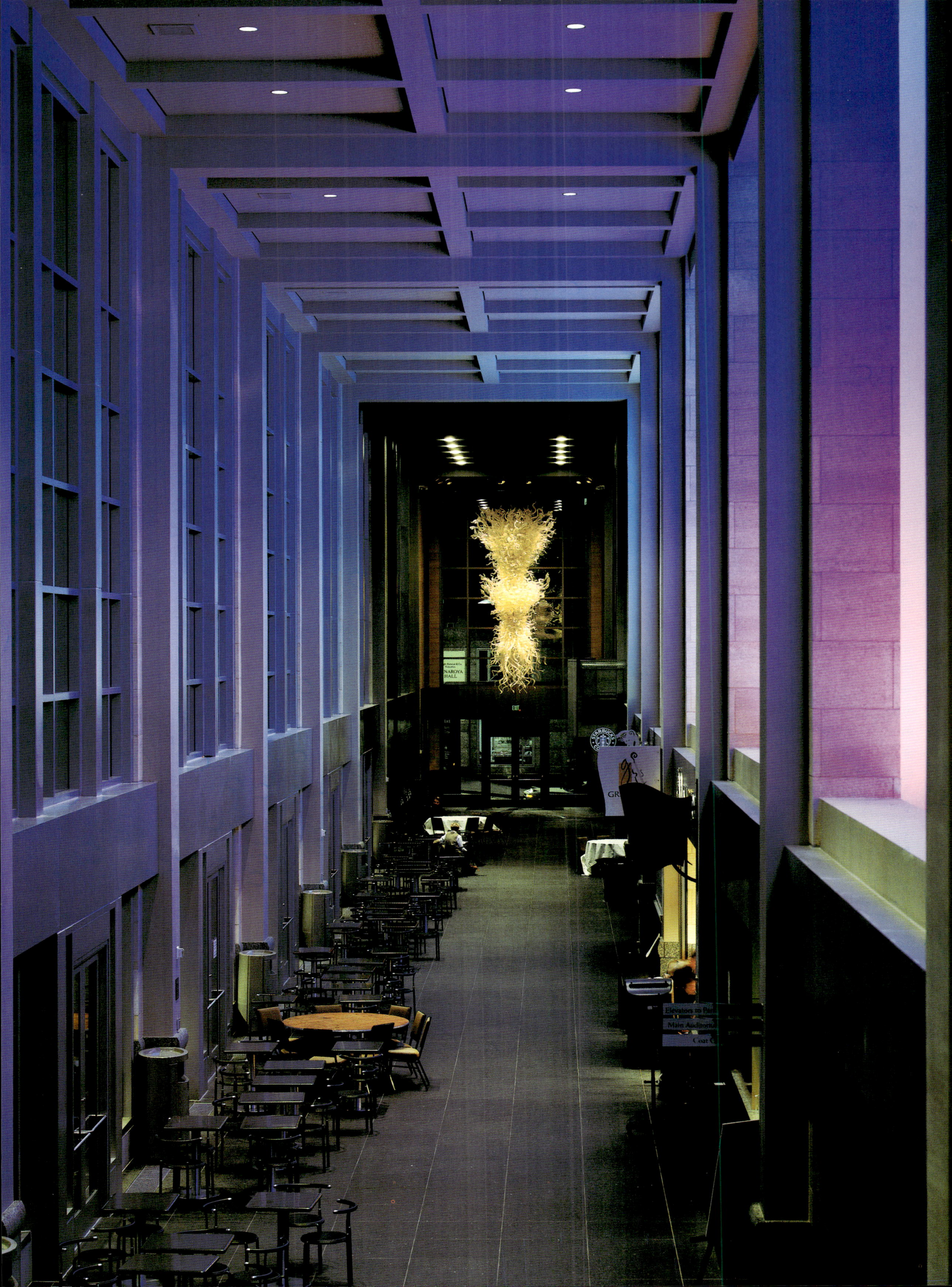

32

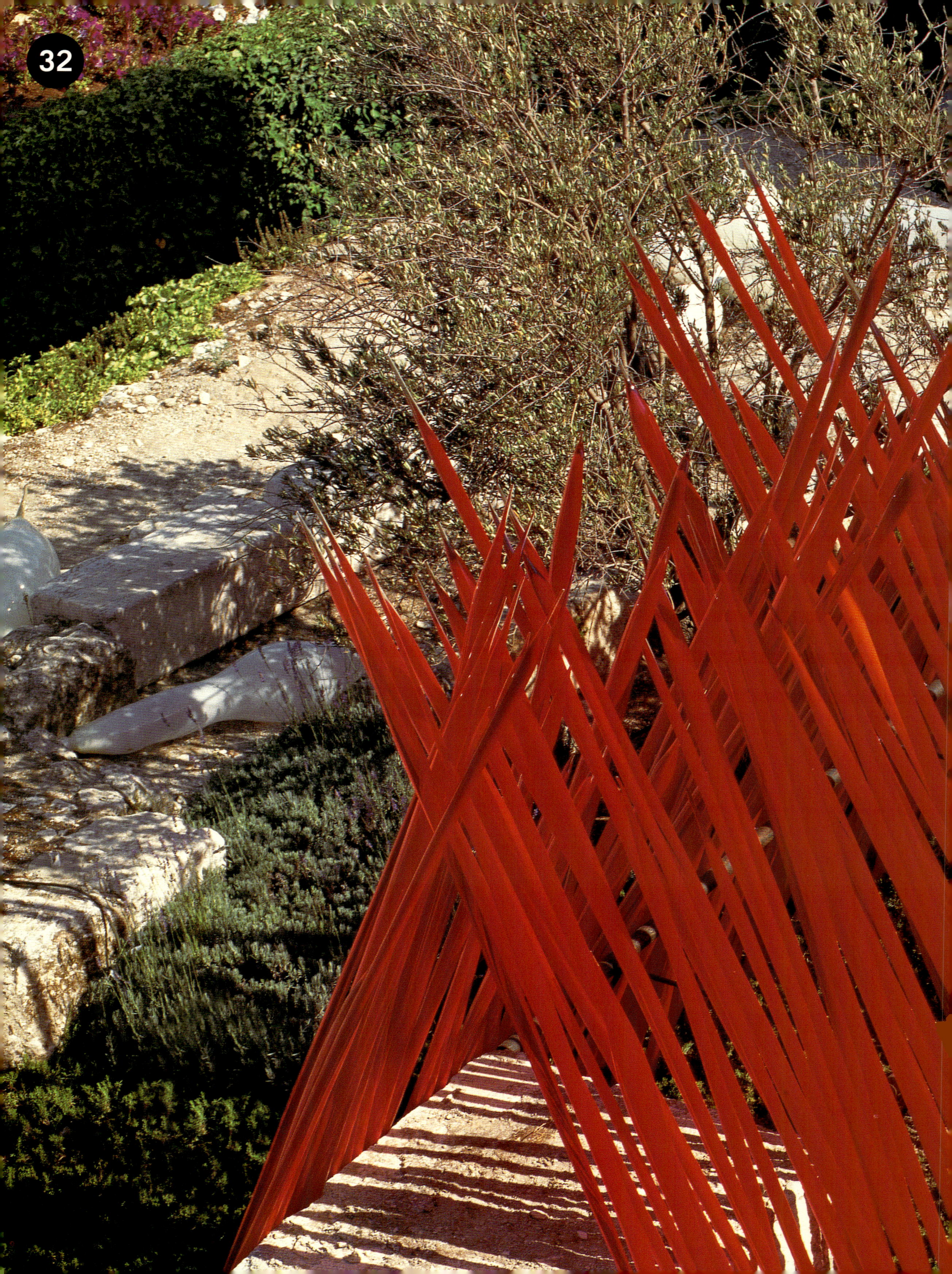

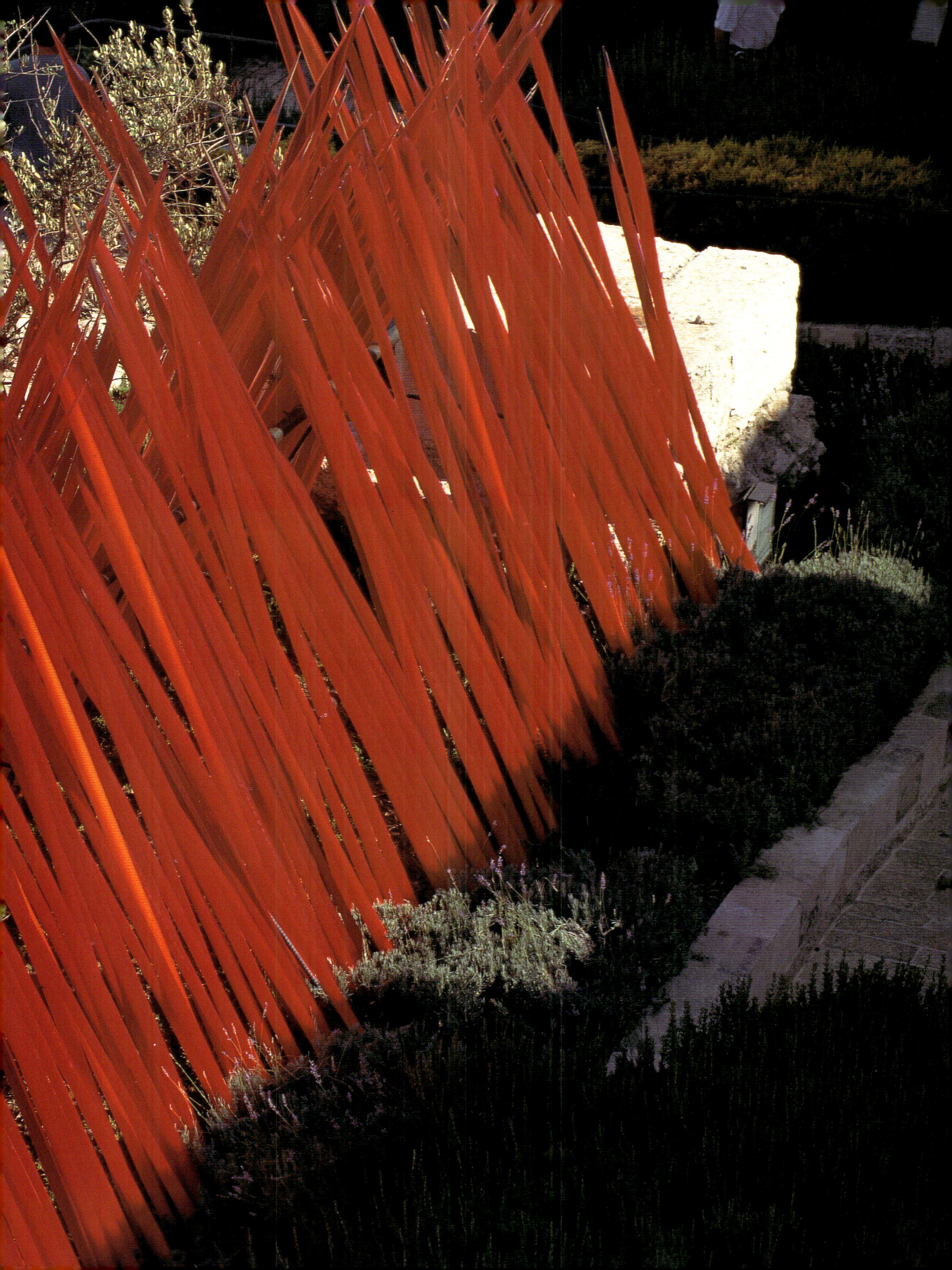

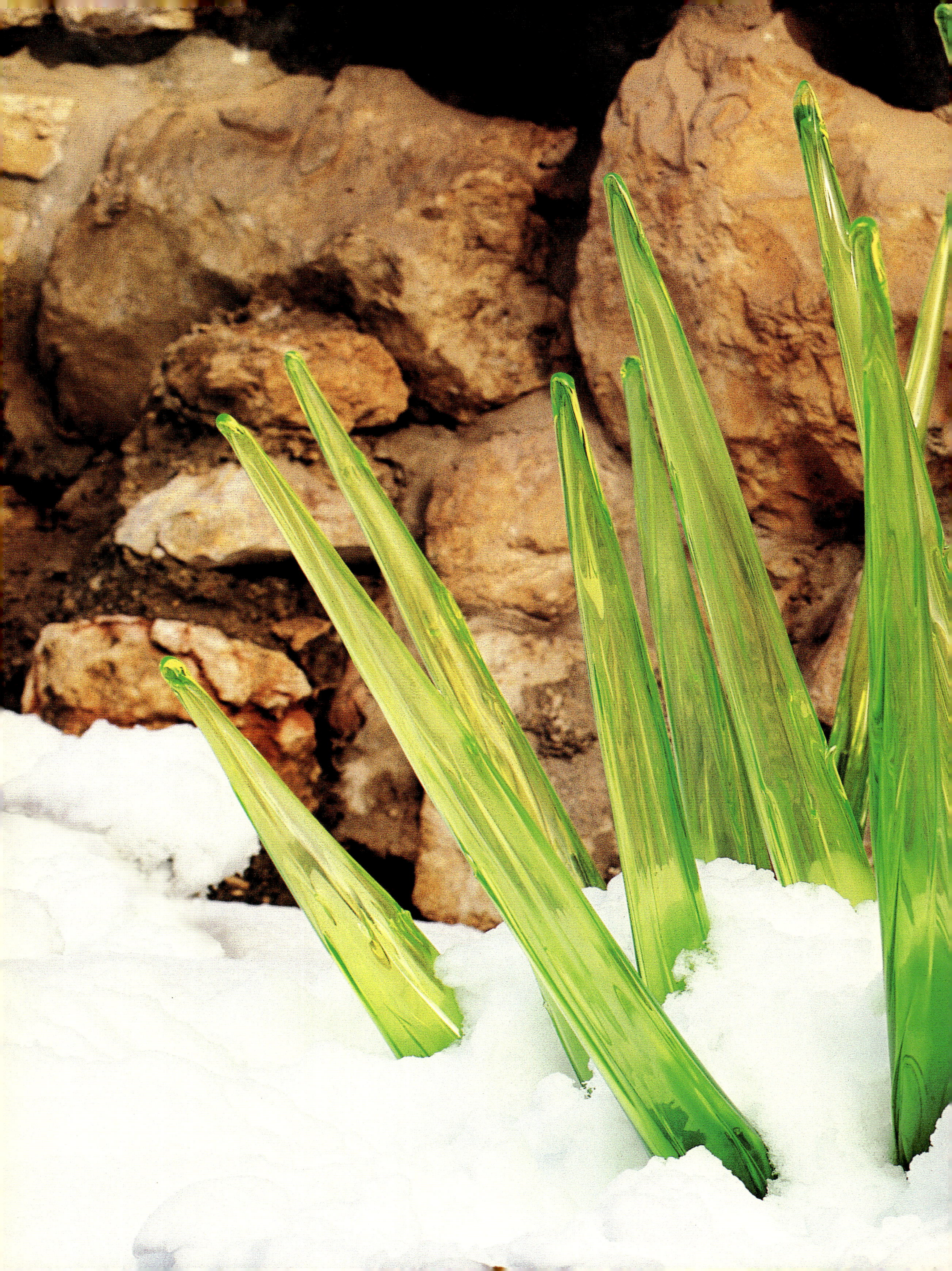

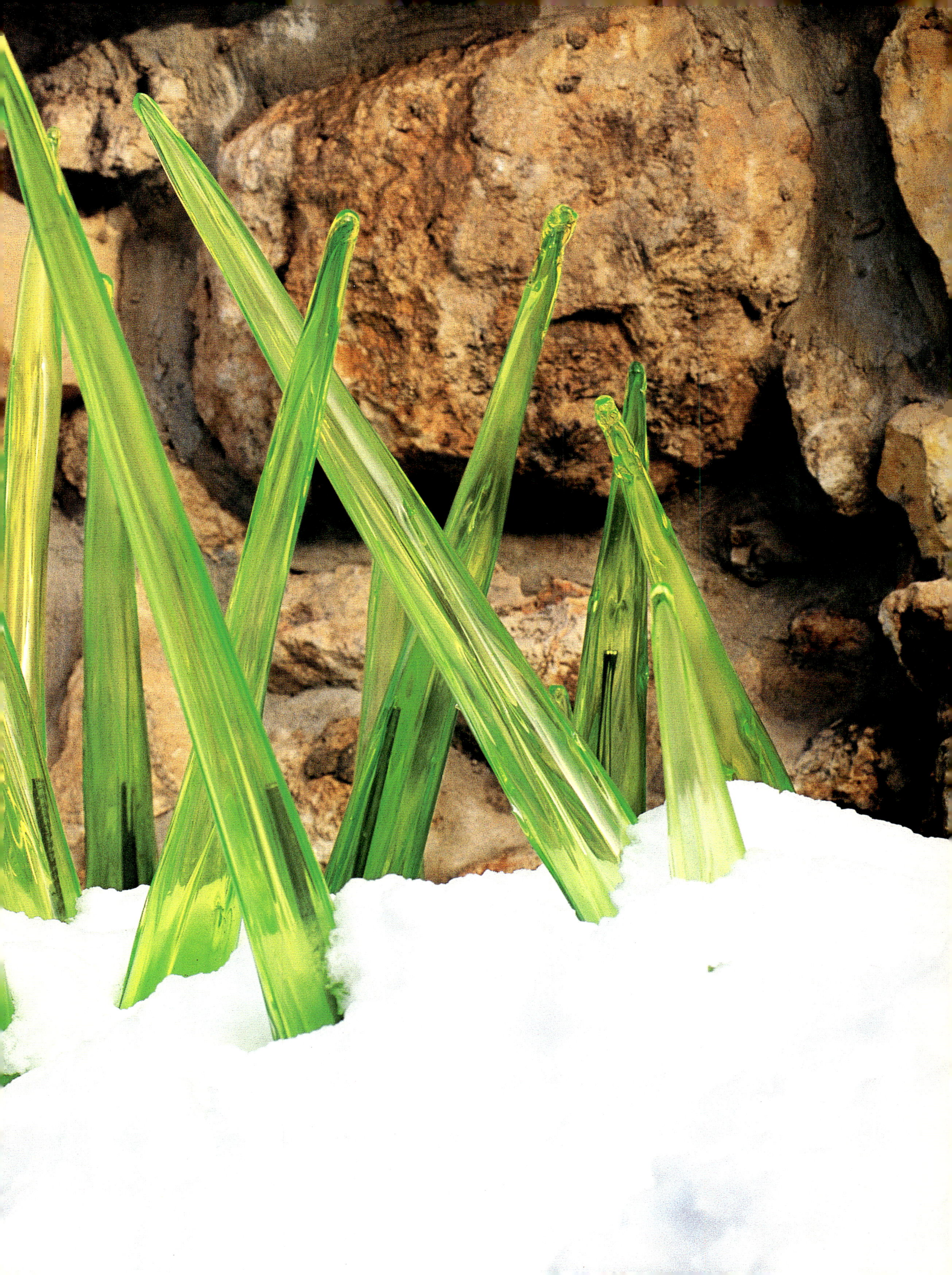

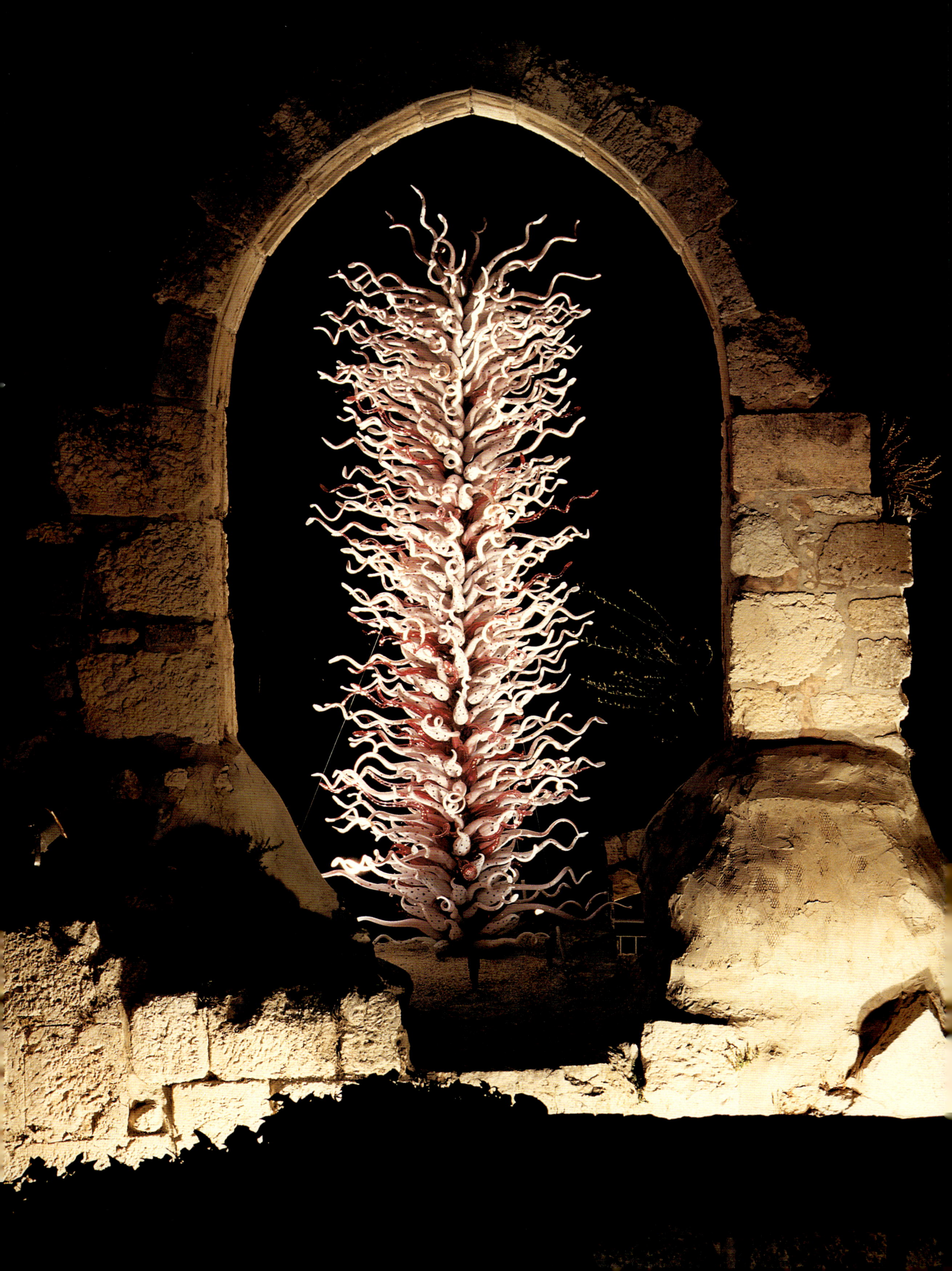

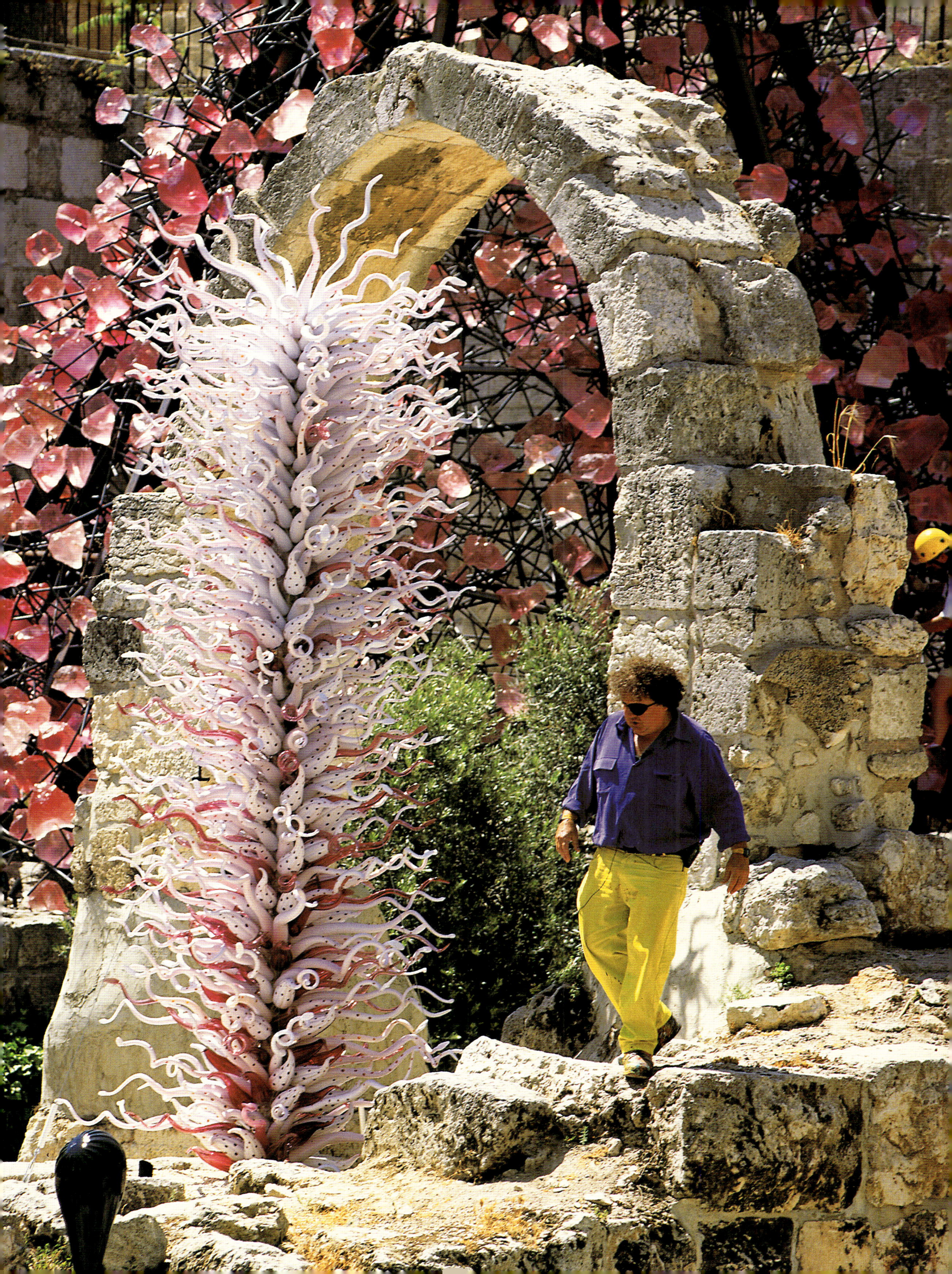

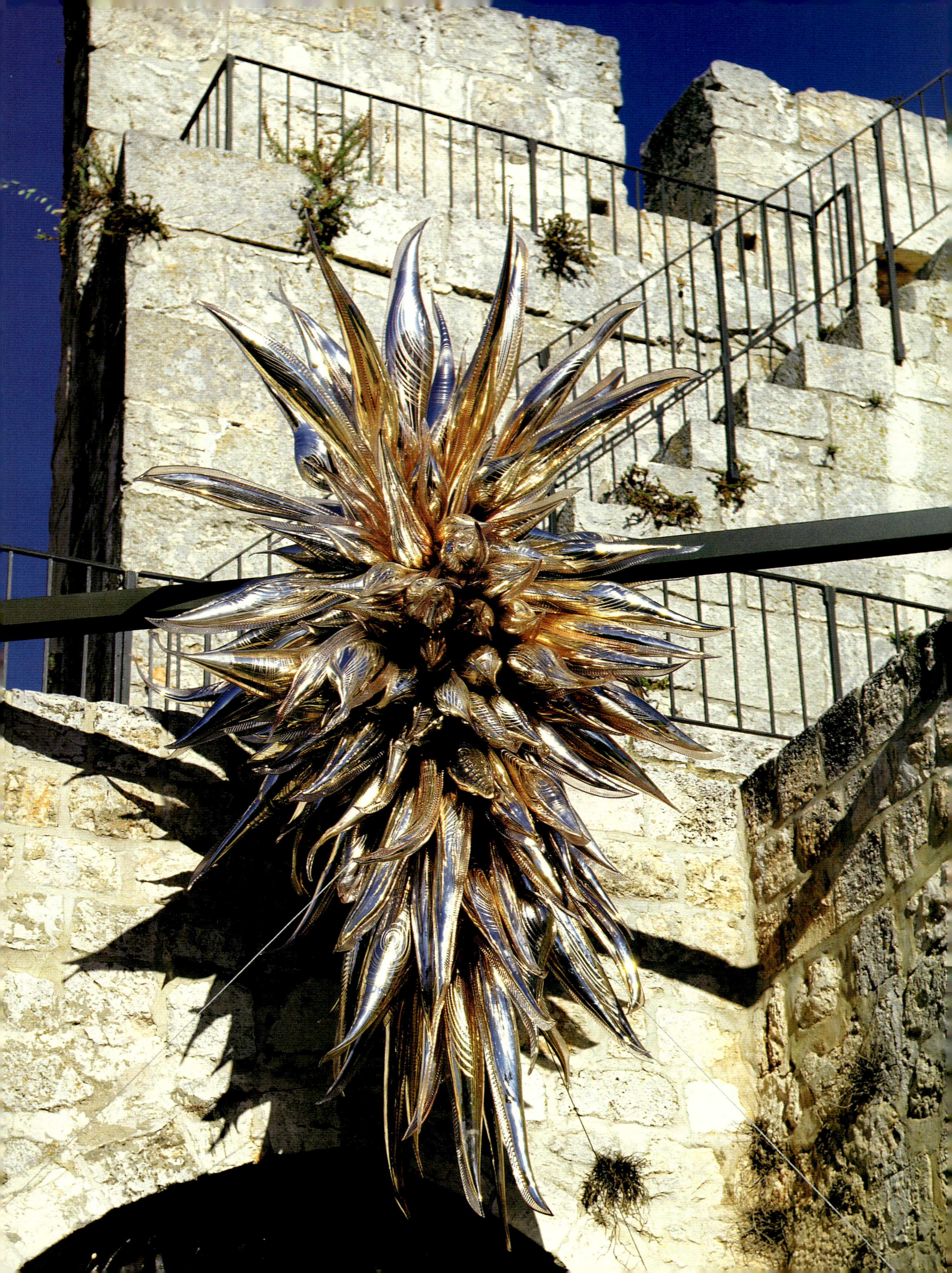

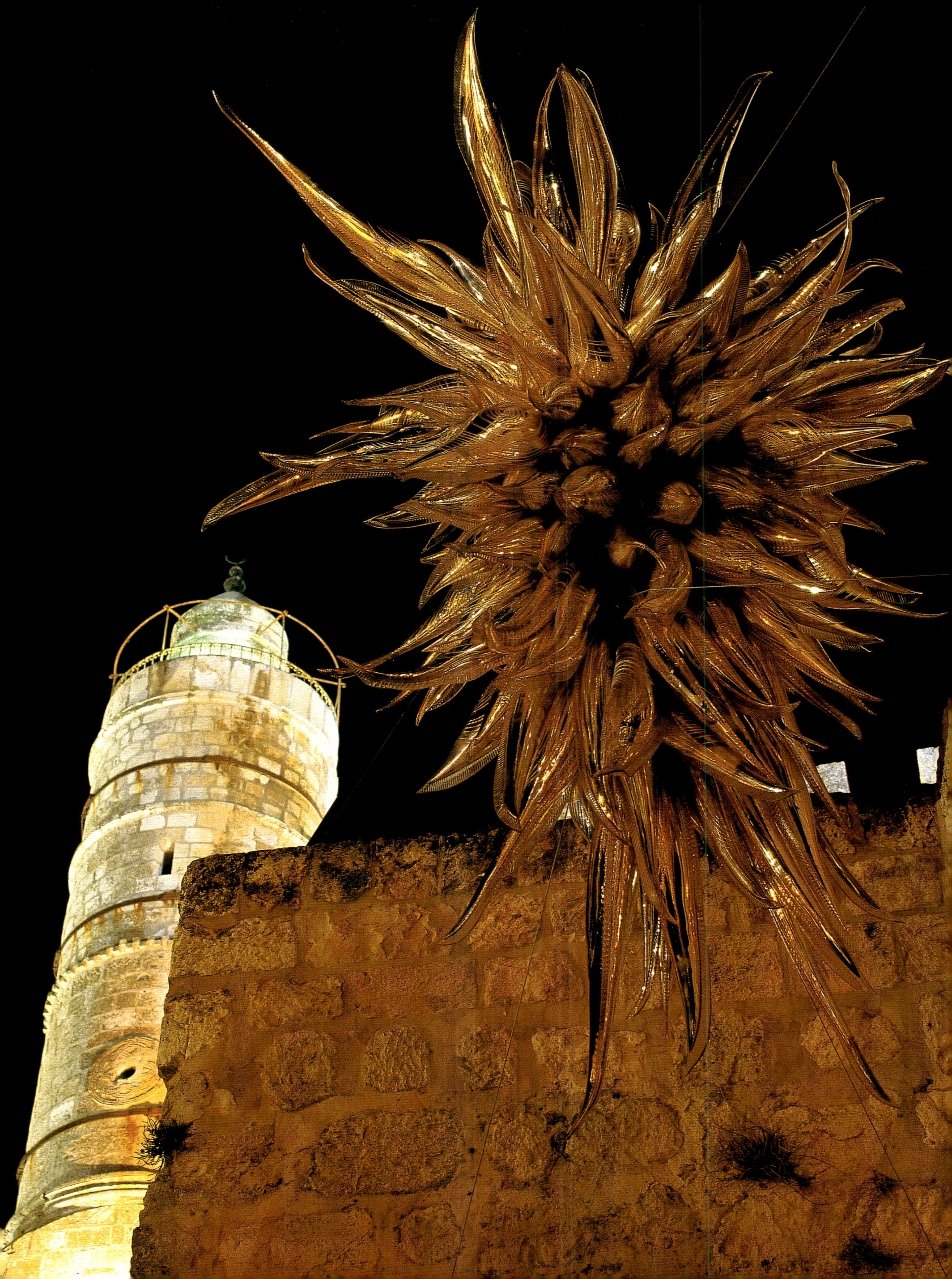

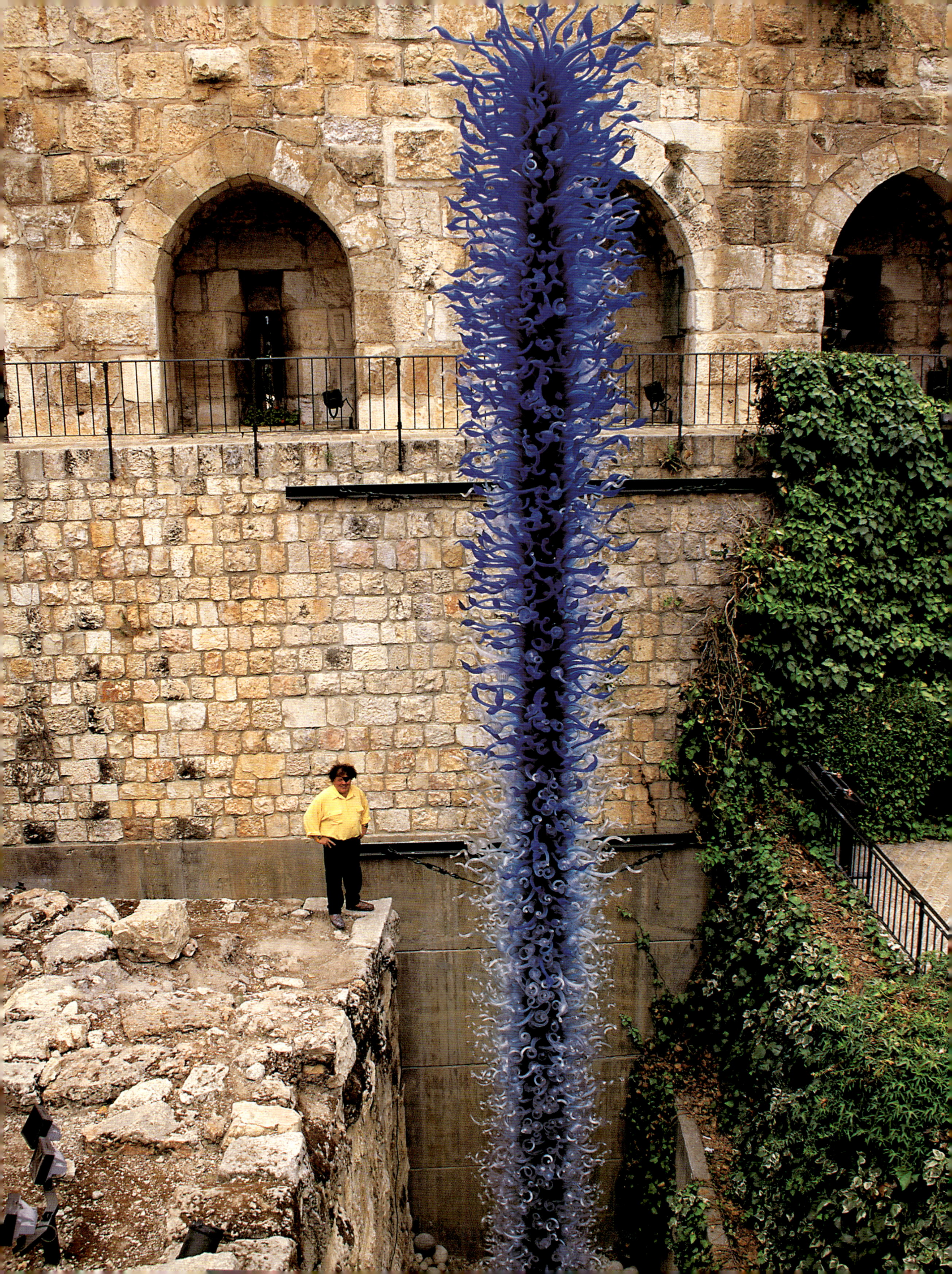

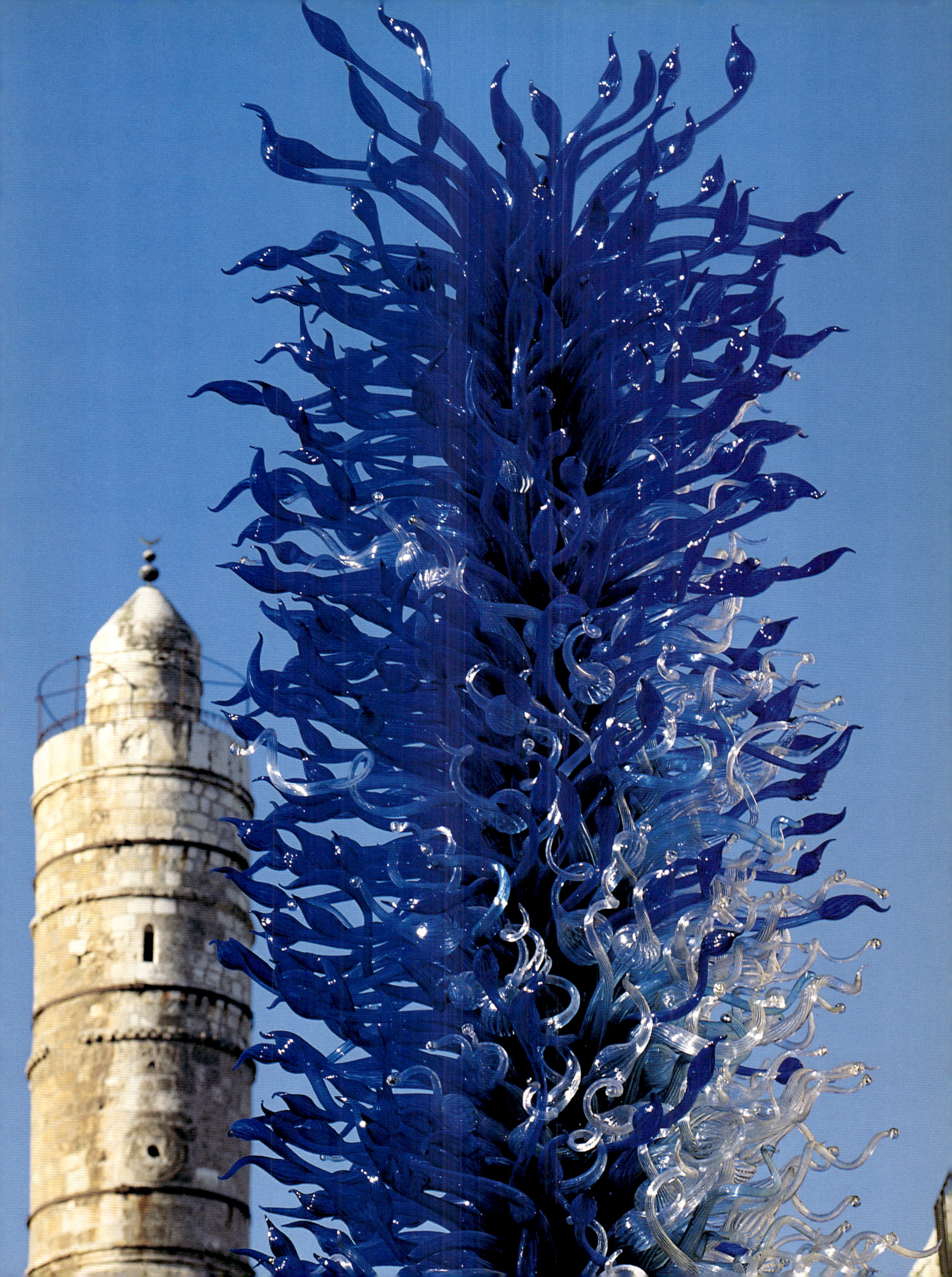

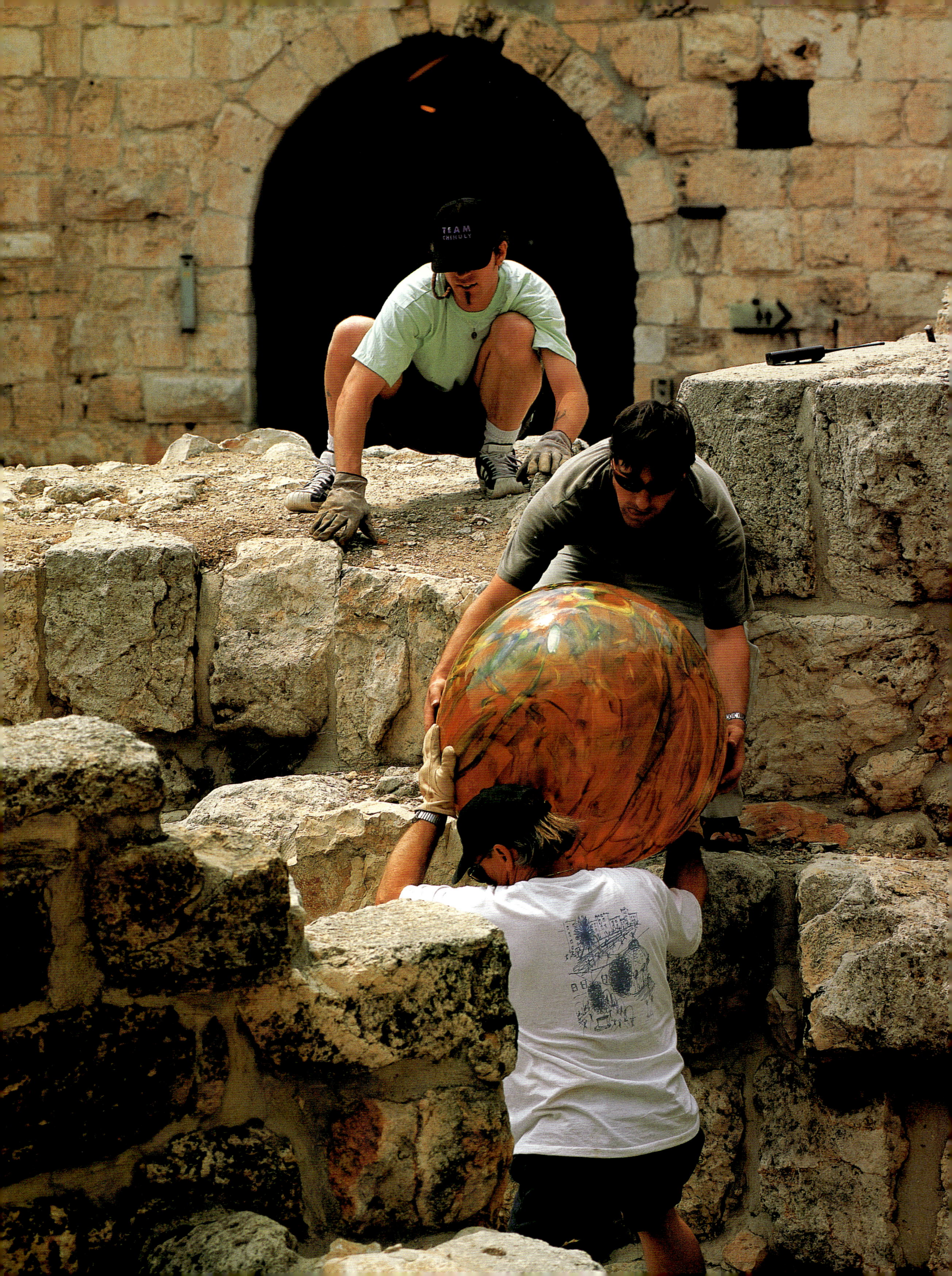
TEAM
CHIHULY

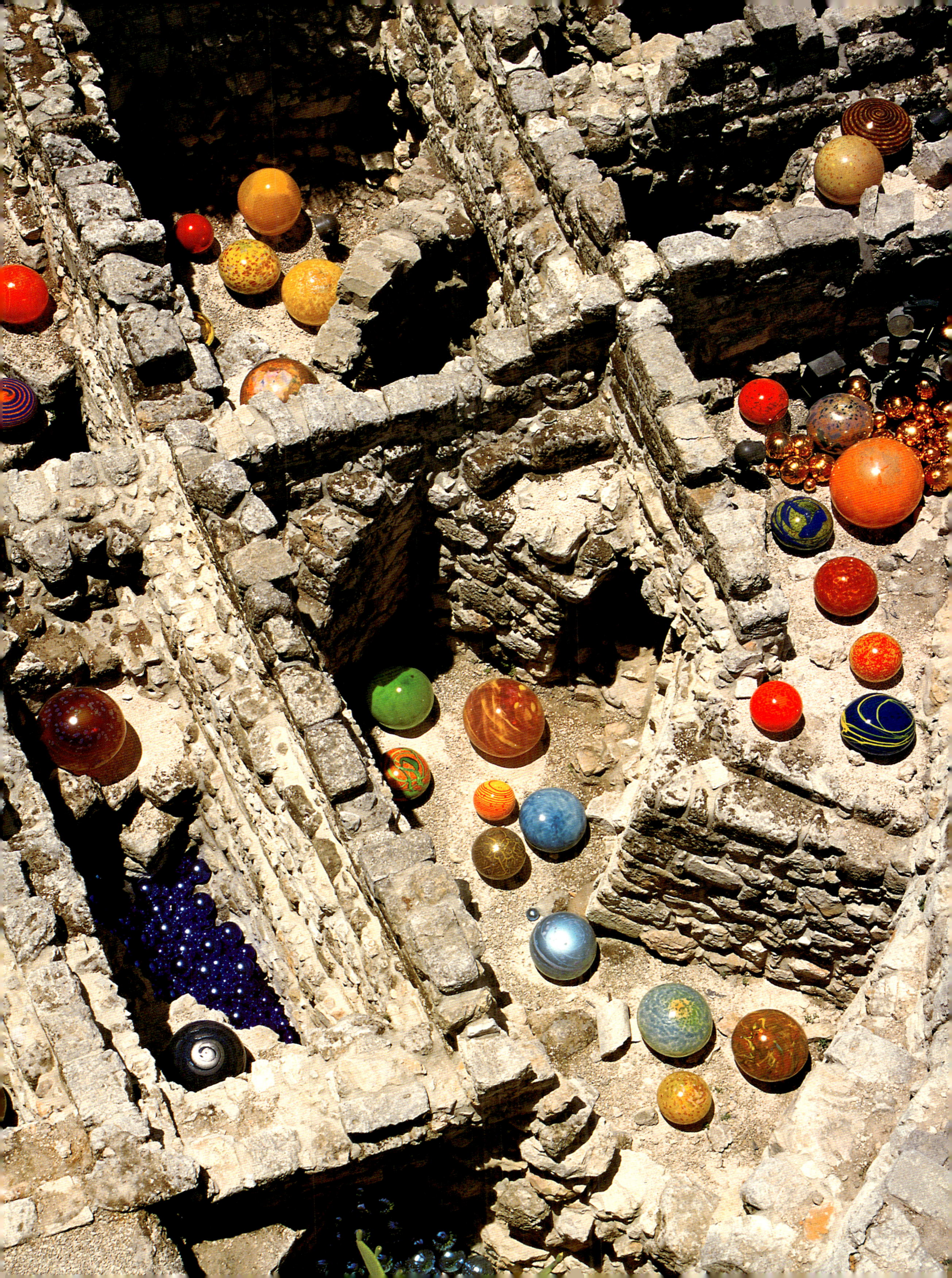

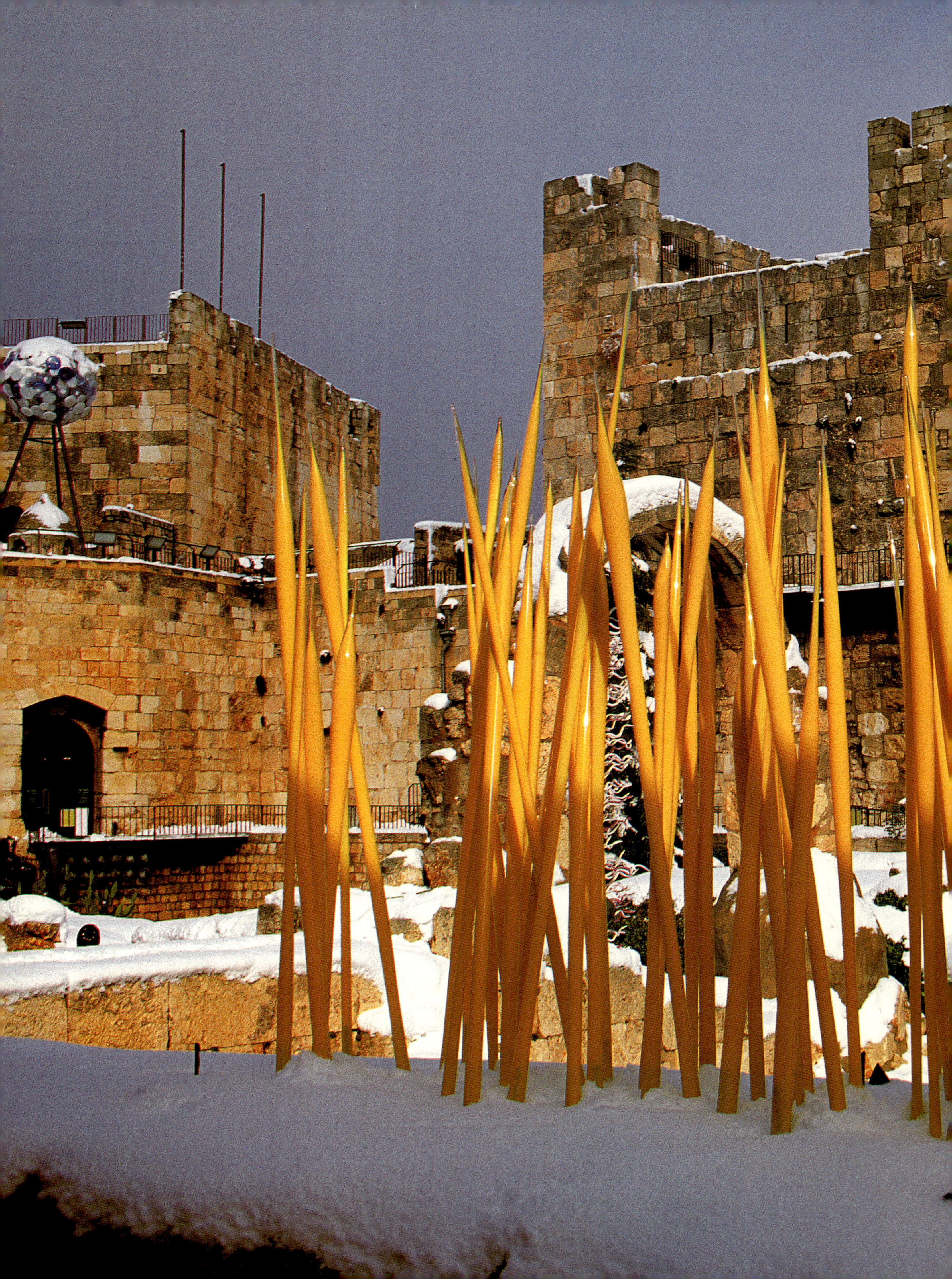

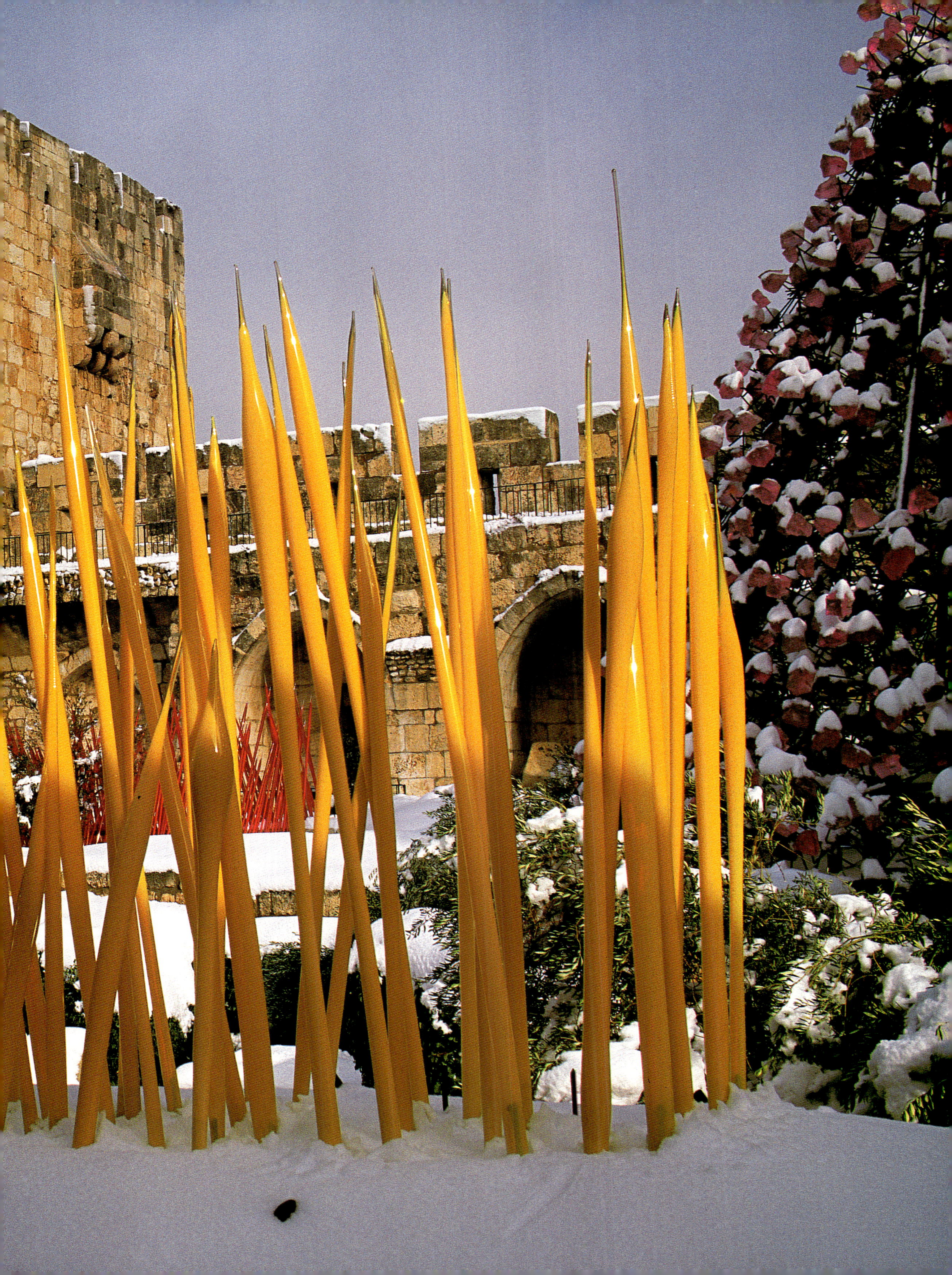

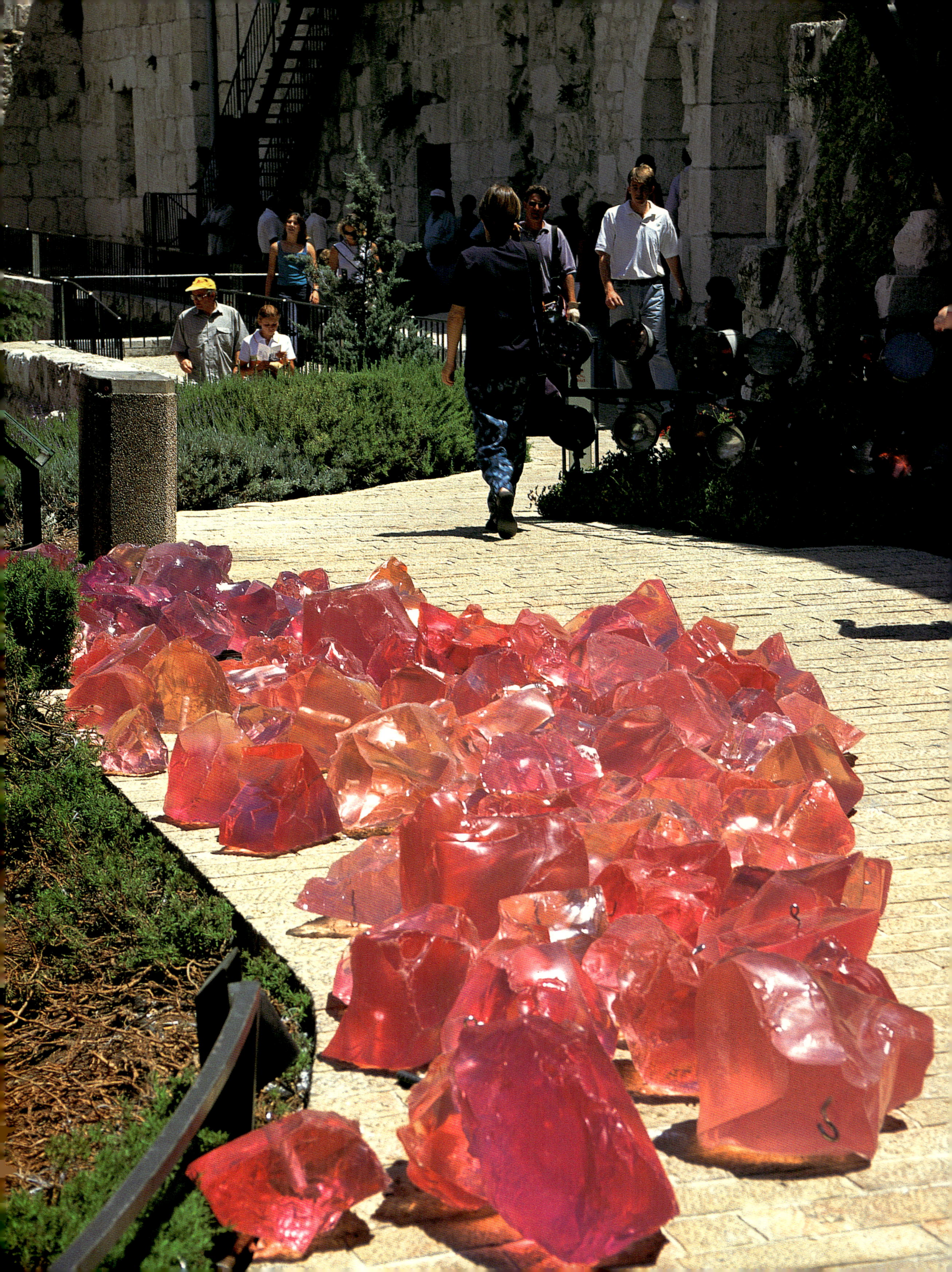

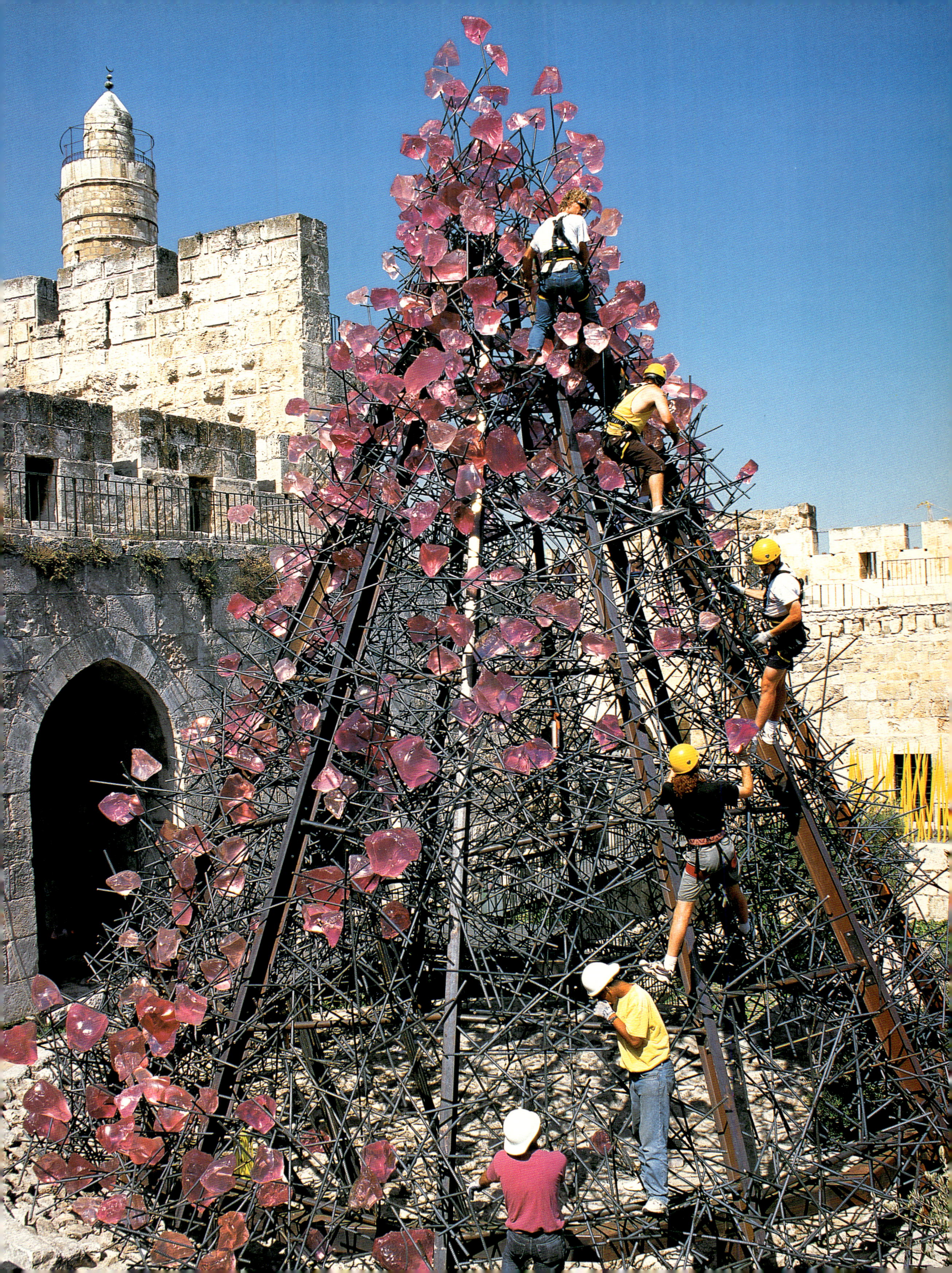

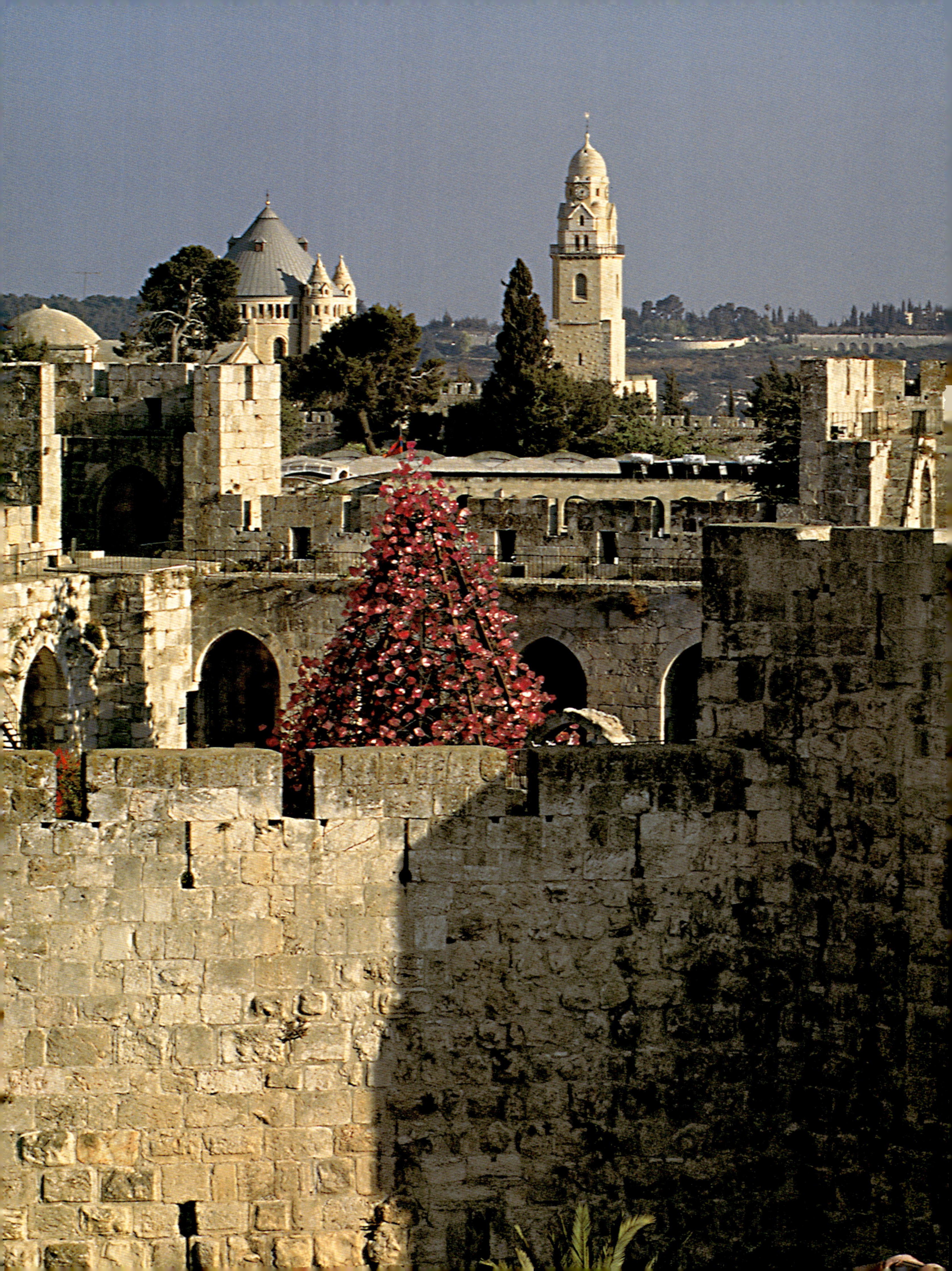

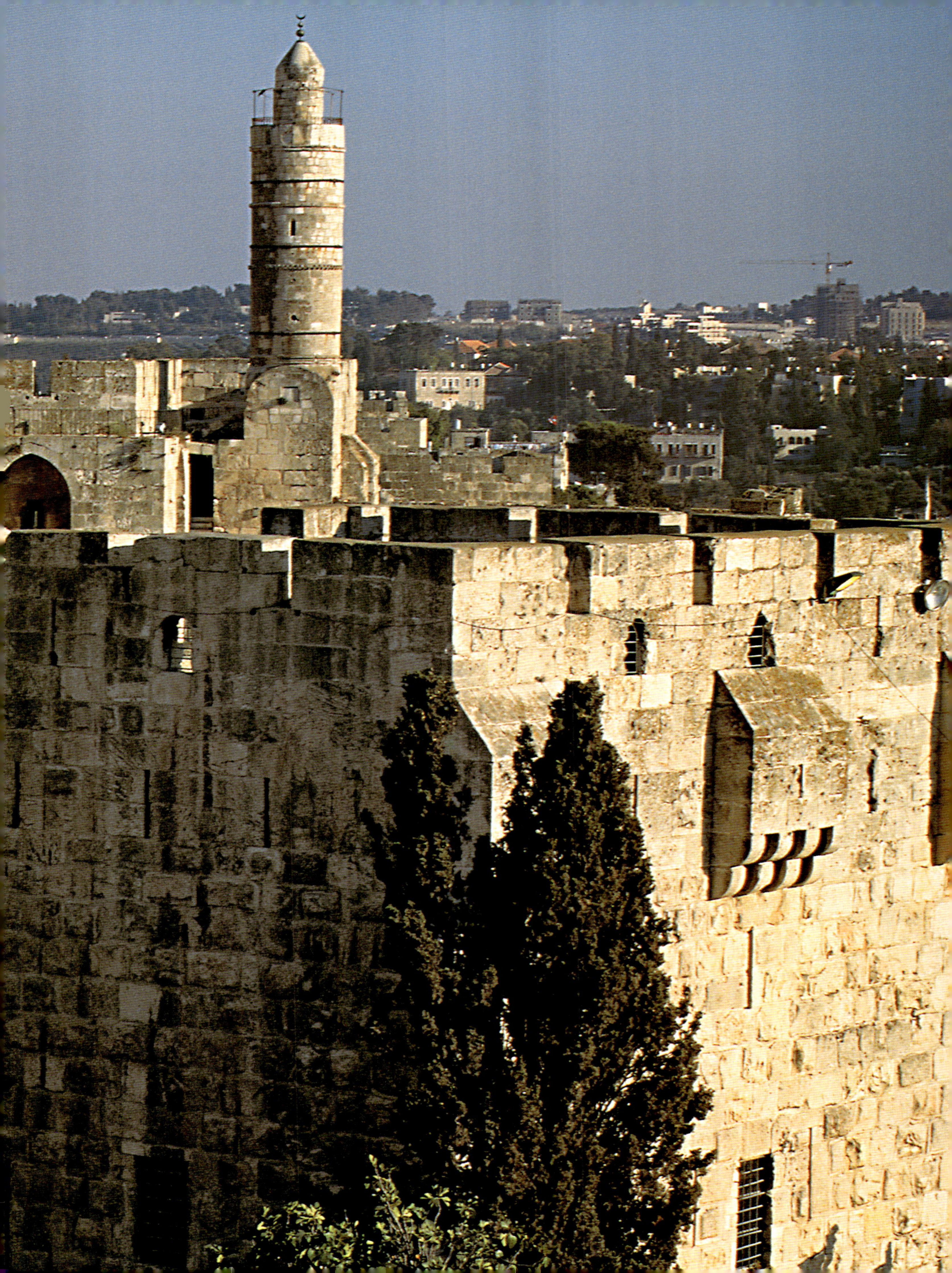

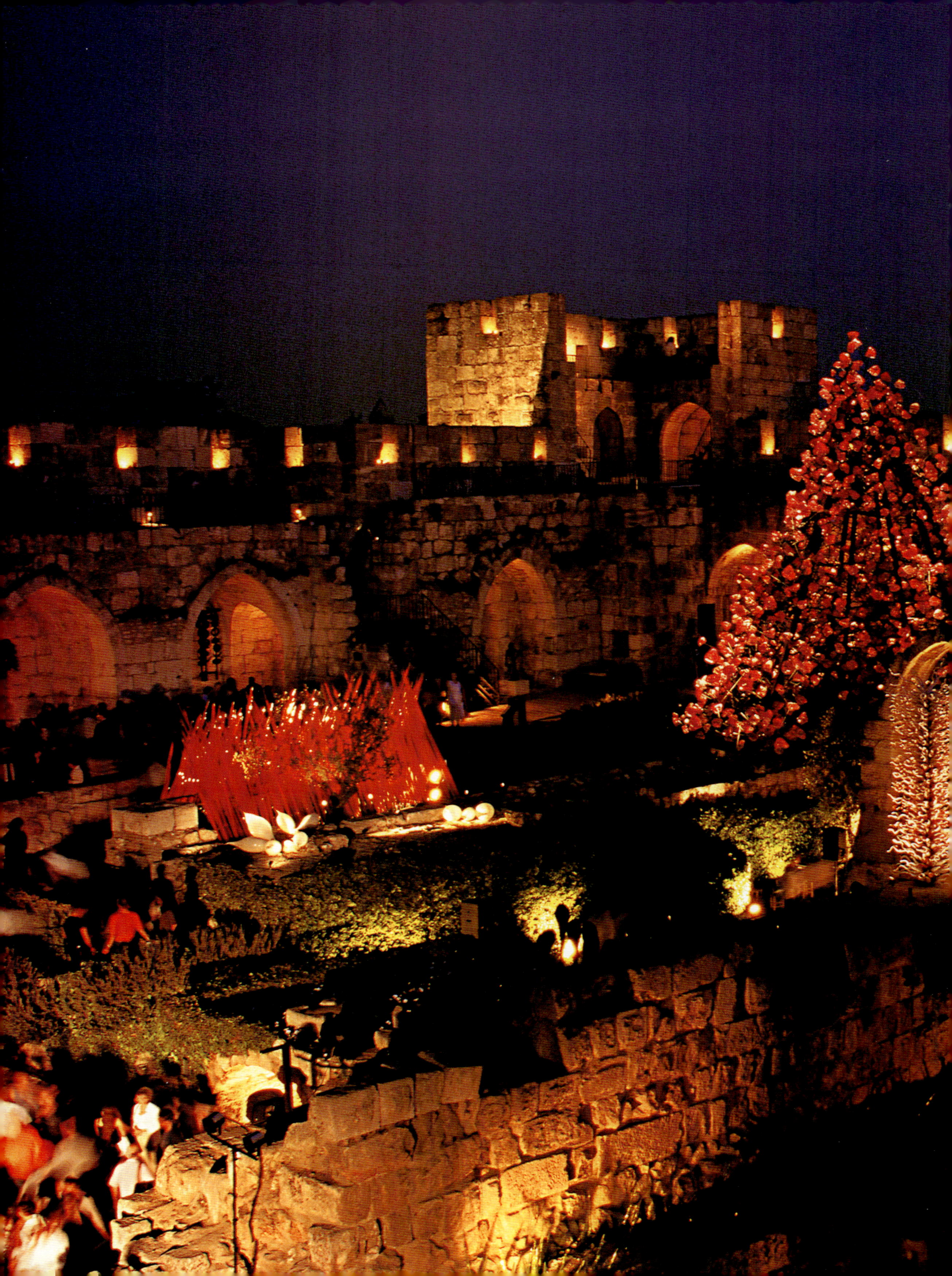

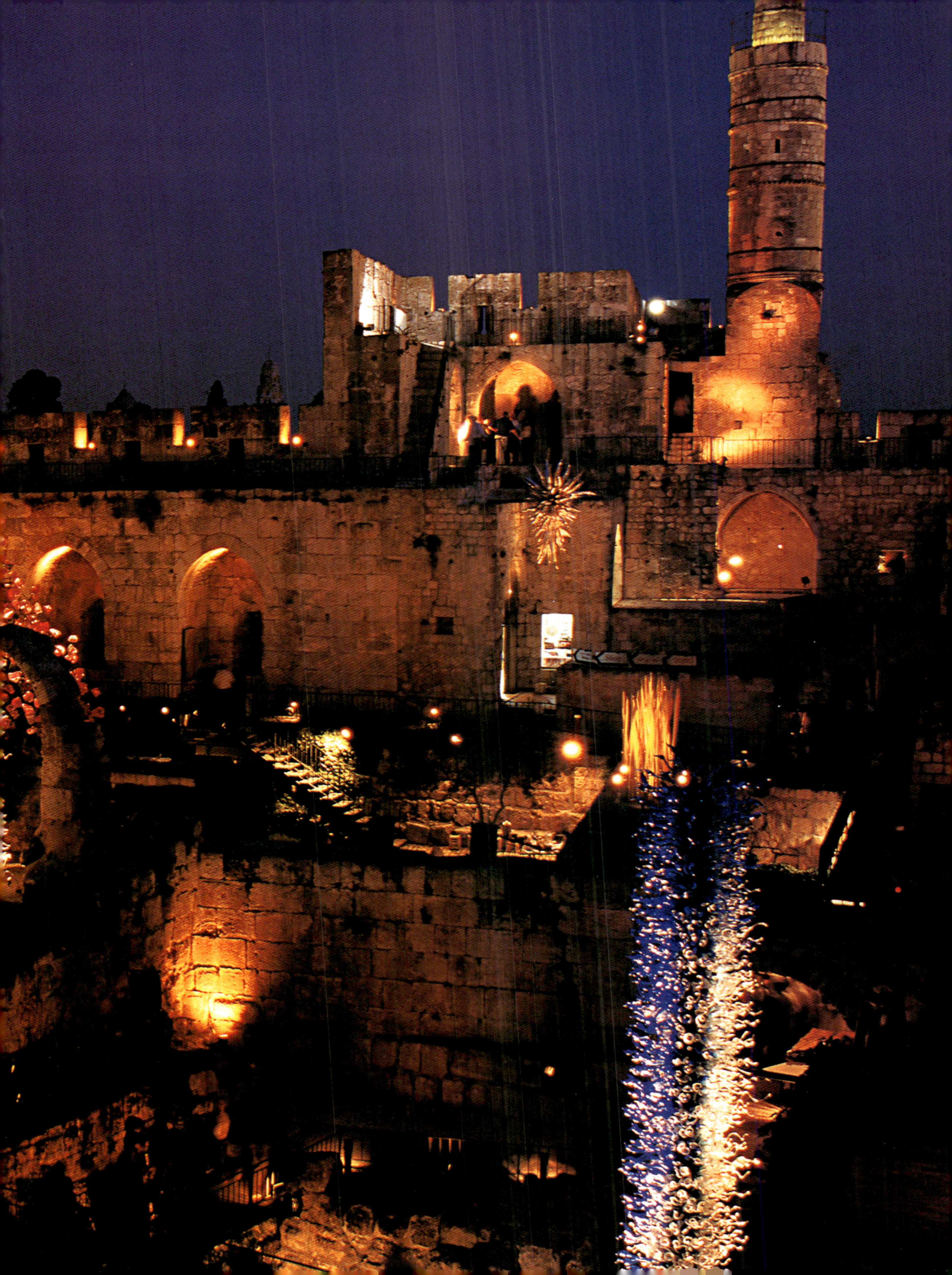

33

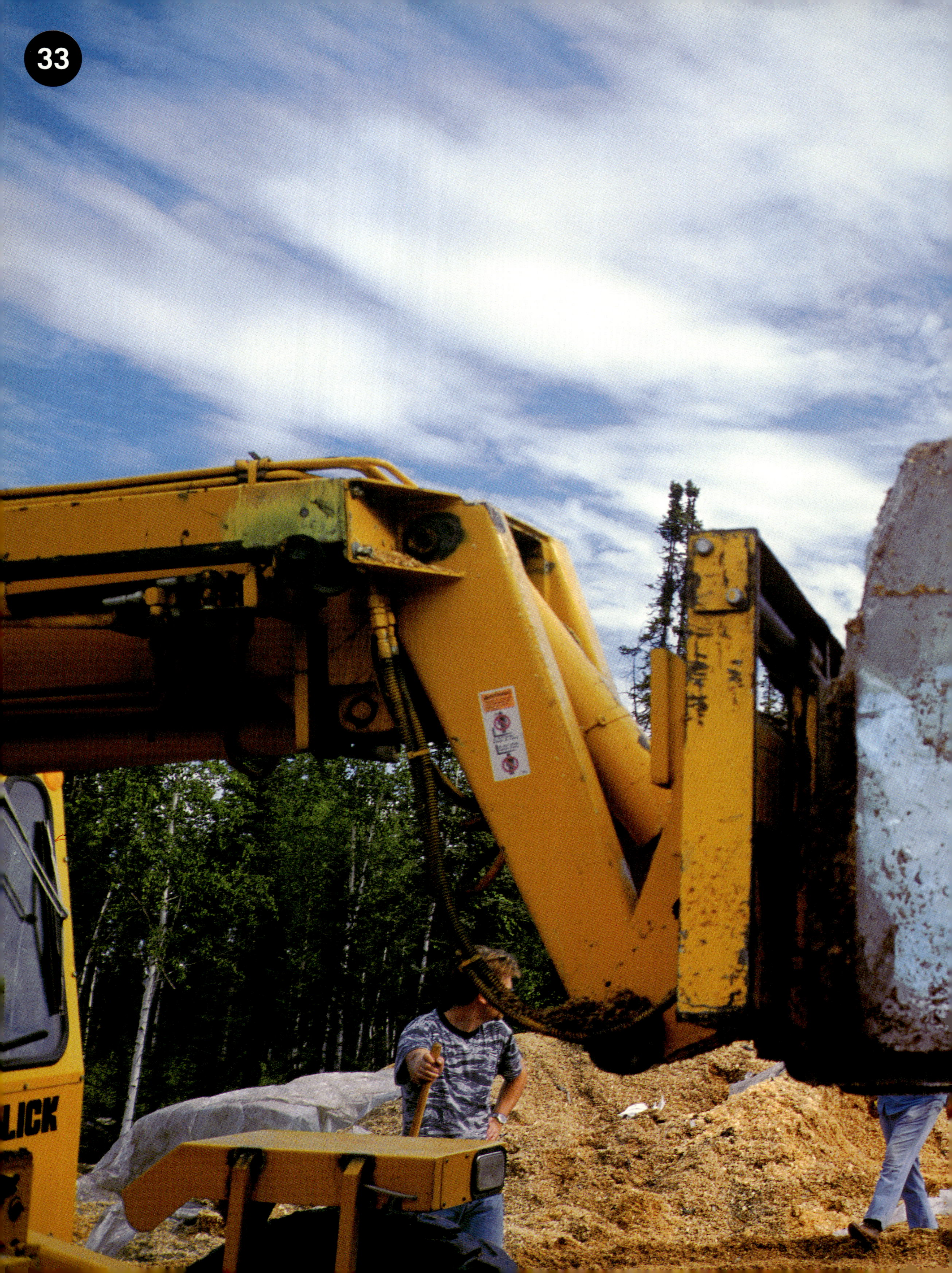

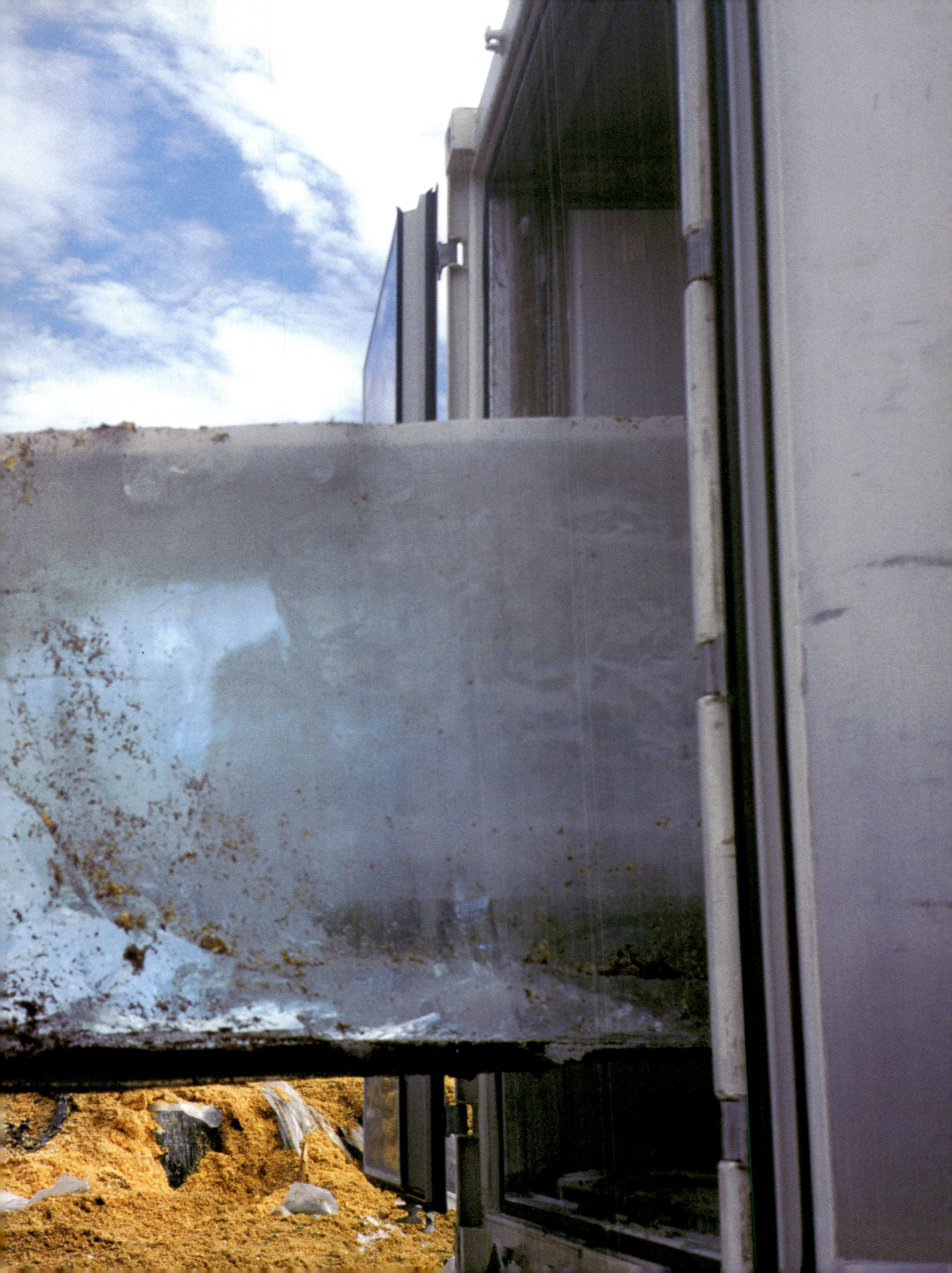

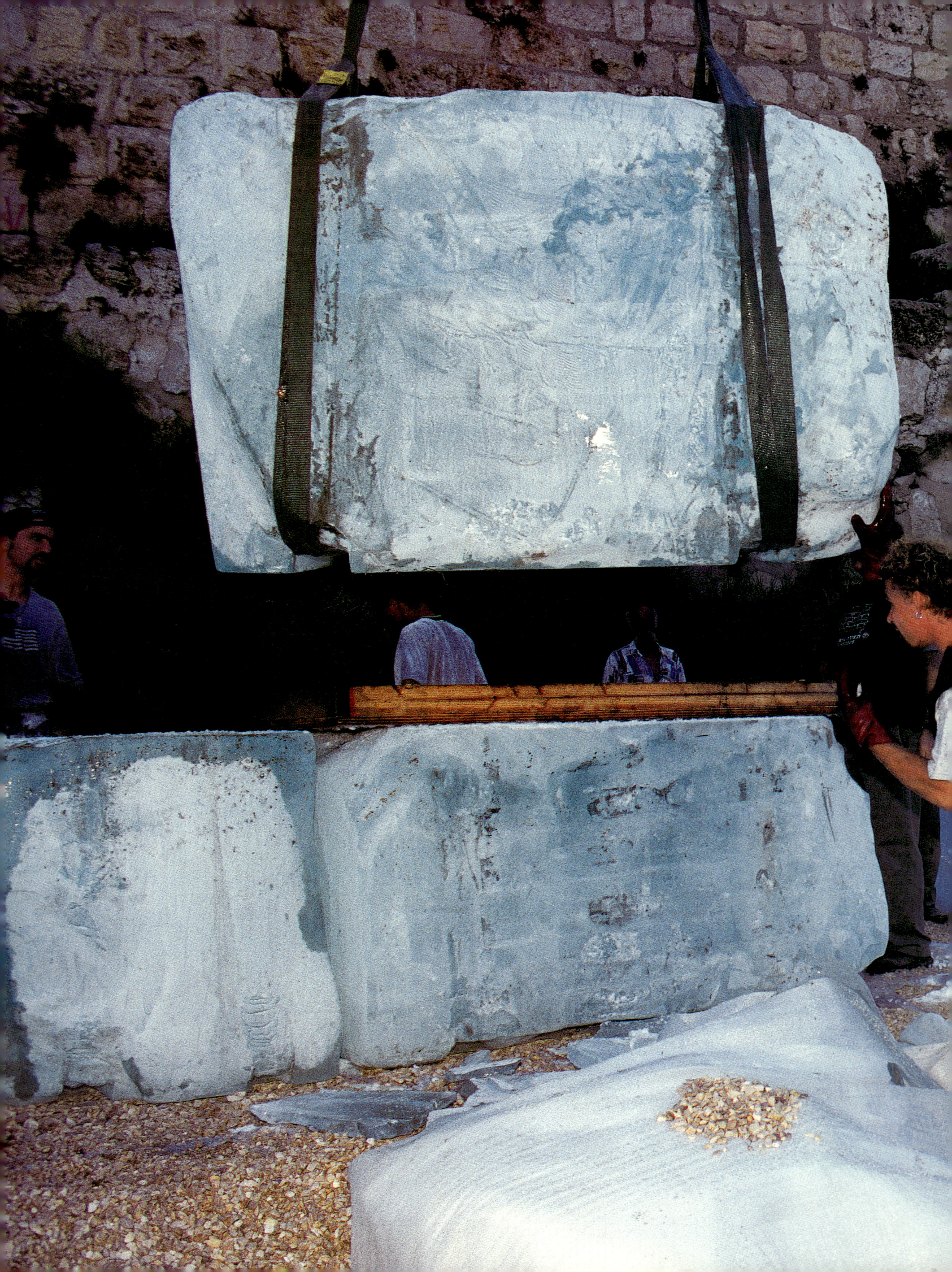

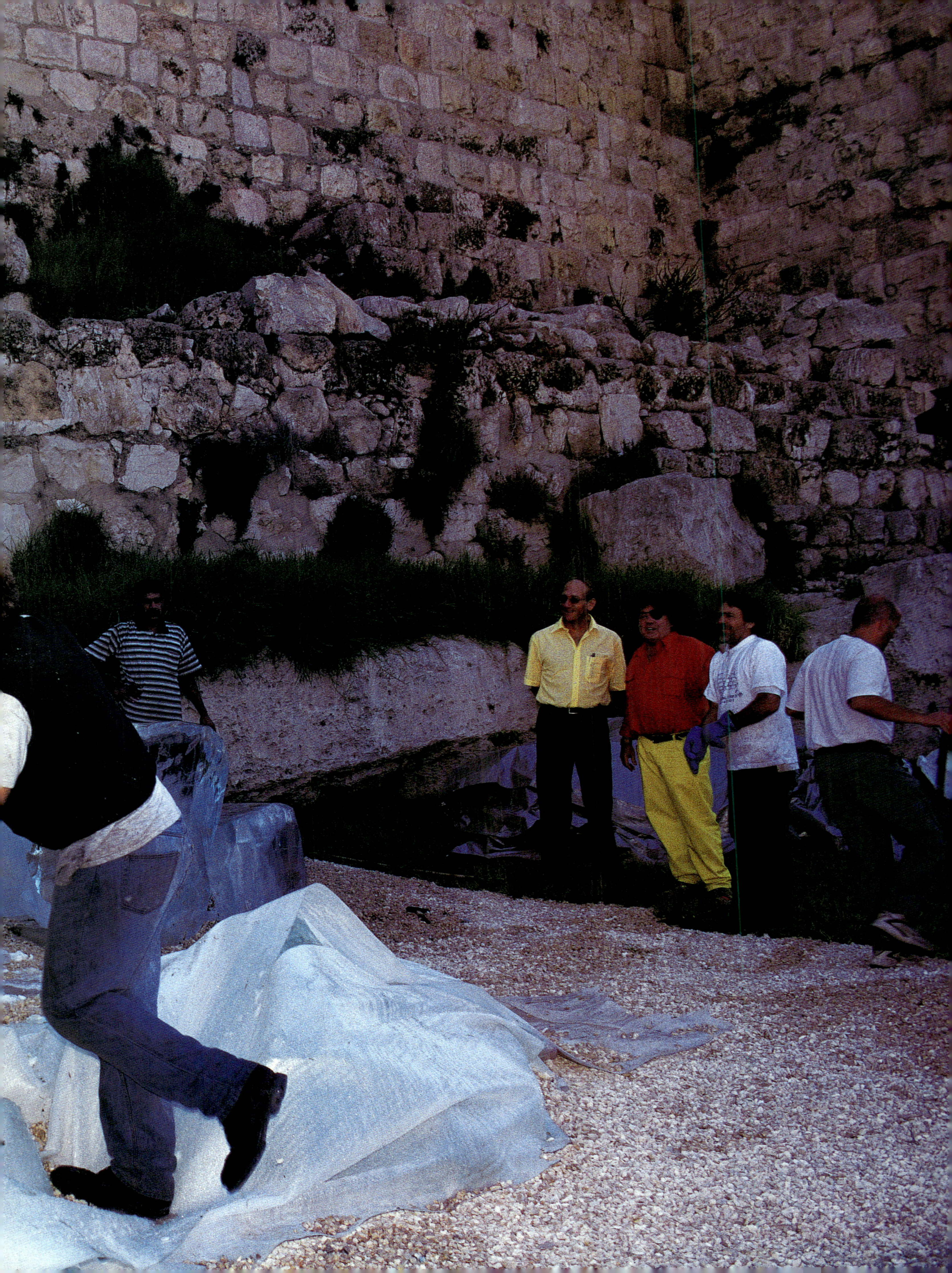

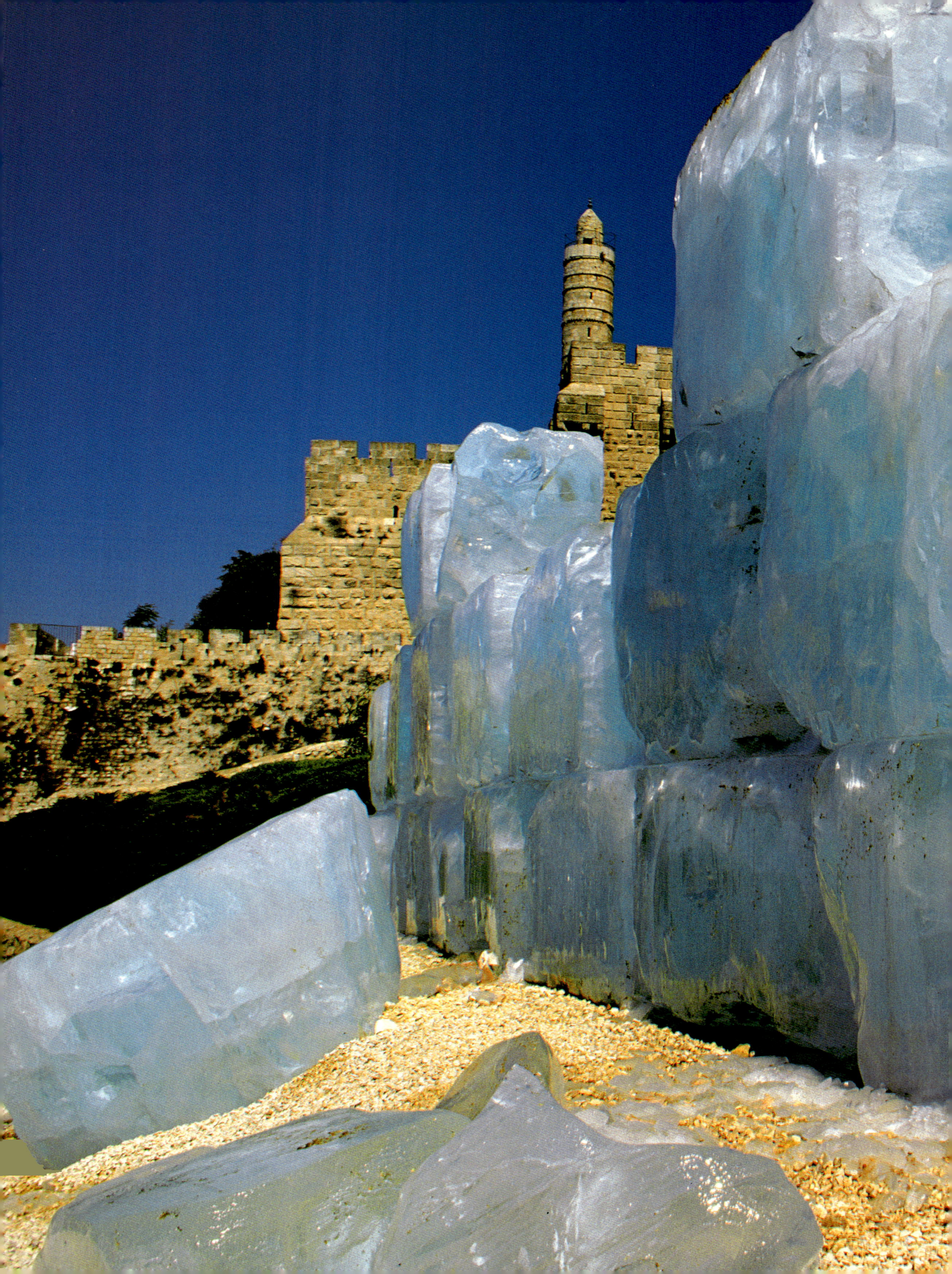

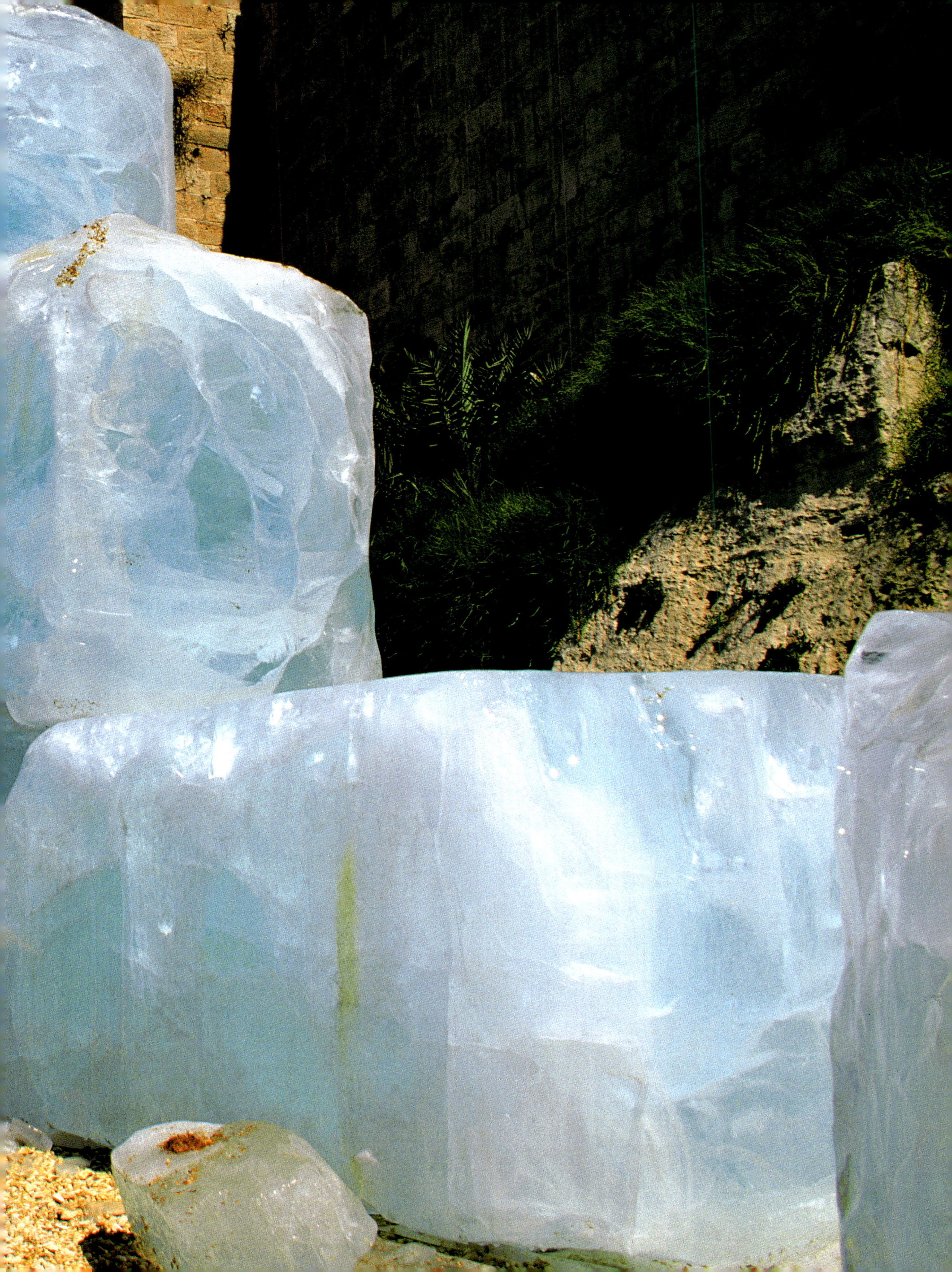

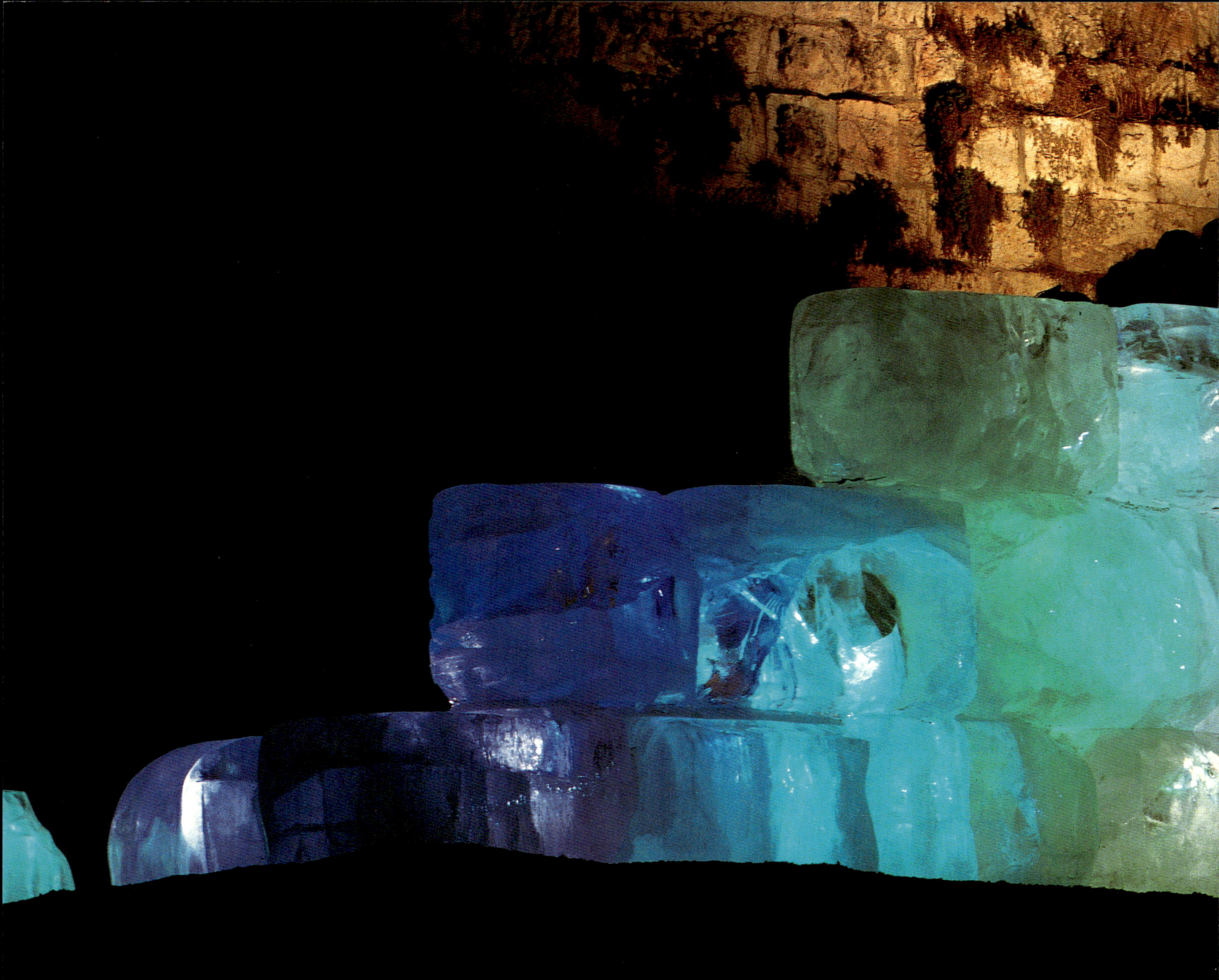

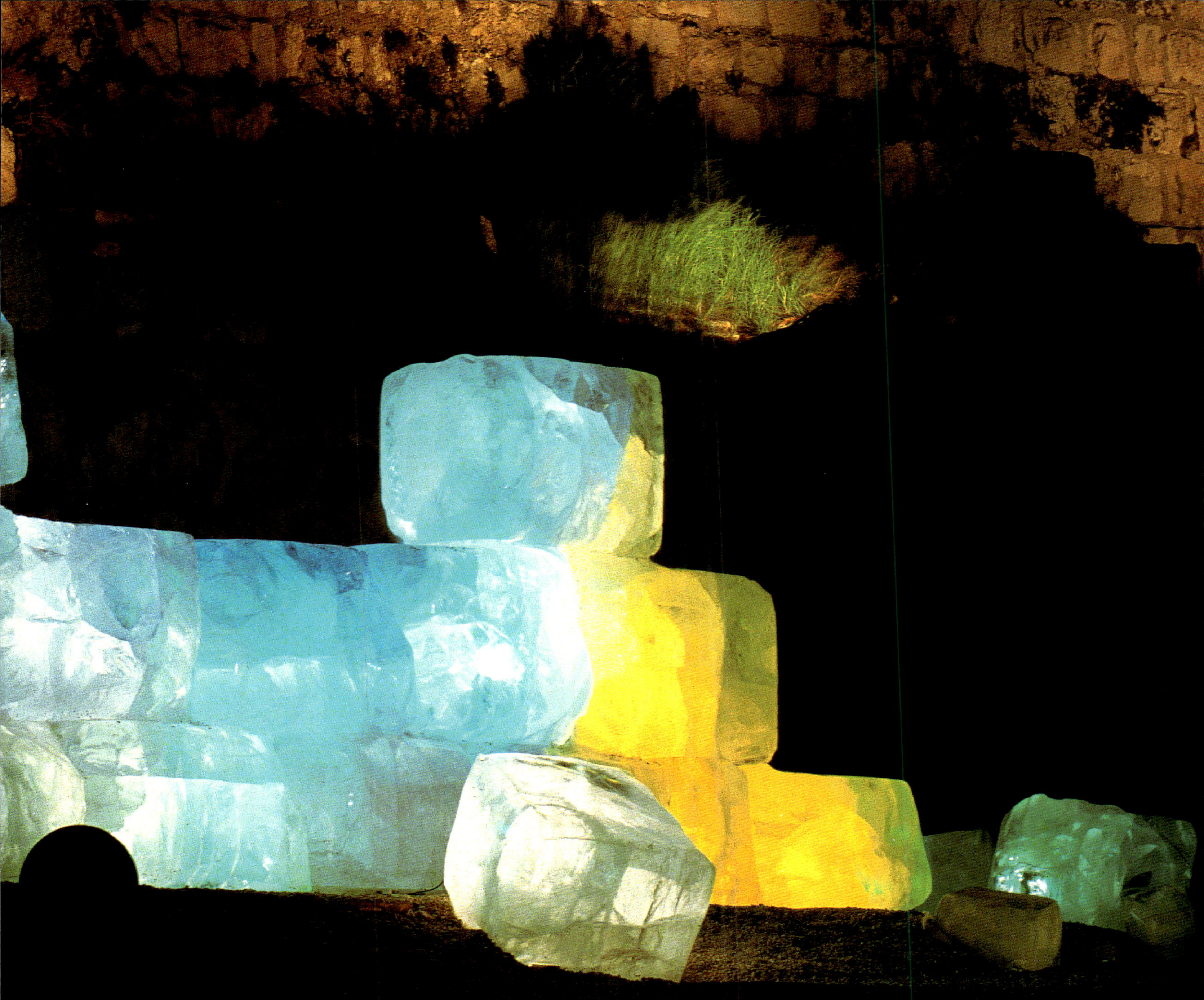

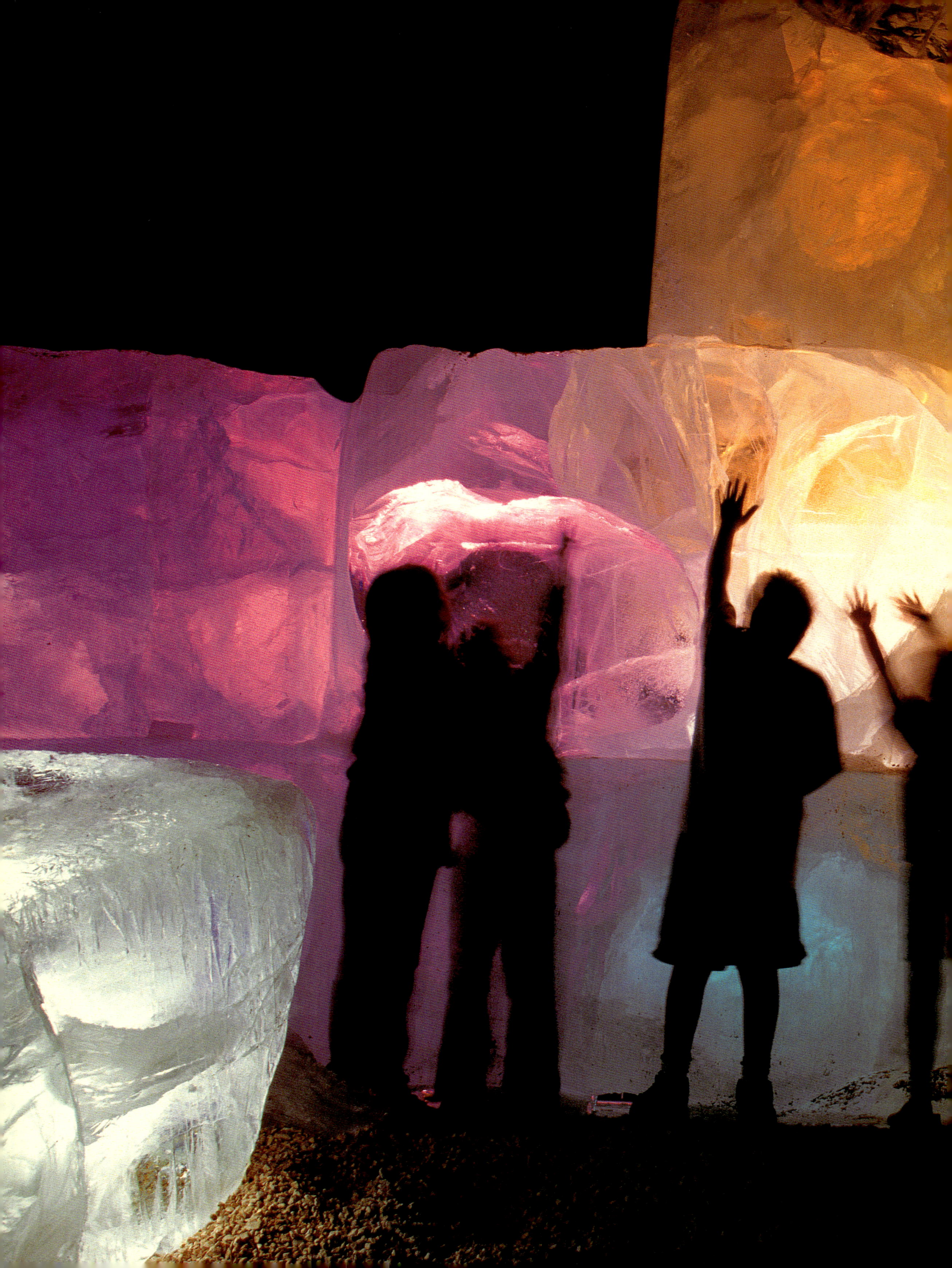

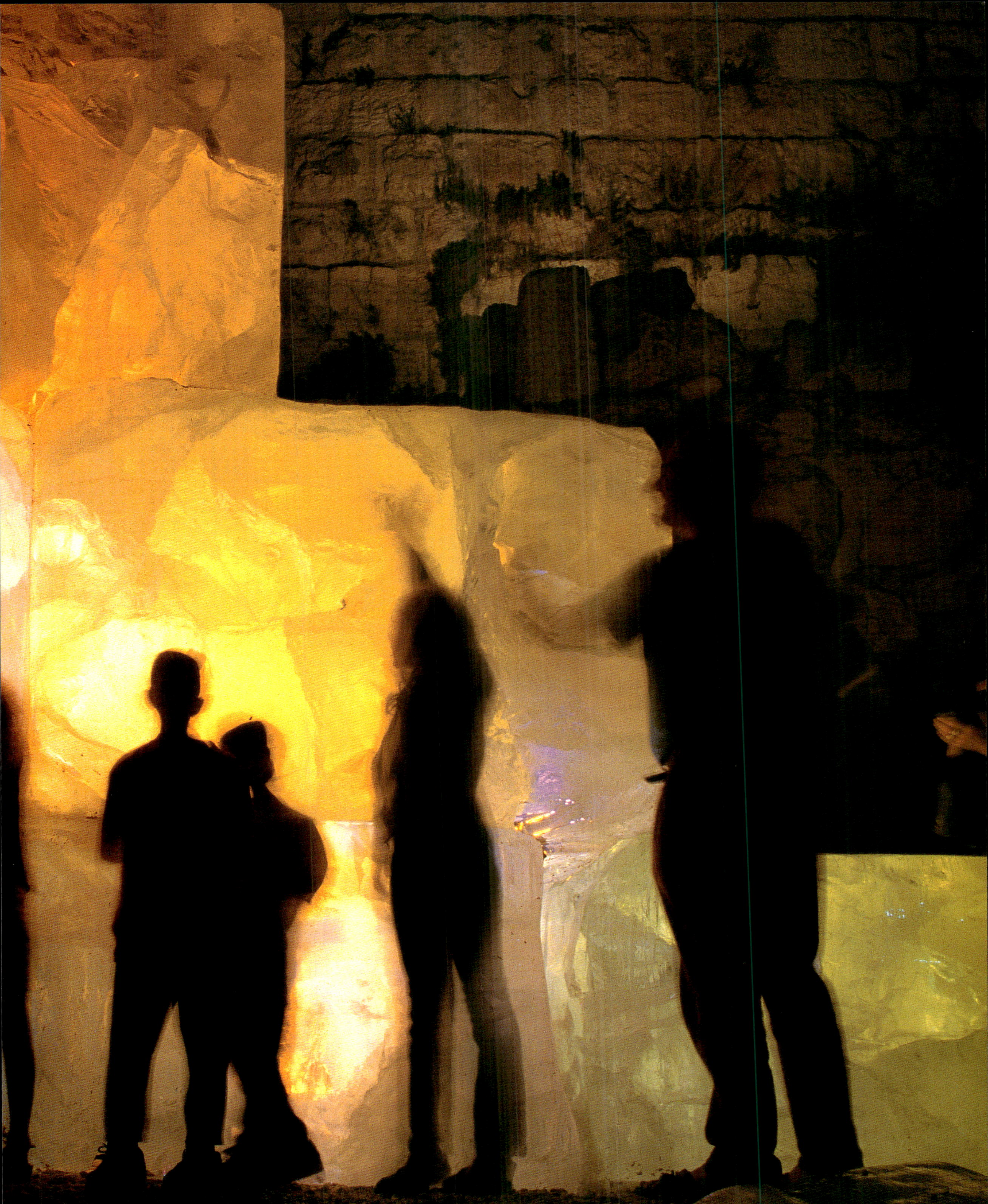

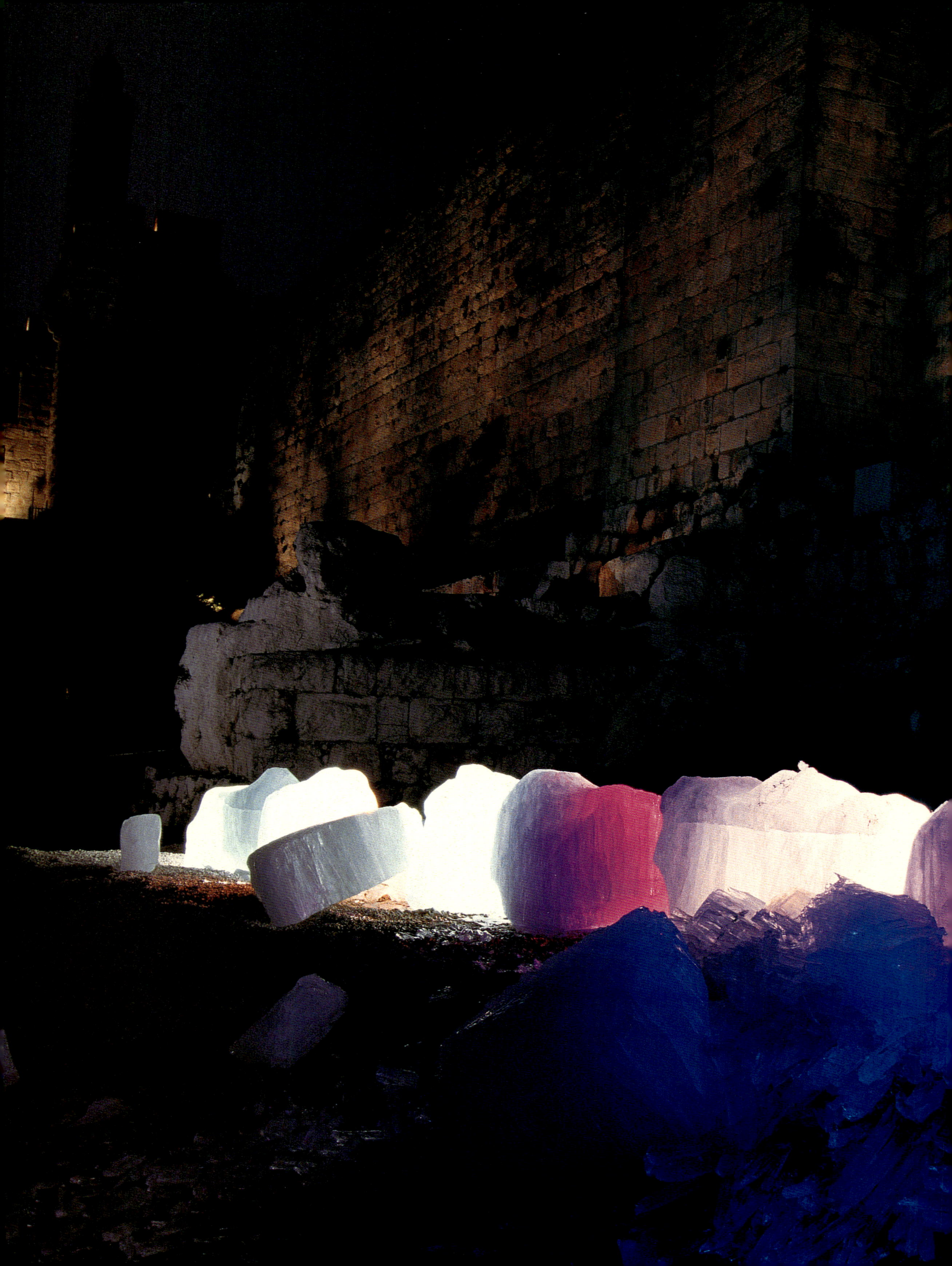

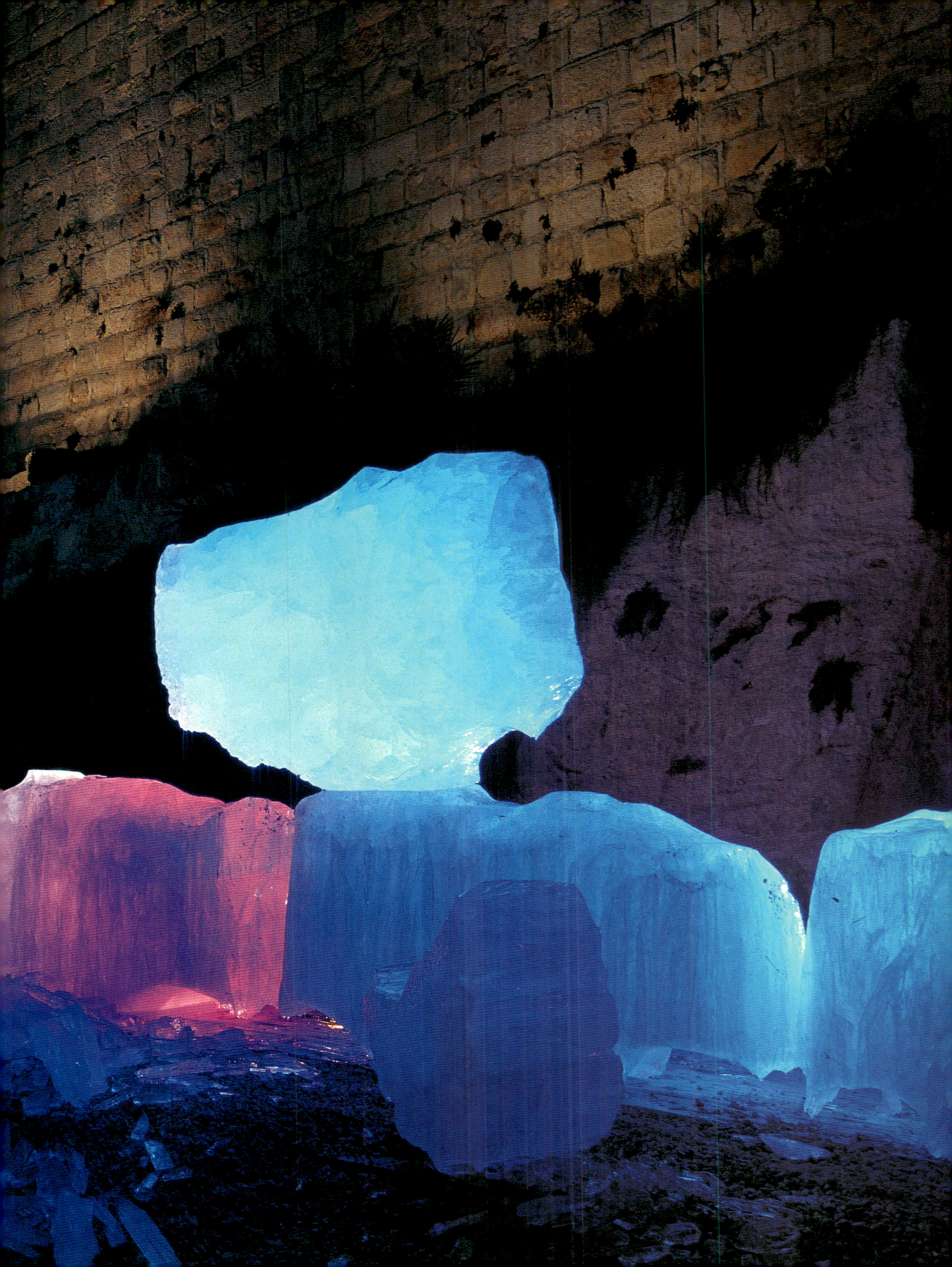

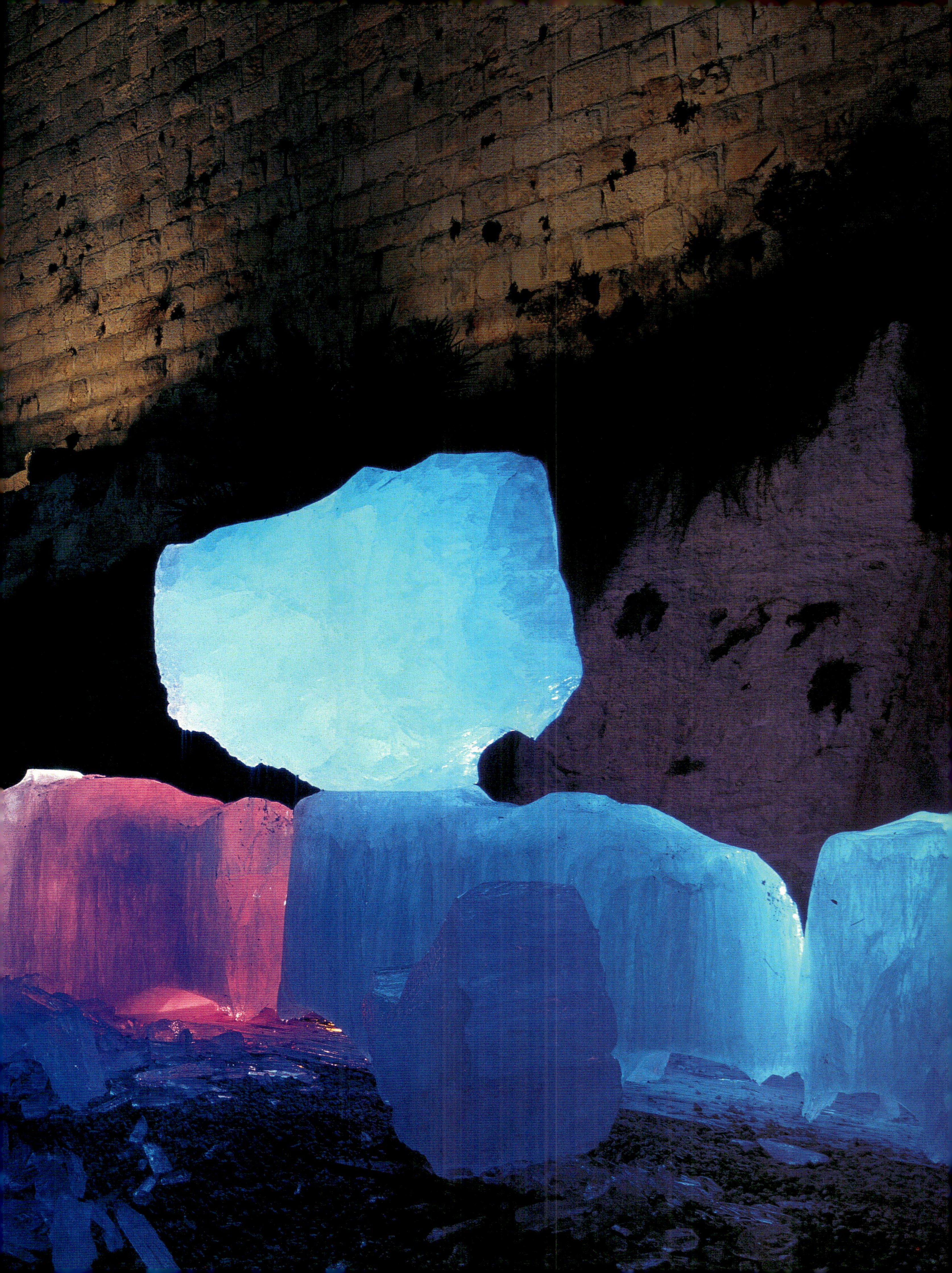

Catalog

Comments by Dale Chihuly and Team Chihuly

1 Rhode Island School of Design, Providence
In collaboration with James Carpenter, 1968–1971

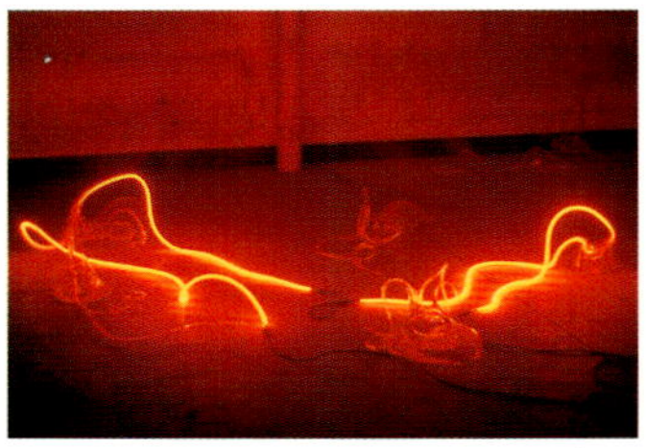

Uranium Neon Installation
Medium: Glass, neon, and argon
Dimensions: 15 x 15 x 15'

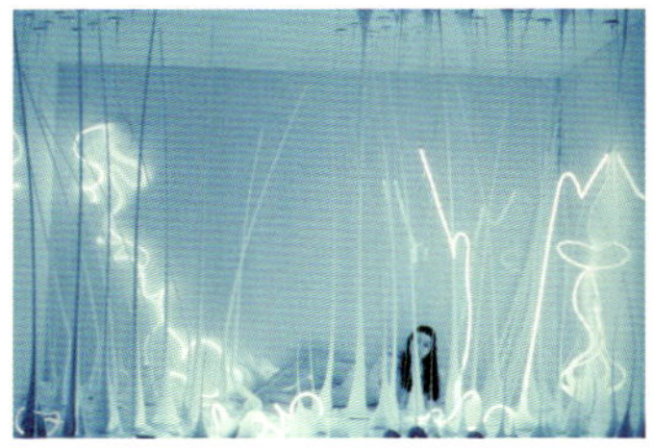

Glass Forest #2
Medium: Glass, neon, and argon
Dimensions: 160 sq. ft., 6–9' high
Elements: Approx. 100

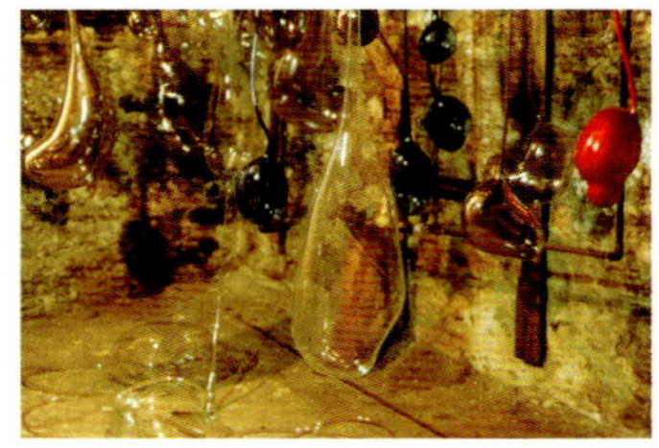

Glass Environment #3
Medium: Glass
Dimensions: 200 sq. ft.

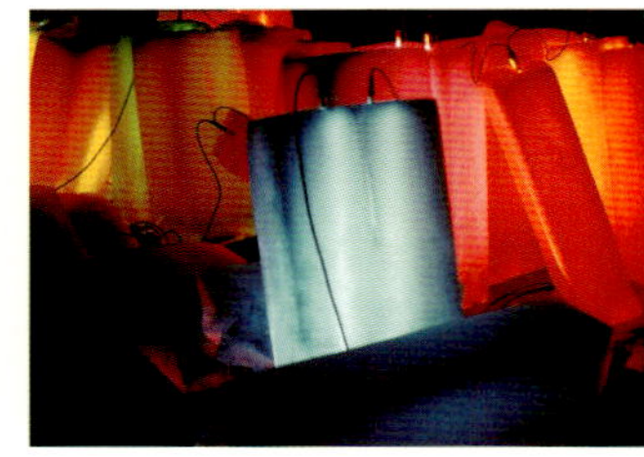

20,000 Pounds of Ice and Neon
Medium: Ice, neon
Dimensions: 600 sq. ft.

I first added neon into my blown forms while in grad school at Madison with Harvey Littleton in 1966–67. The first experiments were inducing neon into organic shapes and using high-frequency energy—without wires or electrodes—to light them up. I made about a dozen of these pieces and they were included in several group shows. The first really major installation with neon—including elements up to nine feet tall—was done with Jamie Carpenter, a RISD student at the time. *Glass Forest* was first shown at RISD and then at the American Craft Museum. It's now in Switzerland at Museum Bellerive in Zurich.

Artpark, Lewiston, New York

In collaboration with Seaver Leslie, 1975

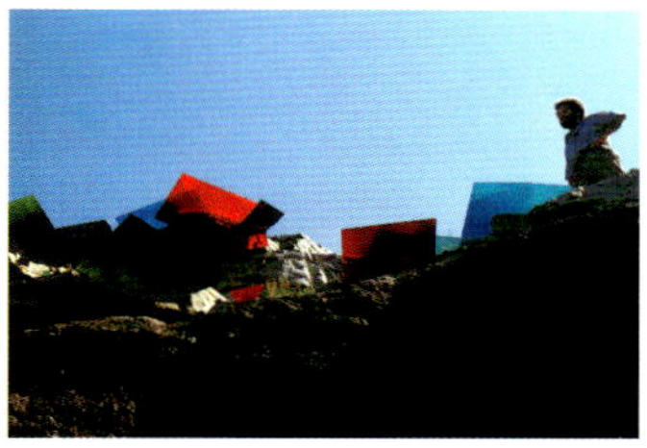

Niagara Gorge Installation
Medium: Stained-glass sheets

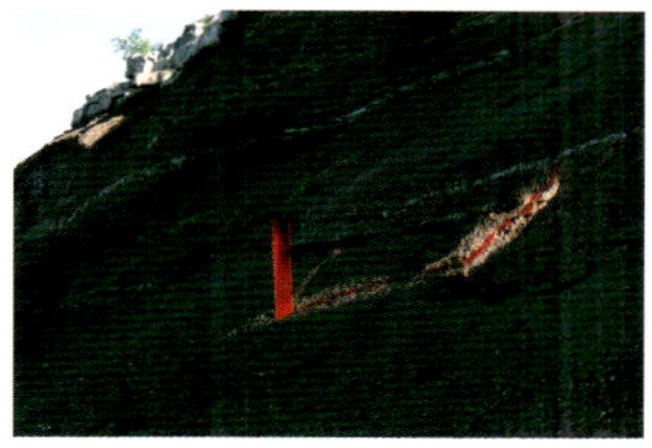

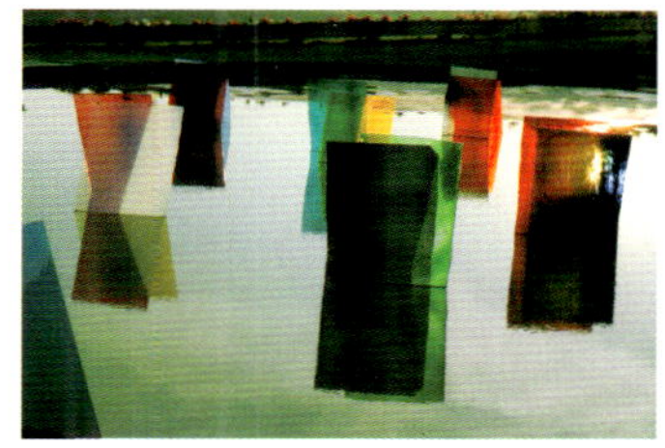

Artpark Installation #4
Medium: Stained-glass sheets

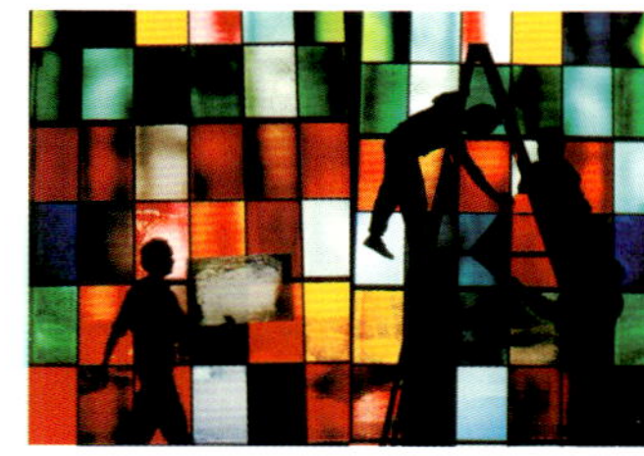

Artpark Installation #7
Medium: Stained-glass sheets
Dimensions: 18 x 10'

Artpark is a fabulous program that invites artists to work outdoors during the summer and make pieces engaging not only the site but the people visiting the park. Lewiston is located on the Niagara River at New York's border with Canada. The challenge was to place the rough landscape *within* the context of art. In 1975, I did a series of site-specific installations in collaboration with Seaver Leslie, another instructor at RISD. Seaver and I used handblown sheets of stained glass in simple arrangements to contrast the material (glass) with the environment (earth) and give physical expression to light (color).

❸ Shaare Emeth Synagogue St. Louis, 1980

Client: Shaare Emeth Synagogue
Architects: Murphy, Downey, Wofford and Richmond

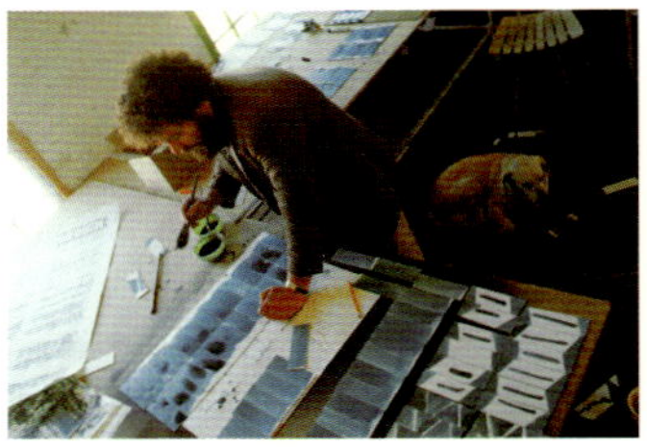

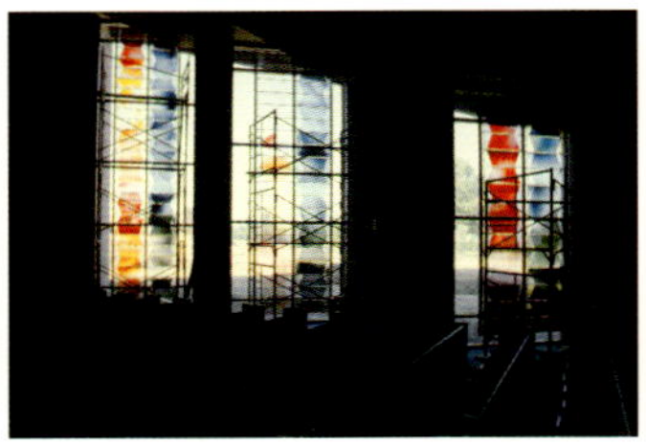

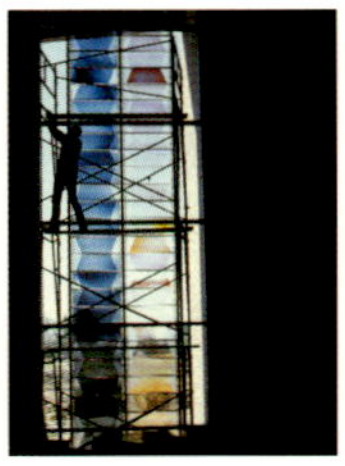

Shaare Emeth Synagogue Windows
Medium: Acid-etched glass, brass
Dimensions: Six panels, two 20' high, two 16' high, and two 12' high
Elements: Six panels

My first architectural commission for a public space, Shaare Emeth, was certainly the biggest project I'd had, with the largest budget, so I hired two RISD students from the glass program (Eve Kaplan and Eric Hopkins) to help me with the project. Eve found a passage in the Torah describing the Israelites led through the desert by a column of smoke by day, and a column of fire by night, and we took this as our inspiration. The stained glass was then acid-etched with linear patterns, and the columns of the window visually lead the congregation to the *bema* (altar) and the synagogue's *ner tamid* (eternal light).

Saint Peter's Church New York City, 1994

Client: Saint Peter's Church
Architects: Hugh Stubbins & Associates
Interiors: Vignelli Associates

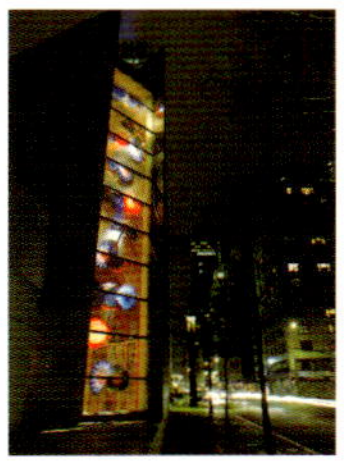

Persian Window
Medium: Handblown glass, steel
Dimensions: 50 x 10'
Weight: 10–15 lbs. each
Elements: 18

Saint Peter's has been a cultural hot spot for decades. Once known as the Jazz Ministry and famous for concerts with the greats, in its new home, a building designed by Hugh Stubbins with interiors by Massimo and Lella Vignelli, Saint Peter's is just as famous for its work with visual artists. The chapel is by Louise Nevelson, while other parts of the church have hosted exhibitions and temporary installations. Asked to work in the sanctuary,

I wanted to make full use of the soaring height there, especially since this was emphasized by a fifty-foot-tall window. It gave me an opportunity to do my first window installation outside of a museum. We also hung one of my first *Chandeliers* over the baptismal font.

❺ **Seattle Art Museum,** 1992

Architects: Venturi, Scott, Brown and Associates

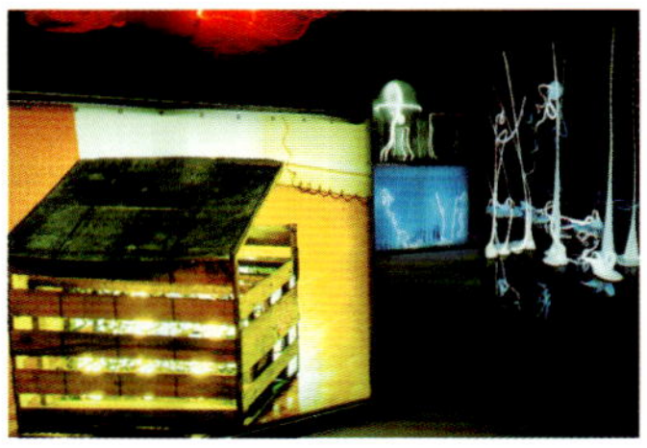

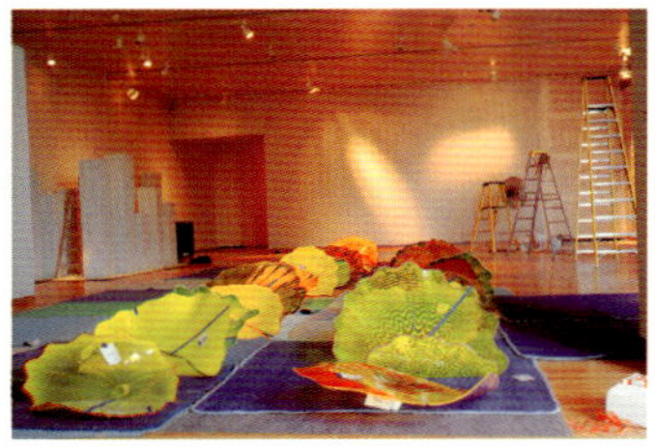

Duratrans
Medium: Photographic Mylar
Dimensions: 5 x 9'
Elements: 12

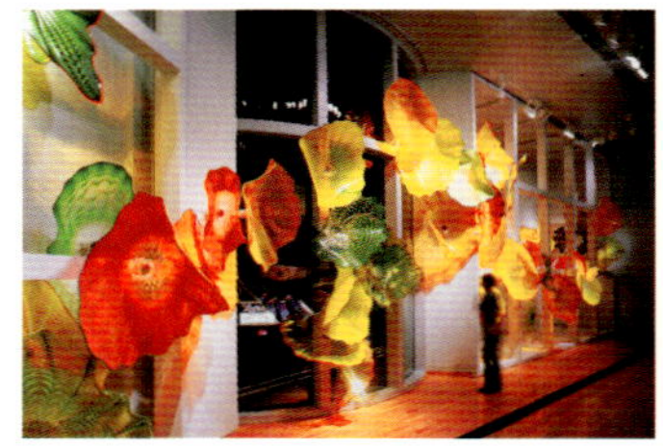

Venturi Window
Medium: Handblown glass, steel
Dimensions: 16 x 48 x 7'
Weight: Up to 20 lbs. each
Elements: 43

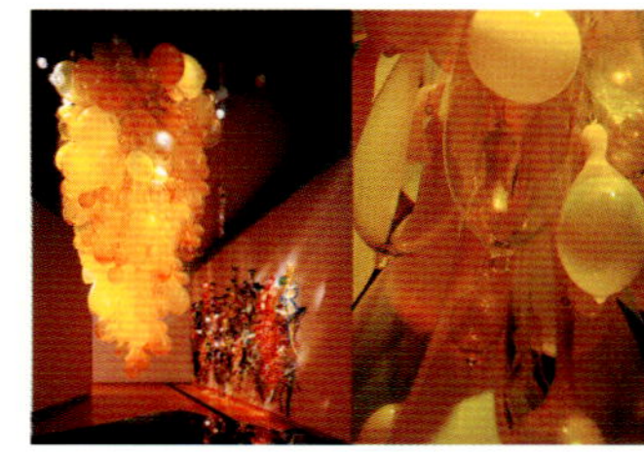

Seattle Art Museum Chandelier
Medium: Handblown glass, steel mesh, wire, filament
Dimensions: 9 x 4 x 4'
Weight: 400 lbs.
Elements: 180

Ikebana Flower Wall
Medium: Handblown glass
Dimensions: 10 x 20'
Weight: 2–6 lbs. each
Elements: 130

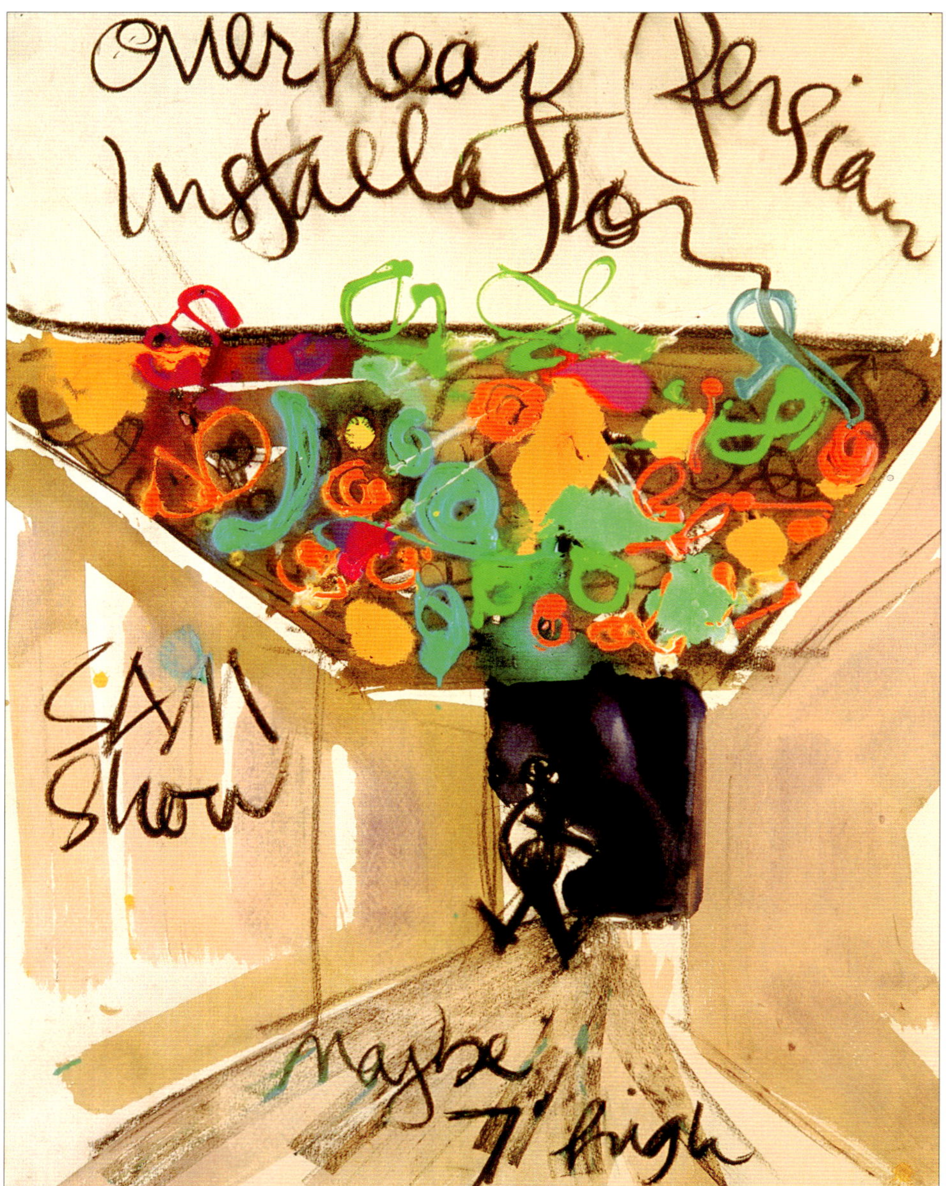

In 1992, the Seattle Art Museum (SAM) moved from Volunteer Park to downtown Seattle into a building designed by Robert Venturi. I was given the first solo exhibition in its brand-new, nine-thousand-square-foot second floor. Together with Patterson Sims, SAM's chief curator at the time, we worked on the plan and the pieces for several months and finally mocked up the whole exhibition, full-scale, at the studio just to make sure.

A lot of new work came from this process, including my first *Chandelier* and a new series, *Pilchuck Stumps*. It even included my first work with plastics, a set for the Debussy opera *Pelléas et Mélisande*. However, the glory of *Dale Chihuly: Installations 1964–1992* was the *Venturi Window*—forty-three blown rondels mounted on an architectural frame set against the museum's impressive central window. I'm proud to say the exhibition was a big hit. About 170,000 people visited SAM that summer, and the show has toured since then to ten cities, and each venue becomes the occasion for new developments in the work as we work to fit the show to each space and institution.

MacMillan Residence
Indian Wells, California, 1996

Client: Donna & Cargill MacMillan
Architect: Guy Drier

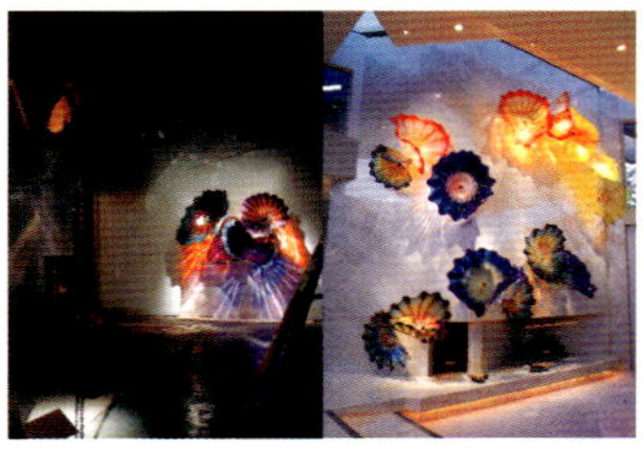

Indian Wells Wall
Medium: Handblown glass, steel
Dimensions: 20 x 17'
Weight: Approx. 15 lbs. each large piece
Elements: 15 large pieces, multiple smaller pieces

It's rare in my experience to find such adventurous patrons as Donna and Cargill MacMillan, and rare, too, to find a site with so many opportunities for creativity. All told, I've done five installations there: two indoors and three outside. I've worked in the garden with *Ikebana* forms, in the pool with *Floats*, and on the river that runs through the dining room. Most spectacular of all, however, is the *Persian* installation on the magnificent marble fireplace wall. Some twenty by seventeen feet, this is my largest commission in a private home.

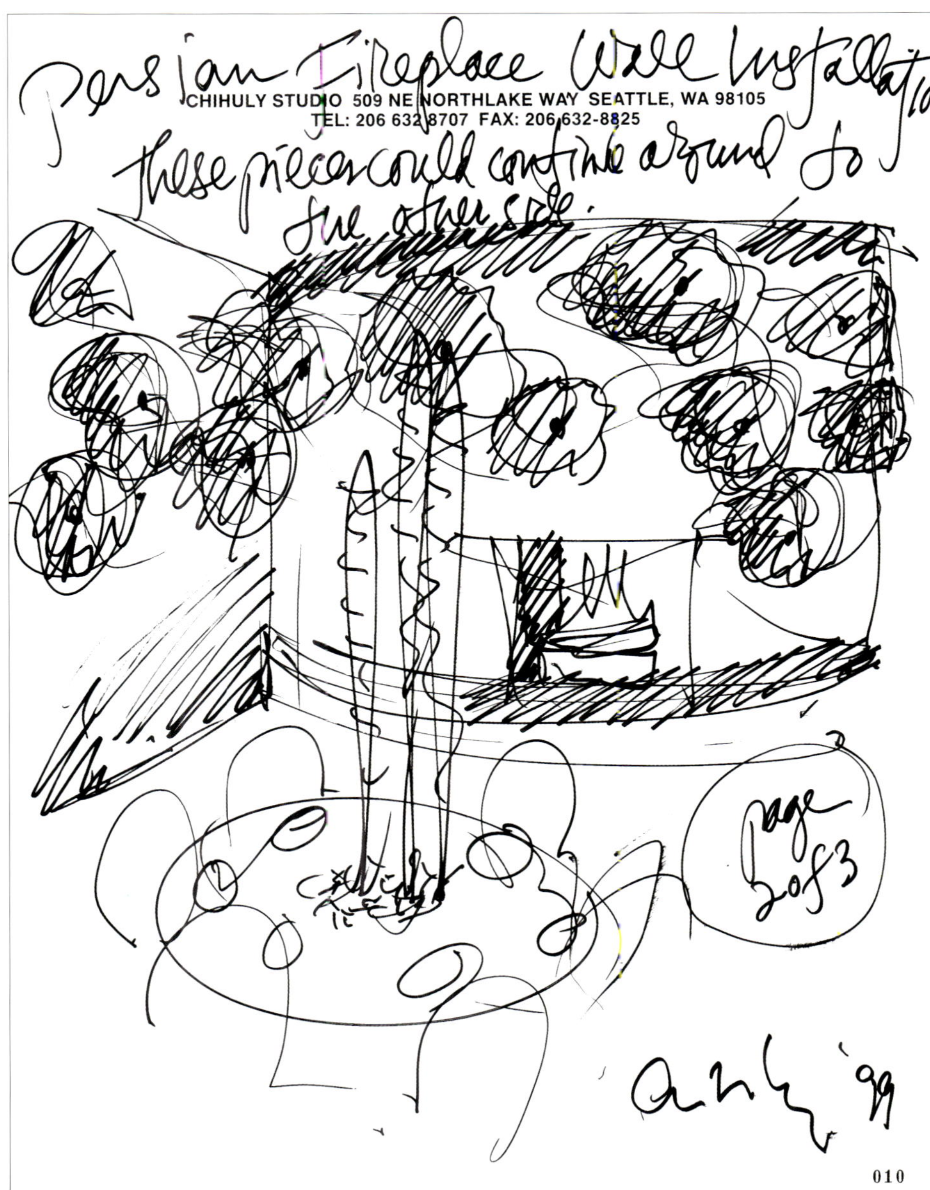

7 Stewart Williams House
Palm Springs, California, 2000

Architect: E. Stewart Williams

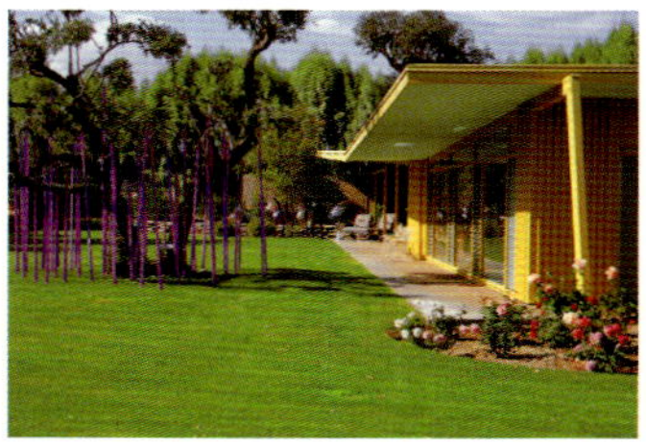

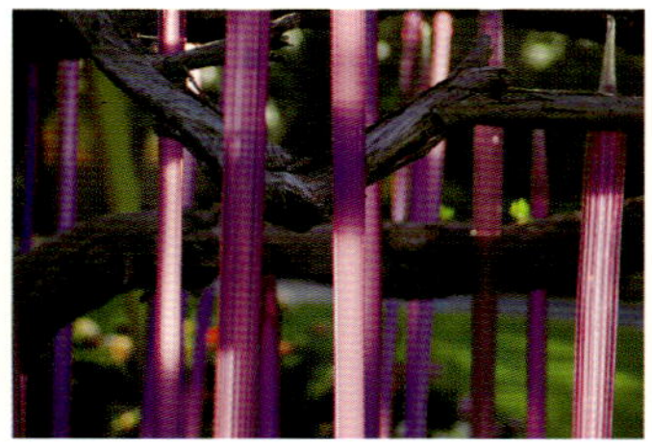

Purple Reeds
Medium: Handblown glass
Dimensions: 10 x 20 x 17'
Weight: Up to 15 lbs. each
Elements: 45

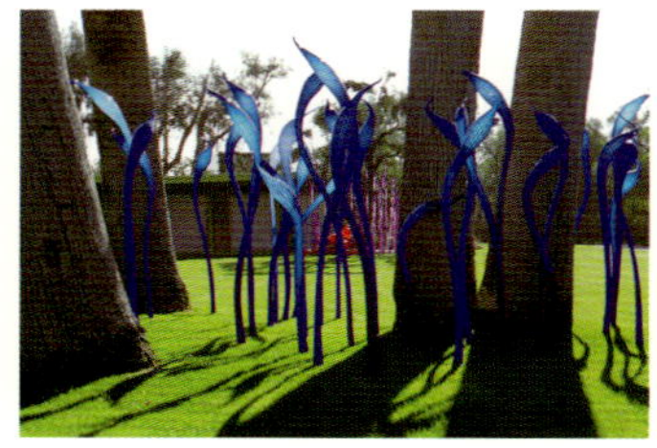

Blue Herons
Medium: Handblown glass
Dimensions: 6 x 17 x 13'
Weight: 5–10 lbs. each
Elements: 31

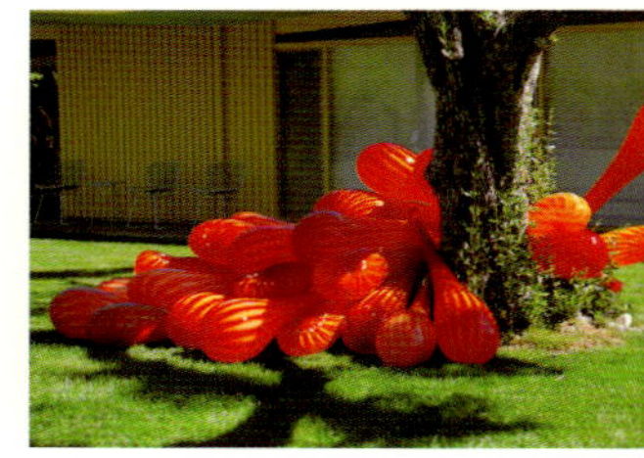

Red Saguaros
Medium: Handblown glass
Dimensions: 4 x 10 x 6'
Weight: Up to 15 lbs. each
Elements: 33

Stewart Williams is one of the most prominent architects in the area, and he built this house for himself and his wife, Mari, in 1955. It is classic 1950s California architecture, with a low-swung "butterfly" roofline, floor-to-ceiling windows and doors, industrial materials, and a great setting. The architecture of the house reflected the expressions of the industrial age after the war. All these new materials, such as plywood and metal, never used before in houses, are all suddenly being used in a very unusual architectural way. I was lucky enough to get the house and it has since become a great place to experiment with outdoor installations—and to enjoy the warm sun.

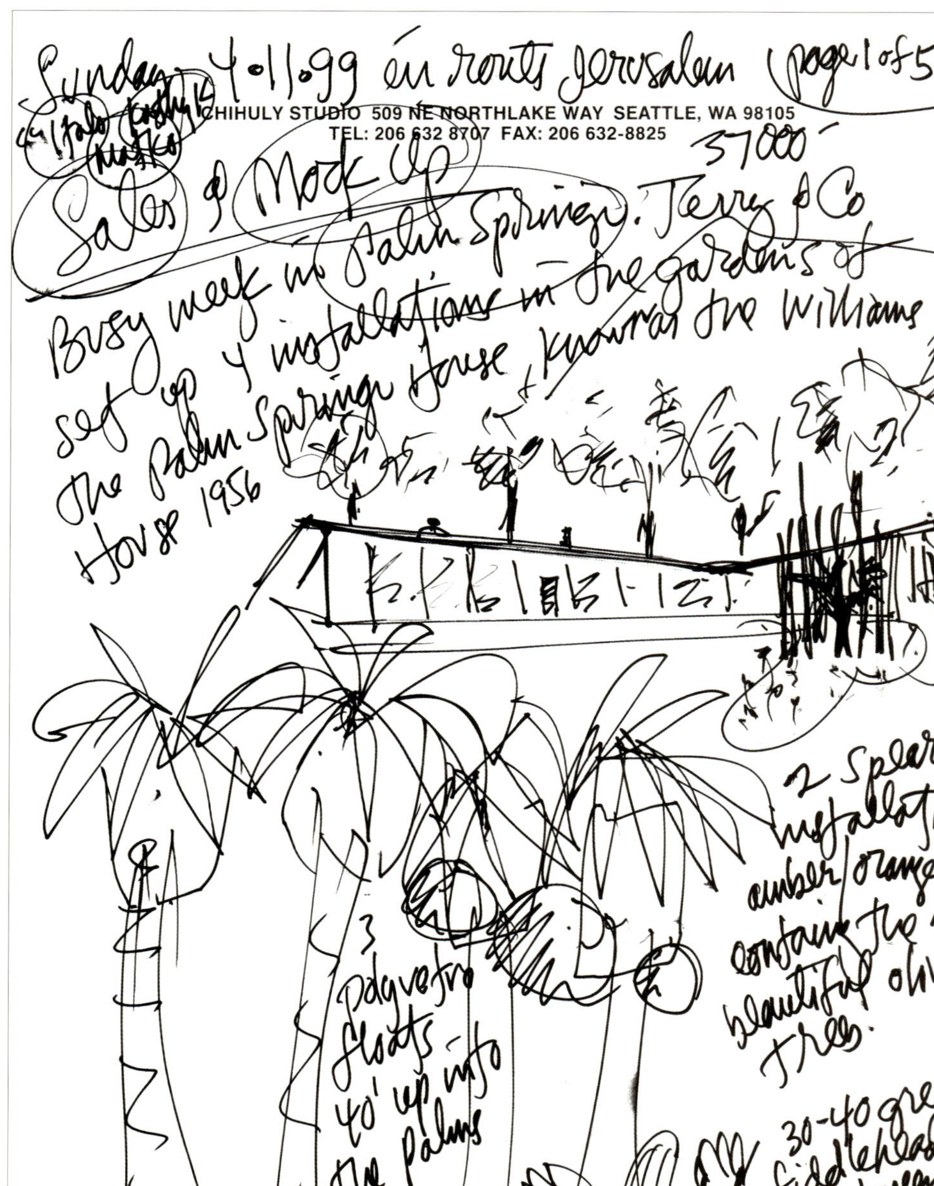

Albright-Knox Art Gallery
Buffalo, New York, 1997

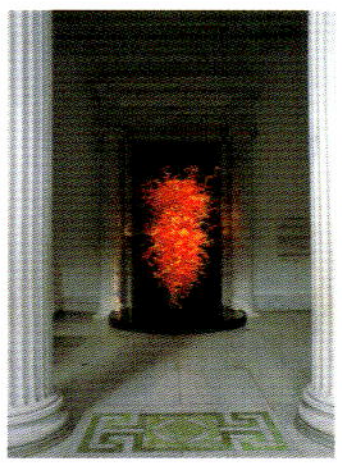

Orange Chandelier with Horns and Bulbs
Medium: Handblown glass, steel
Dimensions: 9 x 5 x 5'
Weight: 665 lbs.
Elements: 244

After a museum signs up for an exhibition, I make a site visit to design the show. The pieces are created around the museum's galleries, courtyards, and exterior spaces. Although many of the installations are similar from one exhibit to another, they are each site specific. The Albright-Knox Art Gallery and other museums often ask for pieces that are unique to their museum. In the lobby of the Albright-Knox there is a pair of columns, and I designed a chandelier centered between these two columns. The essence of an installation show is to evolve the environment into something that transforms the space and excites the viewers.

9 Pillsbury Mansion Wayzata, Minnesota, 1997

Client: Jim & Joann Jundt
Architect: Harrie T. Lindeberg

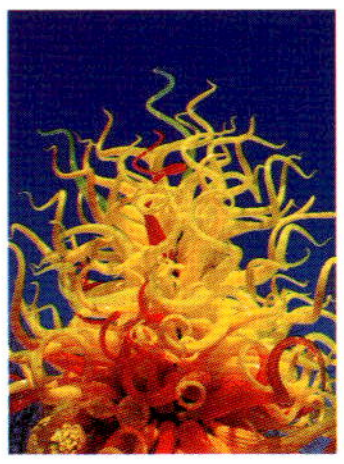

Multicolored Hourglass Chandelier
Medium: Handblown glass, steel
Dimensions: 14 x 8 x 8'
Weight: 2.2 lbs. each
Elements: 600–650

On the occasion of museum exhibitions we sometimes find an adjacent property—a city park or wild land—for installing some outdoor pieces. This time, when the exhibition *Chihuly Installations* toured the Minneapolis Institute of Arts, it was a neighboring historic estate, known as the Pillsbury Mansion. The current owners made the turn-of-the-century gardens on Lake Minnetonka, cloaked in winter's snow, available not just to me, but to museum members.

Dale first met Jim and Joann Jundt when his *Installations* exhibition was mounted at the Jundt Art Museum at Gonzaga University in Spokane, Washington. A year or so later *Installations* was to come to Minneapolis, the home of the Jundts. As part of their generous support of the museum, they were to be hosting a series of opening events for the Minneapolis Institute of Arts at their home in Wayzata. Discussions began, and Dale's vision quickly grew to two containers of glass to be delivered the next Tuesday. He would do a series of installations throughout their home and gardens for these events. On Tuesday two containers, ten people, and Dale all arrived. The Jundts were gracious, surprised, excited, and proud to have Dale install such extraordinary work at their home. The work stayed to see how it would hold up in the depths of the Minnesota winter. How unusual in life for someone's true vision to become reality.

Karin Johnson

At the same time that we were doing a project at the Minneapolis Institute of Arts, we were scrambling to have two semi trucks, filled with glass, arrive at a private residence on Lake Minnetonka. Dale wanted to test the glass in the cold of a Minnesota winter. A second team was flown in to handle that installation, while we finished at the museum. It was about nineteen degrees outside during the day. Over the course of three days, Dale directed us in building two pieces that seemed huge to us back then (about seventeen feet), plus other smaller installations. The owners of the home were good sports, if a little overwhelmed by the full force of the Chihuly road show in action. They funneled ample amounts of chili, hot cocoa, and pizza our way.

Jennifer Lewis

Honolulu Academy of Arts, 1992

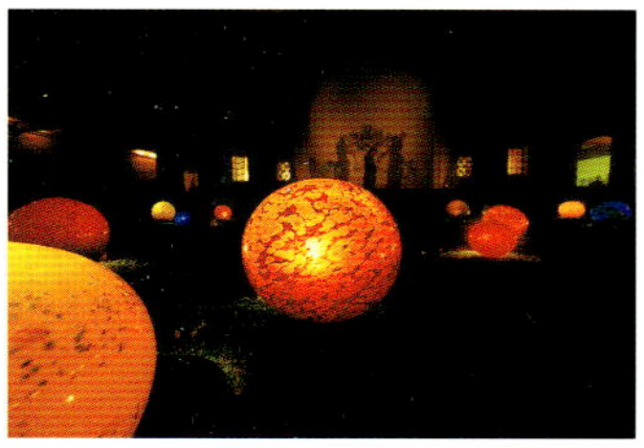

Central Court
Medium: Handblown glass
Dimensions: 20–40" diameter
Weight: Up to 40 lbs.
Elements: 23–26

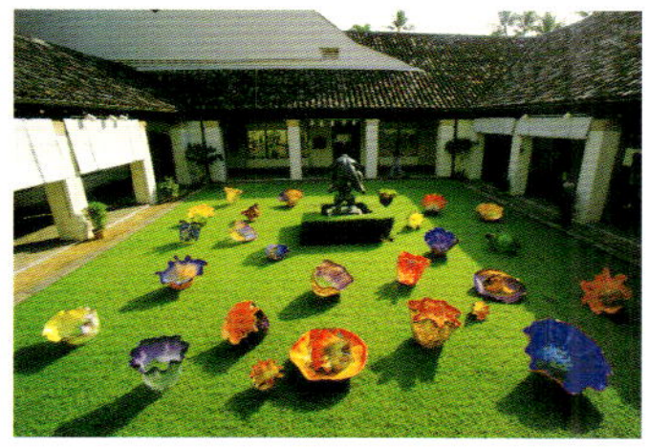

Kinau Court
Medium: Handblown glass
Dimensions: 24 x 40"
Weight: Up to 25 lbs. each
Elements: 25–30

As the first chance to work outdoors at a museum, *Chihuly Courtyards* was a truly unique exhibition. Housed in a gracious turn-of-the-century building surrounding five courtyards, the Honolulu Academy boasts the single most important collection in the Islands. Working hand in hand with George Ellis, the director, and Sarah Bremser, curator for the show, we developed five outdoor installations responding to the architecture and Honolulu's extraordinary light. It was my first museum exhibition with all the pieces exposed to the elements—which included the challenge of lighting at night.

⓫ 100,000 Pounds of Ice and Neon
Tacoma, Washington, 1993

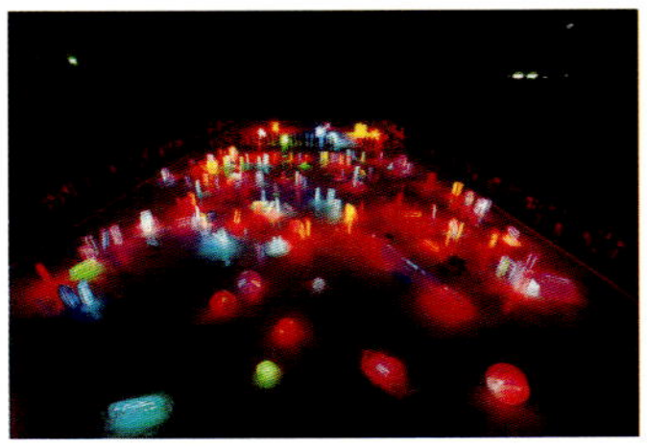

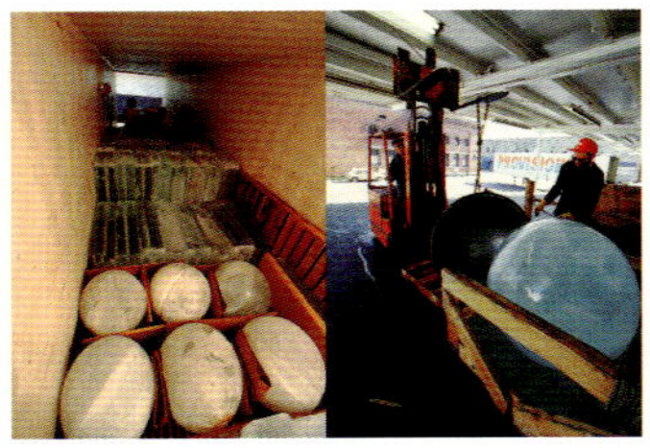

100,000 Pounds of Ice and Neon
Medium: Ice, neon
Dimensions: 85 x 200'
Weight: 10-, 250-, 300-, and 1,000-lb. blocks and spheres
Elements: 300–350

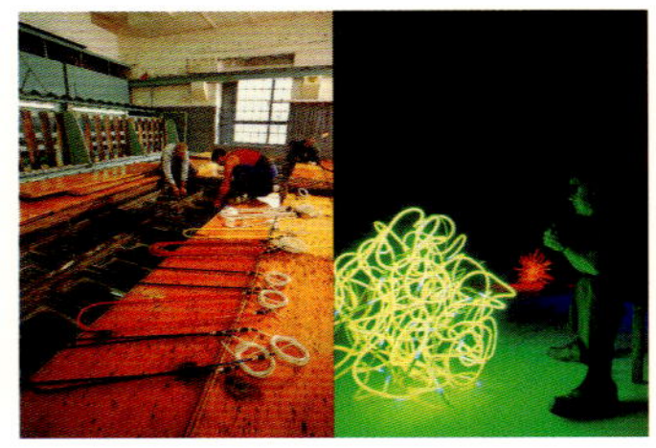

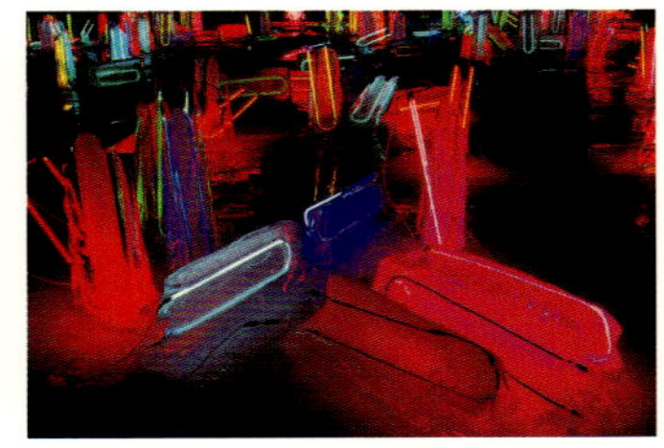

Tacoma Tumbleweed
Medium: Neon
Dimensions: 6' diameter
Elements: 7

After remaking *20,000 Pounds of Ice and Neon* for the opening at the Seattle Art Museum, I decided to experiment. Thinking about making a neon "drawing" in the ice, where else do you turn but to an ice rink. So, I approached my hometown rink at the Tacoma Dome for permission to run the test, and permission was granted. However, the local newspaper heard about it and editorialized that my "experiment" should be open to the public, and so finally it was. Open to the public, yes; an experiment, no. After all, I could not fail the folks of my hometown. We created a spectacle of one hundred thousand pounds of ice in three-hundred-pound blocks with neon of all colors frozen inside, complemented with seven neon tumbleweeds, and an ice-skater to top it all off. Thirty-three thousand people came through that weekend, lots of families came back three or four times, and it made me realize just how interested people—everyday people—are in seeing art and how very much it can mean to children.

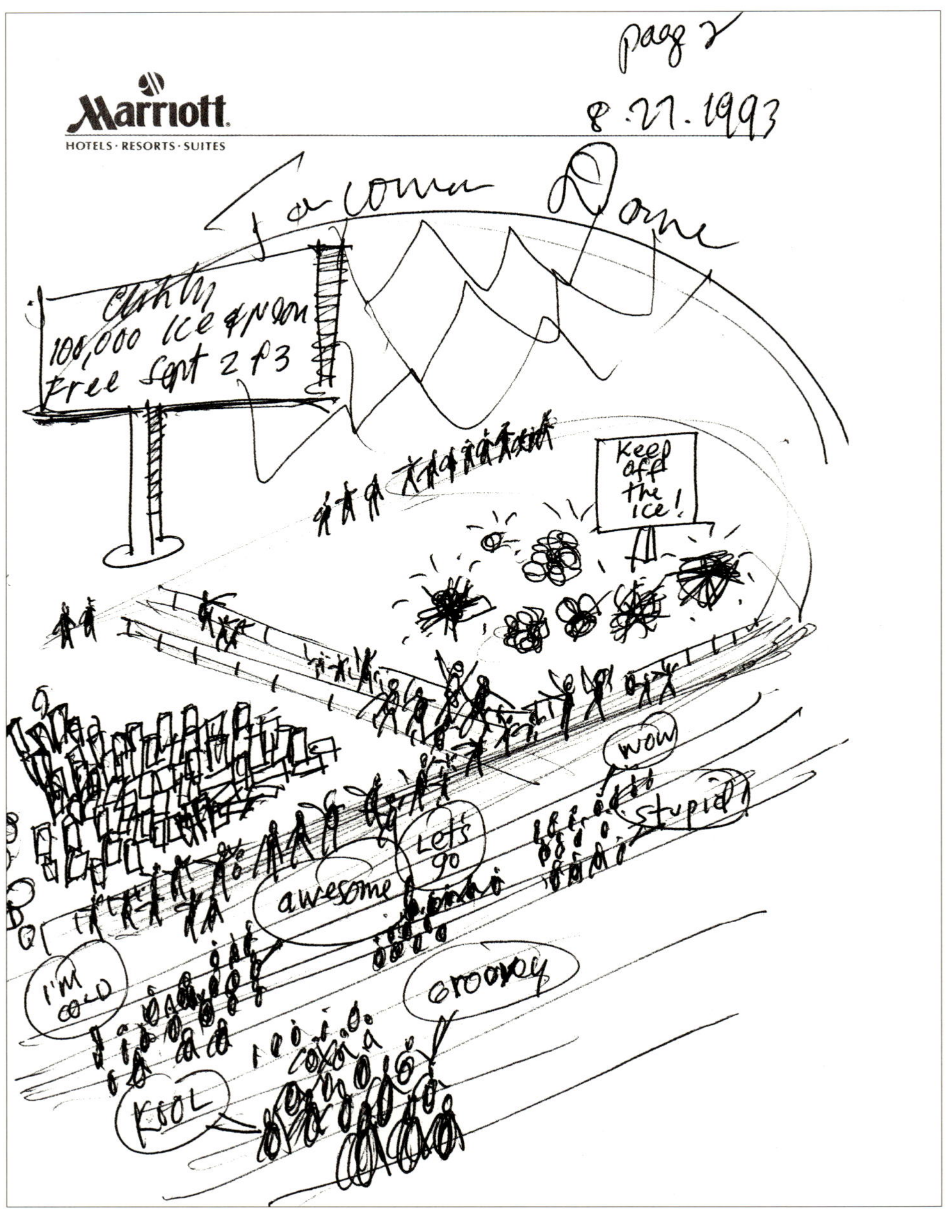

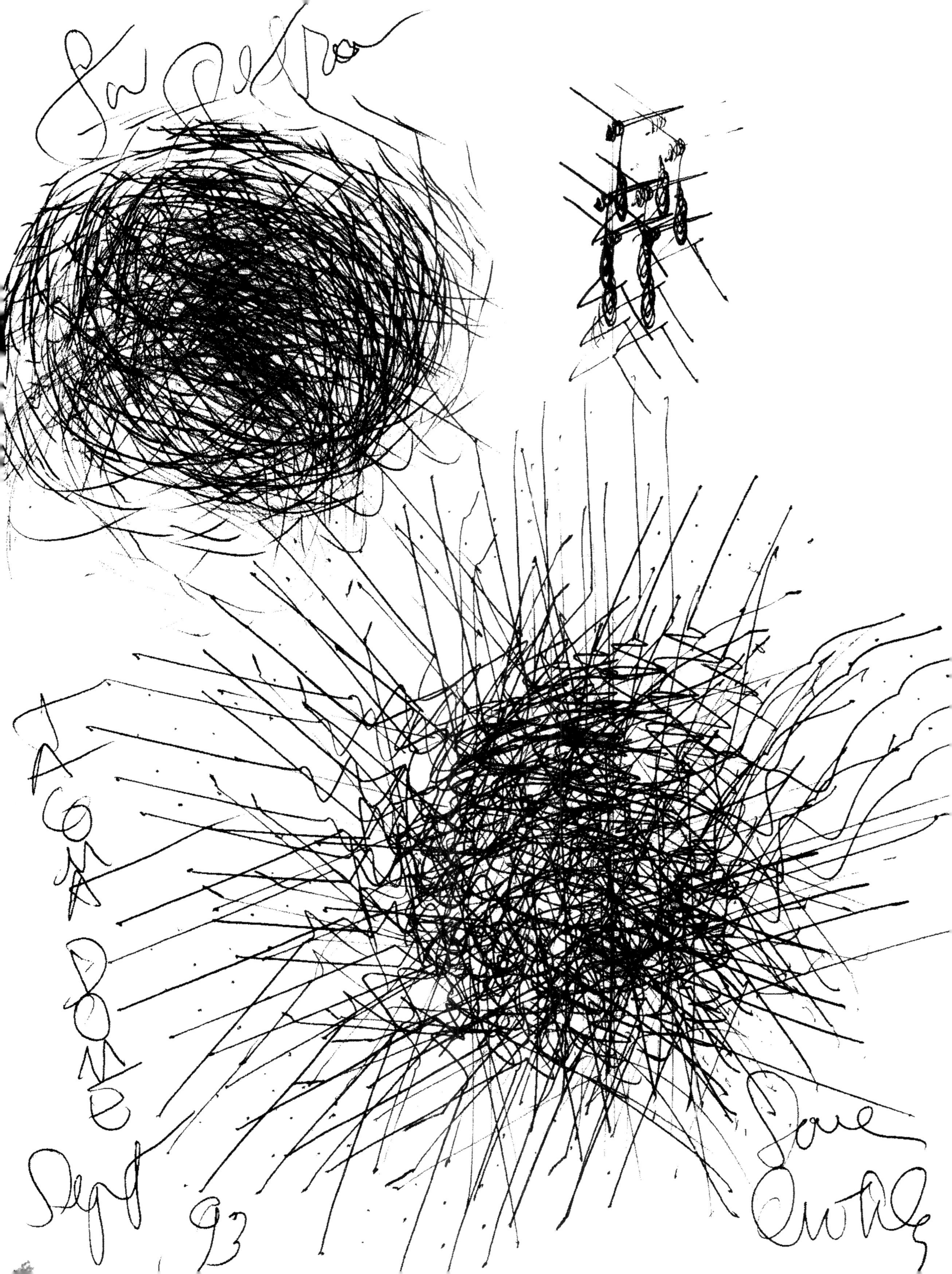
Sept 93

12 Rose Window
Minneapolis Institute of Arts, 1997

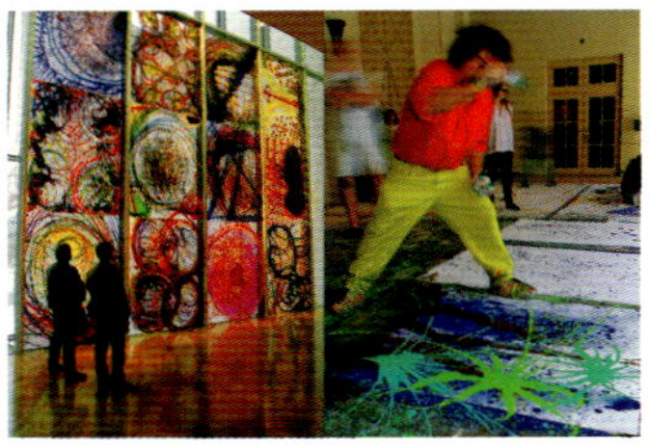

Rose Window
Medium: Glass stain and acrylic on thermoplastic
Dimensions: 21 x 24'
Elements: 12 panels

Drawing is an inspiration for me, and I often draw while the team blows glass. Not just to show them what to make, but just because I like doing it. The first drawing wall was in 1992 when I installed all my drawings—maybe one hundred—made at a workshop with children there while we were putting up the show at the Honolulu Academy of Arts. The wall wrapped around the room. What next? Draw on transparent material, glass or plastic or Plexiglas. For Minneapolis I drew the *Rose Window* on six-by-eight-foot sheets of Plexiglas with special inks and transparent dyes with this special site in mind.

At first Dale wanted to put his opera set of *Pelléas et Mélisande* in the space, but then he decided to do some very large drawings on Plexiglas. We cut each drawing on-site to fit the space, and they glowed beautifully during the day with the Minnesota snow as a backdrop. However, it really bothered Dale that the opacity was lost at night. He wanted to place something opaque behind the drawings for the opening night, a curtain or a scrim. He kept telling us to get some mountain-climbing club to go up inside the space with ropes to put up a scrim, and we kept telling him that it was *Minnesota*, and there were no mountains. Then someone thought of attaching a line to a tennis ball and hitting it over a crossbar with a racket, pulling the scrim up that way.
It was in Minneapolis that I learned not to try to talk Chihuly out of something that he thinks will make his work look the way he wants it to look. There is a great urge sometimes to do just that to avoid a lot of work and trouble. But as soon as you accept that when you're working for him, you are going to go to any length to achieve the effect he wants, it stops being trouble, and is just routine. Call up mountain-climbing clubs and get them inside a window sandwich? Find every square foot of cheesecloth in the city? Not a problem. You can do a lot on the phone. In the end, Dale was able to place the curtain behind the drawings. They looked great.

Jennifer Lewis

CHIHULY STUDIO 509 NE NORTHLAKE WAY SEATTLE, WA 98105
TEL: 206 632 8707 FAX: 206 632 8825

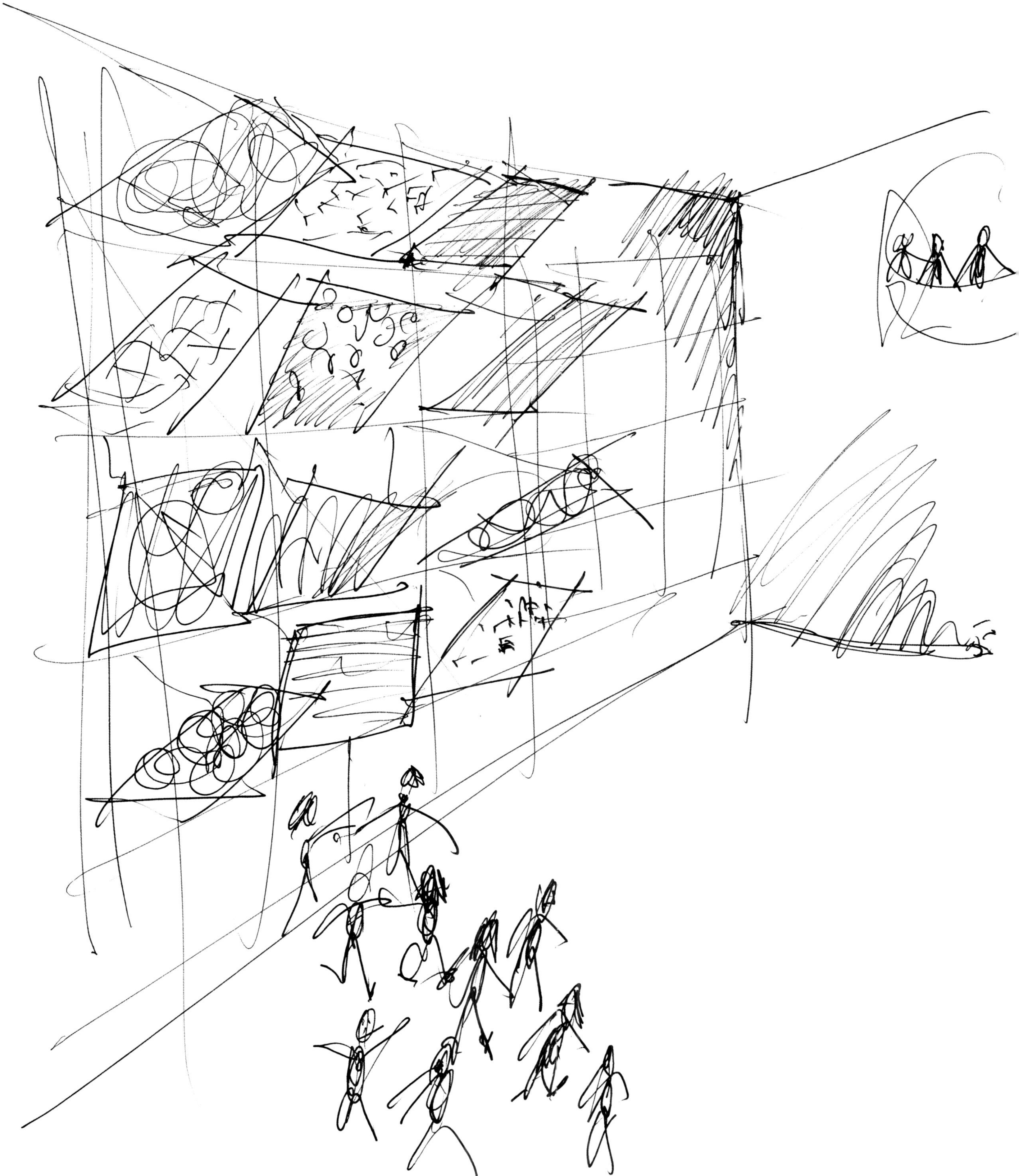

13 Joslyn Art Museum
Omaha, Nebraska, 2000

Client: Joslyn Art Museum
Architect: Sir Norman Foster

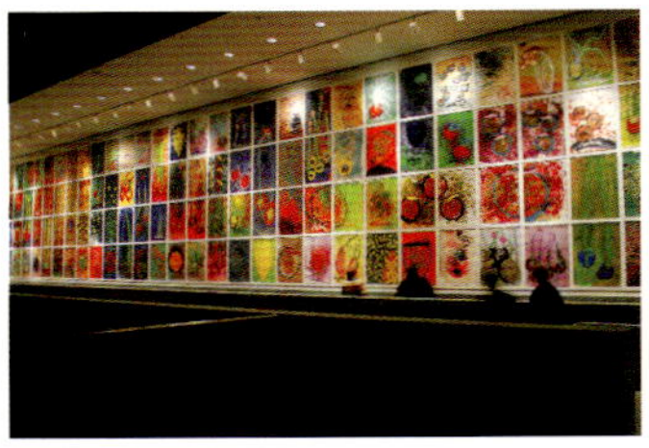

Drawing Wall
Medium: Acrylic on paper
Dimensions: 15 x 77'
Elements: 104

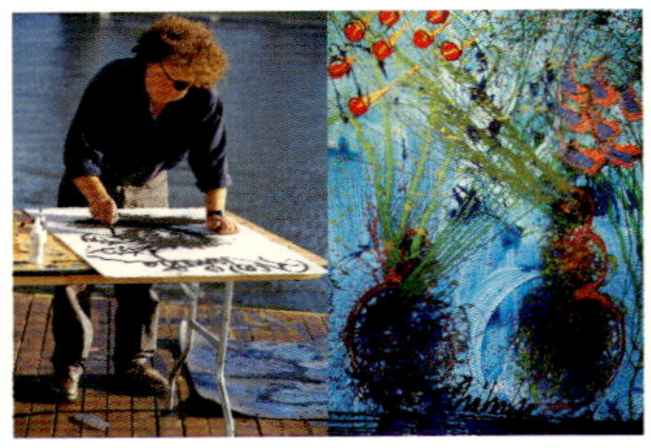

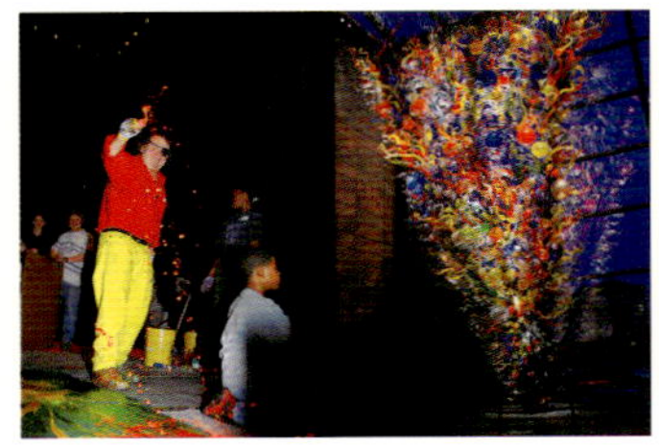

Joslyn Window
Medium: Handblown glass, steel
Dimensions: 33 x 22 (at top) x 8'
Weight: 12,500 lbs.
Elements: 2,084

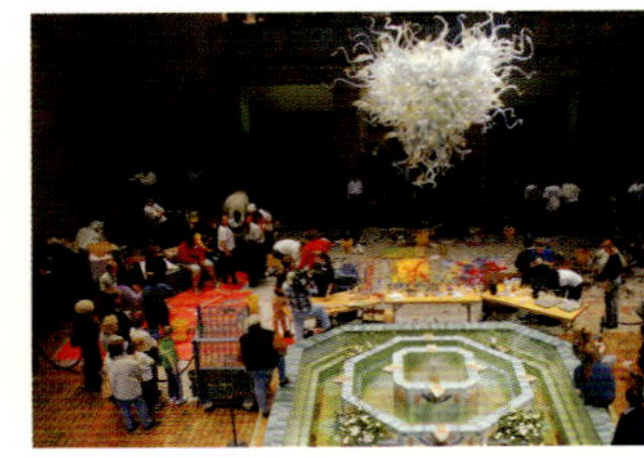

Gilded Silver and Aquamarine Chandelier
Medium: Handblown glass, steel
Dimensions: 24.5 x 10'
Weight: 1,500 lbs.
Elements: 985

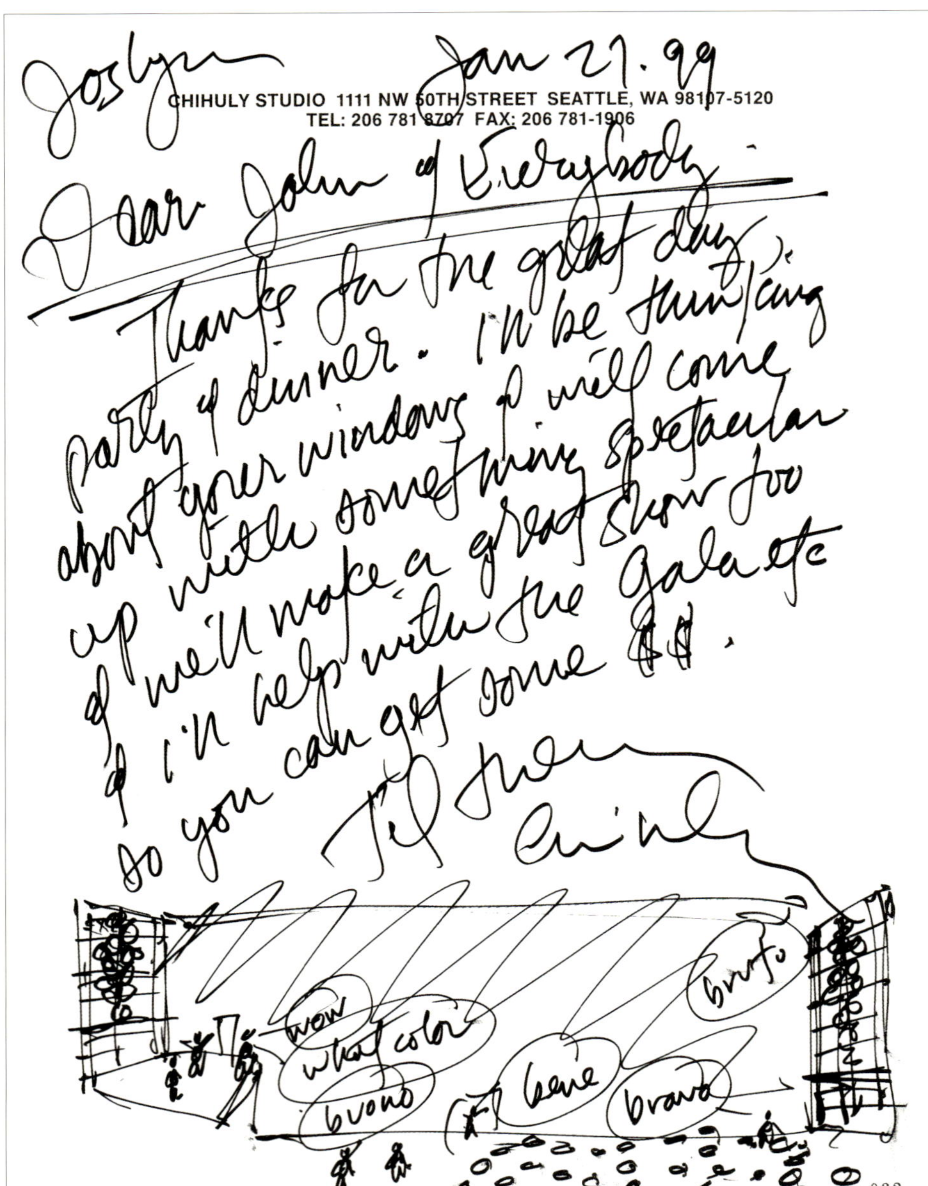

Joslyn Jan 27.99

CHIHULY STUDIO 1111 NW 50TH STREET SEATTLE, WA 98107-5120
TEL: 206 781 8707 FAX: 206 781-1906

Dear John & Everybody –
Thanks for the great day, party & dinner. I'll be thinking about your windows & we'll come up with something spectacular & we'll make a great show too & I'll help with the Gala etc so you can get some $$.
Til then
Chihuly

032

This museum commission for a soaring fifty-foot-high atrium designed by Sir Norman Foster, with a thirty-five-foot window, demanded a singular solution. On vertical struts radiating from a central point, over two thousand handblown parts create a monumental window of color and form. At the same time, *Chihuly Installations* opened at the museum with fifteen new installations, a new drawing wall, and a new ice wall.

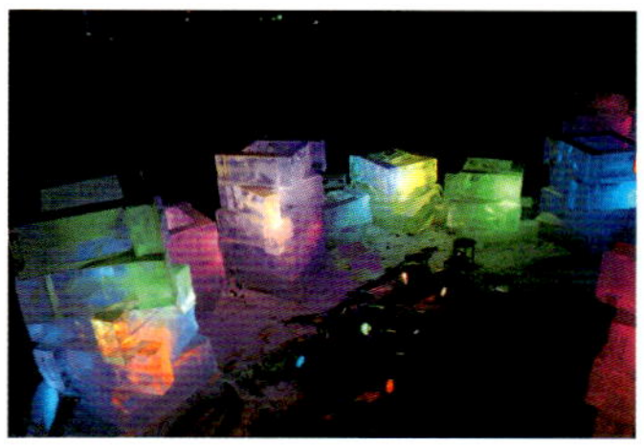

Joslyn Ice
Medium: Ice, stage lights with colored gels
Dimensions: Approx. 14 x 150 x 30'
Weight: 300–340 lbs. each
Elements: 250 blocks

The concept was generated a couple of days before Christmas, developed over the Christmas break, and we went into fabrication around the second or third of January. The scale of the project was quite large, but took only about a month from conception to completion of the piece in Omaha on the 11th of February. Once we decided it was going to be like a sail coming off the window, we worked with engineers to calculate the load bearing. We got to the final designs, but we couldn't build it in our studio because it was too big. We rented the South Seattle shop of a fabricating company that had a crane in it, and worked there. In the course of about a week and a half, we built the primary structure including the armature, exclusive of the gridwork that holds the glass.

Once it was ready to go, it was shipped to Omaha. On-site we started doing the gridwork, which is a stainless-steel bar matrix that you don't really see in the final piece, but is extremely important because it controls the final composition. The other unique thing about this project is that it's the first project where we built the armature as we put the glass on. We had these machines that shoot the spikes on, kind of like a nail gun that welds.

Philip Stewart

14 Lismore Castle Ireland, 1995

Factory: Waterford Crystal Limited

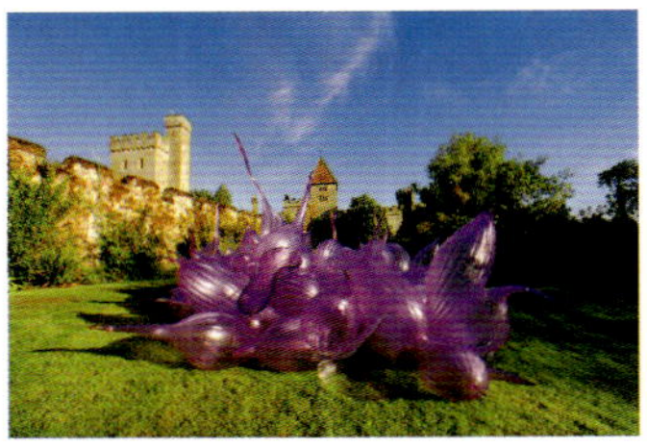

Garden Installation
Medium: Handblown glass
Dimensions: Up to 3 x 2' each
Weight: 3–4 lbs. each
Elements: 15–20

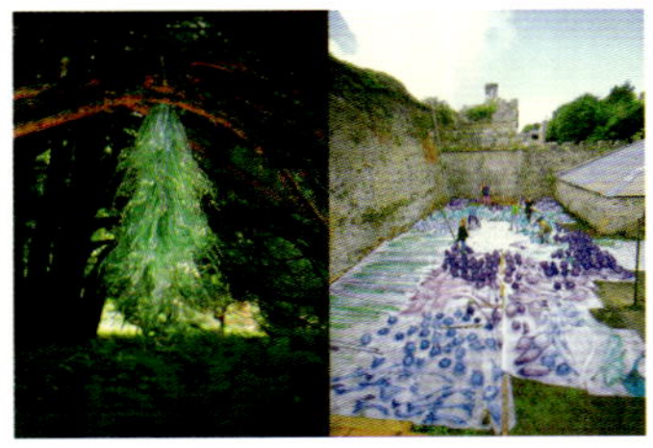

Turquoise Forest Chandelier
Medium: Handblown glass, steel
Dimensions: 8 x 5'
Weight: 608 lbs.
Elements: 76

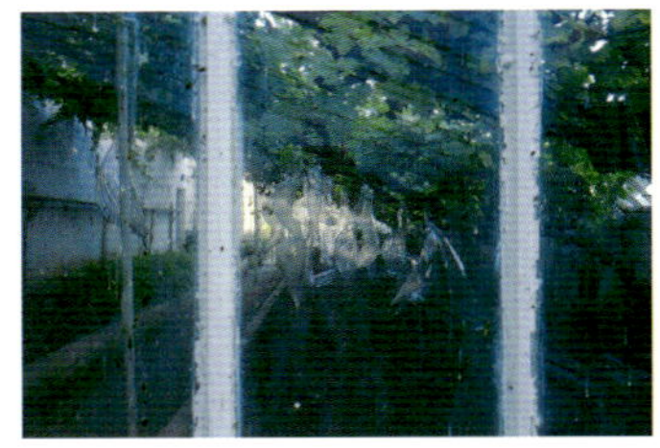

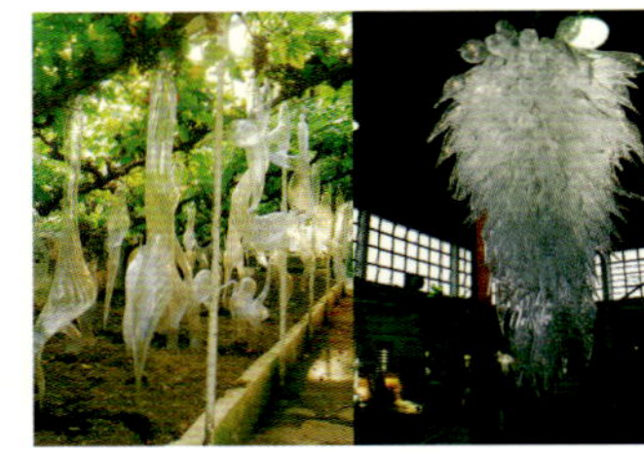

Greenhouse
Medium: Handblown glass
Dimensions: 6 x 10 x 6'
Weight: 2–4 lbs. each
Elements: 33

Cut Crystal Chandelier #1
Medium: Handblown glass, steel
Dimensions: 8 x 4 x 4'
Weight: 1,500 lbs.
Elements: 180–220

I was excited about going with a large team to the famous crystal factory, Waterford, for three weeks to blow glass. We stayed in nearby Lismore and took the opportunity to make about twenty installations on the grounds of Lismore Castle. Owned by the dukes of Devonshire, Lismore Castle and its gardens were redesigned by Sir Joseph Paxton. He also designed the Crystal Palace in Hyde Park, one of the wonders of nineteenth-century architecture. Working at Waterford was a special treat in large part because the people were so great, but also because the glass they use and the opportunities for cutting and engraving the blown glass forms were new to me.

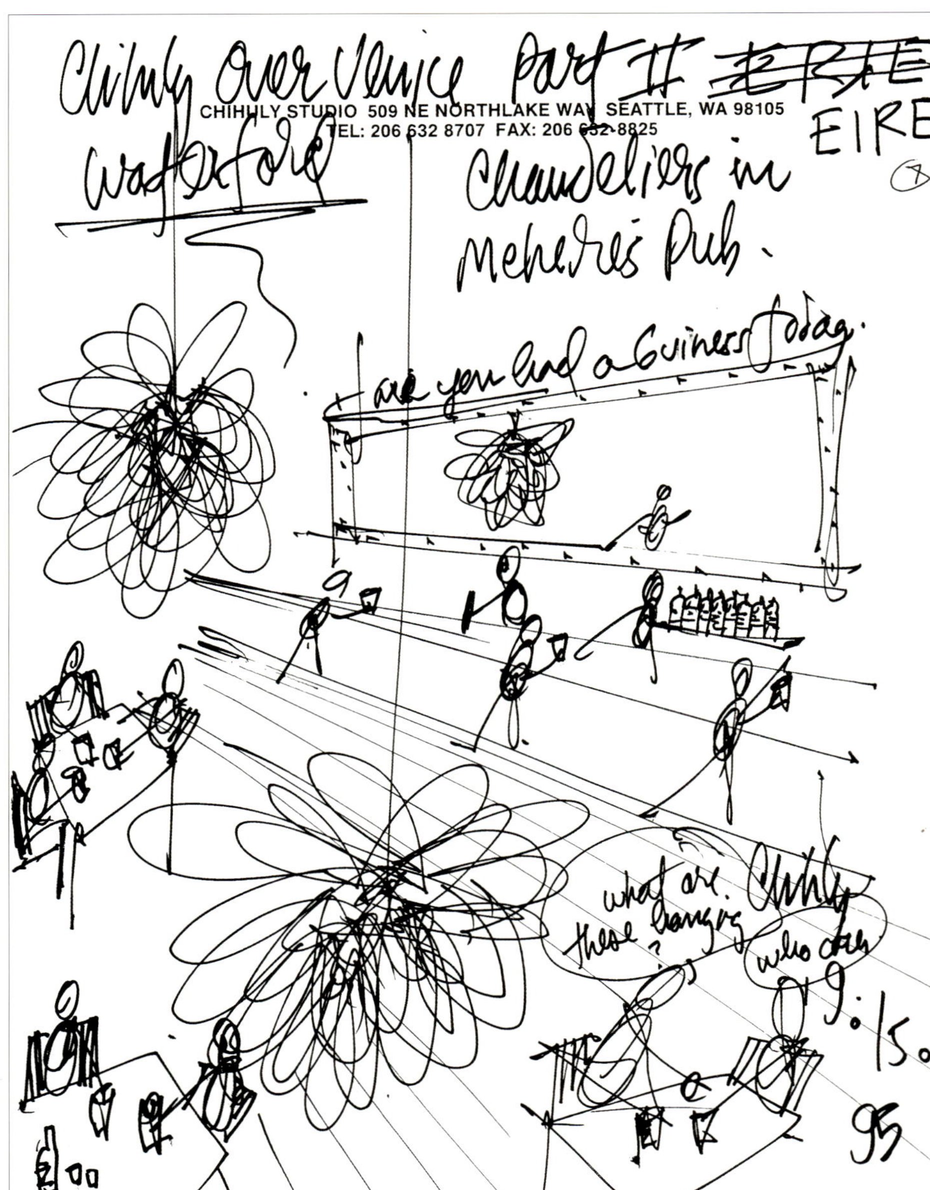

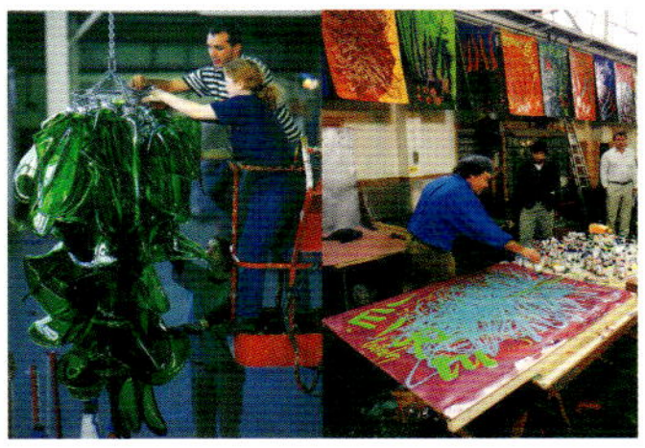

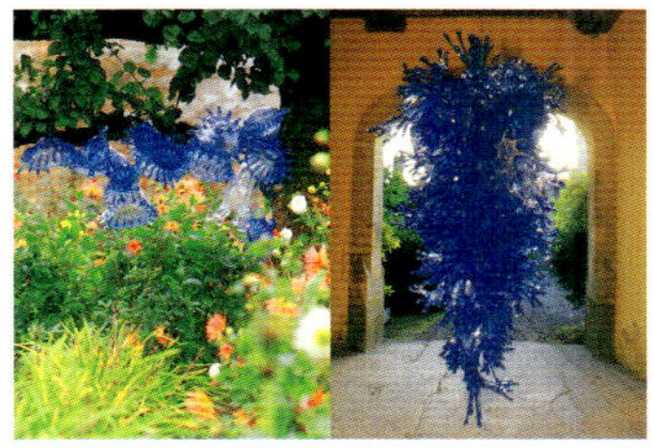

Emerald Green Chandelier
Medium: Handblown glass, steel
Dimensions: 7 x 4 x 4'
Weight: 600 lbs.
Elements: 40–50

Paxton's Garden
Medium: Handblown glass
Dimensions: 6 x 12'
Weight: 340 lbs.
Elements: 75

Frog Foot Chandelier
Medium: Handblown glass, steel
Dimensions: 12 x 6 x 6'
Weight: 1,250 lbs.
Elements: 300

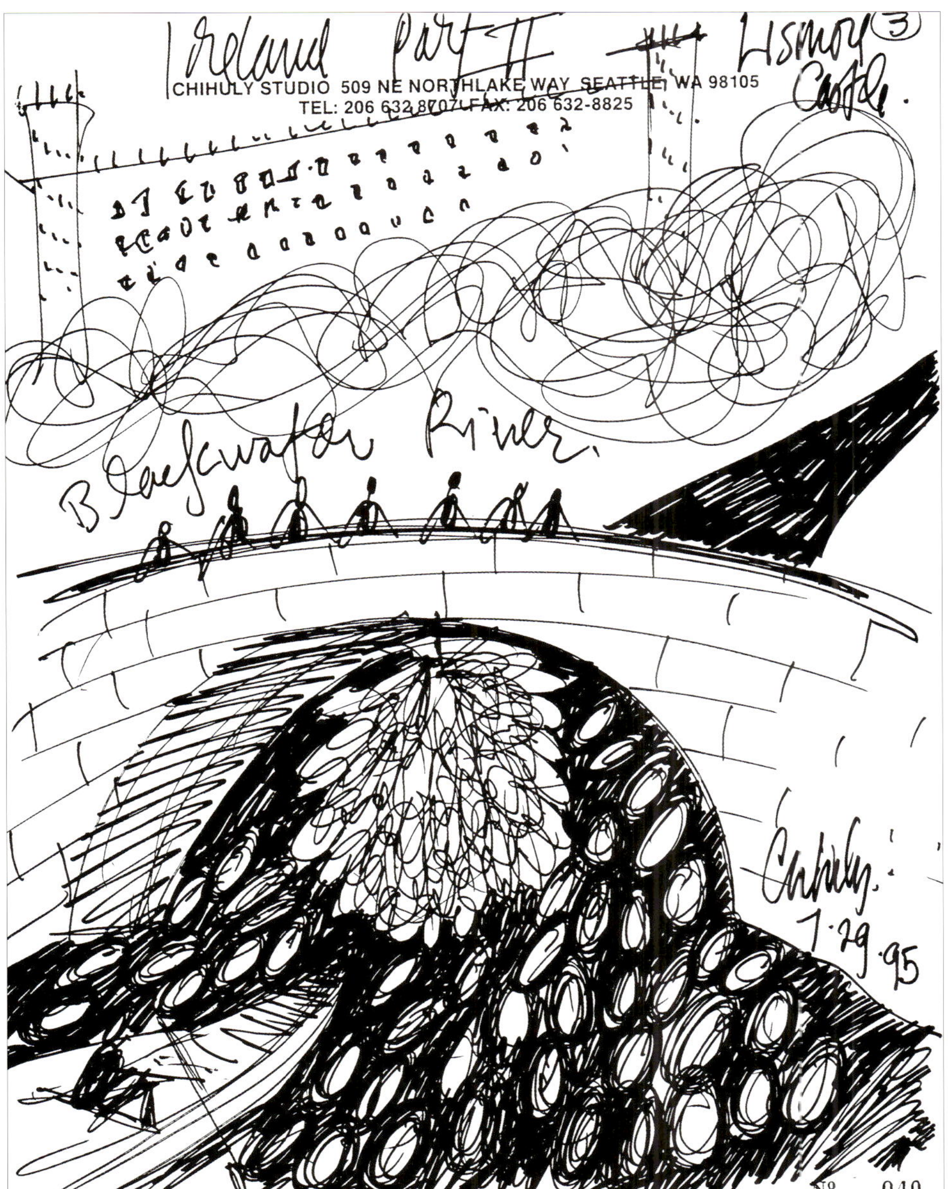

Union Station Tacoma, Washington, 1994

15

Client: Executive Council for a Greater Tacoma
Architects: Reed and Stem

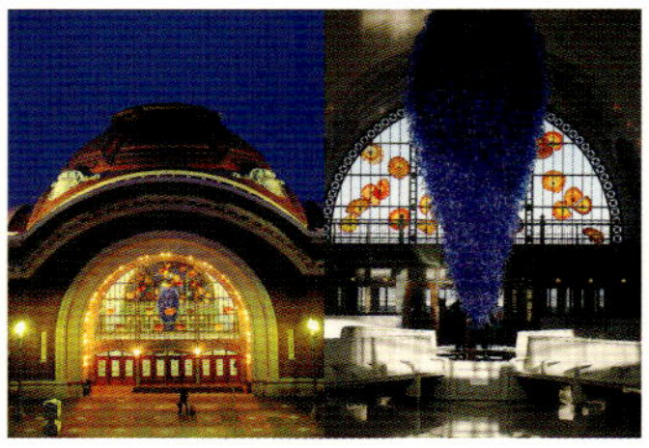

Cobalt Blue Chandelier
Medium: Handblown glass, steel mesh, wire
Dimensions: 20 x 9 x 3'
Weight: 2,700 lbs.
Elements: 2,000

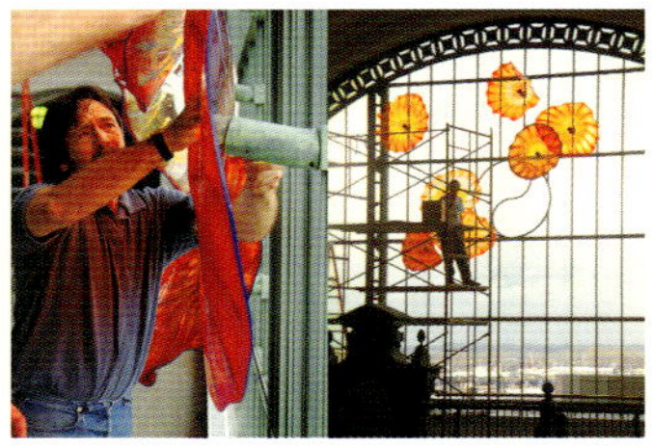

Monarch Window
Medium: Handblown glass, steel
Dimensions: 22 x 40 x 3'
Weight: 10–20 lbs. each
Elements: 27

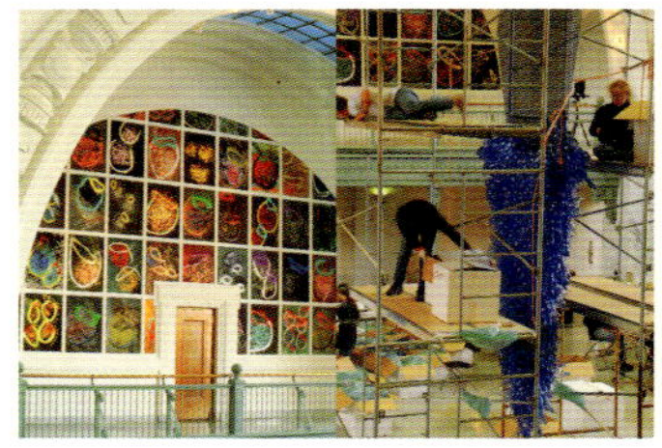

Basket Mural
Medium: Acrylic on paper
Dimensions: 22 x 40' overall
Elements: 50

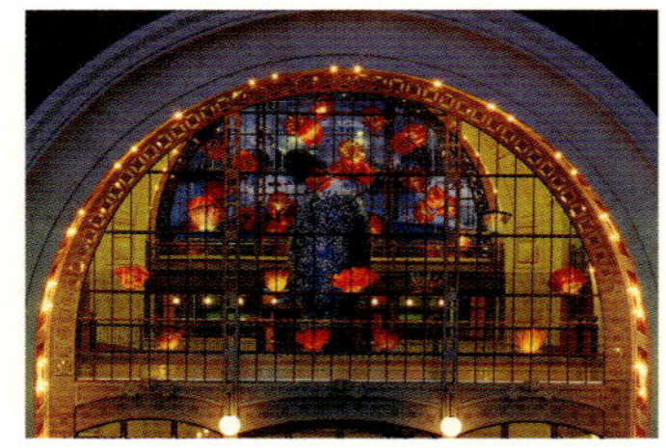

Tacoma Union Station is my favorite train station on the West Coast—well, it *is* my hometown. Built in 1910 by Reed and Stem, architects of Grand Central Station, it was the terminus of the Northern Pacific Railway. The building was opened with much fanfare in 1911, but was later abandoned when the railroad moved the station stop to another location. The future for Union Station wasn't looking too good until 1990, when it was renovated and attached to a new federal courthouse. It was restored to its former glory, pristine white inside, and I jumped at the opportunity to use the space.

The sheer size of Union Station—the central dome is ninety feet high—spurred me to make pieces larger than ever before. These mark the real beginnings of my monumental-scale work. Hanging in the dome is a twenty-by-nine-by-three-foot *Cobalt Blue Chandelier*. Made of about two thousand parts, the piece is basically flat, an interesting element made necessary because of weight restrictions. Behind it the *Monarch Window* looks out on Mount Rainier. The *Basket Mural* at Union Station was the first time we altered the drawings to fit the space, rather than simply "wallpapering" the wall with what would fit.

Union Station also represents an important community collaboration. Brought together for the first time, a local art museum (Tacoma Art Museum), a local artist (me), and local patrons (the Executive Council for a Greater Tacoma) joined with the federal government to present a public art project open to all, with no admission charge.

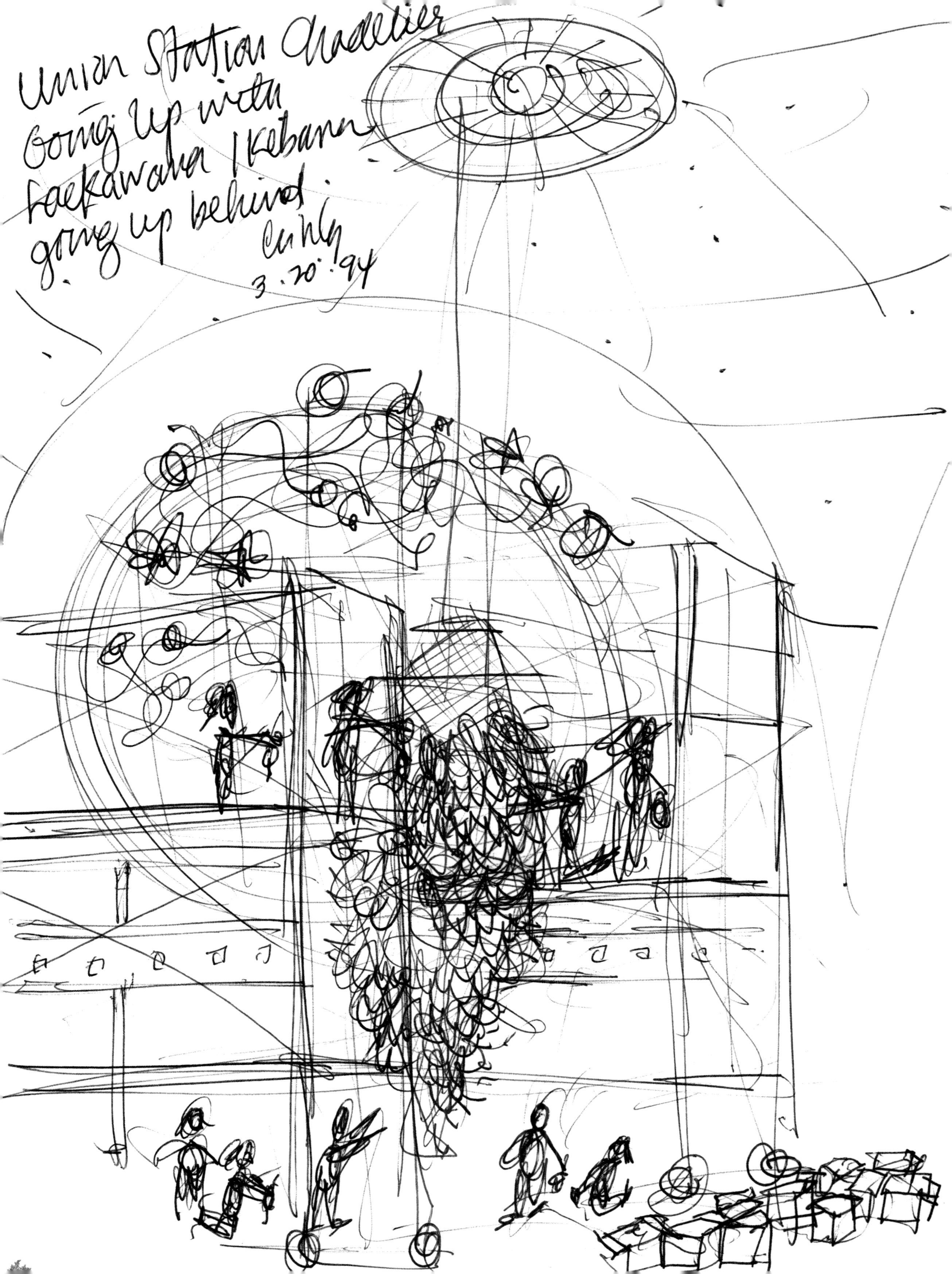
Union Station Chandelier
Going Up with
going up behind
Chihuly
3.20.94

16 Bellagio
Las Vegas, 1998

Client: Mirage Resorts
Architects: Marnell Corrao Associates
Interiors: Atlandia Design

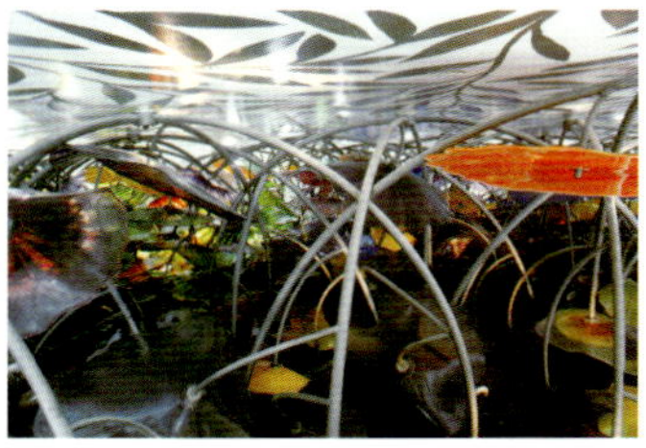
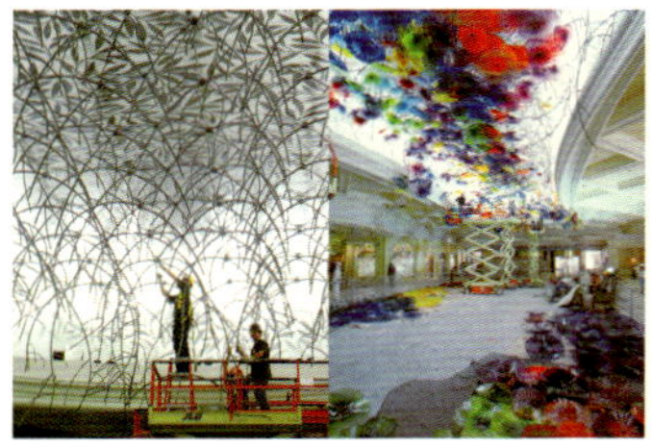
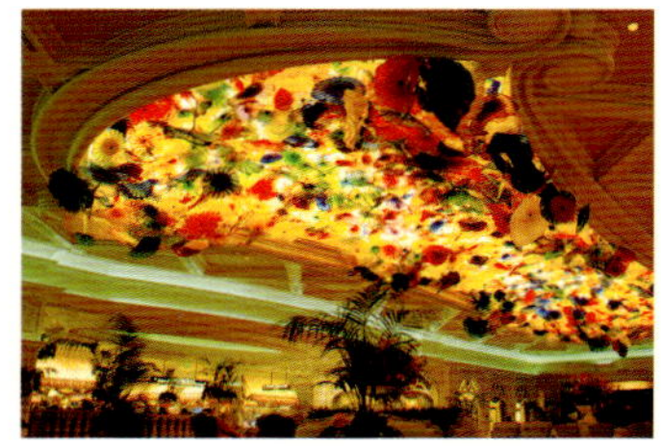
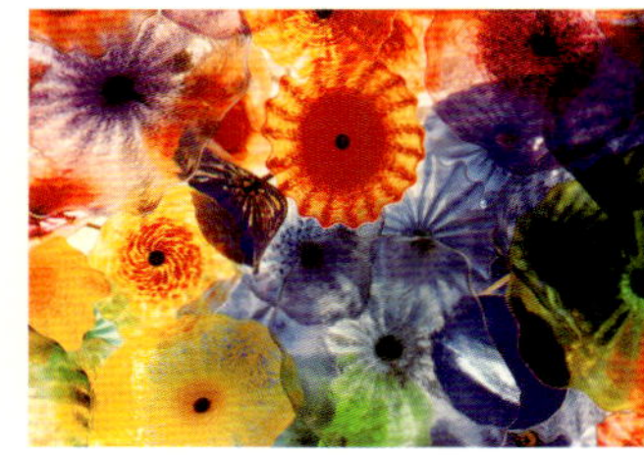

Fiori di Como
Medium: Handblown glass, steel
Dimensions: 70 x 30 x 12',
positioned 15 to 25 ft. overhead
Weight: Approx. 10,000 pounds of steel
and 40,000 pounds of glass
Elements: More than 2,000

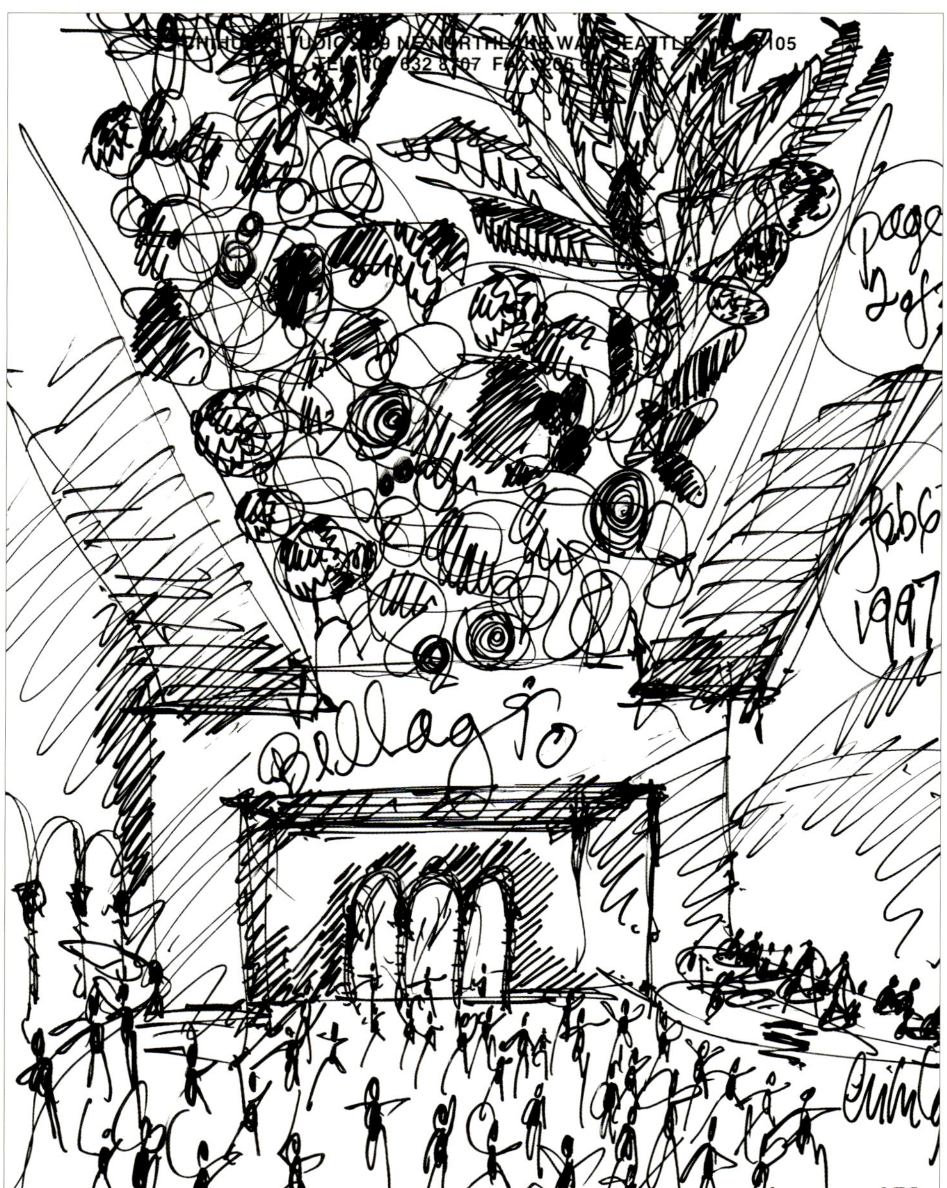

Steve Wynn started talking to me about the ceiling at Bellagio long before construction even began. He wanted me to make a "spectacular" piece in the lobby of the hotel that would rival the aquarium at the Mirage, and generate more interest. Back in Seattle, we built the entire seventy-by-thirty-foot ceiling, full-scale, at my studio. The commission, as contracted, called for a whole new armature type and about a thousand new "flowers." Steve visited several times, loved it, and wanted even more glass. Finally *Fiori di Como* was installed with over two thousand handblown glass elements. It's the glory of Las Vegas.

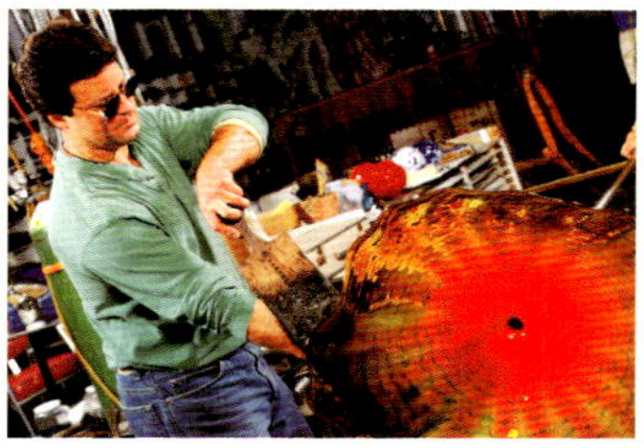

It was a very exciting time, and everyone threw out their ideas for the commission. We mocked up some ideas and went back and forth before narrowing it down. We weren't really addressing the larger picture of how you actually do something of that scale in a style like that. At that stage we just wanted to get the idea across. It's a challenge to compose a steel structure to be organic and weird and all the things Dale wanted. It would take a huge amount of time to compose the piece for such a large space, and this was a stumbling block that drove us to come up with a repeating pattern. It was the first time that we made an armature where the placement of glass could not be flexible, but had to be in a permanent position. It was a very different approach.

We did a mock-up of four different presentations for Steve Wynn, and he picked the one he liked in a half a second. He walked into the room and immediately had us turn off the lights on the other three options. He knew what he liked. It went back and forth, with him saying, "I want more glass," and Dale saying, "No, you can't have any more glass, this is how it should be. The negative space is what's giving us the depth." However, we went back time after time and kept adding glass.

To create this piece we had to build a welding shop. We never, until that time, did any of it in-house. We also created a plastics casting department. Both of these are now integral to most installations and regularly used.

We had to figure out how to make the glass safe. We had never had it in a ceiling. If it was regular, uncoated glass, you could have thrown something up there and it would have just rained down glass. This glass is powder coated with plastic, so if a piece is broken it stays in its casing. It's like safety glass in a car windshield. From the start to the finish all these new elements made the project unique.

The project was started in September of 1997 and finished in July of 1998. The biggest hurdle was going there and actually doing it. Working in an intensely union place, we had major friction. At one point we almost left because there were guys who would come and stare at us, trying to intimidate us. It was really stressful. We were welding until the Bellagio building construction was done, and we were still working while surrounded by a red velvet rope in the middle of the lobby. They had a cocktail party and a fabulous opening and everyone was watching us in their cocktail garb while we continued working. We worked diligently right to the end.

Philip Stewart

17 Malina Window
Detroit, Michigan, 1993

Client: Little Caesar Enterprises, Inc.
Architects: Little Caesars Architecture and Design Department

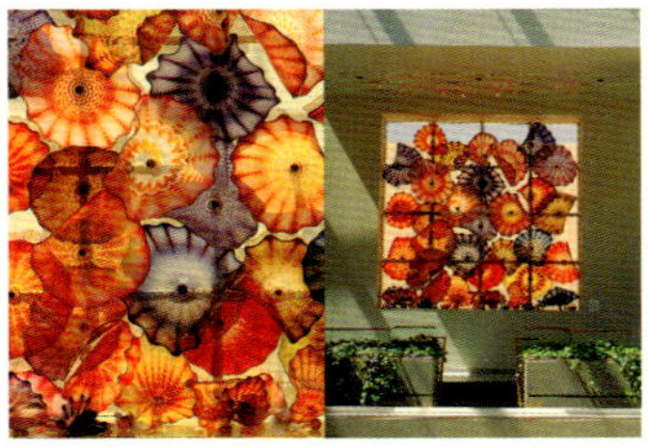

Malina Window
Medium: Handblown glass, steel
Dimensions: 16 x 16'
Weight: Up to 15 lbs. each
Elements: 50–60

The challenge was to make a twenty-foot-square window with a difficult view beautiful. The *Malina Window* was an opportunity to increase the size of the blown elements, and also to develop new hardware for attaching the glass to the armature, hardware we still use.

Lautner House
Palm Springs, California, 2000

Architect: John Lautner

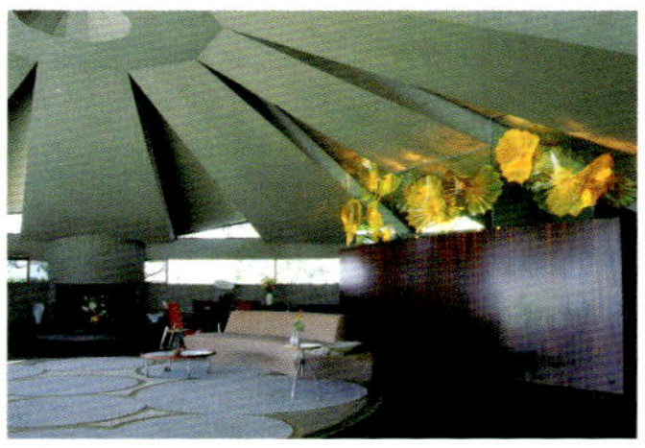

Lautner House
Medium: Handblown glass, steel
Dimensions: 8 x 44'
Weight: 7–15 lbs. each
Elements: 24

Once the set for James Bond's *Diamonds Are Forever*, this Palm Springs classic, designed by John Lautner for Arthur Elrod, was built in 1968 using new concrete techniques. Its poured-in-place concrete and butt glazed windows frame views of Palm Springs and the nearby mountains, creating a dynamic architectural setting to work in. Using a new method of attaching the glass, we worked both sides of a window wall dividing the kitchen and the living room—the first "double" piece I've done.

19

The Boathouse
Seattle, 1990–2000

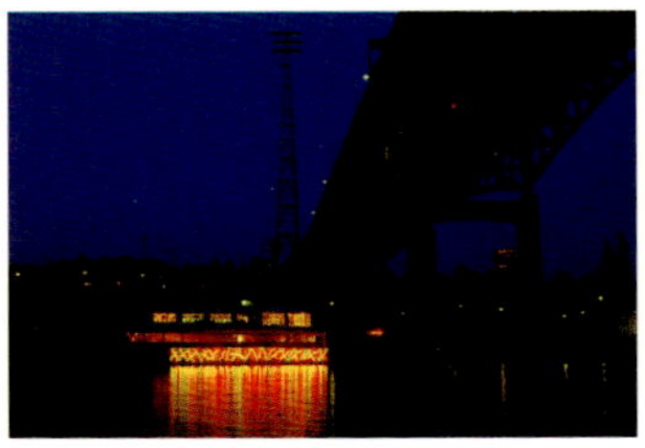

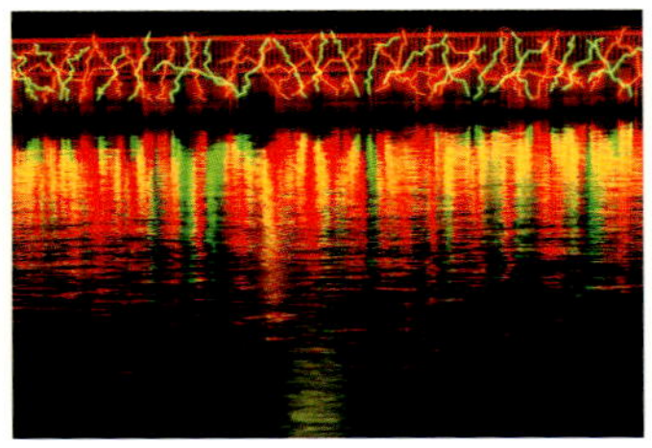

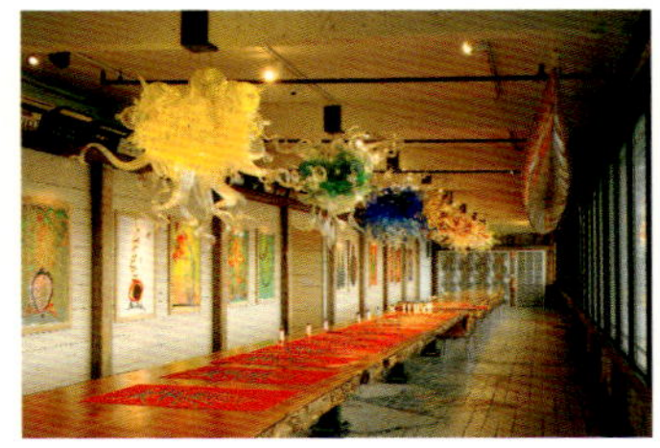

Evelyn Room

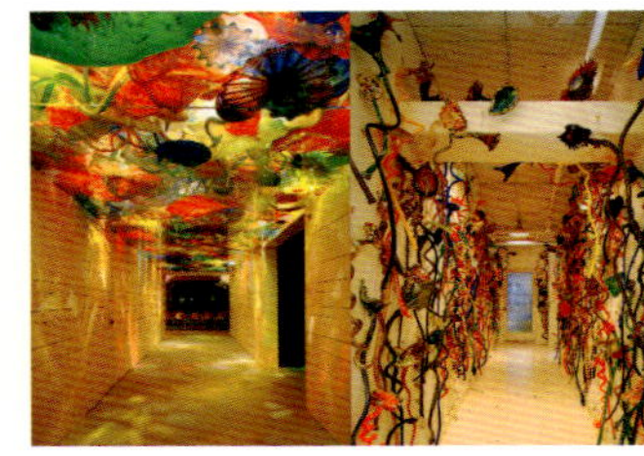

Persian Ceiling
Medium: Handblown glass
Dimensions: 6 x 40'
Weight: 1–15 lbs. per piece
Elements: 900–1,200

Ikebana Hallway
Medium: Handblown glass
Dimensions: 8 x 6 x 15'
Weight: 2–15 lbs. each
Elements: 100–150

Seems like The Boathouse is in a constant state of construction and change. I bought the twenty-five-thousand-square-foot Pocock Building on Lake Union, originally built to fabricate wooden racing shells, in 1990 and we've been working on it ever since. There's always a new project, like the eighty-eight-foot-long table in the Evelyn Room; the Indian Room, built to house my early work, together with a basket collection and several hundred Pendleton blankets; a new *Persian* ceiling; or a lap pool filled with color. But The Boathouse is also, and most importantly, my studio. Glassblowing goes on in the hotshop seven days a week. We do all the experimenting there, and most of my work for the past ten years has been made there. The most notable exception was *Chihuly Over Venice*, when we purposely set out to collaborate with glassworkers in several countries.

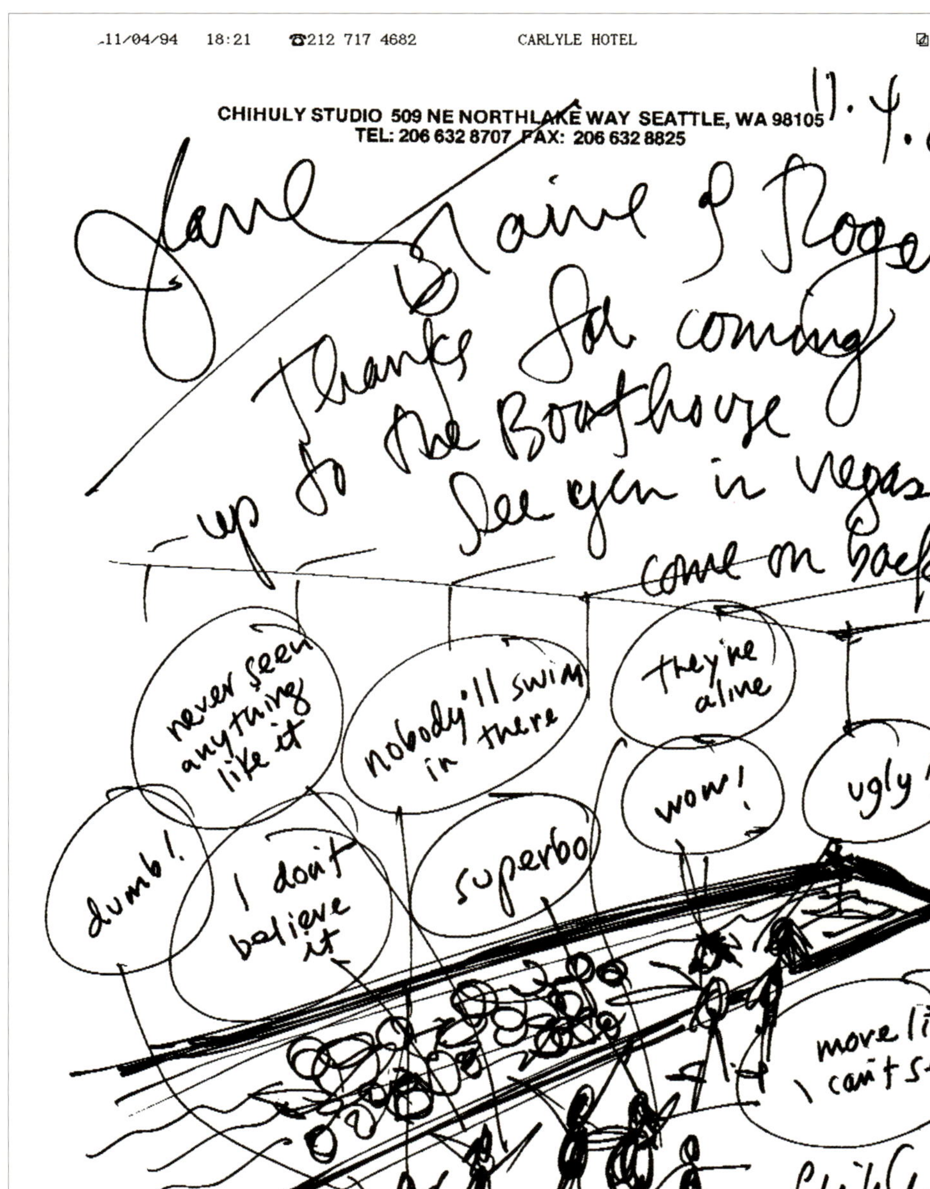

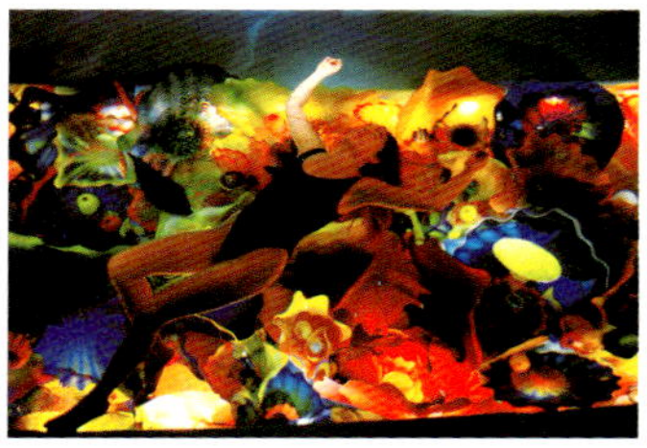

Lap Pool, 1994
Medium: Handblown glass
Dimensions: 12 x 54 x 4'
Elements: Approx. 300–400

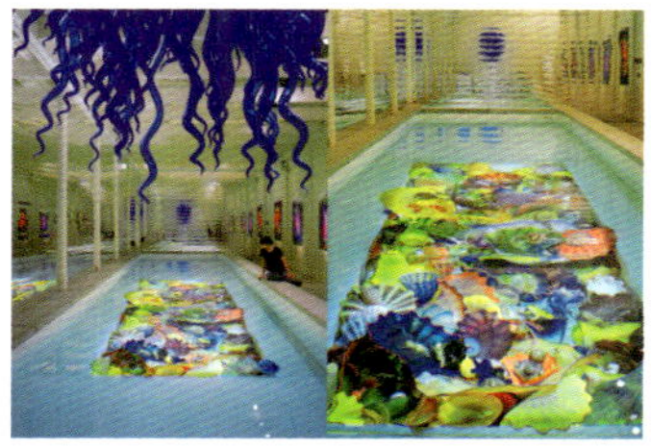

Lap Pool, 2000
Medium: Handblown glass
Dimensions: 12 x 54 x 4'
Elements: Approx. 300–400

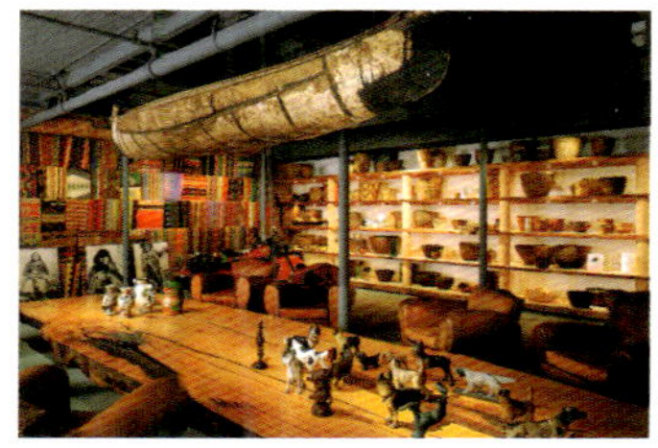

Indian Room

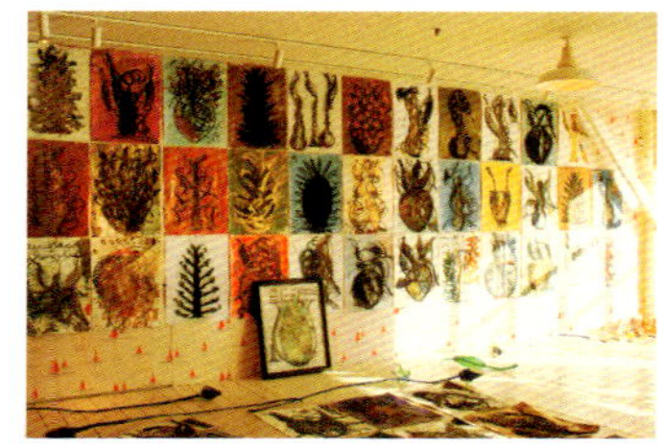

Front Room

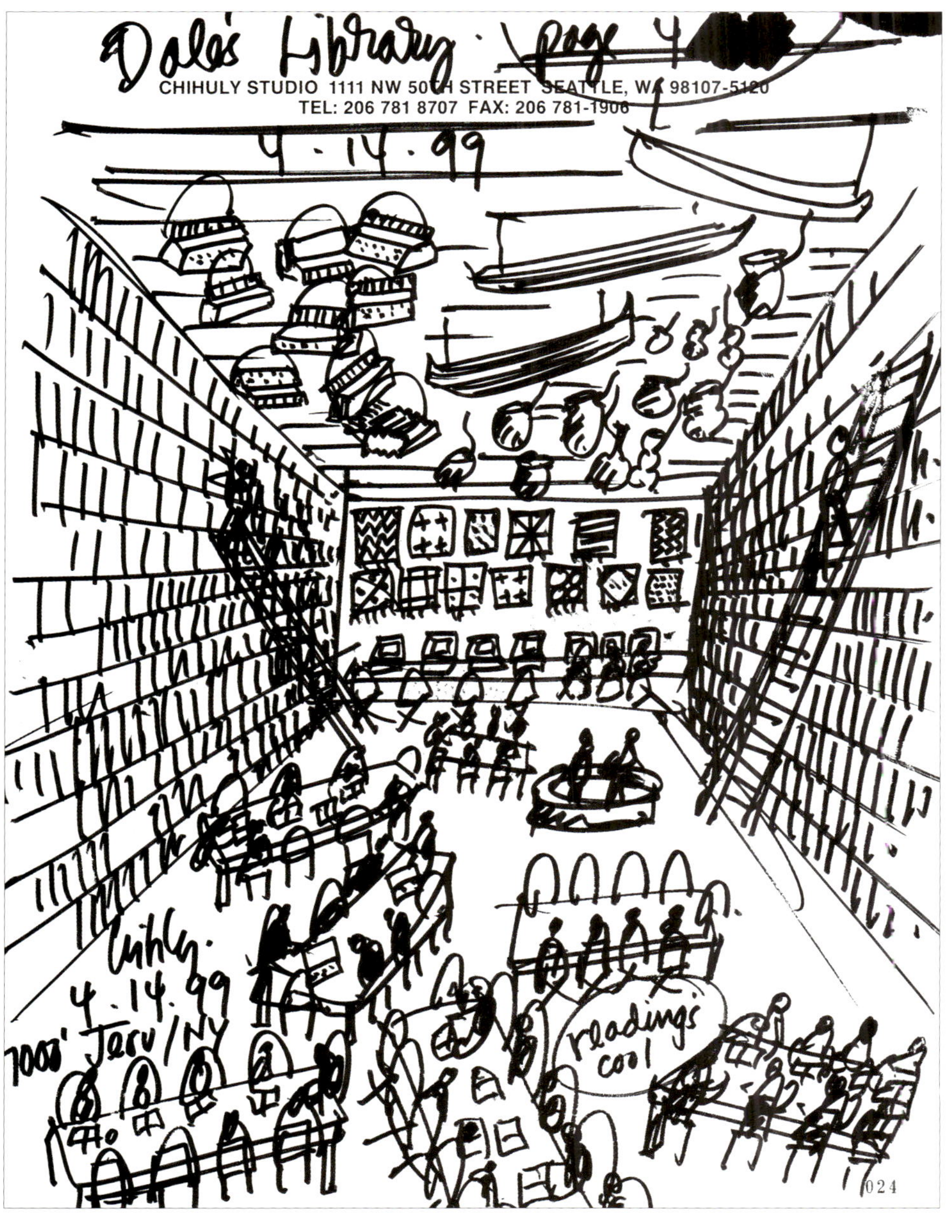

The studio, which had included the hotshop, mock-up space, offices, entertaining space, painting studio, and living quarters, has had many revisions. The entire building is one malleable block of wood that transforms into whatever Dale wants it to be. Nothing remains the same. Even the hotshop has morphed from an intimate scale to an emphasis on production.

Kai-Uwe Bergmann

The Boathouse Hotshop

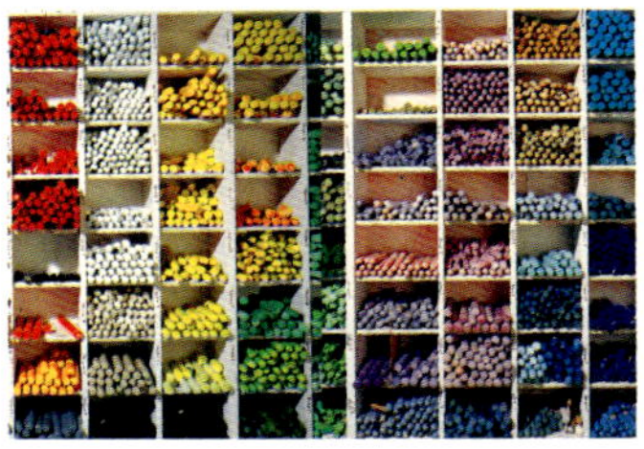

The Boathouse

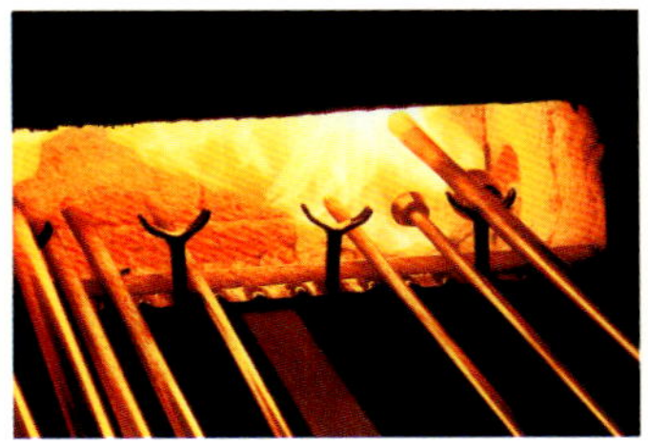

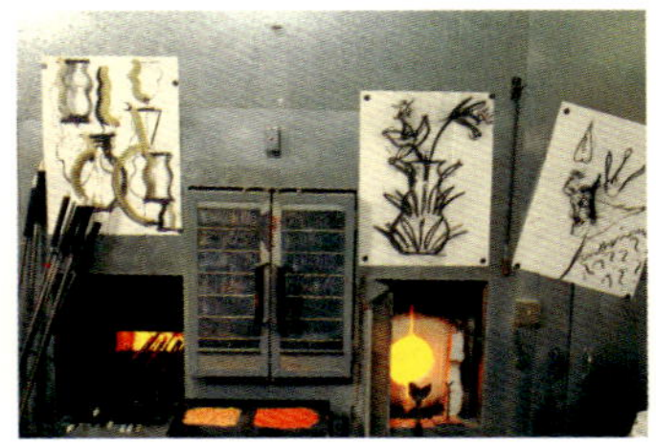

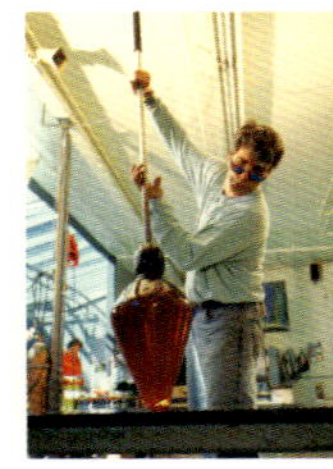

1998

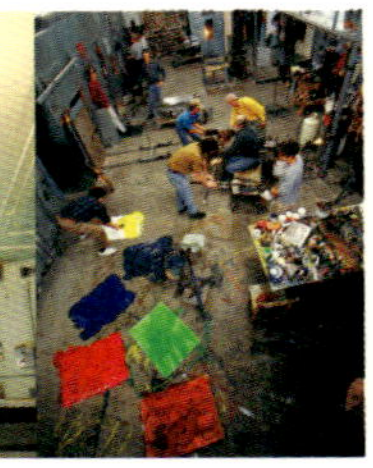

1991

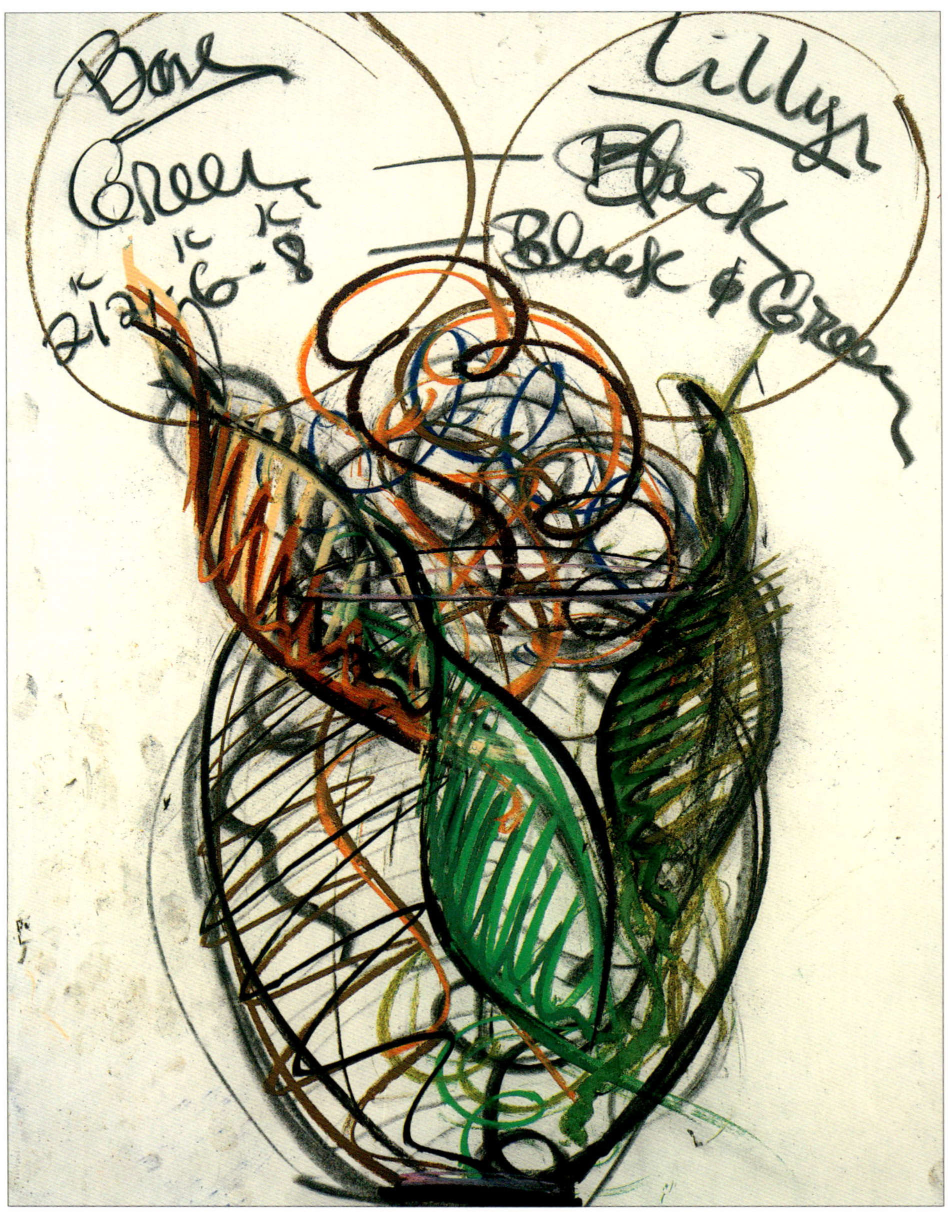

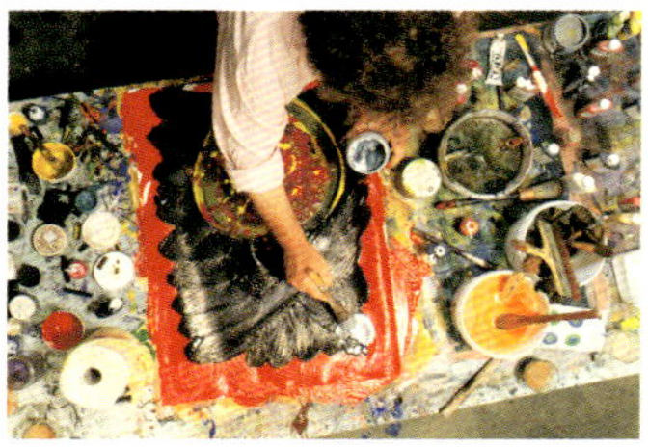

1991

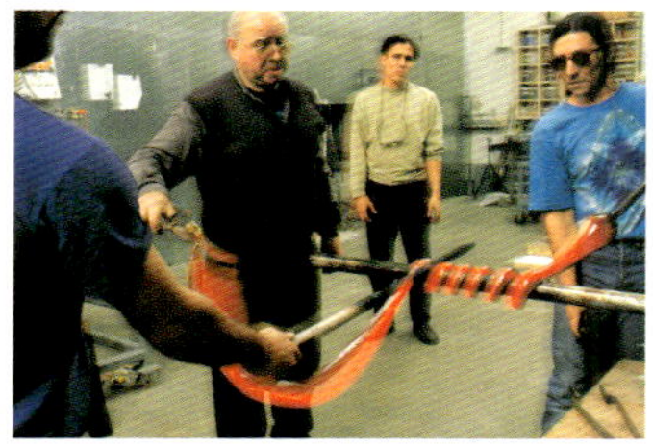

1990

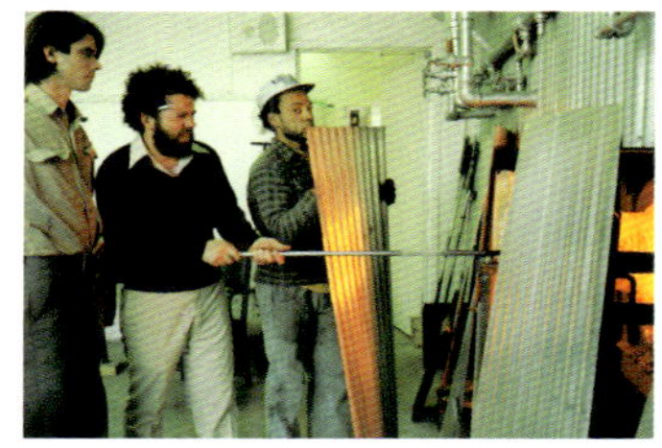

RISD, 1976

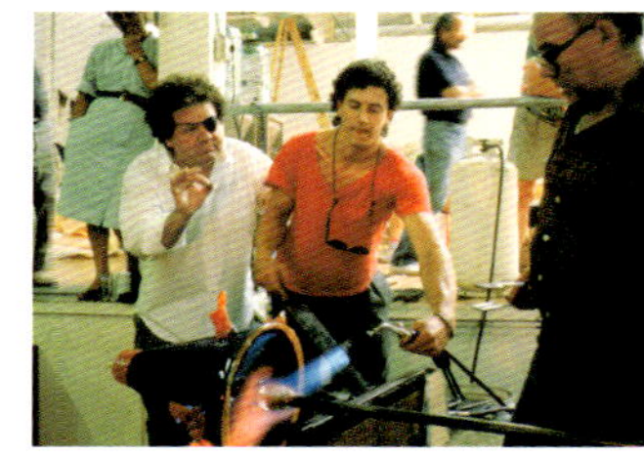

VandeKamp Studio, 1988

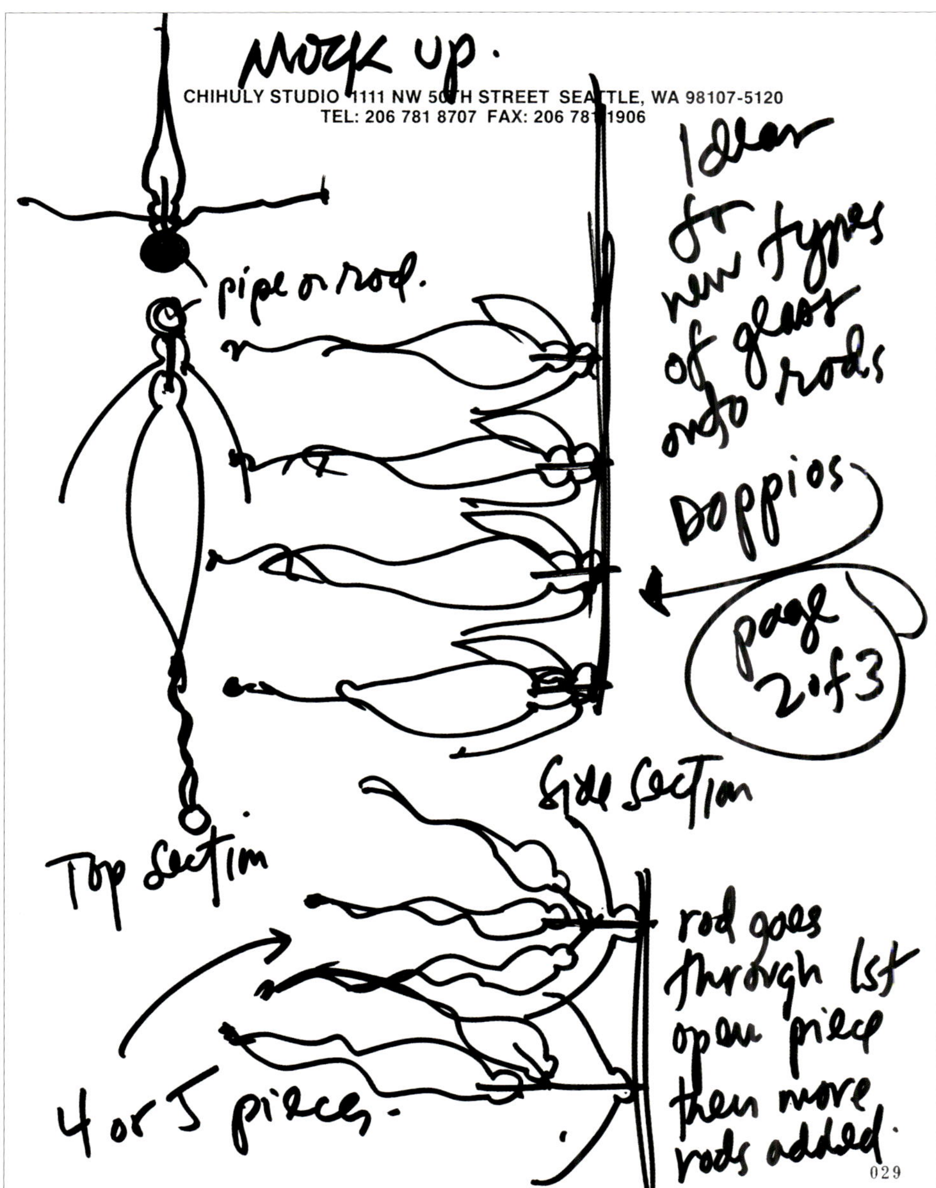

20 Icicle Creek Chandelier Leavenworth, Washington, 1996

Client: Harriet Bullitt
Architects: Jones and Jones

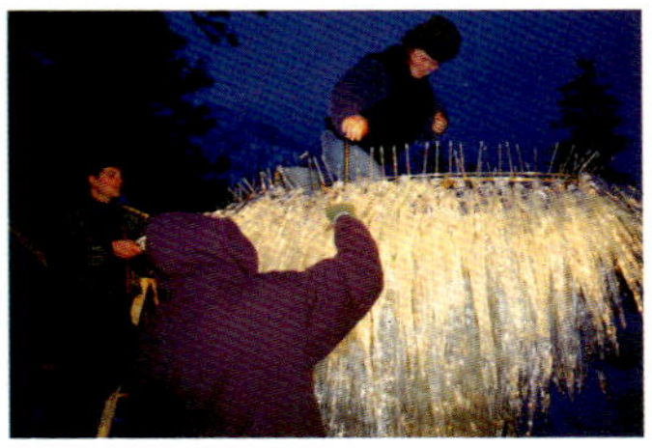
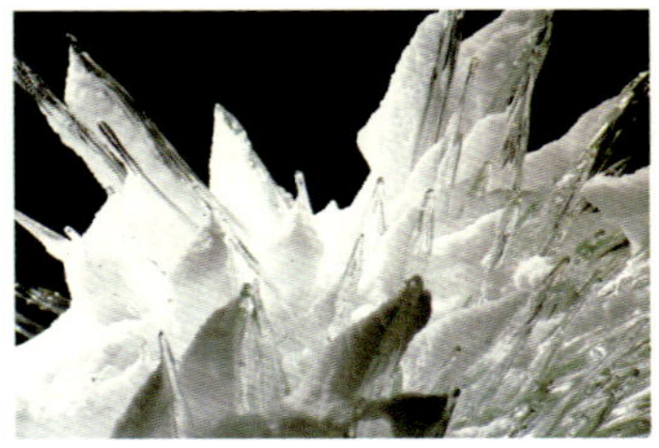
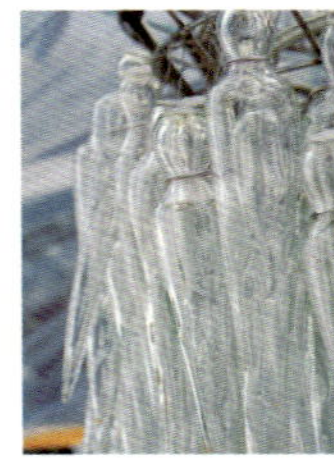
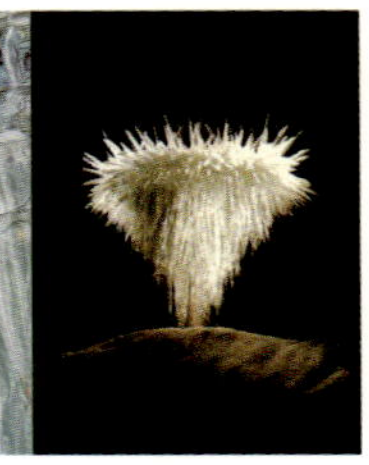
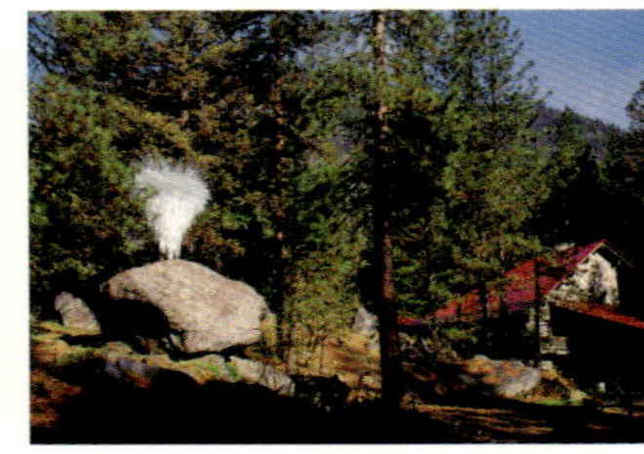

Icicle Creek Chandelier
Medium: Handblown glass, steel
Dimensions: 12 x 9 x 6'
Weight: 2,000 lbs.
Elements: 1,200

When Harriet Bullitt commissioned a piece for her Sleeping Lady Conference Retreat, she gave me total freedom. In one month, a large, outdoor, freestanding sculpture on top of a very large granite boulder was conceived and built.

I worked with my team by fax and the construction took place in sub-zero weather. It snowed six feet the weekend the piece went up. To make full use of winter in the Cascades, I designed an armature with a strip heater built inside it. Staff at Sleeping Lady can warm it up, melt the snow, and form real icicles, which hang from the glass icicles.

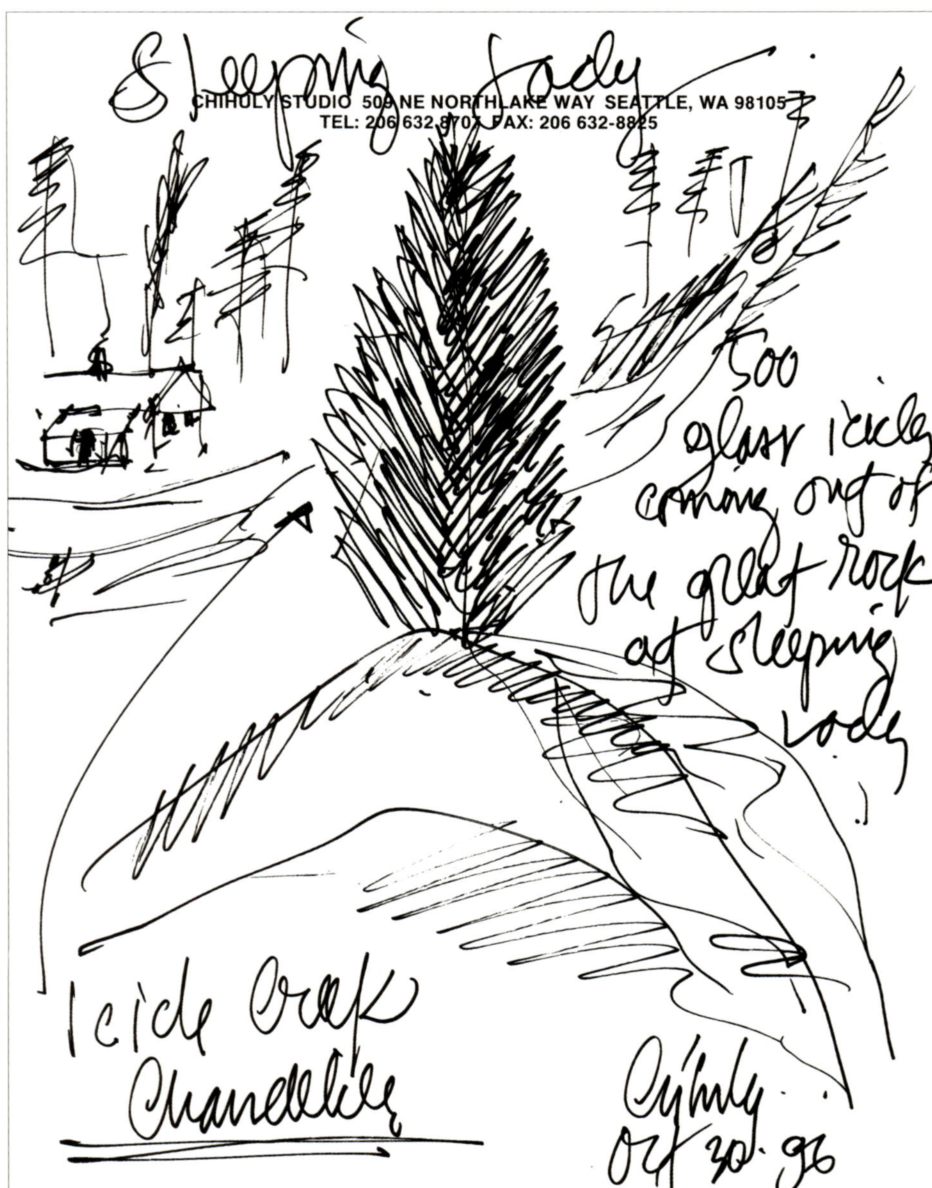

LongHouse
East Hampton, New York, 1996

Client: LongHouse Reserve
Architect: Charles Forberg
Interiors and garden: Jack Lenor Larsen

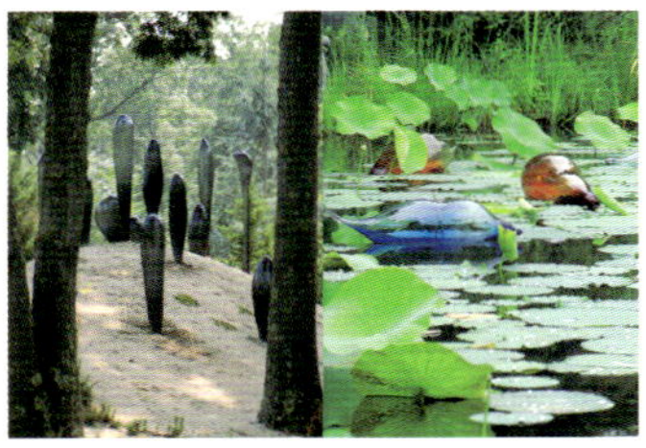

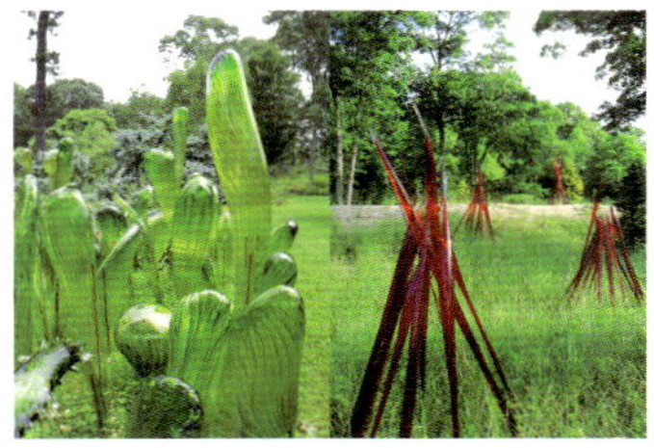

Black Saguaros
Medium: Handblown glass
Dimensions: 2.5–6' tall, up to 8–16" diameter
Weight: 10–15 lbs. each
Elements: 20

Fiddleheads
Medium: Handblown glass
Dimensions: 18–48" high, up to 16" diameter
Weight: 5–15 lbs. each
Elements: 185

Seal Pups
Medium: Handblown glass
Dimensions: 30–48" long, 16" diameter
Weight: 10–15 lbs. each
Elements: 23

Tepees
Medium: Handblown glass
Dimensions: 4–9' tall
Weight: 10–15 lbs. each
Elements: 75

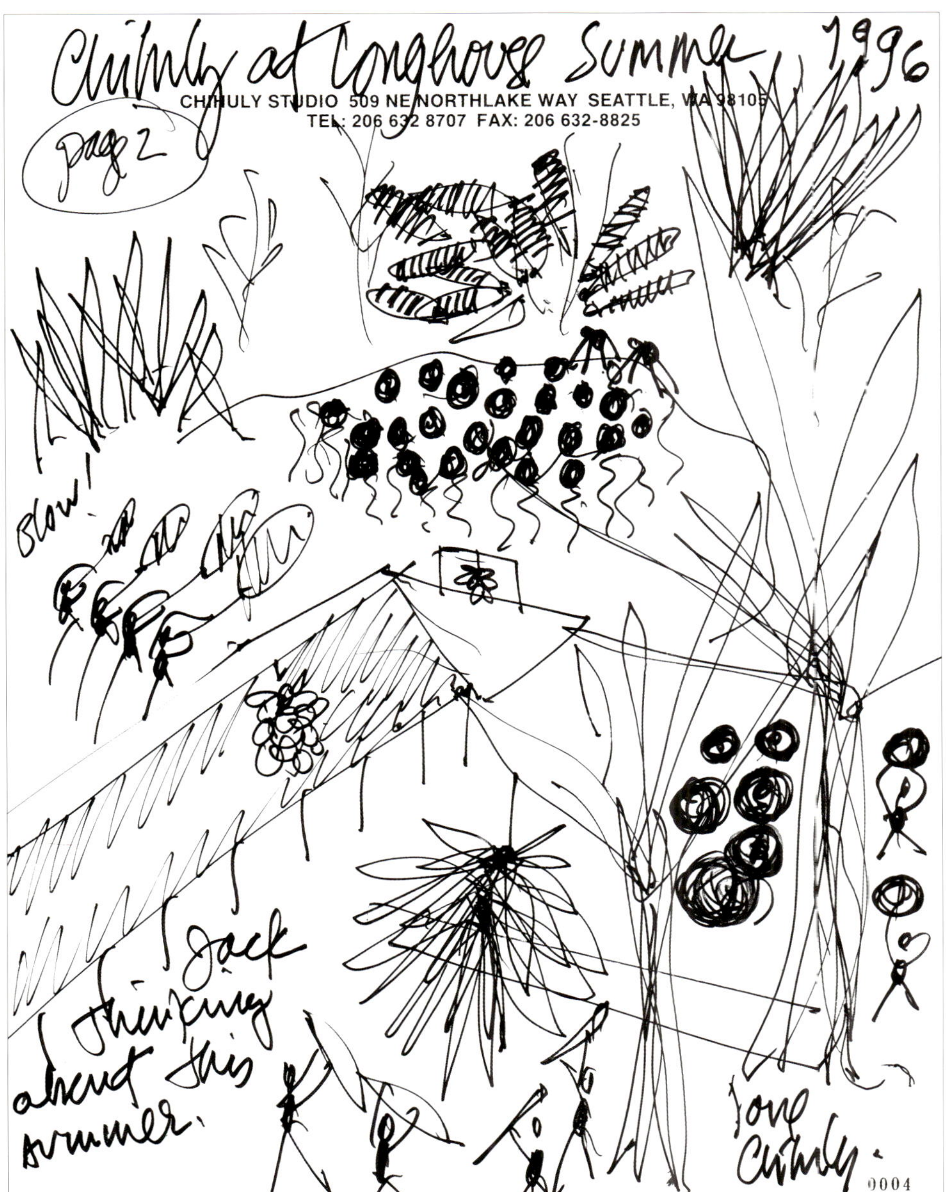

Jack Lenor Larsen, a great friend and mentor, played an essential role in the founding of Pilchuck. A native of Washington, he introduced me to John and Anne G. Hauberg, who became cofounders of the school and its earliest patrons. So when Jack asked me to do an outdoor exhibition in the gardens at LongHouse for the public, we were ready to go. We'd just been working in Finland and had developed many new forms, and this was the first chance to show them. What a setting: I filled the gardens with *Fiddleheads*, *Black Saguaros*, *Tepees*, *Red Reeds, Seal Pups*; hung chandeliers from trees; and set a boat filled with glass on the pond.

22 Vianne, France, 1997

Factory: Les Cristalleries et Verreries d'Art de Vianne

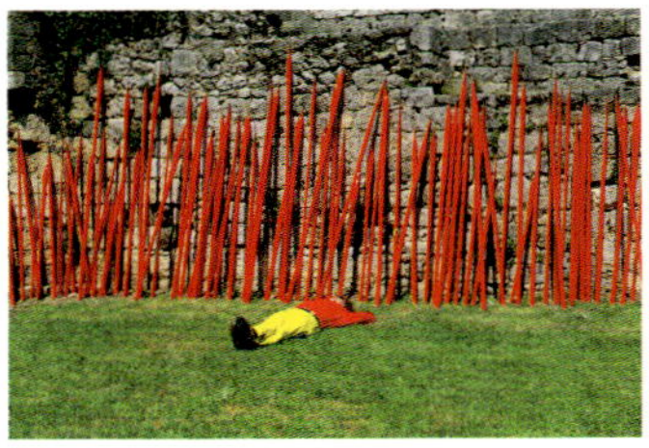

Red Spears
Medium: Handblown glass
Dimensions: Up to 12' tall
Weight: 10–15 lbs. each
Elements: 350

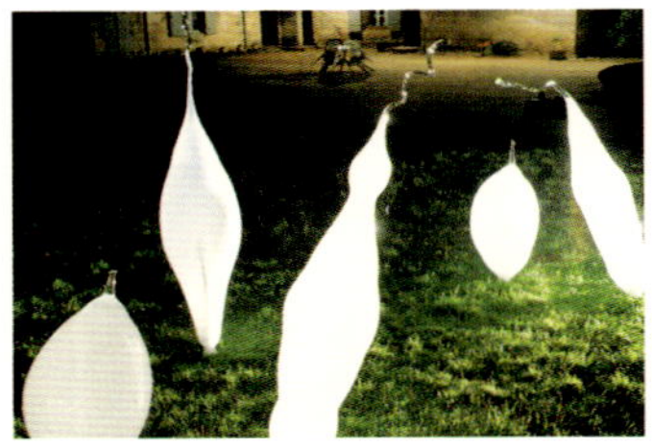

White Seal Pups
Medium: Handblown glass
Dimensions: 2–5' tall, up to 20" in diameter
Weight: 10–20 lbs. each
Elements: 21

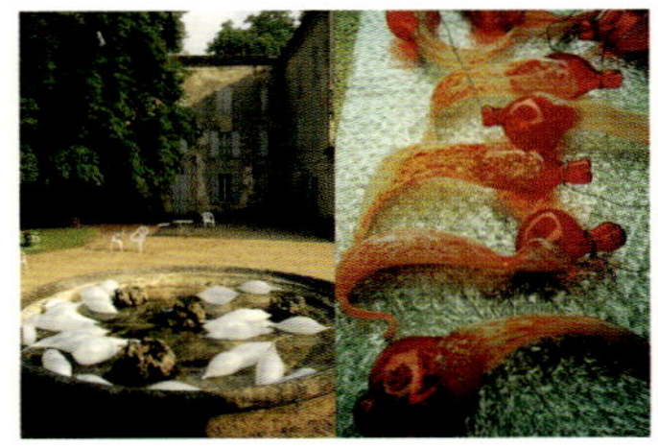

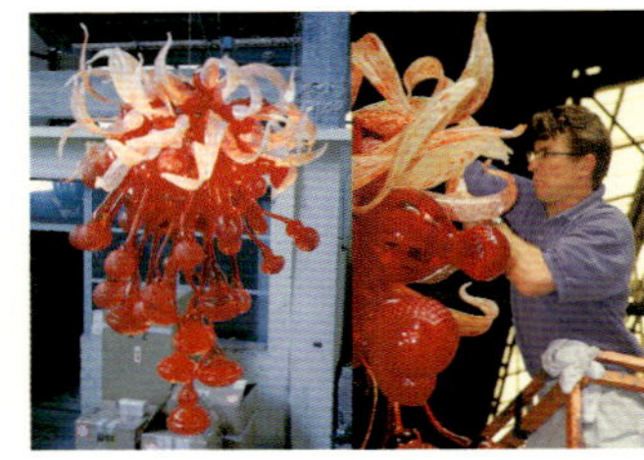

Ruby Red Chandelier
Medium: Handblown glass, steel
Dimensions: 6 x 4 x 4'
Weight: 450 lbs.
Elements: 90

After *Chihuly Over Venice*, Team Chihuly was used to going on the road. Taking on the challenges and chances of working in new environments hand in hand with craftsmen and artisans in other countries only enhanced our work as a team. Factories in Finland, Mexico, Ireland, and this one in Vianne, France, gave us opportunities to work with new glass (not all glass is the same), new techniques, and new colors (some factories work with "pots" of colored glass as a base, while we work at The Boathouse with clear and apply color). Vianne is a beautiful medieval village near Bordeaux in the southwest of France. We took the glass we made out of the factory and into the town, making about a dozen installations all around the area. We made some great glass at the factory and shipped it home by sea. Unfortunately, a storm blew our container into the Atlantic Ocean. Somewhere down there the fish are swimming amongst thousands of pieces of my glass from Vianne.

The trip to Vianne was a challenge. We were just returning from the *Chihuly Over Venice* project in Italy when the opportunity to blow glass in a lamp factory in France presented itself. We had access to many unique molds. The factory was small and crowded. They were still in production, while we were trying to improvise and work around their schedules. The village itself presented many settings for installations, from gardens and fountains to a twelfth-century church.

Tom Lind

We had one afternoon to set up the last installation. It consisted of a hanging chandelier above a reflecting pool in an outdoor park. Tom Lind hung the *Ruby Red Chandelier* over the pool, then left me alone to install the lighting. As I was wading through the water, I had to swing a heavy ladder around without crashing into the delicate chandelier. All the while, curious passersby were asking me questions in French. Dealing with the voltage differences between American and French power sources was the biggest struggle. Wiring transformers and running cable while trying to prevent the circuit breaker from blowing was another. Sundown was our nonnegotiable deadline.

Steve Cochran

The News Tribune
Tacoma, Washington, 1997

Client: The News Tribune
Architects: Merritt + Pardini

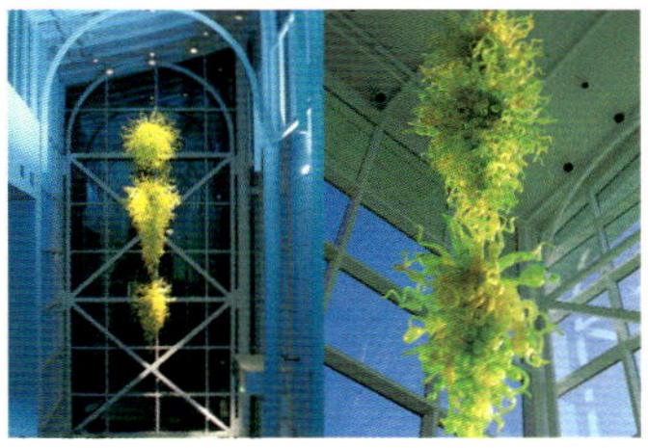

Kelso's Beacon
Medium: Handblown glass, steel
Dimensions: Approx. 22 x 6 x 6'
Weight: More than 1,500 lbs.
Elements: 1,000

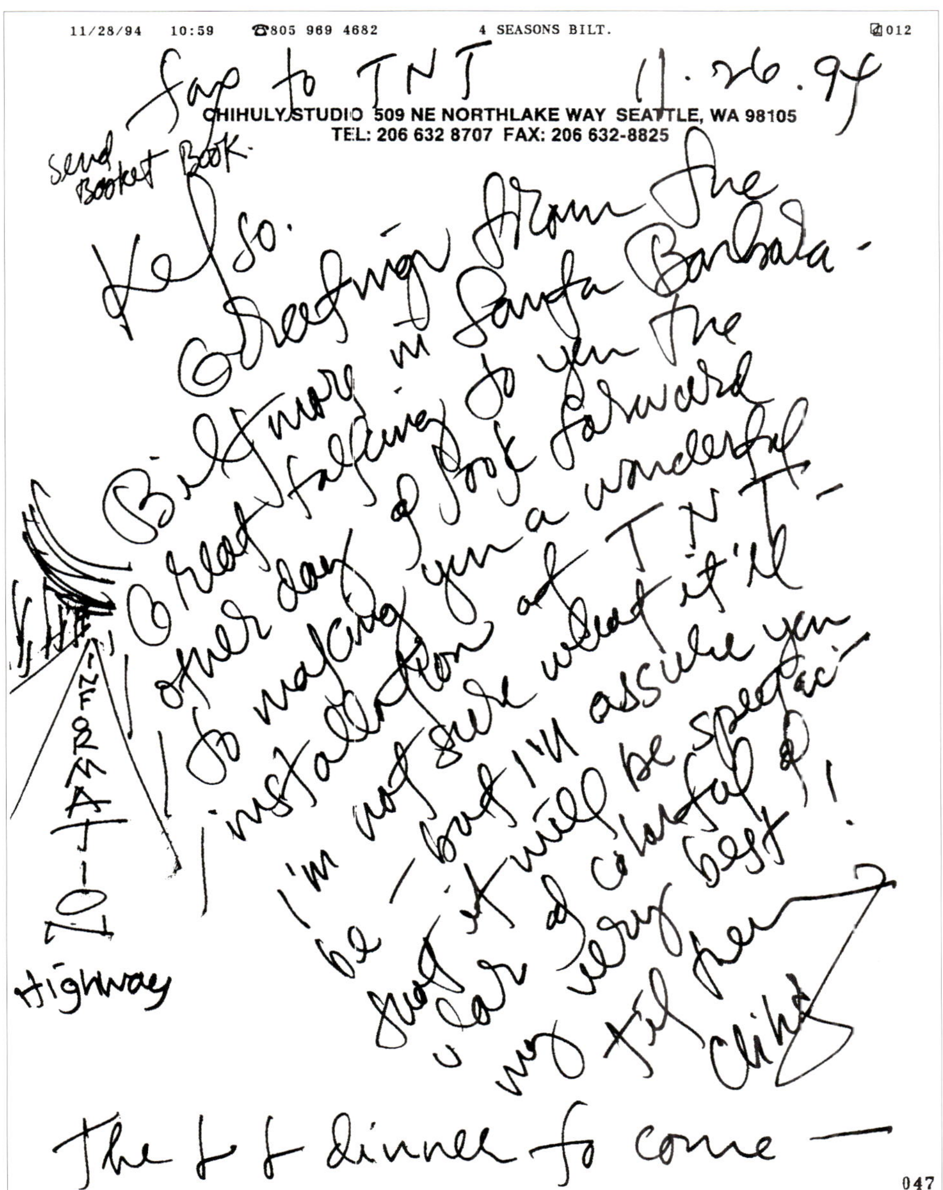

11/28/94 10:59 ☎805 969 4682 4 SEASONS BILT. 012

fax to TNT 11.26.94

CHIHULY STUDIO 509 NE NORTHLAKE WAY SEATTLE, WA 98105
TEL: 206 632 8707 FAX: 206 632-8825

send Booklet Book.

Kelso. Greetings from the Biltmore in Santa Barbara - Great talking to you the other day & look forward to making you a wonderful installation at TNT - I'm not sure what it'll be - but I'll assure you it will be spectacular & colorful & just as very best! can't wait til then

Chihuly

INFORMATION highway

The L & L dinner to come —

047

My very good friend Kelso Gillenwater commissioned a "beacon" for this impressive new building housing Tacoma's main newspaper. For *Kelso's Beacon*—renamed in Kelso's memory—my first tiered chandelier can be seen from three hundred feet away and does serve, as he wanted it to, as a beacon.

24 Victoria and Albert Museum
London, 1999

Client: Victoria and Albert Museum
Dome Architect: Niall Clutton

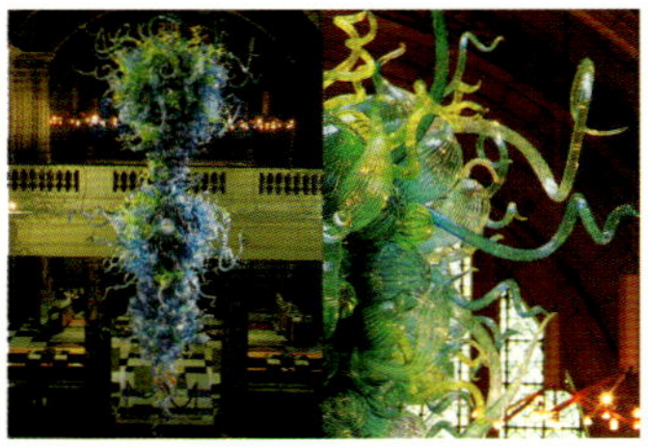

Ice Blue and Spring Green Chandelier
Medium: Handblown glass, steel
Dimensions: 18 x 8 x 8'
Weight: 1,887 lbs.
Elements: 755

You always fret that you may not have enough glass to work with, and in this case it was true. We used all of the largest pieces and grew the chandelier into several sections, spinning the piece as we worked (we could build it only from one side). It was exhausting. After three days we were done, and we stood back to see what we had wrought. Everyone at the museum was thrilled, of course, but it seemed to us that we could have kept going.

Tom Lind

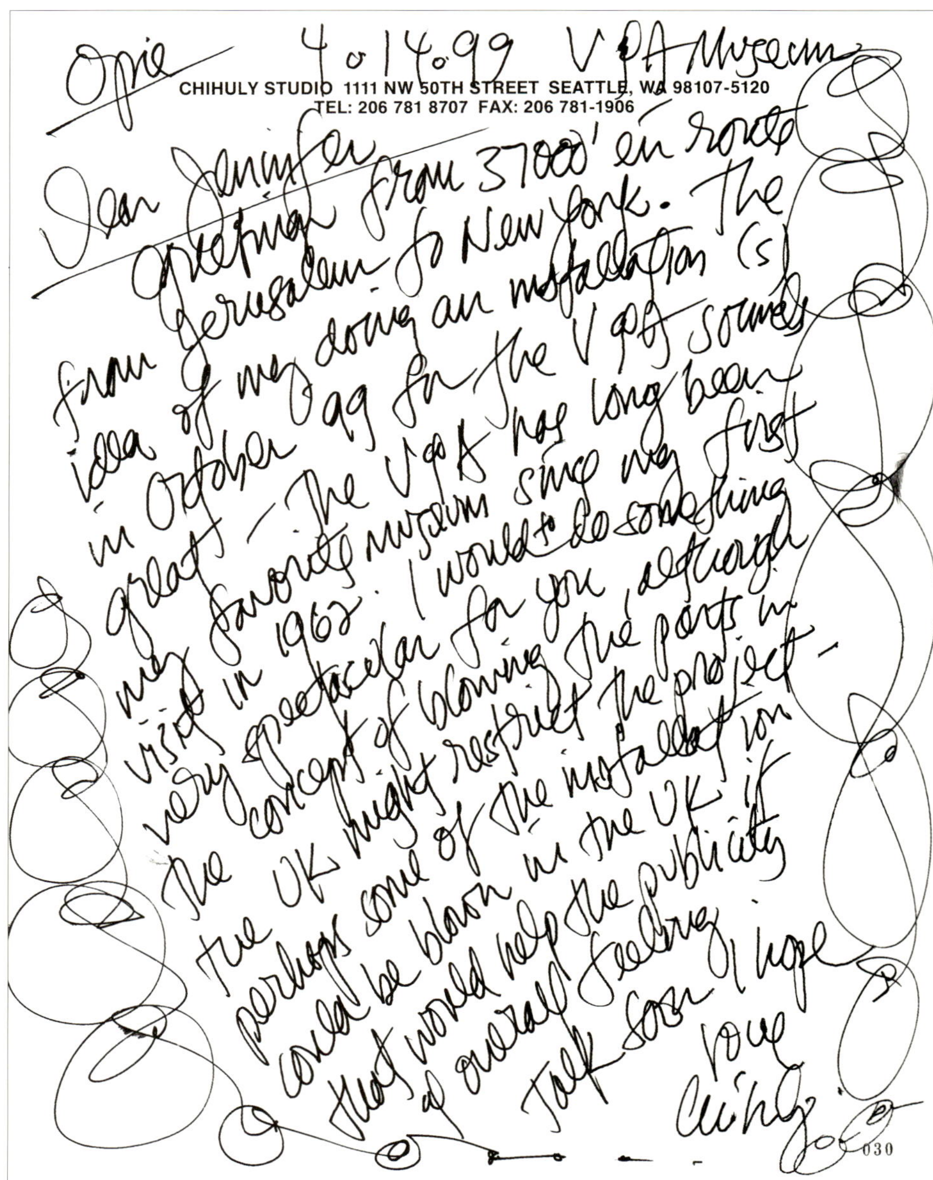

Opie 4.14.99 V&A Museum

CHIHULY STUDIO 1111 NW 50TH STREET SEATTLE, WA 98107-5120
TEL: 206 781 8707 FAX: 206 781-1906

Dear Jennifer
greetings from 37000' en route from Jerusalem to New York. The idea of my doing an installation (s) in October 99 for the V&A sounds great - The V&A has long been my favorite museum since my first visit in 1962. I would do something very spectacular for you although the concept of blowing the parts in the UK might restrict the project - perhaps some of the installation could be blown in the UK if that would help the publicity & overall feeling. Talk soon I hope
love
Chihuly

030

Chrysler Museum of Art
Norfolk, Virginia, 1999

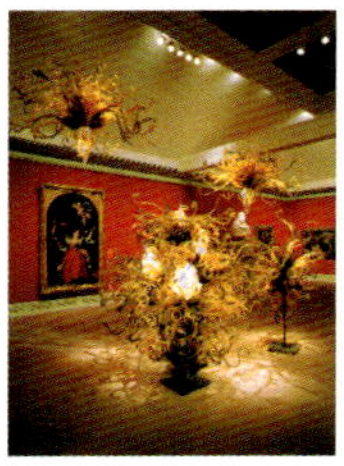

Laguna Murano
Medium: Handblown glass, steel
Dimensions: 12 x 10 x 10'
Weight: 1,430 lbs.
Elements: 600–700

Much of the work in *Chihuly Over Venice* was experimental—we responded to the talents and facilities we found at each factory, rather than arriving with a set program. Venice was the same; installations there took form within available circumstances. At Murano, however, we knew the nature and brilliance of the talents there intimately already, because I'd worked with both Pino Signoretto and Lino Tagliapietra back home for years.

While it is rare for two such great masters to collaborate, I was able to talk Pino and Lino into working together with me on *Laguna Murano*. Along with a team of Americans, we worked for three days with a special opaline glass at Pino's hotshop on Murano.

Lino made the blown forms and Pino modeled the sea creatures that were added onto the blown forms. To finish up, the "kelp" was blown back at The Boathouse and the five-hundred- plus pieces were put together to make this a most complex sculpture.

26 Atlantis
Paradise Island, Bahamas, 1998

Client: Sun International
Architects: HKS Architects
Interiors: Wilson & Associates

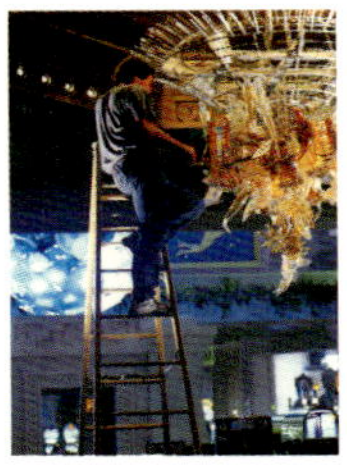

Atlantis Chandelier
Medium: Handblown glass, steel
Dimensions: 12' in diameter
Weight: 2,500 lbs.
Elements: 900

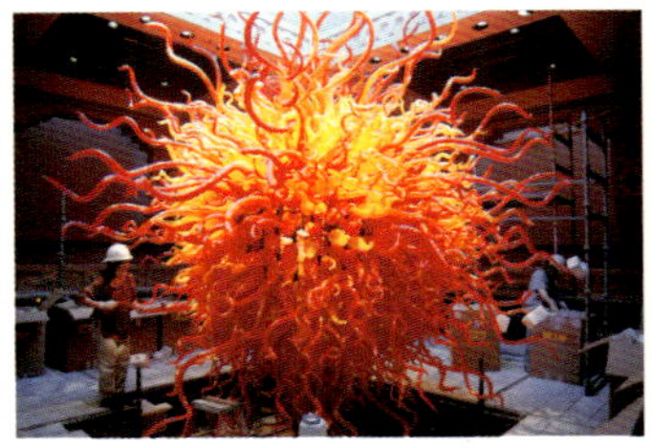

Temple of the Sun
Medium: Handblown glass, steel
Dimensions: 17' in diameter
Weight: 11,200 lbs.
Elements: 2,300

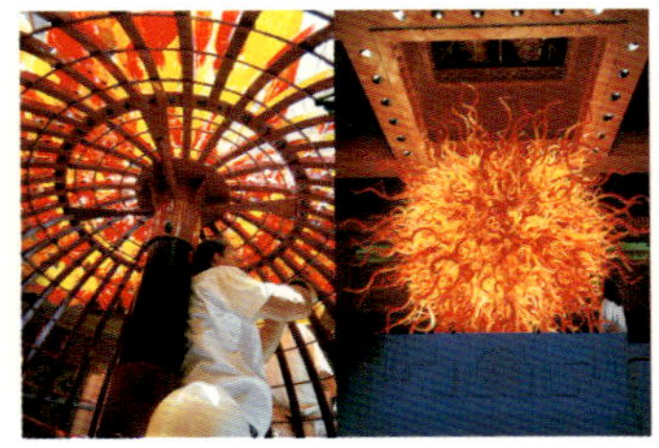

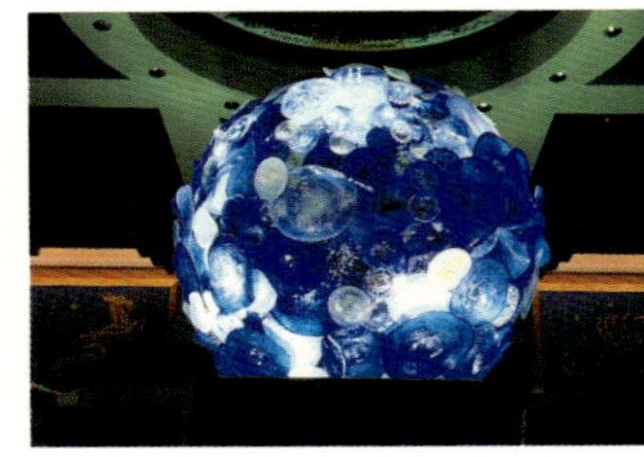

Temple of the Moon
Medium: Handblown glass, steel
Dimensions: 13' in diameter
Weight: 9,000 lbs.
Elements: 900

In one of the more challenging assignments, Sol Kerzner asked me to add my work into a very specific architecture of fantasy. The resort is built to evoke the mythical sunken continent of Atlantis. First were two Mayan temples, *Temple of the Sun* and *Temple of the Moon*, expressing all of creation and the dichotomy of opposition—the fiery sun, the cool moon, day and night. For the entrance, *Crystal Gate* used new forms and glassblowing techniques developed specially for this project. Sol was so happy with these three monumental sculptures that he commissioned a fourth grand piece, *Atlantis Chandelier*. Complex and graceful, expressing the wonders of all life forms, this one goes well beyond anyone's expectations of "a Chihuly."

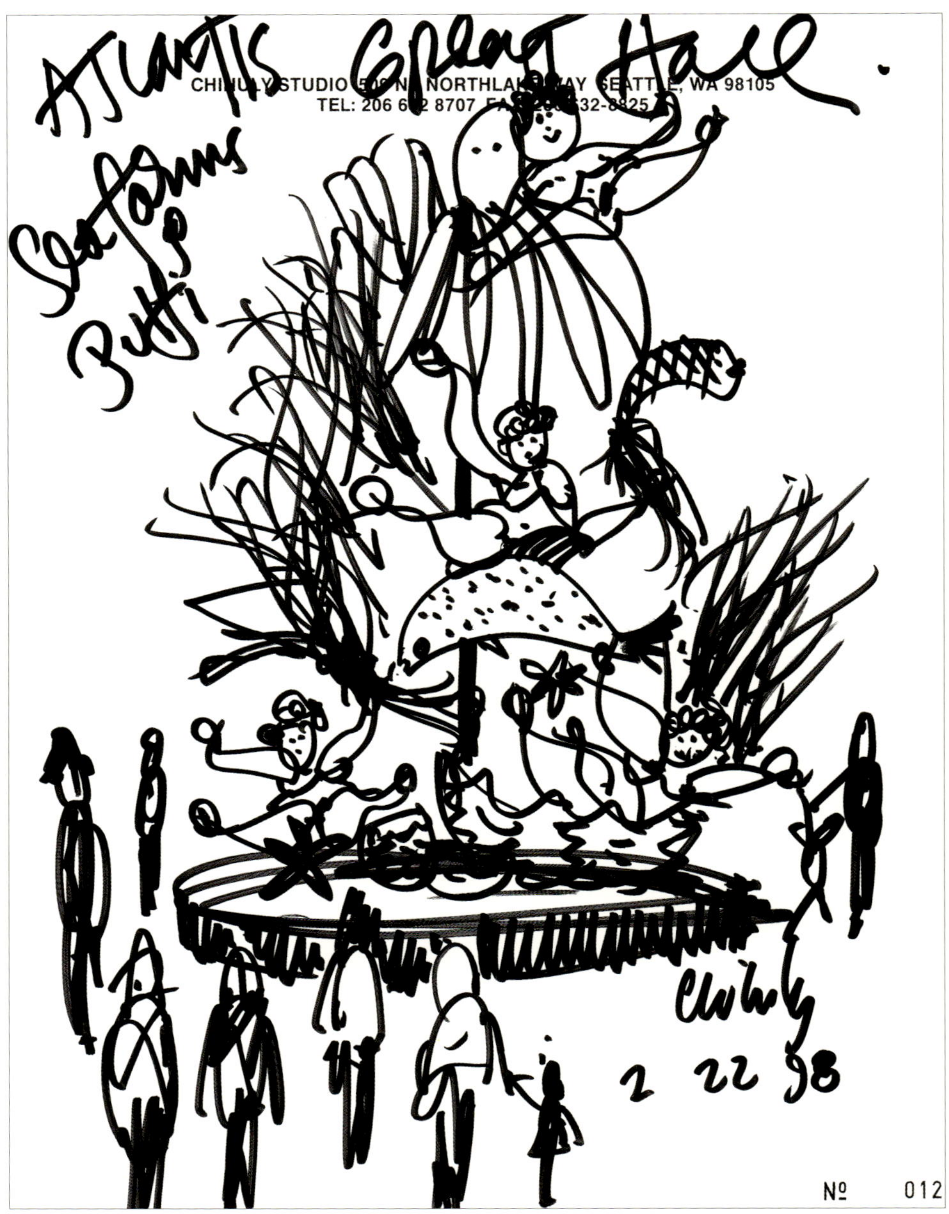

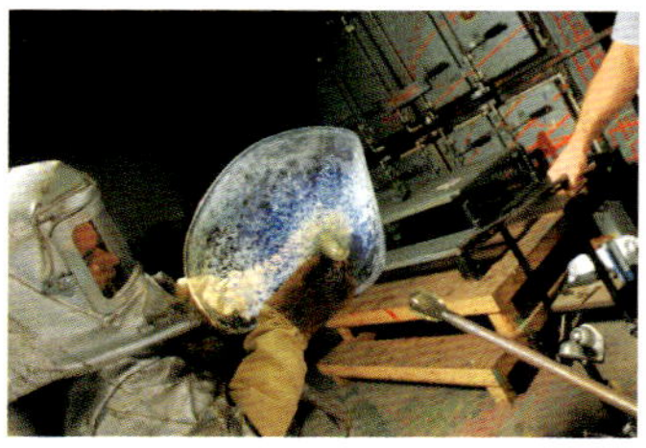

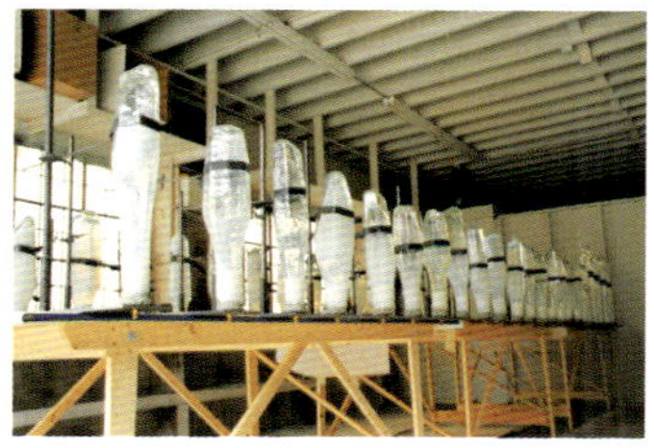

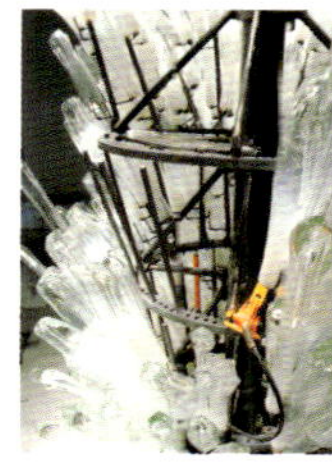

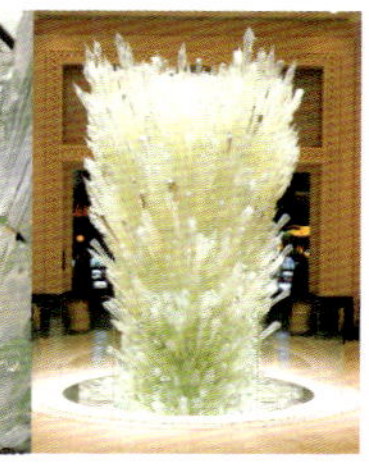

Crystal Gate
Medium: Handblown glass, steel
Dimensions: 18' high, 9' in diameter
Weight: 22,000 pounds
Elements: 3,100

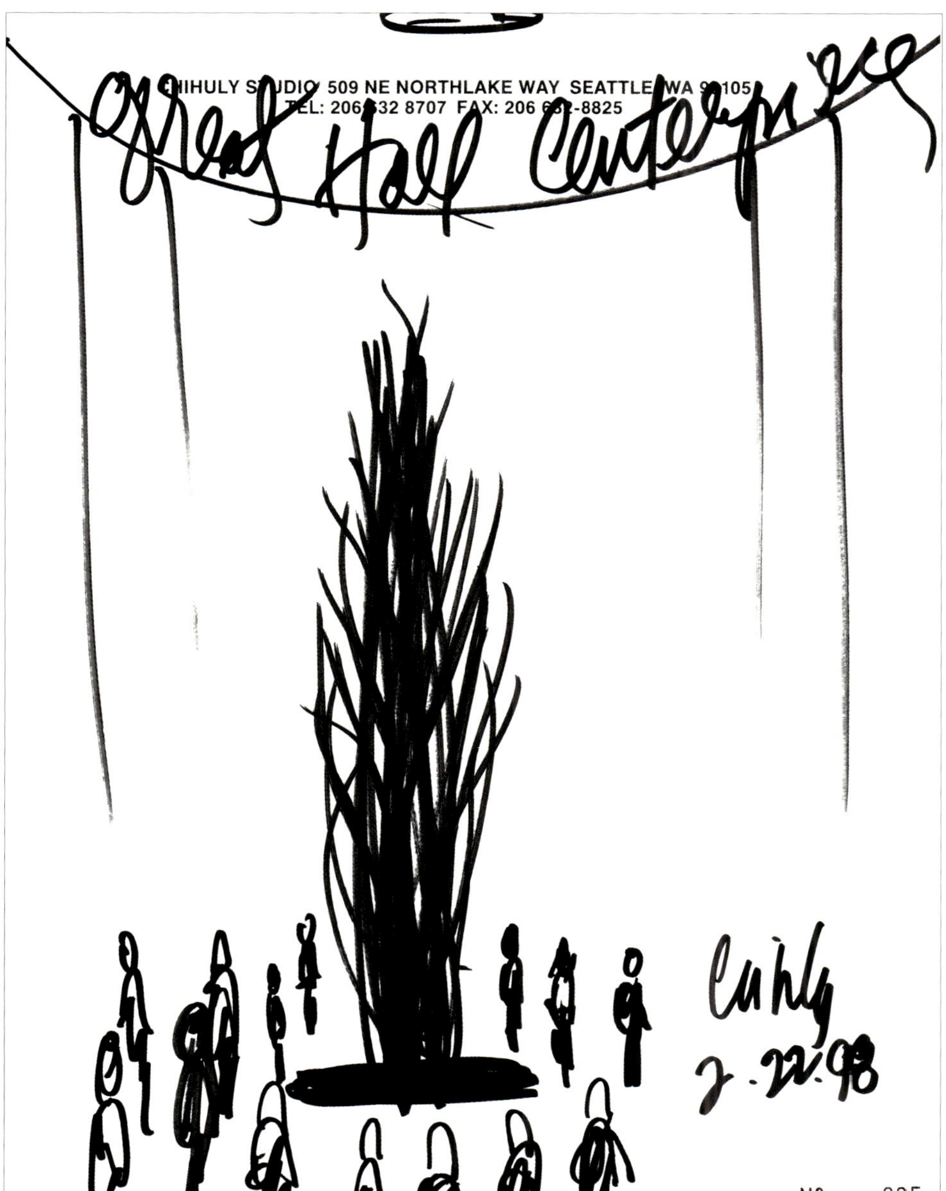

The three largest projects Dale ever undertook up to that time were Bellagio, Benaroya Hall, and Atlantis, which were done simultaneously. I was project manager for the Atlantis and the Bellagio installations, and we were traveling every two to three weeks. We would just trade locales. The team basically commuted back and forth from the Bahamas to Las Vegas. We would go down to the Bahamas and work and work, work, work, work in the steamy tropical storm zone and then tear off back to the Las Vegas dry desert summer. We were working seven days a week for months on end—seven days a week, twelve, fourteen hours a day. Much of the technology we now use did not exist before we started working in such a large scale. I think the scale is the really important thing that delineates these projects from the majority of Dale's previous work.

Philip Stewart

27 Monterrey, Mexico, 1996

Factory: Vitrocrisa

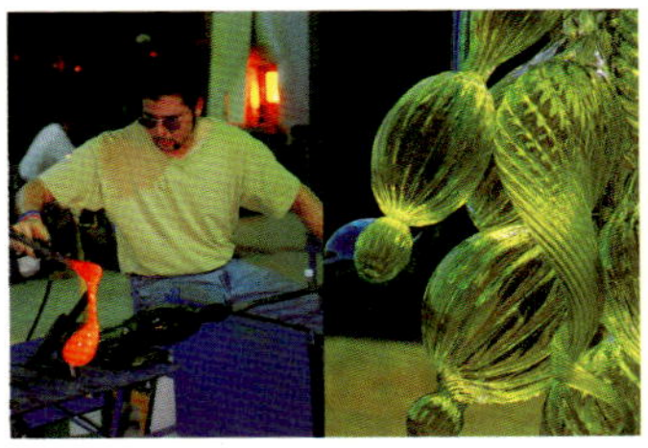

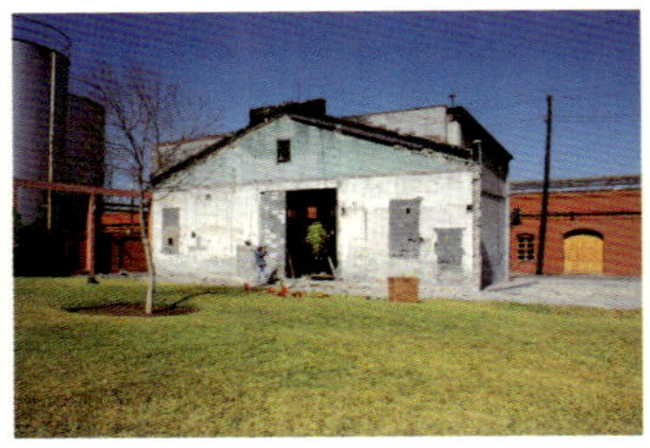

Citron Green Chandelier
Medium: Handblown glass, steel
Dimensions: 8 x 5 x 5'
Weight: 520 lbs.
Elements: 191

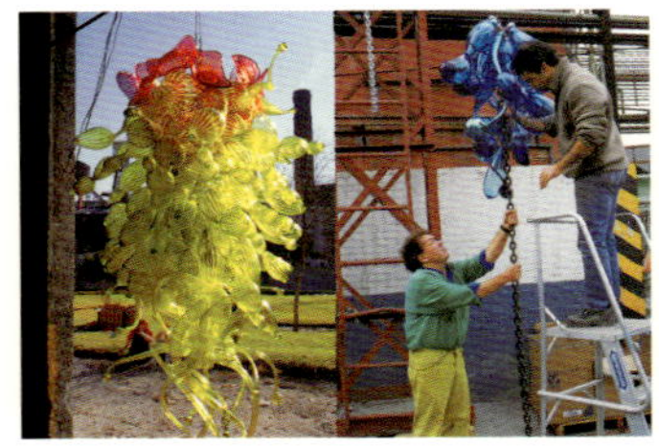

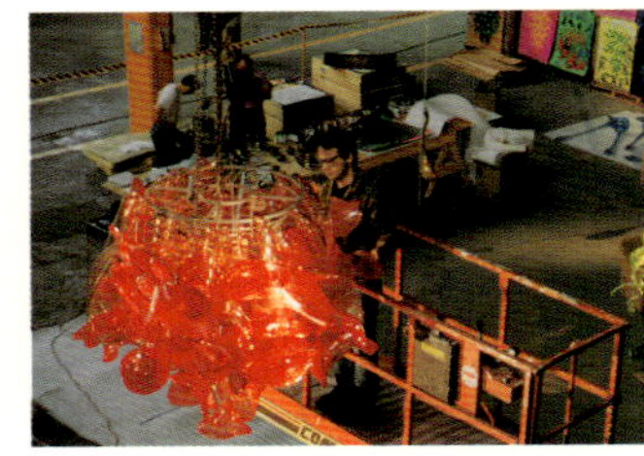

Mexican Hat Chandelier
Medium: Handblown glass, steel
Dimensions: 8 x 7 x 7'
Weight: 780 lbs.
Elements: 120

Vitrocrisa, with some two thousand workers, was the largest factory visited for *Chihuly Over Venice*, and the most prepared for our "invasion." Set up in a corner of the huge turn-of-the-century plant, we were assigned rotating teams of skilled glassblowers and volunteers, and local artists also pitched in. Because of such great preparation, the blow was a dream. We made new forms, hung many chandeliers all around the factory, the town, and into the Sierra Madre. And we made many new friends.

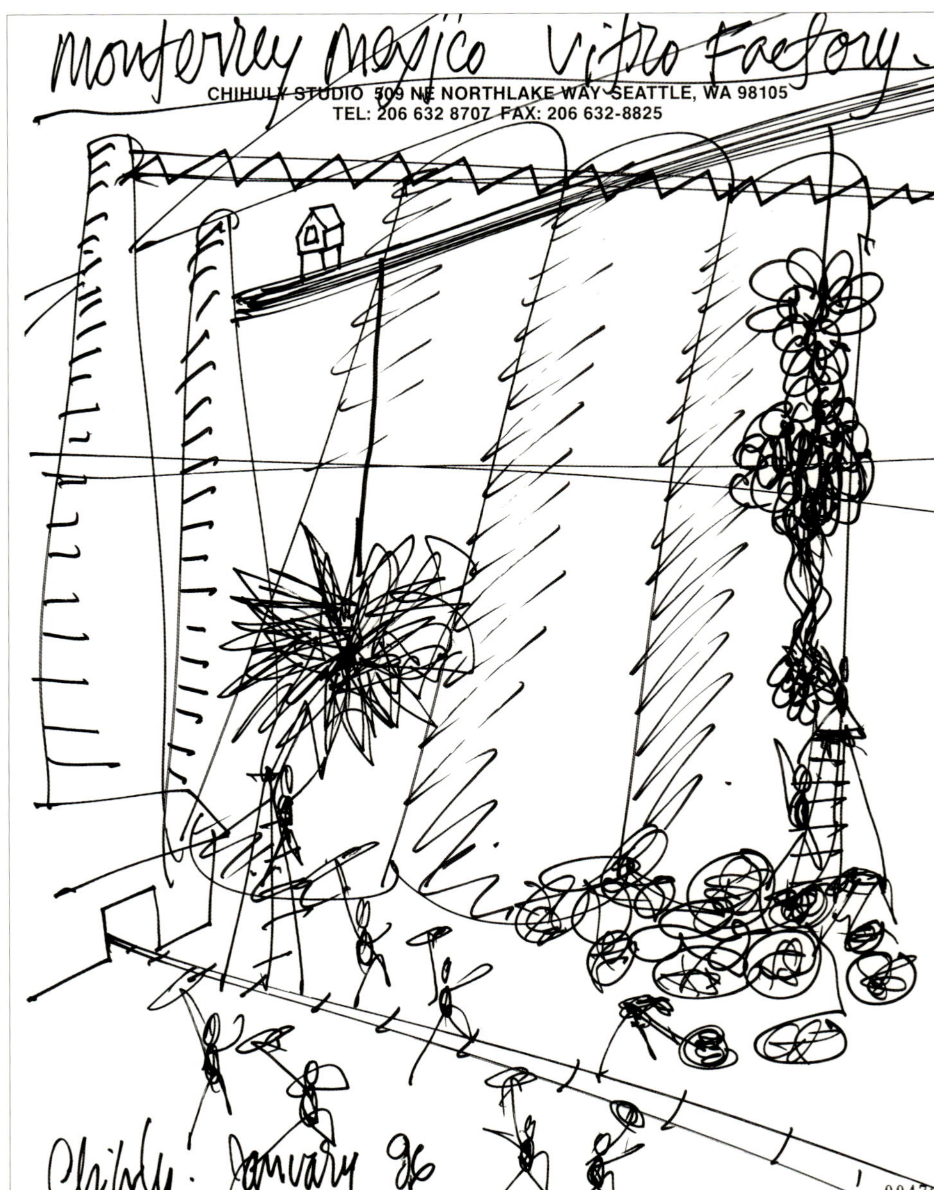

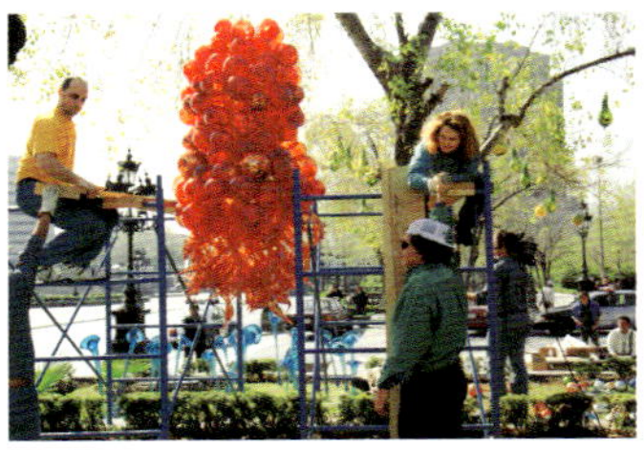

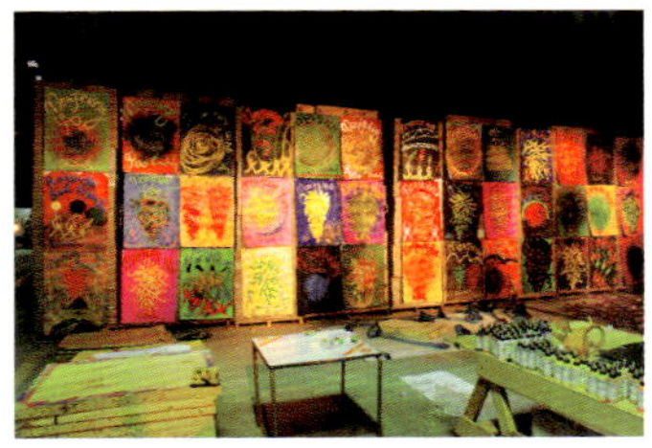

Plaza Chandelier
Medium: Handblown glass, steel
Dimensions: 10 x 5 x 5'
Weight: 972 lbs.
Elements: 333

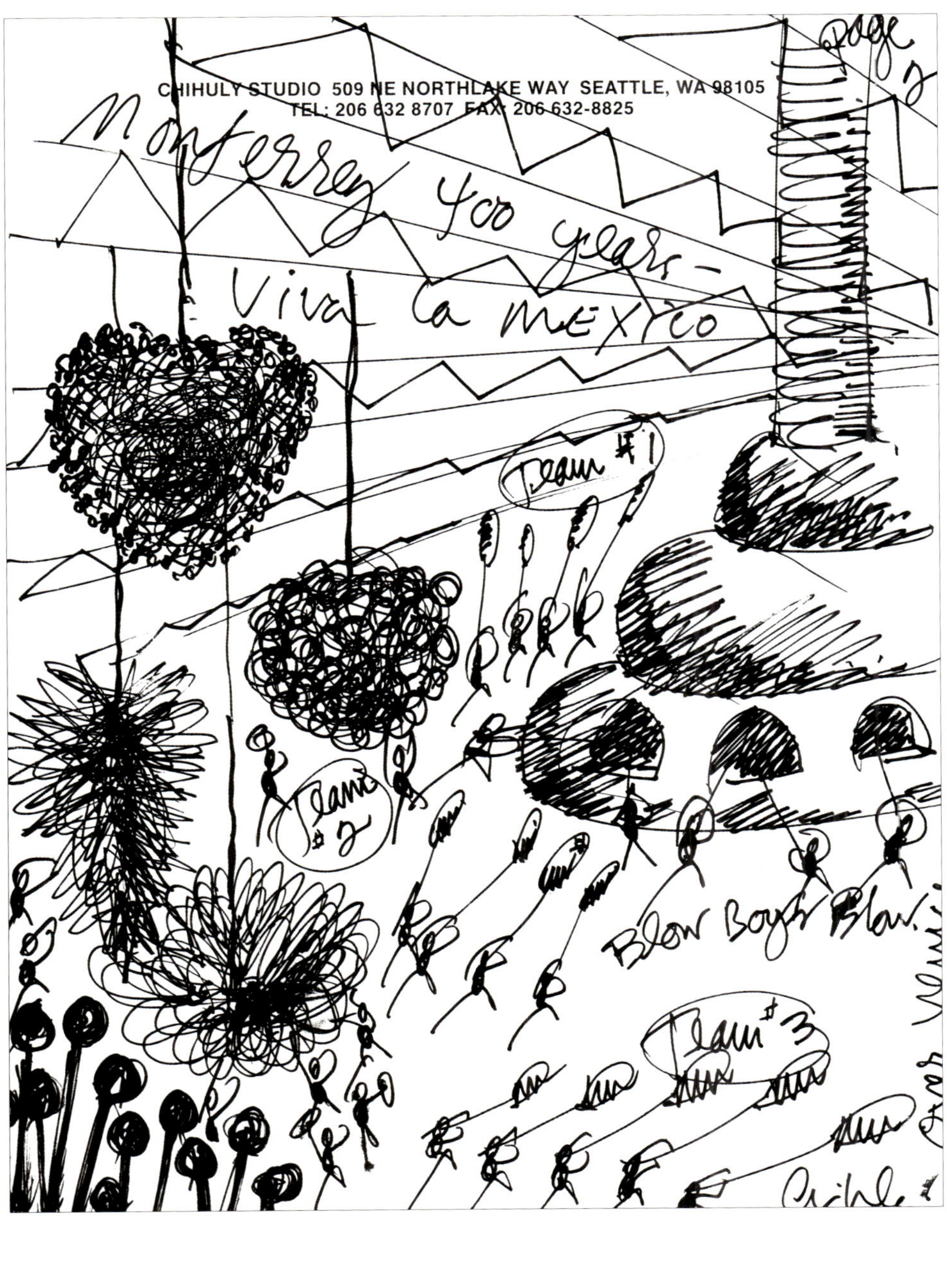

On a high plateau with mountains around, Monterrey is the largest industrial city in Mexico. The people are wonderfully generous and warm. From the glassblowers who work all day in the factory to the owners who supported Dale's efforts in Monterrey at Vitrocrisa, everyone had a genuine love for this project. For two weeks, the floor of the factory was transformed. We would meet every morning with Dale to talk about the day's agenda, what the gaffers were to try and what each team would blow. There was always a pile of glass on the floor that grew each day—those pieces that didn't work, but whose colors and shapes were so interesting. Installations hung from the rafters and Dale's drawings were on the wall. At the end we were invited into their homes to celebrate a wonderful project and something wonderful that had happened here.

Karin Johnson

28 Nuutajärvi, Finland, 1996

Factory: Nuutajärvi Glass Works

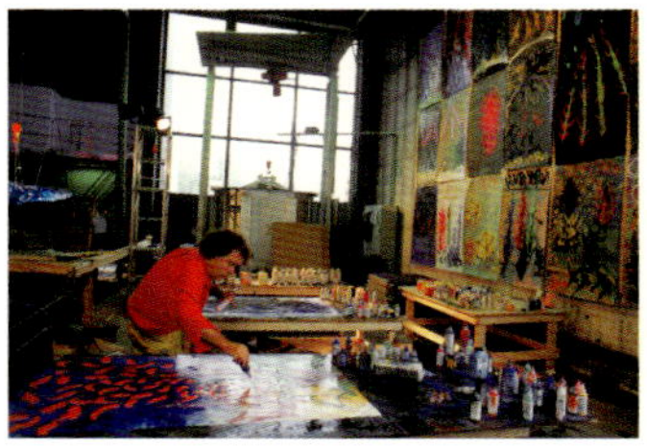

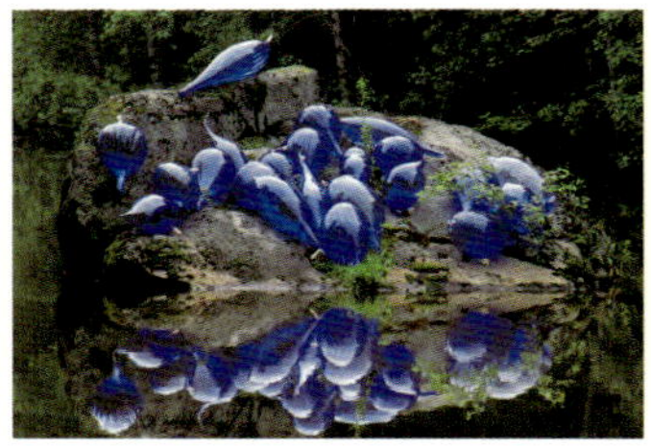

Blue Belugas
Medium: Handblown glass
Dimensions: 5 x 15 x 10'
Weight: 5–15 lbs. each
Elements: 22

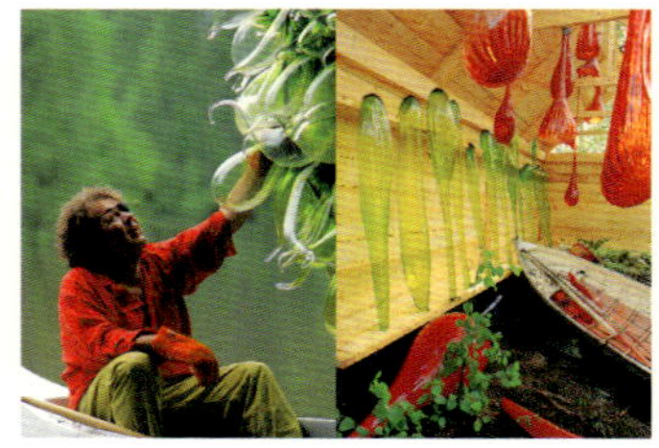

Green Chandelier
Medium: Handblown glass, steel
Dimensions: 8 x 6 x 6'
Weight: 190 lbs.
Elements: 86

The Fish House
Medium: Handblown glass, wood
Dimensions: 12 x 20 x 8'
Weight: 5–15 lbs. each
Elements: 50–60

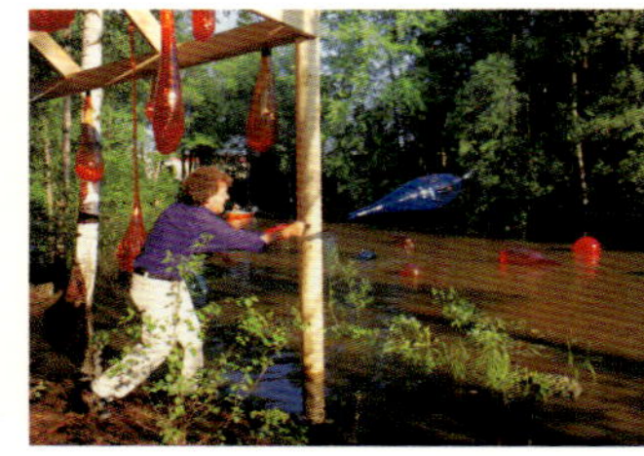

Finland was the first stop on the *Chihuly Over Venice* odyssey, and where we developed new, innovative forms. Well supplied by Ittala with both interesting new equipment and extremely skilled glassblowers, we brought about forty people from Seattle to this tiny village that welcomed us the very first night with a town dance.

We came with a plan—no reheats. That means each part is made and put in the oven in under four minutes. As a result, I discovered many new forms: *Reeds*, *Belugas*, *Seal Pups*, *Saguaros*, *Fiddleheads*, *Antlers*, and the colors were new too, combinations that came from the plant's "pots." But it was the river that really excited me. Before long all the installations were along—and in—the gentle stream connecting two glacial lakes. I think it was the most creative week in my life.

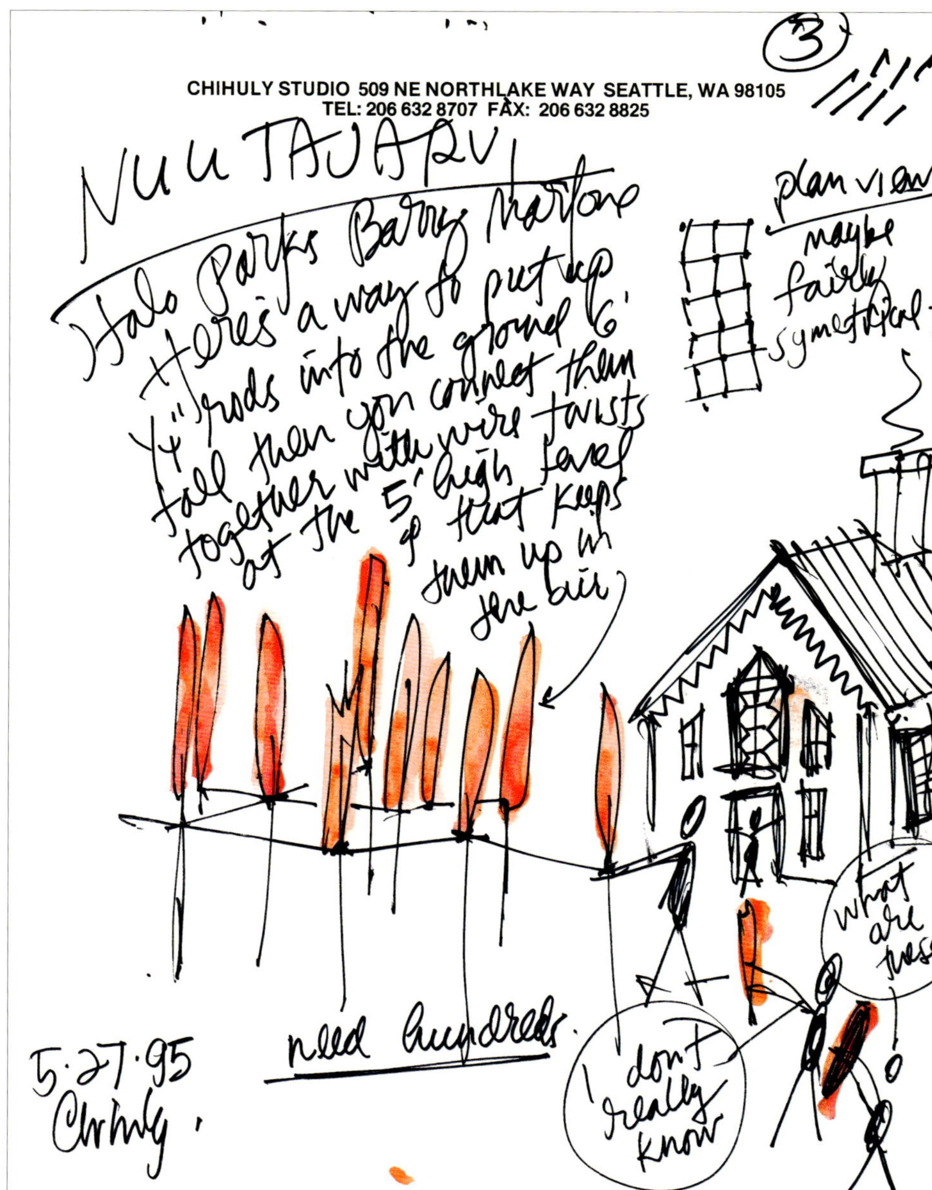

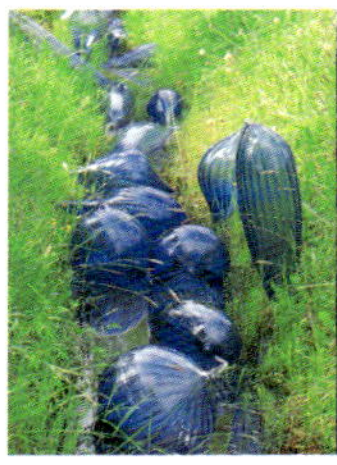
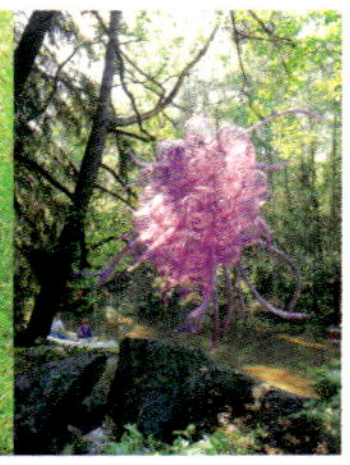
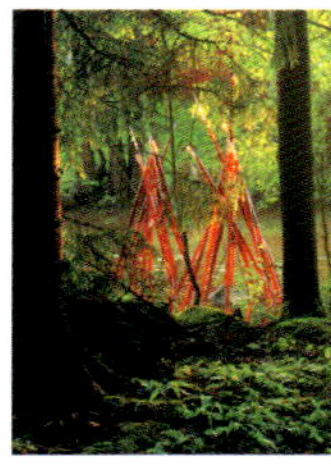
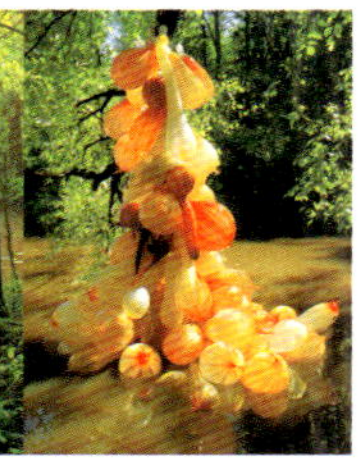
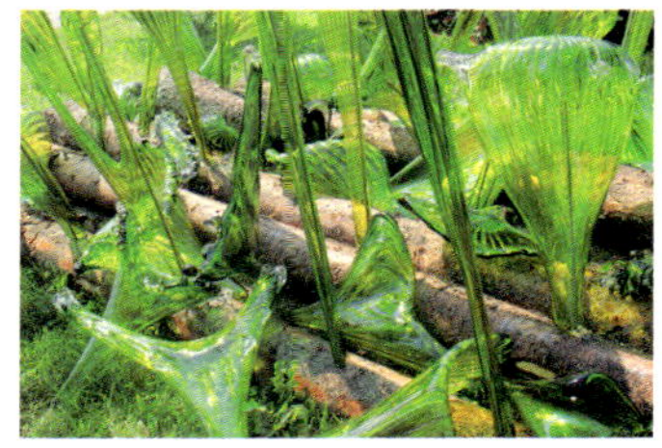

Cobalt Belugas
Medium: Handblown glass
Dimensions: 30 x 6'
Weight: 5–15 lbs. each
Elements: 22

Neodymium Chandelier
Medium: Handblown glass, steel
Dimensions: 7 x 7 x 4'
Weight: 200 lbs.
Elements: 90

Tepees
Medium: Handblown glass
Dimensions: 4–10' tall each
Weight: 10–15 lbs. each
Elements: 22

Gourd Chandelier
Medium: Handblown glass, steel
Dimensions: 10 x 5 x 5'
Weight: 2–3 lbs. each
Elements: 60

Chrome Green Sentinels
Medium: Handblown glass
Dimensions: 7 x 15 x 10'
Weight: 5–15 lbs. each
Elements: 185

Finland was the first step toward Venice. Dale assembled a large group of glassblowers, installation teams, photographers, film and video crews, the Finnish army, and all the resources of the glass factory to launch the *Chihuly Over Venice* project. We had experimented at the studio with new glass forms, all based around the mantra of "no reheats," where the glass object is not returned to the glory hole for continued working but gathered on the blowpipe, formed immediately, and put away.

We arrived in Finland ahead of Dale to set up the hotshop, reconfiguring the factory to our style, and also scouting for installation sites. For many of us, it was going to be a new way of working. The glass we made in the morning could be outside hanging in the trees or floating in the river by the afternoon.

After our first few tentative days we began to hit our stride, and the pace and growth of the work quickly expanded. After all, we were in the Land of the Midnight Sun just prior to summer solstice. Dale's energy seemed not to ebb, but increased with each day's production. We were in the trees; we were in the water; we were in boats; it seemed we were going four directions at once. At one point we took the siding off one section of the factory so we could get better lighting on the *Blue Chandelier*. Another time we hung a chandelier from beneath the only bridge in the village, took the piece down, floated it downstream piece by piece, and reassembled it suspended between two trees, all in nineteen minutes. Of course, Dale held the stopwatch. It was an incredible first step, and I don't know if we ever really have produced that much new and varied work in such a short burst. Those three weeks energized us for the next two years.

Tom Lind

29 Niijima Glass Art Center
Niijima, Japan, 1997

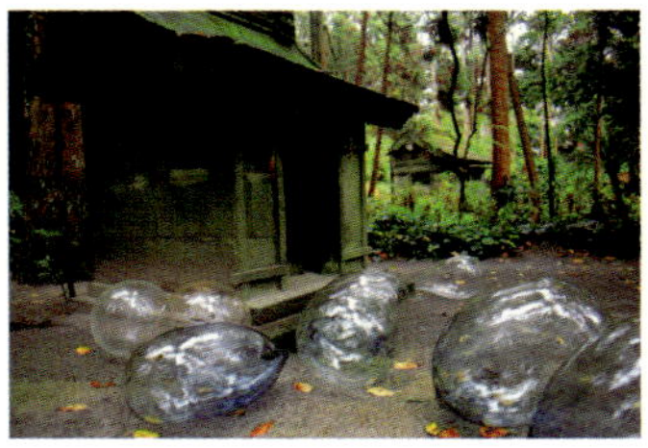

Pale Blue Forms
Medium: Handblown glass
Dimensions: 20–40, up to 18" diameter each
Weight: 3–8 lbs.
Elements: 20–30

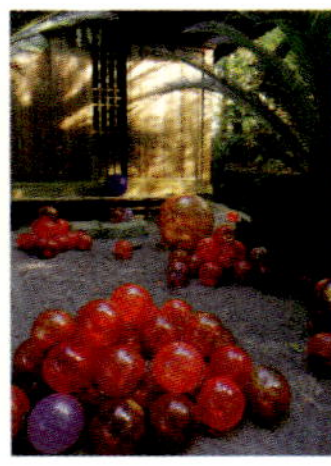

Red Floats
Medium: Handblown glass
Dimensions: 5–20" diameter
Weight: 2–15 lbs. each
Elements: 100–120

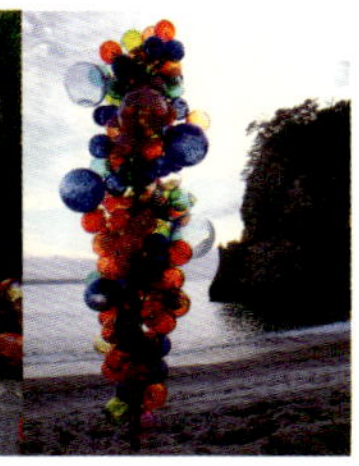

Niijima Tower
Medium: Handblown glass, steel
Dimensions: 8 x 3'
Weight: 2–15 lbs. each
Elements: 100–125

On the tiny island of Niijima, way out in Tokyo Bay (an overnight boat trip), Osamu and Yumiko Noda, former students at Pilchuck, created a glass school perched on a cliff looking out to sea. It was there in 1987 that I started my series *Niijima Floats*—orbs, darkly colored, and amongst the largest free-blown forms ever. Named for both the island and the traditional Japanese fishing floats, my "floats" kept reminding me about the oceans and the oceans' currents.

So, after much discussion, we went back to Niijima in 1997 to experiment with forms—and the sea. Using the local glass made from beach sand, I made variants of the Japanese floats—in my bright colors, of course—and we installed them at the beach and all around the island. We even tried to put them out to sea. Not so easy, and, it turns out that there are literally millions of fishing floats still in the Pacific caught in the trade currents, going round and round. No wonder finding one on the beach is such good luck.

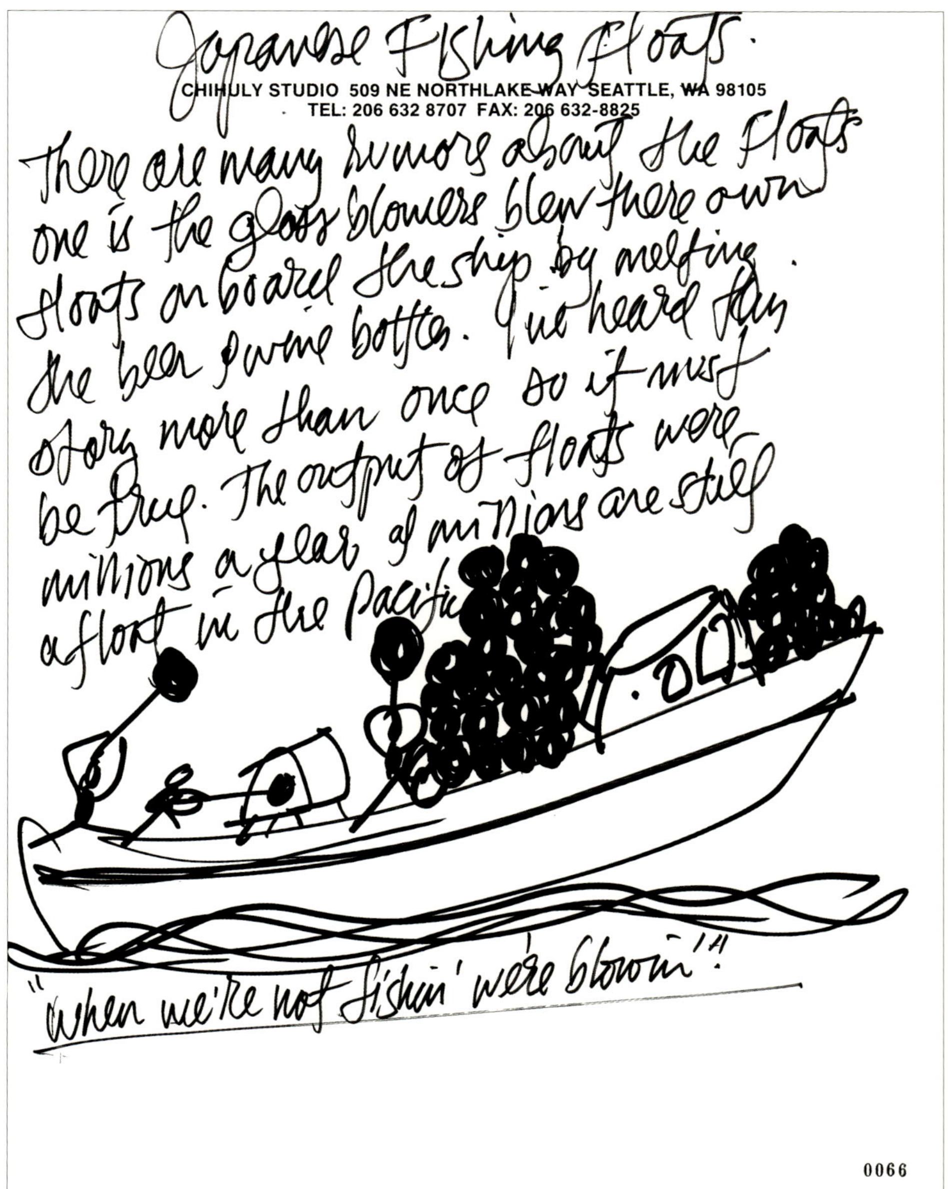

Ukai Museum
Hakone, Japan, 1997

Client: Sadao Ukai
Architect: Yoshiro Ikehara

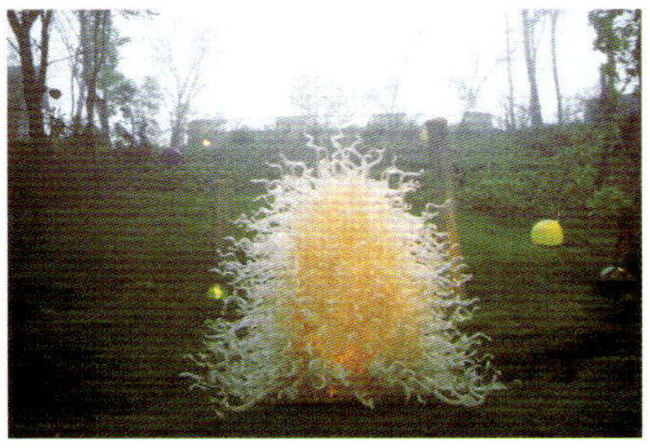

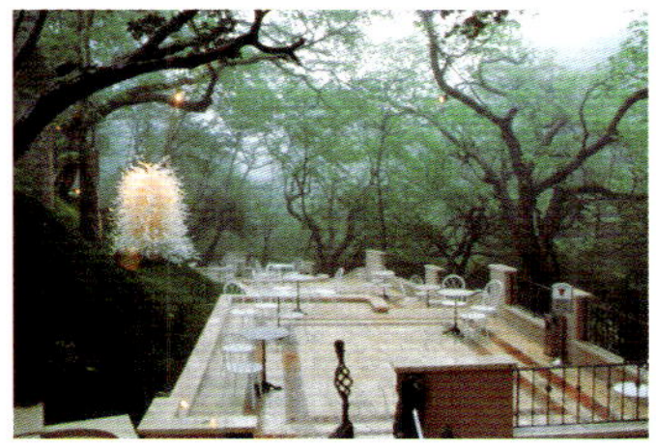

Palazzo Ducale Chandelier
Medium: Handblown glass, steel
Dimensions: 9 x 8 x 8'
Weight: 1,600 lbs.
Elements: 650

This project began when Mr. Ukai met Chihuly in 1996 in Venice at the *Venezia Aperto Vetro* opening at the doge's apartment. Mr. Ukai fell in love with the *Palazzo Ducale Chandelier*, one of the chandeliers for the *Chihuly Over Venice* project.
It was pouring rain when we installed it in the garden at Hakone Glass Forest. The crystal glass covered in gold leaf looked mysterious in the morning mist. The museum has an enormous collection of Venetian glass, which is viewed by eight hundred thousand visitors annually. We have since made many trips to the Ukai Museum to create new installations. We even had a chance to see the baby ducks that were born under the *Ducale Chandelier*.

Etsuko Ichikawa

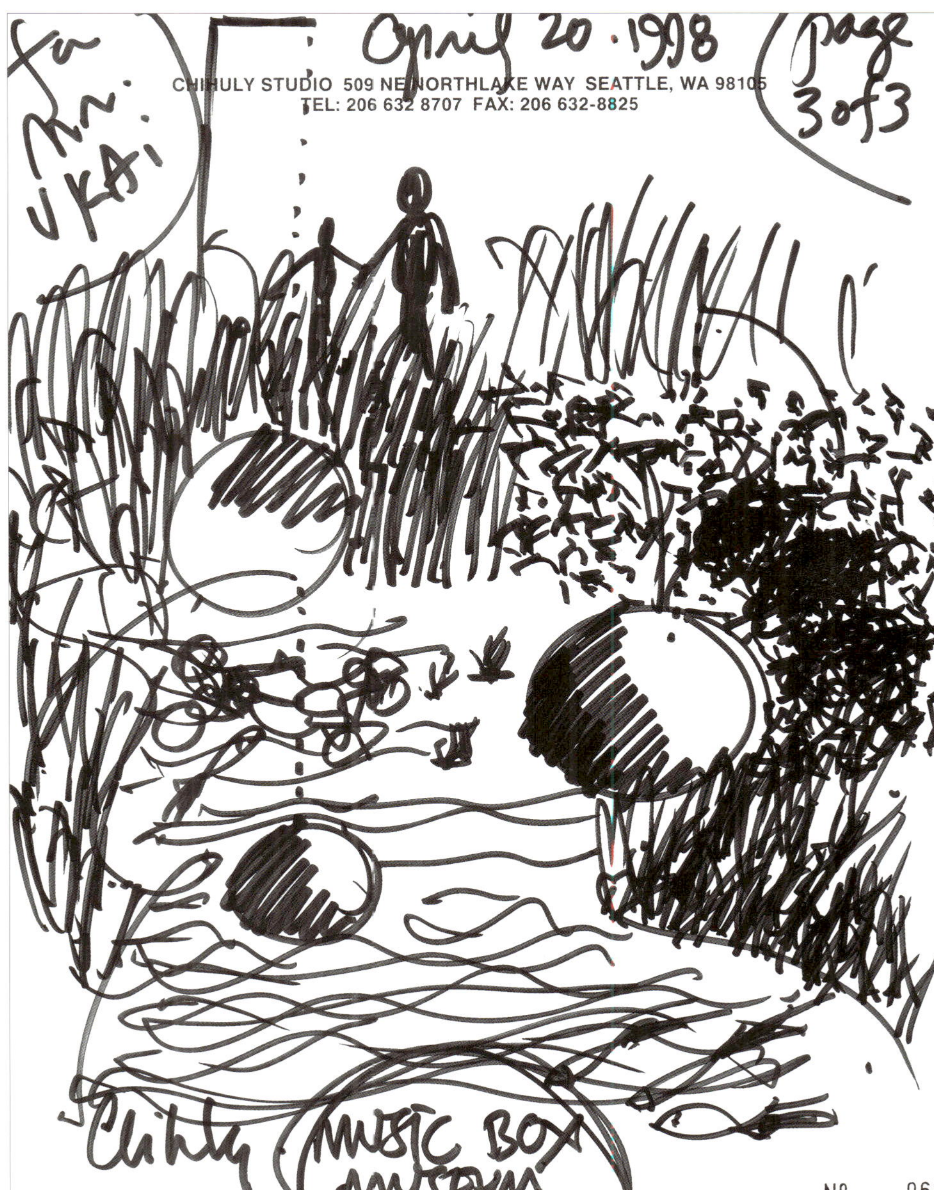

31 Benaroya Hall
Seattle, 1998

Client: Commissioned by Becky and Jack Benaroya for the Seattle Symphony
Architects: LMN Architects

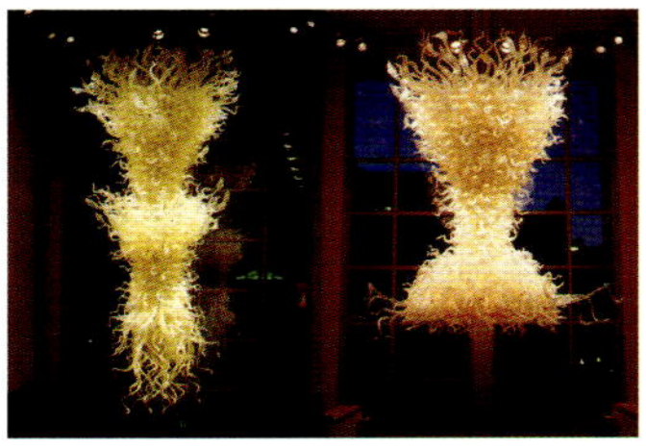

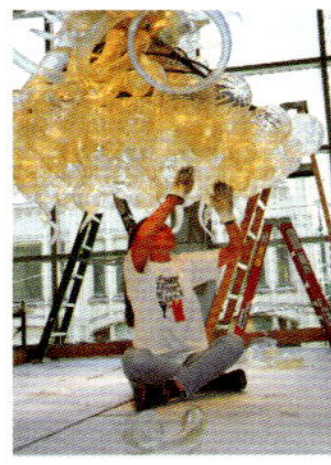

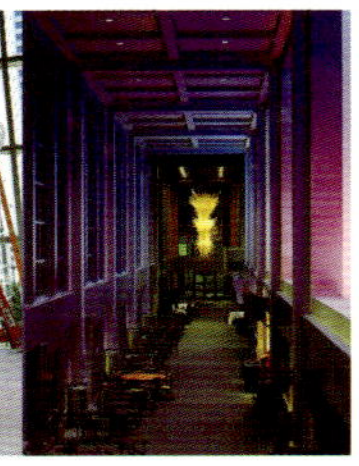

Silver Crystal Cascade Chandelier
Medium: Handblown glass, steel
Dimensions: 20 x 10 x 10'
Weight: 2,000 lbs.
Elements: 1,110

Gold Crystal Cascade Chandelier
Medium: Handblown glass, steel
Dimensions: 15 x 10 x 10'
Weight: 2,200 lbs.
Elements: 1,253

There was a lot of excitement around Seattle's new state-of-the-art Benaroya Hall—for years all concerts had been in a converted public auditorium. So, it was a great honor to be commissioned by Jack Benaroya himself. We were assigned a grand hall the length of a city block. What else to do but place two monumental chandeliers, similar in color, but different in form.

At first it was conceived in the lobby as a series of five or seven pieces that would reflect the columns in the lobby. The *Chandeliers* were built, reviewed, and rebuilt, and several versions later the Boeing Gallery was discussed as a possible site where Dale's works could stand on their own. The scale and length of the space—a full city block—and the vistas from the street and within the building were ideal. We worked with LMN to engineer the hanging and to work out the lighting. For a week our teams were on-site hanging the armature and glass prior to the dedication in September of 1998.

Karin Johnson

Karin please fax Benaroya

CHIHULY STUDIO 509 NE NORTHLAKE WAY SEATTLE, WA 98105
TEL: 206 632 8707 FAX: 206 632-8825

Dear Jack

I love the idea of two grand chandeliers in the lobby – the colors could be subtle or strong or inbetween. I'm thinking they could be rather narrow – maybe 5' wide at the top and 25' to 35' tall? I have other ideas of course! Talk soon

They would be spectacular without conflicting with the architecture.

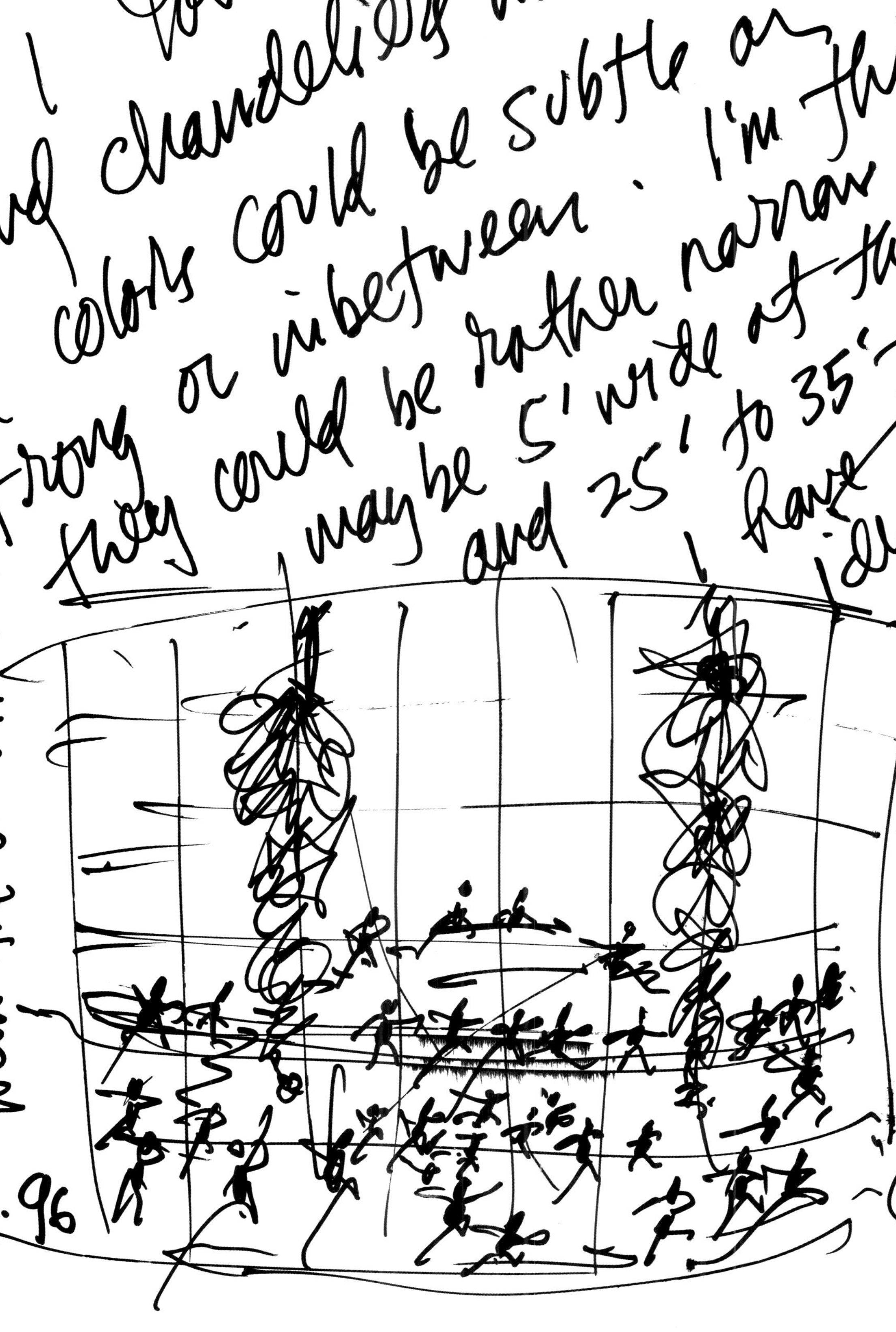

Sept 19. 96 – Chihuly

32 Chihuly in the Light of Jerusalem 2000

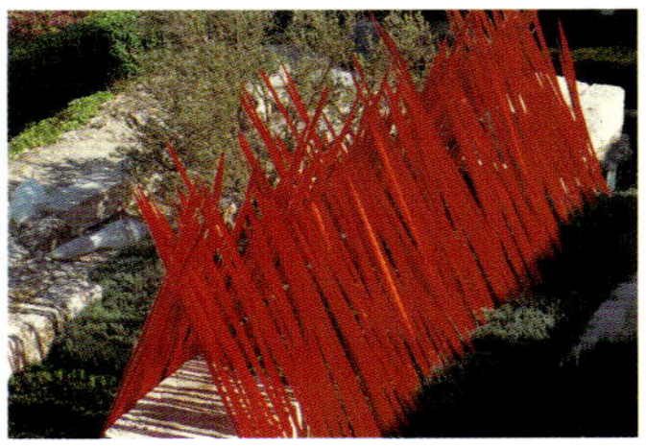

Red Spears
Medium: Handblown glass
Dimensions: 6.5' wide x 29' long, with the tallest spear 12' high
Weight: 10–15 lbs. each
Elements: 247

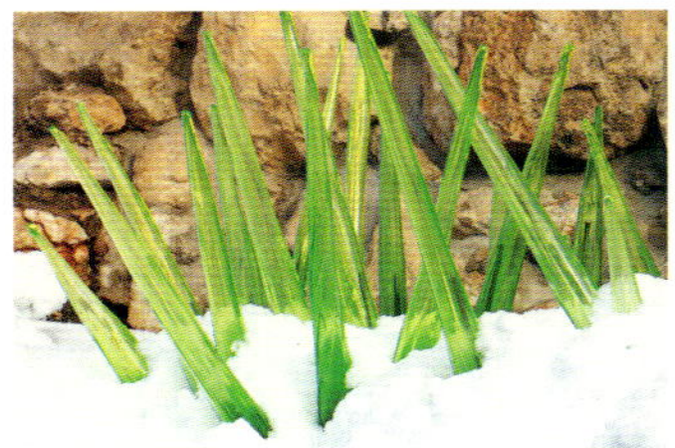

Green Grass
Medium: Handblown glass
Dimensions: 6.5 x 58.5'
Weight: 3–5 lbs. each
Elements: 121

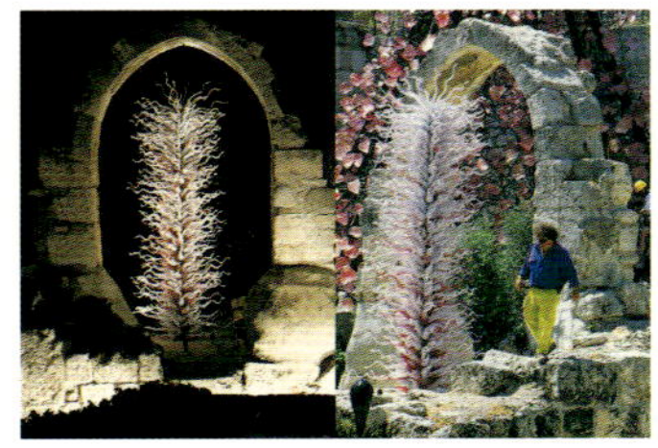

White Tower
Medium: Handblown glass, steel
Dimensions: 15 x 6'
Weight: 1,275 lbs.
Elements: 483

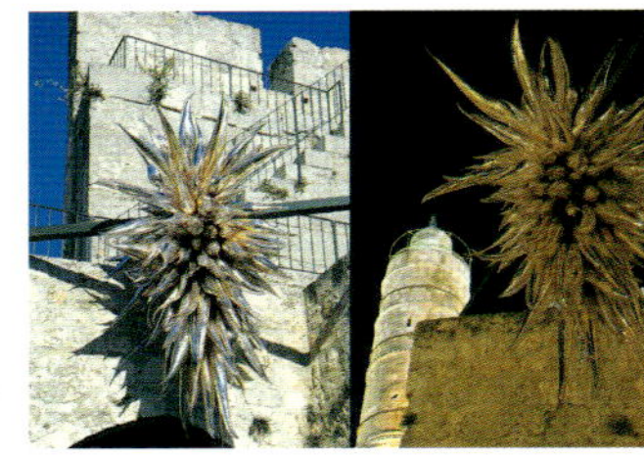

Star
Medium: Polyvitro and steel
Dimensions: 11 x 7 x 7'
Weight: 545 lbs.
Elements: 175

Jerusalem was never intended to be such a large project. After *Chihuly Over Venice* I was not ready to take on another huge project and really couldn't afford to. But every time I visited, I fell more and more in love with the Citadel and my dreams got bigger and bigger. Finally, forty or fifty of us went over for a month in 1999 and installed fifteen monumental installations. *Crystal Mountain*, forty-seven feet high, thirty-three feet wide; *Blue Tower*, forty-seven feet high, six feet wide; *Red Spears*, twelve feet high, twenty-nine feet long.

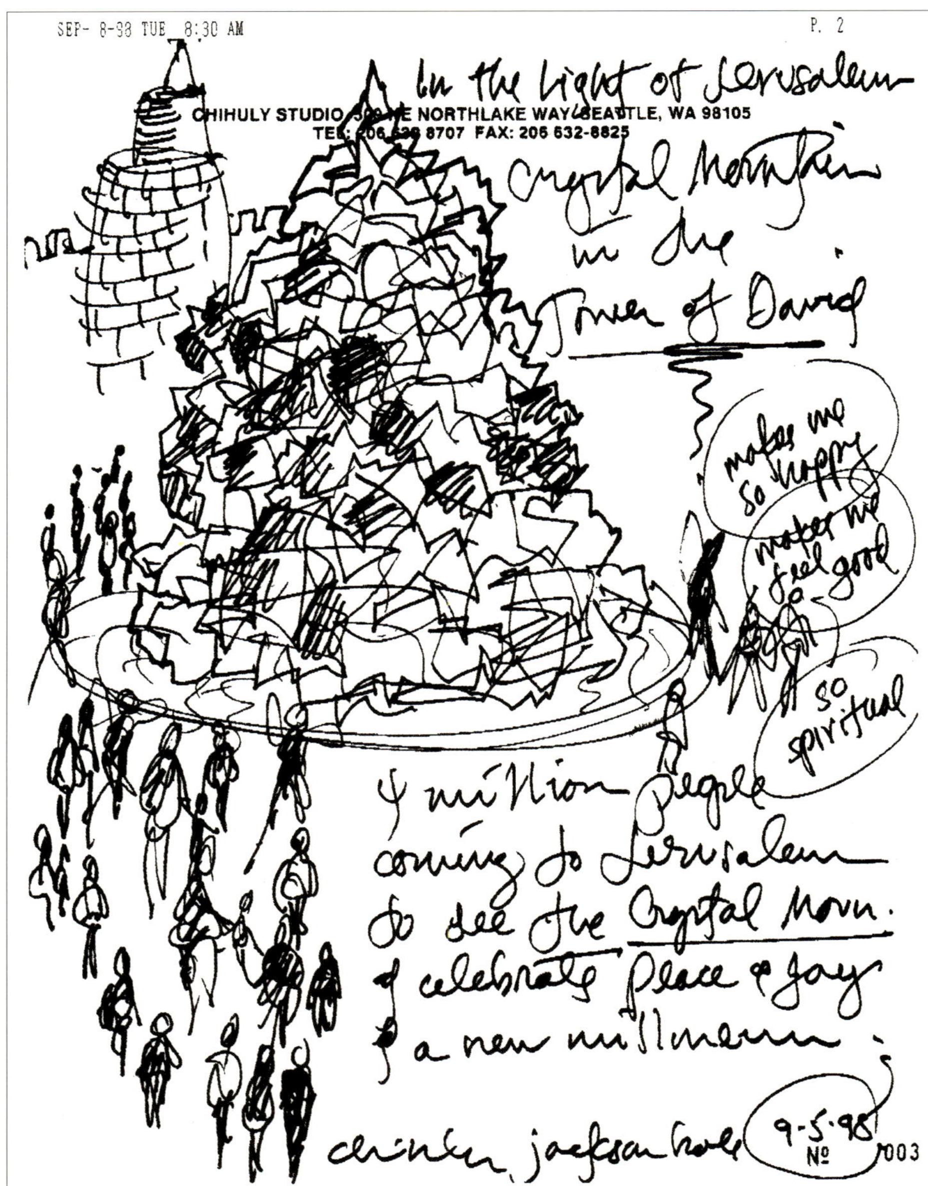

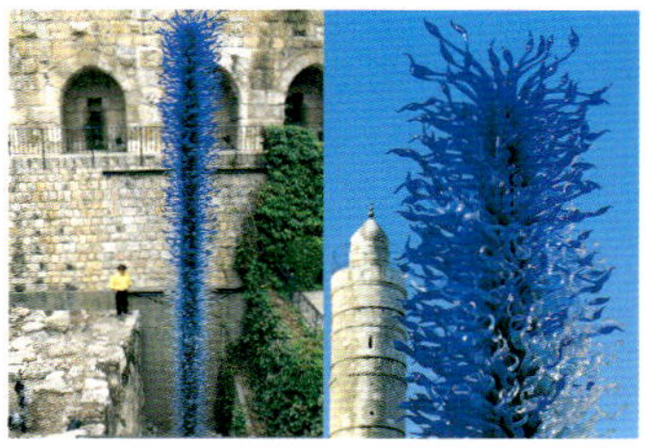

Blue Tower
Medium: Handblown glass, steel
Dimensions: 47 x 6'
Weight: 5,032 lbs.
Elements: 1,966

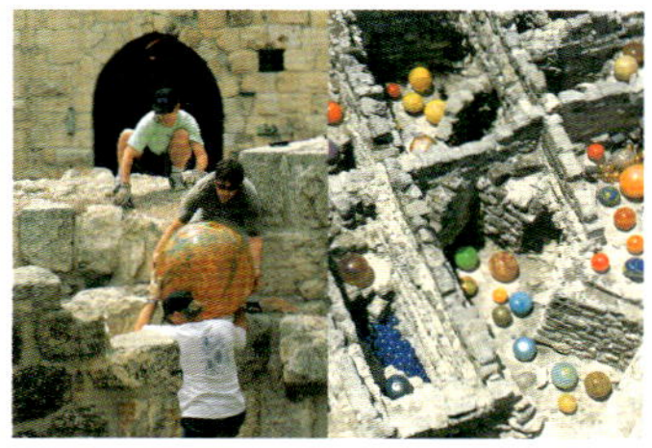

Niijima Floats
Medium: Handblown glass
Dimensions: 19.5 x 39'
Weight: 10–20 lbs. each
Elements: 383

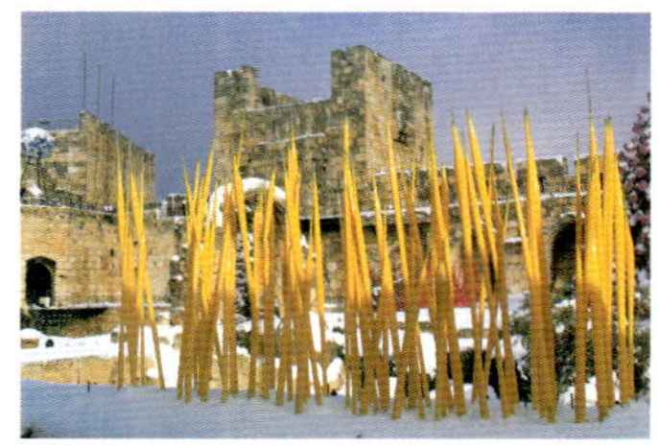

Yellow Spears
Medium: Handblown glass
Dimensions: 10 x 5 x 24'
Weight: 10–15 lbs. each
Elements: 80

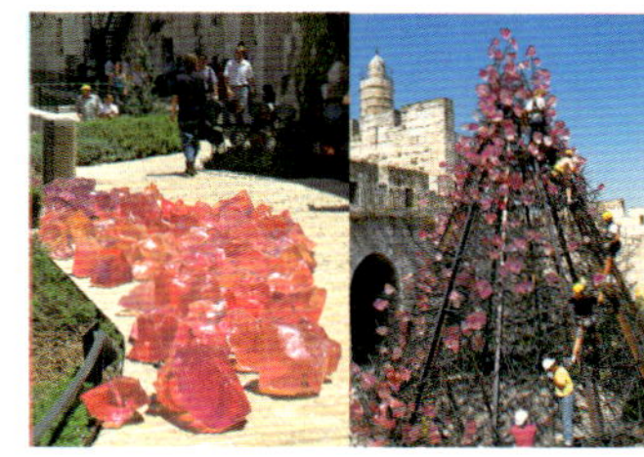

Crystal Mountain
Medium: Polyvitro and steel
Dimensions: 40.5' high x 37' diameter at base
Weight: 60,476 lbs.
Elements: 1,368

Jerusalem—what an undertaking! We worked on the project for two years, but in typical Chihuly fashion, we didn't *really* work on what Dale wanted to make until about two months before the show had to ship. By that time, we had a container load of glass from Vianne stored in Haifa, and Dale knew he wanted to use the glass that had been the *Tower of Tobias* in New York, but he was still working out in his mind a way to match the scale of the fortress. We had just completed a project for a museum in Dale's hometown of Tacoma, an *Ice Cave*, and that had started Dale thinking about big glass crystals and chunks of glass. He had fourteen thousand pounds of these glass chunks mined from a glass factory in Oklahoma, which he used for the *Ice Cave*. But he wanted to cast these chunks in plastic, which would be lighter, more stable, refract better, and be easier to fasten. The museum, in the midst of all of this, had gotten pretty antsy at four months before opening day, with Dale not sure of what he was going to make! They were very plucky, and smart to work with.

We talked about the locations Chihuly wanted to use and the engineering difficulties of each site. Dale had named thirteen installations, thirteen different sites he wanted to use, and the studio started to produce, pack, and ship the parts for the installations. In a big-time hurry. Of course, the things that actually got built were different from what Dale originally decided. Chihuly works by his gut. Once you get used to it, it's an easier way to work. He had us send all the parts he had used in a piece that had hung at the Sydney Opera House and one thousand chandelier parts of all colors, which came in handy. We sent *Niijima Floats* made in Seattle and fishing floats made by a Japanese glassblower in Niijima, and a tower piece that was in storage in the Czech Republic. And he had Charlie Parriott and Joey DeCamp go to a factory in Germany and work with them to produce a bunch of silvered garden balls. Glass from seven different countries was sent, twelve full container loads, over forty-seven tons of material.

Jennifer Lewis

Chihuly in the Light of Jerusalem 2000

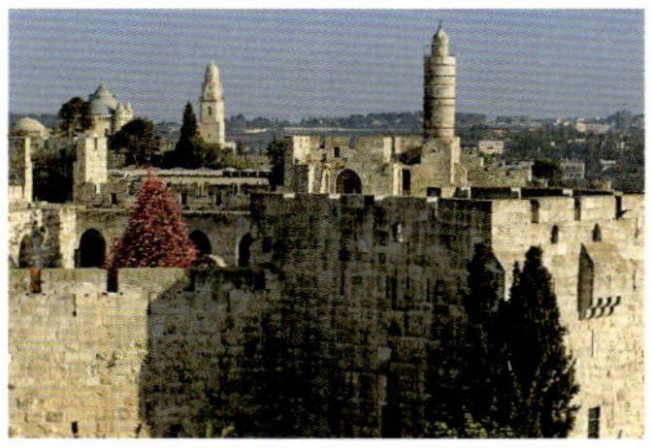

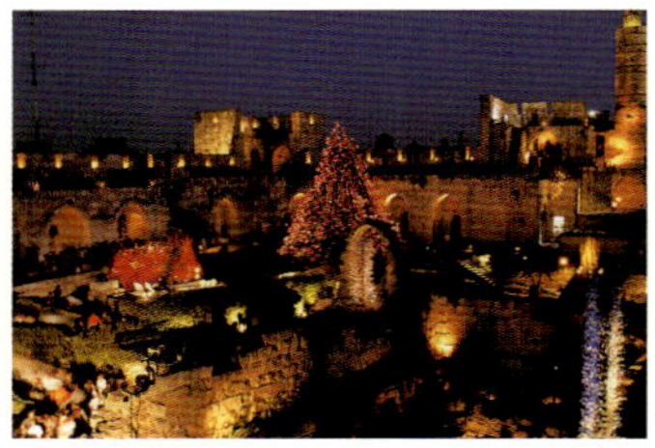

Jerusalem was a funny scenario, because it was actually scheduled and on the calendar. However, no one was talking about it much. We get very wrapped up in trying to keep up with our commission work. We were cruising along and then Dale started to get nervous. God, we're rolling into the start of this and we don't even know what we're doing. We had a couple of meetings, tossed around some ideas, and it became clear from Dale's site visits and the information we had that we didn't really have enough to go on to develop anything. I was going to be in Italy with a crew, so I flew in and met Ryan Smith and Dale in Jerusalem and we worked together to make a plan. We got a grand plan together for the *Crystal Mountain* and the *Blue Tower*. Everything, all the faxes from that show, were all drawn on our second-to-last night. Dale was there for two days. Then Ryan and I tried to stay and deal with the aftermath. Everything got frantic. People were freaking out after Dale left. "You can't build something that big." Then Ryan and I would say, "Oh, it's okay. We'll just do it like this." So it happened very quickly. For probably a month, if I didn't have a good screaming match by the end of the day, something was wrong. It was weird because it's often the way that they deal with people. They would prefer to freak out and air all their grievances and then have a cup of coffee and it's all fine. It's a very different psychology than Seattle. It was tough. I was so excited when the Seattle team finally arrived. I drove to the airport to meet the crew. I was like, *cool, people I know*. It was a very good day. I warned them that I would probably be a jerk from time to time. I apologized up front, because in my mind I had gotten so used to yelling and being really loud because it was the only way that you could really communicate with many people. Not the museum folks, but the people who were physically doing the work.
The project was moving incredibly fast. For me it was amazing because we had the backing there to be able to do all these really incredible things. There were so many people there to help.
We need a giant crane and then a crane appears.
To do the *Moon* installation, we had the largest crane in the Middle East. It was 270 feet tall. When it came in they blocked off the Jaffa Gate, which feeds into the quarter of the Old City. Since the police station is inside the walls, they had to transfer all the terrorist-response units and bomb-response units out for the period of time that we had the Jaffa Gate blocked that night. It was just great. The accommodation by everyone was just tremendous.

Philip Stewart

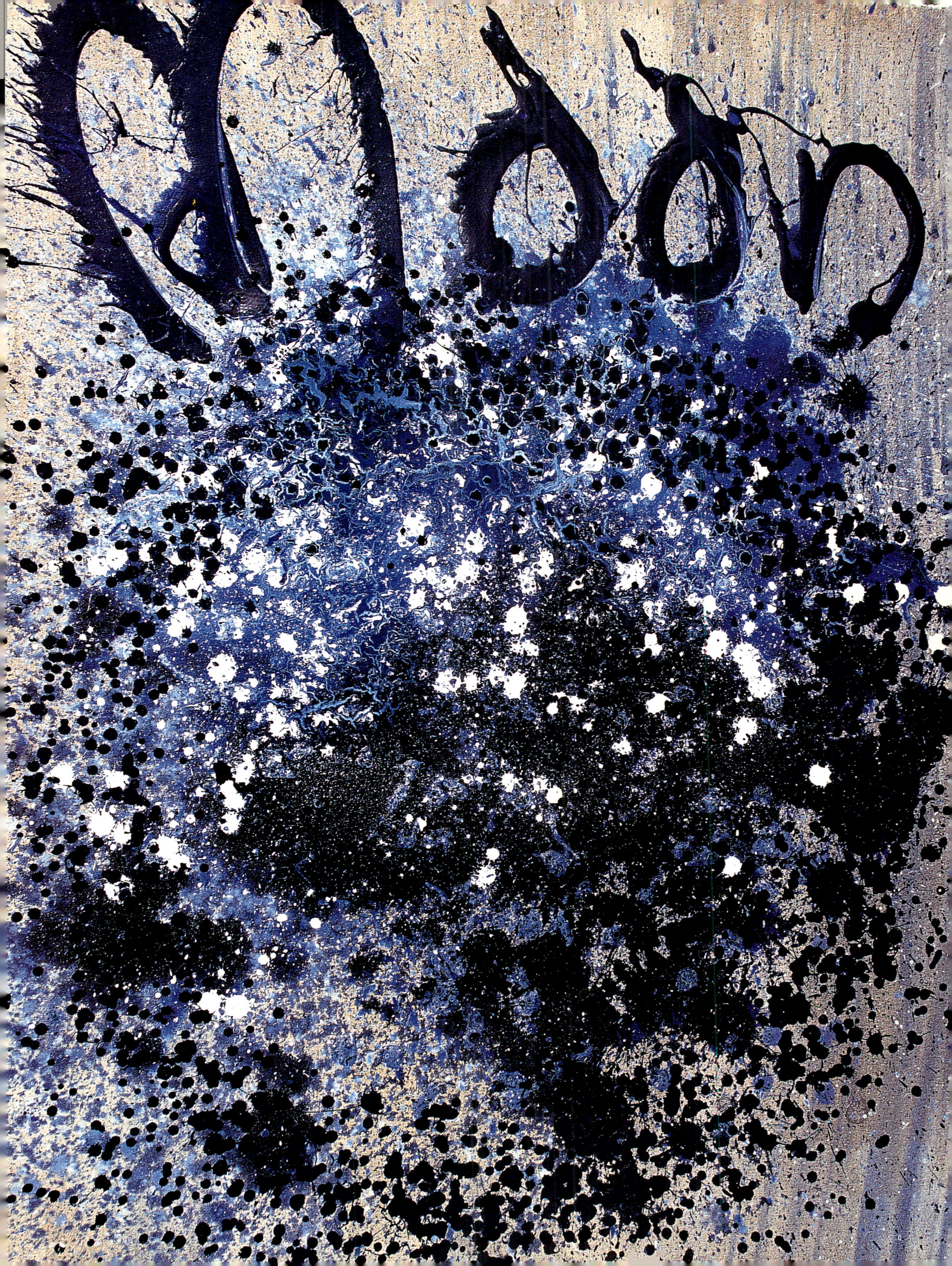

33 **Jerusalem Wall of Ice,** 1999

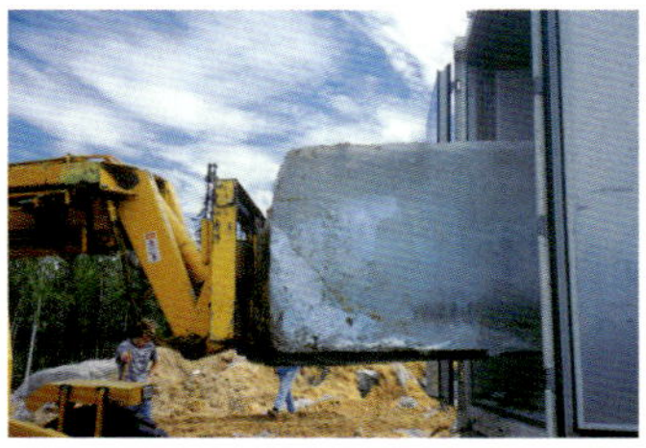

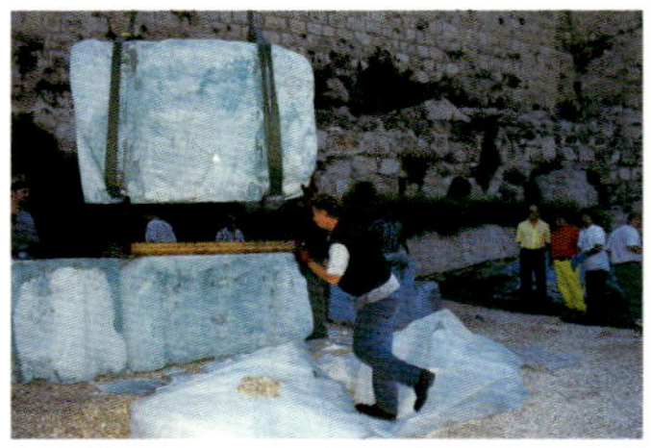

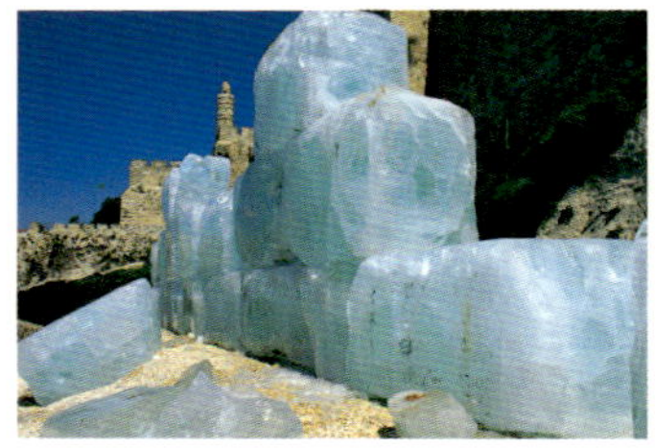

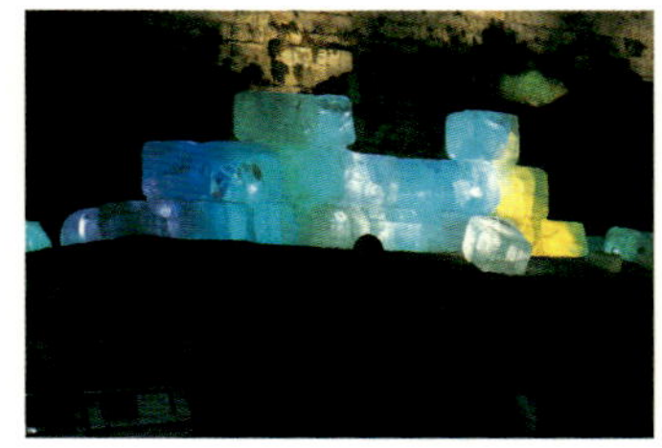

Jerusalem Wall of Ice
Medium: Ice, stage lights with colored gels
Dimensions: Up to 13 x 54'
Weight: 4,500 lbs. per block
Elements: 24 blocks of ice

When I first heard that I could get five-thousand-pound blocks of ice from Alaska, I thought desert—the Negev, to be exact. I'd worked there on a kibbutz in 1962–63, and when I think of deserts, I remember my time in Israel. Five years later I had my chance. We took sixty-four tons of Alaskan ice to Jerusalem to build a wall outside the Citadel as a public thanks to Jerusalem for embracing my exhibition there so enthusiastically—over 700,000 people visited the show in the first six months. But it was also meant as a metaphor and the expression of hope that the new millennium would see a "melting" of tensions between Arabs and Jews, between East and West.

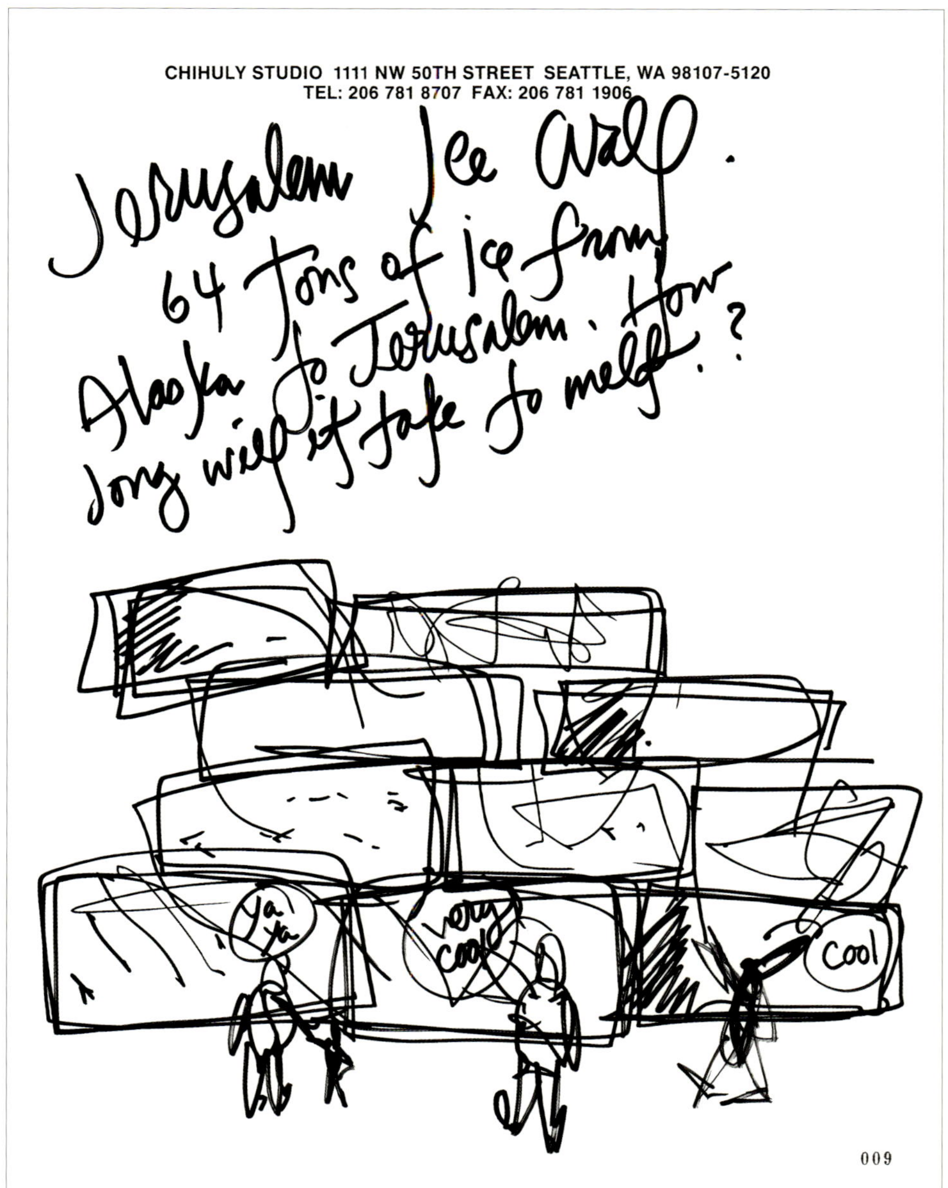

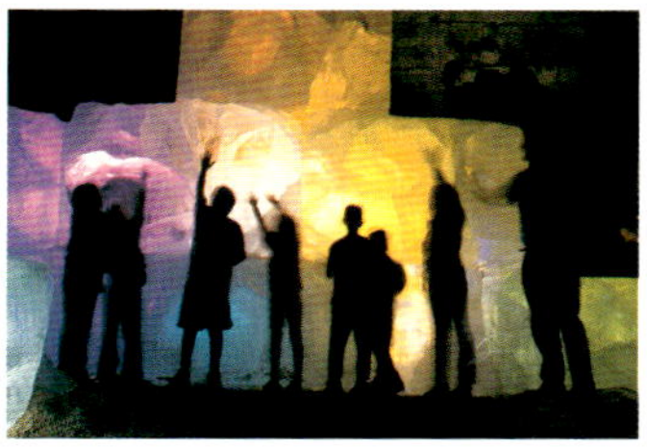 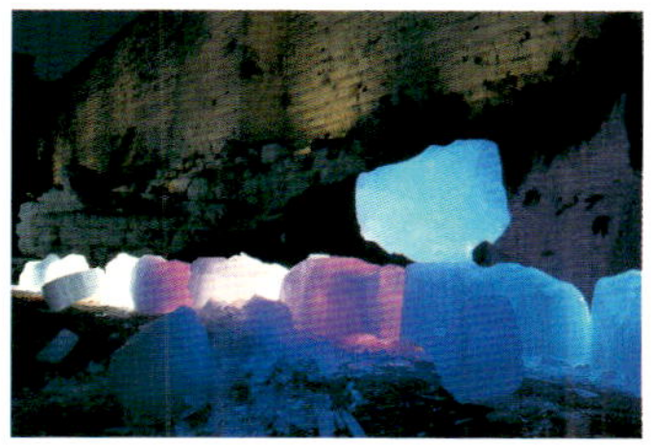

The ice in Jerusalem was fabulous. I think it's my favorite project that we've done, because it was the weirdest. I liked it so much because it was such an absurd notion to take ice from Alaska to the Middle East. I loved being a part of that, coordinating and refining it. I really had a blast with it, because it was such an absurd notion. And everyone's just like, what? Yeah, we've got these containers, we're coordinating all these people and all this stuff, and everyone was in disbelief the whole time. *You're doing what?*

Philip Stewart

Chihuly Bridge of Glass

Completion Date 2002

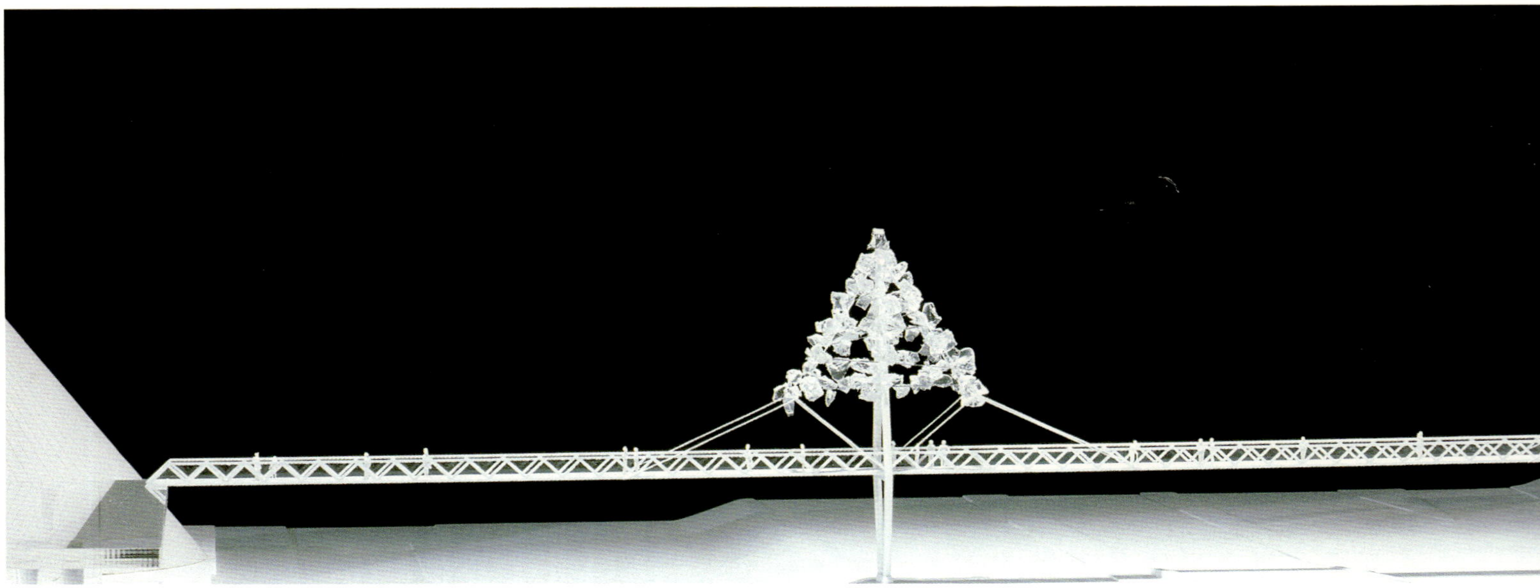

The crystals are of a color and scale that can be seen from miles away. The material is Polyvitro, which can endure the outside elements and not pose a danger to pedestrians or traffic below. The *Chihuly Bridge of Glass* will be a spatial experience of color and light, a transition from object to architecture that has all the qualities of Dale's small-scale work, at a scale that is appropriate for an urban experience.

Ryan Smith

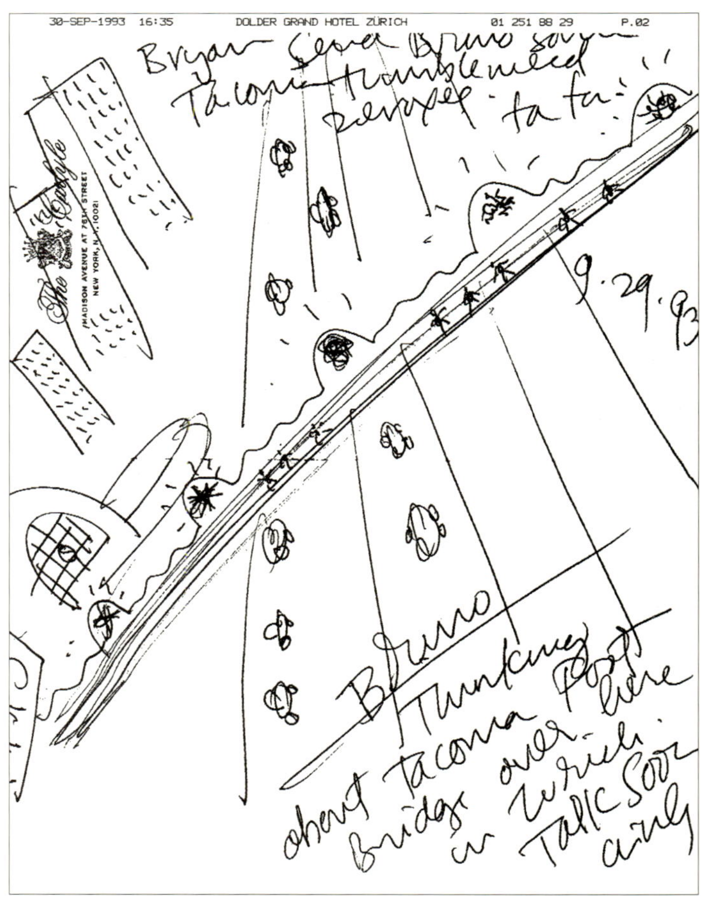

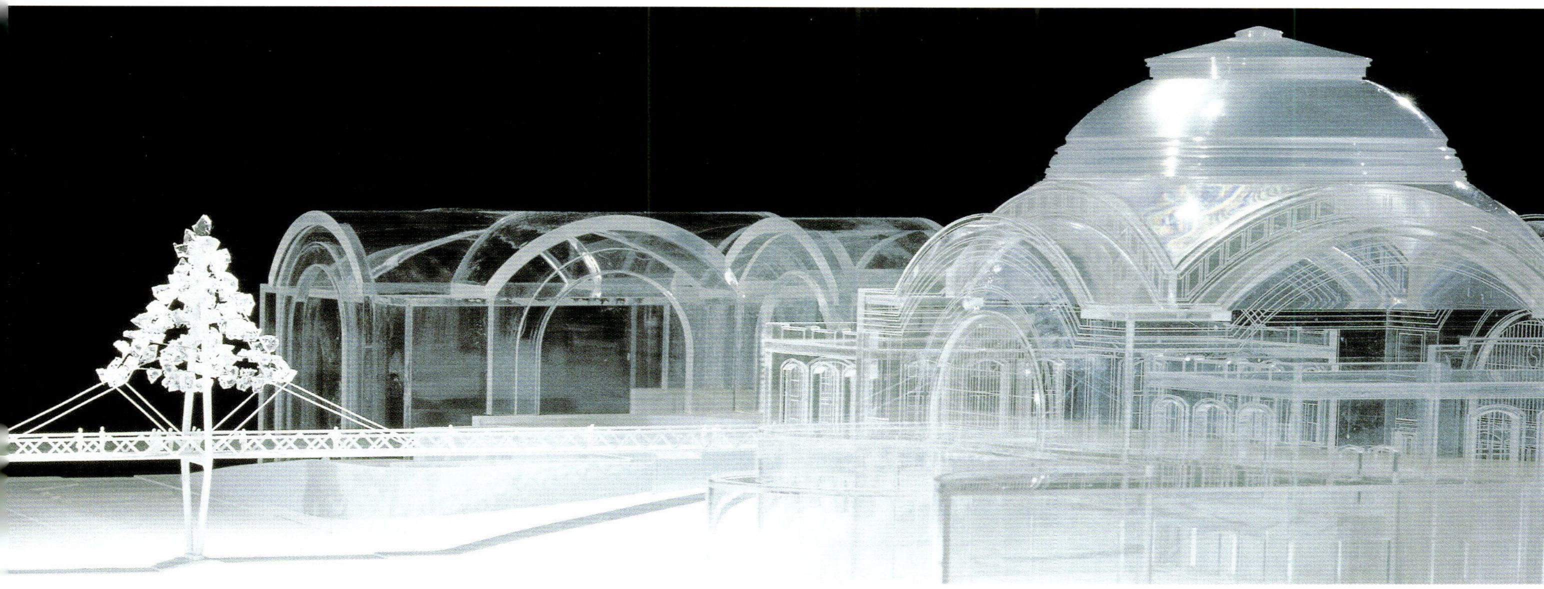

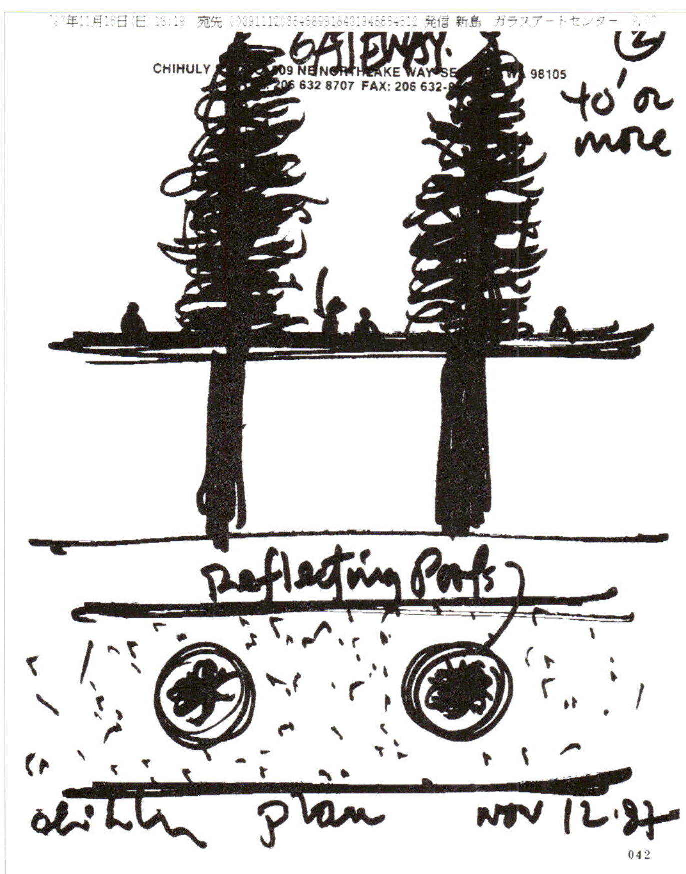
発信 新島 ガラスアートセンター
GATEWAY.
40' or more
Reflecting Pools
plan
NOV 12.'87
042

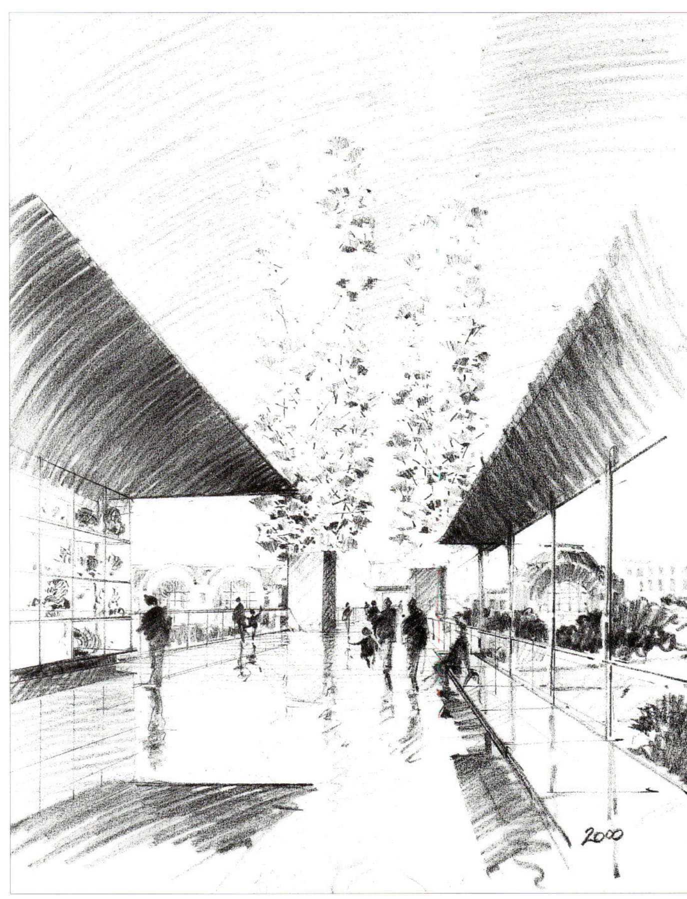
2000

Installations

Public

Academy of Motion Picture Arts and Sciences, Hollywood, California, 1996
Alza Corporation, Mountain View, California, 2000
American Academy of Achievement, Washington, D.C., 1996, 1999
Art in Embassies Program, Washington, D.C.
Atlantis, Paradise Island, Bahamas, 1998
Australian Arts Council, Sydney, Australia, 1974
Bellagio, Las Vegas, Nevada, 1998
Benaroya Hall, Seattle, Washington, 1998
Blue Point Oyster Bar, Providence, Rhode Island, 1978
Bullseye Glass Company, Portland, Oregon, 1998
Chancellor Park, La Jolla, California, 1988
Chase Manhattan Corporation, New York, New York, 1995
City Centre, Seattle, Washington, 1989
Cold Spring Harbor Laboratory, Cold Spring Harbor, New York, 1999
Columbus Visitors' Center, Columbus, Indiana, 1995
Corning World Headquarters, Corning, New York, 1994
DaimlerChrysler Corporation, Auburn Hills, Michigan, 1999
Desert Willows Golf Course, Palm Desert, California, 2000
Disney Cruise Lines, Cape Canaveral, Florida, 1998, 1999
Dreyfus Corporation, New York, New York, 1992
Everett Community Theatre, Everett, Washington, 1993
F. Hoffmann–La Roche Ltd., Basel, Switzerland, 1995
Fleet National Bank, Providence, Rhode Island, 1985
Frank Russell Company, Tacoma, Washington, 1988
Franklin Elementary School, Tacoma School District, Tacoma, Washington, 2000
Glendale Foothills Library, Glendale, Arizona, 1999
GTE World Headquarters, Dallas, Texas, 1991
Guardian Industries Corporation, Auburn Hills, Michigan, 1996
Horizon House, Seattle, Washington, 1995
Hyatt Hotel, Adelaide, Australia, 1988
Kohl Center, University of Wisconsin, Madison, Wisconsin, 1997
Little Caesar Enterprises, Detroit, Michigan, 1993
Liz Claiborne Inc., New York, New York, 1995, 1999
Mattel Corporation, El Segundo, California, 1999
McCormick Place South, Chicago, Illinois, 1997
Microsoft Corporation, Redmond, Washington, 1995

Neiman Marcus, Paramus, New Jersey, 1996
The News Tribune, Tacoma, Washington, 1997
Ohio Arts Council, Ohio State University, Columbus, Ohio, 1992
Pacific Lutheran University, Tacoma, Washington, 1995
Postrio, San Francisco, California, 1996
Ritz-Carlton Millenia Hotel, Singapore, Singapore, 1995
Robins, Kaplan, Miller & Ciresi, Minneapolis, Minnesota, 1990
Rockefeller Center, New York, New York, 1987
Rubicon, San Francisco, California, 1997
Saint Peter's Church, New York, New York, 1994
Seattle Aquarium, Seattle, Washington, 1987
Seay Biomedical Building, Dallas, Texas, 1999
Security Pacific Bank, Los Angeles, California, 1990
Shaare Emeth Synagogue, St. Louis, Missouri, 1980
Simpson Investment Company, Seattle, Washington, 1990
Sleeping Lady Conference Retreat, Leavenworth, Washington, 1996
Spencer Theater for the Performing Arts, Ruidoso, New Mexico, 1997
Spoleto Festival, Spoleto, Italy, 1995
Steelcase North America, Grand Rapids, Michigan, 2000
Sydney Arts Festival, Sydney, Australia, 1998
Tacoma Financial Center, Tacoma, Washington, 1984
Tropicana Products Inc., Bradenton, Florida, 1990
UMB Denver Banking Center, Denver, Colorado, 1995
Union Station, Federal Courthouse, Tacoma, Washington, 1994
United States Border Station, Blaine, Washington, 1979
University of Texas Business Building, San Antonio, Texas, 1997
University of Washington Meany Hall, Seattle, Washington, 1996
University of Washington Tacoma Campus Library, Tacoma, Washington, 1999
Washington Athletic Club, Seattle, Washington, 1999
Washington State Convention Center, Seattle, Washington, 1992, 1993
World Trade Center, Schiphol Airport, Amsterdam, Netherlands, 1996
Yasui Konpira-gu Shinto Shrine, Kyoto, Japan, 1991

Residential

Joan and Stanford Alexander, Houston, Texas
Mr. and Mrs. E.C. Alvord III, Seattle, Washington
Doug and Dale Anderson, Palm Beach, Florida
Edward Anixter, Rancho Mirage, California
Allen Apter, Ambler, Pennsylvania
Christopher Babler, Portland, Oregon
George Barber, Birmingham, Alabama
Dr. Richard and Barbara Basch, Sarasota, Florida
Morris and Sema Belzberg, Rancho Mirage, California
Becky and Jack Benaroya, Seattle, Washington
Marc and Eva Besen, Melbourne, Australia
Irvin J. Borowsky and Laurie Wagman, Philadelphia, Pennsylvania
Mr. and Mrs. Jules Brassner, Palm Beach, Florida
Jeff and Susan Brotman, Bellevue, Washington
Gerard and Cleo Cafesjian, Naples, Florida
Joe and Diana Carter, Leawood, Kansas
Mr. and Mrs. Stuart Cauff, Miami, Florida
Melvin and Ryna Cohen, Bethesda, Maryland
Francine and Marc Cohn, Corpus Christi, Texas
Norman and Suzanne Cohn, Radnor, Pennsylvania
Charles Cowles, New York, New York
Cliff Curry and Delight Stone, Salem, Oregon
Kurt and Leslie Dammeier, Mercer Island, Washington
Andy Davis, Portland, Oregon
Barbaralee Diamonstein-Spielvogel and Carl Spielvogel,
Southampton, New York
Leonard Dobbs, New York, New York
Eric and Barbara Dobkin, Pound Ridge, New York
Roy and Carol Doumani, Venice Peninsula, California
Howard and Marjorie Drubner, Middlebury, Connecticut
Bob Eichler, Bellevue, Washington
Roberta and Eugenio Garza de Elizondo, Monterrey, Mexico
Frank Everett, Sun Valley, Idaho
Leonard and Susan Feinstein, Palm Beach Gardens, Florida
Mr. and Mrs. Lowell Fine, Atlanta, Georgia
Jerome and Mimi Frankel, Delray Beach, Florida

Petra Franklin, Seattle, Washington
Harvey and Doris Friedman, Naples, Florida
Jay and Susan Gates, Washington, D.C.
Kathryn and Norman Gerlich, Seattle, Washington
Irving and Joan Getz, Miami, Florida
Alan and Harriet Ginsburg, Winter Park, Florida
Alan Gleitsman and Sherry Roche, Malibu, California
Steven and Judy Gluckstern, New York, New York
Larry and Jane Goldberg, Aberdeen, Washington
John and Carroll Goodman, Houston, Texas
Meg Goodman and Mike Bonini, Houston, Texas
Bill and Barbara Guinn, Seattle, Washington
Dr. Rahn and Jackie Hall, Houston, Texas
Steve and Roddie Harris, Santa Fe, New Mexico
Mitch and Linda Hart, Beaver Creek, Colorado
Dr. Thomas J. Hawk Sr. and Jodi Hawk, Worthington, Ohio
Marty and Geraldine Hoffman, Aventura, Florida
Doris and Curt Holder, La Jolla, California
David Jenkins, Corona del Mar, California
Elton John, Nice, France
Gene and Jerry Jones, Dallas, Texas
Fred and Gail Jubitz, Portland, Oregon
Jim and Joann Jundt, Wayzata, Minnesota
Sylvan and Doris Kaplan, Longboat Key, Florida
Sara Jane Kasperzak, Columbus, Ohio
Dr. Jeong and Cindy Kim, Potomac, Maryland
Beverly and Irv Lakers, Birmingham, Michigan
Carol and Richard Lane, St. Petersburg, Florida
Carl Lindell, Tampa, Florida
Doron and Marianne Livnat, Savyon, Israel
Cargill and Donna MacMillan, Indian Wells, California
Marty Margulies, Key Biscayne, Florida
Larry and Barbara Marshall, Salina, Kansas
Drs. Doug and Lynn McCorkle, Lutherville, Maryland
Gary and Kathy McLean, Gig Harbor, Washington
Tim and Sherri Meharry, Charlotte, North Carolina

Lester and Jan Mehlman, Morton Grove, Illinois
Frederico and Liliana Melo da Sada, Monterrey, Mexico
Dr. and Mrs. Robert Mendelsohn, Bethesda, Maryland
Edward and Deborah Menin, Boca Raton, Florida
John and Tammy Miller, Los Angeles, California
Linda and Cameron Myhrvold, Bellevue, Washington
Donald and Sue Newhouse, Lambertville, New Jersey
Gerald and Linda Nordberg, Coupeville, Washington
Rowan O'Riley and Bill Kaiser, Wellesley, Massachusetts
Estate of Michael Palm, New York, New York
Shirley Papé, Portland, Oregon
Mr. and Mrs. Benson Pilloff, Beachwood, Ohio
Robert and Jo Pond, Palm Springs, California
Dallas Price, Santa Monica, California
Edward and Madeline Redstone, Rancho Mirage, California
Chapman Root, Ormond Beach, Florida
George and Jane Russell, Tucson, Arizona
George and Dorothy Saxe, Palo Alto, California
Patricia Schaefer, Muncie, Indiana
Manny Schilling, Kirkland, Washington
Thelma and Gilbert Schnitzer, Rancho Santa Fe, California
Gil and Bonnie Schwartz, Bethesda, Maryland
Kris and Scott Selig, Hot Springs, Arkansas
Jon and Mary Shirley, Bellevue, Washington
Barbara and Lloyd Sigel, Minneapolis, Minnesota
Joel and Karyn Silver, Burbank, California
Stuart Sloan, Seattle, Washington
George R. Stroemple, Portland, Oregon
Herb and Isabel Stusser, Mercer Island, Washington
Doug and Shelley Swerland, Kirkland, Washington
Rodney Tan, Singapore, Singapore
Ann Tenenbaum and Tom H. Lee, New York, New York
Steven and Karen Thomas, Las Vegas, Nevada
Ted and Sheila Tierney, Barrington, Illinois
Robert and Marlene Veloz, Montecito, California
Omar and Nicole Vizquel, Issaquah, Washington

Ivan and Linda Volent, Santa Fe, New Mexico
Myra and Hal Weiss, Bloomfield Hills, Michigan
Dr. John and Christine West, Fox Island, Washington
Morris and Paula Westlund, Lake Oswego, Oregon
Malcolm and Carolyn Wiener, Greenwich, Connecticut
Doug and Linda Wood, Montecito, California
Arlene Wright, Kirkland, Washington
Basel and Suzanne Yanes, Dayton, Ohio
Gail and Mike Yanney, Omaha, Nebraska

Museum Collections

Akita Senshu Museum of Art, Akita, Japan
Albany Museum of Art, Albany, Georgia
Albright-Knox Art Gallery, Buffalo, New York
Allied Arts Association, Richland, Washington
American Craft Museum, New York, New York
Amon Carter Museum, Fort Worth, Texas
Anchorage Museum of History and Art, Anchorage, Alaska
Arizona State University Art Museum, Tempe, Arizona
Arkansas Arts Center, Little Rock, Arkansas
Art Gallery of Greater Victoria, Victoria, British Columbia, Canada
Art Gallery of Western Australia, Perth, Australia
Art Museum of Missoula, Missoula, Montana
Art Museum of Southeast Texas, Beaumont, Texas
Asheville Art Museum, Asheville, North Carolina
Auckland Museum, Auckland, New Zealand
Azabu Museum of Arts and Crafts, Tokyo, Japan
Ball State University Museum of Art, Muncie, Indiana
Beach Museum of Art, Kansas State University, Manhattan, Kansas
Bellevue Art Museum, Bellevue, Washington
Berkeley Art Museum, University of California, Berkeley, California
Birmingham Museum of Art, Birmingham, Alabama
Boarman Arts Center, Martinsburg, West Virginia
Boca Raton Museum of Art, Boca Raton, Florida
Brooklyn Museum, Brooklyn, New York
Canadian Craft Museum, Vancouver, British Columbia, Canada
Carnegie Museum of Art, Pittsburgh, Pennsylvania
Charles A. Wustum Museum of Fine Arts, Racine, Wisconsin
Chrysler Museum of Art, Norfolk, Virginia
Cleveland Center for Contemporary Art, Cleveland, Ohio
Cleveland Museum of Art, Cleveland, Ohio
Columbus Cultural Arts Center, Columbus, Ohio
Columbus Museum of Art, Columbus, Ohio
Contemporary Arts Center, Cincinnati, Ohio
Contemporary Crafts Association and Gallery, Portland, Oregon
Contemporary Museum, Honolulu, Hawaii
Cooper-Hewitt National Design Museum, New York, New York

Corning Museum of Glass, Corning, New York
Crocker Art Museum, Sacramento, California
Currier Gallery of Art, Manchester, New Hampshire
Daiichi Museum, Nagoya, Japan
Dallas Museum of Art, Dallas, Texas
Danske Kunstindustrimuseum, Copenhagen, Denmark
Dayton Art Institute, Dayton, Ohio
DeCordova Museum and Sculpture Park, Lincoln, Massachusetts
Denver Art Museum, Denver, Colorado
Detroit Institute of Arts, Detroit, Michigan
Dowse Art Museum, Lower Hutt, New Zealand
Elvehjem Museum of Art, University of Wisconsin, Madison, Wisconsin
Eretz Museum, Tel Aviv, Israel
Everson Museum of Art, Syracuse, New York
Fine Arts Institute, Edmond, Oklahoma
Flint Institute of Arts, Flint, Michigan
Glasmuseum, Ebeltoft, Denmark
Glasmuseum alter Hof Herding, Glascollection, Ernsting, Germany
Glasmuseum, Frauenau, Germany
Glasmuseum Wertheim, Wertheim, Germany
Grand Rapids Art Museum, Grand Rapids, Michigan
Hakone Glass Forest, Ukai Museum, Hakone, Japan
Hawke's Bay Exhibition Centre, Napier, New Zealand
High Museum of Art, Atlanta, Georgia
Hiroshima City Museum of Contemporary Art, Hiroshima, Japan
Hokkaido Museum of Modern Art, Hokkaido, Japan
Honolulu Academy of Arts, Honolulu, Hawaii
Hunter Museum of American Art, Chattanooga, Tennessee
Indianapolis Museum of Art, Indianapolis, Indiana
Israel Museum, Jerusalem, Israel
Japan Institute of Arts and Crafts, Tokyo, Japan
Jesse Besser Museum, Alpena, Michigan
Jesuit Dallas Museum, Dallas, Texas
Joslyn Art Museum, Omaha, Nebraska
Jundt Art Museum, Gonzaga University, Spokane, Washington
Kalamazoo Institute of Arts, Kalamazoo, Michigan

Kaohsiung Museum of Fine Arts, Kaohsiung, Taiwan
Kemper Museum of Contemporary Art & Design, Kansas City, Missouri
Kestner-Gesellschaft, Hannover, Germany
Kobe City Museum, Kobe, Japan
Krannert Art Museum, University of Illinois, Champaign, Illinois
Kunstmuseum Düsseldorf, Düsseldorf, Germany
Kunstsammlungen der Veste Coburg, Coburg, Germany
Kurita Museum, Tochigi, Japan
Leigh Yawkey Woodson Art Museum, Wausau, Wisconsin
Lobmeyr Museum, Vienna, Austria
Los Angeles County Museum of Art, Los Angeles, California
Lowe Art Museum, University of Miami, Coral Gables, Florida
Lyman Allyn Art Museum, New London, Connecticut
M.H. de Young Memorial Museum, San Francisco, California
Madison Art Center, Madison, Wisconsin
Manawatu Museum, Palmerston North, New Zealand
Matsushita Art Museum, Kagoshima, Japan
Meguro Museum of Art, Tokyo, Japan
Memorial Art Gallery, University of Rochester, Rochester, New York
Metropolitan Museum of Art, New York, New York
Milwaukee Art Museum, Milwaukee, Wisconsin
Minneapolis Institute of Arts, Minneapolis, Minnesota
Mint Museum of Craft + Design, Charlotte, North Carolina
Mobile Museum of Art, Mobile, Alabama
Modern Art Museum of Fort Worth, Fort Worth, Texas
Morris Museum, Morristown, New Jersey
Musée d'Art Moderne et d'Art Contemporain, Nice, France
Musée des Arts Décoratifs, Lausanne, Switzerland
Musée des Arts Décoratifs, Palais du Louvre, Paris, France
Musée des Arts Décoratifs de Montréal, Montreal, Quebec, Canada
Musée des Beaux-Arts et de la Céramique, Rouen, France
Museo Contemporaneo de Vidrio Ciudad de Alcorcon, Madrid, Spain
Museo del Vidrio, Monterrey, Mexico
Museum Bellerive, Zurich, Switzerland
Museum Boijmans Van Beuningen, Rotterdam, the Netherlands
Museum für Kunst und Gewerbe Hamburg, Hamburg, Germany

Museum für Kunsthandwerk, Frankfurt am Main, Germany
Museum of American Glass, Millville, New Jersey
Museum of Art, Fort Lauderdale, Florida
Museum of Art, Rhode Island School of Design, Providence, Rhode Island
Museum of Art and Archaeology, Columbia, Missouri
Museum of Arts and Sciences, Daytona Beach, Florida
Museum of Contemporary Art, Chicago, Illinois
Museum of Contemporary Art at San Diego, La Jolla, California
Museum of Fine Arts, Boston, Massachusetts
Museum of Fine Arts, St. Petersburg, Florida
Museum of Modern Art, New York, New York
Museum voor Sierkunst en Vormgeving, Ghent, Belgium
Muskegon Museum of Art, Muskegon, Michigan
Muzeum města Brna, Brno, Czech Republic
Muzeum skla a bižuterie, Jablonec nad Nisou, Czech Republic
National Gallery of Australia, Canberra, Australia
National Gallery of Victoria, Melbourne, Australia
National Liberty Museum, Philadelphia, Pennsylvania
National Museum Kyoto, Kyoto, Japan
National Museum of American History, Smithsonian Institution, Washington, D.C.
National Museum of Modern Art Kyoto, Kyoto, Japan
National Museum of Modern Art Tokyo, Tokyo, Japan
Nationalmuseum, Stockholm, Sweden
New Orleans Museum of Art, New Orleans, Louisiana
Newport Harbor Art Museum, Newport Beach, California
Niijima Contemporary Art Museum, Niijima, Japan
North Central Washington Museum, Wenatchee, Washington
Notojima Glass Art Museum, Ishikawa, Japan
O Art Museum, Tokyo, Japan
Otago Museum, Dunedin, New Zealand
Palm Beach Community College Museum of Art, Lake Worth, Florida
Palm Springs Desert Museum, Palm Springs, California
Palmer Museum of Art, Pennsylvania State University, University Park, Pennsylvania
Parrish Art Museum, Southampton, New York
Philadelphia Museum of Art, Philadelphia, Pennsylvania
Phoenix Art Museum, Phoenix, Arizona

Portland Art Museum, Portland, Oregon
Powerhouse Museum, Sydney, Australia
Princeton University Art Museum, Princeton, New Jersey
Queensland Art Gallery, South Brisbane, Australia
Renwick Gallery, National Museum of American Art, Smithsonian Institution, Washington, D.C.
Robert McDougall Art Gallery, Christchurch, New Zealand
Royal Ontario Museum, Toronto, Ontario, Canada
Saint Louis Art Museum, St. Louis, Missouri
Samuel P. Harn Museum of Art, University of Florida, Gainesville, Florida
San Francisco Museum of Modern Art, San Francisco, California
San Jose Museum of Art, San Jose, California
Scitech Discovery Centre, Perth, Australia
Scottsdale Center for the Arts, Scottsdale, Arizona
Seattle Art Museum, Seattle, Washington
Shimonoseki City Art Museum, Shimonoseki, Japan
Singapore Art Museum, Singapore
Smith College Museum of Art, Northampton, Massachusetts
Sogetsu Art Museum, Tokyo, Japan
Speed Art Museum, Louisville, Kentucky
Spencer Museum of Art, University of Kansas, Lawrence, Kansas
Suntory Museum of Art, Tokyo, Japan
Suomen Lasimuseo, Riihimäki, Finland
Suwa Garasu no Sato Museum, Nagano, Japan
Tacoma Art Museum, Tacoma, Washington
Taipei Fine Arts Museum, Taipei, Taiwan
Tochigi Prefectural Museum of Fine Arts, Tochigi, Japan
Toledo Museum of Art, Toledo, Ohio
Uměleckoprůmsylové muzeum, Prague, Czech Republic
Utah Museum of Fine Arts, University of Utah, Salt Lake City, Utah
Victoria and Albert Museum, London, England
Wadsworth Atheneum, Hartford, Connecticut
Waikato Museum of Art and History, Hamilton, New Zealand
Walker Hill Art Center, Seoul, Korea
Whatcom Museum of History and Art, Bellingham, Washington
White House Collection of American Crafts, Washington, D.C.

Whitney Museum of American Art, New York, New York
Württembergisches Landesmuseum Stuttgart, Stuttgart, Germany
Yale University Art Gallery, New Haven, Connecticut
Yokohama Museum of Art, Yokohama, Japan

Photographs taken by
Parks Anderson, Theresa Batty, James Carpenter,
Shaun Chappell, Steve Cochran, Jan Cook, Claire Garoutte,
Camilio Garza y Garcia, Donna Goetsch, Itamar Grinberg,
Nick Gunderson, Scott Hagar, Russell Johnson,
Ansgard Kaliss, Scott Mitchell Leen, Tom Lind, Teresa Rishel,
Terry Rishel, David Schoales, Leon Shabott, and Julie Stupsker

Rendering by Bill Hook

Designed by
Anna Katherine Curfman, Laurence Madrelle, and Barry Rosen

Typeface Trade Gothic
Paper Lumisilk matt art 150 gsm
Printed and bound in Hong Kong
by Rainbow Graphic and Printing Co., Ltd.

ISBN 0-8109-6708-1 (Abrams)

Library of Congress Card Number: 00-103955

Published by Portland Press
PO Box 70856, Seattle, WA 98127
800 574 7272
www.portlandpress.net

Distributed by Harry N. Abrams, Incorporated
100 Fifth Avenue, New York, NY 10011
www.abramsbooks.com

For more information on the artist, please visit www.chihuly.com

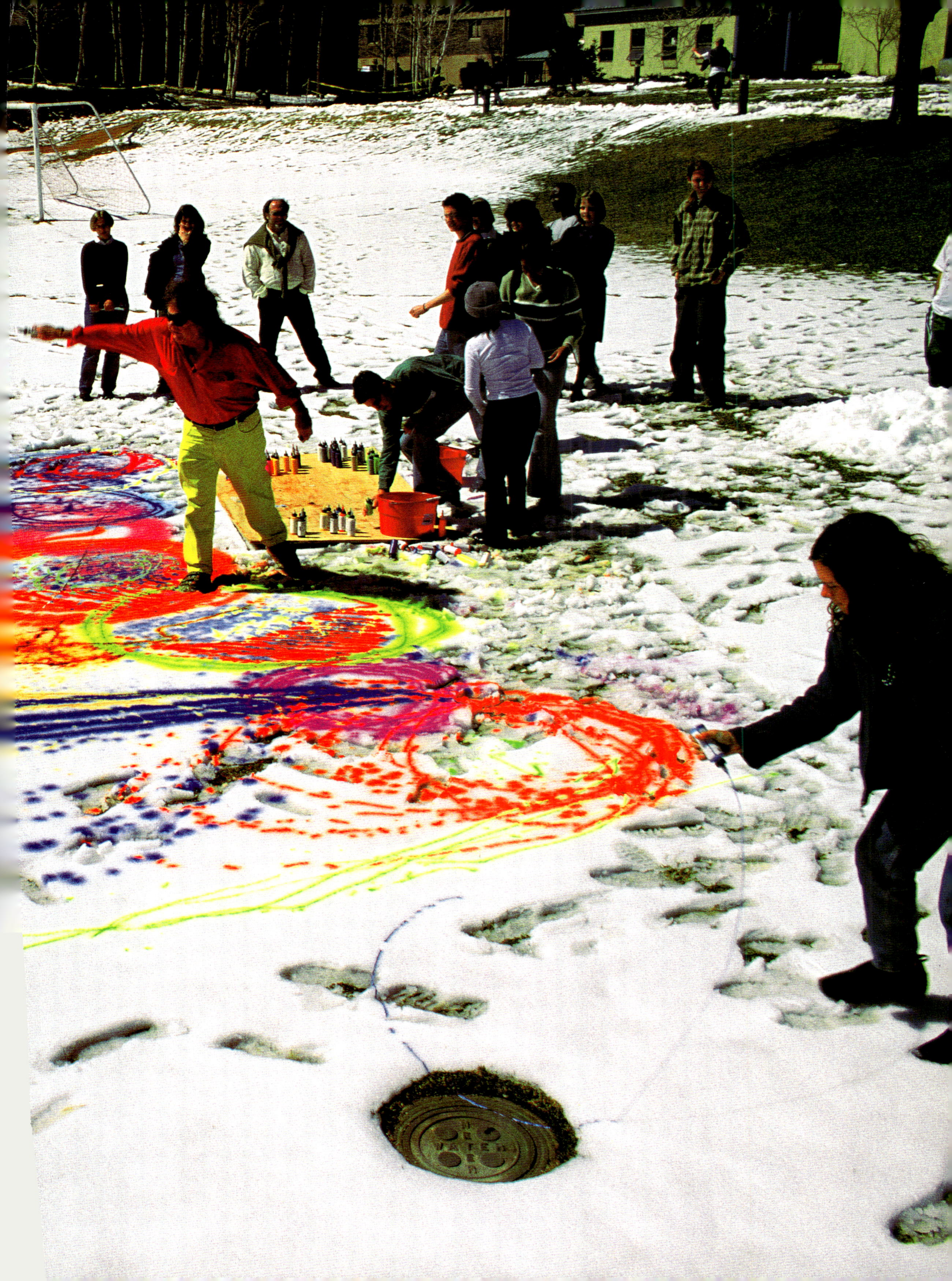

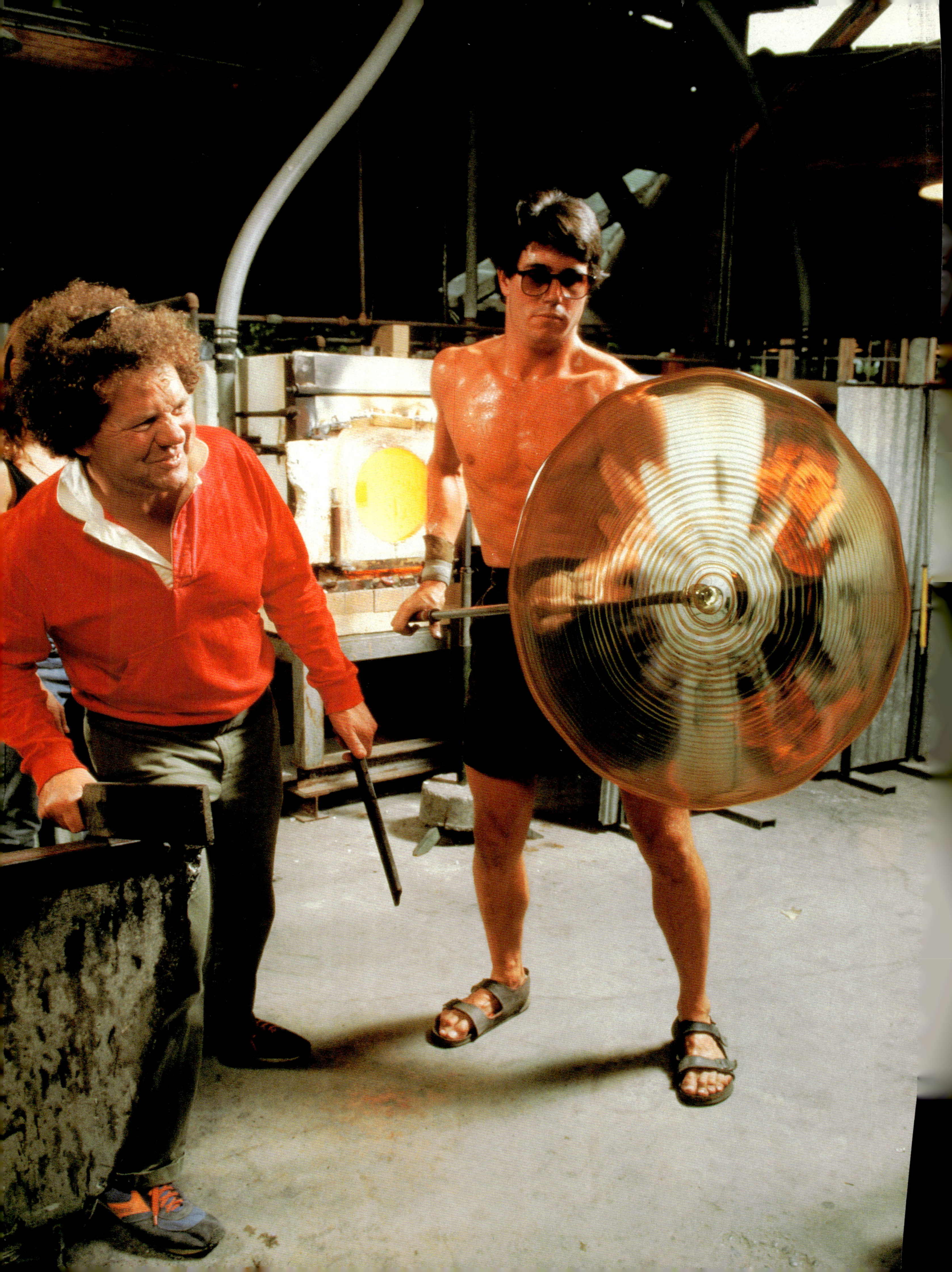